P9-AGA-105

THE
GOOD
STUFF
COOKBOOK

THE GOOD STUFF COOKBOOK

HELEN WITTY

Illustrations by Melissa Sweet

WORKMAN PUBLISHING • NEW YORK

Also by Helen Witty

Mrs. Witty's Home-Style Menu Cookbook

•

Fancy Pantry

•

Mrs. Witty's Monster Cookies

•

Better Than Store-Bought
(with Elizabeth Schneider Colchie)

•

The Garden-to-Table Cookbook
(Compiler and Editor)

•

The Cooks' Catalogue
(Editor)

Published simultaneously in Canada by Thomas Allen & Son Limited.

Library of Congress Cataloging-in-Publication Data

Witty, Helen.
The good stuff cookbook / by Helen Witty.
p. cm.
Includes index.
ISBN 0-7611-0287-6
1. Cookery. 2. Condiments. 3. Confectionery. I. Title.
TX714.W57 1997
641.5—dc21

Cover illustration by Melissa Sweet
Cover and book design by Janet Vicario

Approximately half of the recipes in The Good Stuff Cookbook *have been revised, updated, or expanded since their appearance in* Fancy Pantry *(now out of print).*

Workman Publishing
708 Broadway
New York, NY 10003

Manufactured in the United States of America
First printing June 1997
10 9 8 7 6 5 4 3 2 1

CONTENTS

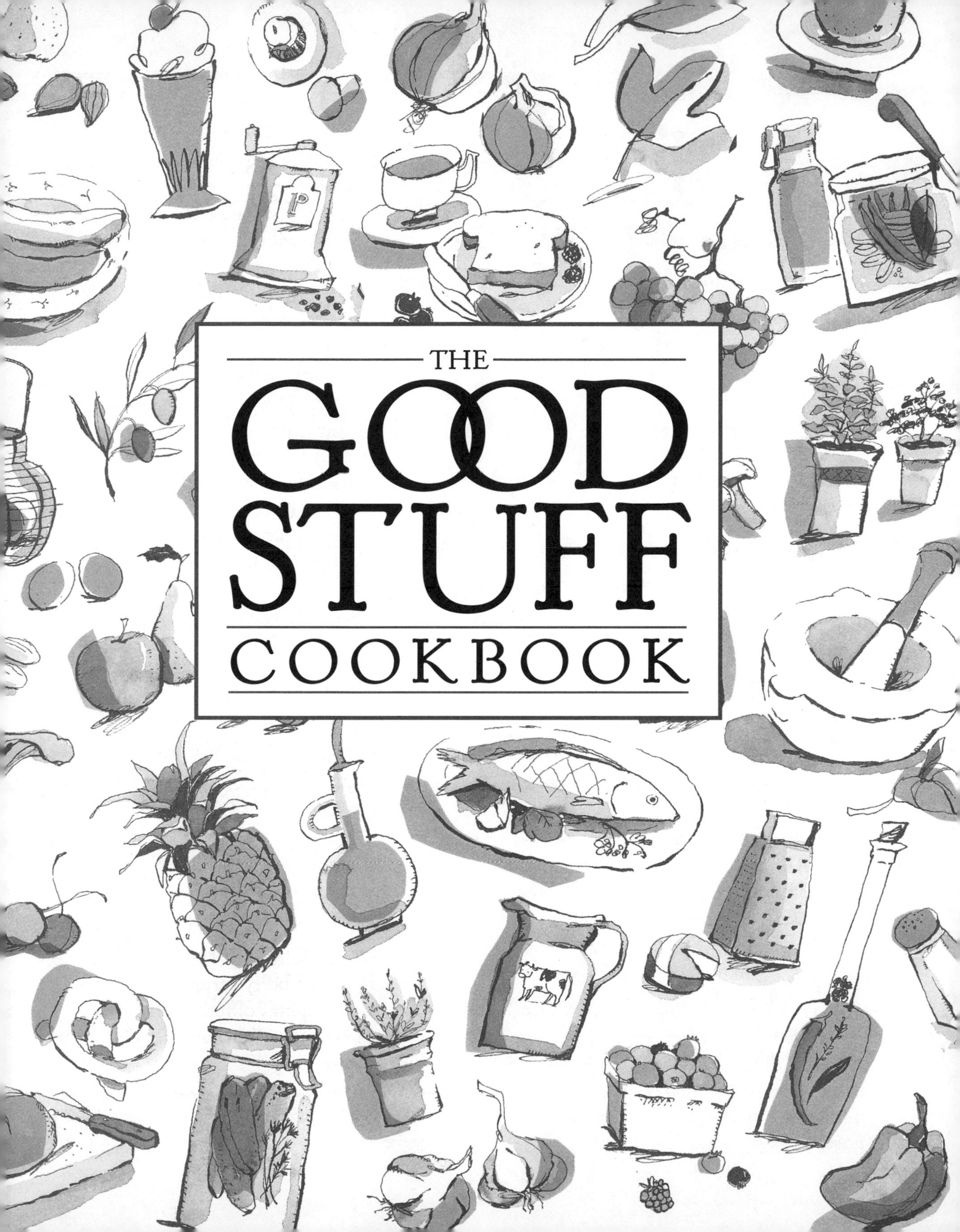
THE
GOOD
STUFF
COOKBOOK

The Good Stuff

In setting out at stove and computer to convert a stack of workbook pages into recipes and a headful of ideas into text for this book, it was my hope to put together a collection that holds up a true and shiny mirror to the author's notions of what's good to eat. (Also, I hoped, a collection written clearly enough, step by step, to guide novice cooks who may not have been lucky enough to spend kitchen time with a skilled grownup in their youth.)

The mirror also needed to be large enough to reflect a wide landscape of culinary traditions—American (there's a whole range of cuisines right there), British, French, Italian, Scandinavian, Middle Eastern, Asian, Caribbean, and points between. To discover just how many geographical points there are, and what we've stopped for at each, see the table of contents in the front of the book.

The good things in *The Good Stuff* have, in short, been chosen mostly because I like them and find that other people like them, too. Nothing is included because it's currently "in"—you'll actually find a few rather retro items here and there. (Consider Nesselrode Sauce, of Victorian vintage and still a deliciously decadent treat.) No recipe is here only because it's newly minted, either—about half of the recipes, if my math skills can be trusted, come from the pages of my earlier book *Fancy Pantry* (now out of print), which was devoted to a great variety of keepable, or pantry, foods. Those recipes—reviewed, updated, tweaked, and buffed, as necessary, with new thoughts added here and there—are among my favorites (and readers' favorites, too) in that book.

The new recipes in *The Good Stuff* are mostly for foods that have begun to interest American palates fairly recently. You'll find in this book (because they're on our tables) such once-obscure or solely store-bought things as aïoli, amaretti, bagels, barbecue sauces, caponata, truffles (the confection), crumpets, digestive biscuits, dried tomato tapenade and pesto, focaccia, garlic and hot pepper jelly, harissa, infused olive oils, an array of nonbasic mustards, onion marmalade, panettone and panforte, porcini or saffron pasta, potted shrimp, roasted garlic or roasted tomatoes, vegetable- and fruit-based peppery salsas, seasoning rubs, salmon pastrami, North African salt-preserved lemons, savory cocktail biscotti (as well as sweet biscotti), seafood sausages, spiced pumpkin and pecan butter, sun-dried tomato bread, tapenades of Mediterranean olives, vinegars infused with fruits or herbs, and white chocolate and hazelnuts made into a scrumptious sauce.

The Good Stuff is thus an eclectic (or maybe motley) collection of recipes ranging from odd-hour snacks to serious eating to smashing desserts, and it includes a lot of things you can squirrel away if you like to be ready for a splurge or the arrival of guests. All these things are "stuff" I enjoy preparing, sometimes because it's challenging to make something verging on the impossible, such as homemade hard pretzels or really crisp amaretti. Some of the recipes are my "takes" on classics, some have been more or less invented. (Caveat: I'm convinced that someone else, somewhere, has also "invented" any dish that a proud begetter is rash enough to claim as an absolutely original and previously unheard-of breakthrough.) Some of the recipes, a few, are a sort of hybrid, grounded in tradition but given some fresh licks just for their own good.

All are offered in the warm hope that you'll truly enjoy using them, as there's really no point in cookery if you don't find pleasure in the process as well as the product—"the attempt, rather than the achievement," in the words of John Thorne, peerless *Simple Cooking* essayist. It must be said, too, that there's not much sense in suiting up for the kitchen if you're really, truly happy with restaurant food, miscellaneous takeout, and frozen meals from the supermarket. Among those who fall—through no fault of their own—into that category, perhaps some who browse through *The Good Stuff* will feel discontented enough with industrialized eats to invest some pleasant time in creating their own good food at home.

Meats & Poultry, Smoked or Made into Pâtés, Sausages, Confits, Spreads, & Wild-Card Chili Bricks

Custom Charcuterie

Anyone who has prepared a simple pâté or a mousse of chicken livers has actually made a foray into the charcutier's art without having had to plunge into the arcana of salting, seasoning, smoking, or otherwise managing the complicated projects of the real pros. In that spirit of modest enterprise, this section offers a sampling of the many good things that can be made from meats and poultry.

The charcuterie here is created from ingredients ranging from leftovers (cooked beef for Brandied Beef & Anchovy Spread, or ham scraps for Potted Ham), to chicken livers thriftily accumulated in the freezer (for a party-perfect Chicken Liver Mousse), or a precious handful of foraged or mail-ordered black walnuts deployed, for their great character, in Country-Style Pâté with Black Walnuts. Should you spy a fine fat goose or a couple of portly ducks in the market, you may want to make a crock of Confit to keep in the fridge. And the several sausages aren't the usual compounds of pork plus fat—they're made with poultry and include a low-fat country-style turkey sausage and a clutch of vividly flavored sausages variously seasoned with touches of smoked meat, dried tomatoes, spinach, Italian herbs, and/or pistachios.

When it's outdoorsy weather, it's enjoyable to smoke a chicken or turkey in the family barbecue in the way described here. When the weather is wintry and it feels like a day for cooking comfort food, try slow-simmering a supply of Chili Bricks, a delicacy unknown to classic charcuterie but worth making if you're any kind of chili-head at all. No one is looking over my shoulder as I place this peppery interloper with the recipes for real charcuterie, so here it is, and *bon appétit.*

Country-Style Pâté with Black Walnuts

Our most remarkable native American nuts are the secret ingredient of this pâté that tastes as if wild game is involved in its compounding, although it is made of everyday meats and poultry. If you don't have access to black walnuts, which have a uniquely rich, deep, earthy savor, they can be omitted, but I do recommend that you include them if you can; they contribute much to this *pâté de campagne* American-style.

This recipe yields a good big loaf, enough for a dozen or more generous servings. Let the pâté ripen in flavor for 2 or 3 days before slicing it, and let it come to room temperature before your guests dig in. To go with it as a first course or a luncheon main dish, you might offer, instead of the customary cornichons, your own Tarragon-Pickled Flame Grapes or Tart Pickled Cherries in the French Style (see the Index), both splendid foils for charcuterie.

⅓ to ½ pound fresh pork fat, preferably fatback, cut into thin, almost transparent sheets
½ pound lean pork, preferably from the shoulder, ground
½ pound lean veal, ground
½ pound skinned turkey breast, ground
¼ pound smoked ham, cooked or uncooked, ground
¼ pound additional fresh pork fat, cut into ¼-inch dice or coarsely ground
¼ pound chicken livers, trimmed and cut into ¼-inch dice
⅓ cup black walnuts, chopped medium-fine (see sidebar)
2 large eggs
3 tablespoons all-purpose flour
3 large cloves garlic, minced very fine
1 tablespoon finely minced mild onion
1 tablespoon salt
½ teaspoon freshly ground pepper, or more to taste
⅓ teaspoon ground allspice
½ teaspoon finely crumbled dried thyme
⅛ teaspoon Powdered Bay Leaves (page 195) or 2 or 3 whole bay leaves
Pinch each of ground cloves, ginger, and nutmeg
¼ cup Cognac or other good brandy, or use half Cognac and half Madeira wine

Makes a 2½ pound loaf

Black Walnuts

These nuts are rich in oil, so they quickly lose flavor after they are shelled. Taste them before purchasing, and store them airtight in the refrigerator or freezer.

Seasoning Note

If you have made a supply of Quatre Epices (see the Index), you can substitute 1½ teaspoons of either version of that mixture for the pepper, allspice, cloves, ginger, and nutmeg listed as ingredients.

Pursuing Pork Fat

If you can't obtain sheets of pork fat (the firmest and best is from the back), salt pork or bacon can be used. Bacon will alter the flavor of the loaf, however. If you opt for salt pork, rinse it well in warm water, then pat it dry, to remove some of the loose salt. Too-thick slices of fat can be pounded out between sheets of waxed paper to suitable thinness, so don't despair if the meat man cuts it too thick, or if you have to slice it yourself.

1. Line a 6-cup loaf pan with the thin sheets of pork fat, letting any loose ends hang over the sides of the pan; reserve part of the fat to cover the top of the pâté. Preheat the oven to 400°F, with a shallow pan, larger than the loaf pan, set on a shelf in the center; pour about 1½ inches of water into the pan and let it heat.

2. Place the ground pork, veal, turkey, and ham, the diced or ground pork fat, the diced chicken livers, and the black walnuts in a large mixing bowl.

3. In another bowl, beat the eggs and gradually stir in the flour. When the mixture is smooth, add the garlic, onion, salt, pepper, allspice, thyme, powdered bay leaves (if you are using them; if you're using whole bay leaves, reserve them), cloves, ginger, and nutmeg. Stir the mixture into the meats for a few strokes, then add the Cognac and mix thoroughly. (A pair of well-washed hands will do the best job.) If you wish to check the seasonings, sauté a spoonful of the mixture in a small greased frying pan until it is well done, then taste. (Don't taste this mixture, or any other mixture containing raw pork, before it's cooked.)

4. Pack the pâté firmly into the lined loaf pan, being careful to eliminate any air pockets. If you are using whole bay leaves, lay them on top of the meat. Cover the loaf with the reserved sheets of pork fat (it isn't vital that the entire top be covered; if you have less than enough fat, lay the pieces down the center). Lay aluminum foil over the pan and press it snugly against the rim all around.

5. Set the loaf pan in the pan of hot water in the preheated oven and bake the pâté for 2 hours, adding boiling water to the outer pan as the level drops below the halfway mark. Remove the foil after 2 hours and check for doneness: If the juices run clear when the pâté is pricked, then pressed with a spatula or spoon, it is done. If longer baking is needed—usually no more than 15 minutes or so—bake the pâté uncovered until it tests done.

6. Remove the inner pan from the oven and set it on a platter or a baking sheet to catch any fat that may spill over during the next operation. Return the foil to the top (or use a fresh sheet) and set a suitable weight on it—a second loaf pan, plus about 3 pounds of weight (such as cans of food), is ideal. Or a wrapped brick will do, or a wrapped section of board, plus weights. Let the loaf cool under the weights, then unweight and refrigerate it, well wrapped, for at least 2 days before serving it; the resting period allows its flavor to develop.

7. ***Making ahead:*** The pâté can be frozen for storage, but it's not the best idea—it might be soggy after thawing. If you'd like to do most of the preparation ahead of time, or perhaps double the recipe with future occasions in mind, pack the batch meant for future use into a loaf pan lined with foil rather than pork fat. Cover the panful with foil, overwrap it, and freeze it until a few days before you'll be needing it; then thaw the unbaked loaf in the refrigerator and transfer it, without the foil, to a loaf pan lined with pork fat as in step 1; you may need to reshape the loaf with your hands to make it fit the new space. Top it with more fat and bake, weight, and chill it as described.

8. To unmold the pâté, run a knife blade all around it, then dip the pan briefly into hot water. Either invert the loaf onto a serving platter or pry it out right side up by using a large rubber spatula. Scrape away any blobs of fat and/or meat juices. The sheets of fat can be removed or not, as you prefer. Slice for serving.

CONFIT OF DUCK, GOOSE, OR RABBIT

Choosing duck or goose as raw material for a classic confit—which is seasoned poultry, meat, or game slow-cooked in abundant fat, then stored in the same fat for long keeping—is the classic move here, but rabbit, too, has its merits when preserved in this way. On the one hand, rabbit meat is naturally low in fat, so a confit of rabbit won't be as unctuous as poultry, but on the other hand, it's a good choice if the high fat content of the traditional birds is a dietary concern. (Naturally, all clinging fat from the confit jar will have been removed from the rabbit pieces before they're served.)

What to do with your confit, after it has rested quietly in its crock for at least a week, better several weeks? It belongs in many versions of the sublime French bean dish called cassoulet, about which regional partisans quarrel regularly (Castelnaudary vs. Carcassone, and so on). Or pieces may be warmed gently in some of the preserving fat, drained, and served with a plateful of assorted seasonal vegetables. Confit may also be served at room temperature with a green salad or coleslaw and plenty of crusty bread. A piece or two will lend terrific flavor to bean or vegetable soups (this is a great use for the bonier cuts), and the flavorful fat is a pantry treasure to be kept for seasoning and sautéing.

CONFIT OF DUCK

1 duck (4½ pounds), defrosted slowly in the refrigerator if necessary
1½ pounds fresh pork fatback

FAT STRATEGY

In order to obtain enough fat to cook and store confit properly, begin with rendering the loose fat of either a duck or a goose, plus the listed quantity of fresh pork fatback. (If you can obtain extra poultry fat from the butcher, use that instead of the pork.) When the meat has been consumed, you'll have plenty of fat for making another confit, perhaps of rabbit or other lean meat (the French also use turkey, veal, and game birds).

SEASONING MIX:
1 tablespoon coarse (kosher) salt
1 tablespoon Quatre Epices, basic version (page 196)
2 teaspoons crumbled dried thyme
½ teaspoon Powdered Bay Leaves (page 195)
1 teaspoon coarsely ground fresh black pepper

FOR MARINATING THE MEAT:
⅔ cup peeled and coarsely chopped shallots

FOR COOKING THE CONFIT:
20 cloves garlic, peeled
Good-quality lard, if needed to augment the cooking fat

Makes about 10 pieces

1. *Preparing the duck:* Rinse and drain the duck. Pull out of the cavity all the fat you can reach and set it aside. Cut off the skin and fat from the neck end and add it to the fat pile. Cut off the wing tips and reserve them for stock, if you wisely save such bits and pieces. Save the liver as a treat for the cook (or freeze it as part of a stash of poultry livers intended for a future pâté). Either prepare the gizzard and neck with the other elements of the confit or add them to the reserve for stock.

With a pair of kitchen shears, a cleaver, or a heavy knife, cut along both sides of the backbone to remove it completely. Work carefully through the area where the thigh bone joins the backbone—it can be tricky. Remove the fat and skin from the backbone, add them to the fat pile, and add the backbone to the pile for stock.

Lay the duck skin side down on the work surface and cut it in half lengthwise, cutting through the breastbone. Cut each half into 5 pieces: cut off the wings; they can be used for stock or prepared with the confit (they are bony, but valuable for seasoning soups and bean dishes). Cut the duck half into leg and breast pieces. Separate the leg pieces at the knee joint and whack each breast portion in half. You now have 8 to 10 pieces (depending on whether you use the wings) plus the gizzard and neck, if they are going into the confit pot. Trim any loose fat from the duck pieces and add it to the fat pile.

2. *Rendering the fat:* Cut all fat and skin into 1-inch pieces. Dice the fatback. Combine the two fats with ½ cup water in a heavy 3-quart saucepan. Heat to boiling over high heat, then reduce the heat to maintain a simmer. Cook uncovered, stirring occasionally, until the duck and pork have rendered their fat and begun to brown lightly. This can take from 2 to 3 hours, and it's important to keep an eye on the heat once the water has evaporated; you want the fat to render slowly and evenly, not to fry. (A slow-cooker, set on Low, is perfect for this job,

Save That Fat

The rich fat that preserves the meat of a confit is tremendously flavorful and shouldn't be discarded when the poultry or rabbit has been consumed. Store it in the refrigerator for use in sautéing (especially potatoes) or for enriching and seasoning bean dishes and hearty soups. Good way to do this: Use the confit fat to gently sauté (or "sweat," covered) the onions and other savory vegetables at the start of soup making.

as it requires little or no watching. I've also rendered fat in a large microwave, operating it at Medium or Medium-Low power and for fairly short increments of time, stirring after each few minutes' cooking. The slow-cooker takes more time but requires no attention; the microwave is faster but does need brief attention at intervals.) Whatever method is used, strain the rendered fat through a fine sieve and refrigerate it until it's needed for cooking the confit.

3. ***Seasoning and marinating the meat:*** While the fat is rendering, stir the ingredients for the seasoning mix in a small bowl. Pat the duck pieces completely dry with paper towels and rub them all over with the seasoning mix. Choose a baking dish or plastic tray that will hold the pieces without overlapping. Sprinkle half the chopped shallots in the dish and place the duck pieces, skin side up, over the shallots. Sprinkle with the remaining shallots. Wrap tightly with plastic wrap and refrigerate for at least 1 day and for as long as 3 days.

4. ***Cooking the confit:*** Melt the rendered fat over low heat. Brush the chopped shallots off the duck pieces and arrange the meat in a heavy pot (a 4-quart enameled iron casserole is ideal), sprinkling each layer with some of the garlic cloves. The pieces should fit snugly without being tightly packed, and there should be ample room for the fat to cover the meat completely without coming within an inch of the rim.

Add the melted fat, which should cover the meat; if an edge protrudes just a little here and there, that will be remedied as more fat melts from the duck and the pieces shrink. If necessary, melt and add enough lard to cover the meat properly. Especially at the beginning, you may want to weight the meat with a heavy plate to hold it under the surface.

Over medium heat, heat the potful to a temperature of 195°F. Use a thermometer if you have one; lacking a thermometer, observe the bubbles. Only an occasional bubble should rise to the surface; a steady bubbly stream means the heat is too high. Adjusting the heat as necessary, cook the confit uncovered until all the pieces in turn have become tender enough to pierce easily with a wooden skewer or paring knife, 1 to 1½ hours. As each piece passes the tenderness test, remove it with a slotted spoon to a baking sheet.

When all the duck is done and removed from the pot, carefully ladle the clear portion of the hot fat into a second heavy pot, working from the top down to leave behind as much as possible of the liquid and debris settled at the bottom. (Consider spooning out and reserving the garlic cloves to enjoy as a special snack.) Discard the dregs of the first pot. Over medium heat, cook the fat until it stops boiling, at which point the residual moisture has evaporated. Be careful not to let the fat overheat and darken—cook it just long enough to get rid of the moisture that would cause spoilage during storage.

Slow-Cooker Note

I'm a big fan of using a crockpot for making confit as well as for rendering the fat. Start with the High setting, then switch to Low once the confit has reached the slow-bubble stage. Goose or duck should be done in about 5 hours; rabbit may take a bit less time, so start testing it for doneness after about 4 hours.

5. ***Storing the confit:*** Choose a heatproof container (crocks are traditional) approximately the size of the original cooking pot (or use two smaller containers, if you prefer). Fill the container(s) with boiling water, leave them to scald for a few minutes, then drain and dry them. Pour in a layer of liquid fat about an inch deep, then add the duck pieces, leaving a little space between the pieces and the sides of the container. Pour in the fat, making sure it penetrates all nooks—there must be no air pockets—and forms a layer an inch or more deep over the meat, rearranging the pieces if necessary. Cool to room temperature, then cover the container tightly with foil and refrigerate the confit for at least a week before using it. It will keep for months, refrigerated under its seal of fat; I've kept confit for a year and found it excellent.

6. ***To use the confit:*** Set the container in a 300°F oven and leave it just until the fat has softened a bit—you don't want to melt it. Remove the required amount of confit, then redistribute the fat and smooth it to form a new sealing layer. Cover and refrigerate as before.

Confit of Goose

For this you proceed exactly as for duck. As a goose has abundant fat, you probably won't need to increase the quantity of extra fat listed for a single duck, but you will need to double the listed seasonings if your goose is of average market size, yielding about 8 to 9 pounds of meat after fat removal and trimming. Goose thighs are large, so I whack them in two with a cleaver. Cooking time will be about the same, but you'll need a larger pot than a duck requires.

Confit of Rabbit

The readiest way to provide fat for confit of rabbit is to make and consume a batch of confit of duck or goose, then reuse the fat for the rabbit. However, it's easy enough to start from scratch if you can obtain enough chicken or duck or goose fat to be rendered as described in the recipe for duck. For a single rabbit, you'll need at least 2 pounds (4 cups) of rendered fat. Good lard can be used to increase the amount of fat if necessary at cooking time.

For the average cut-up young rabbit (about 3 pounds), proceed by defrosting the meat in the refrigerator, if it's frozen, then drain and pat the pieces dry. Chop the saddle (the long back piece) into two sections. Rub the pieces with the seasoning mix (you won't need quite all of it) and marinate them with ½ cup of chopped shallots as described. Cook with a slightly smaller amount of garlic (or use all 20 cloves—it's up to you). Start checking for doneness after 1¼ hours. Complete the recipe and store the confit as for duck. Allow to mellow for a week or more before serving.

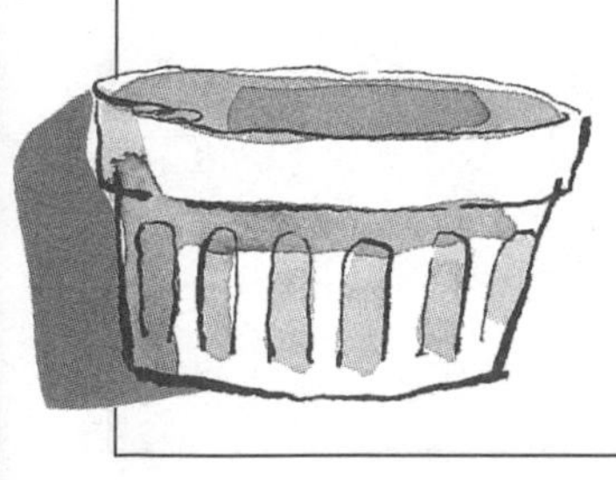

Brandied Beef & Anchovy Spread

(Potted Beef)

Call it brandied or call it potted, by either name this meat mixture is a great thing to have on hand for sandwiches, canapés, or just a snack. It keeps for weeks in the refrigerator, and unlike most pâtés, it freezes well.

The inspiration for this spread was James Beard's mother's enormous recipe for "Strathborough Paste," which son Jim included in his memoirs. Intrigued by that delectable mixture, whose origins he said he had never learned, I did some delving into old British household books that Mrs. Beard could have known in her girlhood and found some very similar preparations, notably one called "Strasburg Potted Meat," whose name could well have been anglicized at some point to "Strathborough." The recipe below is the end result of all this recipe sleuthing. I like it a lot.

Making potted meat is a good use for leftover well-done beef, either potroasted or boiled. The seasonings should be assertive, so taste the compound carefully before storing it.

1½ cups flavorful beef broth (not canned bouillon)
2 slices of a medium onion
1 small bay leaf
Pinch of crumbled dried thyme leaves
2 cups packed (about ¾ pound) cubed lean cooked beef, trimmed of all hard bits, gristle, or fat
1 can (2 ounces) anchovies in oil, drained
3 tablespoons brandy
¾ cup (1½ sticks) sweet (unsalted) butter, sliced into chunks
1 teaspoon, or to taste, Quatre Epices (page 196), either the basic or enhanced version, or see sidebar at right on Alternative Spicing
Salt, if desired
¼ to ⅓ cup Clarified Butter (page 35), for sealing

Makes about 2½ cups

1. Combine the beef broth, onion slices, bay leaf, and thyme in a saucepan. Heat the broth to boiling, then lower the heat and simmer, uncovered, until the liquid has reduced to ¾ cup. Strain the broth

Alternative Spicing

If you don't have on hand either version of Quatre Epices, season the potted beef with freshly ground pepper, a pinch each of ground ginger and nutmeg, and a very tiny pinch of ground cloves. Optionally, add a generous pinch of crushed dried thyme, tiny pinches of ground cinnamon and mace, and a small pinch of Powdered Bay Leaves (page 195). Taste and adjust seasonings.

Packing It In

Potted meat, fish, or cheese that is sealed into crocks with clarified butter—as is Brandied Beef & Anchovy Spread—must be packed into the container with care, a small portion at a time. This prevents air pockets, which would hasten spoilage of these perishable pastes. It's equally important to seal the tops with clarified butter, as described in the recipes, to ensure safe storage for the periods indicated.

into a cup or small bowl; discard the solids. Reserve the saucepan (no need to rinse it out).

2. Grind or chop fine the cubed beef together with the drained anchovies and the brandy; a food processor does this best, as you want a paste, not chunks. Scrape the beef and anchovy mixture into the saucepan. Add the reduced broth and heat the mixture over low heat, stirring constantly, until it is boiling hot. Add the butter chunks, stirring until they melt. Remove from the heat. Stir in the seasoning mixture; taste and add a little salt if needed. Scoop out a small sample of the paste and cool it for further tasting, meanwhile stirring the mixture over the heat until it is again boiling hot. Set it aside and taste the cooled sample for seasoning. Seasonings should be quite pronounced, so add more if they are needed.

3. A spoonful at a time (to prevent air pockets from forming), pack the potted beef, which will be a soft, moist mixture, into small crocks, pottery custard cups, or straight-sided jars and smooth the tops. Let the mixture cool to room temperature, then chill. Melt enough clarified butter to cover the paste in each crock by ¼ inch and pour it over to seal. (If you will be using the paste within a few days, the butter covering may be omitted.) When the butter begins to congeal, cover and/or wrap the crocks for the refrigerator or the freezer and store. Unsealed, the spread will keep for a week in the refrigerator; sealed with the butter, for 3 weeks in the refrigerator or 2 months in the freezer.

4. Frozen potted beef should be thawed in its wrappings. Whether refrigerated or thawed, the beef tastes best at room temperature. Any leftovers should be refrigerated promptly and used within a few days.

Potted Ham

With a milder set of seasonings than deviled ham, this is an old-fashioned English delicacy of a kind that people used to make here too, pounding the meat laboriously in a mortar. Using one or another modern kitchen machine, it's now a snap to make a succulent batch from leftover ham, preferably home-cooked ham of pronounced flavor. (I wouldn't use the bland delicatessen kind.)

Serve your potted ham with crisp toast for Sunday breakfast or with salad for lunch, cutting wedges right down through the potful. Also good for sandwiches.

3 cups (about 1 pound) cubed cooked ham, mostly lean, all gristle and membranes removed
¾ cup Clarified Butter (page 35) at room temperature, plus ¼ to ⅓ cup more for sealing
½ teaspoon fresh lemon juice
¼ teaspoon ground mace
⅛ teaspoon ground hot red (cayenne) pepper
Small pinch of ground cloves
Small pinch of Powdered Bay Leaves (page 195), optional

Makes about 3 cups

1. Grind the ham very fine or, preferably, chop it fine in a food processor. (A blender can also be used, working in several batches.) Add ¾ cup clarified butter, the lemon juice, mace, red pepper, cloves, and powdered bay leaves (if using) and mix very well, but avoid making a puree if you are using a food processor or blender.

2. Taste the potted ham for seasoning and adjust it to taste, remembering that the flavor will develop further. Pack the potted ham tightly into small crocks, pottery custard cups, or straight-sided jars, being careful to leave no air spaces. Smooth the tops and chill.

3. Melt enough additional clarified butter (¼ to ⅓ cup) to seal each pot with a layer ¼ inch thick. Pour the butter over the potted ham, let it cool and begin to congeal, then cover and/or wrap the crocks for refrigerator or freezer storage.

4. Potted ham will keep for 3 weeks in the refrigerator (for about a week if you elect to skip the butter topping) and for 2 months in the freezer. Frozen potted ham should be thawed unopened in the refrigerator. For the best flavor, serve it at cool room temperature. After opening the butter seal, use leftovers within a few days.

Going to the Devil

The seasonings of Potted Ham can be made more incendiary (deviled), if that's your pleasure, by including a pinch or two of ground ginger; a small clove of garlic, minced to a paste; prepared mustard to taste (start with a teaspoonful); and dashes of hot pepper sauce according to liking (use store-bought hot sauce, or see the Index for a recipe).

Chicken Liver Mousse

Not at all complicated to put together even though it's elegant fare for a party, this mousse (or call it a pâté) begins with chicken livers poached with aromatic seasonings instead of being sautéed (I think this produces a better texture). The compound is enhanced with butter, Madeira, and spices—altogether a treat to taste.

Serve the mousse with such a crisp breadstuff as water biscuits, if you're using something store-bought, or check the Index for the possibilities of making your own Oatcakes, Beaten-Biscuit Crackers, Crisp Rye & Wheat Flatbread, or Bagel Chips.

Using Poultry Fat in the Mousse

If you have on hand some rendered chicken fat or duck or goose fat (perhaps seasoned fat from Confit—see the Index), you may want to use it to replace part of the butter. The texture of the mousse will be softer than that of an all-butter version, but there will be a gain in flavor.

Ginning It Up

If you've never cooked with gin, try including it, as suggested, when poaching the livers for Chicken Liver Mousse. And pour some gin into the casserole when cooking sauerkraut with assorted meats in any version of choucroute garnie.

The recipe makes a generous amount, enough to serve as one of the heartier offerings on a cocktail buffet for a good-sized gathering. (I've always found this mousse disappears at a fast clip, which can be frustrating if anyone expects a succulent next-day sandwich made with the leftovers.) If you are sure you won't have immediate need for the whole quantity, part can be stashed away in the freezer for a month or so, as described in step 5 of the recipe.

FOR POACHING THE LIVERS:
2 quarts water
1½ cups sliced celery (about 3 ribs, trimmed)
1 cup pared and sliced carrots (about 2 medium)
⅔ cup sliced onion (about 1 medium)
½ cup gin, dry white wine, or dry vermouth
6 cloves garlic, peeled and cut in half
3 bay leaves
1 small stick cinnamon
2 tablespoons salt
1 tablespoon whole black peppercorns

THE LIVERS AND REMAINING INGREDIENTS:
8 tablespoons (1 stick) sweet (unsalted) butter, at room temperature, cut into 6 pieces
¼ cup Madeira wine
2 teaspoons dark (roasted) sesame oil
1½ teaspoons Quatre Epices, basic version (page 196)
1 teaspoon onion juice (from a slice or two of raw onion pushed through a garlic press), or 2 tablespoons finely snipped fresh chives
¼ teaspoon ground allspice
¼ cup finely minced fresh parsley leaves

Makes about 4 cups

1. Measure the water and the other poaching ingredients into a big saucepan and bring to a boil. Reduce the heat to low, partially cover the pan, and simmer 20 minutes.

2. Raise the heat to medium. Add the chicken livers and cook 5 minutes. Remove from the heat and let stand, uncovered, until cooled to room temperature.

3. Drain the contents of the pot in a colander. Remove the livers to the workbowl of a food processor, picking off and discarding all peppercorns and bits of vegetable as you go. Add to the livers the butter, Madeira, sesame oil, 1½ teaspoons salt, quatre épices, onion juice, allspice, and parsley. Process the ingredients, scraping down the sides of the workbowl repeatedly, until the mixture is smooth. Taste and adjust the seasonings, if necessary.

4. Pack the mousse firmly into a 4-cup crock, ramekin, mold, or loaf pan, smoothing the top. (Or use two smaller containers.) Cover tightly with plastic wrap or aluminum foil and chill thoroughly before serving. Either unmold the mousse onto a plate and smooth the top and sides with a knife dipped into hot water, or serve it in its crock or ramekin.

5. The mousse will keep perfectly for 3 days or so in a properly cold refrigerator. It may be freezer-wrapped and frozen for up to a month. The texture will be less than perfect after thawing (do this in the refrigerator), so I'd pack it into a new serving container before setting it out.

Variation—A Mousse of Duck Livers

When ordinary (not specially fattened) duck livers are available, don't overlook their excellent character in a mousse of this description. Simply substitute them for chicken livers and proceed as described.

A Set of Succulent Chicken or Turkey Sausages

To make your own fresh and flavorful poultry sausages in any of three guises, you begin by preparing the meat as described in the master recipe below, then you marinate it with the additional ingredients as directed in the supplementary information for the version you've chosen—Chicken or Turkey Sausage with Smoked Bacon, Spinach, & Sun-Dried Tomatoes; Chicken or Turkey Sausage with Pancetta, Pistachios, & Orange Zest; or Italian-Style Chicken or Turkey Sausages.

Be sure to read through the list of ingredients and the directions for your chosen version before starting to make the sausage, as you'll have to allow for overnight marination of ingredients.

The wrong raw material: Ground turkey and chicken are now supermarket staples, but they aren't called for in these recipes. The reason is this: Most commerically packed ground poultry contains the very fatty skin of the bird, plus a generous complement of the fat that clings to the meat, all of which boosts the poultry onto a quite high level of calories and cholesterol. Unless ground poultry is available under a label that assures its low fat content (such brands have been sighted here and there), it's best to strip chicken or turkey of its skin and surplus fat and grind or chop it as described in the recipe.

Master Recipe for Poultry Sausages

½ pound boneless, skinless chicken or turkey breast, any tendons removed, cut into 1-inch cubes (about 1 cup)
1 pound boneless, skinless turkey thighs, cut into 1-inch cubes or 5 bone-in chicken thighs (about 2 pounds), skinned, boned, and cut into 1-inch cubes (see the sidebar on page 19 for how-to's), (about 2 cups of either)
2 teaspoons coarse (kosher) salt
¼ teaspoon freshly ground pepper, white or black
Additional ingredients as listed for your choice of the three variations below
About 4 feet of sausage casings, soaked in cold water to cover while the sausage mixture is being made

The yield will vary a little from version to version. Expect to finish up with about 2½ pounds of sausage made with spinach and dried tomatoes, or a little under 2 pounds for either of the other two. All recipes produce 8 sausages about 4 inches in length.

1. Mix the cubed chicken or turkey meat, salt, and pepper with the additional marinating ingredients of your chosen recipe. Mix everything thoroughly with a rubber spatula or your hands. Cover and marinate in the refrigerator overnight, or for at least 8 hours.

2. Add any remaining ingredients your chosen recipe directs you to grind with the meat. Grind the mixture, using the medium disk of a meat grinder or, lacking a grinder, a food processor, operated in short on-off bursts. (Be careful not to overprocess the mixture, which should retain some texture.) Stir in any remaining ingredients. Keep the mixture cold while preparing the casings, or for several hours or up to overnight if more convenient.

3. To check the balance of seasonings before stuffing the sausages, cook a small patty of the sausage mixture in an oiled pan until lightly browned and cooked through, then taste.

4. *Making the sausages:* Remove the sausage casings from the soaking water and rinse them thoroughly. To do this, fit one end of a section of casing over the faucet and turn on the cold water very slowly, increasing the flow as the casing straightens out. Note whether there are any tears (small holes are no problem); if there are larger holes, cut the casing where they occur and use the good portions, or choose another length of casing. Drain the casings well.

To fill the casings, follow the manufacturer's directions for using a grinder attachment or other machine designed for stuffing sausages. Otherwise, choose a large pastry bag fitted with a large plain tip. Fill the bag about three-fourths full with the sausage mixture and fold over

Handling Raw Poultry

The advice here has been around for a long time, but it's now more important than ever, because outbreaks of illness caused by Salmonella *bacteria in both poultry and eggs have been giving concern. These bad bugs are destroyed by cooking, but they may remain on utensils used to prepare poultry. Boring as it may seem, it's now basic good sense to scrub boards, knives, cutting boards, grinders or food processor bowls and blades, and anything else (including hands) that has touched the raw poultry. Use soap, and rinse everything well.*

the top. Lay the filled bag on its side and work about 2 inches of casing slowly onto the tip. Tie the opposite, open end of the casing firmly closed with a short length of string.

Pipe the sausage mixture into the casing, filling it loosely—it should be only about four-fifths full. Don't worry if the filling is unevenly distributed—you'll adjust that in a minute. Just be sure not to overfill the casing or the sausages will burst during cooking. When the casing contains enough filling to make as many 4-inch sausages as its length will accommodate, slide the remaining casing off the pastry bag tip and tie it with string where the filling ends. Press and stroke the filled casing on a work surface to equalize the filling, then twist it firmly at 4-inch intervals to divide it into links; optionally, tie with string over the twists. Pierce each sausage several times with a fork (or do this just before cooking). Continue filling casings until all the filling has been used.

5. *Storing:* Refrigerate the sausages, lightly wrapped, until you are ready to cook them. They may be refrigerated for up to 24 hours or frozen for up to a month in suitable freezer wrappings.

6. *Cooking poultry sausages:* Preheat the oven to 350°F. Pierce each sausage several times with a sharp fork or a knife tip, if you haven't done this earlier. Oil a heavy ovenproof skillet lightly (cast iron is best) and set it over medium heat on the stovetop. Cook the sausages, turning them often until they are lightly browned all around, about 6 minutes. Place the pan in the oven and cook the sausages, uncovered, until no trace of pink remains in the center, about 15 minutes. Remove any strings, cut apart, and serve hot with generous wedges of lemon or, for an interesting change, wedges of orange.

SAUSAGE CASINGS

Natural casings for small sausages are sold (as are large casings, and synthetic substitutes) by suppliers of sausage-making ingredients (see Mail-Order Sources, page 390). Before sending off for a supply, try a local butcher department or deli that sells house-made sausages—chances are good that the shop will be willing to sell you a few yards of casings.

CHICKEN OR TURKEY SAUSAGES WITH SMOKED BACON, SPINACH, & SUN-DRIED TOMATOES

¼ pound (about 4 slices) thick-sliced bacon, cut crosswise into ½-inch strips

3 cloves garlic, peeled and minced (about 1½ teaspoons; optional but good)

1 teaspoon crumbled dried basil leaves

Ingredients as listed in the Master Recipe, on page 17

1 pound fresh spinach, stemmed, washed repeatedly until free of sand, and well drained

½ cup (about 2 ounces) drained sun-dried tomatoes in oil, cut into ½-inch dice

1. Add the bacon, garlic (if used), and basil to the ingredients listed in the Master Recipe and marinate the meats overnight.

REPLACING PANCETTA

As a substitute when pancetta is unobtainable, dice relatively lean (streaky) salt pork and sprinkle it lightly with black pepper.

2. When ready to make the sausages, steam the washed spinach leaves in their own moisture in a large covered pot over high heat just until they wilt but are still bright green, about 1 minute. Turn the spinach into a colander and rinse it quickly under cold water. Using your hands, squeeze out all possible liquid from the spinach, then chop it coarsely.

3. Grind the meats as described in the Master Recipe, then stir in the chopped spinach and diced tomatoes. Proceed to fill the casings and complete the recipe as described.

Chicken or Turkey Sausages with Pancetta, Pistachios, & Orange Zest

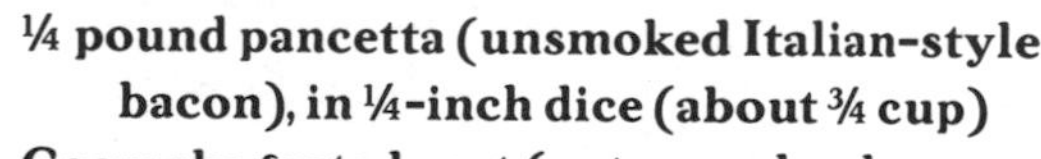

¼ pound pancetta (unsmoked Italian-style bacon), in ¼-inch dice (about ¾ cup)
Coarsely grated zest (outer peel only, no white pith) of 1 orange (about 1 tablespoon)
½ teaspoon ground ginger
¼ teaspoon ground cloves
Ingredients as listed in the Master Recipe, on page 17
¼ pound (about 1 cup) pistachios in the shell

1. Add the pancetta, orange zest, ginger, and cloves to the ingredients listed in the Master Recipe and marinate the mixture overnight as directed.

2. When ready to make the sausages, shell the pistachios and place them in a heatproof bowl. Pour in boiling water to cover and let the nuts stand 5 minutes. Drain them and slip off as much of the skin as will come off easily.

3. Grind the meats as directed in the Master Recipe, then stir in the pistachios. Proceed to fill the casings and complete the recipe as described.

Italian-Style Chicken or Turkey Sausages

Ingredients as listed in the Master Recipe, on page 17
¼ pound salt pork, cut into ½-inch dice (about ¾ cup)
3 medium cloves garlic, peeled and minced (about 1½ teaspoons)
1½ teaspoons fennel seed, lightly crushed
½ teaspoon hot red pepper flakes

Combine all the ingredients and marinate the mixture overnight. Grind the mixture and complete the sausages as described in the Master Recipe.

How to Bone Poultry Thighs

If you can't purchase boned thigh meat of chicken or turkey, here's how to proceed from scratch: Remove and discard the skin, leaving as much of the fat in place as possible. Place the thigh(s), with the outer (round) side down, on a cutting board. You'll see a line of fat that follows the path of the bone through the meat. Cut along this line down to the bone and use the tip of your knife to scrape the meat free. Cut the final attachments of bone to meat, making sure to remove bits of miscellaneous gristly tissue wherever you spot any (mostly around the joints). Strip out the tendons (the tough, silvery strips). Cut the meat into 1-inch pieces for marination.

Low-Fat Country-Style Turkey Sausage

Seasoned in the style of traditional pork sausage (which is about one-third pure fat), this poultry version contains a fraction of the fat of the porky original but is satisfactorily succulent, thanks to a little cheatin' with soft-cooked rice.

If your sausage is made with packaged ground turkey from the supermarket, be aware that its fat content may be much higher (read the label of the turkey package) than the recommended mixture here—half skinless turkey breast and half skinless turkey thigh meat, trimmed of all visible fat and ground by the butcher or yourself. (Use your food processor for a quick and effortless job.)

We like patties of juicy turkey sausage for breakfast, with fried apples or broiled or pan-fried green or ripe tomatoes; or we serve the links alongside eggs, or grits, or pancakes. For lunch, tuck a patty into a split and toasted bagel (especially a big homemade one; see the Index) for an offbeat "hamburger."

1 medium onion, peeled and chopped
2 pounds turkey meat, preferably half breast meat and half thigh meat, without skin or visible fat, or 2 pounds of purchased ground turkey, prepared without seasonings and preferably low in fat content
1 cup very soft cooked rice, sieved or mashed (1/3 cup before cooking)
2 teaspoons coarse (kosher) salt or 1½ teaspoons fine salt
2 large bay leaves, torn up
2 teaspoons sweet Hungarian paprika
1½ teaspoons crumbled dried leaf sage or rubbed sage, or more to taste
1½ teaspoons crumbled dried thyme leaves, or more to taste
½ teaspoon hot red pepper flakes, or pinch of ground hot red (cayenne) pepper
½ teaspoon crumbled dried sweet marjoram leaves
½ teaspoon white or black peppercorns, or to taste
½ cup ice water
About 5 feet of sausage casings, soaked in cold water while the sausage mixture is being made (optional)

Makes 2¾ to 3 pounds

Cheatin' Fair

The strategy of adding moisture to lean ground turkey by including soft-cooked rice instead of fat can be extended to making any other kind of fresh (not cured) sausage you fancy—about ½ cup of mashed soft rice per pound of meat has been about right in my experiments.

Paprikas with a Difference

Whether sweet, medium, or hot—there are great differences between them—the best paprikas come from Hungary, often in colorfully decorated tins. Good supermarkets usually offer at least one or two grades of the Hungarians' great contribution to the spice trade. Spice specialists will have all stages of sweetness and hotness to offer.

1. Cook the onion in water just to cover until soft, about 5 minutes on the stovetop or 2 minutes in the microwave. Sieve or mash the onion with its liquid and scrape it into a mixing bowl to cool to room temperature.

2. If you are preparing your own ground turkey, grind it medium fine in a meat grinder or dice it, then chop it in a food processor, using quick on-off pulses of the motor just until it resembles pale hamburger—be careful not to reduce it to a pulp. Add the turkey and the mashed rice to the onion.

3. Combine the salt, bay leaves, paprika, sage, thyme, pepper flakes, sweet marjoram, and peppercorns in a spice mill or the container of a blender and grind to a powder. Add to the mixture of onion, turkey, and rice.

4. Stir in the ice water and mix until well combined and rather fluffy. To test for seasoning, cook a small patty in a skillet over medium heat, then taste. When adjusting seasonings, remember that the flavor will develop further with time, so don't overdo the additions. If you plan to cook thc sausage in patties, wrap it in plastic or foil and refrigerate for 12 to 24 hours. (This allows the sausage to cure a bit, to let the flavors blend and mellow.)

5. ***Shaping link sausages:*** If you prefer to fill sausage casings, follow the directions accompanying your sausage-stuffing equipment, or follow the directions on pages 17 and 18 for using a pastry bag to stuff casings. Place the filled and tied sausages on a cake rack and refrigerate them, uncovered, to cure for about 24 hours.

6. ***To store:*** The bulk sausage or the links will keep in the coldest part of the refrigerator for at least 3 days, well wrapped. For longer keeping, wrap the links or formed patties of bulk sausage (see size below) in plastic, then overwrap in foil or freezer wrap, seal, and freeze for up to 2 months. Thaw frozen sausage, still in its wrappings, in the refrigerator.

7. ***To cook:*** Form bulk sausage into patties about ½ inch thick and as large or small as you choose. Cut links apart. Film a cold heavy skillet with oil or cooking spray. Arrange the patties or links in the cold pan, add about ¼ inch of water, and set over medium-low heat. Cover and cook for 10 minutes, uncovering two or three times to turn the sausage. After 10 minutes, uncover and continue to cook, turning often, just until the liquid has evaporated and the sausage has browned *lightly* and become attractively glazed by the reduced liquid. Overcooking should be avoided because it will cause the sausage to become dry.

Smoked Chicken or Turkey

Smoked poultry was an expensive rarity until quite a lot of people twigged to the basic simplicity of what is involved in preparing it. Home-smoking a whole chicken, small whole turkey, or a whole turkey breast is quite feasible in any of several types of smokers.

Box Smokers: Box smokers, which produce only moderate heat, can be used to smoke-flavor a large chunk of food, such as poultry, that has been precooked. If that's the kind of smoker you have, brine the bird (directions are below), then roast it in a 325°F oven for 20 to 30 minutes per pound until it's done enough for the table. Switch to the smoker and smoke the bird for 2 or 3 hours, or longer for deeper flavor. Cool it promptly and store it as described in the detailed recipe below.

Smoke-Cookers and Barbecues: The instruction booklet provided by the manufacturer is the best guide, but here are some general pointers:

The *smoke-cookers* found in many if not most backyards today are much more versatile than specialized box smokers, as they produce enough heat for grilling as well as the more moderate heat needed for roasting or smoke-cooking big hunks of meat or poultry. For smoke-cooking, a temperature between 225° and 300°F does the job beautifully; if your appliance lacks a thermometer, set an oven thermometer near the meat and check it occasionally. Regulate the heat and smoke in the way recommended by the manufacturer and continue the smoke-cooking until the poultry tests done (see the detailed recipe below).

A *covered barbecue grill* can also be used for smoke-cooking: Place the coals (charcoal, not briquettes) well away from the bird, either in a distant circle or in two bands set well apart, and roast the poultry slowly (between 225° and 300°F), turning it occasionally. When you judge the bird to be about half done, begin adding a few soaked and drained hickory or other smoking chips to the coals from time to time. Continue the smoke-cooking until the poultry tests done (see details that follow).

All this isn't much more complicated than grilling a few steaks, although it takes longer. There is a wide choice of smoke-producing chips and sawdust, sometimes sold in assortments that make for easy experimentation: hickory, maple, cherry, or maple plus corncobs, or another kind of smoking chips altogether, such as pungent mesquite.

I recommend the brining formula on the facing page if you'd like to cure the poultry lightly before smoking it—this improves both texture and flavor. However, if time is limited, the bird can just be rubbed generously with salt and pepper (some like to add a little brown sugar), then with vegetable oil, and smoke-cooked at once.

Stovetop Shortcut

Owners of the small box smokers called "stovetop smokers"—they may be quite small, or large enough for a small chicken—can prepare smoked poultry on the fast track. Rub the portion of poultry with salt, pepper, and a little oil and bake it, basting often, in a 325°F oven until three-quarters done. (When a thick portion is tested, the juices will still be pale pink.) Fire up the smoker according to the manufacturer's directions and smoke-cook the chicken until done, about 15 minutes for a small half, a little longer for a thicker piece. Cool, store, and serve as described in the recipe.

Bay Leaves Sorted Out

Recipe writers mean the true Mediterranean bay, the oval-leaved Laurus nobilis, *which has a flavor both sweetly aromatic and resinous, when they call for a bay leaf. Also called "bay," however, is the California-grown tree* Umbellularia californica, *with long slender leaves, which has its admirers despite tasting a bit like the fragrance of eucalyptus. Both sorts may be labeled simply "bay leaves," so check the leaf shape if you want one kind and not the other.*

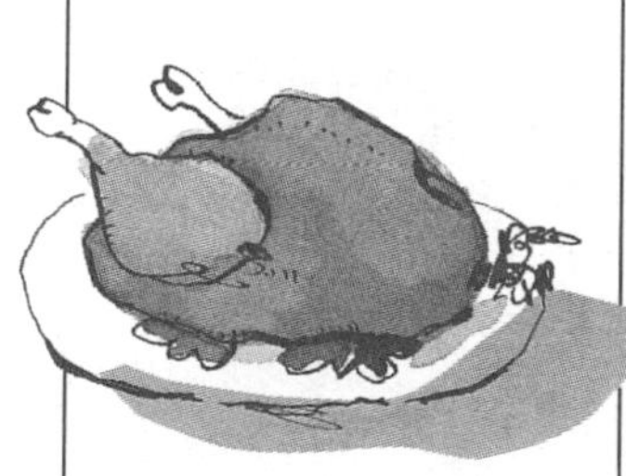

A Curing Brine & General Smoke-Cooking Method

1 whole chicken, small whole turkey, or whole turkey breast
Enough cold water to cover the poultry

FOR EACH QUART OF WATER:
3 tablespoons (packed) dark brown sugar or 2 tablespoons (packed) brown sugar plus 1 tablespoon honey
¼ cup noniodized fine salt or ⅓ cup coarse (kosher) salt
2 generous pinches of freshly ground white pepper
Pinch of Powdered Bay Leaves (page 195) or a medium bay leaf, crumbled
Vegetable oil

1. Rinse the poultry, cleaning the cavity of a whole bird thoroughly. Pull off all possible fat that can be reached. Drop the bird into a plastic bag. Tie the neck of the bag, pressing out the air, then drop it into a bowl or crock that will hold it and still leave room at the top. Run cold water into the bowl until the bag, held with the tied neck above the surface, is covered by at least an inch. Remove the bird and de-bag it.

2. Measure the water, return it to the bowl, and add the listed brine ingredients, multiplying them as necessary. Stir until the sugar and salt have dissolved. Drop the bird into the brine, cover it with a small plate to hold it under the surface, and refrigerate for at least a day, better two. If you think of it, turn it once or twice.

3. When you are ready for smoke-cooking, remove the bird from the brine, rinse it briefly, and dry all surfaces thoroughly, giving particular attention to the cavity of a whole bird. Rub the outside lightly with vegetable oil. Truss a whole bird as you would for roasting. (That is, skewer the neck skin neatly over the opening, fold the wings behind the back, and tie the drumstick tips together with string, looping the string about the tail and tying it firmly.)

4. Following the general pointers above as well as the smoker or grill manufacturer's suggestions, slow-cook and smoke the poultry until a meat thermometer inserted in the center of the thickest part of the thigh or breast registers 165° to 170°F. If the skin appears dry at any point, brush it lightly with a little more oil. The time needed for smoking will vary according to the size of the bird, its temperature when cooking begins, and the ambient temperature in the cooker. (Try to maintain a temperature between 225° and 300°F). As a timing guide, count on about 3 hours for a medium-size roasting chicken and proportionately more for larger specimens. In general, slower rather than faster smoke-cooking makes for more succulent poultry.

5. Cool the smoked poultry to room temperature for immediate serving, or cool it completely and wrap it in foil or plastic for the refrigerator or freezer-wrap it for freezer storage. Expect to keep it for up to 5 days, refrigerated, or for up to 3 months frozen.

6. *To serve:* For the best flavor and texture, serve smoked poultry at room temperature. (Refrigerate any leftovers promptly.) If it has been frozen, thaw it in the refrigerator, then wrap it loosely in foil and freshen it in a low oven (325°F) for about half an hour. Cool to room temperature before serving. Again, refrigerate leftovers promptly and plan to use them within a day or so.

CHILI BRICKS

For chili aficionados, here's a way to have on hand a time-saving, space-saving, industrial-strength supply of chili con carne (no beans) for occasions when there isn't time for a slow-simmered masterpiece from scratch. Just extract a brick of concentrated chili from the freezer, thaw it, add liquid, make the stew piping hot over low heat, check the seasonings, and there you are.

This recipe makes mildly hot chili. For more piquancy, use more chili seasoning at the outset, or add a bit of cayenne (ground hot red pepper) or ground chile of an extra-hot variety to the pot along with the custom-made chili seasoning. Hot pepper sauce(s) on the table let the eater season to taste at the moment of truth.

One school of chiliheads serves seasoned pinto beans on the side; another group holds with folding them into the chili. Take your pick, or accompany the piquant stew with hot brown rice or even plain pasta.

2/3 cup bacon drippings, melted beef fat, or vegetable oil
4 pounds trimmed lean beef, cut into 1/2-inch cubes
2 pounds trimmed lean pork, cut into 1/2-inch cubes
4 cups chopped white or yellow onions (3 to 4 large)
8 or more large cloves garlic, peeled and minced
2 or 3 sweet red (bell) peppers, roasted, peeled, seeded, and diced (see page 60, Roasted Red Antipasto Peppers), optional
1/2 cup tomato paste
6 cups plain canned beef broth or beer, or a combination
3/4 cup Custom-Made Chili Seasoning (page 184), or more or less to taste
1 1/2 tablespoons salt, or to taste

Makes 2 bricks, 6 to 8 servings each

CHILI COOL-OFF

In Cooking: A Dictionary, *Henry Beard and Roy McKie define the chile pepper as an "extremely hot-tasting plant of the genus* Capsicum, *usually added in powdered form to a dish made of shredded cattle."*

The two wags could have added that "hot-tasting" understates the case for people born with low tolerance for piquancy but a liking for chili. For them, it's necessary to know how to cool a burning tongue when the chile-seasoned shredded cattle is too incendiary. Some swear by cold beer (water doesn't work), but it seems that cold milk is the best cooler for a scorched palate. (Milk proteins interact helpfully with capsaicin, the stuff that makes chile peppers hot, hotter, or hottest.) Evidently, chili parlors like those I remember in pre-chic California were onto something when they offered cold milk as the beverage of choice with their bowls of red.

CHILE OR CHILI?

Both spellings are used, sometimes discriminatorily, sometimes not. Wordsmiths who are fussy about usage point out that chile designates any of many chile peppers, all native American plants, nearly all very hot, but all possessing distinguishing characteristics to the palate of a true chilihead. Some, unpersuaded, write "chili pepper." Chili or chili con carne rightly means the dish of that name, which is of course seasoned with chiles (or chilies, if you insist). Chili powder is what you put into chili, but the powder is based on chiles.

1. Heat the fat in a large heavy pot (cast iron for choice). Add enough of the meat to cover the bottom and stir over medium-high heat until all surfaces have lost their pinkness and are very lightly browned. Remove and reserve the batch and repeat until all the meat has been sautéed and set aside. Add the onions and garlic and cook over low heat, stirring frequently, until softened and pale gold, about 10 minutes. Return the meat and any juices to the pot. Stir in the roasted peppers (if using), the tomato paste, and enough broth to barely cover the meat. Bring to a boil, lower the heat, and simmer the meat very slowly, uncovered, for 1 hour.

2. Add the chili powder and salt and continue to simmer for another hour, adding any remaining broth and additional water, if needed to prevent sticking, as the chili cooks. Toward the end of cooking the consistency should be dense and the meat very tender. Taste for seasoning, adding more chili powder and/or salt if needed, remembering that the flavor will develop as the chili rests; it should mellow at least overnight before use. If you're making bricks, go to step 4.

3. ***To serve:*** After the chili has been refrigerated at least overnight (it can be kept this way for up to a week), remove any surface fat, if you wish, and add liquid (beef broth, beer, water, or tomato juice) if it's needed to make chili of the consistency you like, then reheat it slowly.

4. ***To store in brick form:*** Spoon the chili into two foil-lined 6-cup loaf pans, cool, wrap, and freeze solid. Remove the bricks from the pans, overwrap them, and store them in the freezer for up to 3 months. Thaw the chili slowly in the refrigerator or defrost it fast (unwrapped) in the microwave, then add liquid and heat. As freezing can affect the level of seasoning, taste again and adjust the seasonings before serving.

GONE FISHING

Seafood Feasting

Fishy delicacies of several sorts, some to be found in good delicatessens and some to be met with only in fine restaurants (unless you make them yourself), are marshaled in this section to pique the palate of anyone who admires seafood, whether with fins, legs, or a shell.

Seafood sausages and pâtés have come into their own since the publication of recipes for the several other fishy dishes that are reprised here from *Fancy Pantry*. This culinary good news is celebrated by the first recipe, for a compound of shrimp, salmon, and scallops that can either be stuffed into sausage casings or baked in small molds as individual pâtés.

You'll also find a splendid Gravlax (dill-cured salmon), together with a variation made with mackerel, and a classic mustard sauce excellent with both; delicate Potted Shrimp; and Salmon Pastrami, an improbable but delectable melding of the traditions of spicy cured beef and smoked fish.

Among the *Fancy Pantry* recipes that play a return engagement are Marinated or Pickled Salmon or Herring, offered both "straight" and in cream sauce; salt-cured and smoked fish; and directions for turning your own or store-bought smoked fish into a spread for canapés or sandwiches.

Seafood Sausages or Little Seafood Pâtés

Delicate seafood sausages have become deservedly popular in circles where creative chefs make them with the freshest possible seafood and the most cunning complementary ingredients. Putting together the delicious compound of scallops, salmon, and shrimp that follow is a relatively straightforward home-kitchen project, and either the sausages or the miniature pâtés are sure to delight as a change from meaty sausages, however delicate those may be.

This recipe, perfected in the kitchen of friend and talented chef Chris Styler, is a double-barreled one—you may make pearly sausages studded with bright nuggets of shrimp and salmon and flecked with parsley, or you may opt to bake the sausage mixture in individual ramekins or loaf pans to make pâtés to serve as the first course of a special dinner or as the main dish at luncheon.

¼ pound shrimp, peeled and deveined
¼ pound skinless fillet of salmon
1 tablespoon Cognac or other good brandy
1¼ pounds sea scallops, well chilled
1 large egg white
¼ cup (packed) fresh parsley leaves, chopped fine
½ to 1 teaspoon grated or minced lemon zest (outer peel only, no white pith), to taste
½ teaspoon salt, or more to taste
⅛ teaspoon freshly ground white pepper
Pinch of freshly grated nutmeg
Pinch of ground hot red (cayenne) pepper
½ cup heavy cream, very cold
½ cup unseasoned very fine, dry white bread crumbs

FOR SAUSAGES:
About 4 feet of sausage casings, soaked in cold water to cover while the sausage mixture is being made
½ cup water or ¼ cup each water and dry white wine
2 tablespoons sweet (unsalted) butter

Makes about 2 pounds sausages (8 or more 4-inch sausages) or 8 seafood pâtés (about ½ cup each)

1. Cut the shrimp and salmon into ¼-inch dice. Toss the seafood with the Cognac and refrigerate it for at least 30 minutes or up to 3 hours.

2. Dry the scallops well on paper towels, place in a food processor, and process until coarsely pureed. Add the egg white, parsley, lemon zest, salt, white pepper, nutmeg, and ground hot red pepper. Process until very smooth, scraping down the sides of the workbowl once or twice. With the machine running, add the heavy cream in a thin stream. Scrape down the workbowl again and process until the cream has been incorporated. Scrape the mixture into a bowl and fold in the diced shrimp and salmon and the bread crumbs. Cover and chill thoroughly, at least 1 hour and for as long as 3 hours.

3. ***To check the seasonings*** (this is an optional step): Spoon 2 or 3 tablespoons of the sausage filling onto a square of plastic wrap, making a small cigar shape. Roll the mixture up in the plastic and twist the ends of the wrap firmly. Drop the mini-sausage into simmering water and cook for about 8 minutes, or until the "sausage" is very firm. Let it cool a few minutes, then remove the plastic wrap, taste the "sausage," and adjust the seasonings of the sausage mixture if necessary.

Seafood Sausages

1. Remove the sausage casings from the soaking water and rinse them thoroughly. To do this, fit one end of a section of casing over the faucet and turn on the cold water very slowly, increasing the flow as the casing straightens out. Note where there are any tears (small holes are no problem); if there are larger holes, cut the casing where they occur and use the good portions, or choose another length of casing. Drain the casings well.

2. ***To fill the casings:*** Follow the manufacturer's directions for a grinder attachment or other machine designed for stuffing sausages. Otherwise, choose a large pastry bag fitted with a large plain tip. Fill the bag about three-fourths full with the seafood mixture and fold over the top. Lay the filled bag on its side and work about 2 inches of casing slowly onto the tip. Tie the opposite, open end of the casing firmly closed with a short length of string.

Pipe the sausage mixture into the casing, filling it loosely—it should be only a little more than three-quarters full. Don't worry if the filling is unevenly distributed—you'll adjust that in a minute. Just be sure not to overfill the casing or the sausages will burst during cooking.

When the casing holds enough filling to make as many 4-inch sausages as its length will accommodate, slide the remaining casing off the tip and tie it with string where the filling ends. Press and stroke the casing on a work surface to distribute the filling uniformly but not allowing the casing to be filled more than about three-quarters. Lop off any leftover casing. Continue filling lengths of casing until all the mixture has been used. To divide the long sausages into 4-inch lengths,

Freshness Is All

Don't even think of making seafood sausages unless you're proud to bursting of the quality of the seafood available to you. Salmon, scallops, and shrimp must all be impeccable when sniffed inquisitively. Using the olfactory nerve (well, all right, nose) is still the best way to judge freshness of any item except a whole fish, whose bright eye and bright gills are the indicators to look for.

twist the casing several times between sausages. Optionally, tie over each twist with a short bit of string.

3. Coil the sausages on a plate and pierce each link once or twice with the tip of a sharp knife (this provides for the release of steam during cooking.) Cover with waxed paper or plastic wrap and refrigerate until cooking time, preferably no more than a few hours. If it's necessary to make the sausages a day ahead, poach them immediately as described in step 4.

4. ***To parcook sausages for brief storage:*** Place the sausages in a heavy skillet or sauté pan and add lukewarm (not hot) water to cover. Cover with a round of waxed paper cut to fit inside the pan. Bring to a simmer slowly over medium heat, then lower the heat and simmer gently for 10 minutes, basting the sausages once or twice. (Or you can turn them very gently after they have become firm.) Leave to cool in the water for a few minutes, then drain and refrigerate, covered. The sausages may be refrigerated for up to 2 days, or they may be freezer-wrapped and frozen for up to a month.

To complete the cooking of parcooked sausages, thaw them in the refrigerator if frozen. Follow the cooking directions in step 7, cooking them gently until they are hot through and lightly browned and glazed, which will take less time than for raw sausages.

5. ***To cook the sausages:*** Pour ½ cup water or ¼ cup each water and white wine into a 12-inch skillet. Add the butter, cut into thin slices, and place the pan over medium heat. Coil the sausages into a spiral and place the coil in the skillet. Cover partially and cook for 5 minutes over medium heat; beware of too much heat, or the sausages may burst. Remove the cover, turn the sausage coil over, and continue cooking until the liquid has evaporated and the butter begins to sizzle, about 8 minutes. (If the liquid vanishes in less than 8 minutes or so, add a little hot water.) When the butter sizzles, turn the heat to low and brown the sausages lightly, about 2 minutes, then turn the whole works and brown the second side about 2 minutes. Let the sausages rest in their pan, off the heat, for 5 minutes before cutting them apart for serving.

6. Serve the sausages hot, accompanied by a simple sauce. Try sour cream or lightly whipped heavy cream blended with some well-drained horseradish and a speck of Dijon mustard. For garlic lovers, a little aïoli (see the Index) would do nothing but good, and some would vote for hollandaise, especially if steamed asparagus and/or tiny boiled new potatoes were also on the plate. Other possibilities are Mustard Sauce for Gravlax or Dill-Cured Mackerel (page 33), with its fresh dill, or mayonnaise blended with a generous proportion of drained and pureed Roasted Red Antipasto Peppers (page 60).

Wise Words

Food for pleasure, and not just nourishment, is best cooked in one's own kitchen and eaten with the feet under one's own table.
—Nicolas Freeling, The Kitchen

Little Seafood Pâtés

1. Make the sausage mixture and chill it as directed.

2. Preheat the oven to 325° F, with a shelf in the center position.

3. Oil lightly 8 ramekins (6-ounce size) or small heatproof glass custard cups or miniature loaf pans of about the same capacity. Divide the seafood mixture among the ramekins, smoothing the tops. Cut pieces of parchment or waxed paper to fit the tops of the pâtés; brush a piece lightly with oil and press it, oiled side down, directly over one of the pâtés.

4. Place the pâtés in a baking pan at least 2 inches deep and set the pan in the oven. Pour in enough hot water to reach halfway up the sides of the ramekins. Bake 25 minutes, or until a knife blade emerges clean after piercing the center of a pâté.

5. Let stand 5 to 10 minutes, then run a thin paring knife around the edges before unmolding each pâté onto a plate. Serve hot with one of the sauces suggested above as platemates for the sausages.

Gravlax (Dill-Cured Salmon) & Dill-Cured Mackerel (Gravmakrell)

A cut of choice salmon, a fat bunch of fresh dill, a seasoning or two, and some time in the refrigerator produce a buttery-textured seafood delicacy that's hard to beat, even in its native Scandinavia. Served with the traditional mustard sauce, gravlax (sometimes spelled *gravad lax*) is a fixture of the classic smörgasbord, and at dinner it's a starter that wins the hearts of even inveterate smoked-salmon partisans.

Fillet(s) of fresh salmon, backbone out, 2 to 2½ pounds, or use a center cut, split and boned
3 tablespoons coarse (kosher) salt
2 tablespoons (packed) light or dark brown sugar
2 teaspoons white peppercorns
1 to 2 teaspoons whole coriander seed, to taste
3 tablespoons aquavit or vodka
A generous bunch of fresh dill

Makes 2 to 2½ pounds

1. Scrape any stray scales from the skin side of the salmon and wipe the fish with a paper towel (don't rinse it).

2. Combine the salt, sugar, peppercorns, and coriander seed in a small spice mill or a mortar and run the mill or crush the ingredients with a pestle until medium-fine, not a powder. Add the aquavit and stir to make a paste. Rub all surfaces of the salmon with the mixture.

3. Trim the roots from the dill, sort and rinse the sprigs, and shake them free of excess water. Chop the dill coarsely. Select a glass, enamel, or ceramic dish that will hold the salmon snugly. Spread half of the dill in the dish, then lay the seasoned salmon on the dill, skin side down. Spread the remaining dill over the fish. Slip the dish into a large plastic food bag, or cover it loosely with plastic. Set a section of board or a baking pan or some other flat object on top of the salmon and weight it with cans of food or capped jars of water weighing 2 to 3 pounds.

4. Set the whole works in the refrigerator and marinate the salmon for at least 2 or as long as 4 days, turning the fish over and basting it with its juices daily. You can dispense with the weights after 24 hours. A piece of fish about 1½ inches thick seems perfect, to me, after 36 hours, but you can sample at any point and form your own opinion; some experts cure gravlax for only 12 to 18 hours.

5. When you find the gravlax seasoned to taste, scrape off and discard the seasonings and pour off the brine. Wrap the fish in fresh plastic and keep it in the coldest part of the refrigerator, where it will keep for at least a week from the beginning of the cure. (For longer storage, I've experimented with the suggestion of slicing surplus gravlax and storing it in olive or vegetable oil to cover. This works very well, adding 10 days to 2 weeks to its refrigerator life. The oil must be blotted from the slices with paper towels before the salmon is served.)

6. ***To serve:*** Lay the gravlax skin side down on a cutting board. Using a long, very sharp knife, cut across the grain into thin, wide bias slices, turning the knife at the end of each cut to free the slice from the skin. Serve with the mustard sauce below, or with sour cream into which a little vinegar, sugar, and chopped dill have been stirred, or simply with generous wedges of lemon and plenty of dark rye bread or pumpernickel and sweet butter.

Dill-Cured Mackerel (Gravmakrell)

Treated like salmon, very fresh mackerel turns into a delicious variation of gravlax. Season 2 or 3 cleaned and split mackerel as described for salmon, then arrange them on a bed of dill with dill between the halves and on top. Proceed as for salmon, but cure the fish for about 12 hours only. Scrape off the seasonings and serve with the mustard sauce on the facing page, or wrap and refrigerate for a few days.

Other Ways to Serve Your Gravlax

Do as they do in Sweden and have gravlax with hot potatoes for supper, or offer it at lunch with a potato salad, or make superb sandwiches on buttered grainy bread. Dice or sliver a generous helping of gravlax and toss the pieces with freshly boiled thin pasta plus cubed cream cheese, minced dill, fresh-ground pepper, and a few drops of lemon juice; add a little of the hot pasta water to give the "sauce" its correct consistency, and feast on a dilly stand-in for pasta with smoked salmon.

Gin, Again

Instead of rubbing aquavit or vodka into the salmon or mackerel you're going to cure with dill, try substituting gin. Very good, and a handy substitution when the liquor cupboard isn't overflowing with variety.

Mustard Sauce for Gravlax or Dill-Cured Mackerel

3 tablespoons mild mustard, Dijon or other
1½ tablespoons sugar
2 tablespoons white wine vinegar or Asian rice vinegar
½ teaspoon salt, or more to taste (optional)
½ cup corn or other vegetable oil
Water, if necessary
3 tablespoons chopped fresh dill or 2 tablespoons dried dill weed

Makes about 1 cup

Whisk together the mustard, sugar, vinegar, and optional salt. Add the oil slowly, whisking constantly. Add the dill. Taste and adjust seasonings, adding more mustard, sugar, vinegar, or salt if indicated. The sauce may be made a day or two ahead. Whisk again before serving.

Cheatin' version when calories count: Blend the mustard, sugar (or the equivalent amount of a sugar substitute), vinegar, and optional salt with ⅔ cup low-fat or fat-free mayonnaise; taste and add more mustard and/or vinegar and sugar if needed. (This will depend on the seasoning of the mayonnaise base.) If too thick—the sauce should be pourable—add a little water. Add the dill.

Potted Shrimp

Starting with very fresh shrimp home-cooked in the shell is the best point of departure for this classic delicacy, but *good* cooked shrimp from the fishmonger may be a more realistic option. (Canned or frozen shrimp are not recommended.)

This delicate paste is good around the clock, not just with champagne for a celebration—the British have been known to serve potted shrimp with toast as part of a lavish breakfast. Try a slice or a wedge of this buttery composition on slices from a good brown loaf (and more sweet butter, if you want) to complement a large green salad for lunch.

Seasonings can be varied. One compatible addition is a touch of anchovy paste or mashed anchovy fillets, 1 to 2 teaspoons to this quantity of shrimp. Instead of the hot red pepper and white pepper, add finely minced hot green jalapeño pepper—I'd start with 1 teaspoonful and put in more only after tasting, remembering that the hotness of the pepper will become more apparent as the seasonings kick in during the mellowing period.

1 pound medium or small shrimp, in shells (to make 2 cups cooked and shelled)
1 tablespoon fresh lemon juice
1 cup (2 sticks) sweet (unsalted) butter
Scant ½ teaspoon freshly grated nutmeg or ground mace, or scant ¼ teaspoon of each
Pinch or two ground hot red (cayenne) pepper
Pinch or two freshly ground white pepper
½ teaspoon salt
¼ cup Clarified Butter (recipe follows)
Cucumber slices, dill sprigs, sprays of watercress, for garnish

Makes about 2½ cups

1. Line a small loaf pan (about 6 x 3 inches) with plastic wrap. Alternatively, line with plastic a straight-sided bowl of about 3-cup capacity.

2. Drop the shrimp into lightly salted boiling water to cover, return to a boil, lower the heat, cover, and cook for 3 minutes (for medium shrimp) by the clock. Remove from the heat and pour into a colander to cool. When cool enough to handle, remove the shells and, if you wish, any veins. (Some individual shrimp will have veins, some won't). Dice half of the shrimp small (¼ inch) and chop the rest coarsely. Toss with the lemon juice.

3. Melt the butter in a sauté pan over low heat with the nutmeg, hot pepper, white pepper, and salt, swirling it in the pan until quite hot but not anywhere near browning. Add the shrimp, stir to coat, and heat for a moment or two more, stirring a little, until barely warmed through.

4. Let the mixture cool slightly, then taste it carefully for seasoning and add more drops of lemon juice, or more nutmeg, hot pepper, white pepper, or salt as your tastebuds suggest. (The seasonings will strengthen later, remember.) Scrape the shrimp and butter into the prepared pan or bowl and smooth the top. Set in the refrigerator until completely cold.

5. Melt the clarified butter and pour it over the potted shrimp, making sure it covers the top completely if you plan to keep the paste for a few days. (This step may be skipped if you're going to serve the shrimp within 2 days.) Cover closely with foil and chill at least overnight before serving. The potted shrimp will keep in the refrigerator for at least a week if the butter topping has not been broken, or in the freezer, removed from the container and freezer-packaged, for up to 2 months. If frozen, thaw in the refrigerator. Don't plan to refreeze any leftovers. Leftovers will keep in the refrigerator for 2 or 3 days.

6. *To serve:* Turn the potted shrimp out on a plate, remove the plastic wrap, and garnish with whatever strikes your fancy—thin-sliced

To Devein or Not to Devein

In a given batch of shrimp, some specimens will have veins (they're dimly visible through the translucent flesh) while others won't. To get rid of veins, hold a peeled shrimp between the fingers, back upward. With a small, very sharp knife, cut ¼ inch deep the length of the back and use the tip of pry out the vein—no special gadget is needed. If you feel you should rinse the shrimp, do so in a small bowl of water, not under the tap, in order to preserve flavor.

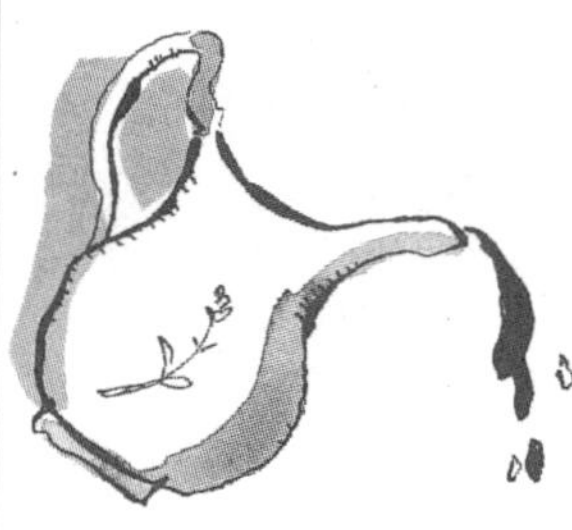

cucumber, sprigs of dill, or watercress sprays, for instance. Slice and serve with thin-cut rye or whole-wheat bread or crisp thin toast and, if you like, wedges of lemon.

Clarified Butter

If you clarify a pound of butter at a time, you'll always have a supply on hand in the refrigerator. It is the very best fat for sautéing delicate foods, both for its flavor and because it won't burn easily (unlike unclarified butter), and it's indispensable for sealing pots of meat or fish paste such as Potted Shrimp.

Makes about 1½ cups

1. Place 1 pound (4 sticks) sweet (unsalted) butter in a heavy saucepan and set it over low heat. Heat, checking from time to time to make sure it isn't heating too fast, for 15 minutes. It will bubble and look foamy, showing that its moisture is being cooked away. Simmer the butter for 20 to 25 minutes in all without stirring or disturbing it. It has been clarified enough when the boiling action lessens and the foamy top crust begins to look dry. Be alert not to let the butter get hot enough to brown even the slightest bit.

2. Remove the butter from the heat and leave it for 5 to 10 minutes to settle. Skim off the top crust, reserving it, if you like, to season vegetables (it has a lot of flavor). Carefully pour the clear golden liquid into a completely dry jar or crock; stop pouring before the sediment in the pan is disturbed. (These good dregs, like the foam, can season vegetables, if you are of the waste-not school.)

3. Cool the clarified butter until it begins to congeal, cover it airtight, and refrigerate it. It keeps indefinitely.

Salmon Pastrami

The Alice who famously visited Wonderland learned on her travels that words meant just what the speaker wanted them to mean; so Alice, for one, would not have been surprised to discover that salmon is being turned into something called by the same name—pastrami—as garlicky, smoky, spicy beef pastrami. Salmon pastrami, wherever it started (in California?) is a delicious morsel, and here is a good way to create it.

Producing this savory stuff at home requires smoking equipment, which is discussed in connection with Smoked Chicken or Turkey (see the Index). The directions here are for a covered charcoal grill. If another kind of outdoor equipment is used, consult the manufacturer's directions; be sure to watch the heat level and provide plenty of smoke. Following the main recipe is an outline for preparing the pastrami in a stovetop smoker. For either smoking method, it's helpful to have an instant-read thermometer to check doneness.

This is great stand-up party food as well as a delicious starter, so the recipe produces a generous chunk.

A salmon fillet, skin on, about 1½ inches thick and weighing about 2 pounds
6 cups water
3 tablespoons coarse (kosher) salt
3 tablespoons finely chopped garlic
2 tablespoons (packed) light or dark brown sugar
A few dashes Tabasco or other hot red pepper sauce, optional
Vegetable oil
6 tablespoons coarsely cracked coriander seed
4 tablespoons coarsely cracked black peppercorns
1 teaspoon ground ginger, optional

Makes about 2 pounds

1. Inspect the salmon and remove any fine bones (use tweezers) or scales the fishmonger may have missed. Lay the fillet flat in a nonreactive container just large enough to permit it to be covered comfortably by brine. In a medium-size bowl, stir together the water, salt, garlic, brown sugar, and optional hot pepper sauce. Pour over the fish, cover tightly with plastic wrap, and refrigerate. Brine the fish for at least 4 hours or as long as 6 hours, turning it over once or twice.

2. Lift the fish from the brine, drain it thoroughly, and pat it dry. Rub the fish with a few drops of vegetable oil, then place it on a work surface. Strain at least a tablespoonful of the garlic from the brine and mash it with the coriander seed, peppercorns, and optional ginger. Press the mixture firmly into all surfaces of the fish.

3. Allow the fillet to come to room temperature on a cake rack while preparing a charcoal (not briquette) fire in a covered grill, with the air vents open. Soak in water a double handful of mild-flavored wood smoking chips—hickory, mesquite, mixed maple and corncobs, or whatever type you prefer. (We like hickory here.)

4. When the bed of coals is well covered with gray ash, check the temperature at grill level; you want a reading of 200°F or a few degrees less. Grease the grill. (If you possess a cage-type fish grilling basket,

Coriander Come-On

Coriander seed is a revelation to tasters who think of "coriander" as the green herb with a distinctive savor that's either adored or detested by those who meet it for the first time. The ripening seeds develop a distinctive citrus fragrance that makes them a delightful addition to baked goods, pickling brines, and, of course, classic pastrami. Other recipes to look up in the Index, if you're a fan, are Coriander Seed & Honey Jelly and Tomato Jam with Ginger and Coriander.

grease that too—it makes handling the fish simpler.) Close the vents. Lay the fish (in the cage grill, if used) on the grill, strew the soaked chips on the coals, and close the cover at once; you want a lot of smoke. Smoke-cook the fillet for 5 minutes if it's 1½ inches thick, a couple of minutes longer if it's thicker; turn it carefully and cook the second side the same length of time. Check the internal temperature with an instant-read thermometer; I find 120°F to be about right; the inside should be on the rare side and the outside somewhat moist under the spicy crust. If necessary, smoke the pastrami a minute or two longer and recheck the thermometer reading. Remove the pastrami to a sheet of foil, skin side down, and let it cool to lukewarm. Wrap it snugly in the foil, place it on a plate or pan, and weight it with something flat and heavy (a loaf pan weighted with a can or two of food will do the trick). Refrigerate the weighted fish for several hours or up to 24 hours before serving.

***5.** To serve:* Lay the fish skin side down on a cutting board. Optionally, scrape off most of the spicy coating. Use a very sharp knife to cut not-too-thin slices slightly on the bias, cutting all the way through the skin (which is good to eat) or cutting the fish free of the skin after slicing. Either place the sliced pastrami on buttered pumpernickel or other firm bread to make open sandwiches, or arrange the slices on plates and pass homemade mayonnaise blended with a good deal of mustard. (The Mustard Sauce for Gravlax or Dill-Cured Mackerel—see the Index—is good with this, too.) Refrigerate any leftovers promptly and use within 2 or 3 days. Unsliced, well-chilled pastrami keeps for several days. Any crumbly scraps make a delicious sandwich filling when mashed into cream cheese with a few drops of lemon juice.

Been Fishing, Caught Fish

Smoking the catch is a time-honored way of preserving it, especially when luck has been good and the fisherperson has run out of neighbors willing to accept a share. Smoking is an especially good way to add allure to mackerel and bluefish, because their natural oiliness makes them good for smoking, although it isn't to every taste when they are served fresh. Note that smoked fish freezes well, too.

Smoked Salmon Pastrami on the Stovetop

To use a stovetop smoker and fine smoking sawdust, adjust the recipe as follows

Use salmon fillets no more than 1 inch thick (the thin end of an average-size fish, filleted, is just right). If the fillets are too long for your smoker, divide them and plan to smoke in batches, resupplying the smoker with sawdust for each batch.

Brine the fish, following the main recipe. Set up the smoker with plenty of sawdust and smoke the fillet without turning it for about 8 minutes, starting the timing after traces of smoke appear. Check for progress with an instant-reading thermometer inserted into the thickest part of the fillet; the "done" reading is 120°F (overcooking will cause the fish to fall apart). Until that temperature is reached, continue smoking the fish, checking every couple of minutes. I find 15 minutes, total, is about par for the course.

Marinated or Pickled Salmon or Herring

Both of these sea-born preparations rate high among European seafood delicacies in general and New York–style "appetizers" in particular. Marinated or pickled salmon, also called marinated or pickled lox, is a specialty offered by relatively few purveyors, whereas pickled herring is widely available. However, the herring is also worth preparing at home if you want custom quality, so directions for herring follow the three steps for marinated salmon—salt-curing the fish, pickling it in spiced vinegar with a tangle of sweet onions, and adding a sour-cream sauce.

For the salmon, you can skip the curing step if you wish to start with store-bought belly lox (the choicest cut) or other salted salmon, being sure you don't get by mistake the smoked salmon that is sometimes loosely but erroneously called lox. Salt-cured herring can be purchased, or you can salt your own.

Whether you start from scratch or with the pickling stage, both pickled salmon and herring will be choice, and they keep well enough to reward you for the time (but little work) required. Although you must make them well ahead of time, at each stage of the process the fish is keepable: Salmon or herring packed in salt keeps well for months (connoisseurs insist that either is at its best only after 3 to 6 months' salting). Pickled, either fish keeps for a few weeks, and after being "creamed," herring or salmon can be stored for an additional week.

Salt-Cured Salmon

If you'd like to start from scratch and salt-cure your own supply of salmon to be pickled at a future date, you need an impeccably fresh fish or two, scaled, beheaded, and split and with the backbone removed; or you can use only the less choice portion of the fish lying between the "steak" and the tail, split and with the tail and backbone removed.

About 2 pounds, or amount needed, pure (noniodized) pickling or dairy salt
4 quarts cold water
5 to 6 pounds split and boned very fresh salmon, weight after trimming

Makes 3 to 4 pounds

1. Dissolve 1 cup of the salt in the 4 quarts of water in a large nonreactive bowl (stainless steel is okay) or crock. Rinse the salmon pieces,

Salt Salmon

Salt-cured Pacific salmon was a staple food in Alaska and the Pacific Northwest from the mid-nineteenth century onward, and shipping the salt fish to the rest of the country, to Hawaii (where it was, and is, called lomi-lomi), and to Europe was an early and important industry. Northwest-

erners fixed their native salt salmon in various ways after freshening it in cold water; it could be steamed, then served with a sauce, perhaps melted butter and dill, or a cream sauce with chopped hard-cooked eggs folded in. The salmon was also poached, flaked, and creamed or scalloped, and it was made into hearty soups and chowders. Back East and in Europe, people didn't need to be told twice that they could pickle the Northwestern salt salmon in such good ways as the one detailed here.

add them to the brine, and soak for 1 hour to free them of diffused blood and to prepare them for curing.

2. Rinse the pieces of fish and drain them well. Make a few shallow slashes about 2 inches apart in the flesh side of the thickest area.

3. Choose a flat-bottomed ceramic, enameled, plastic, or stainless-steel container that will hold the fillets in layers with depth to spare; if the fillets are too long for the container, cut them in halves or thirds. Spread a generous ¼ inch of salt in the dish. Make a layer of fillets on the salt, skin side down and slightly apart. Cover the fish pieces with a layer of salt, rubbing salt into the slashes, and fill the spaces between the pieces with salt. Make more layers of fish and salt, placing each succeeding layer at right angles to the preceding one; for the final layer of fish, place the skin side up and finish with salt, being sure all spaces are filled. The total quantity of salt needed will depend on the shape of the container and the size of the fish pieces. Cover the dish loosely with plastic wrap, then add a light weight (a glass or ceramic pie plate or baking dish, for instance) to press the fish down slightly. Slip the whole works into a large plastic bag and close it, or overwrap the container with plastic. Refrigerate the container for 2 weeks, checking every few days to assure that the fish is covered with the brine that will have formed. If necessary, rearrange the pieces to keep them submerged and re-weight them.

4. Drain off the brine, measuring it to discover how much fresh solution you'll need to replace it. Wash and dry the container and repack the fish in it, making layers as before, but scattering salt only lightly between the layers. Make the necessary quantity of fresh brine, using ¼ cup of salt to each quart of water. Boil the brine for 3 minutes, cool it completely, and pour it over the fish to cover the pieces. Cover and refrigerate the fish as before.

5. The salt-cured salmon will be ready to use 2 weeks after step 2 has been completed, but it will be all the better if left to cure longer. If you remove a share of the fish, transfer the remaining pieces, with brine to cover, to a smaller container. It will keep under refrigeration for at least 6 months.

Marinated or Pickled Salmon

This second-stage recipe gets down to the actual pickling after the salt curing. Store-bought salt-cured salmon may be used if you haven't cured your own.

The spiced pickling liquid for this step is sufficient for 4 to 6 cups of fish pieces, plus 2 to 3 cups of onion rings. A half-gallon glass jar or two quart jars will hold the batch.

2 to 3 pounds (to make 4 to 6 cups of pieces) Salt-Cured Salmon, above, or salt-cured but unsmoked salmon ("lox" or "belly lox") from a delicatessen
1 quart distilled white vinegar
1 cup water
¾ cup sugar, or more to taste
1 to 1½ tablespoons peppercorns (black and white mixed or all black or all white), to taste, slightly bruised in a mortar or with a rolling pin
1 tablespoon mustard seed
12 whole allspice, slightly cracked in a mortar or with a rolling pin
8 whole cloves
4 bay leaves, crumbled
⅛ teaspoon ground hot red (cayenne) pepper, or 1 or 2 small dried hot red peppers, optional
2 medium-large red onions or other mild onions, optional

Makes about 2 quarts

1. *If you use Salt-Cured Salmon:* Drain it and place in a large ceramic, enameled, plastic, or stainless-steel bowl. Cover the fish with cold water, cover the bowl, and refrigerate it for 2 to 3 days, changing the water twice a day. (To speed up the removal of excess salt, set the container under a barely running cold tap for part of the soaking period.) When the soaking water is no longer particularly salt, the fish has been freshened enough.

If you use commercially prepared lox: When buying, ask whether it has been freshened by soaking; if it has, omit the soaking in step 1. Instead, place it in a bowl under the cold tap and let the water run slowly over it for 15 minutes.

2. Combine the vinegar, 1 cup water, sugar, peppercorns, mustard seed, allspice, cloves, bay leaves, and hot pepper in a saucepan. Bring the mixture to a boil, cover it, and simmer gently for 20 minutes. Let the pickling mixture cool completely.

3. Drain the freshened fish and remove the skin by laying each piece skin side down on a cutting board. With a long, thin, very sharp knife, cut the flesh free of the skin, starting at the tail end and pressing the edge of the knife down against the skin as you move the blade forward beneath the flesh. Decide whether you want the marinated salmon in long strips, slices, or cubes. For inch-wide strips, cut the flesh lengthwise; for slices, cut crosswise, slightly on the bias, into pieces at least ½ inch thick. Cubes should be about an inch square. As you cut the pieces, feel with the fingertips for any bones and remove them with tweezers.

4. Peel the onions, if you are including them, halve them from top to bottom, and slice them crosswise about ⅛ inch thick.

5. Layer the fish and the sliced onions in a nonreactive bowl or crock or a wide-mouthed jar or jars. Pour the cooled spiced vinegar through a sieve over the fish and onions. If you wish, add a few pieces of the strained-out bay leaves and some of the spices to the fish. Cover the picked salmon and refrigerate it for 3 days or more before serving it. It will keep for 3 weeks in the refrigerator.

6. The salmon (and the now-pickled onions, if included) can be drained and served as is, but a sour-cream sauce (below) is a delicious enhancement.

Marinated Salmon in Cream Sauce

At least a day ahead of serving time, arrange drained pieces of Marinated or Pickled Salmon and the accompanying onions in layers in a glass or ceramic bowl, crock, or straight-sided glass jar.

Using 1 cup of dairy sour cream for about 3 cups of fish and onions, sauce the fish: Stir the sour cream with 1 to 2 tablespoons, or more to taste, of the pickling liquid. Pour the sauce over the pieces, making sure it filters down among them. Cover closely and refrigerate at least overnight.

Serve with bread and butter as a first course or a light lunch, or (why not?) for breakfast with the Sunday papers.

Balancing Opposites

Sweetness set off by tartness isn't found only in Chinese dishes dubbed "sweet and sour," as demonstrated by this originally European way of pickling salmon (or herring, as on this page). Seasonings both piquant and aromatic are added with great cunning to a pickling liquid in which vinegar plays standoff against sugar, and the "hot" elements—peppercorns, cayenne, and mustard seed—are counterpointed by the "sweet" character of allspice (pimento in its native Caribbean), bay leaves, and whole cloves. A delicate and delectable balance.

Herring Pickled Like Salmon

Anyone who has tasted classic New York–style pickled herring in cream sauce, often called creamed herring, will notice that the marinated salmon described above is prepared in exactly the same way. Here's how to fix a batch.

Salt-curing fresh herring: If you can buy fresh herring, you can salt your own. Before they are cured they should be beheaded, split up the belly, and emptied. From that point open the fish like a book, leaving the sides attached by the skin of the back, and remove the backbone. Rinse and drain, then salt the herring exactly like Salt-Cured Salmon, above. They will be ready to use after 2 weeks and will keep under refrigeration for at least 6 months.

Starting with purchased salt herring: Substitute the salt herring, beheaded but not emptied of innards, that are found in small kegs at well-stocked delicatessens and fishmongers. Use the directions for Marinated or Pickled Salmon, above.

Remove 2 to 3 pounds of herring from the brine (10 to 15 fish weighing 3 or 4 ounces each). Use heavy, sharp kitchen shears to slit the bellies and scoop out the skimpy innards. Soak the herring in abundant cold water in the refrigerator for 12 to 24 hours, changing the water twice. Drain the fish and cut off their fins and tails. Slit the herring fully open and, optionally, cut out the backbones with the scissors tips and pull out any small bones you'd like to get rid of. Cut the herring crosswise into 1-inch pieces.

Use the same ingredients as for salmon to pickle the herring pieces and to add the cream sauce. In the pickle without the cream, the herring will keep, refrigerated, for 3 weeks or so. After the cream sauce has been added, count on a week's refrigerator storage.

Smoked Mackerel, Bluefish, Bonito, Tuna, or Swordfish

All of these fine rich fish make an appetizing delicacy when cured briefly in seasoned brine and smoked at a temperature high enough to cook the flesh while the smoke flavors it.

Most home barbecues with a cover, as well as specialized smoke-cookers, can serve as hot-smokers. I have also converted a box-type smoker, normally heated only moderately by its small electric element, into a hot-smoker by burning charcoal or briquettes in it as well. (This strategy is described in the recipe.) Small cuts of fish can be quickly smoked in the stovetop smokers that burn fragrant sawdust prepared for the purpose. When using this recipe, consult the manufacturer's directions for tips on using the type of smoker you own.

3 to 3½ pounds fillets (with skin) or 1- to 1½-inch steaks of very fresh mackerel, bluefish, bonito, tuna, or swordfish
2 quarts water
⅔ cup coarse (kosher) salt
½ cup (packed) light brown sugar
½ teaspoon Powdered Bay Leaves (page 195) or 6 large bay leaves, crumbled
¼ teaspoon freshly ground white pepper
⅛ teaspoon ground allspice
Pinch of ground hot red (cayenne) pepper, optional
Vegetable oil

Makes 2 to 2½ pounds smoked fish

Using a Stovetop Smoker

These handy little boxes come in small and not so small sizes and with a supply of fine sawdust, rather than wood chips, for smoke production. The directions accompanying the stovetop smoker should be followed for the hot-smoking process.

1. Fish fillets should be cut from fish with the skin left on but with scales removed. Steaks shoud be at least 1 inch thick; 1½ inches is better. Optionally, cut out with a sharp knife the lengthwise strip of very dark and strongly flavored flesh in mackerel or bluefish fillets and cut out the very dark roundish section of swordfish slices. (The family cat will appreciate these trimmings.) Rinse the fish quickly in cold salted water to remove any scales and blood.

2. Stir together the 2 quarts water, salt, brown sugar, bay leaves, pepper, allspice, and hot red pepper, if used, in a large ceramic, glass, or stainless-steel bowl until the salt and sugar have dissolved. Add the fish, placing fillets skin side up. Weight the fish with a plate, cover the bowl, and set it aside for 3 hours, or refrigerate it for as long as 6 hours if more convenient.

3. Rinse the pieces of fish briefly under cold running water and lay them on a wire rack (or hang each fillet up by means of a loop of string threaded through with a needle) to dry until a slight membrane forms on the flesh, which should not feel sticky to a light touch. This takes about 2 hours, depending on the humidity of the air. (An electric fan speeds this stage along.)

4. Meanwhile, soak several handfuls of mild-flavored wood smoking chips in water. I like a mixture of chipped corncobs and maple for this, but hickory chips are fine. Preheat your smoker according to the manufacturer's directions. When the temperature reaches the level for hot-smoking (at least 125°F), sprinkle a small handful of drained chips onto the coals or the sawdust pan, as appropriate to your smoker. (If you use a smoker that doesn't ordinarly produce the level of heat needed for hot-smoking, such as a box smoker, ignite a supply of charcoal (preferable) or briquettes separately and bed them down in improvised "pans" of heavy foil in the bottom of the smoker. Replace the charcoal with a new, separately ignited supply when necessary.)

5. Brush the fish lightly with vegetable oil and hang fillets in the smoker or lay either steaks or fillets on lightly oiled racks. Smoke the fish, maintaining the heat and the supply of soaked chips as necessary, until the pieces are golden and cooked through (test a thick portion with a skewer). The smoking temperature should be kept between 125°F and a high of no more than 180°F; try to keep it between 160° and 170°F. During smoking, brush the fish once or twice with a little more oil. The time required for smoking will depend upon the temperature of the smoke and the thickness of the pieces; from 2 to 3 hours is average for fish 1 to 1½ inches thick.

6. Cool the fish (this allows its texture to settle down), then either serve it or wrap the pieces closely in foil, enclose them in plastic bags, and refrigerate or freeze them. Thaw frozen smoked fish in its wrappers to prevent sogginess. The smoked fish will keep for up to a week in the refrigerator or up to 6 months in the freezer.

7. *To serve:* Cut the fish slightly on the bias into thin slices and serve at room temperature. Broken bits can be made into Smoked Fish Paste (the recipe follows), or you may want to dedicate a whole chunk to this purpose.

Smoked Fish Paste

For this savory pâté (or just call it "paste") for parties, you can use any of the fish smoked as described in the preceding recipe for smoked fish. Or start with deli-bought finnan haddie, kippered herring, smoked salmon, or smoked trout.

If the kippered herring (kippers) are on the dry side, cover them with boiling water and soak 5 minutes, then drain and proceed. If you want to use smoked salmon, ask your delicatessen if trimmings are available—the price is much lower than that of whole slices. If your pâté is made with smoked trout, you may want to add to the other ingredients a bit of well-drained horseradish, just a teaspoonful or so.

½ pound smoked fish (about 1½ average fillets)
¾ cup (1½ sticks) sweet (unsalted) butter, softened at room temperature
Few drops of fresh lemon juice
Freshly ground black pepper
Salt, if needed
Pinch of Powdered Bay Leaves (page 195), optional
About ¼ cup Clarified Butter (page 35), if needed

Makes about 1½ cups

1. Flake the fish, eliminating all bones, skin, and bits of hard or dark flesh. You should have about 1¼ cups.

2. Cream the butter in an electric mixer. Add the fish and beat well. Taste, then beat in a few drops of lemon juice, pepper to taste, a little salt if needed, and, if desired, a small pinch of powdered bay leaves

3. Pack the fish paste firmly into small ceramic crocks, pots, or custard cups that have been scalded, then drained until dry and cool. In

Been Fishing, Got Skunked

You can start with store-bought kippers or other "deli" smoked fish for this versatile spread, which is delightful eating with crisp crackers or with Oatcakes (see the Index). Or, to make it, the fortunate fisher can delve into the freezer for any of the fish smoked and stored away according to the recipe preceding this one.

filling the pots, be careful to eliminate any air pockets. Smooth the top of the paste

4. Refrigerate the paste, covered airtight with plastic wrap or foil, if it will be consumed within a few days. If it is to be refrigerated or frozen for longer storage, melt enough clarified butter to cover the paste at least ¼ inch deep and pour it into the pot(s) to form a seal. Cover and/or wrap the container(s) for the refrigerator or the freezer and store. The paste keeps unsealed in the refrigerator for up to a week; sealed with butter, for up to 2 weeks in the refrigerator or 2 months in the freezer.

5. Frozen fish paste should be thawed in its wrappings. Once the butter seal has been broken on either refrigerated or thawed paste, use the contents of the pot within a few days.

Transforming Olives, Tomatoes, Nuts, Mushrooms, & Red Peppers into Great Beginnings

SAVORY WHETS
FROM THE VEGETABLE KINGDOM

One of the best things to happen to food lately, according to me, is the rediscovery of vegetables as fascinating edibles in their own right. What or who is to be thanked for this new appreciation I don't know, but I'm ready to cheer for *any* food person who greatly esteems the fruits of the earth (without, I speedily say, sacrificing any regard for the fruits of the sea or the pasture).

A "whet," including those that follow, may or may not be an appetizer, depending on when it's offered in the meal (or between meals). As it happens, most of the vegetable loves in this section are first-class first courses. Some, such as the dried tomatoes, are used in many ways besides "as is," notably as the base of Dried Tomato Tapenade and Dried Tomato Pesto. Other preparations, such as the seasoned nuts, Olivata, Potted Mushrooms, and the two versions of tapenade, are useful as cocktail companions as well as starters; and one confection, Broiled & Baked Summer Vegetables, manages to preserve the flavor and much of the character of grilled and oil-bathed vegetables with only a fraction of the fat grams.

A bonus: Except for the broiled and baked vegetables, all the dishes in this section are good keepers and so are eligible items for stashing away for impromptu entertaining.

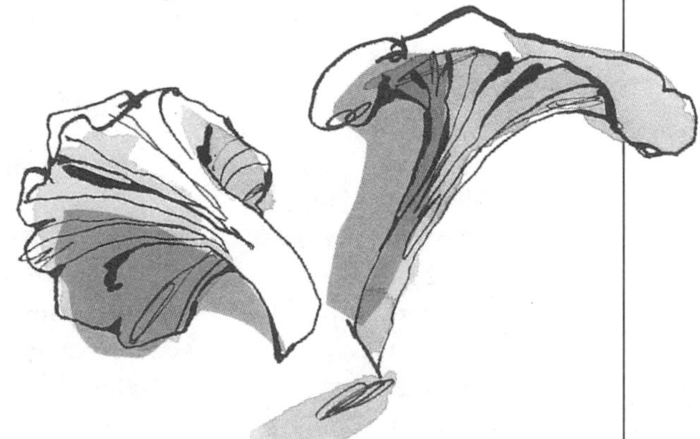

DEVILED PEANUTS OR ALMONDS

The firepower of deviled nuts is easily increased by stepping up the hot red pepper and/or by including the optional hot pepper sauce; but be warned—as written, the recipe supplies enough heat for most palates (as does the following recipe for Curried Peanuts).

2 tablespoons Worcestershire sauce
2 tablespoons soy sauce, preferably imported
2 cloves garlic, peeled and sliced
1 teaspoon salt, plus more for sprinkling if desired
3/8 teaspoon ground hot red (cayenne) pepper, more if desired
1/4 teaspoon ground cumin
Large pinch of freshly ground black pepper
2 dashes Tabasco or other hot red pepper sauce, optional
2 large egg whites
1 jar (16 ounces, about 3 cups) unsalted dry-roasted peanuts or 3 cups blanched almonds

Makes about 3 cups (1 pound)

1. Combine the Worcestershire sauce, soy sauce, garlic, 1 teaspoon salt, ground red pepper, cumin, black pepper, and the hot pepper sauce, if used, in a blender. Run the motor until the garlic has been completely pureed. Add the egg whites and run the motor until the ingredients are blended.

2. Place the peanuts in a bowl and pour the pureed mixture over them. Let the peanuts stand for 30 minutes, stirring them several times.

3. Preheat the oven to 250°F and oil two jelly-roll pans or baking sheets, or use nonstick pans if you have them.

4. Pour the nuts into a sieve set over a bowl and drain them for a moment or two; reserve the liquid. Spread the nuts in the prepared pans.

5. Bake the nuts on two shelves of the oven until they have dried slightly, about 10 minutes. Stir them and break apart any clumps, then drizzle the reserved liquid over them, mix well, spread them out, and sprinkle lightly with additional salt if desired. Return the nuts to the oven, exchanging shelf positions, and continue to bake until the glaze is dry, about 20 minutes. Turn off the oven and leave the nuts in it, with the door ajar, until they have cooled completely.

6. Store the nuts in an airtight container in a cool cupboard for a few days, in the refrigerator for up to 2 weeks, or in the freezer for as long as 3 months. If the nuts have been chilled or frozen, refresh them (no need to thaw them first) in a 200°F oven for a few minutes. Cool and serve.

DEVILING SALTED NUTS

If salted peanuts are what you have and you'd like to bedevil them, proceed as the recipe describes, but leave out the salt when preparing the seasonings.

RECYCLING NUTS

If frozen for storage, Curried Peanuts may be thawed, refreshed (as described in the recipe), and any leftovers refrozen with good success. Equally true of Deviled Peanuts or Almonds (opposite).

CURRIED PEANUTS

This formula produces hotter or milder nuts, according to your choice of curry seasonings. Those especially fond of fiery tastes may also want to check the following recipe.

1½ cups (about ½ pound) unsalted dry-roasted peanuts
1 large egg white
1 teaspoon salt, or more to taste
3 to 4 teaspoons hot (Madras-style) curry powder, or more to taste; or use the basic Mild Curry Powder on page 193
½ teaspoon pure garlic powder or 1 teaspoon finely minced or pressed fresh garlic, optional

Makes about 1½ cups (½ pound)

1. Measure the nuts into a bowl. In a second bowl beat the egg white until foamy, then beat in the salt, 2 teaspoons of the curry powder, and the optional garlic powder or fresh garlic. Pour the liquid over the nuts, stir, and marinate them for 30 minutes, stirring once or twice.

2. Meanwhile, preheat the oven to 250°F and oil a jelly-roll pan or baking sheet.

3. After the nuts have marinated, spread them in the prepared pan. Bake the nuts about 10 minutes, then scrape up and break apart the clumps they will have formed. Bake another 10 minutes or so, until the nuts feel dry to the touch. Turn off the oven and let them cool in the oven with the door ajar. They should be crisp when cool. If not, turn on the oven and bake them again for a few minutes.

4. Scrape the nuts into a storage jar or plastic container. Add the remaining curry powder and shake to coat the nuts. Store the nuts tightly covered; they will keep at room temperature for a week or so, in the refrigerator for twice as long, or in the freezer for up to 3 months. If the nuts have been chilled or frozen, refresh them (no need to thaw them first) in a 200°F oven for a few minutes. Cool and serve.

CAPONATA

Caponata, a rich compote of vegetables with sweet-and-sour saucing, is an ancient dish known in so many versions in its native Italy that it's almost impossible for food sleuths to define a "real" caponata.

However that may be, I like the mainly Sicilian caponatas on which this recipe is based. The touch of unsweetened cocoa, first come across in Mary Taylor Simeti's book *Pomp and Sustenance* (a wondrous exploration of Sicilian life, history, and cuisine), both deepens and enhances the other flavors without calling attention to itself.

In whatever version you make (you're sure to experiment sooner or later), caponata served with crisp-toasted rounds of Italian bread makes a lusty first course or party snack. It's also splendid as a side dish with plainly grilled or roasted meat, fish, or fowl, in lieu of more conventional vegetable preparations. Summer seems the perfect time for this refreshing and intricately flavored dish, although it may be made at any season when eggplants are to be had.

2 to 4 small eggplants (about 1¼ pounds in all), the smaller and more tender-skinned the better
Salt, as needed
3 or 4 ribs celery
½ cup olive oil, or more to taste
1 large or 2 medium red onions (about ½ pound in all), trimmed, peeled, and sliced
1½ cups plain tomato sauce or well-drained and pureed canned plum tomatoes
¼ cup red or white wine vinegar, or more to taste
¼ cup water
½ cup brined green olives, preferably the Sicilian type, pitted and left in chunks (brined black olives, or a combination of green and black, may be used if preferred)
2 to 4 tablespoons drained capers preserved in vinegar, to taste
1 tablespoon sugar
2 teaspoons unsweetened cocoa powder, optional but recommended
***Optional additions:* 4 to 6 anchovy fillets, drained of oil, patted dry, and cut coarsely; or a tablespoonful or so of raisins plus an equal quantity of pine nuts (*pignoli*)**
Additional salt and freshly ground black pepper, to taste

Makes about 5 cups

1. Trim both ends from the eggplants and cut into ¾-inch cubes without peeling; you should have about 6 cups. Sprinkle generously with salt, mix, and drain in a colander, weighted down with a small plate and a jar of water or another heavy object, for 1 hour.

2. While the eggplant is draining, scrape the coarse strings from the celery and cut it into slim sticks about an inch long. Drop the celery into boiling salted water and blanch for 4 or 5 minutes. Drain and pat dry; reserve.

A Note on Calories

The quantity of olive oil has been kept moderate in this recipe; some cooks would use twice as much, and the caponata can be made quite deliciously with as little as 3 tablespoons. However much you decide to use, make sure your oil is flavorful, not blah (like so-called light olive oils).

Choose Your Caponata

In the infinite variety described by culinary authorities, caponata can seem a bit far out. Sometimes it is based on potatoes in place of the eggplant in this recipe, or it may be even more oddly made with bread or sea biscuits. It may include cauliflower, hard-cooked eggs, garlic, anchovies, raisins, pine nuts, green beans, almonds, or carrots in addition to the ingredients I've used, or it may be composed of all manner of seafood. However it has been played with by regional cooks in Italy, its origins are Sicilian, and, not surprisingly, the firm, strongly flavored Sicilian-style green olives work best in the recipe.

3. Rinse the eggplant pieces well, drain them, and dry by rolling them in a tea towel and squeezing the roll.

4. In a wok or a skillet large enough to hold all the ingredients, heat ¼ cup of the olive oil over medium-high heat. Add the eggplant and fry, tossing and stirring almost constantly, until the cubes are browned and softened just a bit. Add the drained celery and stir-fry for a minute or two more. Scoop out the vegetables and reserve.

5. Pour the remaining ¼ cup oil into the wok or skillet, heat over medium-high heat, and add the onions. Sauté, stirring often, until just beginning to turn golden, about 4 minutes. Add the tomato sauce, stir, cover, and cook over low heat for 5 minutes.

6. Add the vinegar, water, olives, capers, sugar, and cocoa and mix. Add the eggplant and celery, mix well, and simmer 5 minutes or a bit longer, just until the sauce has reduced somewhat. The vegetables should retain shape and texture—caponata isn't meant to be a mush, but it's sometimes made with vegetables cut smaller than this recipe suggests.

7. Add either of the optional trimmings, then taste carefully and season with salt, if needed, a little fresh black pepper, and a little more wine vinegar and/or sugar if needed. Cool and store in the refrigerator at least overnight before serving. Refrigerated, the caponata will keep for weeks. It tastes best if allowed to come to room temperature.

Dried Tomatoes Italian Style

Among the good things that come in small jars at large prices are Italian sun-dried tomatoes packed in olive oil. Undeniably delicious but undeniably costly, they can be equaled by your own home-prepared supply. If you prefer your dried tomatoes without oil, they're even simpler to prepare; see the directions following the main recipe.

The right kind of tomatoes are the meaty, oblong paste or Italian-type tomatoes, also called plum or Roma tomatoes, that are ready in late summer. Count on the tomatoes giving up about 90 percent of their moisture; you'll need about 10 pounds in order to end up with a pound or so as your winter's supply.

If you'd like to dry the tomatoes in the sun, be aware that the process may take several days; they have to be brought indoors at night or when the weather turns damp. For indoor drying a dehydrator is excellent, but it isn't essential; an ordinary oven or (even better) a convection oven does very well.

When you're through with either outdoor or indoor drying, you'll have leathery, dark red pieces with intensely tomatoey flavor, ready to use as soon as you wish. After they have been packed in oil (with herbs, if you like), the tomatoes will develop more flavor for weeks, so don't be in a hurry to serve them.

4 pounds ripe but not soft Italian-type (Roma) tomatoes
Salt, optional
Distilled white vinegar
Sprigs of fresh rosemary or a little dried rosemary, optional
Olive oil

Makes 6 to 8 ounces (more if packed with oil)

1. Rinse the tomatoes and dry them. Cut a slice from the top, removing the stem scar, and a thin slice from the bottom (to facilitate the drying of the bottom slice). Cut the tomatoes crosswise into 3 slices if they are average size, into 4 if they are large. (Alternatively, halve or quarter them lengthwise and use the tip of a knife to scrape out most of the seeds without removing the flesh.)

2. Arrange the tomatoes, one cut surface upward, on the drying racks (cake racks with closely set wires are fine). Sprinkle them lightly with salt if you are using it.

3. *Drying tomatoes in the sun:* Set the racks in the sun and cover them with cheesecloth, draped over jars or some other objects in order to keep it from touching the tomatoes. Dry the tomatoes until they are leathery, which may take as long as 2 or 3 days; turn the pieces twice a day, and take the racks indoors at night or when the weather turns damp. After they have partially dried, flatten the pieces gently with a rubber spatula. If the weather is uncooperative at any point, switch to an oven (see below). Proceed with step 4 when the tomatoes are dry.

Drying the tomatoes indoors: If you have a dehydrator, follow the manufacturer's directions. Otherwise, place the racks in an oven or convection oven. Turn the heat control to 200°F and leave the tomatoes for 30 minutes. Reset the heat control of a conventional oven to 140°F (or its keep-warm setting, whichever is lower) and leave the oven door ajar. Reset the control of a convection oven to the drying temperature recommended by the manufacturer, or leave it at 200°F (this works very well with my particular oven) and leave the door slightly open. Dry the tomatoes until they are decidedly leathery but not rock-hard, switching the shelf positions of the racks occasionally. When the tomatoes are about half dry, flatten the pieces with a rubber spatula. The drying time required will depend on your oven and the size of the

Ways to Use Dried Tomatoes

Although dried tomatoes are sometimes seen on salad plates, this isn't their best use; they are both too chewy and too dominant in flavor to be so presented. Some better ideas:

- *Dried tomatoes are an effective flavor intensifier for pizza and pasta sauces. Drain a handful of the pieces (save the oil), snip them into bits, and simmer them in a little water or some of the sauce until they are soft. Puree or not, as you wish.*
- *Add snipped-up dried tomatoes, either straight from the jar or simmered as described, to the topping of a pizza; drizzle some of the tomato oil over the topping before baking.*
- *Make Dried Tomato Tapenade or Dried Tomato Pesto (forms of* essenza di pomidori; *recipes begin on the facing page).*
- *Don't fail to use the delicious oil from oil-packed tomatoes in salads or sauces as well as on pizzas.*
- *Bake a round loaf of Sun-Dried Tomato Bread (see the Index).*

pieces, but as a rule the tomatoes should be ready in about 6 to 8 hours. (The drying can be done in more than one session, if you like.)

4. Cool the tomatoes completely. Place them in a bowl and sprinkle them quickly with a little vinegar. Toss the pieces rapidly (best done with the hands) to moisten them lightly. Immediately empty the bowl onto a double layer of paper towels and pat the tomatoes thoroughly dry with more towels.

5. Pack the tomatoes lightly into a clean, dry pint jar, including a sprig or two of fresh rosemary or a pinch or two of dried rosemary if you wish. Pour in enough olive oil to cover the tomatoes generously, being sure that no bits protrude. Cap the jar tightly and shelve it at cool room temperature for at least a month before serving the tomatoes. After removing the tomatoes from the jar, add more oil if necessary to keep the remaining pieces covered. Tomatoes in oil will keep for up to a year in a cool cupboard or the refrigerator.

Dried Tomatoes Packed Without Olive Oil

Follow the preceding directions through step 3 (drying). Omit step 4 (vinegar). Spread the dried tomatoes on a baking sheet and leave them in the freezer until frozen hard. Working quickly, pack the pieces (with or without rosemary) into a clean jar, cap it tightly, and store it in the freezer. Pieces can be removed as needed without allowing the batch to thaw. They'll stay in fine condition for a year or more.

Dried Tomato Tapenade & Dried Tomato Pesto

Sun-dried tomatoes have come fairly recently to America from Italy, where they are nothing new. They have become a supermarket item here, but they are still pricey enough to encourage me to sun-dry (or oven-dry) my own supply of summer tomatoes (see the preceding recipe).

Whether you use your own dried tomatoes or some from the market, you can quickly produce either version—tapenade or pesto—of this rich, dark, and pungent pantry asset. The recipes derive from the Italian preparation known as *essenza di pomidori.* The first, a "tapenade" only by courtesy, is a relish or condiment or ingredient, according to how it's used.

- Spread it on toasted slices of baguette or on rounds of raw zucchini or thin slices of fennel as an appetizer.

• Include some in a tomato-based pasta sauce for a deeper and darker flavor.

• Slather it on hot pasta.

• Enrich a pizza topping with dabs here and there.

• If you're in a hurry, make a fake pizza by spreading a layer of dried tomato tapenade on split and lightly toasted English muffins, adding shreds of mozzarella, and broiling.

Beyond these notions, let your imagination roam. Imagination may lead you to eat the essence (as does one fancier I know) with a spoon.

The "pesto" version of this compound skips the capers and vinegar but adopts pine nuts and Parmesan. I use it in the same ways suggested for the basil-based Pesto farther along (see the Index).

TAKING LIBERTIES

Writing a cookbook would be less fun if lexicographers held foodies to the literal meaning of words; so I've opted for fun over precision in dubbing this pair of recipes "tapenade" and "pesto." Scholars are welcome to sue, but only after making and tasting.

DRIED TOMATO TAPENADE

1 cup (moderately packed) Dried Tomatoes Italian Style (page 51) or purchased dried tomatoes, drained if packed in oil (reserve the oil)
2 medium cloves garlic, peeled
1 tablespoon drained capers packed in brine
1 tablespoon minced fresh basil or frozen basil Pesto (page 140), or scant 1 teaspoon crumbled dried basil
½ to 1 teaspoon salt, to taste
⅛ teaspoon crumbled dried oregano
½ teaspoon minced fresh rosemary leaves or ⅛ to ¼ teaspoon crumbled dried rosemary
3 to 5 tablespoons olive oil, including some of the oil in which the tomatoes were packed, if available
1 tablespoon red wine vinegar

Makes about 1 cup

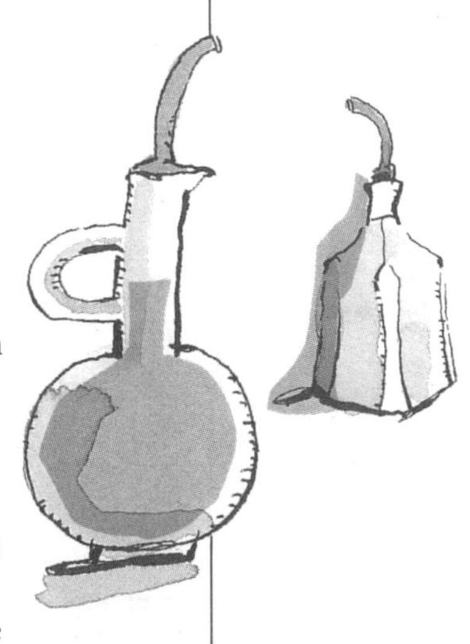

1. Place the tomatoes in a food processor and chop to a coarse puree. Remove and reserve them.

2. With the motor of the processor running, drop in the garlic and chop it fine, scraping down the workbowl once or twice. Add the capers and process the mixture to a coarse puree. Turn off the machine.

3. Return the chopped tomatoes to the processor. Add the basil, ½ teaspoon salt, the oregano, rosemary, 3 tablespoons oil, and the vinegar. Process the ingredients briefly, just long enough to mix them well; the texture should be slightly rough. Taste the mixture and add more seasonings and, if desired, more oil, stirring in the additions by hand to avoid overprocessing.

4. Scrape the tomato essence into a clean, dry jar and store it, covered, in the refrigerator; it will keep indefinitely. Let it come to room temperature before serving.

DRIED TOMATO PESTO

Use the ingredients listed for the Dried Tomato Tapenade, but omit the capers and vinegar.

In step 3, add 2 to 3 tablespoons of pine nuts (*pignoli*) and 3 to 4 tablespoons of freshly grated imported Parmesan cheese (Parmigiano-Reggiano, the real stuff). Puree the mixture until quite smooth. Refrigerate, covered, for indefinite keeping.

TWO TAPENADES

A gleaming bowlful of Provençal tapenade made with black olives looks like caviar, but on the palate it's quite different though equally zesty—an olivaceous, anchovy-salty, and capery-tart waker of the taste buds that was probably born somewhere around Marseilles. (When you try the originally Italian recipe for Olivata—see the Index—you'll note its kinship with tapenade, although it lacks anchovies.) However tapenade came to be devised, whether with black olives or green (see the second recipe), it has been widely adopted over southern France and beyond in its century or so of existence.

To count the ways to consume tapenade:

• As part of an hors d'oeuvre tray or as an accompaniment for a glass of wine or iced vodka, or any properly dry cocktail or aperitif, offer it with toasted French bread (or Semolina Bread—see the Index), or Melba toast, or warm focaccia (see the Index).

• Tapenade is slightly grainy when made from this recipe; just process it longer for a smoother, saucelike texture and bed halved hard-cooked eggs upon it for a more substantial hors d'oeuvre (Elizabeth David's suggestion), or serve the smooth sauce as a dip for raw vegetables or small breadsticks or lightly salted crackers.

• Smooth or grainy, tapenade is also an authentic Provençal addition to the mashed yolks of what would otherwise be deviled eggs (perfectly delicious) and for a salad of cooked small potatoes (use red-skinned or waxy yellow spuds) and fresh tomatoes.

• I have also tossed it with freshly cooked thin pasta and a little extra oil for a quick hot meal. Very good.

Black Olive Tapenade

2 jars (6½ ounces each) black Mediterranean-style oil-cured olives (brined olives are not suitable), or about ¾ pound bulk olives
2 tins (2 ounces each) flat fillets of anchovies, drained (see sidebar opposite)
¼ cup drained capers (rinsed if packed in salt)
½ cup fine-quality fruity olive oil, or as needed
2 or 3 large cloves garlic, or to taste, peeled and minced to a pulp or forced through a press
½ teaspoon crumbled dried thyme, or half dried thyme and half dried rosemary
1 tablespoon strained fresh lemon juice, or more to taste
Freshly ground black pepper, to taste
Additional oil for storing the tapenade

Makes about 2½ cups

1. Pit the olives (most easily done by squeezing each between fingers and thumb) and place them in a food processor or blender. (If you feel muscular and possess a large mortar and pestle, using those implements is the authentic way of dealing with the olives.)

2. Add the anchovy fillets, capers, ⅓ cup of the olive oil, the garlic, and the thyme. Turn the machine rapidly on and off repeatedly to chop the ingredients to a grainy texture, or continue to process the mixture if you want a smooth sauce. Blend in 1 tablespoon of lemon juice and freshly ground pepper; taste the tapenade and add more seasoning if you wish; no salt will be needed because of the olives and anchovies. Stir in the remaining olive oil, or even more if the mixture seems to need it—it should be unctuous.

3. Serve the tapenade, or pack it into a crock or jar, pressing it down to eliminate air pockets. Smooth the top and pour on enough additional olive oil to cover it well. Cap the jar and refrigerate it.

4. Serve tapenade at room temperature. Refrigerate leftovers, covering the top with a little more oil to exclude air. Tapenade improves with mellowing, and will keep for 6 months in the refrigerator.

Changing a Tapenade

Some recipes for black olive tapenade contain such ingredients as tuna canned in oil—which is most harmonious—and Dijon-style mustard, which seems to my palate to be superfluous. Such dried herbs as thyme, powdered bay leaf, rosemary, oregano, or summer savory are sometimes added without harm, as is a little brandy, but adding dried figs and even tea, as described by some writers, may be going too far.

Green Olive Tapenade

A spread of a different color, adapted here from my *Home-Style Menu Cookbook*. Like the preceding recipe, this is a pattern, not a prescription, so feel free to up the ante when you're seasoning it, possibly adding more capers, anchovies, garlic, or lemon juice, or herbs other than those suggested. I like the Green Olive Tapenade made with half

For Anchovy Enthusiasts

For more anchovy flavor in tapenade, include the oil from the can, reducing the quantity of plain olive oil accordingly.

green and half California black olives, too—a good use for the canned olives from my home state, which otherwise aren't all that great.

Makes about 2½ cups

Follow the directions for Black Olive Tapenade, substituting large pitted but unstuffed green Spanish olives, well drained, or half green olives and half California black olives, for the oil-cured olives listed. To pit the green olives, you'll need a sharp paring knife.

You may reduce the capers, if you wish, and use only half as much anchovy if you're not a big fan. Add lemon juice at the end only if it's needed, as green olives are quite tart. The addition of pepper is optional.

Store and serve exactly as for Black Olive Tapenade. The color of this version is drab, but the flavor isn't.

Olivata
(Black or Green Olive Spread)

These pungent olive pastes redolent of Mediterranean seasonings are most useful appetizers, either spread on toasted French bread or Melba toast or served as a dip with a collection of raw vegetables. The black olivata (or olivada) also steps in handily as a quick sauce for pasta in the same fashion as its richer kissin' cousin, Tapenade (see the Index), which is made with anchovies and capers in addition to olives.

Olivata Made with Black Olives

2 jars (6½ ounces each) oil-cured black olives, or about ¾ pound loose oil-cured olives, either with or without added herb and red pepper seasoning
¼ to ⅓ cup full-flavored olive oil, plus more for topping
1 to 2 large cloves garlic, peeled and minced
Herbs to taste: ½ to 1 teaspoon crumbled dried oregano plus a pinch or two of crumbled dried rosemary (or twice as much minced fresh rosemary); or up to 2 tablespoons chopped fresh basil leaves; or a combination of ½ to 1 teaspoon crumbled dried thyme (or twice as much minced fresh thyme leaves) and a pinch of hot red pepper flakes
Freshly ground black pepper, to taste
A little strained fresh lemon juice, if needed
Additional oil for topping the olivata

Makes about 2 cups

1. Pit the olives (most easily done by squeezing each between fingers and thumb). Combine the olives, ¼ cup of the oil, the garlic, and your chosen herbs in a food processor or blender (or use a large mortar and pestle and pound the ingredients if you feel like getting physical). Turn the machine rapidly on and off repeatedly to chop the ingredients to a grainy puree, or pound away if you are wielding a pestle; don't let it become too smooth. Taste the olivata and add more herbs, if needed, plus freshly ground pepper and a little lemon juice, if you think a touch of tartness is a good idea. (Bear in mind that the flavor of the mixture will develop further.) Add the remaining olive oil if the mixture needs it to become properly unctuous.

2. Pack the olivata firmly into a jar or crock and smooth the top. Cover the puree with a thin layer of olive oil, then cover the container tightly and refrigerate it. It will keep for months.

3. Let the olivata come to room temperature before serving it. Refrigerate leftovers, first adding a fresh topping of oil.

Green Olivata

Substitute green olives, either Sicilian, Spanish, or Italian, for the black olives in the main recipe. As the herbal seasonings, use basil, thyme, and a little oregano plus a very little hot pepper. Optionally, include a handful of blanched almonds before pureeing everything together. Store as described for the black olivata. Serve at room temperature.

Potted Mushrooms

(Mushroom Paste)

Enjoy this buttery, dusky spread, pungent with the flavor of both dried and fresh mushrooms, on canapés or in thin-cut sandwiches, especially good when a few leaves of watercress are tucked in. It is also a fine snack on crackers. Use the paste as the "butter" for substantial sandwiches of chicken or cheese, or swirl spoonfuls into hot noodles as sauce and seasoning, or slather it over a broiled steak.

To achieve the most intense mushroom flavor at the most reasonable cost, choose dried fungi labeled "European mushrooms" or, if you can find them, the otherwise anonymous dried mushrooms imported from Chile. You can also use dried mushrooms identified as boletes (boletus mushrooms), which have marvelous flavor but carry a high price tag. These will be found under such names as *cèpes secs, porcini, funghi secchi porcini,* and *Steinpilze.* Chinese and Japanese dried mushrooms are not suitable.

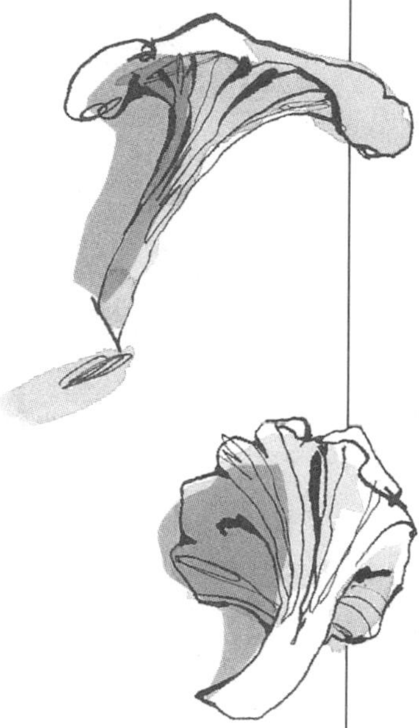

1 ounce (about ⅔ cup) imported dried mushrooms
⅔ cup warm water
2 tablespoons Madeira wine, plus more if needed (a full-bodied sherry may be substituted)
2 medium shallots, peeled and sliced
1 medium clove garlic, peeled and sliced
½ teaspoon salt, or to taste
¼ teaspoon ground mace
Large pinch (⅛ teaspoon) of crumbled dried thyme leaves
Scrap of bay leaf about 1 inch square, or large pinch of Powdered Bay Leaves (page 195)
Tiny pinch of ground cloves
¾ pound firm, fresh cultivated mushrooms, stems removed (about ½ pound after trimming)
Freshly ground black pepper or ground hot red (cayenne) pepper, to taste
½ to ¾ cup (1 to 1½ sticks) sweet (unsalted) butter, cut into ¼-inch slices
About ½ cup Clarified Butter (page 35), for sealing containers

Makes about 2½ cups

1. Soak the dried mushrooms in the warm water, covered, for several hours or overnight, until the mushrooms are very soft.

2. Lift the mushrooms from their liquid with a slotted spoon and place them in a food processor or blender; let the soaking liquid settle for a moment, then pour it carefully into the food processor, leaving behind any sand that may be at the bottom. Add the Madeira, shallots, garlic, salt, mace, thyme, bay leaf, and cloves, and process the mixture to a puree. Scrape the puree into a bowl and reserve it.

3. Preheat the oven to 300°F.

4. Working in batches, if necessary, chop the fresh mushroom caps very fine in the processor or blender (no need to clean the container first). Add the puree and blend everything together well.

5. Scrape the mixture into a small baking dish (a 3-cup soufflé dish is just right) and set it into a slightly larger baking dish or pan. Cover the inner dish tightly with foil and add a metal lid or ovenproof plate to hold the foil in place. Pour enough boiling water into the outer dish to come within an inch of the rim of the inner dish.

6. Bake the mushroom mixture in the preheated oven, adding hot water to the outer dish as necessary to maintain the level; uncover and

Mushroom Season

Dried mushrooms are always available, but cultivated fresh mushrooms can be pricey out of season; so the time to make this delicious compound is late winter and early spring, when supplies in the market are greatest and bargains most likely.

stir the mushrooms after 1½ hours, then re-cover. Check the mushrooms again after another hour; the fragments should be tender, almost jellylike. When this point is reached, leave the inner dish uncovered and let the mixture bake for an additional ½ hour. Remove the whole business from the oven and set the inner dish on a rack to cool to lukewarm.

7. Taste the mushroom mixture and add pepper to taste, plus a little more of any of the seasonings you think may be needed; the flavor should be pronounced, as the butter you're about to add will dilute its impact.

8. Using at least 1 stick of butter or as much as 1½ sticks, add the butter slices, about one third at a time, whisking after each addition until the butter disappears. Taste the mixture again and make any final additions to the seasonings.

9. Pack the potted mushrooms into two or three attractive small crocks suitable for serving and smooth the tops. Chill the paste, uncovered, until it is firm; as it cools, it will develop an attractively marbled appearance.

10. Melt the clarified butter and pour a layer about ¼ inch thick over the paste, being sure that the butter layer is sealed to the sides of the containers. Cover the containers tightly and refrigerate for up to 3 weeks. Before serving, allow the potted mushrooms to soften slightly at room temperature. Leftovers should be used within a few days after the butter seal has been broken.

Roasted Red Antipasto Peppers

Red-ripe sweet peppers, roasted for an edge of smokiness and packed in olive oil with plenty of fresh garlic, make a robust appetizer to pull from the refrigerator or freezer whenever an Italianate first course sounds good. We like them arranged on a bed of greens on either an antipasto platter or solo on individual plates, with a topping of crisscrossed anchovy fillets and a strewing of fresh parsley. Using both yellow and red sweet peppers makes an especially attractive mixture, and purple and orange peppers can be treated this way, too.

The peppers are endlessly useful as an ingredient, adding zest to salads and sandwiches as well as to sauces, soups, and other cooked dishes.

. . . AND THE OSCAR GOES TO . . . :

Among all the broiled and roasted vegetables we enjoy these days, red peppers are among the most delicious and beyond doubt one of the most useful as an ingredient, with Roasted Tomatoes (recipe follows) as runner-up. (Or perhaps Roasted Garlic? See Index.) Suggestion: Puree some peppers and fold the puree into mayonnaise for use in sandwiches (I vote for a filling of thickly sliced beefsteak tomato) or in a salad of cooked, chilled, and drained vegetables.

4 pounds (about 9) large, fully ripe sweet red (bell) peppers or a mixture of red and yellow
1 tablespoon salt
½ cup mild red wine vinegar
⅔ cup olive oil, preferably a full-flavored type
4 to 6 large cloves garlic, or to taste, peeled and sliced
***At serving time, optional garnish:* Minced fresh parsley**

Makes about 4 cups

1. *Roasting the peppers on the stovetop:* Rinse the peppers to remove any grit or soil. Set a metal rack over a stove burner (I keep a retired cake rack just for pepper roasting) and arrange several peppers on it, keeping them within the area of the gas flame or electric heat. Turn on the flame or heat at the medium-high setting. Roast the peppers until they are charred black all over, turning them often with tongs (a fork causes juice to escape and the peppers to collapse). As each pepper is ready, drop it into a pot and cover the pot with a lid. Continue until all the peppers are sweating in the pot. Let them cool, covered, until they can be handled. (If left until completely cool, the peppers will be even smokier in taste.)

Broiler method: Alternatively, broil the peppers about an inch below a preheated broiler element. Turn them frequently, using tongs, until they are well blackened, then put them into the pot to steam and even cool as described.

2. Using your fingers and a short sharp knife, strip off the loose charred skin from the peppers (don't rinse them at this stage), cut out the stems and cores, and remove the seeds. Tear the peppers lengthwise into strips about an inch wide, dropping them into a bowl as you finish. For the moment, disregard any stray clinging seeds.

3. Sprinkle the salt over the peppers and mix it in thoroughly (most easily done with your hands). Let them rest for 10 minutes.

4. Pour about a cupful of water into another bowl and rinse the pepper strips quickly, a few at a time. As they are rinsed, drop them into a clean bowl. Add the vinegar and mix it well with the peppers, then mix in the olive oil and sliced garlic.

5. *For refrigerator storage:* Spoon the peppers, garlic, and oil into clean, dry pint or half-pint canning jars (or use plastic food containers), settling them well to eliminate air pockets. Cover airtight and refrigerate for a day or two before serving the peppers with a garnish of minced parsley. When using the peppers, make sure the remaining pieces are covered with oil, adding more if necessary.

For freezer storage: Do not add garlic to peppers you plan to freeze. Pack them in clean canning jars or plastic freezer containers, eliminating air pockets, and cover them with oil as described; leave ½ inch of headspace. Cap the jars with two-piece canning lids and store at 0°F or less. Frozen, they'll keep for 6 months.

To serve after freezing: Thaw the peppers in the refrigerator, then shower them with thinly sliced garlic, at least 1 large clove to each cup of pepper strips. Toss everything together and leave the peppers out at room temperature for at least an hour, better more, before they are served with the optional garnish of parsley. It's a good idea to check the seasoning and add more vinegar, salt, and/or oil if indicated—freezing may have altered the balance of flavors. Any leftovers will keep in the refrigerator as long as peppers that haven't been frozen, but they shouldn't be frozen again.

Roasted Tomatoes

Done this way, thick slices of red-ripe tomatoes shrivel gently to a state of concentrated lusciousness that is both intense and fresh in taste. Wonderful warm or at room temperature as a first course or "side" to grilled foods or a composed salad, they're also versatile as an instant sauce for pasta (just add oil, fresh herbs, and fresh or sautéed garlic, and toss with hot, chunky pasta). You can use roasted tomatoes instead of fresh in a salsa (see the Index), or scatter them as a pizza topping, or chop or puree them as the base for a great cold soup. Or tuck slices into a summer sandwich as a change from fresh tomato.

We like our own August tomatoes roasted without added seasoning and served with a sprinkle of basil or other fresh herbs, a drizzle of oil, or a spritz of balsamic vinegar.

Fully ripe large tomatoes
Optional Seasonings: **Olive oil, salt and freshly ground black pepper, minced garlic, or Italian-Style Herb Blend (page 191)**
At serving time, optional sprinklings: **Fresh parsley leaves, snipped basil leaves or chives, or other herbs; olive oil or balsamic vinegar**

1 large tomato makes about 1 serving

LOOKING AHEAD

In seasons of great plenty in the tomato patch, making a great stash of roasted tomatoes for the freezer is a fine idea—they keep, frozen, for the many months we must survive without acceptable fresh tomatoes, and they add great flavor to off-season cookery.

1. Cover one or two baking sheets with aluminum foil. Preheat the oven to 325°F.

2. Rinse and dry the tomatoes; cut and discard (or save to add to the soup pot) a slice from the top and one from the bottom, then from the rest make crosswise slices about 1 inch thick. Arrange the slices on the foil-covered pan(s).

3. If you like, brush a very little olive oil over the slices and sprinkle them with a little salt and freshly ground pepper. (They will still be delicious if this step is omitted.) Place in the upper part of the preheated oven and bake for 1 hour, then check progress and exchange shelf positions of the pans if you are using two baking sheets. After another half-hour or so, begin checking for doneness. The tomatoes are at their best, to my way of thinking, when they stay in the oven until the juice on the pan is caramelized and the slices have become a bit chewy; others may prefer them shrunken but still juicy. If slices are cooking at different rates, remove them to a plate as they reach the doneness you prefer. Optionally, sprinkle a little finely chopped garlic and/or Italian-Style Herb Blend on the slices toward the end of roasting.

4. Serve the tomatoes warm from the oven, as is or with further seasonings of your choice. Alternatively, cool the tomatoes and refrigerate them, covered, until they're wanted. They keep for at least a week. Let them come to room temperature before serving.

BROILED & BAKED SUMMER VEGETABLES

Vegetables grilled (over the heat) or broiled (below the heat) and bathed in olive oil with plenty of lively seasonings are undeniably delectable as part of an antipasto, but the dish has almost as many calories as vitamins, and more's the pity. This version of "grilled" vegetables is broiled and then baked with only a moderate blessing of oil, so you'll want to use olive oil with plenty of character.

The recipe is for a big batch because the vegetables taste even better the next day or on the day(s) after that, and they can be frozen for future reference. If you don't have a stash of roasted tomatoes on hand, start the proceedings by preparing some (see preceding recipe) before broiling the other vegetables for this succulent Mediterranean mélange.

2 sweet red (bell) peppers, or about 1 cup Roasted Red Antipasto Peppers (page 60)
2 small to medium eggplants (1½ pounds), unpeeled, sliced ½ inch thick
2 medium-large onions, peeled and sliced ¼ inch thick
2 zucchini or yellow summer squash, scrubbed, trimmed, and sliced ½ inch thick
Olive oil, as needed
Salt, as needed
3 large cloves garlic, or more to taste, peeled and finely chopped
1 teaspoon crumbled dried oregano
2 teaspoons chopped fresh thyme leaves or 1 teaspoon crumbled dried thyme
About 8 large slices Roasted Tomatoes (see preceding recipe)
1 teaspoon cumin seed, lightly crushed
4 to 6 bay leaves
Fresh lemon juice, as needed
***Garnishes:* Extra-virgin olive oil (optional), chopped fresh parsley, lemon wedges**

Makes 8 to 12 servings

1. Preheat the broiler. Cover a large baking sheet with foil and brush the foil with olive oil.

2. If using fresh red peppers, set them on a rack close to the broiling element and broil, turning them often, until their skins are well blackened. Set them aside in a covered bowl or a plastic bag until slightly cooled, then strip off the scorched skin and remove the stems and seeds. Cut into broad strips.

3. Arrange the eggplant, onion, and zucchini slices close together on the foil. Brush or spray them lightly with olive oil, and sprinkle lightly with salt. Broil the vegetables 4 or 5 inches from the broiling element for about 10 minutes, or until the first side is nicely browned, then turn the pieces, again oil them lightly, and brown on the second side. If the vegetables brown at different rates, remove the slices from the pan as they are ready.

4. Reset the oven to 350°F. Mix together the chopped garlic, oregano, thyme, and cumin seed.

5. Choose a shallow baking dish (an 8-inch square dish is just right for this quantity) and place the bay leaves in it, together with a sprinkle of the chopped garlic and herbs. Construct layers of vegetables with the remaining bay leaves tucked here and there, beginning with eggplant or zucchini and finishing with red pepper strips and then the roasted tomato slices. Sprinkle each layer with a few drops of lemon juice, a little of the garlic and herb mixture, a little salt, and, if

CALORIE NOTE

The relatively low calorie count of vegetables broiled and baked this way is achieved by keeping an eye on the measure of olive oil. The amount used is left to the cook, but I've found that it can be unbelievably modest—2 or 3 tablespoons, for the whole dish—if a really assertive, fine oil is chosen.

you wish, a little olive oil. Pour a few tablespoons of liquid (if any) from the roasted tomatoes (or use water) over the top and press the vegetables down evenly. Cover the dish tightly with foil and bake in the 350°F oven until the vegetables are just tender when probed with a fork, 45 minutes to an hour.

6. Cool the vegetables to lukewarm or room temperature, then cut down firmly through the layers and serve in squares as a starter, with or without a drizzle of extra-virgin olive oil. Garnish with chopped parsley and lemon wedges and pass crusty bread or breadsticks. Refrigerated leftovers will keep for a week and may be reheated or simply allowed to return to room temperature before serving. For longer storage, the vegetables may be frozen, well wrapped, for 2 or 3 months.

Part I: Bread in Loaves & in Special Shapes

Part 2: Crisp & Savory Breadstuffs & Biscotti

Bread & Beyond

Home Baking for the Joy of It

When the moment came to choose the breads to include in this section, oh me oh my, what a quandary. The list, which of course *had* to include some favorites from *Fancy Pantry*, grew long and longer, after which the pruning job required a very sharp bread knife indeed. Even so, the trimmed-back recipe roster had to be divided into noncrisp and crunchy breadstuffs to make it more user friendly.

Accordingly, Part I of this section serves as the breadbox for actual loaves of interesting breads as well as for not-crisp breads of special character or in special shapes, such as chocolate-filled rolls, bagels, soft pretzels, crumpets, tortillas, English muffins, and focaccia.

Part II contains the crisp and crunchy specialties, including hard pretzels, corn chips, oatcakes, a variety of crackers, super-crisp grissini, and a collection of savory biscotti sporting such ingredients as herbs, dried tomatoes, chile peppers, and pesto.

For an introductory discussion of what's involved in baking bread (or a brushup, if that's all you require), see Breadmaking, which follows.

Getting hungry? Ladies and gentlemen, light your ovens. Let's bake.

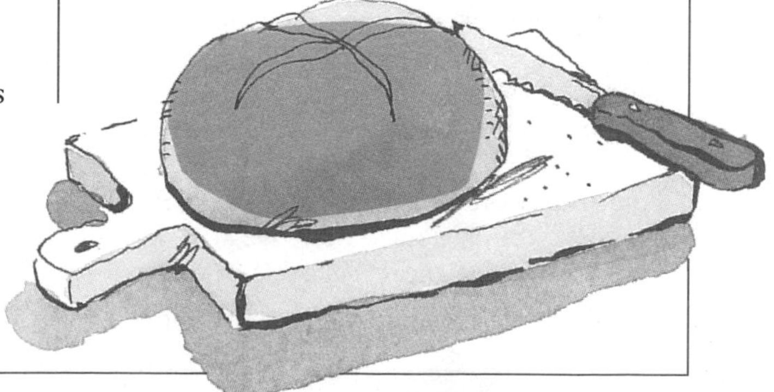

Breadmaking–A Primer or a Brushup

For anyone who hasn't had the pleasure of making yeast bread, or perhaps has forgotten some how-to's, here are some pointers. The idea of baking with yeast—actually one of the most satisfying of kitchencrafts—terrifies some otherwise well-rounded cooks, and that's a pity. Once a few basics are understood, baking with yeast is no more daunting than many other enterprises, such as making fudge, that don't seem to frighten much of anyone. Making a yeasted loaf—or breadsticks, pretzels, English muffins, crackers, or bagels—is simpler to do than to write about. Some background notes can help.

Yeast

The Good Stuff recipes call for and tell how to use regular active dry yeast, available everywhere in packets or small jars and, from specialist suppliers, in larger quantities or even by the pound, a wise choice if you bake a lot. There are other useful kinds of dry yeast, among them instant yeast (a faster-acting form that is mixed first with the dry ingredients rather than a liquid) and certain special yeasts. Some of these are for use in bread machines or in doughs rich in fat, eggs, and/or sugar, all ingredients that inhibit the action of regular yeast when they are used lavishly, as in fancy pastries. In general, though, regular active dry yeast will be all you need. I prefer it to instant yeast because it allows doughs, since they rise at a slower rate, to develop more flavor. If you substitute another type of yeast for standard active dry yeast, follow the package directions for adapting your mixing procedures and timing.

Yeast in cakes: My recipes don't call for compressed yeast, sold fresh in small cakes, because it is hard to find and quite perishable. If you want to try it, one approximately ½-ounce cake equals 1 envelope (or 1 tablespoon) active dry yeast. Reactivate it by crumbling it into the warm water listed for yeast preparation in recipes, leave it to dissolve and become foamy (about 10 minutes), then stir it before proceeding.

How yeast works: When the tiny hibernating yeast organisms are revived by liquid and provided with food (the starch in flour), they metabolize the starch into the sugar they need to reproduce rapidly and give off the carbon dioxide gas bubbles that make a yeast dough rise. (This process also produces a little alcohol, which vanishes in the baking.)

Most doughs are allowed to rise twice before baking; however, some quickie breads rise only once, and some rich doughs require as many as four risings, including a preliminary "sponge" stage, to reach their potential. Rising stops after oven heat has expanded the gas bubbles in the dough to their utmost, at the same time killing the yeast. As baking continues, the structure of the dough "sets" and the loaf takes its final form.

Storing yeast: Dry yeast will keep, either in its package or an airtight jar, in a cool cupboard for a considerable time (expiration dates are stamped on packages), or for an even longer time—at least a year—in an airtight jar in the refrigerator or freezer. (I'm still working with a frozen batch that's more than two years old, and it's fine.)

Testing yeast: If you doubt the liveliness of yeast that's been around for a while, test by stirring a pinch of sugar into 2 or 3 tablespoons of tepid water, add a big pinch of yeast, and let matters take their course. Within 5 to 10 minutes the yeast should be foaming into a fluffy cap. If nothing happens, the yeast is defunct. Testing isn't necessary every time you bake, despite what some older recipes advise; yeasts are more reliable than they used to be.

Flours

If you can, use the kind of flour specified in a recipe or its suggested substitute; not all flours are interchangeable. In general, however, plain all-purpose flour can be used for any basic white loaf.

Some flours: Among the flours you'll come to know if you find breadmaking to your taste are all-purpose flour, milled from a blend of hard (high-gluten) and soft wheats; bread flour, milled from hard wheat, which is high in gluten; bread flour labeled for use in bread machines, which is even higher in gluten and fine for any recipe calling for bread flour if the dough is kneaded with an electric mixer or a food processor, in the absence of a bread machine; white and whole-wheat pastry flours; whole-wheat flour and a newcomer, white-wheat flour, a sweeter, lighter-flavored variant available from the King Arthur Flour people (see Mail-Order Sources); durum (or semolina, or pasta) flour; pumpernickel (coarse rye) and other rye flours; potato flour; oat flour; barley flour; cracked wheat, bulgur, bran, oats, cornmeal, and wheat germ (not actually flours); "and more besides," including seeds, nuts, malt flakes, dried fruits and vegetables, and countless other intriguing additions to a basic loaf. Bread experts agree that all-purpose, bread, and pastry flours that have been neither bleached nor bromated (treated with a chemical) are best, because yeasts work best with them.

Why bread flour? The higher content of gluten (the stuff that builds the internal structure of the loaf) in bread flour makes it the first choice for many recipes, but all-purpose flour may be substituted if that's what's available. The label of a bag of flour lists its protein content (which indicates the potential strength of gluten) as grams of protein per quarter-cup of flour. The higher the number, the more gluten strength (and consequent better rising and final volume) you may expect. Most all-purpose flours have 3 grams of protein (although a few have more), while bread flours have about 4 grams and some special flours, for bread machines and for professional use, have even more.

To Measure Flour Consistently

Stir or whisk the flour in its canister, scoop it up with a dry-measure cup (don't use a glass measuring cup meant for liquids), and level the top by sweeping off the excess flour with the back of a knife blade or other straight-edged utensil.

Other Ingredients

Liquid: Most commonly water or milk is used, but bread may be made with buttermilk, broth, yogurt, whey drained from yogurt cheese, vegetable or fruit juice, and sour cream, for example.

Salt: Salt improves the flavor of bread and slightly slows its rate of rising. Some great bakers swear by sea salt; *Good Stuff* recipes call for coarse salt, which may be either the kosher type or medium-grain sea salt. Reduce the measurement of salt by one third if fine salt is substituted.

Sweetening: Putting sugar or another sweetener in plain breads is not essential, and according to a major school of thought, it detracts from the wheaty intensity of flavor a good loaf should have. (Many great breads contain only flour, yeast, salt, and water; fancy breads are another story.) Adding sugar to a dough speeds up rising (because the yeast can feast on it without having to first convert starch into sugar), and it pleases many palates accustomed to commercial breads.

Malt: Another common but not essential addition to doughs, barley malt powder of various types (see the discussion on page 81) is used in baking to improve flavor, boost rising, and/or improve the looks of a loaf. I like to use malt powder in certain loaves and such specialties as pretzels and bagels.

Shortening: If fat is used, it may be an oil—olive oil is especially good in such breads as Focaccia—butter, margarine, solid vegetable shortening, or lard.

Eggs: Fresh eggs or powdered whole eggs (page 139), reconstituted according to package directions, are fine for any recipe calling for eggs.

Making the Bread Dough

Mixing the dough: No special hints are needed for the first mixing of bread dough, whether by hand or in a mixer; the recipes describe the process.

Kneading

Here's where some art comes in. Kneading is manipulating dough vigorously enough—by pounding, thumping, pressing, folding, and/or knocking it about in general—to force the gluten in the flour to develop a strong internal structure capable of trapping the gas produced by the yeast that causes the dough to rise. (Without gluten, the dough would be unable to contain the gas bubbles and would, sooner or later, inevitably collapse).

Kneading can be done by machine: If you use an electric mixer equipped with a dough hook, run it at the "kneading" speed of your machine for the time specified in the recipe. If you knead in a food processor fitted with a dough-kneading blade, follow the manufacturer's instructions, as it's easy to overprocess a dough in these powerful machines. Although I often use my big mixer to knead, kneading by hand, when time allows, is my favorite way. Here's how.

The art of hand kneading: Dust a dry, smooth work surface with flour and have extra flour on hand. Turn the dough out of the mixing bowl, dust it with flour, flour your hands, and flatten the dough into a more or less smooth blob. Lean into the dough with the heel of one or both hands, pushing it out and away from you. Fold it in half toward you, give it a quarter-turn on the board, and repeat the pushing, folding, and turning of the dough, which will feel increasingly lively as you work. As necessary, dust the dough and board with a little flour to keep the dough from sticking as you work. Dough has been kneaded enough when it is smooth and elastic and has a satiny surface (unless it has nubbly ingredients, in which case it should be judged for liveliness and elasticity). Hand kneading can scarcely be overdone; 10 minutes is about average, but you can go on longer if you find it, as many do, a soothing occupation.

Another way to knead by hand: This one is fun. Scoop the just-mixed dough onto the floured work surface, flour it lightly, then grab one end of the mass, lift it quickly, and slam it down hard on the board with an overarm movement, causing it to stretch away from you. Fold the stretched dough end to end, grasp it at one side, and repeat the slamming and folding until your dough has pulled itself together into a coherent mass that is lively, elastic, and smooth-surfaced. If it tends to stick as you knead, dust a little flour onto board and dough.

The Rising

After kneading, dough is formed into a cannonball shape and placed in a lightly oiled bowl, covered with plastic wrap, and allowed to rise. If your kitchen is quite cool and you want to move along without undue delay, wrap the whole works in a towel or a small blanket.

Dough will rise successfully within a surprisingly wide range of temperatures, from the chill of the refrigerator to room temperature (normally around 70°F), to a *slightly* warmer spot, such as an oven warmed only by the viewing light or a bowl of hot tap water placed near the dough (too much heat will kill the yeast stone dead). So don't worry about finding the classic "warm, draft-free spot" unless you are in a hurry; the dough will rise eventually even though mistreated, so long as the yeast cells haven't been killed by too much heat. Slow rising actually produces better flavor in the finished bread.

Refrigerating doughs: Chilling a dough (retarding it) for a time during its rising is standard practice among artisanal bakers. The chill, by promoting slow fermentation and slow rising, develops more flavor and character in the bread; additionally, for the home cook it can serve the purpose of interrupting a baking session to permit attention to other matters. You can refrigerate dough at any point after it has been kneaded, even after it's in the baking pans (but not risen more than slightly) and come back to the job after several hours or even the next day. If dough has risen more than a very little in its bowl before you prepare to stash it, punch it down by plunging a fist into it until it is deflated, then turn it over, cover it with plastic wrap, and refrigerate it.

Time limits: A dough will rise slowly in the refrigerator, even to double its original volume, so check on it by pressing a finger into the mass if it has been left as long as 12 hours. (A dough that's allowed to overrise will collapse and become sour in taste and hopeless in structure.) If a dough has risen fully but must remain in the refrigerator, punch it down as before and try to get to it as expeditiously as you can.

When you are ready to proceed, punch down the dough (if in a bowl) and resume the recipe where you left off. If you have refrigerated loaves in pans, they can go right to the preheated oven if they have risen fully; if not, just let them complete their rising at room temperature.

How high the loaf? Always read and heed recipe indications of how much a dough should rise at a given stage—to not quite double its volume, or to double its volume, or even to triple volume, depending on the type of dough. Until you are accustomed to gauging the rise by eye, it's helpful to mark the original level of the dough on the outside of the bowl with a wax pencil or crayon. Rising of a bowlful of dough can be tested by poking a finger an inch or so into the top; if the dent remains instead of beginning to fill up, the dough has risen enough. To test in pans, press the side of the loaf just above the pan rim.

Baking

Oven times: Recipes indicate baking temperatures and approximate baking times, but it's a good idea to check bread for doneness a few minutes before the end of the indicated time. That's because ovens perform very differently, some even eccentrically, and an actual oven temperature can turn out to be much higher or lower than the setting you've chosen.

Testing a loaf: The classic test for doneness is to turn the loaf out of its pan onto the oven shelf (or turn it over, if it's a hearth loaf) and rap on the bottom crust with your knuckles. A hollow note means it's done, a dull sound means baking should continue. (No need to return the loaf to the pan for the last lap.) You can also test for doneness with an instant-reading thermometer; in general, a reading of 200° to 210°F indicates doneness, depending on the density of the bread; denser loaves, such as those made with whole grains, are done at a somewhat lower reading than lighter ones.

Gumshoeing the Oven

Buying an oven thermometer for checking the reliability of your oven control is a small investment with a large payoff. Many oven controls can be adjusted on the spot, so consult the oven manual before calling for service if you find the oven is overshooting or falling short of its setting. (Even 25°F one way or the other makes a serious difference in baking results.)

Cooling and Mellowing

Fresh bread smells irresistibly good but it will taste better when it has had a chance to complete the transformation of grain into manna by cooling completely. The day after it's baked, bread has begun to ripen into its full flavor and will become better and better as long as it lasts, so don't be in a hurry to tear into that tempting creation, if you can help it—it will be good to the last crumb.

PART 1: BREAD IN LOAVES & IN SPECIAL SHAPES

"Loaf" is the word that usually defines bread, but not always, as demonstrated here. The following recipes for noncrisp breadstuffs include directions for some specialties—bagels, soft pretzels, focaccias, crumpets, English muffins, and tortillas—that are all over the map in terms of shape. However, the pleasingly holey English Muffin Bread and Ultimately Cheesy Cheddar Bread are baked in classic bread pans, while Semolina Bread and Sesame-Topped Bulgur Bread are shaped and baked as long, slim free-form loaves. Sun-Dried Tomato Bread, with or without rosemary, produces a big, nubbly hearth-style loaf, most appetizing to behold, worthy of a place of honor on a table indoors or out.

Falling on the borderline between a sweet treat and the staff of life, there's something a bit different—Chocolate-Filled Bread Rolls, the French *petits pains au chocolat,* fat finger rolls enclosing a mother lode of soft, dark chocolate. To be eaten warm, they're perfectly delicious with a cup of something hot, or just a glass of milk.

CHOCOLATE-FILLED BREAD ROLLS

(PETITS PAINS AU CHOCOLAT)

Bread rolls stuffed with delectably soft and warm chocolate are mouthwatering to hear and read about as an armchair traveler, and a little experimental baking has established that this delight of French children lives up to its billing. *Petits pains au chocolat,* in other words, are not for kids only.

My version uses a tender milk, egg, and butter dough I usually turn into a panful of soft rolls. (Brioche dough, which is much richer, could be used, or you could go the other way and use any plain bread dough.)

Try to use excellent bittersweet chocolate—Merckens is one label I like a lot. For the filling you either cut crosswise fingers from 3-ounce bittersweet chocolate bars, or chop squares or disks of sweet dark baking chocolate into pea-sized chunks, or use the best available chocolate chips or bits (no fake chocolate will do the job). Note that the recipe lists 8 to 12 ounces of chocolate, allowing for a degree of indulgence—I usually opt for 12 ounces.

AN UNLIKELY COMBINATION?

Until you try it, the pairing of simple bread and chocolate sounds odd, but curious bakers really should try these buns with the surprise in the middle. Less fatty and less sweet than Danish pastries, they are wonderful with coffee.

4 tablespoons (½ stick) sweet (unsalted) butter
1½ cups milk (or half milk and half water)
¼ cup warm (110° to 115°F) water
2 teaspoons (⅔ envelope) active dry yeast
1 large egg, at room temperature, beaten to mix
1 tablespoon nondiastatic malt powder (see page 81) or 2 teaspoons sugar, optional
1½ teaspoons salt
About 4½ cups unbleached all-purpose flour, or more if needed

FILLING:
8 to 12 ounces fine bittersweet or semisweet chocolate

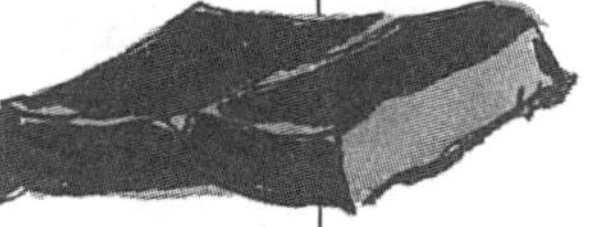

GLAZE:
1 large egg beaten with 1 tablespoon milk

Makes 1½ dozen

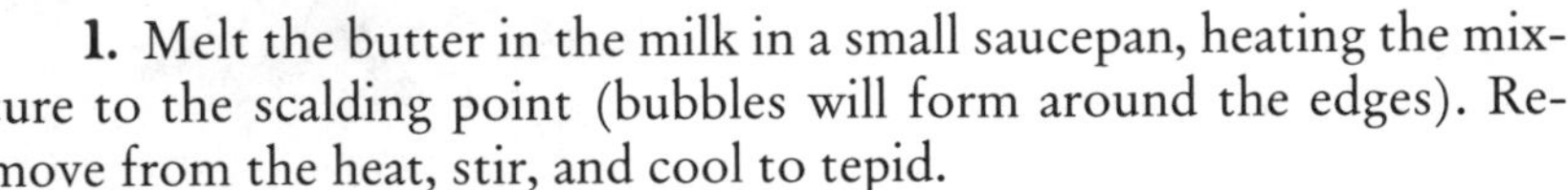

1. Melt the butter in the milk in a small saucepan, heating the mixture to the scalding point (bubbles will form around the edges). Remove from the heat, stir, and cool to tepid.

2. In the large bowl of an electric mixer, stir the yeast into the warm water and let stand until completely dissolved, about 10 minutes.

3. Stir the buttery milk into the yeast mixture, then mix in the egg, malt powder, and salt. Gradually beat in enough flour to make a dough that cleans the sides of the bowl. If you have a dough hook, change to it and knead the dough for about 3 minutes; or turn the dough out onto a floured surface and knead it for about 5 minutes by hand. Form the dough into a ball, return it to the wiped-out bowl, cover with plastic wrap and a towel, and leave in a warm spot until approximately tripled in volume, about 2 hours.

4. Meanwhile, grease two baking sheets and measure the chocolate for the filling as follows: *If chocolate is in 3-ounce bars:* Cut 3 or 4 bars into 18 equal crosswise strips a scant 1¼ inches wide. *If chips are used:* For 8 ounces, measure out about 1⅓ cups; for 12 ounces, 2 cups. *If chocolate is in disks:* Chop 8 ounces to equal about 1½ cups; 12 ounces, about 2¼ cups. Set the chocolate aside.

5. Turn the dough out onto a lightly floured surface and divide it in half; return one half to the bowl and cover it. Roll out the portion on the board about ½ inch thick, making a rough square. Cut it into 9 equal pieces (2 cuts in each direction). Roll each piece into an oblong approximately 4 by 5 inches in size.

6. Divide the chocolate in half and set aside one share. Place the remaining chocolate on the pieces of dough as follows: Lay one of the

Choosing Yeast

The recipes have been written for standard active dry yeast, not the fast-rising type or the "European-style yeasts" now available. (The latter are produced by a manufacturing method that keeps more of the cells viable, and so gives quicker and livelier rising action.) If using quick-rise or another special yeast, read the label for special instructions.

Chocolate Bulletin

Just in time to be slipped into these pages, news of the availability of slim chocolate bars for making petits pains au chocolat *has arrived via the Baker's Catalogue, a great source for special flours and unusual ingredients. See Mail-Order Sources for the address.*

prepared bars or 1 to 1½ tablespoons of chopped-up chocolate (or chips or bits) in a lengthwise strip down the center of each oblong, leaving half an inch clear at either end. Bring the long edges together over the chocolate and pinch them closed; pinch the ends closed, then lay each roll seam side down on one prepared baking sheet, smoothing it into a pleasant shape with your fingers. Leave 1½ inches between rolls on the pan. Shape the second half of the batch in the same way.

7. Cover the baking sheets with towels and let the rolls rise until almost doubled, about 45 minutes. About 15 minutes before the rising is complete, preheat the oven to 375°F, with a shelf in the upper third and one in the lower.

8. Brush the rolls with the glaze and bake them until firm and golden brown, about 25 minutes, exchanging shelf positions halfway. Cool the rolls on a rack, serving some, if you like, while the chocolate is still warm and soft.

9. After they have cooled, bag the chocolate rolls for room-temperature storage for a few days, or freezer-wrap and freeze them for up to 2 months. Thaw frozen rolls in their wrappings.

10. ***To serve:*** As the charm of these rolls lies in the soft chocolate inside, the rolls that have been stored must be rewarmed. Either enclose them in a paper bag and warm them in a moderate oven (350°F) for a few minutes, until the chocolate has softened; or wrap 2 to 4 rolls at a time in slightly moistened paper towels and microwave them for 30 seconds, check on progress, and microwave them again in very short bursts (10 or 15 seconds) until you judge they are warmed through—check them by touch, remembering that the outsides will be cooler than the chocolate in the center.

English Muffins, Updated

Treated to a helping of texture (a.k.a. fiber) by way of this recipe, English muffins are even more toothsome than usual, especially if you like breadstuffs with a lot of character. Wheat bran (my preference), oat bran (which creates a slightly softer and creamier texture than wheat), or a portion of whole-wheat flour does the fiber trick. Lacking these ingredients or the desire to use them, just replace them with additional all-purpose or bread flour.

As muffineering methods have evolved at our house, the size of muffins, as well as their fiber content, has increased. These extra-large muffins, a bit denser and less rough-textured than commercial sorts, make a marvelous foundation for a burger or sandwich of any kind when fork-split and lightly toasted. Needless to say they remain highly eligible for breakfast, with marmalade or jam.

Four-inch-round cutters for really big muffins aren't easily come by—I don't possess one—so I use a recycled tall coffee can, which is exactly right, or dig out one of the 4-inch "muffin rings" necessary for baking crumpets (page 82) but curiously enough not much used for baking muffins. If a smaller round cutter is used, you'll have more muffins than the yield indicates.

English Muffins with Wheat or Oat Bran

1½ teaspoons (½ envelope) active dry yeast
1½ cups warm (110° to 115°F) water
¾ cup low-fat yogurt or buttermilk, at room temperature (or use milk, scalded and cooled, or water, or the liquid drained from yogurt made into Yogurt Cheese, page 216)
1 tablespoon nondiastatic malt powder (see page 81) or 2 teaspoons sugar, optional
1 tablespoon vegetable oil
1 to 1½ teaspoons salt, to taste
½ cup plain unprocessed wheat bran (not bran cereal) or oat bran
About 4¼ cups all-purpose or bread flour, or more as needed
Cornmeal for the "rising" pan(s)

Makes from 10 to a baker's dozen extra-large muffins

1. In the large bowl of an electric mixer, stir the yeast into ½ cup of the warm water and let stand until completely dissolved, about 10 minutes.

2. Mix in the remaining cup of warm water, the yogurt or buttermilk, malt powder, oil, salt, and bran. Gradually beat in the flour, starting with 1 cup, then adding flour ½ cup at a time. Change to the dough hook, if you have one, and knead the dough (which will be soft) very thoroughly, at least 6 minutes. (If you choose to knead by hand on a board, you'll need a baker's dough scraper and twice as much time to knead the soft mixture, which you do by scraping and folding it repeatedly.) If the dough sticks to the bowl unduly, sprinkle in a very little more flour until it cleans the bowl. Cover with plastic wrap and let the dough rise in a warm place until fully doubled, about 1½ hours.

3. Beat down the dough to deflate it, cover it again, and let it rise again until doubled, 30 to 45 minutes.

Bran

In this book's recipes, "bran" means the unprocessed form, not a breakfast cereal. Wheat and oat bran are stocked by supermarkets as well as health-food emporiums.

4. Meanwhile, sprinkle a generous layer of flour over a work surface. Beat down the dough again and divide it in half. At this point, decide whether you can bake all the muffins at once—at our house, this takes two griddles, each spanning two burners, but one griddle and a couple of skillets would also do. If you plan to bake in batches, refrigerate half of the dough, covered with plastic. Flatten the remaining half of the dough into an even ½-inch layer, using your hands or a rolling pin; keep plenty of flour under the layer (to prevent sticking) without working it into the dough. Let the piece relax for a few minutes.

5. Sprinkle cornmeal generously over one or two baking sheets, depending on whether you're shaping all the muffins at once. Cut out muffins with a 4-inch round cutter. Lift the cut rounds onto the cornmeal surface, placing them at least an inch apart. Press together the scraps, incorporating as little additional flour as possible, and cut more muffins. Repeat with the remaining dough if all the muffins are to be baked at once; otherwise, begin shaping the second batch when the baking of the first muffins is almost finished.

6. Cover the muffins with a towel and let them rise until they have doubled in height, which will take from 20 to 30 minutes. When they are ready, you will glimpse bubbles under the top skin.

7. When the muffins are almost ready, heat one or two large griddles or a griddle plus a heavy skillet or two (cast iron is ideal) over medium-low heat until a few drops of water sizzle quite slowly before evaporating. If you are using an electric griddle or skillet, heat it with the control set at 325°F.

8. Transfer the muffins carefully to the cooking surface(s), using a wide pancake turner to avoid deflating the soft dough. Reduce the stovetop heat to low and bake the muffins slowly for 10 minutes, then check the progress of the undersides: the bottoms should have taken on only a tinge of color. If they are beginning to brown, reduce the heat. Check baking progress in the same way if using an electric appliance. Continue cooking for about 5 minutes more, or until the bottoms are pale gold and the tops are firm to a light touch. Turn the muffins, squash each lightly against the griddle with the spatula, and bake them for about 15 minutes more, until their sides are firm and they feel relatively light when lifted. Turn off the heat, turn the muffins again, and leave them on the cooling griddle for another 15 or 20 minutes, turning them once or twice if convenient.

9. Cool the muffins completely on racks, then split some (use a fork, not a knife, to separate the halves), toast them lightly, butter, and serve; or bag the muffins in plastic until wanted. The muffins keep well at room temperature for 3 or 4 days. For longer storage, package them for freezer keeping for as long as a month to 6 weeks; thaw them in their wrappings. For convenience, the muffins may be split, ready for

Better Batter

The softer you make the dough for English muffins, the more lovely holes, crannies, and crevices you'll have in the finished product. If holeyness is your preference, try for the softest dough you can handle successfully.

toasting, before they're frozen; they can then be toasted directly from the frozen state.

English Muffins Made with Whole-Wheat Flour

Makes about a dozen extra-large muffins

Use the preceding recipe, but omit the bran. Use about 3 cups all-purpose or bread flour and about 2 cups whole-wheat flour, or 1½ cups whole-wheat flour and ½ cup wheat germ. I use either regular dark whole wheat or the delicious white (or "sweet") whole-wheat flour available by mail order from the King Arthur Flour people (see Mail-Order Sources, page 390).

An English Muffin Loaf

A slice of this bread has the flavor, holeyness, and attractive rough texture of an English muffin, but the loaves are quicker to make than muffins. (See the preceding recipe for English muffins and page 82 for crumpets, if those are your pleasure.) The loaf is for toasting and slathering with butter, or cream cheese, or jam, or a combination to suit. If you like the traditional rough texture of a split English muffin, "slice" the loaf as described in the final step.

Shortening or pan coating for the pans and cornmeal for the pans and topping
1 tablespoon (1 envelope) active dry yeast
⅓ cup warm (110° to 115°F) warm water
1¼ cups milk
1 cup cold water, or more as needed
1 tablespoon nondiastatic malt powder (see page 81) or 2 teaspoons sugar, optional
2 teaspoons salt
2 tablespoons vegetable oil
5 cups all-purpose flour, or as needed

Makes 2 loaves

1. Grease two 6-cup loaf pans (8½ × 4½ × 2½ inches). Sprinkle cornmeal into the pans, shake to coat the inside of the pans, and tap out the excess.

Instant Assistance

An instant-reading cooking thermometer is worth its weight in truffles, at the very least, to either the constant or occasional cook. Using this tiny instrument, there's no need to guess whether the water is lukewarm or not, or the roast done to taste. Highly recommended.

For Holey Bread

The method used to produce An English Muffin Loaf is unusual—the "dough" is actually a thick yeast-leavened batter, and you beat it vigorously, instead of trying to knead it (which would be almost impossible) to develop the desired holeyness and roughness of texture.

2. In the bowl of an electric mixer, stir the yeast into the warm water and let stand until dissolved, about 10 minutes.

3. Meanwhile, scald the milk (heat in a small saucepan until small bubbles gather around the edges), then add the 1 cup cold water and let cool until the temperature of the mixture is 110° to 115°F. Add the liquid to the dissolved yeast, together with the malt powder, salt, and oil. Beat in the flour gradually, beginning with a cupful, then adding ½ cup at a time. Beat the dough, which will actually be more like a gloppy batter, for an additional 3 or 4 minutes. If the batter is on the stiff side, add up to ¼ cup more water. Scrape down the sides of the bowl, cover it with plastic wrap, set in a warm place, and let the dough rise until doubled and about to collapse, about 1½ hours.

4. Beat the dough a few strokes and scrape it into the prepared pans. Smooth the tops with a rubber spatula dipped in water, then sprinkle them generously with additional cornmeal. Cover loosely with plastic wrap and let rise until the dough comes just above the pan rims, about 45 minutes (the time will depend on the ambient temperature).

5. Shortly before the loaves are ready to bake, preheat the oven to 375°F, with a shelf in the center position.

6. Bake the muffin bread for 30 minutes, then reduce the oven setting to 325°F. Turn the loaves out of the pans, lay them on their sides on the oven shelf, and bake them 10 to 15 minutes longer, or until a knock on the bottom of a loaf produces a hollow sound. Cool completely on a rack. To store, bag in plastic and keep at room temperature for a few days, or double-bag and freeze for up to 2 months. A frozen loaf should be thawed in its wrappings.

7. ***To serve:*** Slice the bread with a serrated knife and toast until golden; serve with butter and any embellishments you prefer. For rough-surfaced slices resembling a split muffin, with plenty of nooks and crannies to hold melting butter, I use an angel-cake divider to tear the loaf apart.

The Bagel Shop

Since I first began making bagels just for the fun of it, bagel bakeries have sprung up all across the map, even in such formerly deprived places as the eastern end of Long Island, where we now live, breathe, and enjoy good food. But home-crafted bagels still get our vote as chewy, dense, inimitable items that are rewarding to make once in a while, especially if you live in the hinterlands in terms of bagel availability. (Supermarket bagels don't count, dosed as they are with sugar, or gussied up with cinnamon, raisins, and other extraneous whatsits.) You'll notice that the recipe here takes notice of such toppings as sea salt and various savory seeds, all of which are compatible with the plain, chewy nature of the bagel.

Water Bagels–The Real Thing

This recipe makes a dozen and a half bagels of standard size, or it will make 8 to 10 giant bagels, or two dozen modest-size rings, or as many miniature bagels as you have the patience to form.

If you do not have the malt powder called for, sugar may be substituted when the bagels are boiled, but they won't be as glossy and tasty as those boiled with malt.

1 tablespoon (or 1 envelope) active dry yeast
2 cups warm water (110° to 115°F)
3 tablespoons nondiastatic barley malt powder, optional (see sidebar opposite)
1 tablespoon coarse (kosher or sea) salt
About 5½ cups bread or all-purpose flour, or more if needed

WATER BATH:
3 quarts water
¼ cup nondiastatic barley malt powder (see sidebar opposite) or 3 tablespoons sugar

OPTIONAL GLAZE AND TOPPINGS:
1 egg white, beaten until foamy with 1 tablespoon water
Coarse (kosher or sea) salt; caraway seed; sesame seed; chernushka ("black caraway"); poppy seed

Makes about eighteen 3½-inch bagels

1. In the large bowl of an electric mixer or a mixing bowl, stir the yeast into the warm water and let stand until dissolved, a matter of a few minutes. Stir in the malt powder, then the salt. Beating at slow speed, start adding 5½ cups flour; continue to mix until the dough comes cleanly away from the sides of the bowl. Switch to the dough hook, if you have one (or turn the dough out onto a floured kneading surface) and knead very thoroughly (5 minutes or more by machine, twice as long by hand), adding more flour as necessary to make a nonsticky, elastic dough. This dough can scarcely be kneaded too much.

2. Form the dough into a smooth ball and return it to the bowl (which I don't bother to clean and grease). Cover the bowl with plastic wrap and leave the dough to double in bulk, about 1 hour.

How to Slice a Bagel

Hospital emergency rooms report a plethora of wounds to bagel slicers who don't tackle the job with care. (The unwary seem to hold a bagel in one hand and a knife in the other.) There are many gizmos on the market for holding the bagel (and cluttering the cupboard), but the human hand does very well, rightly used: Hold the bagel flat on a cutting surface, pressing it with the palm of one hand, while the bread knife in the other hand halves it horizontally.

Barley Malt Powder

One bagel ingredient, nondiastatic barley malt powder, makes a difference both in the character of bagel dough and in the shininess of the crust. (I've made many a bagel without it, but they're much better with.) Malt powder for baking is sold in two forms, both of whose names are a mouthful: the nondiastatic form used here (for flavor and gloss) and diastatic malt, containing live enzymes and used to assist leavening as well as taste. Malt is stocked by sellers of baking supplies and by health-food stores.

3. As the dough rises, combine the water bath ingredients in a wide pan (a large sauté pan is ideal) and set it over a burner, ready to turn on the heat.

4. Punch down the dough to deflate it and turn it out onto a floured work surface. Divide it in half; return half to the bowl and cover with plastic wrap. Divide the working half into approximately equal-size pieces—4 or 5 for monster bagels, 8 or 9 for classic dimensions, 12 or more for smallish or miniature bagels. Cover the pieces with a towel and let the dough rest for a few minutes.

5. Meanwhile, preheat the oven to 425°F, with a shelf in the center position, and begin heating the water bath. Prepare the glaze and any toppings if you're using them.

6. ***Form the bagels:*** If you've divided the dough to make the standard size, roll one piece of dough on the board, pressing it very firmly with the palms (important for a smooth surface) and stretching it to about 10 inches in length. To make a ring, moisten one end of the "snake" and press it firmly onto the other end; smooth the joining with your fingers, and stretch the center hole if necessary. Place each bagel on a spare baking sheet as it is shaped. (At this point, choose whether to let the bagels rise a little—allow about 20 minutes—before they're boiled; if you do, they'll be lighter in texture than bagels that are boiled at once. Lovers of chewy bagels will opt for immediate boiling.) When the portion of dough you're working with has been shaped (and allowed to puff up a little, if you wish), proceed to the water bath.

7. ***Boiling the bagels.*** Have the water bath at a full boil. Slip in several bagels (don't crowd the pan) and begin timing at once. Boil exactly 1 minute (30 seconds for miniatures), flip the bagels gently, and boil the second side for a minute or half a minute as before. Lift out and place on a nonstick baking sheet, or a regular baking sheet covered with parchment. Repeat until all the shaped bagels have been boiled. Brush them with the optional glaze and sprinkle generously with salt or seed, if you wish.

8. Bake the bagels for 15 to 20 minutes (for the standard size; a little less for miniatures, more for monsters), until they are a rich golden brown and firm when pressed. Meanwhile, shape and boil the second portion of dough. Bake the second batch while the first batch cools on a rack.

9. Store fully cooled bagels at room temperature, bagged in plastic, for up to several days; or freezer-wrap and freeze for up to 3 months or more. Thaw frozen bagels in their wrappings. Refresh them, unsliced, in a moderate oven for a few minutes if they're not to be toasted; or slice them and go straight to the toaster.

Bagel Chips

The only trick here is to avoid slicing oneself instead of the bagel, but the trick is a simple one. Cut plain bagels across the center to make two fat horseshoes of each. Stand a half-bagel on its cut ends and hold it firmly while making the thinnest possible slices with a sharp serrated knife. When you reach the position for the last cut, lay the piece flat, press it with the palm of the holding hand, and slice it horizontally. Result, about 6 very thin slices per bagel half.

Spread the slices directly on the oven shelf and bake them in a low oven (about 175°F), until the chips are very lightly colored and completely crisp. The time required will depend on the thickness of the chips. (Just keep an eye on them.)

Stored in a canister at room temperature, any chips not served at once with dips, spreads, or whatnot will keep for several weeks. If the chips should require refreshing after a spell of storage, warm them for a few minutes in a 300°F oven.

Bagel Bruschetta

Slice the bagels as for chips, above, but make only 3 slices instead of 5 or 6. Rub the slices with a cut clove of garlic, then brush on the lightest possible film of olive oil. If you like, add a few grains of coarse salt. Bake the slices on a baking sheet for 5 minutes or so in a 300°F oven, until crisp and hot. Serve warm.

Real Crumpets

Curiously named and curiously cooked, crumpets are one of those odd things to eat that are either liked a lot or not at all. (Essayist John Thorne has called them "an evolutionary dead end, a muffin trying to find its way back to the flapjack and getting lost.") These low-rise, holey griddle breads are fun to make, though, and anyone who dotes on the cousinly English muffin is likely to like them at teatime or breakfast, especially if plenty of butter is the day's allowable indulgence. (And marmalade.)

Try to acquire a set of "muffin" rings, hoops about 4 inches across and 1 inch deep, for shaping crumpets. (The rings are not much used for English muffins, despite their name.) Lacking the rings, you can make do (and make smaller crumpets) by using small food cans, tuna or pineapple size, with bottoms as well as tops removed.

CRUMPETS OF TWO SEXES?

John Ayto's delightful Diner's Dictionary *(Oxford University Press, 1993) ruminates on the etymology of the word "crumpet," learnedly going back to the fourteenth century. The author then points out that crumpet, which since the 1930s has been British slang for an attractive girl, is now also applied to sexually attractive males. Authority? A BBC broadcast, no less, crumpetizing the actor Paul Newman.*

2 teaspoons (⅔ envelope) active dry yeast
½ cup plus ⅓ cup warm (110° to 115°F) water
1 cup milk
1 cup cold water
2 tablespoons vegetable oil or melted and cooled sweet (unsalted) butter
2 teaspoons salt
1 tablespoon nondiastatic malt powder (page 81) or 2 teaspoons sugar
3½ cups all-purpose flour, or use half all-purpose flour and half unbleached pastry flour
½ teaspoon baking soda
Sweet (unsalted) butter for greasing the muffin rings and griddle

Makes 15 to 18 crumpets

1. In the large bowl of an electric mixer, stir the yeast into ½ cup warm water and let it stand until the yeast has completely dissolved, about 10 minutes.

2. Heat the milk to scalding in a small saucepan (bubbles will appear around the edges), then add the cup of cold water; the final temperature should be around 110°F. Stir the milk and water into the yeast mixture together with the oil, salt, and malt powder. Beat in the flour gradually, starting with a cupful and tapering down to half a cup at a time. Beat vigorously, using the flat paddle if you have one, until you have an elastic and just-pourable batter, not thick enough to be called a dough. If it is too thick, add a little more water.

3. Cover the bowl and let the batter rise until the top is very bubbly and the whole mass is about to collapse, about 1½ hours at usual room temperature. Stir the batter down.

4. Dissolve the baking soda in the ⅓ cup of warm water and stir it into the batter. Cover and let rest until again very bubbly, about 30 minutes.

5. Heat a griddle, preferably a thick one, over medium-low heat, or heat an electric griddle or skillet with the control set at 375°F. Rub the insides of the muffin rings with butter and heat as many of them as the griddle will accommodate until they are hot.

6. Rub the griddle lightly with butter, pushing the rings aside as necessary. Using a ¼-cup measure for each crumpet, ladle batter into the warmed rings, filling them about halfway. Bake the crumpets slowly until the top bubbles have broken, the tops have dried, and the rings become loose, in 7 to 10 minutes. Lift off the rings and turn the crumpets; bake the second side 3 to 4 minutes, until freckled and firm. If the crumpets are to be served at once, keep them warm in a napkin-lined basket; otherwise let them cool on a rack. Repeat until all the batter has been used, buttering and warming the rings before re-using them.

7. To keep cooled crumpets for up to 3 days or so, bag them in plastic and leave them at room temperature. For longer storage, double-bag and freeze them for up to 2 months. They may be warmed (see below) from the frozen state.

8. *To serve:* Toasting crumpets (do not split them) lightly before serving is a matter of taste; putting a *lot* of butter on the holey side is a matter of custom. (Asked, I'd say toast, by all means, but toast lightly just to warm them through and crisp the outside.) If you don't toast your crumpets, rewarm them, wrapped in damp paper towels, for a few minutes in a low oven. The general idea is to replicate their just-baked character.

Focaccia~Savory Italian Flatbread

As one of the rustic Italian foods that have crept into our hearts in the years since spaghetti became merely all-American, flattish loaves of focaccia are sliced up for restaurant bread baskets far and wide, but the commercial kind is seldom as good as focaccia of your own baking because this bread is best served while fresh, even still warm.

Focaccia can be thick or thin (just like, come to think of it, pizza, surely a close cousin), and like pizza it can be basic—for focaccia, that means a topping of nothing more than good olive oil and salt—or enriched with uncounted authentic add-ons—cheese, ham, herbs, onions, tomatoes, even mushrooms, zucchini, and eggplant, olives, garlic, anchovies.

Research has been tantalizing: I've hesitated over the setting down of each possible recipe and over each tasting, wondering if this focaccia is in fact the one I like best of all. What came out of this pleasing perplexity is the following basic recipe, plus an outline of alternative additions and toppings. Beyond these, only your creativity sets the limits.

However you make your focaccia, you'll have a wonderful snack bread, but don't overlook slices as a substantial accompaniment for a salad or soup lunch, or as the dinner bread to complement meat, fish, or fowl. Good for sandwiches, too.

Bread of Many Savors

The introduction to the focaccia recipe offers a basketful of suggestions for flavoring this flatbread. Don't be limited by Italian-style variations—a sprinkle of mixed poppy, caraway, and sesame seed, plus a little coarse salt, over the loaf after it's brushed with olive oil, is a great topping for an all-purpose breadstuff.

Simple Focaccia

1 tablespoon (1 envelope) active dry yeast
1¼ cups warm water (110° to 115°F)
1 tablespoon nondiastatic barley malt powder (see page 81) or 2 teaspoons sugar, optional
3½ to 4 cups all-purpose flour, as needed
2 teaspoons coarse (kosher or sea) salt
3 tablespoons fruity olive oil

TOPPING:
2 tablespoons additional fruity olive oil, or more if desired
A little additional coarse (kosher or sea) salt

Makes a 12-inch round loaf

1. In the large bowl of an electric mixer, stir the yeast into ¼ cup of the warm water and let stand until completely dissolved, about 10 minutes. Add ½ cup more of the warm water, the malt powder, if using, and 1½ cups of the flour. Beat well, using the flat paddle of the mixer. Let it rise in the bowl, covered, until doubled in volume, about 1 hour.

2. Punch the dough down to deflate it. Dissolve the 2 teaspoons salt in the remaining ½ cup warm water and beat it into the dough together with the olive oil. Gradually add enough of the remaining flour to form a stiff dough. Change to the dough hook (or turn onto a floured board) and work in enough more flour to make an elastic, nonsticky dough. Continue to knead until the dough is smooth and elastic, about 5 minutes by machine or 7 to 8 minutes by hand. Return the dough to the bowl (no need to grease it) and let it rise again until doubled, 45 minutes to 1 hour.

3. Turn the dough out onto the floured work surface and roll it out into an 11-inch round. Dust a baking sheet with flour and transfer the flat loaf to it. Poke deep dimples all over the top with your fingertips, cover with a damp towel, and let rise until doubled, about 30 minutes. Shortly before rising is complete, preheat the oven to 400°F. Have ready a plant mister or another kind of spray bottle containing fresh water.

4. *Adding the topping:* Drizzle or paint the additional oil over the focaccia, using a larger quantity if you wish. Sprinkle the coarse salt on top.

5. Bake for about 25 minutes, spraying a good blast of mist into the oven immediately after putting in the loaf and twice more at 4-minute intervals. The focaccia is done when it is golden-brown and firm. Slip it immediately onto a rack and serve while still slightly warm, if possible. Leftovers should be wrapped in plastic (for up to a day or two) and refreshed in a paper bag placed in a moderate oven (350°F) for a few minutes.

Focaccia Enhancements

Herbs: In step 2, knead either sage or rosemary into the dough. Use 2 teaspoons crumbled dried leaf sage or 1½ tablespoons coarsely chopped fresh sage leaves; 1½ teaspoons crumbled dried rosemary or 1 tablespoon chopped fresh rosemary leaves. Top with oil and salt as described and decorate with sprigs of fresh sage or rosemary if available. My friend, expert chef Chris Styler, kneads in a teaspoonful of crumbled dried oregano, another of crumbled dried basil, and half a teaspoon of crumbled rosemary—delicious. (You might also like to use 2 to 3 teaspoons of Italian-Style Herb Blend, page 191, in this way.)

Italian-style ham with herbs: Knead 3 ounces (or more, for a richer flavor) of diced prosciutto into the dough in step 2. Top the focaccia with about 1 tablespoon of chopped fresh rosemary leaves plus 2 tablespoons of either chopped fresh thyme or sweet marjoram leaves and press the herbs lightly into the dough before brushing on the oil. Added salt is optional.

Olives: Pit a big handful of oil-cured black olives and strew them onto the focaccia after it has risen and is ready to bake; press them lightly into the dough and brush with the added oil but don't add salt.

Onions: Sometimes thin-sliced raw onions are pressed lightly onto the risen dough and sprinkled with oil and salt. For milder flavor, sauté 2 medium onions, sliced, plus a little chopped garlic if you like, until soft in a little olive oil. Cool before spreading onto the risen loaf, then brush on the additional oil and sprinkle lightly with additional salt.

Tomatoes: Thin-sliced, these are laid on top of the risen dough, strewn with chopped fresh basil, and brushed or sprinkled with oil and topped with a little salt.

Two Kinds of Tortillas

Making your own soft, warm, fragrant tortillas with the help of a good thick griddle plus a rolling pin (for flour tortillas) or a tortilla press (for corn tortillas) is an enjoyable project that takes longer to write about than to do. Naturally, experience leads to expertise in tortilla making, but even the irregularly shaped or imperfectly baked examples turned out in your first effort will be eatable and may well lead to addiction, so I'd encourage anyone who can't buy good locally made tortillas to scorn the supermarket kind in favor of a homecrafted supply.

These south-of-the-border flatbreads are a delicious alternative to everyday breads at the table, and both corn and flour tortillas figure as elements of countless Mexican or hyphenated-Mexican dishes served nowadays all over North America. (Think of quesadillas, tostadas, tacos, enchiladas, burritos.)

So here are basic directions for flour tortillas (originally from northern Mexico) and all-Mexican (and now all-American) corn tortillas made from masa flour, which is also called masa harina or masa mix.

Flour Tortillas (Tortillas de Harina)

The dough for flour tortillas is as easy to make as dough for baking-powder biscuits. The expertise comes in rolling them out into neat rounds, but fortunately for cooks who are still learning, they'll taste the same even if raggedy. *Tortillas de harina* can be made ahead of time if necessary, but they're at their best if fairly fresh from the griddle. Any leftovers make great giant "crackers" if dried until paper-crisp directly on the shelf of a 175°F oven.

Tortilla experts debate the question: Baking powder or no baking powder? This recipe using baking powder works well and has the merit of requiring less shortening than one for flour tortillas made without leavening. If you'd like to try the higher-fat alternative, omit the baking powder and double the shortening.

3 cups all-purpose flour
1½ teaspoons baking powder
1 teaspoon salt, or more to taste
3 tablespoons lard (preferred by many) or solid vegetable shortening
¾ to about 1 cup lukewarm water, as required

Makes about 1½ dozen flour tortillas

1. Sift or whisk together the flour, baking powder, and salt in a large bowl. Using a pastry blender, the fingers, or two knives wielded scissors fashion, cut in the lard or shortening until the mixture is uniform, like fine meal. Stir in ¾ cup of the water, plus more if required to make a pliable dough (the exact amount will depend on the dryness of the flour). Knead the dough about 2 dozen times on a lightly floured work surface, until smooth and elastic. Cover with a dampened towel and let rest 10 minutes.

2. Divide the dough into 18 pieces weighing about 1½ ounces each (the size of a smallish egg) and form each into a ball. Cover the dough again with the dampened towel and let it relax for another 10 minutes.

3. Set a griddle or large heavy skillet, preferably cast iron, over moderately high heat; do not grease. Before starting to bake the tortillas, test the pan—drops of water should bounce and evaporate immediately.

4. Roll out the first tortilla between two sheets of heavy plastic (cut open a good-sized freezer bag), making a round 8 inches in diameter and as thin as you can manage. It doesn't matter if it's lopsided, but you can trim it if you're feeling particular. To remove from the plastic, lift off the upper sheet; invert the tortilla onto your hand, and peel off the second piece of plastic. Lay the tortilla in the pan and cook it for about half a minute or until brown spots appear on the underside, then flip it and cook the second side until similarly freckled (a few darker spots are okay, in fact authentic). Shape and bake the rest of the dough in the same way, stacking the tortillas on a sheet of foil and covering them with foil or plastic between additions to the stack. Serve warm with butter, or proceed to the making of the Mexican dish you have in mind.

5. If the tortillas are not to be served immediately, they'll keep warm for an hour or two wrapped in foil and placed in an oven at its lowest setting. If they are being made for later use, cool the finished stack of tortillas, wrap it airtight, and store in the refrigerator for a day or two. (They don't freeze particularly well, in my experience.) To reheat, rub or brush a very little water over each if they seem at all dry, then bake them briefly on a medium-hot griddle, turning them rapidly and repeatedly, for about 30 seconds. As each tortilla becomes warm and soft, put it into a pot or dish and cover the container closely.

Corn Tortillas (Tortillas de Maiz)

Corn tortillas can be shaped with a rolling pin (we won't even *talk* about trying to pat them out by hand), but a tortilla press is a small luxury that I wouldn't give up. Lacking such a device, roll out small balls of dough (step 3) as symmetrically as possible between two sheets of plastic. Peel off the upper plastic, invert the tortilla onto your palm, and peel off the second sheet. (The plastic-peeling procedure is the same when using the tortilla press, opposite.)

The raw material for the corn tortillas made by the fortunate few is fresh masa dough, which is sold in some corners of the country, but for everybody else it's instant masa flour or masa mix. This specially processed, fine-textured corn flour—not actually a mix—has been treated with lime to create the unique "tortilla" flavor and requires only the addition of water. It's worth seeking out a locally favored brand in a Latin American market—I've found one in particular that's noticeably paler and more aromatic than the supermarket brand labeled "masa harina."

Tortillas North of the Border

If you like all-American corn bread—and who doesn't—consider tortillas as an alternative when you're having fried chicken, or soup, or a hearty bean dish or stew, or a salad lunch. Gently heated and served with a spread of butter or its equivalent, tortillas are cockle-warming and quick to produce from a frozen or refrigerated supply.

1 to 1½ cups warm water
2 cups instant masa (also called masa flour, masa mix, or masa harina)

Makes about a dozen corn tortillas

1. Stir 1 cup of the water (which can be quite hot if you like) into the instant masa, then slowly add a little more water, stirring vigorously, until a pliable dough has been formed; it should be neither crumbly nor wet. (If it turns out to be either, just add more water or more masa flour and mix again; you can't hurt this dough by working it.) Cover the dough with plastic and let it rest at room temperature for a few minutes.

2. Set out a tortilla press and two plastic sandwich bags, or two sheets of heavy plastic recycled from food storage bags, trimmed to a size a little larger than the face of the tortilla press. Set a heavy griddle or a heavy skillet, preferably of cast iron, over medium-high heat; grease the pan lightly.

3. To form a tortilla, make a ball of dough about 1½ inches in diameter. Lay one sandwich bag on the lower face of the press, place the dough on it somewhat closer to the hinge than the handle, cover with the second bag, close the press, and press slowly until the tortilla is as thin as it can be made. Lift off the upper plastic, turn the tortilla onto the palm of your hand, and peel off the remaining plastic. Invert the tortilla on the hot griddle and bake it for half a minute or less, until the round has puffed or bubbled (don't be discouraged if this doesn't always happen) and the top looks firm, then flip to the second side and continue to bake just until the underside is lightly speckled with brown. Finally, turn back to the first side and cook a few seconds longer. With practice, your tortillas will come out handsomer and handsomer, with freckled faces. Just don't overcook them or they'll be dry.

4. As the tortillas are finished, stack them on a sheet of foil and fold it over to retain heat; or stack them on a casserole and cover it closely. If the tortillas are not to be served immediately, they'll keep warm for an hour or two if enclosed in foil and placed in an oven at its lowest setting. If you are producing them for another day, cool the tortillas as they're finished, wrap them airtight, and store in the refrigerator for a few days or in the freezer (double-wrapped) for up to 3 months.

5. To reheat, thaw the tortillas at room temperature if frozen. If they seem at all dry, brush a very little water over each. Reheat on a medium-hot griddle, turning repeatedly, for about 30 seconds. As each tortilla becomes warm and soft, put it into a pot or dish and cover the container tightly. Alternatively, bundle the tortillas in foil and reheat them in a 350°F oven until the stack is heated through.

Sesame-Topped Bulgur Bread

Bulgur bread has a lot of whole-grain character but it is less chewy than regular cracked-wheat bread because bulgur is precooked before it goes into the package. However, if regular cracked wheat is what you have or can get most readily, by all means use it. Simply cook it for an additional 2 minutes in step 1.

Let bulgur bread rest for 24 hours before serving it to allow the flavor to bloom as the texture mellows.

2 cups water
1 cup bulgur (or regular cracked wheat, if preferred)
1 to 3 tablespoons honey or brown sugar, as desired
2 tablespoons (2 envelopes) active dry yeast
1½ cups warm water (110° to 115°F)
½ cup yellow cornmeal
⅓ cup hulled sesame seed
¼ cup corn oil or other vegetable oil
1 tablespoon salt
1½ cups whole-wheat flour
4½ to 5 cups all-purpose or bread flour, as needed

FOR THE PANS:
A little cornmeal

GLAZE AND TOPPING:
1 large egg white
2 tablespoons water
¼ to ⅓ cup additional sesame seed

Makes 4 long loaves, about 1 pound each

1. Bring the 2 cups of water to boil in a saucepan and stir in the bulgur. Lower the heat and simmer the bulgur, uncovered, for 7 minutes, stirring once or twice. Cool the bulgur mixture. Drain off any remaining liquid.

2. In a mixing bowl or the large bowl of an electric mixer, stir the honey, then the yeast, into ½ cup of the warm water, and let stand until the yeast is completely dissolved, about 10 minutes.

3. Add the cornmeal, sesame seed, oil, salt, the cooled bulgur mixture, and the remaining cup of warm water and beat until smooth. Beat in the whole-wheat flour, then beat in the all-purpose flour, 1 cup at a

Bulgur, Defined

Plain cracked wheat is wheat that has been broken up, not milled. The whole grain that becomes bulgur (or bulgur wheat) is first boiled, then dried, then cracked. The precooking makes it possible to use bulgur in such preparations as tabbouleh without additional cooking, and makes it especially toothsome for this bread.

time, until the mixture is too stiff to stir. Either turn the dough out onto a floured kneading surface and knead it by hand, or change to the dough hook for machine kneading and knead in as much of the remaining flour as needed to make an elastic dough that is no longer sticky. Knead the dough well, about 5 minutes by machine and twice as long by hand.

4. Form the dough into a ball and return it to its bowl (no need to wash, dry, or grease the bowl). Cover the bowl with plastic wrap and set it in a warm spot to rise until the dough has doubled, about 1 hour.

5. Punch the dough down with your fist, turn it over in the bowl, re-cover it, and let it rise again until doubled, about 45 minutes.

6. Divide the dough into four pieces and knead each briefly to deflate it. Flatten each piece into an oval about 1 inch thick. Cover the dough with a towel and let it rest for 10 minutes before continuing.

7. Sprinkle two baking sheets with cornmeal.

8. One at a time, flatten each piece of dough on a lightly floured surface into an oval about 12 inches long. Roll each up from one long side, pinching the seam together as you roll; pinch the ends closed and shape the loaves to smooth ovals about 14 inches long. Place the loaves seam down on the cornmeal-strewn baking sheets, placing them well apart, two loaves to a sheet. Cover the loaves with towels and let them rise until doubled, about 45 minutes.

9. Shortly before the rising is complete, preheat the oven to 400°F, with a shelf in the upper third and one in the lower. Prepare a glaze by beating the egg white briefly with the water.

10. Brush the loaves with the glaze and sprinkle them generously with sesame seed. Using a very sharp knife or razor blade held almost horizontally, cut three shallow slashes diagonally in the top of each.

11. Place each pan on a shelf in the oven and bake the loaves for 20 minutes, lower the oven setting to 350°F, then exchange the shelf positions of the pans, and bake the loaves 15 minutes longer, or until they sound hollow when thumped on the bottom.

12. Remove the loaves to wire racks and cool them completely, then wrap them in plastic wrap and store for at least 24 hours before serving. They will keep at room temperature for up to a week, or in the freezer, properly wrapped, for 3 months or more. To prevent sogginess, thaw frozen loaves in their wrappings. It's worth the extra minutes to refresh a thawed and unwrapped loaf by treating it to 10 minutes or so on the shelf of a 325°F oven before it is served.

ULTIMATELY CHEESY CHEDDAR BREAD

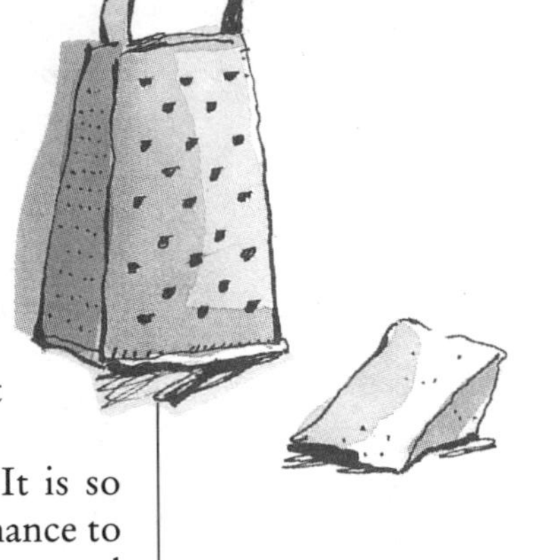

My warm thanks go to Ella Elvin, one of New York's most knowledgeable food writers, for permission to play with a bread recipe of hers that has been adapted here. The flavor intensity has been increased by using extra-sharp Cheddar that has been dehydrated to concentrate its flavor. If you want to skip that step, be sure to use the most flavorful natural Cheddar you can find.

As it's a substantial bread, this is best when sliced thin. It is so good with butter alone that a loaf can vanish before there's a chance to toast any of it, but do try toasting it (*lightly*—it should just warm and crisp a bit) to serve for breakfast, or for lunch with a salad. Toasted or not, it makes champion ham or chicken sandwiches.

To prepare Cheddar-flavored Melba toast, see the Index. This will keep for many weeks in a covered canister.

2 cups milk
6 tablespoons (¾ stick) sweet (unsalted) butter
2 teaspoons salt
½ teaspoon sugar
1 tablespoon (1 envelope) active dry yeast
½ cup warm water (110° to 115°F)
1 large egg, beaten
6 to 7 cups all-purpose flour, as needed
2 cups Dried Cheddar Cheese (see the directions following this recipe) or 2½ cups finely grated sharp natural Cheddar
⅛ teaspoon ground hot red (cayenne) pepper, optional
A little melted butter for brushing the finished loaves

Makes 2 large loaves, about 2 pounds each

1. Combine the milk, butter, and salt in a saucepan and heat the mixture, stirring, over low heat until the butter melts; set it aside to cool to warm (110° to 115°F).

2. Meanwhile, in a mixing bowl or the large bowl of an electric mixer, stir the sugar, then the yeast, into the warm water and let stand until the yeast is completely dissolved, about 10 minutes.

3. Combine the milk mixture with the yeast mixture, add the egg, and beat to mix.

4. Stir 2 cups of the flour thoroughly together with the dried cheese and add the mixture gradually to the liquid mixture, beating by hand or with an electric mixer until well combined. Add the hot red

YEAST IN BULK

Even the occasional baker will find it worthwhile to purchase yeast in a jar, either at the supermarket (for smallish jars of standard active dry yeast) or from a specialist in baking supplies (for both standard and special types, often sold by the pound). This is a sensibly frugal way to buy yeast, which keeps a long time when it's refrigerated or frozen in a capped jar. (I've found freezer-stored two-year-old yeast perfectly fine.) Frozen yeast needn't be thawed—just spoon it from the jar.

Instead of Mold, Gold

Keeping Cheddar and similar cheeses on hand if you use "cooking" cheese only occasionally can be a problem, because all cheeses tend to mold and/or become rock-hard in time. However, if Cheddar is grated, dried, and kept in a capped jar in the refrigerator, it is cook's gold, always ready to enrich a dish or flavor a loaf.

pepper, if you are including it. Then gradually beat in more of the remaining flour, mixing until the dough is too stiff to beat further.

5. Either turn the dough out onto a floured kneading surface and knead it by hand, or change to the dough hook for machine kneading; knead in enough of the remaining flour to make a satiny and elastic dough. Knead the dough very well, about 5 minutes by machine, twice as long by hand.

6. Form the dough into a ball and place it back in its bowl (no need to wash, dry, or grease the bowl). Cover the bowl with plastic wrap and set it in a warm spot until the dough has doubled in volume, about 1 hour. Punch the dough down to deflate it, turn it over in the bowl, re-cover it, and let it rise again until approximately doubled, about 45 minutes.

7. Turn the dough out onto a lightly floured work surface and knead it a few strokes to deflate it. Cut it into two equal portions. Pat each out into a rectangle measuring about 10 x 7 inches and roll up the dough from a short side, pinching the layers firmly together as you roll. Fit each roll, seam down, into a buttered 8-cup loaf pan (9¼ x 5¼ x 2¼ inches). Cover the pans with a towel and let the loaves rise in a warm spot until they are doubled, 45 minutes to 1 hour.

8. Shortly before the rising is complete, preheat the oven to 375°F, with a shelf in the center position.

9. Brush the tops of the loaves with melted butter and bake them for 15 minutes, then lower the oven setting to 350°F and continue to bake the loaves until they are golden brown and sound hollow when turned out of the pan and given a thump on the bottom; total baking time is about 45 minutes. Brush the tops with butter again and cool the loaves on racks, then wrap and store them at least overnight before serving (the flavor grows in that period). The bread will keep for a few days at cool room temperature or in the refrigerator; freezer-wrapped and frozen, it keeps for several months. To prevent sogginess, thaw a frozen loaf before unwrapping it.

Dried Cheddar Cheese

Since I first figured out the how-to's of drying cheese, commercially dried cheese for home use has become available from bakers' suppliers, but it isn't an everyday item, and I have stayed with this recipe because the home-dried cheese tastes better than the factory stuff.

Cheese dried as outlined here is a great thing to have on hand, ready to add zingy flavor to a roster of things, from macaroni to the Ultimately Cheesy Cheddar Bread above or the Cheese-Flavored Beaten-Biscuit Crackers on page 110. It adds no unwanted moisture to doughs and has, incidentally, lost some of its calorific butterfat.

2 pounds sharp or extra-sharp natural Cheddar cheese

Makes about 1¼ pounds (3½ to 4 cups)

1. Using a fine grater, reduce the cheese to the finest possible bits. Strew the cheese over two or more baking sheets.

2. *Drying cheese in an oven:* Place the baking sheets in a convection oven with the control set at 130° to 140°F or in a conventional oven that has been preheated for a few minutes at its "keep warm" setting and turned off. Leave the conventional oven light on to furnish gentle heat, and turn it on briefly at "keep warm" from time to time; don't let any kind of oven get too hot. (The drying can be done in more than one session if you have other uses for the oven.)

Dry the cheese, turning it with a spatula once in a while, until it is crumbly (it will also be oily, thanks to the butterfat oozing out), which will usually take at least 6 hours.

Spread the cheese on paper towels and blot up as much of the fat as possible, using additional towels. If the cheese has formed clumps (likely), whirl it in a food processor or blender until it is well pulverized. Stored in a tightly covered jar in the refrigerator or freezer, it keeps indefinitely.

Using a food dehydrator: This works like a charm. Put the cheese on the solid trays intended for drying fruit leathers and other purees. Keep the temperature setting low; 110° to 115°F is about right for my machine. Dry the cheese until it is crumbly, stirring it occasionally. Blot the butterfat at intervals or at the end of drying, and pulverize the cheese as described if it's clumpy.

SEMOLINA LOAVES

Classic semolina bread is creamy yellow in color, delicate in texture inside and crusty outside, and considerably richer in flavor than other long loaves. Pale-golden semolina flour—not to be confused with coarse semolina, which is like farina in texture—is the essential ingredient. (It's also the key to the wonderful homemade pastas listed in the Index.) If there is no source of *good* semolina bread near by, it's worthwhile to seek out the flour and adopt this recipe.

Semolina flour can be found in good supermarkets and health-food stores, or obtained by mail through sellers of flours and other special ingredients (see Mail-Order Sources, page 390). It is often labeled "pasta flour," and sometimes it's called "durum flour," just to keep you on your toes.

Good Bread Defined

Semolina bread is deservedly popular, but not all store-bought semolina loaves are equal. A good loaf is crusty, not limp, and has a crumb that's delicate in texture—almost creamy on the tongue—without being squishy (like Wonder Bread). If local loaves don't measure up and you like to make bread (or would like to learn), get some semolina flour (discussed in the recipe headnote) and bake the real thing.

2½ cups warm water (110° to 115°F)
¼ teaspoon sugar
4 teaspoons (1⅓ packages) active dry yeast
1 tablespoon salt
¼ cup olive oil or vegetable oil
1 large egg
4 cups semolina flour
2½ to 3 cups bread flour or all-purpose flour, as needed

FOR THE PANS:
A little cornmeal

GLAZE:
1 teaspoon cornstarch
⅔ cup cold water

Makes 4 long loaves, about 1 pound each

1. In a mixing bowl or the large bowl of an electric mixer, stir the sugar, then the yeast, into 1 cup of the warm water and let stand until the yeast is completely dissolved, about 10 minutes.

2. Add the remaining warm water, then mix in the salt, oil, egg, and semolina flour. Beat by hand or with an electric mixer until a smooth dough is formed, then beat in about a cup of the bread or all-purpose flour and beat until the dough is smooth and elastic. If mixing by hand, turn the dough out onto a floured kneading surface, or switch to a dough hook if mixing by machine. Knead the dough vigorously, adding as much as necessary of the remaining flour to make an elastic and moderately stiff dough; knead the dough well, 7 minutes by machine or twice as long by hand.

3. Form the dough into a ball and return it to the mixing bowl (no need to wash, dry, or grease the bowl); cover it with plastic wrap and set it in a warm spot until it has tripled in volume, about 1¼ hours.

4. Punch down the dough to deflate it, turn it over in the bowl, recover it, and let it rise again until it has doubled, about 40 minutes.

5. Turn the dough out onto a lightly floured work surface and knead it a few strokes to deflate it, then divide it into four equal parts. Let the dough rest, covered with plastic wrap or a dampened towel, for 5 minutes.

6. Sprinkle cornmeal generously on two baking sheets.

7. One at a time, flatten each piece of dough into an oval about half an inch thick. Roll the dough up from one long side, pinching the layers firmly closed as you go; pinch the final seam firmly, then roll the dough under your palms into a tapering shape about 12 inches long, with smoothly rounded ends. Place the loaves, two to a pan, well apart on the baking sheets. Brush surplus cornmeal from the baking sheets (if left, it will scorch).

8. Cover the loaves with towels and let them rise in a warm spot until they have doubled, about 35 minutes.

9. Shortly before the rising is complete, heat the oven to 425°F, with a shelf in the upper third and another in the lower. Prepare a glaze by combining the cornstarch and cold water in a small saucepan, stirring the mixture over medium-low heat until it bubbles and becomes translucent, about 2 minutes. Let the glaze cool.

10. When the loaves have risen completely, brush them with the glaze, and then, using a razor blade or very sharp knife held almost horizontally, cut three or four shallow slashes diagonally in the top of each.

11. Place each pan on a shelf in the oven and bake the bread for 15 minutes, then lower the oven setting to 375°F, exchange the shelf positions of the pans, and again brush the loaves with the glaze. Bake the loaves until they are golden brown and firm and sound hollow when thumped on the bottom, about 15 minutes longer.

12. Remove the loaves to wire racks and cool them completely, then wrap them in foil or plastic and store them at room temperature for a few days; or wrap them for the freezer and freeze for up to 6 months. To prevent sogginess, thaw frozen bread in its wrappings. Before serving, you may want to refresh the loaves, whether or not they have been frozen, in a preheated 325°F oven for 10 minutes, or until they are warm and crisp-crusted.

Big Soft Pretzels Made Three Ways

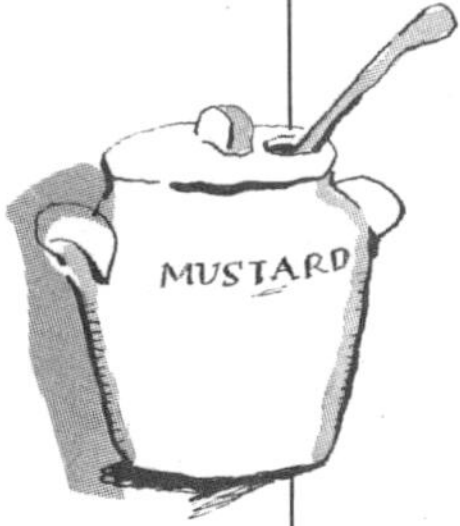

Soft pretzels go way back at our house, although this is a delicacy I had never met in my West Coast youth. But once I'd learned to make them I was hooked. Lately I've upgraded my earlier pretzel recipes by using malt powder, which improves both the flavor and the finish of the big twists. It may be omitted, but it's highly recommended and easily obtained from surveyors of baking supplies (see Mail-Order Sources, page 390).

This set of recipes turns out giant pretzels, each 5 or 6 inches across. All are delicious in place of rolls with a meal, or as a snack with butter, cream cheese (or a cheese spread), or, in classic Philadelphia fashion, a few squirts of mild yellow mustard.

Downsizing Pretzels

You can make more and smaller pretzels from this recipe if you divide the dough into 18 pieces instead of 12 and make somewhat shorter ropes than specified. Proceed as the recipe directs for shaping, rising, boiling, and baking the pretzels, which may need a little less baking time than bigger twists.

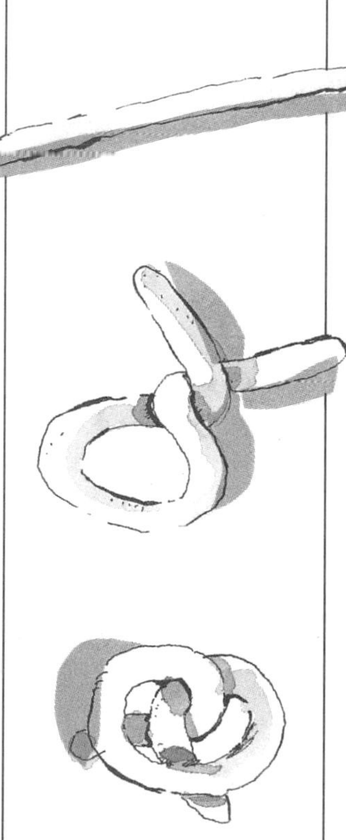

Basic Soft Pretzels

2 tablespoons (2 envelopes) active dry yeast
2¼ cups warm water (110° to 115°F)
2½ tablespoons nondiastatic malt powder (see page 81) or 2 teaspoons sugar, optional
2 tablespoons vegetable oil
1 teaspoon salt
5½ cups bread flour, or as needed

WATER BATH:
3 quarts water
¼ cup nondiastatic malt powder or 5 tablespoons baking soda plus 2 tablespoons sugar

TOPPING:
Coarse (kosher or sea) salt, if desired

Makes 1 dozen giant pretzels

1. In the large bowl of an electric mixer equipped, if possible, with a flat beater and a dough hook, stir the yeast into ½ cup of the warm water and let stand until completely dissolved, about 10 minutes.

2. Add the remaining 1¾ cups warm water, then stir in the malt powder, oil, and salt; mix well. Gradually beat in about two-thirds of the flour to make a dough that cleans the bowl. Change to the dough hook (or turn the dough onto a kneading surface) and knead in enough of the remaining flour, adding more if needed, to make a smooth, elastic dough. Form the dough into a ball, return it to the bowl, cover, and let rise until doubled, 45 minutes to 1 hour.

3. When dough is almost risen, heat the 3 quarts of water in a big skillet or sauté pan and stir in the malt powder (or soda and sugar) until dissolved. Remove from the heat and set aside until needed. Preheat the oven to 425°F. Grease two large baking sheets lightly.

4. *Shape the pretzels:* Turn the dough out onto a lightly floured work surface. Punch it down to deflate it, divide it in two, and refrigerate one half, wrapped in plastic. Cut the dough from the remaining half into 12 equal pieces. For each pretzel use two pieces, forming each into a smooth 12-inch rope by rolling the dough under your palms, moving your hands apart as you roll. Moisten one tip of each rope and join the two, pressing and rolling the seam to smooth it. Form the long rope into the classic pretzel twist (this may take a couple of minutes' practice), flip it over so the ends are on the bottom, and lay it on a floured baking sheet or other flat surface to rise while you shape pretzels from the remaining cut pieces and the refrigerated half of the dough.

5. When all the pretzels from this batch have been shaped, reheat the water bath to simmering and spread one or two kitchen towels on a surface near your stove. Starting with the first pretzel you made, lift it gently with your hands and slip it into the water bath. Counting, cook for 20 seconds, then flip the pretzel over and cook 20 seconds more. Using a slotted spatula, lift the pretzel onto a towel to drain briefly, then place it on a greased baking sheet. Repeat with the remaining shaped pretzels, placing them well apart on the pan.

6. If you like, sprinkle the pretzels with a little coarse salt. Bake them for 10 minutes or a bit more, until well browned. Cool on racks. Repeat steps 4, 5, and 6 with the remaining dough, beginning by dividing the dough into 12 pieces.

7. When all pretzels have cooled, store in canisters or, bagged, in the freezer. They will keep for several days at room temperature or for at least a couple of months in the freezer.

8. Before serving, refresh unfrozen pretzels by heating them in a low oven for a few minutes. From the frozen state, they'll need at least 15 minutes at 325°F to regain their just-from-the-oven character.

Wheaty Giant Pretzels

No need to beguile eaters with promises of high-fiber health—the fine flavor of these speaks for itself.

Follow the preceding recipe, with the following changes:

For the 5½ cups bread flour called for, substitute 1½ cups whole-wheat flour (use the white whole-wheat kind if you can find it), plus ½ cup unprocessed wheat bran and 3½ cups bread flour (or amount needed for mixing and kneading).

Rye & Caraway Giant Pretzels

Caraway seeds stud these twists adapted from a classic rye bread, and you can add a topping of more seeds before baking if you like.

Follow the recipe for Basic Soft Pretzels, with the following changes:

For the 5½ cups of bread flour called for, substitute 2½ cups bread flour, or amount needed to mix and knead the dough, plus 2 cups rye flour and 1 cup whole-wheat flour. Add 2 to 3 tablespoons caraway seeds to the dough as it is mixed, and sprinkle additional seed on the pretzels before baking, if you wish.

SUN-DRIED TOMATO BREAD & DRIED-TOMATO BREAD WITH ROSEMARY

The sunset coloration and exceptional flavor of the first hearty loaf below are contributed by sun-dried tomatoes plus a complement of orange zest and black pepper. (For custom drying your own tomatoes, see the Index.) Pungent rosemary is added to the tomatoes and other seasonings for the second loaf, which may possibly taste even better than the first.

At our house we make this bread two loaves at a time and store the "spare" in the freezer.

SUN-DRIED TOMATO BREAD

⅓ to ½ cup (packed) sun-dried tomatoes prepared without oil
2 teaspoons (⅔ envelope) active dry yeast
¾ cup warm water (110° to 115°F)
2 tablespoons honey
1 cup whole-wheat flour
¼ cup cornmeal
2 tablespoons plus 2 teaspoons flavorful (not "light") olive oil
2½ teaspoons coarse (kosher or sea) salt
3 tablespoons oat bran (or raw quick-cooking oatmeal that has been coarsely chopped in a food processor)
1 tablespoon nondiastatic malt powder (see page 81), optional
2 to 2½ cups bread flour, plus more if needed for kneading
1 to 2 teaspoons, to taste, finely minced or grated orange zest (outer peel only, no white pith), or half as much dried orange zest, or ½ teaspoon orange oil (not extract)
¼ to ½ teaspoon coarsely ground or crushed black pepper, to taste

FOR THE PAN:
A little cornmeal

GLAZE:
1 large egg white
2 tablespoons water

Makes a round hearth-style loaf weighing about 2 pounds

TOMATO BREAD, STONE-BAKED OR IN A PAN

To bake Sun-Dried Tomato Bread on a baking stone, let the dough rise on a baking sheet (no sides) generously coated with cornmeal. Preheat the oven and baking stone for at least 30 minutes. Slip the risen loaf from the baking sheet onto the stone and proceed to bake the bread as described.

For a pan loaf you'll need a bread pan of the old-fashioned size, about 9½ × 5½ inches (holding 6 cups), which will make a really big loaf with this amount of dough. Or you can bake two less lofty loaves in pans measuring about 8 × 4 inches and holding 4 cups.

1. Cover the dried tomatoes with hot water and leave them to soak for 15 to 30 minutes, depending on their degree of dryness.

2. In the large bowl of an electric mixer, stir the yeast into the warm water and let stand until completely dissolved, about 10 minutes. Add the honey, whole-wheat flour, and cornmeal, beating in well, then cover the bowl and let the batter rise and then fall, about 45 minutes.

3. Drain the soaked tomatoes, reserving the liquid and tomatoes separately.

4. Add to the batter ¾ cup of the tomato soaking water (make up the difference with tap water if there isn't enough), the oil, salt, oat bran, and malt powder (if using). Beat in enough of the bread flour to make a dough that cleans the bowl. Change to the dough hook (if you've got one) and knead the dough very thoroughly, about 5 minutes by machine (twice as long if you turn the dough out onto a floured board and knead by hand), adding enough bread flour to make a moderately firm and elastic dough. Cover the bowl with plastic wrap (and a towel, if the room is cool) and let the dough rise until doubled, about 1 hour.

5. While the dough rises, pat the soaked tomatoes dry with paper towels and place them on a chopping board, sprinkling them with the orange zest, pepper, and the 2 teaspoons olive oil. Chop the tomatoes into ¼- to ½-inch bits, mixing them well with the seasonings.

6. After the dough has risen, punch it down to deflate it and turn it out onto a floured kneading surface. Flatten the dough with your hands, then let it rest for a few minutes before spreading the dried tomato mixture over the surface. Fold, cut, and knead the dough until the tomatoes are well distributed. Let it rest again briefly, covered with a bowl, then form into a round loaf and place it on a baking sheet lightly sprinkled with cornmeal. Cover with a towel and let rise until not quite doubled—a little springiness will remain in the hollow when a finger is pressed into the dough near the base of the loaf.

7. Meanwhile, preheat the oven to 375°F and prepare a glaze by beating the egg white briefly with the water.

8. When the loaf has risen, brush it with the glaze and bake it in the center of the oven for 15 minutes. Lower the oven setting to 325°F, brush the loaf with the glaze again, and bake for about 35 minutes longer, or until the loaf sounds hollow when thumped on the bottom.

9. Cool the loaf on a wire rack, wrap loosely in plastic or foil, and let it mellow (ideally for 24 hours) before serving. The tomato bread will keep at room temperature, bagged in plastic, for a week, or for at least 3 months, freezer-wrapped, in the freezer. Thaw frozen bread in its wrapper to prevent sogginess, then refresh it by placing the unwrapped loaf on the shelf of a moderate (350°F) oven for about 10 minutes.

Dried-Tomato Bread with Rosemary

Proceed exactly as for Sun-Dried Tomato Bread, but while the dough rises (step 4), chop enough dried rosemary leaves to make a generous tablespoonful and soak them in a little warm water. When you begin step 5, drain off the water and add the herb to the tomatoes, orange zest, pepper, and olive oil; chop everything together and go on with the recipe. Optionally, press extra rosemary sprigs or leaves into the top of the loaf before it is put to rise.

PART 2: Crisp Bread-stuffs & Savory Biscotti

When it comes to breadmaking, shaping and baking a perfect loaf (or a batch of bagels or crumpets) is wonderfully satisfying, but exploring the byways of crisp and crunchy things that begin with a dough may be even more rewarding for curious cooks.

Not all the specialties in this section are made with yeast, although some are. (Consult Breadmaking, page 68, for basic or brushup information.) The yeast-leavened pleasures are Grissini (quite addictive breadsticks), Handmade Hard Pretzels (for soft pretzels, see page 96), and Crisp Rye & Wheat Flatbread.

Non-yeast items abound, from Beaten-Biscuit Crackers through corn chips (including a baked version and another with chile flavoring), Digestive Biscuits, Ginger Crackers, Oatcakes, and Wine & Parmesan Crackers. Then there is the collection of savory biscotti, twice-baked cocktail crunchies packed with such tasty things as sun-dried tomatoes, pesto, herbs, or chile. Looking to the East, finally, we have Salted Sesame Crackers, flavored with toasted sesame salt, a traditional Japanese seasoning you can prepare in a minute or two and use for many purposes.

Handmade Hard Pretzels

Hard pretzels aren't just soft pretzels that have been left to dry out and become crisp. No indeed. They must be designed from the start to become crisp as a twig, which is why most hard pretzels come from the ovens of professionals.

But not these particular twists, with which I'm rather pleased after years of off-and-on fiddling with hard-pretzel ways and means. (Soft pretzels were much simpler to figure out—see the Index for the recipe.)

If you enjoy making really good crunchy snacks, get the right kind of flour—unbleached pastry flour—and some nondiastatic malt powder and you'll succeed with these. (The malt—and high-quality pastry flour, too—are most readily obtained from a specialist in baking supplies.) Shiny and full of crunch, these custom-crafted whirligigs lack nothing but the deep color and glassy finish commercial pretzels gain from a bath of lye or washing soda.

2 teaspoons (⅔ envelope) active dry yeast
2 tablespoons warm water (110° to 115°F)
3 cups unbleached pastry flour (or substitute 2¾ cups all-purpose flour sifted with ¼ cup cornstarch)
2 tablespoons nondiastatic malt powder (see page 81)
½ teaspoon salt (may be omitted if pretzels are baked with a salt topping)
⅜ teaspoon baking soda (to measure, use the tip of a knife to remove ¼ of the soda in a measured level ½ teaspoonful)
1 tablespoon vegetable oil, preferably corn oil
Warm water (110° to 115°F) as needed to make dough, usually about ½ cup

GLAZE:
1 large egg white
2 tablespoons water

OPTIONAL TOPPINGS:
Coarse (kosher) salt; poppy, caraway, or sesame seed; or mixed salt and seed; or Toasted Sesame Salt (page 198)

Makes about 2 dozen pretzels

1. In a small bowl, stir the yeast into the 2 tablespoons warm water and let stand until completely dissolved, about 10 minutes.

2. Measure the flour, malt powder, salt, and baking soda into the workbowl of a food processor and pulse the machine to mix them well. With the motor running, pour the oil through the feed tube and process until well mixed. Again with the motor running, add about ¼ cup warm water, then the yeast mixture. Add a little more water very gradually; when the dough begins to hold together as it whirls, continue to process until it forms a ball on the top of the blade, then process for 20 seconds longer. If the dough doesn't readily form a ball, add a little more water but don't overdo it; the dough should be stiff. (Lacking a food processor, the dough may be mixed in an electric

CRUNCH TIME

Because of their crispness, these merry bites are perfect light snacks with something to drink. For more substantial entries in the pretzel lineup, see Big Soft Pretzels Made Three Ways on page 96.

mixer equipped with a flat paddle, then kneaded very well either by hand or with a dough hook.)

3. Transfer the dough to a greased bowl, cover it with plastic, and let it rise until doubled, about 1 hour. Punch the dough down to deflate it, turn it out on a work surface, and let it rest for 5 minutes.

4. Preheat the oven to 500°F, with a shelf in the center position. Set out two large nonstick baking sheets, or brush regular large baking sheets lightly with oil or spray with baking spray. Prepare a glaze by beating the egg white briefly with the water.

5. Cut the dough in half; wrap one portion in plastic. Shape the half you're working with into a cylinder and cut it into 12 portions. Cover the pieces with plastic or a dampened kitchen towel while you begin to form the pretzels.

6. *Shaping the pretzels:* Place a piece of dough on an unfloured work surface. Roll and press it under the spread fingers of both hands, moving your hands slowly apart to stretch the dough; press as firmly as you can while doing this, to prevent cracks. Repeat the motion until you have a thin rope about 16 inches long (to make a finished pretzel about 3½ inches across). Loop the rope into a pretzel, then invert it onto a baking sheet with the ends underneath. Repeat, spacing the pretzels at least an inch apart.

7. Cover the panful with a dry towel and let the pretzels rise for about 15 minutes, or until puffy. Meanwhile, shape the remaining half of the dough.

8. Brush the first panful of pretzels sparingly with the glaze. Sprinkle them with salt, seeds, or salt plus seeds, or sesame salt, if you wish. Place in the center of the oven and bake for about 5 or 6 minutes, adding another coat of glaze after 3 minutes.

9. When the pretzels are shiny, fairly firm, and lightly browned, remove them from the oven and bake the next panful.

10. Remove the pretzels to a large wire rack or racks. Turn the oven off and open the door. When it has cooled down considerably, turn it on again with the control set at 200°F. Slip the rack(s) of pretzels into the oven, close the door, and bake them again for an hour or so, checking occasionally to make sure all is well (an unreliable oven may overbrown them). When a sample is very light and completely dry throughout and of a good golden brown color, remove and cool the pretzels. (The final low-heat baking may be done in more than one session, if necessary.)

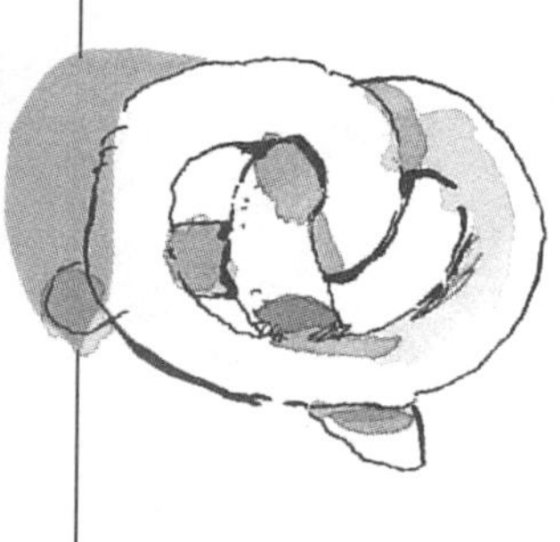

11. Stored in a canister at room temperature, they'll keep for weeks. If dampness should creep in, refresh them by a brief baking in a low (250° to 300°F) oven until they are again bone-dry.

Pretzel Sticks

Form the dough into very thin ropes and cut it into short lengths. Let rise on baking sheets, glaze, add topping, bake, and rebake in the same way as shaped pretzels. The baking and drying time will be a bit shorter than for pretzel twists.

Cocktail Biscotti with Sun-Dried Tomatoes, Green Peppercorns, & Rosemary

Ruddy in color and robust in flavor, these savory biscuits ring a change on traditional sweet biscotti. They beg to accompany a mild cheese, from cream to Edam to Monterey jack, as a snack, and they are a lively bite with wine or other drinks.

¼ cup (packed) sun-dried tomatoes prepared without oil
2 cups all-purpose flour or 1 cup each all-purpose and light rye flour
2½ teaspoons baking powder
½ teaspoon salt
1 teaspoon dried green peppercorns, or well-drained peppercorns packed in brine, crushed
1 teaspoon crumbled dried rosemary
1 large egg
¼ cup olive oil
Additional crumbled dried rosemary for topping, optional

Makes 2 to 2½ dozen biscotti

1. Preheat the oven to 350°F, with a shelf in the center position. Cover a baking sheet with foil and grease the foil.

2. Snip the tomatoes into ¼-inch pieces, then cover with hot water and leave them to soak until soft, 15 to 30 minutes, depending on their degree of dryness.

3. Meanwhile, sift together the flour, baking powder, and salt into a mixing bowl. Stir in the crushed peppercorns and the 1 teaspoon dried rosemary.

Savory Biscotti

When it's drinks time, nonsweet biscotti ring a change on the more usual crisp things to eat, and they have the merit of carrying their flavors with them and being good matches for cheese as well. Besides the biscotti made with sun-dried tomatoes here, you'll find, further along, Pesto Biscotti and Smoky Chile & Corn Biscotti.

4. Drain the tomatoes, reserving the soaking liquid. Pat the pieces between paper towels to remove surplus moisture. Reserve the liquid and tomatoes separately.

5. In a small bowl, beat the egg with ¼ cup of the soaking liquid (add water if there isn't enough). Add the oil and mix. Stir the liquid into the dry ingredients until just combined, then stir in the tomato pieces. Mix with a spoon (or, even better, the hands) to make a firm dough.

6. Divide the dough in half. Form each half into a compact loaf on the prepared baking sheet, making the loaves about 10 inches long and 2½ inches wide and placing them at least 2 inches apart. Using a pastry brush and cold water, smooth the surface with firm strokes. Optionally, sprinkle the tops with a little more crumbled rosemary.

7. Bake the loaves in the center of the oven for about 25 minutes, or until firm to the touch and deeper in color but not overbrowned. Remove from the oven and cool the loaves on a wire rack for 10 to 15 minutes. Meanwhile, lower the oven setting to 275°F.

8. Slice the loaves on a diagonal into strips ½ inch thick, using a sharp serrated knife. Lay the strips flat on the cooling rack or baking sheet, using a second rack or sheet (ungreased) if necessary, and return to the oven for 20 minutes. Turn off the oven and leave the biscotti for 30 minutes more with the oven door slightly open. Remove from the oven, still on the racks, and cool completely. The biscotti should be quite dry throughout; if by some chance they aren't, dry them as long as necessary in the oven set at "warm" (or its lowest setting), then cool again.

9. Place the biscotti in an airtight canister and store for a few weeks, or wrap them for the freezer and freeze for up to 3 months. If frozen, thaw without unwrapping, spread on a baking sheet and then refresh in a 300°F oven for 10 minutes or so and cool them again.

Corn Chips Three Ways

After their sizzling in corn oil, chips made by the first recipe taste like the best of the professionally made article, but they're more tender to the tooth and, naturally, fresher. Fans of so-called tortilla chips don't need to be told twice to dip these into their salsa of choice, or to munch on them straight.

The chile-seasoned version can taste only gently hot, or the chips may be made hotter if you like. The dough for either kind of corn chips may be baked, in thin shards, as described in the third recipe, for a low-fat but still flavorful version. All three recipes are easily doubled—a good idea for chip-hungry households.

The basic chip recipe here is adapted from one developed for my earlier book *Better Than Store-Bought* (with Elizabeth Colchie); the others are new. The masa flour is the same specially processed corn flour (*not* cornmeal) used to make tortillas. (See the Index for recipes for both corn and flour tortillas.)

CLASSIC CORN CHIPS

1 cup warm water (100°F)
1 large egg yolk
¾ teaspoon salt
¾ cup masa flour (specially processed corn flour for tortillas), plus more if needed
Corn oil for deep frying

Makes about 7 ounces chips

1. In a medium-size bowl, beat together the warm water, egg yolk, and salt to mix. Stir in the masa flour to make a soft dough that won't stick to your fingers when touched, adding more flour if needed.

2. In a wok, an electric skillet, or a wide saucepan, slowly heat 2 inches of corn oil to 375°F. Meanwhile, scoop the dough into a cookie press or pastry bag fitted with the tip designed to shape a broad but thin corrugated ribbon.

3. When the oil is ready, press out a few short lengths of dough, to cover no more than half of the surface, directly into the oil. Fry the ribbons until golden brown, turning them once. Using a slotted spoon, lift them from the oil onto several layers of paper towels to drain. Repeat until all the dough has been used.

4. Check the texture of the chips—they should not bend when tested. If any chips are still pliable, reheat the oil to frying temperature and refry them a few at a time until they are very crisp. Drain again.

5. Serve the chips fresh and warm, or cool them and bag them for airtight storage at room temperature. Stored chips will benefit from a brief warming in a low (250° to 300°F) oven before they're served. They keep very well for several days.

CHILE CORN CHIPS

Makes about 7 ounces chips

1. Make the dough for Classic Corn Chips, above, adding 1 to 2 teaspoons of Custom-Made Chili Seasoning (page 184) or other mild

CHIPPING AWAY AT THE FAT

Free-form Baked Corn Chips are just the ticket when fat calories are being counted, so don't overlook the third recipe in this set. Baked chips can be either straightforwardly corny (the Classic Corn Chip recipe) or zipped up with your choice of chile, mild to hot (Chile Corn Chips).

chili powder. (As alternative flavoring, for the equivalent of 2 teaspoons of the chili seasoning, add 1 teaspoon of pure ground mild chile, such as ancho, plus ½ teaspoon ground cumin, 2 or 3 big pinches of crumbled dried oregano, and ⅛ teaspoon of high-quality granulated garlic, or about ½ teaspoon of fresh garlic pushed through a press.)

2. Fry the chips as described in the preceding recipe, but heat the cooking oil to 360°F instead of 375°F, or the chile-seasoned chips will be overbrowned while still undercooked.

3. Cool and store as described for Classic Corn Chips.

Baked Corn Chips

Makes about 5 ounces

1. Prepare the dough for either Classic or Chile Corn Chips, adding 2 teaspoons of corn oil to the dough.

2. Preheat the oven to 400°F, with a shelf in the upper third. Grease one to three unrimmed baking sheets lightly, or grease the backs of jelly-roll pans or large pizza pans.

3. Flatten a handful of dough in the center of each pan. Cover the dough with a large sheet of plastic wrap and roll it paper-thin with a rolling pin, or press it into a thin sheet by rubbing the plastic with the heel of your hand. Remove the plastic and slash the dough into free-form wedges, strips, rectangles, or diamonds, using a knife or a pizza wheel. Repeat with any remaining baking sheets.

4. Bake the chips, one panful at a time, in the upper third of the oven until golden in color and beginning to peel away from the pan, about 5 minutes. Remove the pan from the oven, lift off the chips with a pancake turner, and cool them on a rack. Bake the remaining chips, if necessary reusing sheets after they have cooled.

5. Test the cooled chips for crispness by trying to bend any that look doubtful; if they are pliable, a second baking is needed. For this, reset the oven to 175°F. When it has cooled down to that temperature, bake the pliable chips again, on their rack, for about 10 minutes with the oven door slightly open. Check often to prevent overbrowning and to judge dryness. Cool again. If any chips are still leathery (unlikely), lower the oven setting to 140°F and bake those specimens further, checking them often, until the crunch-test is met.

6. Cool the chips on their rack(s) and store as described for deep-fried chips. These keep even better than the originals because of their low fat content. Refresh them in a low oven (250° to 300°F) if necessary before serving.

Grissini, Long & Thin & Crisp

(Breadsticks With or Without Seeds or Coarse Salt)

Grissini might be called honorary peanuts, for no one has ever been able to eat just one from the spiky bouquet of breadsticks on a properly generous Mediterranean table. So this recipe makes an opulent basketful of long, crisp, airy cylinders of crust with a little bread (also crisp) in the middle.

When made commercially, grissini are mostly texture, pencil-thin and pale in color. They're okay, but even bread beginners can turn out these more flavorsome sticks, which are enjoyable to make. They keep excellently, in case avid eaters have left some for you to put away.

If you don't require long breadsticks, make them half-length or shorter (cigar-sized); just cut the dough into lengths that suit. If you admire the pencil style, use your plain pastry wheel (or pizza cutter) to create very thin strips, stretch them further, and bake them a shorter time, without the optional glaze and toppings.

1 tablespoon (1 envelope) active dry yeast
1½ cups warm water (110° to 115°F)
2 tablespoons nondiastatic malt powder (see page 81)
4 tablespoons olive oil
2 teaspoons salt
4½ cups all-purpose flour, or as needed

GLAZE AND TOPPINGS (OPTIONAL):
1 large egg white
2 tablespoons water
Seeds—sesame, poppy, caraway, cumin, and/or "onion" (*chernushka*)—or coarse (kosher) salt, for sprinkling

Makes from 2 to 3 dozen long breadsticks or more short or very thin ones

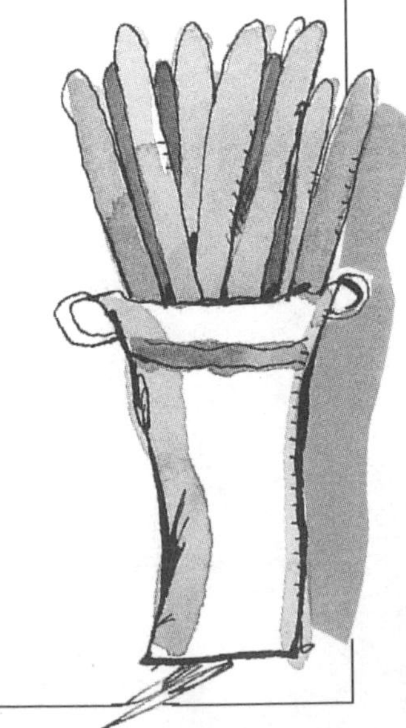

1. In a mixing bowl or the large bowl of an electric mixer, stir the yeast into ½ cup of the warm water and let stand until completely dissolved, about 10 minutes.

2. Beat in the remaining cup of warm water, the malt powder, 3 tablespoons of the oil, the salt, and 2 cups of the flour to make a smooth batter. Gradually beat in the remaining flour, then turn the resulting

A Word of Thanks

I am indebted to Carol Field, author of the splendid book The Italian Baker *(Harper & Row, 1985), for describing how an Italian artisan baker shapes the sticks; I've borrowed the shaping method for this recipe. Until that information caught up with me, I'd always divided my breadstick dough into chunks and rolled and pulled each into shape by hand. That method works, but as Carol indicates, no professional baker has time for such shenanigans.*

dough out onto a floured kneading surface, or change to the dough hook if you are mixing by machine, and knead it until smooth and elastic, adding more flour only if necessary to make an easily handled dough. Knead well (4 minutes by machine, or 8 minutes by hand). Finish by kneading machine-kneaded dough a few strokes by hand on a floured work surface.

3. Being sure your work surface is well coated with flour, pat the dough out in a rectangle until it is about ¼ inch thick. Brush with the remaining tablespoon of olive oil, cover with plastic wrap or waxed paper, and let rise until doubled, about 1 hour, depending on the room temperature. Alternatively, form the dough into a ball, return it to its bowl (no need to wash, dry, or grease the bowl), cover it with plastic wrap, and leave to rise until doubled in volume, about 1 hour.

4. Meanwhile, preheat the oven to 375°F, with a shelf in the upper third and one in the lower. Grease two or more rimless baking sheets. Prepare a glaze by beating the egg white briefly with the water.

5. ***Shaping the breadsticks the Italian baker's way:*** Dust the top of the dough rectangle with flour (semolina flour, in Italy). Using a plain (uncrimped) pastry wheel or a pizza cutter, cut the dough into quarters or cross-sections, depending on the length of breadsticks you plan to make, then cut strips from ¼ to ½ inch wide. Pick up and stretch each strip to about half again its original length and lay them about an inch apart on the prepared pans. When the baking sheets are full, place the remaining breadsticks on greased sheets of foil to be slipped later onto the cooled baking sheets for baking. Let the sticks rise for a few minutes more, then brush them with the glaze and, optionally, sprinkle them with seeds or salt. Bake as described in step 6.

Rolling and stretching the breadsticks by hand: This is for dough that has risen in the bowl. Without punching it down, remove the dough to a lightly floured work surface and divide it into two portions. Wrap and refrigerate one piece. Form the other piece into a cylinder 18 inches long; cut the cylinder into 12 to 18 equal pieces depending on whether you want thicker or thinner breadsticks. Cover the pieces with a kitchen towel and let them rest 5 minutes. Shape each into a rope 12 to 15 inches long, rolling the dough under your palms while stretching it by moving your hands apart. (For shorter breadsticks, cut each piece of dough into 2 or 3 pieces before shaping.) As they are shaped, place the breadsticks on a greased baking sheet, leaving at least 1 inch between them. You'll need two baking sheets for each half of the dough; so, if you have only two, place the breadsticks shaped from the remaining dough on greased sheets of foil to be slipped later onto the cooled pans. Let the breadsticks rise, covered with a towel, until doubled, about 20 minutes. Brush with the glaze and add optional seeds or salt, then bake as described in step 6.

6. Bake the breadsticks on two shelves of the preheated oven for 8 to 12 minutes, depending on whether they're thin or thick, then exchange shelf positions and bake for another 8 to 12 minutes, or until the breadsticks are a good golden brown. Optionally, turn the breadsticks on the baking sheets after the first baking period. Remove from the baking sheets to cool on racks.

7. Bake the foil sheets of breadsticks in the same way after slipping them onto the baking sheets after they have cooled.

8. ***Final crisping:*** When all the sticks have been baked, reset the oven to 200°F. Lay the breadsticks directly on the oven shelves, bake for 5 minutes, and turn the oven off. Leave the breadsticks in the oven with the door closed for 15 minutes, then open the oven door and let them cool completely.

9. Store the breadsticks, bagged tightly closed in plastic or in an airtight canister, for 2 weeks or more at room temperature, or wrap them for the freezer and freeze them for up to several months. At serving time, refresh frozen breadsticks in a 300°F oven, leaving them for 5 minutes; there is no need to thaw them first.

VARIATIONS

Cheese-Flavored Grissini: When the dough is ready for rising, knead in 6 to 8 tablespoons of grated Parmesan or combined Parmesan and Romano cheese, or use the same amount of Dried Cheddar Cheese (page 93) plus a pinch of ground hot red (cayenne) pepper—the pepper is optional but good. Omit the seeds or salt. These brown more quickly than plain or whole-wheat breadsticks, so keep an eye on the baking and reduce the time as necessary.

Whole-Wheat Grissini: Substitute 2¼ cups of whole-wheat flour (regular or white wheat) for the same quantity of the all-purpose flour. Increase the oil in the dough to ¼ cup. Use the glaze and, optionally, seeds or salt.

LARD NOTE

For high-quality lard (the commercial kind is sometimes pretty sorry stuff), you may want to try your hand at preparing your own. (Lard makes the best piecrusts, too, by common consent.) Use fresh, sweet pork fat, which can be supplied by most butchers if they're given a little notice.

Grind or chop the fat and place it in a heavy saucepan with 3 or 4 tablespoons of water per pound of fat. Simmer the mixture over low heat (you don't want either the solid or liquid fat to brown) until all possible liquid lard has been obtained. Spoon the clear liquid from the top of the panful frequently and strain it into a storage jar. Cool the lard, cover it, and refrigerate it indefinitely. Discard the cracklings, or hang them outdoors in a mesh onion or citrus bag for the delectation of the birds.

If you have an electric slow-cooker, it's perfect for extracting the lard.

BEATEN-BISCUIT CRACKERS, PLAIN & CHEESE-FLAVORED

Basically a borrowing from Southern beaten biscuits, these crackers are pale, rather dense but crisp, very good indeed with a sliver of fine country ham, cheese of any kind, or a savory spread (I'm thinking particularly of Potted Ham—see the Index for this porky pleasure). The cheese-flavored crackers have enough oomph to stand on their own as a snack, but they're doubly delicious with more cheese on top.

The thoroughly modern method of making beaten biscuits dispenses with the traditional lengthy thumping of the dough with a club or a similar implement by using a food processor or a heavy-duty mixer. Either machine "beats" the dough to the requisite state of exhaustion while the cook rests. If you use your mixer, or if you have a large-capacity food processor, this recipe can be doubled. Whole-grain fans can substitute whole-wheat pastry flour for the unbleached kind; this makes for a more textured biscuit.

Beaten-Biscuit Crackers

2 cups unbleached pastry flour or 1 cup all-purpose flour plus 1 cup cake flour
¾ teaspoon salt
½ teaspoon baking powder
2 tablespoons sweet (unsalted) butter
2 tablespoons fine-quality lard, preferably homemade (see the sidebar opposite)
About ½ cup ice water

Makes about 3 dozen crackers

1. Preheat the oven to 350°F, with a shelf in the center position.

2. *Using a food processor to make the dough:* Combine the flour, salt, and baking powder in the workbowl of a food processor. Pulse the motor two or three times to mix, then add the butter and lard and run the machine in short bursts until the fats are incorporated; the mixture should be mealy. With the motor running, pour most of the ice water (reserve 2 tablespoons) through the feed tube. If a dough mass doesn't form atop the blade within a few seconds, add as much more of the water, with the motor running, as necessary.

When the dough ball has formed, process ("beat") it for several minutes longer in short sessions (about half a minute each session), letting the dough cool each time before resuming. (The total time of beating will depend on the power of your machine. Cooling between spells of beating is necessary because considerable heat develops in the dough as it wallops around the workbowl.) During the cooling times, turn the ball of dough top for bottom and break it up with your fingers. When the dough has been "beaten" sufficiently, it will be quite relaxed, not elastic. You can hardly overbeat it.

Alternatively, using an electric mixer: To mix the dough in an electric mixer equipped with a flat paddle beater, follow the preceding steps; the paddle will cut in the fat and form a dough when the liquid is added. Then beat the dough for 15 minutes at moderately low speed. Again, the finished dough should be velvety and relaxed.

Roots

Our Southern beaten biscuits are of British descent, on the evidence of an old recipe unearthed while researching things breadlike and British. Called "flead biscuits," these morsels were made with flead (a fatty membrane from the innards of a porker), which served as the shortening; the dough was then thumped to a fare-thee-well, just as for beaten biscuits, to incorporate the fat and develop a distinctive texture.

3. ***To shape the crackers:*** Roll the dough out to a thickness of ⅛ inch on a lightly floured surface. Either cut out 2½- to 3-inch crackers with a fluted round cutter and arrange them slightly apart on ungreased baking sheets, or trim the rolled-out dough to a rectangle that will fit on a baking sheet. Place the dough on the pan and cut it into oblong crackers with a plain or fluted pastry wheel. Prick each cracker just two or three times with a table fork if you'd like them to puff a bit, or prick them all over for flatter crackers.

4. Bake the crackers, one panful at a time, in the center of the oven until they are very pale buff-gold, about 15 minutes. Cool on a rack. For extra crispness, return the cooled crackers to a 200°F oven, bake them again for 8 to 10 minutes, then cool them again. Stored in a canister at room temperature, the crackers will keep for at least a week. Freezer-wrapped, they can be frozen for up to 3 months.

5. Frozen crackers should be thawed in their wrappings. However stored, the crackers will gain taste and crackle from a freshening session, about 5 minutes in a 250°F oven. Watch to prevent overbrowning, and cool the crackers or not, as you prefer, before serving them.

. . . Or Call It Hardtack

Whether dubbed "flatbread" or "hardtack," these savory, gently spiced wedges of crispbread are a great addition to the snack repertory. For cooks who haven't baked with yeast, the recipe is a rewarding introduction to the art.

Cheese-Flavored Beaten-Biscuit Crackers

Make the biscuits as described in the preceding recipe, adding ⅓ cup finely grated Parmesan cheese or Dried Cheddar Cheese (page 93), plus a pinch of ground hot red (cayenne) pepper, before incorporating the lard and butter. "Beat" or knead the dough and shape the crackers as described.

Bake them at the reduced temperature of 300°F just until they are very pale gold in color, about 30 minutes; don't let them take on more than a tinge of color, as overbrowning will spoil their flavor.

After the crackers have cooled, if you'd like more crispness, return them to a 200°F oven for a few minutes, watching them carefully. Store as for the plain crackers.

Crisp Rye & Wheat Flatbread

Not exactly what you'll get in a paper packet from the grocer's shelf, wedges of this crunchy yeasted flatbread are deeply flavorful, thanks to rye and whole-wheat flours and a hint of anise and caraway. Splendid with cheese, sausage, smoked fish, cold meats, or savory spreads, or as the cracker of choice with a big bowl of hearty soup for supper.

2 teaspoons (⅔ envelope) active dry yeast
¾ cup warm water (110° to 115°F)
¾ cup all-purpose flour
¾ cup coarse (pumpernickel) or medium rye flour, or more as needed
¾ cup whole-wheat flour, or more as needed
1 teaspoon anise seed, ground (see sidebar)
1 teaspoon caraway seed, ground (see sidebar)
1 tablespoon dark corn syrup
1 teaspoon salt
2 tablespoons sweet (unsalted) butter, melted
Additional rye flour for rolling the dough

Makes 2 dozen wedges

1. In a small bowl, stir the yeast into the warm water and let it stand until completely dissolved, about 10 minutes. Meanwhile, whisk together the three flours and the ground anise and caraway seeds in the large bowl of an electric mixer fitted with a flat paddle.

2. Stir the corn syrup, salt, and melted butter into the yeast mixture, operating the mixer at low speed. Increase the speed slightly and beat the dough briefly, just until it cleans the sides of the bowl; it should be firm, not wet. If it doesn't clean the bowl, beat in about a tablespoonful of rye or whole-wheat flour at a time until it passes the bowl-cleaning test.

3. Form the dough into a ball with your hands, return it to the bowl, cover with plastic wrap, and leave it to rise until doubled in bulk, 45 minutes to an hour.

4. Preheat the oven to 350°F, with a shelf in the upper third and one in the lower if you'll be baking two panfuls at a time. Grease three large baking sheets, the backs of jelly-roll pans, or the backs of pizza pans (or any combination of pans).

5. Divide the risen dough into three parts. If you're using round pans, form each part in turn into a ball, pat it flat on a work surface generously dusted with rye flour, and roll it into a thin (about ⅛ inch) round about 12 to 13 inches in diameter. For oblong pans, roll out either rounds or oblongs of dough. Transfer the dough to the pans and prick it closely all over with a fork. Using a pastry wheel, mark rounds into 8 equal wedges and oblongs into large or small rectangles, as preferred. Let the dough rise on two of the pans until doubled in thickness, from 20 to 30 minutes, refrigerating the third portion of dough for the time being.

Ways & Means—Grinding Seeds & Spices

When anise, caraway, or other seeds, or any hard spice, must be ground, one way to do it is to whiz them in a small spice or coffee mill dedicated to grinding only seeds, spices, and dried herbs. When you're making a dough such as that for Crisp Rye & Wheat Flatbread, a blender works as a grinder if you increase the bulk of the seeds by adding about ½ cup of the flour used in the recipe.

6. Bake the flatbread two pans at a time for 10 to 12 minutes, reversing the shelf positions midway. When the edges and undersides are golden and the flatbread feels firm, remove it from the oven and let it cool on the pans. Meanwhile, let the refrigerated dough rise at room temperature until it has doubled in thickness, then bake it as described above.

7. When all the flatbread has been baked, turn off the oven to cool with the door open. When the oven has cooled to warmish, turn it on again at 140°F (or its warm setting), slip the flatbread onto wire racks, and return it to the oven for the drying-out phase. After 20 minutes, check for progress, turning any pieces that are deepening in color. Continue to dry the flatbread until it is very light and crisp, being careful to avoid overbrowning (some ovens overshoot their settings). The final phase of the second baking can be finished with the oven turned off and the door open.

8. Cool the flatbread completely, then store it in an airtight canister at room temperature for 2 weeks or so. (For longer storage, it freezes well.) If it has become at all damp in storage, or if it has been frozen, refresh the pieces (without thawing, if frozen) in a low (140° to 150°F) oven until they are again crisp.

OATCAKES

Not exactly crackers and certainly not "cakes" in the teatime sense, these grainy biscuits, native to Scotland, are just the thing to savor all on their own with good butter, or with cheese or preserves or as a base for any other spread you fancy. Crammed with oaty flavor and texture, these particular oatcakes are also rich in bran, which adds healthful fiber to the diet without proclaiming its presence as something that's "good for you."

Serve oatcakes straight from the canister, or warm them for a few minutes in a moderate oven to restore the freshness of their truly excellent flavor.

3½ cups old-fashioned rolled oats
½ cup oat bran or unprocessed wheat bran
1½ teaspoons salt
1½ tablespoons sweet (unsalted) butter
1 tablespoon solid vegetable shortening
½ cup warm water (110° to 115°F)

Makes about 5 dozen oatcakes

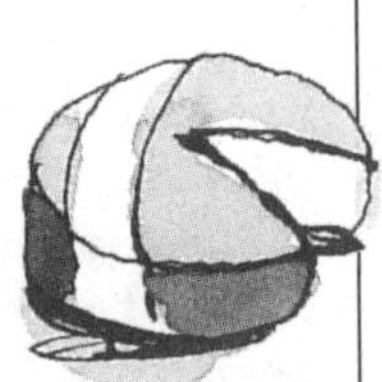

NEIGH TO DR. JOHNSON

Dr. Samuel Johnson, in his great Dictionary, *defamed oats as something usually eaten by horses, except in Scotland, where humans consume the grain because they have nothing better to eat. Oatcakes do their bit to demonstrate the depths of his innocence on this particular subject.*

1. Preheat the oven to 350°F, with a shelf in the upper third and one in the lower.

2. Grind the oats to a coarse meal—there should be small flakes as well as fine bits—using a food processor, a blender (work in batches), or a coffee or spice mill (work in even smaller batches). Measure 2 cups of the meal into a food processor workbowl or a mixing bowl and reserve the remainder for scattering on the work surface on which you'll roll out the oatcakes.

3. Add to the meal the oat bran and salt and mix them thoroughly. Cut in the butter and shortening, using the processor or, if working by hand, a pastry blender or two knives; the bits of fat should disappear into the mixture. Add the warm water and mix the dough, by machine or by hand, until it forms a coherent ball. Depending on the degree of moisture in the oats, the dough may seem wet at first, but it will soon become firm.

4. Divide the dough into two equal portions. Spread a thin layer of the remaining ground oatmeal over a work surface and flatten half of the dough on it. Sprinkle the top with a little more of the meal and roll the dough out ⅛ inch thick, lifting it from the board and sprinkling more meal under it if necessary to prevent sticking. If the dough should crack during rolling, dip a fingertip into water and paint the cracked areas, then press them together and continue rolling. Cut the dough into rounds with a 2-inch cutter. Lay the rounds on ungreased baking sheets, leaving an inch of space between them. Gather together the scraps and reroll and cut them, first working in a few extra drops of water if necessary (the dough may be too dry because of the ground oats it has picked up from the board). In the same fashion, make oatcakes from the second half of the dough. (If you have only two baking sheets, lay the rest of the oatcakes on a sheet of foil of the proper size to fit a baking sheet, and slip the foil and its cargo onto a *cooled* pan for baking after the first two panfuls are done.)

5. Run the rolling pin back and forth over the oatcakes on the pan, shaping them into ovals. Prick each oatcake several times with a fork.

6. Bake two panfuls of oatcakes 10 minutes on two shelves of the oven, then exchange shelf positions and bake the cakes until they have turned pale gold around the edges, 7 to 8 minutes longer; watch them carefully during this time—they should not actually brown.

7. Remove the oatcakes to wire racks and let them cool; meanwhile, bake and cool the third panful.

8. Store the oatcakes in an airtight canister at room temperature for up to 2 weeks. For longer storage, double-bag them and freeze them for up to 2 months. Thaw frozen oatcakes in their wrappings. Refresh either stored or frozen cakes by warming them for a few minutes in a 325°F oven.

Digestive Biscuits

Despite their odd name, these crisp, grainy, and slightly sweet crackers are tremendously appealing with a cup of coffee. In their native Britain, where they are sold everywhere, they're often served with the cheese course, too.

6 tablespoons rolled oats, any kind
1½ cups whole-wheat flour
½ cup all-purpose flour
½ cup (packed) dark brown sugar
1 teaspoon baking powder
½ teaspoon salt, or to taste
6 tablespoons cold butter, either salted or sweet (unsalted), cut up
About ½ cup cold milk, as needed

Makes about 2 dozen biscuits

1. Preheat the oven to 350°F, with a shelf in the upper third and one in the lower. Grease two baking sheets.

2. Grind the rolled oats in a food processor or blender until reduced to medium-coarse meal. Measure out ¼ cup of the ground oats and return any surplus to the oatmeal box.

3. In the workbowl of a food processor or an electric mixer equipped with a flat paddle, combine the ground oats, whole-wheat flour, all-purpose flour, brown sugar, baking powder, and salt and run the machine to mix everything well. Add the cut-up butter and again run the machine (in pulses, if you're using a food processor) until the butter is finely chopped throughout—the mixture will look like coarse meal. With the machine running, slowly pour in ⅓ cup of the cold milk. If the dry ingredients don't form a crumbly dough almost at once, slowly add the rest of the milk, plus a bit more if it's needed (but you don't want a wet dough; the dough should just hold together when pinched; if made in the food processor, it will form a ball whirling around on top of the blade when it is ready).

4. Divide the dough into three or four portions. Roll out one portion at a time between two sheets of plastic wrap until it is a scant ¼ inch thick.

To check the thickness of rolled-out dough, pierce it with the tip of a skewer or something similar, mark the depth on the skewer with your fingertip, and measure against a ruler.

Cut out rounds with a 3-inch round cutter—use a scalloped cutter for the authentic look. Transfer the rounds to a prepared baking sheet,

Chocolate Biscuits

For a touch of highly compatible sweetness, polka-dot the tops of Digestive Biscuits with chocolate morsels or chopped chocolate (try dark sweet or bittersweet chocolate) immediately after taking them from the oven. Spread the dots of chocolate over the biscuits after they soften, or leave them as is.

placing them about an inch apart. Prick all over with a table fork. Repeat rolling and cutting until all the dough has been used.

5. Bake one panful of the biscuits at a time in the center of the preheated oven, or bake two panfuls on two shelves, exchanging shelf positions after 5 or 6 minutes. The biscuits should look pale golden-brown in about 12 minutes (for one pan), in perhaps a minute or two longer if two pans are in the oven. Slide the biscuits onto a rack to cool completely and reuse one of the baking sheets, cooled, to complete baking the batch, if necessary.

6. Stored in an airtight canister at room temperature, digestive biscuits keep for weeks.

Ginger Crackers

Cookies? Crackers? Or biscuits, which is what the British would call them? Whichever, these unsweet crackers are good with cream cheese or with thin slices of Cheddar, or Monterey Jack, Edam, Gouda, or other firm cheese. Preserves, too, are perked up by their light gingeriness.

⅔ cup milk, plus a little more if needed
3 tablespoons sweet (unsalted) butter
1 tablespoon vegetable oil
1¼ cups whole-wheat pastry flour
¾ cup all-purpose flour
2 tablespoons cornstarch
2 teaspoons sugar
2 teaspoons ground ginger
¾ teaspoon salt
¼ teaspoon baking powder

Makes about 3½ dozen crackers

1. Preheat the oven to 325°F, with a shelf in the upper third and one in the lower. Grease two baking sheets lightly.

2. Heat the milk and butter together in a saucepan over low heat just until the butter has melted. Remove the mixture from the heat and stir in the oil. Set aside to cool slightly.

3. Sift the pastry flour, all-purpose flour, cornstarch, sugar, ginger, salt, and baking powder together into a mixing bowl. Make a well in the center. Pour the warm milk mixture into the well, then stir the liquid into the drys from the center, mixing gradually and thoroughly

More Ginger

These crackers become more cookie-like and enticing when finely minced Crystallized Ginger (see the Index) is mixed into the dough. Use from 2 tablespoons to ¼ cup, depending on the degree of your ginger-mania.

to make a crumbly dough that just holds together when squeezed; if the dough is too crumbly (this will depend on the moisture content of the flour), gradually add up to a tablespoonful more of milk and blend it in thoroughly. Form the dough into a ball.

4. Divide the dough into two parts. One portion at a time, roll the dough out ⅛ inch thick between sheets of plastic wrap. Cut the dough into rounds with a 2½-inch scalloped cookie cutter; transfer the rounds to the prepared baking sheets, placing them half an inch apart. Gather the scraps, reroll them, and cut more crackers until the portion of dough has been used. Repeat with the second half of the dough, adding any dough scraps left from the first half. Brush the crackers with a little additional milk, then prick them all over with a sharp fork.

5. Bake the ginger crackers on two shelves of the oven for 10 minutes, then exchange shelf positions and continue to bake the crackers until they are firm and very light golden brown, 6 to 8 minutes longer. Be careful not to overbake the crackers.

6. Cool the crackers on wire racks, then store them in an airtight canister at room temperature for up to 2 weeks or freezer-wrap them and freeze for 3 months or so. Frozen crackers should be thawed in their wrappings and refreshed briefly in a 300°F oven.

Melba Toasts & Homemade Croutons

Unsliced bread, either homemade or store-bought, is what you need for properly thin Melba toast. Good choices from this book are Semolina Bread, Sesame-Topped Bulgur Bread, and Ultimately Cheesy Cheddar Bread (see the Index). For croutons, ready-sliced bread is fine; leave the crusts on or trim them off, as you wish—I leave the crusts on because I like the added texture.

Basic Melba Toast

Slice good firm bread, not too fresh, as thin as you can manage, no more than ¼ inch and preferably ⅛ inch. Preheat the oven to 200°F and bake the slices directly on the shelf, turning them occasionally until they are dry and pale golden, not actually brown. If you are Melba-ing the Cheddar bread, stop the toasting as soon as the pieces are crisp; for the truest flavor, they should not brown at all. Cool the toasts and store them airtight at room temperature; they'll keep for weeks.

To the Last Crumb

Odds and ends of bread, especially good homemade bread, shouldn't be wasted. Tear up or dice the bread, including end pieces; spread the bits on a baking pan and place them in a turned-off oven (turn on the oven at "warm" for a while if the weather is damp). The bread will dry gently at its own pace and is then ready to whirl in a food processor to crumbs of the preferred texture. Alternatively, make crumbs of the bread first, then dry them on a baking sheet in a turned-off or "warm" oven (this takes less time). Stored in a capped jar at room temperature, crumbs will keep well so long as they are kept dry.

How to Spritz

Olive oil for spraying onto food or cooking pans is sold in pressurized cans, but if the notion of aerosol propellants in olive oil isn't pleasing, you can have both the convenience of spray application and the quality of oil you prefer. Just pour a couple of inches of olive oil into a small pump-style "mister" bottle and keep it handy but not too near the heat of the stove. There you are, ready to gild the surface of croutons, focaccia, kebabs, or what-have-you with the oil of your choice, without additives.

Melba Toast Bruschetta Style

Rub one side of Melba toast slices lightly with fresh garlic, brush very lightly (or spray) with good olive oil, and bake for about 5 minutes in a 300°F oven. Serve warm.

Also good: Brush melba toast slices with olive oil and sprinkle them lightly with coarse (kosher or sea) salt, then bake in the same way. Also best made fresh, these aren't suitable for storage.

Basic Croutons

Cut not-too-thick slices of firm bread, crusts removed or not as you prefer, into ½-inch squares (with luck, the croutons will be approximately square, but it doesn't matter if they're not). Spread them on a baking sheet or sheets and bake in a 200°F oven until they are crisp and dry, stirring them occasionally. Cool and store airtight at room temperature.

Herbed Croutons

Especially good on salads, these can be seasoned with any combination of herbs you like.

Cut bread cubes as described. For each 2 cups of cubes, mix at least 2 tablespoons of good olive oil with a generous ½ teaspoonful of crumbled mixed dried herbs of your choice, such as equal parts of thyme and tarragon or thyme and basil, plus generous pinches of oregano, Powdered Bay Leaves (page 195), a little salt and fresh pepper. (Or use the Italian-Style Herb Blend, page 191, plus salt and pepper.) Optionally, add freshly pressed or minced garlic according to conscience. Drizzle the seasoned oil over the cubes, toss them very well, then bake and cool the croutons as described.

Stored in a covered jar in the refrigerator, they keep for up to 3 weeks. Return to room temperature and/or refresh them by a brief stay in a moderate (325°F) oven before serving them.

Zesty Pesto Biscotti

All the good things in pesto—fresh basil, olive oil, *pignoli,* and garlic—flavor these twice-baked savory biscuits, pistachio-green in color. Just right with drinks, especially a glass of wine, and commendable as a crisp sidekick for salad.

4 tablespoons solid vegetable shortening
⅔ cup Pesto (page 140), made with plenty of garlic (do not use the cheater's pesto described)
2 large eggs
2⅔ cups all-purpose flour
¼ cup cornmeal
2 teaspoons baking powder
½ teaspoon salt
⅛ teaspoon freshly grated nutmeg
⅛ teaspoon freshly ground white pepper, or more to taste
2 tablespoons pine nuts *(pignoli)*

GLAZE:
1 large egg white
1 teaspoon water

Makes about 3 dozen biscotti

1. Preheat the oven to 325°F, with a shelf in the center. Grease a baking sheet.

2. In the large bowl of an electric mixer fitted with the flat paddle, if you have one, beat the shortening until light. Beat in the pesto, then the eggs.

3. Sift together the flour, cornmeal, baking powder, salt, nutmeg, and white pepper. With the mixer running, gradually add the dry ingredients, then the pine nuts, to the pesto mixture. Beat just until well mixed.

4. Turn the dough out onto a work surface and divide in half. Using floured hands, squeeze one half into a compact cylinder, then place it on one side of the prepared baking sheet and pat it into a loaf about 11 inches long and 2½ inches wide, pressing to eliminate air pockets or cracks. Form the second loaf in the same fashion, leaving at least 2 inches between them on the pan. Dip a pastry brush into water and smooth the loaves to eliminate any remaining cracks. Prepare the glaze by beating the egg white briefly with the water. Brush the tops and sides of the loaves with the glaze.

5. Bake the loaves in the center of the oven about 25 minutes, or until firm to the touch and deeper in color but not overbrowned. Remove from the oven and cool the loaves on a wire rack for 10 to 15 minutes. Meanwhile, lower the oven setting to 275°F.

6. Slice the partially cooled loaves on the bias into strips, ½ inch thick, using a serrated knife. Lay the strips flat on the baking sheet, using a second sheet (ungreased) if necessary to accommodate all of them. Bake 15 minutes, turn the slices, and bake 15 minutes longer, or until the edges are a delicate gold. (These biscotti are not meant to be bone-dry.) Cool completely on racks, then store in an airtight canister

Familiar Flavor, New Crunch

Pesto is not just for pasta, according to the thinking behind this invention. Be sure the basil is flavorful, and use plenty of garlic.

at room temperature for a few days, or in the refrigerator for up to 2 weeks, or, packaged for freezing, in the freezer for up to 3 months. If frozen, thaw without unwrapping, then spread on a baking sheet and refresh in a 300°F oven for 10 minutes or so and cool them again.

Wine & Parmesan Crackers

White wine secretly tenderizes these little crackers gently flavored with good Parmesan cheese. If you wish, water may replace the wine, but in that case be sure to omit the baking soda and increase the baking powder to 1 teaspoon.

2 cups all-purpose flour
½ teaspoon salt
½ teaspoon baking power
½ teaspoon baking soda
3 tablespoons fresh finely grated imported Parmesan cheese
4 tablespoons solid vegetable shortening or lard
About 6 tablespoons dry white wine

Makes about 3 dozen 2-inch crackers

1. Preheat the oven to 350°F, with a shelf in the upper third and one in the lower.

2. Whisk together thoroughly the flour, salt, baking powder, baking soda, and Parmesan in a mixing bowl.

3. Divide the shortening into several chunks, toss them in the dry ingredients to coat them, then rub the fat into the flour, using your fingertips to make a crumbly mixture. Sprinkle about 4 tablespoons of the wine over the mixture and mix with a fork, tossing lightly and adding more of the wine as necessary to make a dough that just holds together when squeezed. Gather the dough into a ball and let rest for a few minutes.

4. On a floured surface, roll out a third of the dough ⅛ inch thick. Prick the dough all over with a fork, then cut into 2-inch squares, using a knife and a ruler or, more simply, a pizza cutter. Place the crackers close together on ungreased baking sheets. Cut more crackers from the remaining dough and the trimmings.

5. Bake the crackers two panfuls at a time for 12 to 15 minutes, exchanging shelf positions midway. The crackers should be pale gold

Variations

To play around a little with this cracker recipe, add a little fresh-ground coarse pepper or a pinch of ground hot red (cayenne) pepper to the dry ingredients. Or substitute dry vermouth for the white wine, or strew the top of the rolled-out dough with coarse sea salt or aromatic seeds (cumin, sesame, caraway, or poppy). Run the rolling pin over the topping to anchor the salt or seeds before pricking the dough and cutting out the crackers.

rather than actually browned. Cool the crackers on a rack and store them in a covered container for up to 2 weeks or so. If they should soften in storage, refresh them in a low oven for a few minutes and cool them before serving.

SALTED SESAME CRACKERS

Tender little oblongs topped with Toasted Sesame Salt (the Japanese *goma shio;* see the Index), these are delectable on all crackery occasions. Serve with a spread or a topping if you must, but these are remarkably good without embellishment.

2 cups unbleached pastry flour
1 teaspoon baking powder
½ teaspoon salt, optional if the sesame seed topping is used
¼ cup butter-flavored solid vegetable shortening
¼ cup water, or more as needed
2 tablespoons roasted (dark) sesame oil

GLAZE (OPTIONAL):
1 large egg white
2 tablespoons water

TOPPING:
½ cup Toasted Sesame Salt (page 198) or hulled white sesame seed, plain or lightly toasted

Makes about 4 dozen crackers

1. Preheat the oven to 400°F, with a shelf in the upper third and another in the lower. Lightly grease two large unrimmed baking sheets.

2. Sift together the flour, baking powder, and salt, if used. Cut in the shortening. (Both steps may be done most handily in a food processor, or do it all in a mixing bowl, using a pastry blender or two knives to cut in the shortening.) Combine ¼ cup water with the sesame oil and add to the dry ingredients (pour the liquid through the feed tube with the machine running, if you're food-processing this; or make a well in the center of the dry ingredients in the bowl and stir from the center outward). Add a little more water as needed; you will almost certainly need more in order to make a not-too-dry dough (in the food processor, the dough will form a ball on top of the blade).

OPEN, SESAME

The oil of roasted sesame seed is rich, dark, and aromatic, a far cry from the rather nondescript oil pressed from raw seed. Unroasted sesame oil is good for frying and dressing salads; oil from roasted sesame seed, often called Asian sesame oil, is mainly a flavoring rather than a cooking medium, as it loses its charm rapidly when overheated. In these crackers it reinforces the flavor of the topping of Toasted Sesame Salt.

3. Divide the dough in half. Place one half on one prepared baking sheet, cover it with a sheet of plastic wrap, and roll it out to a thickness of about ⅛ inch. Remove the plastic, trim the edges to make an oblong, and reattach the trimmings along one side in a more or less straight strip; roll the trimmings to the same thickness as the body of the dough and trim the edge again to make an oblong measuring about 12 x 9 inches. If you're using the glaze, beat the egg white briefly with the water and brush the dough lightly with the mixture. Sprinkle half of the sesame salt or sesame seed on the dough, brush the topping into an even layer with a pastry brush, and go over the dough lightly with the rolling pin to press the topping into the dough. Using a ruler and a pastry wheel, cut the dough into crackers of the size you like (3 x 1½ inches is a good size and shape). Prick each cracker several times with a table fork. Repeat, using the remaining dough.

4. Bake the crackers on two shelves of the oven for about 9 to 10 minutes, reversing shelf positions midway in the baking; the crackers are done when puffed, firm, and lightly browned. Remove the crackers to wire racks immediately and turn off the oven.

5. When the crackers have cooled slightly, put the racks of crackers back into the oven; leave the door open until the oven has cooled down to fairly warm, then close it and leave the crackers to continue to dry. When the oven is cold, if the crackers aren't as crisp as you'd like them, turn the oven on at its "warm" setting, leave the door ajar, and let the crackers dry until they suit you.

6. Store in an airtight container at room temperature. These will keep their good character for a week or two and may be refreshed before serving, if they have lost crispness, by spending a few minutes in a 300°F oven.

Smoky Chile & Corn Biscotti

Biscotti, a word meaning "twice-baked," usually describes the sweet, often crisp, cookielike bars of Italian heritage that are wildly popular wherever they have become known. (See the Index for recipes suitable for tea or snack time). Savory or cocktail biscotti, such as these chile-seasoned bars, though newcomers to the food scene and quite different from the sweet versions, are indeed double-baked and so entitled to their name.

Smoke-dried and powdered red chipotle chiles, which begin life as the familiar green jalapeños, give kick and warmth to these corn-studded biscotti. They are spicy enough for most tastes as written, but feel free to make them really incendiary if you're sure you know what you're doing. If ground chipotle chile isn't readily available, use the same quantity of other pure ground chile or about twice as much Custom-Made Chili Seasoning (see the Index).

1 cup young, crisp corn kernels, either freshly cooked, canned, or frozen
3 large eggs
3 tablespoons corn oil or other vegetable oil
2¼ cups all-purpose flour
6 tablespoons cornmeal
2 teaspoons baking powder
1½ teaspoons salt
1½ teaspoons ground dried chipotle chile, or more if you're sure you know what you're doing
1½ teaspoons crumbled dried oregano, preferably the Mexican kind
½ teaspoon pure garlic powder, optional

GLAZE:
A little milk, or 1 egg white beaten with 2 teaspoons cold water

Makes about 3 dozen biscotti

1. Preheat the oven to 325°F. Grease a baking sheet.

2. Using the pulsing action of a food processor (or a large heavy knife on a cutting board), chop the corn coarsely and scrape it into the workbowl of an electric mixer fitted with the flat paddle, if you have one. Add the eggs and the oil to the corn and beat until the ingredients are well mixed.

3. Sift together the flour, cornmeal, baking powder, salt, chile, oregano, and garlic powder, if used. With the mixer running, spoon the dry ingredients into the corn base and mix until a dough has been formed. (It will be a bit sticky.)

4. Divide the dough in half. With floured hands, form one portion into a compact cylinder, then place it on one side of the prepared baking sheet and pat it into a loaf about 11 inches

A Special Chile

Chipotle chiles, which are jalapeño chiles dried over smoke, aren't found in every fancy grocery, perhaps, but they are offered by specialists in Southwestern and Latin American foods. Choose whole, crumbled, or ground chipotles, or buy them pickled or canned in adobo sauce. In these corn-studded biscotti the hot, smoky chipotles contribute more oomph than other kinds of chiles, I think, but it's cook's choice, and the cook's choice sometimes depends on the grocer.

long and 2½ inches wide, pressing to eliminate cracks and air pockets. Form a second loaf in the same fashion, leaving at least 2 inches between the loaves on the pan. Dip a pastry brush into water and smooth the loaves to eliminate any remaining cracks. Brush the loaves with the glaze, pressing the loaves firmly with the brush to smooth the surface and make the dough more compact.

5. Bake the loaves in the center of the oven about 25 minutes, or until firm to the touch and a deeper gold than before baking. Remove from the oven and cool the loaves on a wire rack for 10 to 15 minutes. Meanwhile, lower the oven setting to 275°F.

6. Slice the partially cooled loaves on a diagonal into ½-inch strips, using a sharp serrated knife. Lay the strips flat on the cooling rack or baking sheet, using a second rack or sheet (ungreased) to accommodate all of them. Bake 15 minutes, turn the slices, and bake 15 minutes longer. Turn off the oven, leave the door ajar, and leave the biscotti until completely cool. If the biscuits are not very dry throughout, return them to the oven, heat it to "warm" (or its lowest setting), and leave them until they are dry throughout. Cool them again before they are served or stored.

7. Store the biscotti in an airtight canister at room temperature for up to 2 weeks or, packaged for freezing, in the freezer for up to 6 months. If they have been frozen, thaw them in their wrappings, then spread them on a baking sheet or a rack and refresh them in a 300°F oven for 10 minutes or so. Cool them before serving.

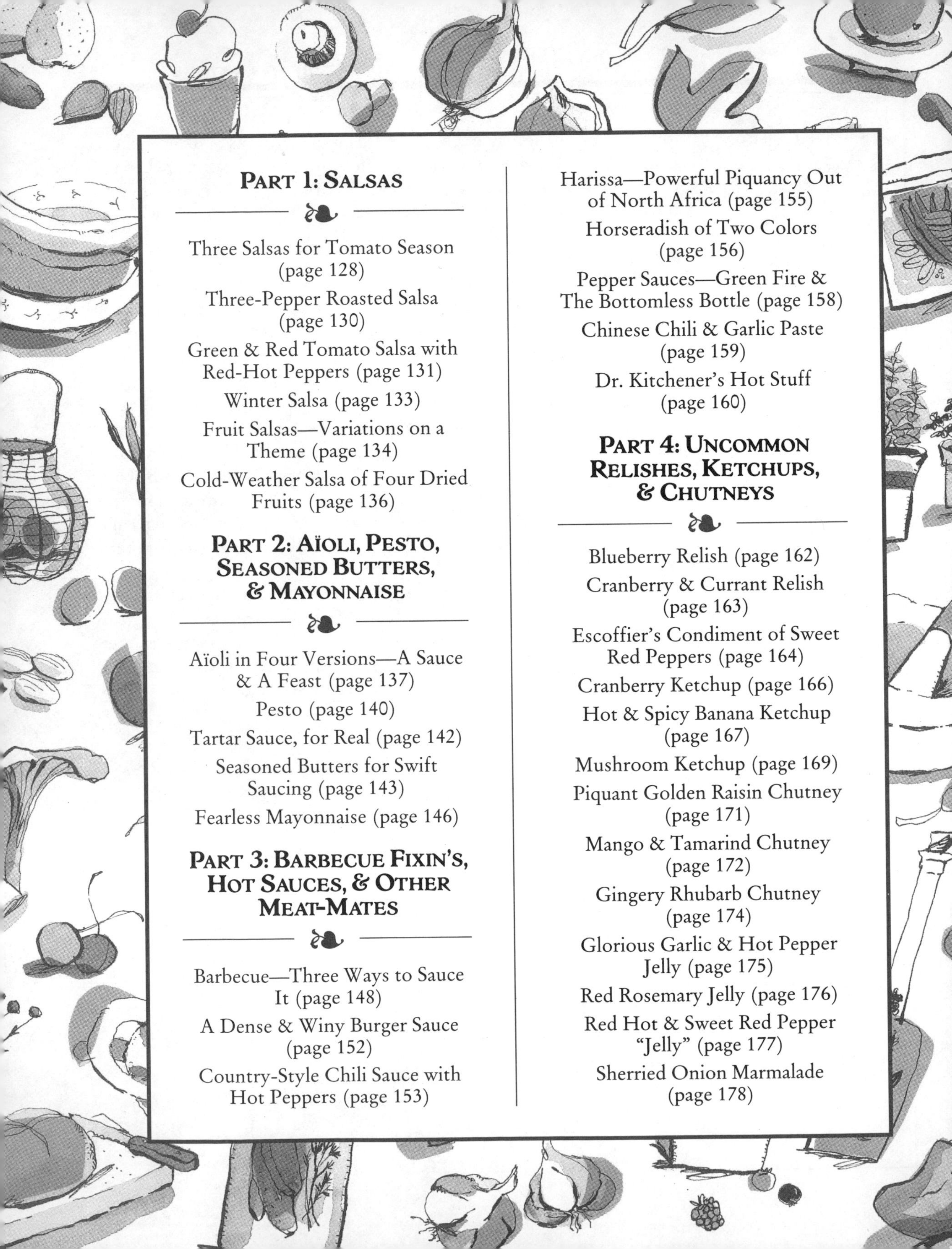

Part 1: Salsas

Part 2: Aïoli, Pesto, Seasoned Butters, & Mayonnaise

Part 3: Barbecue Fixin's, Hot Sauces, & Other Meat-Mates

Part 4: Uncommon Relishes, Ketchups, & Chutneys

Savory Saucery

A lively recipe basketful, this, a cornucopia of sauces, relishes, and condiments variously sharp and mellow, hot and soothing, sweet and sour. Look in the four groupings that follow for piquant salsas of fruits and vegetables; aïoli, pestos, and other oil- and butter-enriched cold sauces; an array of relishes that includes savory jellies based on garlic, rosemary, or hot pepper; uncommon chutneys and fruit or vegetable ketchups; some really hot items (harissa, Chinese chili paste, Dr. Kitchener's Hot Stuff); and other kickshaws to enhance the appeal of main-event edibles.

Salsas, in the first set of recipes, are no longer seen only on Southwestern and Western tables. These Mexican-born sauces have been embraced with gusto across the nation, and a good thing, too, according to anyone who delights in zesty extras. So long as salsas stay within reasonable gastronomic bounds, as these do (the farther-out "fusion-food" cooks, who make salsa from *anything*, are bound to settle down someday), salsas will be giving the more traditional American-style relishes a vigorous run for their money, both in the market and on the plate.

Recipes for sauces that include aïoli, pesto, seasoned butter, and updated mayonnaises begin on page 137. Barbecue and hot sauces and others of that savory sort begin on page 148; and the relishes, ketchups, and chutneys starts on page 162.

PART 1: SALSAS

Salsas have quite recently exploded onto the American gastronomic scene in regions far from the Southwest and West, where piquant table sauces adopted from Mexico have been great favorites for generations. (Wherever you live, just check the salsa shelves in any supermarket for evidence of this nuclear event, then try making your own salsas for a better and fresher outcome.)

The big-bang arrival of salsas has been especially welcome to those who delight in hot stuff, but not all salsas need to be incandescently spiked with hot peppers; one of the bonuses of making your own, for immediate use or for keeping, is matching the chile-pepper content of the sauce to your own palate.

You'll notice that the recipes on the following pages are made with both vegetables and fruits, but they do not include some of the fartherout ingredients encountered in some modish "fusion" versions. Which doesn't mean I'm against new wrinkles—salsas are fun to experiment with, as is done in the Fruit Salsas recipe, which is a pattern, not a prescription. All in all, these new-old sauces are adding a great deal to the American repertoire of zingy relishes.

THREE SALSAS FOR TOMATO SEASON

Summer tomatoes ripened on the vine can't be matched by those produced in any other season and "ripened" in a gas chamber, so the very good uncooked salsa that comes first below is, naturally, called Summer Salsa. As it's not a keeper for the storage cupboard, I extend the season by freezing a supply of it to keep on hand, as described in the second recipe below. Like the many store-bought salsas that have invaded the condiment section of groceries, it has the merit of being ready to use when you are ready to eat.

When tomatoes are piled high in markets and farm stands, I like to roast an ovenful to make the unusual and tasty salsa described in the third recipe of this set.

SUMMER SALSA TO SERVE RIGHT NOW

Mild is the word for this salsa, which can be a mere starting point for those who choose more emphasis on heat or onion and garlic or cilantro. Salsa experts like to make use of toasted, skinned, and pureed dried chiles of various kinds; some use roasted garlic; some include cumin and/or oregano or a bit of oil or a bit of brown sugar in the sauce, so the beginner should feel free to build on the basic formula here.

3 cups skinned, seeded, chopped, and briefly drained ripe fresh tomatoes
½ to 1 cup finely diced red or other mild onion or sliced white part of scallions, to taste
1 tablespoon seeded and chopped fresh jalapeño peppers (pickled jalapeño peppers can be substituted), or chopped roasted and peeled green chiles (such as serrano), or chopped and drained canned green chiles
1 teaspoon very finely minced or pressed garlic
¼ to ½ cup chopped fresh cilantro (coriander) leaves
2 tablespoons fresh lime juice (unsweetened bottled lime juice or fresh lemon juice may be substituted)
Salt, to taste

Makes about 4 cups

Combine the ingredients and let the sauce stand at room temperature for half an hour or so, then taste and adjust the seasonings as desired. Leftovers will keep for up to 3 days, but may need to be drained and reseasoned before use as a sauce.

An unorthodox but successful notion: Add leftover salsa to an extemporaneous pot of vegetable soup, or make it part of a tomato-based spaghetti sauce.

Summer Salsa to Keep on Hand

Though it has necessarily been cooked, you'll find this version to be fresher-tasting than salsas born in supermarket jars. It's a pleasure to have this ready for use.

4 cups peeled, seeded, and diced very ripe fresh tomatoes
2 tablespoons seeded and chopped fresh jalapeño peppers, or chopped and drained canned green chilies, or chopped and drained pickled jalapeños
3 or 4 large cloves garlic, minced, to taste
2 tablespoons tomato paste
1 to 2 teaspoons ground cumin, to taste
½ teaspoon crumbled dried oregano, optional
1 cup finely diced onion
¼ to ⅓ cup chopped fresh cilantro (coriander) leaves, to taste
3 tablespoons fresh lime juice (unsweetened bottled lime juice or fresh lemon juice may be substituted)
Salt, optional

Makes about 5 cups

Creating a "Keeper"

There's nothing wrong with most of the bottled salsas that jostle each other on the grocery shelves, but there can be a lot more right with your own salsas, seasoned to taste and kept on hand for seasons of no tomatoes. Freezing is the recommended way to store both Summer Salsa to Keep on Hand and Roasted Tomato Salsa; no preserving procedures are called for.

1. Combine the tomatoes with the hot peppers, garlic, tomato paste, cumin, and oregano in a nonreactive saucepan or wide skillet or sauté pan, bring to a boil, and reduce the heat to medium; cook, with frequent stirring, for about 10 minutes, or until a good deal of the liquid has evaporated. Add the onion and cook about 5 minutes longer, stirring often. Remove from the heat.

2. Cool the salsa to lukewarm, then fold in the chopped cilantro and lime juice. Taste for seasoning and add salt, if desired, and more hot peppers, lime juice, and cumin and/or oregano if you wish.

3. This may be served after an hour or two of mellowing at room temperature, or refrigerate it, covered, for several days. To keep it longer, freeze it. After thawing, check the seasonings and add a bit of additional chopped fresh cilantro, if you have it, to brighten the flavor. Serve the revived salsa at room temperature.

CHILE CHANGE

Canned or bottled chipotle chiles packed in adobo sauce may be substituted for the ground chile. Scrape off the sauce before chopping the peppers and add them with caution—they are a high-BTU type of chile.

ROASTED TOMATO SALSA

To make a modest batch of this intensely flavored offshoot of the cooked-salsa tree, chop enough roasted tomato slices (see Roasted Tomatoes, page 62) to measure 2 cups. Add ½ cup tomato juice plus one half of the amounts of hot peppers, garlic, cumin, oregano, and onion listed in the preceding recipe. Omit the tomato paste.

Cook the mixture in a nonreactive wide pan just long enough, perhaps 8 to 10 minutes, to soften the onions and produce a sauce of the consistency you want; the time will depend on the moisture level of the roasted tomatoes. Cool slightly and add one half of the listed amounts of cilantro and lime or lemon juice and season with salt to taste.

This keeps for several days, or may be frozen for future use. Recheck the seasonings after thawing it and, if possible, add some chopped fresh cilantro leaves.

THREE-PEPPER ROASTED SALSA

A spoonful of this snappy crimson relish does a lot for grilled or roasted meat or an everyday casserole or pot of beans, and it's also a grand pick-me-up for a sandwich, salad, or impromptu cheese-and-cracker snack. Folded into mayonnaise, low-fat or high-, it puts vaguely Southwestern oomph into a seafood or vegetable or chicken salad, and it can even be stirred into vegetable soup that's suffering from the blahs.

⅓ cup diced red or other mild onion
1 cup well-drained roasted sweet red (bell) pepper strips (see Roasted Red Antipasto Peppers, page 60)
2 tablespoons chopped pickled jalapeño peppers or stemmed, seeded, and chopped fresh jalapeños, or more to taste
2 tablespoons balsamic or sherry vinegar, or to taste
1 tablespoon full-flavored olive oil, optional
2 teaspoons honey or dark corn syrup
1 to 2 teaspoons Roasted Garlic Paste (page 260), to taste, or 1 or 2 large cloves garlic, or more or less as you choose, minced fine or pressed
½ teaspoon ground dried chipotle chiles or any other ground pure chile, or a few drops Tabasco or other hot pepper sauce, or ¼ to ½ teaspoon Chinese Chili & Garlic Paste (page 159)
½ teaspoon salt
2 tablespoons chopped fresh cilantro (coriander) leaves

Makes about 1¾ cups

1. Steep the diced onion in a heatproof bowl with boiling water to cover for 3 or 4 minutes, then drain and return to the bowl; cover with very cold water and cool completely; drain again.

2. Chop the sweet red peppers coarsely and combine them with the onion, jalapeños, vinegar, oil, honey, garlic paste, chipotle chile, and salt. Taste attentively and adjust the seasonings, adding more vinegar, oil, sweetening, garlic, chile, and/or salt to reach the balance you want. Fold in the chopped cilantro.

3. Let the salsa mellow at room temperature for an hour or two to meld flavors before serving. Leftover salsa will keep, refrigerated, for 3 days or so; let it come again to room temperature before serving it.

Green Tomato Futures

Green tomatoes aren't hard to get in summer and early fall, but they are rare at any other time of year because they're not a "market" item. So, to have a supply on hand for making chutney, green-tomato mincemeat, or this salsa, just wash, dry, and freeze the tomatoes whole in freezer bags. Thawed, they're fine for any use for which you chop them up, but they're not good for slicing and frying—the freezing toughens their texture, which isn't apparent when they're chopped and cooked.

Green & Red Tomato Salsa with Red-Hot Peppers

Green tomatoes can be an autumn puzzlement—what to do with an abundance of fruits that won't have time to ripen on the vine? Among the answers is a keepable salsa, cheerfully green and red in color, made as mild or hot as you prefer. As written, the recipe produces a gentle salsa; it can be made more piquant, as suggested in the directions, even after cooking is finished. If you have a lot of raw material as well as a great big cooking pot, the recipe may be multiplied.

2 cups cored and coarsely chopped completely green fresh tomatoes
1 cup peeled, seeded, and coarsely chopped ripe fresh tomatoes, or drained, seeded, and coarsely chopped high-quality canned Italian-style plum tomatoes
½ cup diced onion
¼ cup distilled white vinegar
¼ cup diced sweet red (bell) pepper
1 to 2 tablespoons seeded, deribbed, and minced fresh hot red peppers, or more to taste
1 tablespoon minced garlic
1 teaspoon salt
1 teaspoon ground cumin
Ground hot red (cayenne) pepper, hot red pepper flakes, or Tabasco or other hot pepper sauce, optional

AT SERVING TIME (OPTIONAL):
Diced sweet onion and/or chopped fresh cilantro (coriander) leaves

Makes about 3 cups

1. Combine the green tomatoes, ripe tomatoes, onion, vinegar, sweet red pepper, hot peppers, garlic, and salt in a nonreactive wide skillet or large saucepan. Bring to a boil, then lower the heat to medium and cook at a brisk simmer, stirring often, for 30 minutes, or until the green tomato pieces are tender and translucent and very little liquid emerges when a sample of the salsa is spooned onto a saucer. If the salsa tends to stick before the pieces are tender, stir in a little boiling water as needed until the tomatoes are done, then continue the cooking until any surplus liquid has been reduced and the salsa passes the saucer test.

2. Add the cumin. Transfer the salsa to a bowl and let it rest at room temperature, covered, for a few hours or overnight. Taste the salsa and adjust the seasonings with more vinegar, salt, cumin, and/or ground hot red pepper, pepper flakes, or hot pepper sauce to taste. (Keep in mind that the seasonings will continue to "bloom" as the salsa mellows, and such additions can be made at any point as long as the salsa lasts.)

3. Store the salsa, covered, in a glass or plastic container in the refrigerator, where it will keep (and improve) for many weeks.

Alternatively, seal the salsa in jars: Return the salsa to a nonreactive saucepan and heat, stirring it until boiling hot throughout. Ladle it into hot, clean half-pint canning jars, leaving ¼ inch of headspace. Seal with new two-piece canning lids according to manufacturer's directions and process for 10 minutes in a boiling-water bath (page 283). Cool, label, and store the jars. The relish will keep for up to a year in a cool cupboard.

4. *At serving time:* The salsa is ready to go onto the table from the jar (and that's the way we like it best), but you may want to add a bit of texture in the form of diced sweet onion, and/or introduce another flavor note by folding in a small quantity of minced fresh cilantro (coriander) leaves. After tasting, you may want to adjust the other seasonings.

Winter Salsa

Making the best of it in the long months when no decent fresh tomatoes are to be had, this mild-mannered salsa is fresher tasting than most bottled salsas even though it starts with canned tomatoes. (If that looks like a put-down, it isn't meant to be—Italian-style plum tomatoes, whether domestic or imported, are among the few glories of the canned-food shelves. Picked ripe and well flavored, they are a much better choice for cooking than the rubbery pink spheres that pass for fresh tomatoes in the off season.)

Winter Salsa can be made as fiery as you please by adding more hot pepper, and the cook should not be timid about upping the sweet pepper, onion, cilantro, or lime juice. To go further beyond the recipe as written, consider such additions as minced or pressed garlic, chopped parsley, or a little crumbled dried oregano.

1 can (28 ounces) fine quality Italian-style plum tomatoes
½ cup diced mild onion
¼ cup chopped sweet red or green (bell) pepper
2 teaspoons minced jalapeños or other hot peppers, or to taste, (if fresh peppers are unavailable, drained pickled jalapeños or a generous pinch or two of ground pure chile peppers—not chili powder—can be substituted)
¼ cup chopped fresh cilantro (coriander) leaves or 2 to 3 tablespoons drained frozen cilantro (see sidebar)
1 to 2 tablespoons fresh lime or lemon juice, or more to taste (mild wine vinegar may be substituted)
Salt, if needed

Makes about 3 cups

Freezing Cilantro

Frozen cilantro is quite satisfactory when a fresh bunch can't be had. To freeze a supply, pull the leaves from the stems, rinse them, then chop them briefly with a little water in a food processor or blender. Freeze the chopped cilantro, with the water, in an ice-cube tray or small custard cups. Unmold the frozen blocks, bag them airtight, and store in the freezer. After thawing, drain the pulp or not, as the dish requires; the cilantro water is full of flavor.

1. Drain the tomatoes, reserving the juice. Squeeze each tomato gently over the bowl of reserved juice, removing as much of the seedy juice as possible without mashing the flesh too much. Chop the tomatoes into coarse chunks.

2. Strain and discard the seeds from the reserved juice, then boil it rapidly in a nonreactive wide pan (or in a large glass bowl in the microwave) until reduced to about ½ cup. Add the juice to the chopped tomatoes.

3. Add all the remaining ingredients except the lime juice and salt. Sample the salsa and add lime juice to taste plus salt if needed (canned tomatoes are sometimes well salted).

4. Mellow the salsa at room temperature for an hour or two before serving, if possible, then taste again and adjust seasonings, if necessary. This can be refrigerated for several days.

Fruit Salsas~ Variations on a Theme

Now that the term "salsa" is emblazoned on countless labels in fancy-food shops and supermarkets as well as on the pages of cookbooks, the original Southwestern/Mexican definition of the dish has stretched to cover a lot of new ingredients and styles. "Salsa" is now applied to chefs' inventions involving beans and corn and zucchini and peanuts and olives and whatnot, relishes more like a salad than a sauce, some of them almost impossible to categorize. They taste good, but are they *salsas*?

Never mind: When the salsa excitement dies down a little, we'll be left with a number of good things we'll want to keep for our tables. Besides the estimable tomato-based salsas you'll find farther along, among the "keepers," to my palate, are the several fruit salsas presented below and a few pages farther along. The fresh-fruit versions here are fun to improvise and near foolproof, too, if you taste as you fool with them. Use this recipe as a pattern, letting your own tastes and preferences guide your choices of embellishments.

Fruit Salsas

Amount to make: Fruit salsas don't keep their charm intact (though they'll still be quite edible) for more than a few hours, so I'd make just

Key Lime Juice

The real thing is squeezed from small yellow limes once widely grown in the Florida Keys but now hard to obtain. Mexican limes are similar, if not actually identical (a question for fruit experts). Bottled "Key lime juice" may be exactly that, but read the label to make sure; I've seen such wording as "Key West lime juice," which raises the question: Why not "Key lime juice," if that's what's in the bottle?

enough for the upcoming meal. And I'd allow as much as a third of a cup of this refreshing compound per person, based on the rate of consumption observed around our table. With the additions suggested below, a cupful of prepared fruit should make four helpings for diners with a healthy but not obsessive liking for relishes.

Fruit: Begin with something in season—one or more kinds of melon, not overlooking watermelon; berries, mangoes, oranges, pineapple, peaches or nectarines, halved grapes, kiwi fruit, papaya, for openers. From the pantry shelf, unsweetened canned pineapple makes excellent salsa. Dice or chop the fruit you're using and drain it well. If you like, combine any of the more assertive fruits with an equal measure of skinned, seeded, diced, and well-drained ripe tomatoes, which are, come to think of it, also a fruit.

Additional ingredients for each cup of prepared fruit:

Acid: For tartness, add 1 to 1½ tablespoons of lime, Key lime, or lemon juice; or orange or grapefruit juice concentrate; or use 1½ teaspoons mild vinegar, such as rice or white wine vinegar.

Heat: For piquancy, fold in 1 tablespoon minced fresh or canned or pickled (in a pinch) jalapeño peppers. Also consider including a little grated or minced fresh ginger if you have a root on hand.

Pungency: Add 2 tablespoons finely diced mild red or sweet white onion or half that amount of snipped chives. Some might include a whisper of garlic, minced to a pulp or squashed through a press.

Crunch: Fold in 2 tablespoons of diced sweet red or yellow (bell) pepper (this is for flavor too), or jicama or water chestnuts or a crisp kind of apple. Try seeded cucumber if its flavor is compatible with the fruit you're using.

Cilantro (fresh coriander): If you can obtain this most characteristic salsa ingredient, by all means include it. Chop the leaves only, skipping the coarse stems, and fold in about 2 tablespoons per cup of fruit. The same amount of fresh mint can be substituted for cilantro; half as much dried mint as fresh is okay in the off-season, but dried cilantro, in my view, isn't worth bothering with. Frozen chopped cilantro (see the Index) is second-best to fresh, but it's quite good).

Seasonings, all to taste: Add a little salt and freshly ground pepper, a little sweetening if needed (honey or brown sugar or corn syrup); a scattering of grated zest of orange, lemon, or lime; for more piquancy, dashes of hot pepper sauce (see the Index for some custom-made pepper sauces).

Method: Toss everything together and let the salsa macerate for about half an hour; then taste it, adjust the seasonings, and serve it within an hour or two of its making.

Cold-Weather Salsa of Four Dried Fruits

You could call this compound a chutney and no one would argue, but "salsa" recognizes the presence of hot peppers—without which salsa just isn't salsa—in the sweet-and-sour matrix of fruit.

Duck, turkey, chicken, pork, and ham are all perked up by the company of this tracklement. Its fruitiness and fire add interest to a dressing for chicken, ham, or pasta salad, and you can build quick piquant canapés by slathering crackers with cream cheese (or thickened yogurt—see the Index) and adding a dollop of the salsa.

1 medium red onion, diced
Water as needed
¾ cup raisins, dark or golden
½ cup diced pitted prunes
½ cup diced dried apricots
½ cup diced dried light figs
1½ to 2 cups water
¼ cup cider vinegar
¼ cup sugar
2 tablespoons chopped fresh or pickled jalapeño peppers, or more or less to taste
½ teaspoon salt, optional
½ teaspoon ground ginger or 1 teaspoon grated or minced fresh ginger

Makes 3 cups

1. Combine the onion with water to cover in a small saucepan. Bring to a boil, then simmer for 5 minutes. Drain and reserve.

2. Place the raisins, prunes, apricots, and figs in a saucepan and add 1½ to 2 cups water, just to reach the top layer of fruit. Bring to a boil, reduce the heat to low, and simmer the fruit 15 minutes. Add the onion, vinegar, sugar, jalapeño peppers, salt, and ginger. Bring to a boil again, then reduce the heat and simmer for 5 minutes. The mixture may look too liquid, but the salsa will further thicken as it cools.

3. Let the salsa mellow for a few hours before serving it at room temperature. The salsa keeps indefinitely, refrigerated in a covered jar.

Consider Also . . .

substituting such dried fruits as peaches (for apricots), currants, cherries, or blueberries (for raisins), and pears (for figs) in this recipe. Dried or glazed pineapple can also stand in for apricots. So long as the general proportions are kept, any of these work delightfully.

PART 2: AÏOLI, PESTO, SEASONED BUTTERS, & MAYONNAISE

The eggy, buttery, and oil-rich sauces in this section are meant to serve various culinary purposes. Some are heavy hitters that set the character of the meal—aïoli is the linchpin of a whole feast, and pesto has been adopted on this side of the water as a sauce for pasta served as a main dish, not a first course as in Italy.

Other sauces in this section have a double role, serving as both a table sauce and kitchen standby. In this category, basic mayonnaise, in a version designed to avoid the dangers of raw egg, is presented with many variations, and seasoned butters appear in great variety. For good measure, there's a tartar sauce that returns to the classic outlines of a sauce that can be wonderful, or not so, when encountered here and there.

AÏOLI IN FOUR VERSIONS—A SAUCE & A FEAST

"Sauce" or even "garlic mayonnaise" seems an inadequate descriptive for this succulent compound of garlic—lots and lots of wonderful garlic—egg yolks, fine olive oil, and a few drops of lemon juice. Okay, so you think it will overpower everything in sight. In Provence, its native heath, the tradition has been to dollop it onto just *about* everything in sight, for every Friday's dinner and especially for the feast known as *le grand aïoli* (an opulent spread of salt cod, various other kinds of seafood, simmered meats, hard-cooked eggs, endless vegetables, and, when available, snails cooked artfully with herbs. All anointed with aïoli and consumed with gusto).

For most aficionados of garlic, a more manageable aïoli feast might be a beaker of sauce plus baked or boiled potatoes in their jackets and some vegetables—steamed green beans, artichokes, boiled carrots and beets, cauliflower, broccoli, whatever is good and in season, for a meat-free meal. Or simply lavish your aïoli on poached fresh fish or poached salt codfish, plus vegetables of your choice, or have it with "boiled" beef and vegetables (a.k.a. boiled dinner). In Provence, I gather, the sauce is served in the mortar in which it is made. I hope to go and see (and taste) for myself one of these days.

The measure of garlic: The recipe demands good, big, juicy cloves of garlic, really the only kind to use, without any sprouting hearts or rubbery texture. If you are sure you like garlic a *lot,* increase the number of cloves. Anyone who feels timid can cut way back. (French cookbooks will call for a larger number of cloves, as Provençal garlic is milder than American.)

The egg yolks: Health authorities have been telling us to be cautious about consuming uncooked eggs, which harbor dangerous salmonella bacteria in some localities. If eggs in your geographical region are under suspicion, you may want to make the alternative aïoli based on (salmonella-free) powdered dried eggs, or either of the two eggless aïolis that follow it.

The olive oil: The recipe for Eggless Low-Fat Aïoli is supplied for anyone who can't afford to consume the fat grams in aïoli made entirely with olive oil. This is a passable substitute, generously garlicked.

The utensils needed: A large mortar and pestle are traditionally used for making the sauce, but most mortars (like mine) are too small for the job. If you're in the same boat, use the small mortar for crushing the garlic with the salt and blending in the egg or egg substitute. Then transfer the sauce to a sturdy bowl and complete the job, using the pestle for stirring. If you have no choice, a blender may be used to make the sauce, but its texture will be less authentic. Proceed just as you would when making blender mayonnaise.

Lower fat note: Aïoli has never appeared anywhere *near* anyone's list of diet foods, but the version on the opposite page—eggless and made with nonfat or low-fat mayonnaise and only a smidgen of oil—might qualify. Purists (and noncounters of calories) would scorn it, but others might well prefer it to no aïoli at all.

Classic Aïoli

3 large, juicy cloves garlic (no green sprouts inside), peeled
¼ teaspoon salt, or to taste
4 large egg yolks, lightly beaten, at room temperature
2 cups fruity olive oil, at room temperature
Room-temperature water, as needed
About 2 teaspoons strained fresh lemon juice

Makes about 2½ cups

1. Crush the garlic and salt to a smooth paste in a mortar. (Alternatively, push the garlic through a press into the mortar or mixing bowl, then blend it with the salt, using the pestle.) Stirring in one direction only, blend in the egg yolks until thoroughly mixed. (If your mortar won't hold the entire amount of sauce, transfer the mixture to a bowl at this point and continue using the pestle to mix, stirring in the same direction as before.)

2. Adding it a drop at a time, begin stirring in the oil. After a few spoonfuls have been incorporated, you can add oil in a very thin stream, never ceasing to stir. The sauce may become very thick before all the oil has been added; if that happens, stir in a teaspoonful or two of tepid water to make the sauce more receptive to the remaining oil. When all the oil has been worked in, stir in the lemon juice. Check for seasoning. Serve at room temperature.

3. *Troubleshooting:* As when making mayonnaise, the oil in aïoli may separate from the body of the sauce, usually because one or another ingredient is too cold or the oil has been added too fast. *Remedy:* Empty the mortar or bowl, saving the sauce; wash and dry the bowl; put an additional yolk in it with a half-teaspoonful of water and a tiny pinch of salt; stir, then start afresh by adding the failed aïoli a small dribble at a time, stirring vigorously as before. This should pull everything together again.

The Glories of Garlic

Those who admire garlic and use it generously may be healthier than most of us—the scientific jury is still out on that—but they certainly have great things to eat, such as aïoli, while waiting for the verdict. The time for a feast of aïoli is summer, after the main garlic crop arrives, crisp and bursting with juice, incomparably better than tired-out late-season heads, with acrid sprouting hearts, that have been languishing in a warehouse. Earlier in the year than the main crop, pink heads of garlic grown in warmer regions arrive in the market, and they're good, too. At either season, I like to bake a big batch of the glorious bulbs for Roasted Garlic Paste, (see Index), which keeps excellently.

Aïoli Made with Dried Whole Eggs

For the 4 egg yolks called for in the recipe for Classic Aïoli, substitute 3 tablespoons of dried and powdered whole eggs blended with 4 tablespoons of water. To mix the two, measure the water into a bowl, then stir in the powder until all lumps disappear. Proceed with the recipe as if using fresh egg yolks.

The egg powder is available from dealers in baking supplies and may be used, after being reconstituted, in any recipe calling for whole eggs or, as here, in place of egg yolks in mayonnaise (see Fearless Mayonnaise, page 146).

Eggless Aïoli

This aïoli is made without egg yolks, but the boiled potato is an authentic ingredient, not an upstart notion. If you feel any doubt about consuming uncooked eggs, here is another aïoli answer.

Makes 2 to 2½ cups

To replace the egg yolks in Classic Aïoli, boil a smallish (3 to 4 ounces) waxy potato (not a "baker") in its jacket. Peel and cool until just tepid, then crush until smooth in the mortar containing the garlic and salt. Proceed to add oil and lemon juice as for classic aïoli, incorporating the tepid water if it seems to be needed. Taste and adjust the seasonings to your liking.

Eggless Low-Fat Aïoli

Here we push the aïoli envelope a bit, but this impudent version has a good reason for being: It is for those who love the garlicky sauce but are legitimately concerned about fat intake. In this recipe a good brand of nonfat (or slightly more caloric low-fat) mayonnaise dressing replaces most of the oil and all of the egg yolks . (Do not use a dressing of the Miracle Whip type.)

Makes about 2 cups

Use the garlic, salt, and boiled potato called for in Eggless Aïoli. Crush them together as described in that recipe. When you've made a smooth paste in the mortar, gradually work in 1½ cups of a good brand of nonfat or low-fat mayonnaise dressing in place of most of the olive oil. Then stir in 3 tablespoons of fruity olive oil. Add the tepid water if needed for good consistency. Season the sauce with lemon juice to taste. Optionally, stir in a dab of Dijon-style mustard and a pinch of ground hot red (cayenne) pepper. Taste and adjust the seasonings.

Pesto

Pesto, one of the world's most splendid fresh sauces, can never be better than the basil it's made from, which is why the Genoese, who invented pesto, sniff at all versions that haven't been made with their superb local basil. (But they do unbend enough to use parsley when it isn't basil season.) Never mind, just pick your basil wisely in garden or greengrocery and proceed. Excellent basil is unbruised and unwilted and should be kept no longer than necessary. (Stick the cut ends into a jug of water and cover the top loosely with a plastic bag if the herb must wait for a few hours.)

When you slather this brilliantly green delight over hot, tender-cooked pasta you'll experience one of summer's greatest pleasures. But it's not just for pasta: pesto is a splendid dollop for a bowl of vegetable soup (classically, a minestrone), and I like it as a lively last-minute topping for a zucchini or spinach frittata, or as a filling for a plain rolled omelet. Try it spread on broiled tomato halves or, as peerless essayist and food friend John Thorne suggests, as a sauce for poached fish.

Pine Nuts, Pignoli, Pignolias

These piñon seeds, like the true nuts, should be kept in a jar in the freezer or fridge. Basically soft and sweet, with a faint resinous edge, pine nuts are essential to a genuine pesto and delightful in biscotti and other cookies. Get them as fresh as possible from a specialist supplier. If you like, just before use, toss them very briefly in a skillet over medium heat, just until pale gold, to intensify their flavor.

The formula that follows began a long while back when I tried a recipe by Marcella Hazan, who knows what's what in Italian food; it has evolved as my preferences have been blended in. Experiment to suit yourself, bearing in mind that several other ingredients are authentically added to pesto in Italy—butter, cream, even pancetta (unsmoked, peppered bacon). Just keep basil as the dominant note.

A lower-calorie version for freezing follows the main recipe.

3 to 3½ cups fresh, unblemished basil leaves (no stems), rinsed, patted dry, and packed gently into the measure
1 cup fine-quality olive oil
3 large cloves garlic, peeled and sliced, or more to taste
3 tablespoons pine nuts *(pignoli)* or chopped toasted walnuts (see page 305), or 2 tablespoons pine nuts and 1 tablespoon walnuts
½ cup freshly grated imported Parmesan (preferably Parmigiano-Reggiano), or more to taste, or 6 tablespoons Parmesan plus 2 tablespoons Pecorino Romano or Pecorino Sardo
½ teaspoon salt, or to taste
Few grinds of pepper, black or white, optional
Sweet (unsalted) butter, optional

Makes about 2 cups

1. Combine everything in the workbowl of a food processor (preferred), or divide the ingredients into batches and use a blender. Run the machine, stopping to scrape down the sides of the container occasionally, until the pesto has reached the texture you like, either smooth or more or less finely chopped. If using a blender, mix the batches.

2. Use immediately, or cover and refrigerate for up to a week. (For pesto to be frozen, see below). One cup of pesto will sauce enough pasta for 4 to 6 servings. Toss the sauce with the hot pasta and, if you like, a chunk of sweet butter. Pass additional cheese at the table.

Pesto for the Freezer

Follow the Pesto recipe but omit the cheese. Pack the pesto into half-pint canning jars, or use small freezer containers leaving ½ inch of headspace. Cap the jars and freeze at 0°F or less for two months or so.

To use frozen pesto: Thaw it (in the refrigerator if time permits). Blend 3 to 4 tablespoons of freshly grated cheese into each cup of sauce. If the pesto is too stiff to mix easily with the hot pasta, thin it with a spoonful or two of the pasta cooking water.

Cheatin' with Pesto

If the richness of the sauce is a concern far dietary reasons, I venture to suggest an acceptable cheater's version I've devised.

Adapt the Pesto recipe by reducing the oil according to conscience (I've left out as much as half). Skimp a little on the cheese and nuts, and blend in enough chicken broth, white wine, or water to compensate for the missing oil. Still very good, but don't tell Marcella Hazan.

Tartar Sauce, For Real

Some versions of this famous fish sauce are more estimable than others (see any two cookbooks), because the original formula has suffered deletions and additions over the years. The tartar sauce I like best is close to what a buttoned-up chef might make in a kitchen grounded in the French classics. (Some chefs might add chopped green olives to this recipe, and some might omit the hard-cooked egg yolk.)

This recipe calls for real mayonnaise; but low-calorie (or even fat-free) "mayonnaise dressing" may be substituted when there's good reason to dodge extra fat grams. If such a lesser type of mayo is used, you may need to step up the seasonings to compensate for its blandness.

If you'd like to use homemade mayonnaise but consuming uncooked eggs is questionable in your region, see the Index for Fearless Mayonnaise and use that as a base.

1½ cups mayonnaise
Yolks of 2 hard-cooked large eggs, sieved
1½ to 2 tablespoons finely sliced chives (minced scallions may be substituted)
1 to 1½ tablespoons chopped drained cornichons or other sour cucumber pickles
1 to 1½ tablespoons chopped fresh parsley, leaves only, no stems
1 to 1½ tablespoons drained and coarsely chopped capers
1 teaspoon Dijon-style mustard, optional
Pinch of ground hot red (cayenne) pepper, or a few drops of Tabasco or other hot pepper sauce, optional
Salt and freshly ground black pepper, to taste
Drops of fresh lemon juice, if needed

Makes about 2 cups

The Temper of a Tartar

The name of tartar (or tartare*) sauce seems to have been chosen by the French to indicate a certain ferocity of character. To the palates of the time the mildly piquant sauce must have seemed quite fiery, leading one to wonder what contemporaries of its inventor would have thought of Harissa (see Index), or of a Southwestern salsa crammed with the hottest of chiles.*

1. Fold together all the ingredients except the lemon juice and taste for seasoning. After perfecting the seasonings and adding the lemon juice if you feel it's needed, allow the sauce to mellow for half an hour before serving.

2. Serve with broiled or fried fish or other seafood. The sauce is also good in the dressing for tuna (or other fish) salad, and it can be pressed into service as a robust spread for sandwich bread and canapés. Leftover sauce will keep, refrigerated in a covered jar, for several days.

Seasoned Butters for Swift Saucing

Chefs have traditionally made great use of *beurres composés,* or flavored butters, when making complicated hot sauces that have mostly gone the way of the dodo thanks to today's simpler tastes and the lack of time and kitchen help to devote to their compounding. But good cooks have long used seasoned butters as instant sauces in their own right, and that is a notion worth preserving. The time-pressed cook—meaning any cook, today—can make these delicious butters ahead and refrigerate or freeze them.

The cold seasoned butters that follow do fine things for broiled or baked or plainly sautéed fish, meat, or chicken, as noted with the recipes. Some are great spreads for the bread for canapés or sandwiches—try Anchovy Butter, Mustard Butter, or Curry Butter with savory fillings or toppings, or spread Horseradish Butter on whole-wheat bread for sandwiches of thin-sliced roast beef. A small float of any of the herbal butters can perk up hot soup, and, to kick over the traces even more, garlic, herb, shallot, red pepper, or anchovy butter can be the spur-of-the-moment sauce for a quick dish of piping-hot angel-hair pasta.

Seasoned Butter Basics

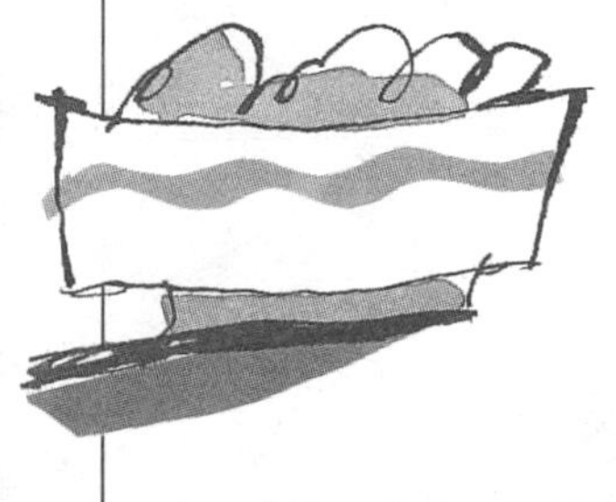

To make about ½ cup of any of the butters suggested on the following pages, let ½ cup (1 stick) of sweet (unsalted) butter soften at room temperature, then beat it until creamy, using an electric mixer.

Work in the ingredients for the specific butter, then decide whether or not to take the additional step of pushing the butter through a fine sieve to perfect its texture and appearance (I don't usually bother). Scrape the butter onto a sheet of plastic, wrap it loosely, and chill it until firm enough to shape into a cylinder (roll the package on a work surface, pressing with your palms). Add another layer of wrapping and refrigerate for use within a day or so, or freeze for up to 2 weeks, enclosed in a freezer bag for additional protection against the off-flavors that can develop in a freezer.

To serve the butter: Let it thaw in the refrigerator if frozen, then slice it into ½-inch pats if it is to be placed on steak, fish, or other hot food. Keep the butter pats firm in a bowl of cold water and ice until serving time, then drain at the last minute.

To use as a spread: Let the butter soften at room temperature, then fluff it with a fork, if you like, to lighten the texture.

Building on Butter

There are times when flavor is more important than calories, and on many such occasions butter is involved. Basic butteriness is delicious, but sweet (unsalted) butter gains new interest when seasonings are added to transform it into a sauce or a special spread.

An Alphabet of Butters

Anchovy: Work in about 1 tablespoon anchovy paste or mashed anchovies packed in oil, plus fresh lemon juice to taste and a pinch of ground hot red (cayenne) pepper. For ham, beef, fish; excellent for canapés and sandwiches.

Caper: Blend in 2 tablespoons minced drained capers, a tiny bit of minced garlic, and fresh lemon juice, salt (if needed), and pepper to taste. For grilled pork and fish, canapés.

Chive, Thyme, & Parsley: 2 tablespoons chopped chives, 1 tablespoon chopped fresh thyme leaves, and 1 tablespoon chopped fresh parsley leaves; a very little finely minced or pressed garlic (optional); a few drops of fresh lemon juice; salt, pepper. For steaks, burgers, fish, chicken, vegetables.

Curry: Stir in your choice of curry powders, mild or hot, to the pungency you like. (See the Index for a custom-made curry seasoning.) Optionally, add drops of fresh lemon juice. For fish, shellfish, chicken.

Garlic: Peel 4 to 6 large cloves of garlic, drop into boiling water and blanch at a simmer for 3 or 4 minutes. Drain, pat dry, pound to a paste in a mortar (or use a mini-food processor), and work into the butter together with salt and pepper and, if you like, a few drops of fresh lemon juice and a few grains of ground hot red (cayenne) pepper to lend point to the proceedings. For steaks, burgers, broiled shrimp; or spread on sliced crusty bread, press the slices back into loaf form, and oven-bake, uncovered, until very hot.

Horseradish: 2 to 3 tablespoons grated fresh horseradish, or the same quantity of drained and pressed bottled horseradish from a fresh batch; pound to a paste in a mortar before blending with the butter. For beef and for canapés and sandwiches.

Lemon: Pare the zest (outer peel only, no white pith) from half a lemon, using a swivel peeler; simmer it in water 3 minutes, drain, and mince fine. Blend it into the butter with the

juice of half a lemon; add a pinch of ground hot red (cayenne) pepper if you like, plus a little salt and freshly ground white pepper. For fish, chicken, hot vegetables, canapés, sandwiches.

Mustard: Choose a fine-quality mustard, flavored with tarragon if you wish, and blend 2 to 3 tablespoons of it into the butter, plus salt and pepper. For broiled meats and fish; for canapés and sandwiches.

Parsley: 1½ tablespoons finely chopped fresh parsley leaves, 1 tablespoon fresh lemon juice, salt, and pepper. For chicken, fish, hot potatoes, other vegetables.

Roasted Tomato: Puree enough Roasted Tomatoes (see the Index) to make ¼ cup; place in a fine sieve and drain off excess liquid. Blend into the butter with salt, pepper, lemon juice, and a little finely crumbled dried basil or chopped fresh basil; optionally, add a tiny bit of garlic minced to a paste. For broiled chicken, fish.

Rosemary: 1½ teaspoons chopped tender fresh rosemary leaves and 2 tablespoons chopped fresh parsley leaves; few drops of fresh lemon juice; salt and pepper to taste. For steaks, chicken, burgers, fish of strong character (bass, bluefish).

Sage: 1½ tablespoons minced fresh parsley leaves, 1 tablespoon minced fresh sage leaves, plus fresh lemon juice, salt, and pepper. For poultry.

Shallot: Peel a good handful of shallots; drop into boiling water and blanch at a simmer for 3 minutes. Drain and pat dry. Pound to a paste in a mortar (or use a small food processor); blend into the butter together with a little salt and pepper; taste and decide whether to add a few drops of fresh lemon juice. Optionally, include a teaspoonful of mild or medium Hungarian paprika. For broiled beef, veal, or fish.

Sweet Red Pepper: Drain ¼ cup of roasted red peppers, from a jar or custom-made (see the Index); pat dry on a paper towel, then pound to a paste in a mortar or puree in a small food processor. Blend into the butter with a tiny bit of minced garlic, ½ teaspoon mild or medium Hungarian paprika, salt to taste, and a few drops of fresh lemon juice. For any broiled meat or fish, or for canapés.

Tarragon: 1½ tablespoons chopped fresh tarragon leaves and 2 tablespoons chopped fresh parsley leaves; few drops of fresh lemon juice; salt and pepper to taste. For chicken, fish, veal.

Alternative Butters

If medical considerations dictate the use of a low-fat or no-fat spread instead of butter, any reasonably firm margarine or "spread" can be seasoned in the same way as the butters above. The gussied-up nonbutter may not be moldable into neat pats (some substitutes are too soft), but it can be a decent substitute if real butter is off the menu.

FEARLESS MAYONNAISE

I've made mayonnaise with fresh eggs all my life and would be happy to continue in that groove, but now come the food-safety experts telling us to stay away from raw eggs. (Why? See the sidebar.)

What to do about this cherished sauce? We can settle for safe store-bought mayo, which is made with pasteurized eggs; or we can adopt recipes for the cooked dressings our foremothers freely called "mayonnaise"—not very satisfactory—or we can use this recipe calling for dried whole eggs (perfectly safe). It is lighter in texture than stiff yolk-only versions but it's also fresher tasting than something from a jar and it's as easy to make as the conventional kind. The only secret is to add the oil very slowly at first, as described.

2 tablespoons cold water
1½ tablespoons powdered whole eggs
1 teaspoon tarragon or plain white-wine or rice vinegar
1½ teaspoons smooth Dijon-style mustard
Salt, to taste (start with ¼ teaspoon)
Freshly ground white pepper, to taste
Pinch of sweet (mild) paprika, optional
1½ cups oil (all olive oil or vegetable oil, or half and half olive oil and corn, peanut, or safflower oil)
2 tablespoons strained fresh lemon juice, or to taste, or 1 to 2 tablespoons additional vinegar, to taste
Pinch of sugar, optional

Makes about 2 cups

1. Measure the cold water into a deep bowl or the container of a blender. Stir in the powdered whole eggs until completely dissolved. Add the teaspoon of tarragon vinegar, the mustard, salt, a little white pepper, and the optional paprika. Beat or blend just to mix.

2. Whisking constantly or running the machine at moderately low speed, add the oil in drops at first, then in a tiny, slow stream. When the sauce has become fairly stiff, which will happen after only part of the oil has been beaten in, beat in the lemon juice. Add the remaining oil in a small steady stream. When all the oil has been added, continue to beat briefly to perfect the texture of the sauce.

3. Taste and adjust the seasonings with more salt, pepper, lemon juice or vinegar, or mustard. For some tastes, a pinch of sugar smooths and pulls together the flavors. This is your sauce, so suit yourself.

BUT NO FEAR OF FRYING

Cooked eggs are perfectly safe, but raw or undercooked eggs have caused serious or even fatal gastroenteritis, in certain regions of the country, according to experts working on the problem of salmonella contamination. (Why does this happen? Ask the poultry people.) That's why I devised the recipe for Fearless Mayonnaise, which is made with dried, powdered whole eggs; and why you'll find a version of Aïoli (on page 139) that's also made with dried eggs. Beyond these two uncooked sauces, such lightly cooked egg-based sauces as hollandaise and béarnaise may pose salmonella risk in some areas, so making them with reconstituted dried eggs is a good idea if you're at all in doubt about the eggs available to you. If you use a hollandaise recipe calling for 3 egg yolks, reconstitute 3 tablespoons of egg powder in ¼ cup of water (1 tablespoon of egg powder equals 1 fresh yolk).

A 19TH-CENTURY "MAYONNAISE"

This recipe for Bottled Salad Dressing from The Buckeye Cookbook *(1883) shows how eggs, cream, and butter once substituted for oil in the dressing many cooks called "mayonnaise" (the* Buckeye *editors were more accurate in their title):*

"Beat yolks of 8 eggs, add 1 cup sugar, 1 tablespoon each of salt, mustard, and black pepper, a little cayenne, and half a cup of cream; mix thoroughly; bring to a boil a pint and a half vinegar, add 1 cup butter, let come to a boil, pour upon the mixture, stir well, and when cold put into bottles, and set in a cool place. It will keep for weeks in the hottest weather, and is excellent for cabbage or lettuce."

VARIATIONS

Mayonnaise is the base for uncounted cold emulsion sauces, as any big fat classic cookbook will tell you. Here are some of the most useful quick changes.

Aïoli: See page 138 for this ultimate garlic mayonnaise.

Anchovy Mayonnaise: Blend in anchovy paste to taste, starting with a teaspoonful to a cup of mayonnaise and ratcheting up the quantity according to the food to be sauced. (Alternatively, mash 3 or 4 drained anchovy fillets packed in oil as replacement for a teaspoonful of anchovy paste.) This is especially good with salads involving meat, fish, or cooked vegetables, or as a spread for the bread used for canapés or sandwiches.

Chili Mayonnaise: Season basic mayonnaise with Custom-Made Chili Seasoning (see the Index), or a spoonful of imported paprika plus drops of hot pepper sauce (store-bought or made from one of the recipes listed in the Index), or Chinese Chili & Garlic Paste (see the Index). Add any of these gradually, tasting as you go. Optional additions: a little ground cumin; lime juice. This can be a dip on its own, or a sauce for broiled or sautéed fish.

Curry Mayonnaise: Stir in your favorite curry powder to taste, starting with a teaspoonful or so. For a custom-made curry seasoning, see the Index. Excellent in salads of cold poultry or fish.

Herbed Mayonnaise: Fold in chopped fresh herbs of your choice, from 1 to 3 tablespoons of herbs per cup of sauce. Try equal parts of minced parsley, chives, and tarragon or chervil. Add a little minced thyme, basil, and/or sweet marjoram, if you like, and optionally blend in a touch of minced or pressed garlic to support the green herbs.

Sweet Red Pepper Mayonnaise: Puree enough drained roasted red peppers to make ½ cup (see the Index for Roasted Red Antipasto Peppers). Fold into 1 cup mayonnaise and season with a squeeze or two of fresh lime or lemon juice, a little minced or pressed garlic, and, if you like, drops of hot pepper sauce, purchased or custom-made (the Index lists possibilities). This rings a real change on a potato or pasta salad and is a great tastemaker when tossed with a collection of cooked, drained, and chilled vegetables, with chopped celery, radishes, or jicama added for crunch.

Tartar Sauce: See the Index for this sauce for fish and other seafood.

Tomato Mayonnaise: Tint and flavor the mayonnaise with tomato paste, starting with 1 tablespoon for a cup of sauce. Optionally, add a little crumbled dried basil or minced fresh basil.

PART 3: Barbecue Fixin's, Hot Sauces, & Other Meat-Mates

As you'll see as you browse along, the barbecue sauces devised for this section reflect my personal choices, meekly made. (Heaven forbid that a Californian now resident on the East Coast should argue with the barbecue-meisters of the South and Midwest—they argue quite enough among themselves. I have refrained from joining any barbecue faction but my own.)

My advice about barbecue saucing (a very loose term indeed), if I were asked, would be: Use these barbecue sauces as a take-off point for your own embellishments, once you've made them more or less as described. After that, a hotter, sweeter, thicker, thinner, or more tangy sauce is all up to you.

With kind intentions, I've also included here a throw-together sauce for rescuing over-bland burgers, and also Country-Style Chili Sauce with Hot Peppers, an old favorite from *Fancy Pantry.* Harissa, Dr. Kitchener's Hot Stuff, Chinese Chili & Garlic Paste, and the other hot sauces are for connoisseurs of real heat.

Barbecue~Three Ways to Sauce It

Of the devising of barbecue sauces (and methods of barbecuing) there is no end (and no end to arguments, either). Tastes run from heavily sweetened sauces for such viands as ribs to thin, very peppery and vinegary Carolina-style slathers for completely cooked and pulled-apart meat, and a lot of terrain is crossed in between. (I've lost count of the wildly various ingredients in the sauces I've met while working out my own ways of preparing home-style "barbecued" foods.) So we're not tackling the full subject of barbecuing here, but choosing three bastes or finishing sauces I happen to like for chicken, pork (especially ribs), or beef cooked on backyard equipment, whether open grill, covered barbecue, or rotisserie—or, for that matter, in the oven (think of slow-baked brisket, or oven-baked ribs, or broiled chicken). These are "mop" sauces, meant to be brushed on food several times during the last half or third of cooking; they aren't meant to be marinades.

A nonregional cookout sauce, savory but neither sticky sweet nor incendiary hot, is produced by the first recipe; it's good on any barbecuable meat or poultry. Smoky Barbecue Sauce is as aromatic as advertised, thanks to judicious use of liquid smoke, but it's tangy as well; it's my choice for beef ribs (sometimes hard to find) or pork ribs, or hamburgers. Citrus Barbecue Sauce works its wiles by means of citrus peel and citrus juices plus hot peppers, honey, onion, and a jolt of wine vinegar; it's especially good on oven-baked or kettle-barbecued baby back or country ribs, pork chops or tenderloin, and chicken.

I don't believe in gussying up a great steak (thick, finely marbled and well trimmed) with anything much beyond a rub of oil plus salt and pepper and perhaps the benison of a seasoned butter (see page 143) added when the meat is ready to carve. That's why you won't notice any steak-barbecuing recommendations in these pages.

Cookout Sauce

3 tablespoons vegetable or olive oil, or more if desired
1½ cups finely chopped onion
2 tablespoons chopped garlic
3 cups pureed and strained canned Italian-style plum tomatoes (a 28-ounce can)
½ cup water
¼ cup tomato paste
¼ cup red wine vinegar or cider vinegar
¼ cup (packed) dark brown sugar or molasses
2 tablespoons Worcestershire sauce
1½ teaspoons steak sauce (A.1. or similar)
2 teaspoons dry mustard powder, preferably imported (such as Colman's)
1½ teaspoons seafood seasoning (Old Bay or similar), or chili powder (see the Index for a home-blended mix), or Cajun-style blackening spice, optional
1 teaspoon salt, or more to taste
1 teaspoon crumbled dried thyme, optional
½ teaspoon Tabasco or other pepper sauce
½ teaspoon Powdered Bay Leaves (page 195), optional
½ teaspoon celery seed, optional
¼ teaspoon freshly ground black pepper, or to taste

Makes about 3 cups

1. Heat the oil in a heavy-bottomed pot and sauté the onion over medium-low heat, stirring almost constantly, until golden, about 10 minutes. Add the garlic and stir-cook for another minute. Add the remaining ingredients. Bring to a boil, lower the heat, and cook at a simmer, stirring often, for about 40 minutes, or until about the consistency of light spaghetti sauce.

2. Puree the sauce in a blender for a few seconds only—it should not be completely smooth—or press it through a food mill fitted with a medium disk. Taste and adjust the seasonings toward more hotness, tartness, or sweetness, according to what you like.

3. Brush the sauce at intervals over meat or poultry during the last half or third of its cooking time, watching the heat and turning the viands often to prevent the coating from scorching. Leftover sauce may be kept for a week or two, refrigerated, or for 2 months in the freezer. After thawing, adjust the seasonings, which can become unbalanced after time spent at 0°F.

Smoky Barbecue Sauce

Liquid smoke lends a smokehouse edge to this quick "mop" sauce based on handy bottles of *good* ketchup and chili sauce. Like Cookout Sauce, it's used as a baste during the second half or last third of outdoor cooking. Slosh it onto partially cooked beef ribs (if you can find them) or pork ribs, or chicken, or, especially, hamburgers. Also dandy for oven-baked brisket or ribs.

1 tablespoon vegetable oil, or more if you wish
¼ cup minced onion
1 tablespoon minced garlic
1½ cups excellent store-bought ketchup (or use the contents of a 14-ounce bottle without further measuring)
1½ cups excellent chili sauce, homemade (page 153) or store-bought (a 12-ounce bottle will be close enough)
½ cup water
¼ cup cider vinegar or red wine vinegar
2 tablespoons honey
1 tablespoon Worcestershire sauce
1 tablespoon steak sauce (A.1. or similar)
½ teaspoon liquid smoke (sometimes called "smoke sauce")
½ teaspoon Tabasco or other hot pepper sauce, or to taste, optional (see the Index if you'd like to make your own)
Salt, if needed
Freshly ground black pepper, to taste

Makes about 3 cups

1. Heat the oil briefly in a heavy saucepan; add the onion and stir over medium-low heat until golden and soft, about 10 minutes; add the garlic and cook 1 minute longer, stirring.

2. Add the ketchup, chili sauce, water, vinegar, honey, Worcestershire sauce, and steak sauce. Bring to a boil, lower the heat, and cook over low heat, stirring frequently, until thickened to the consistency of

Smoke Comes into It, Mildly

Liquid smoke, used with discretion, can be a useful seasoning, but be aware that this preparation, which captures the flavor of condensed hickory smoke, is strong. *Start with the amount listed in the recipe when making Smoky Barbecue Sauce, and don't add more until the sauce is complete enough to be tasted. (Read skeptically any label instructions that recommend slathering liquid smoke liberally on meats before grilling them.)*

ketchup, about 20 minutes. Add the liquid smoke, hot pepper sauce (if using), salt if needed, and pepper to taste. Puree the sauce briefly in a blender, or press it through a sieve or food mill.

3. Cool the sauce and check the seasonings before using or storing it. If a *little* more smokiness is desirable, add a drop or two of liquid smoke and taste again; it's easy to overuse this extract, so caution is in order.

4. Brush on the sauce as a baste during the latter part of cooking your meat or fowl. Extra sauce keeps for weeks if refrigerated in a covered jar. It may also be frozen if you don't expect to need it for the next month or so. After thawing, taste it and adjust the seasonings.

Zesty Oil

Citrus oils, extracted from the peel of fresh fruit, are among the commendable items recently made available to home cooks, and all three kinds—orange, lemon, and lime—are dandy, true in flavor and very potent. In this barbecue sauce, orange oil can substitute for the dried or fresh citrus zest. Start with ¼ teaspoon of the oil and add more drops, if needed, only after the sauce has been tasted—this stuff is potent. Available from specialist suppliers (The Baker's Catalogue, Williams-Sonoma, etc.).

Citrus Barbecue Sauce

Great for oven-baked or kettle-barbecued baby back ribs, pork chops or tenderloin, or chicken halves. Mop it onto the meat during the last half of cooking, turning often to prevent scorching. In nonbarbecue weather, I use this on oven-baked or broiled meat and fowl, too, especially meaty country-style pork ribs.

Defatted drippings from roasted poultry or meat blended with chicken or beef broth to make 2 cups, or 2 cups fine-quality chicken or beef broth (not bouillon) or stock
⅓ cup sweetened lime juice (bottled sweetened juice such as Rose's, or unsweetened bottled or freshly squeezed lime juice plus a big pinch of sugar)
¼ cup olive oil
¼ cup tomato paste
¼ cup honey
¼ cup vegetable oil
3 tablespoons dried onion bits, soaked until soft, or ⅓ cup minced fresh onion, sautéed until soft in a little oil
2 tablespoons red or white wine vinegar, or more to taste
1 tablespoon ground dried orange peel (see sidebar next page), or 6 chunks (1½ x ½ inch) of home-dried orange or tangerine peel, soaked in water to cover until soft and drained; or 2 tablespoons grated fresh orange zest (no white pith)
4 teaspoons ground coriander seed, preferably freshly ground
¾ teaspoon Tabasco or other hot pepper sauce, or to taste
2 tablespoons strained fresh lemon juice, or more to taste
Salt, if needed (this depends on the saltiness of the drippings and/or broth)
Freshly ground pepper, black or white, to taste

Makes about 2½ cups

1. Simmer the combined drippings and broth, or the broth or stock, in a wide saucepan until reduced to about ¾ cup.

2. Combine the liquid in a blender or food processor with all the remaining ingredients except the lemon juice, salt, and pepper and process until smooth.

3. Empty the sauce into a skillet and bring it to a boil; lower the heat and simmer, stirring, for about 4 minutes. Remove from the heat and add the lemon juice, salt, and pepper. Taste carefully and add more of any ingredient needed for the balance you like. (Some like a hotter or sweeter or more acidic sauce.)

4. Brush the sauce liberally on meat or poultry during the second half of cooking, repeating several times. Be sure to keep the heat moderate; too much heat will scorch the surface while it toughens the flesh beneath.

5. Surplus sauce keeps for 2 or 3 days, refrigerated. For longer keeping (up to a month or two) it should be frozen. After thawing, check and adjust the seasonings.

A Dense & Winy Burger Sauce

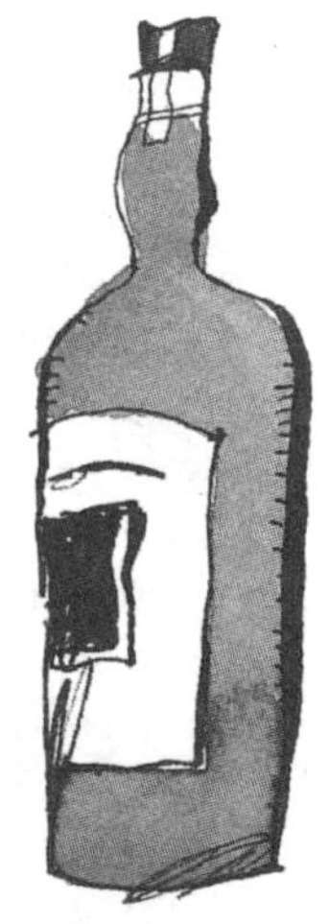

A great steak or standing rib roast doesn't need a sauce like this one, but burgers are another story. Sadly enough, they need all the help they can get, unless you've been able to find a source of chopped beef with actual beefy flavor, a great rarity. So this tasty toss-together is offered without apology—what it does is blend into a velvety puree some of this and that from various jars and bottles to make a condiment that works very well as a rescuer of anemic beef patties. (It's also good with hot dogs.)

As lagniappe, the sauce is fine with crumb-coated and fried fish and shellfish, too, if such dishes are your pleasure.

An excellent variant of this sauce born in the cupboard is made with chili sauce in place of ketchup. I use either a good store-bought kind (the brand name Heinz inevitably comes to mind), or the Country-Style Chili Sauce with Hot Peppers that follows this recipe. Half chili sauce and half ketchup works well, too.

Immortal Flavor

For a supply of citrus flavoring that keeps on the shelf almost forever, scrub an orange or two (or tangerines, or both), strip off the peel, and use the edge of a teaspoon to scrape the white pith from the inside. Dry the peel in an oven warmed only by its light, or let the peel dry at room temperature. When it's hard, no longer leathery, store it at room temperature in a jar with a tight cap.

Chili-Sauce Sermon

Home-made chili sauce is a glory of traditional American preserving, and it's a cause I'm willing to preach for. Your own chili sauce won't be a carbon copy of sauce in a bottle—it will be excellent in a different way. I like to make a lot of it when tomatoes of the Italian type are in season; and as we prefer a chunky texture, I cut the tomatoes up roughly instead of chopping them.

1 bottle (28 ounces) best-quality tomato ketchup (about 2⅔ cups)
½ cup full-bodied red wine
¼ cup well-drained prepared horseradish, homemade (page 157) or freshly purchased
2 tablespoons bottled steak sauce (preferably A.1. brand)
2 tablespoons Worcestershire sauce
1 teaspoon Tabasco or other hot pepper sauce
½ teaspoon ground pure mild chile, optional
½ teaspoon granulated dried garlic or 1 teaspoon minced or pressed fresh garlic
Several grinds of fresh pepper, black or white
½ cup water or vegetable or fat-free beef broth (not bouillon) or use additional red wine
Pinch or two of sugar, optional
Drops of fresh lemon juice, if needed

Makes about 4 cups

1. Combine all the ingredients except the water, sugar, and lemon juice in a blender or food processor and whiz together until velvety. Add as much of the water, broth, or additional wine as you need to make a substantial but not stiff mixture.

2. Taste carefully and blend in, if needed, more horseradish or any other seasoning, plus, if needed, the sugar as a flavor-smoother and the lemon juice to add tartness.

3. Store leftover sauce in a covered jar in the refrigerator, where it will keep for weeks. It may be almost solid after refrigeration. Use it in that state, or beat in a little additional wine and/or water or broth if you prefer it spoonable.

Country-Style Chili Sauce with Hot Peppers

The seasonings of this hotted-up version of classic chili sauce can be ratcheted up with more hot peppers for a condiment of real authority; or you can make a mild sauce by omitting the hot peppers or substituting for them just a dash of ground hot red (cayenne) pepper, added at the end of cooking.

Substitutions: If you have to use tomatoes of the slicing type, which have more seeds and juice than Italian-type tomatoes, cut them crosswise after skinning and squeeze out most of the seeds and their surrounding watery pulp, then chop them. If sweet green (bell) peppers are what you have, they can replace the red ones; the sauce will not be the same vivid red, however, nor will the flavor be quite the same.

This recipe can be doubled, if you have a really large pot.

2 quarts skinned, cored, and coarsely diced ripe Italian-type (plum) tomatoes (about 4 pounds)
2 cups finely chopped stemmed, seeded, and deribbed sweet red (bell) peppers
1½ cups finely chopped onion
½ cup finely chopped celery
1 fresh long hot red pepper, stemmed, seeded, deribbed, and minced, optional
1 large clove garlic, peeled and minced, or more to taste
1½ cups cider vinegar
2 tablespoons pickling salt or other fine noniodized salt, or 2½ tablespoons coarse (kosher or sea) salt
½ cup (packed) light brown sugar or granulated sugar
¼ cup light corn syrup
1½ teaspoons mustard seed
¾ teaspoon ground cloves
¾ to 1 teaspoon ground cinnamon, to taste
Ground hot red (cayenne) pepper or Tabasco or other hot pepper sauce, optional

Makes 6 to 7 cups

1. Combine the tomatoes, sweet peppers, onions, celery, hot pepper, garlic, vinegar, salt, sugar, and corn syrup in a preserving pan. Bring the mixture to a boil, stirring occasionally; then lower the heat and simmer it briskly, uncovered, for 1 hour. Stir it occasionally.

2. Stir in the mustard seed, cloves, and cinnamon. Continue to cook the sauce, stirring occasionally, until it releases scarcely any liquid when a spoonful is tilted on a plate. Final cooking should take from 1 to 1½ hours. Taste the sauce and add, if desired, a little more vinegar or sweetening or salt; for a hotter sauce, add ground hot red pepper or hot pepper sauce.

3. Ladle the boiling-hot sauce into hot, clean pint or half-pint canning jars, leaving ¼ inch of headspace. Seal the jars with new two-piece canning lids according to manufacturer's directions and process for 15 minutes (for either size jar) in a boiling water bath (page 283). Cool, label, and store the jars. The sauce will keep for at least a year in a cool cupboard and is best if allowed to mellow for a few weeks before being served.

To Skin Tomatoes

Drop ripe tomatoes a few at a time into a pot of boiling water and let them heat for about half a minute. Scoop them out, drain, and slip off their skins with the help of a small sharp knife for cutting out the core. If any skins won't yield after the first scalding, drop them in again for a second try, but don't let them begin to cook and turn mushy.

Toasted Caraway or Coriander Seed

Toasting these seeds (and cumin, too) is a traditional step in harissa country, as it intensifies their flavor and adds an indefinable nuttiness.

Simply heat a cast-iron or thick aluminum skillet until a drop of water dances slowly when flicked onto its bottom. Add enough caraway or coriander seed to cover the bottom of the pan and shake and stir over medium heat for a few minutes, until the seeds deepen in color slightly and release their fragrance. Pour them from the pan into a dish at once and let them cool. Store in a covered jar out of light and heat, or grind immediately for use.

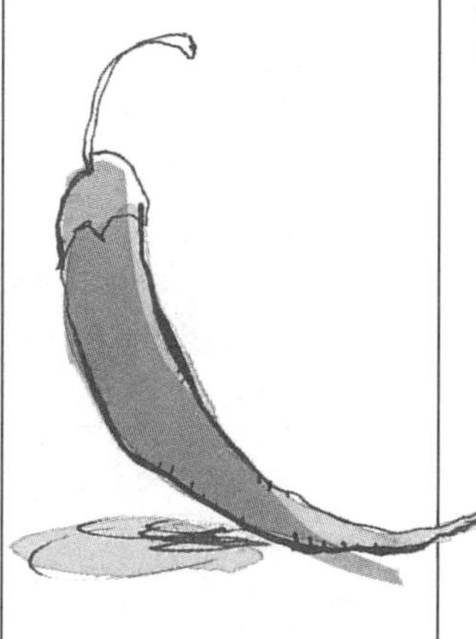

Harissa–Powerful Piquancy Out of North Africa

The ubiquitous chili pepper (or chile) enlivens cuisines in both hemispheres and on both sides of the Equator, and here's the way the enlivening is done in the countries of North Africa, most especially in Morocco. The rust-red seasoning paste called harissa or hrisa contains chiles or cayenne pepper, olive oil, and a little salt as constants, but it's often more intricately compounded to include garlic and such spices as cumin and/or toasted coriander and caraway seed (as here). You may encounter harissa spiked with a touch of mint or lemon juice, too, and some commercial versions contain many more spices. In other words, the formula for harissa is nowhere engraved in stone.

A jar of harissa will keep for 2 or 3 months, refrigerated, which will give you plenty of time to try it. For openers, see how you like it as a marinade for lamb, poultry, or fish to be broiled, or as a table sauce with real authority, or as a seasoning used exactly like any other powerful pepper-based condiment found in a well-furnished pantry. Harissa is traditionally added to the pot liquor of the many-splendored North African stew called couscous—an indication of its talent for peppering up any stew or soup, not only pottages from the southern shore of the Mediterranean.

A relatively mild variety of dried chile, such as Anaheim or New Mexico, is my own choice when making this sauce. (Nature hasn't blessed me with much tolerance for piquancy). Those who want more heat will use hotter peppers (such as guajillo), or add the optional cayenne pepper after the chiles have been pureed as directed.

4 ounces dried chiles (about 12 dried New Mexico chiles, for example) of a mild or hot variety, according to taste
2 cloves garlic, peeled
½ teaspoon salt, or more to taste
1 tablespoon coriander seed, toasted (see sidebar)
1½ teaspoons caraway seed, toasted (see sidebar)
3 to 4 tablespoons olive oil, as needed, plus more to cover the finished paste
Ground hot red pepper (cayenne), optional

Makes about 1 cup

1. Stem and seed the chiles, rinse them briefly, drain them, and tear them up. (It's a very good idea to wear rubber gloves for this job, being sure to wash the gloves with soap before taking them off). Cover the chiles with boiling water and let them soak for 1 hour. Drain the chiles in a colander, then scrape them into the container of a blender (or into a big mortar, if you're going to pound the paste with a pestle the old-fashioned way).

2. Chop the garlic on a board with the salt until fine. Add to the chiles.

3. Grind the toasted coriander and caraway seed together in a spice mill (or a well-cleaned coffee mill) and add the powder to the chiles. Add 3 tablespoons of the olive oil and run the blender until you have a puree, scraping down the sides of the container often and adding more oil if it is needed to make a paste. Tough bits of skin may remain in the puree; if so, sieve it.

4. Check the balance of flavors and add the cayenne, if you wish, and/or more salt or ground caraway and coriander. Scrape the harissa into a clean jar, cover the surface with additional olive oil, cap it snugly, and refrigerate it for storage. The harissa will keep for 2 months at least. After spooning harissa from the jar, be sure the remaining condiment is completely covered with a layer of oil to seal out air, which would shorten its shelf life.

Harissa as a Table Sauce

Prepare this just before it's wanted. Either mix Harissa, above, with olive oil and a few drops of fresh lemon juice to make a sauce of a consistency you like, or stir the paste with an approximately equal quantity of water, then a smaller quantity of olive oil, and point up the flavors with drops of lemon juice.

Horseradish of Two Colors

Horseradish, ubiquitous in angular little jars in the grocer's cold case, is supposed to be good for you (it's believed to cure ailments ranging from the common cold to hangovers, perhaps because it's rich in vitamin C), but never mind, what's *really* good about it is its whopping flavor when prepared fresh. Serve it on its own, or blend it into sour cream for saucing fish (especially smoked fish) or

Frightful Horseradish

This was Bertie Wooster's term for an outrageous notion or utterance, as recorded in the immortal Jeeves stories by P. G. Wodehouse. A jar of horseradish that has languished too long on the shelf can indeed be frightful, but quite another story is a batch of the condiment made from a fresh root and kept properly cold.

boiled beef, or blend it into horseradish butter (see the Index for seasoned butters) or use it to pick up other savory cold sauces, especially those for shellfish.

Here's how to prepare this ancient root, sinfully ugly but full of distinctive flavor.

Prepared Horseradish

Look for a fresh horseradish root that is relatively smooth and grayish-brown in color, preferably not green-tinged. Spring is the best supermarket season for horseradish, because it is in demand at the time of Easter and Passover. It's feasible to prepare part of a root and keep the rest in the vegetable drawer of the refrigerator for several weeks. (This herb is also easy to grow, persisting year after year once established; most nursery catalogs offer the roots.)

1 fresh horseradish root
White wine vinegar or distilled white vinegar as needed
Sugar, to taste
Salt, to taste

1. If the horseradish root is tinged with green, the outer flesh may be bitter. To deal with such a root, pare it very deeply, removing the thick outer layer of tissue just under the skin (you can see it as a distinctive ring in cross-section).

2. Cube the horseradish and chop it in a food processor or blender with enough vinegar to moisten the mass. Stir in additional vinegar for the consistency you like and season the condiment with a little sugar and salt. (Alternatively, grate the horseradish, most easily done with the fine-toothed grating disk of a food processor. Fair warning: Grating horseradish by hand is a chore that provokes copious tears.)

3. Store prepared horseradish in a tightly closed jar in the refrigerator, where it will keep for many weeks, gradually losing some of its pizzazz. Real fans like to make it fresh as needed.

Red Beet Horseradish

Combine Prepared Horseradish, above, with an approximately equal quantity of finely grated cooked beets (canned beets are fine). Taste carefully and add more vinegar (red wine vinegar is good with this version), sugar, and salt as needed.

Red Beet Horseradish will keep for several weeks, refrigerated in a tightly closed jar.

Pepper Sauces–Green Fire & The Bottomless Bottle

For an exquisitely hot condiment to sprinkle on cooked greens in time-honored Southern American style, or for seasoning any dish of any kind that needs a touch of tart torchiness, these two simply made vinegar-based sauces are hard to beat.

As written, the Green Fire recipe produces a moderately hot vinegar; add more peppers if you're sure that your palate would be grateful.

What can be said about The Bottomless Bottle? It can be a real firecracker, depending on the kind of peppers you use. And as long as you replenish the vinegar in which the peppers repose, you have a sauce you can bequeath to your descendants—good little peppers don't quit.

Green Fire Pepper Sauce

9 to 12 small fresh hot green peppers, any shape
3 cups distilled white vinegar
Small dried hot red peppers (optional)

Makes about 3 cups

1. Rinse and dry the fresh peppers. Protecting your hands with rubber gloves, stem the peppers and chop them, veins, seeds and all, into medium-coarse pieces. Place the peppers in a clean, dry heatproof quart-size jar with a snug lid.

2. Heat the vinegar to simmering in a nonreactive saucepan and pour it over the peppers. Cool the peppers and vinegar, uncovered, then cap the jar with an enamel-lined canning lid, or use a recycled lid (from mayonnaise, etc.) screwed over two layers of plastic wrap. Let the mixture stand for at least 2 weeks or for as long as 3 months, shaking the jar occasionally.

3. When you think it might be sufficiently flavored, taste the liquid cautiously—it's wise to sample it on a bit of bland food rather than directly. If it is fiery enough to suit, strain it through a very fine-meshed sieve, pressing lightly on the debris of the peppers to extract all possible flavor.

4. Funnel the sauce into clean, dry bottles and cap it airtight. Optionally, place a single whole dried hot red pepper in each bottle, or tie one or two hot peppers to the neck to indicate the heat quotient of the contents. Alternatively, label the bottles explicitly, especially if the sauce is to be a gift.

Two-Minute Wonders

These two sauces are utterly simple to make, and The Bottomless Bottle is remarkable for its longevity. As long as the peppers are kept covered with vinegar they continue to yield up their fiery flavor; our household bottle, of an old vintage, is still going strong.

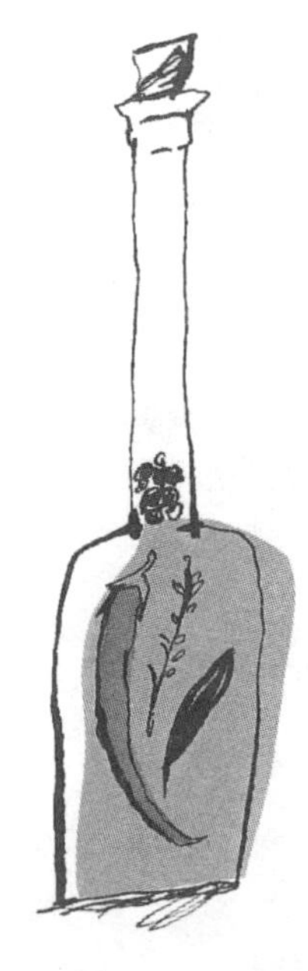

The Bottomless Bottle of Classic Pepper Sauce

This isn't really a recipe, just a suggestion to acquire your choice of tiny fresh red peppers—I lean to the kind called "Thai," which are among the hottest. Trim the stems short, rinse the peppers, blot them dry, and drop a good handful into an impeccably clean and good-looking bottle that can go to the table. Fill 'er up with your choice of vinegars: Some choose cider, some like malt, and distilled white vinegar will be fine, too. Leave this to gather strength for a few weeks, then put it into service. As the liquid level drops, add vinegar, and there you are. Immortality for saucing the greens.

Chinese Chili & Garlic Paste

In one mutation or another, zesty condiments based on hot peppers with lashings of garlic are enjoyed all over Asia but especially in China. Here's my take on the valuable sauce called chili garlic paste, great for cooking (put dabs in stir-fries, soups, sauces, whatever) and widely used, too, as a table sauce to be spooned sparingly onto the side of the plate. It's fiery, so don't make the mistake of ladling it over *anything.*

¼ pound long, thin fresh hot red peppers, cayenne or other
1 medium head (about 2 ounces) garlic
2 large ripe plums or medium nectarines (in winter, use well-drained canned purple plums, skins and all)
¼ cup vinegar, preferably half balsamic, half red wine (or use red Chinese vinegar)
2 teaspoons sugar
1 teaspoon ground roasted Sichuan peppercorns (see sidebar)
1 teaspoon salt
1 teaspoon cornstarch blended with 1 tablespoon water
½ teaspoon dark (roasted) sesame oil

Makes about 1 cup

Toasting Sichuan Peppercorns

To prepare them for use, Sichuan peppercorns, also called fagara and flower pepper, should be shaken over medium heat in a dry heavy skillet until the grains become very fragrant and just begin to darken a little—don't let them scorch. Cool and grind in a spice mill or with a mortar and pestle.

1. Rinse the peppers and remove the stems and caps, leaving the cores and seeds intact. Place in a small saucepan, add 1 cup water (or enough to cover the peppers), and bring to a boil. Lower the heat, cover, and simmer for about 30 minutes, until the peppers are almost tender.

2. Meanwhile, separate the garlic cloves. Flatten each by smashing lightly with the flat of a big knife blade, then remove the papery peel and chop the garlic. Reserve. Skin the plums and cut the flesh from the stones. Reserve.

3. When the peppers are tender, add the garlic, plums, and vinegar. Stir, cover partially, and simmer 10 minutes more.

4. Scrape the mixture into a blender or food processor and puree until fairly smooth (some pepper seeds will remain). At this point, decide whether to keep the seeds (as is done with some imported brands) or sieve the paste to remove them (my choice). Return the puree to the saucepan and stir in the sugar, Sichuan pepper, and salt. Reheat to simmering and stir in the cornstarch and water. Stir over the heat until slightly thickened, about 2 minutes. Remove from the heat, cool for a few minutes, then stir in the sesame oil.

5. At this point, a cautious tasting (this is *hot!*) may suggest the need for a little more vinegar, sugar, Sichuan pepper, salt, or sesame oil. Make additions accordingly, bearing in mind that the sauce will pull itself together further as it rests in the jar.

6. Funnel the chili paste into a clean, dry jar and cover it airtight. This will keep in a cool cupboard for a while, but if it is refrigerated it keeps next to forever.

CHINESE CHILES

Spice specialists offer a dizzying selection of hot peppers for various styles of cooking. My favorite purveyor sells thin, medium-size hot red peppers he calls "Tientsin peppers," the kind often used in Sichuan-style cooking and, perhaps, in China's commercial versions of Chili & Garlic Paste. However that may be, they're what I use for the paste, but any equally hot peppers should be fine too.

DR. KITCHENER'S HOT STUFF

Requiring only the work of moments (and a blender or food processor) to prepare, this quite piquant (well, *very hot*) pepper sauce provides a reason for buying Scotch bonnet chiles (small, round, and crumpled looking, said to be the hottest of all), or beautiful little bird peppers (round), small pointed cayenne, Tabasco, or Thai (*very* hot) peppers, or the somewhat less fiery long, thin red peppers of various kinds that appear, usually anonymously, in markets.

Let this seasoning ripen in peace for a few weeks before it is served. To discover how hot it is, sample a drop or two on a bland food—it's impossible to know in advance the exact firepower of any batch of peppers, though some kinds are never less than torrid.

As for Dr. Kitchener (a.k.a. Kitchiner), he was the author of *The Cook's Oracle,* one of the most delightful of nineteenth-century cookbooks. He is believed to have been the first to publish, at least in Britain, a formula for this Caribbean condiment, known in many versions in its home territory. Made as described here, Kitchener's mixture is a relish of real authority.

4 to 5 ounces small fresh hot red peppers
½ cup dry sherry
½ cup fine-quality brandy
½ cup strained fresh lime juice
½ teaspoon salt
¼ teaspoon ground hot red (cayenne) pepper, optional

Makes about 1 cup

1. Taking due precautions (see the sidebar), rinse and drain the peppers. Cut out and discard the stems, being careful to retain the cores and seeds. Slice the peppers roughly into a blender or food processor.

2. Cover the container and chop the peppers. With the machine running, gradually add the sherry and brandy and continue to operate the blades until a rough puree has been achieved, then add the lime juice, salt, and optional ground hot red pepper.

3. Scrape the puree into a clean, dry pint-size canning jar. Cover the top with a square of fine nylon net or two layers of cheesecloth, held in place with the band portion of a canning lid or a rubber band. Set the jar in a warm spot in the kitchen and allow the sauce to ripen and swap around its flavors for at least 2 weeks, better 3, giving it a gentle shake or swirl now and then.

4. Taste the sauce (carefully, preferably on a bite of something bland) and judge its hotness. Add more ground hot red pepper if you think it's needed. Puree the sauce again in a blender or food processor, this time making it as smooth as possible; some skin and seed fragments will remain. Press the sauce through a fine-meshed sieve, then funnel it into a clean, dry bottle suitable for table use. Cap and store in the refrigerator (to preserve its hotness more effectively) or in a cool cupboard. Either way it keeps indefinitely.

Hot Pepper Warning

When preparing any kind of fresh hot peppers, work at arms' length, or at least not close to your face, to avoid fiery fumes. Wear rubber gloves if possible. Never, never touch your face (most especially the eye area) after handling peppers until your hands have been most thoroughly washed and dried. Soap and rinse rubber gloves and any utensils and cutting surfaces that have come in contact with the peppers.

PART 4: UNCOMMON RELISHES, KETCHUPS, & CHUTNEYS

Revisited with good appetite, polished here and there, and retested with pleasure, most of these recipes come from *Fancy Pantry*. That's both because I'm greatly attached to them and because I'd be in trouble with persons who shall be nameless if I were to leave certain things out of this book.

Highly recommendable, if you're looking for unusual condiments, are the banana and cranberry ketchups, Glorious Garlic & Hot Pepper Jelly, Red Rosemary Jelly, and the chutneys, especially Piquant Golden Raisin Chutney, which is quickly made with pantry staples. Mango & Tamarind Chutney follows classic lines for this useful and delectable condiment adopted from India.

BLUEBERRY RELISH

Lightly spiced and gently tart, this whole-berry relish points up the charms of chicken, duck, turkey, ham, tongue, or roast pork as well as such snacks as fresh soft cheese on a crisp cracker.

Because the berries are cooked only briefly, the relish has the consistency of a preserve, not a jam. I make this with cultivated berries, not wild ones, whose elusive flavor would be submerged in the spicing (though it's delicate) of this condiment.

3 cups sugar
1½ cups water
3 pint baskets (about 9 cups) firm-ripe cultivated blueberries, picked over, rinsed, and drained
1½ cups cider vinegar
Zest (outer peel only, no white pith) of 2 oranges, cut into ¾-inch-wide strips
3 sticks (about 2 inches each) cinnamon, coarsely broken
1½ teaspoons whole allspice
1 teaspoon whole coriander seed
½ teaspoon whole cloves

Makes about 6 cups

1. Combine the sugar and 1½ cups water in a preserving pan. Bring to a boil over medium heat; boil 1 minute. Add the blueberries and return the mixture to a boil. Reduce the heat to medium-low and cook the berries, uncovered, at a hard simmer just until they break open, about 5 minutes. Remove from the heat.

Raiding the Freezer

Blueberries freeze perfectly if their baskets are overwrapped in freezer plastic and sealed; they keep for up to a year with little loss of character. A frozen supply makes it possible to toss together this spicy relish at any season, a point to keep in mind if you like to offer little gifts of edibles during the winter holidays.

2. Pour the berries into a sieve set over a bowl and drain off the syrup. Set the berries aside and return the syrup to the preserving pan.

3. Add the vinegar, orange zest, cinnamon, allspice, coriander, and cloves to the syrup and bring it to a boil over medium-high heat. Boil the syrup, uncovered, stirring occasionally, until it registers 220°F on a candy/jelly thermometer or passes the jelly test (page 282); this will take about 50 minutes, after which the syrup will be reduced by about half. Remove from the heat.

4. Strain the spices from the syrup and discard them. Return the syrup to the pan. Add the berries and any juices that have accumulated in their bowl and bring the relish to a boil over medium-high heat. Reduce the heat to medium and boil the relish gently until the syrup again registers 220°F or passes the jelly test, 3 to 5 minutes.

5. Ladle the boiling-hot relish into hot, clean pint or half-pint canning jars, leaving ¼ inch of headspace. Seal with new two-piece canning lids according to manufacturer's directions and process for 15 minutes (for either size jar) in a boiling-water bath (page 283). Cool, label, and store the jars. Sealed, the relish will keep for at least a year in a cool cupboard.

Alternative strategy: Instead of sealing and processing the relish, store it in clean and tightly capped jars in the refrigerator, where it will keep for at least 3 months.

Cranberry & Currant Relish

Cranberries have been around North America—and not just in New England—even longer than the Native Americans, who acquainted the Pilgrims with this scarlet autumn fruit. Since then, on the whole, North Americans have been content with the standard cranberry sauce or jelly with their Thanksgiving turkey, and that has been the cranberry story, except for an occasional glass of cranberry juice or a pie.

To ring a change on the old standard, here is a very red relish that's crunchy with both cranberries and mild onion, a bit sweet (currant jelly and raisins), and a bit tart. It keeps well without any special fuss, emerging better than ever after weeks in the refrigerator or months in the freezer. Try having it instead of chutney with a curry, and think of it when you are serving hot or cold ham, roast pork, or any poultry.

3 cups (a 12-ounce bag) cranberries, fresh (picked over and rinsed) or frozen (thawed)
2 tablespoons chopped red onion or other mild onion, or substitute shallots
¾ cup golden raisins, soaked briefly in warm water if not quite soft, then drained
¾ cup red currant jelly
⅓ cup sugar
1½ teaspoons salt
Generous pinch of ground hot red (cayenne) pepper
⅛ teaspoon ground ginger
3 tablespoons strained fresh lemon juice

Makes about 3 cups

1. Chop the cranberries fairly coarsely (this can be done in the food processor), then scrape into a mixing bowl and add the onion.

2. Chop the raisins fairly coarsely, by hand or in the processor; add to the cranberry-onion mixture.

3. Combine the currant jelly, sugar, salt, ground red pepper, and ginger in a small saucepan. Heat the mixture, stirring, over medium heat until the sugar and salt have dissolved and it is smooth and is quite hot; it need not boil. Pour the hot jelly mixture over the cranberries, onion, and raisins. Add the lemon juice and stir the relish to mix it well.

4. Scrape the relish into a clean, dry jar, cover, and refrigerate at least overnight before serving it. It will keep for many weeks refrigerated, or for 6 months or more in the freezer.

Cranberry, Currant, & Horseradish Relish

To vary Cranberry & Currant Relish, add from 1 to 3 teaspoons of well-drained plain bottled horseradish to a cupful. Especially good with cold meat—beef, pork, veal, or ham.

And Now for Something Somewhat Different . . .

A relish of raw cranberries and oranges has been percolating through American home cooking for a long time and very good it is, but this one is a bit more intriguing to the tongue. Try, you'll like.

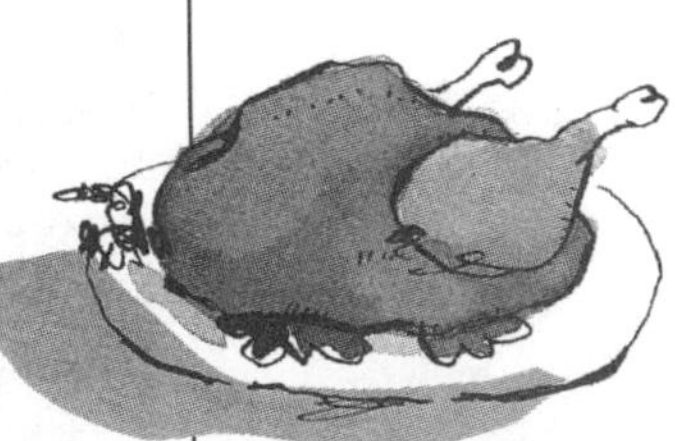

Escoffier's Condiment of Sweet Red Peppers

Adapted from various formulas for a condiment he called a "pickle" (now we'd say relish) written down generations ago by the King of Chefs, this compound contains sweet peppers, onions, raisins, aromatics, a touch of oil for suavity, and a dousing of wine vinegar for zest. It's absolutely scrumptious with cold meat or poultry.

Small liberties have been taken with the recipe—I've reduced Escoffier's measures of oil, sweetening, and spices, and I've found that the condiment is better if made ahead of time instead of being served at once. It keeps admirably under refrigeration and in fact improves for several months.

½ cup fine-quality olive oil
1⅔ cups chopped onion
1½ to 1¾ pounds sweet red (bell) peppers
1½ cups red wine vinegar
1½ pounds ripe Italian-type (plum) tomatoes
1 to 1½ cups sugar, to taste
1 cup golden raisins
2 medium to large cloves garlic, minced
1 teaspoon finely minced fresh ginger or ¼ teaspoon ground ginger
½ teaspoon salt
⅛ teaspoon freshly ground black pepper
¼ teaspoon ground allspice
2 small dried hot red peppers, optional

Makes 3 to 4 cups

1. Measure the olive oil into a large heavy saucepan; add the onions and cook them over medium-low heat, stirring often, until the pieces are golden, about 10 minutes.

2. Meanwhile, blanch the sweet red peppers in boiling water for 3 minutes, then plunge them into cold water to cool. (Reserve the blanching water for reuse in step 4.) Strip the skins from the peppers, quarter, core, and seed them, then slice the quarters crosswise into ¼-inch strips. You should have about 2 cups, packed.

3. Add the peppers to the onions. Stir, cover, and cook the mixture over low heat for 10 minutes. Add the vinegar and boil the mixture, uncovered, until it has reduced by half.

4. While the pepper mixture cooks, scald the tomatoes in boiling water for about 30 seconds, then plunge them into cold water. Strip off the skins, cut up the tomatoes, puree them in a food processor or blender, then force the puree through a sieve or food mill to remove the seeds. (The tomatoes may be chopped roughly and pressed through the food mill, but the job will take longer.) Measure 2 cups of the puree and reserve any surplus for another use.

5. Add the tomatoes to the pepper mixture in the saucepan. Add 1 cup of the sugar and the raisins, garlic, ginger, salt, pepper, allspice, and optional dried red peppers. Bring to a simmer, cover, and cook over low heat until thick, about 1½ hours, stirring the pot occasionally and

THE CONDIMENT OF THE KING OF CHEFS

Escoffier, like other great cooks, devised many recipes that he changed over time—his ideas seldom, if ever, failed to change with time. His condiment made with sweet red peppers was recorded in various versions, several of which have been drawn on for the recipe here.

uncovering toward the end. Taste; adjust seasonings, adding more sugar or other seasonings if you like. Remove and discard the dried red peppers.

6. Ladle the condiment into hot, clean glass canning or storage jars. Let the relish cool, then cover and store in the refrigerator, where it will keep for at least 6 months. Best if allowed to mellow for at least a day or two before serving.

Cranberry Ketchup

More versatile than conventional cranberry sauce because it is spicier and less sweet, this quickly made table sauce goes beautifully with all the foods traditionally accompanied by cranberries, and with others besides. Try it with an otherwise plain hamburger in place of tomato-based ketchup, or with roast pork or pork chops, and especially with baked beans. Cranberry ketchup zips up dressing for a fruit salad, too, and to my mind belongs on the Thanksgiving table in its own pretty bowl alongside the traditional cranberry sauce.

1 cup chopped mild onion
5 cups water
4 strips orange zest (outer peel only, no white pith), 1 inch wide, cut from top to bottom of orange
9 cups (three 12-ounce bags) cranberries, fresh (picked over and rinsed) or frozen (thawed)
1 cup cider vinegar, or more if needed
1 cup (packed) light brown sugar, or more if needed
1½ teaspoons salt, or to taste
1½ teaspoons ground cinnamon
1½ teaspoons ground allspice
1 teaspoon ground ginger
¼ teaspoon ground cloves

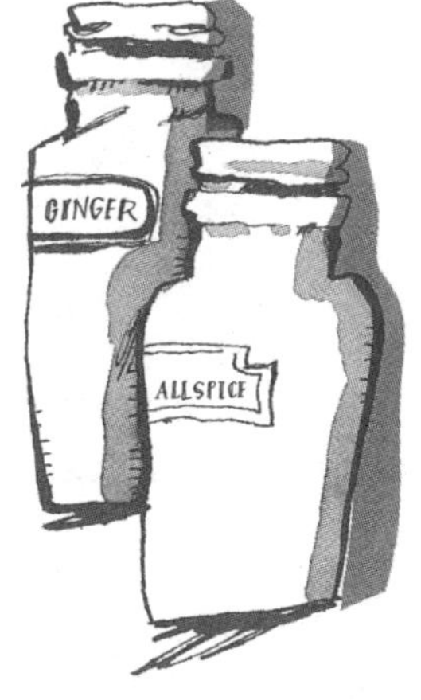

Makes about 6 cups

1. Combine the onion with the water and orange zest in a preserving pan. Bring to a boil, then lower the heat and simmer, covered, until the onion pieces are translucent, about 10 minutes.

2. Add the cranberries to the pan and return to a boil. Partially cover the pan, and cook the mixture, stirring occasionally, until the berries are quite soft, about 10 minutes. Pour into a bowl and cool slightly.

THE SECRET'S OUT

Cranberry ketchup has been made here and there for a long time by cooks who either adore cranberries or adore supplying their tables with good things, but only lately has its manufacture become a cottage industry. To make your own instead of mail-ordering it, round up some bouncing-fresh cranberries as soon as they appear in the autumn and devote a really very short time to turning out a batch. If you've been forehanded and chucked bags of fresh cranberries into the freezer (they keep for a remarkably long time), you can make ketchup at any season that suits you.

3. Scrape about half the cranberry mixture at a time into a food processor or put a smaller quantity into a blender (or use a food mill fitted with a fine disk) and puree the batches to a moderately fine texture. Pour the puree into the rinsed-out preserving pan.

4. Add the vinegar, brown sugar, salt, cinnamon, allspice, ginger, and cloves and bring to a boil over medium-high heat. Boil the mixture, stirring almost constantly, until it is thick, 3 to 5 minutes. It should be obvious when the mixture has reached ketchup consistency—in fact, some batches of berries are inclined to turn into a jelly—but you can test the ketchup for doneness (first taking the pan from the heat) by spooning a little onto a chilled saucer and setting it in the freezer or refrigerator until it is cold. If a track remains when a fingertip is drawn through the sample, the ketchup has cooked enough.

5. If the ketchup is jellylike, thin it with a little extra vinegar and water, half and half. Taste and add more sugar and/or salt if desired. Press the ketchup through a fine-meshed sieve and return to the pan.

6. Reheat the ketchup to boiling and ladle it into hot, clean half-pint canning jars, leaving ¼ inch of headspace. Seal the jars with new two-piece canning lids according to manufacturer's directions and process for 15 minutes in a boiling-water bath (page 283). Cool, label, and store the jars. The ketchup will be ready to serve in a few days, but it continues to mellow for weeks and will keep for at least a year in a cool cupboard. Refrigerate after opening. If the solids and the liquid should separate slightly in storage, just stir.

HOT & SPICY BANANA KETCHUP

Piquant, smooth, and red-brown in hue, this Caribbean-spiced, rum-touched, fruit-based condiment was inspired by a nameless hot sauce I tasted and admired in Jamaica. It is highly compatible with roast or grilled pork or poultry as well as a simple hamburger or cold meats, and I like to beat a little into the butter for what would otherwise be a bland cheese or chicken sandwich, or stir a spoonful into mayonnaise to create a subtly spicy dressing for cabbage slaw, fruit salad, or chicken salad.

For this ketchup, choose completely ripe but not mushy bananas, with well-freckled skins and decided fragrance. The spicing in the recipe produces moderately hot ketchup; for more zip, the red pepper can be increased. (However, I'd taste a cooled sample carefully before adding more red pepper; a well-balanced flavor will let the fruitiness come through.)

If fresh hot red peppers are available, they can be substituted for the ground red pepper. Use 3 or 4 peppers about 4 inches long, cored, seeded, and pureed with the other ingredients in step 1.

1 cup raisins, either dark or golden
¾ cup coarsely chopped onion
3 or 4 large cloves garlic, peeled
⅔ cup (6-ounce can) tomato paste
2⅔ cups distilled white vinegar or cider vinegar
3 pounds (about 8 large) very ripe, fragrant bananas
4 to 6 cups water
1 cup (packed) light or dark brown sugar
1 tablespoon salt
1 teaspoon ground hot red (cayenne) pepper
½ cup light corn syrup
4 teaspoons ground allspice, preferably freshly ground
1½ teaspoons ground cinnamon
1½ teaspoons freshly grated nutmeg
1 teaspoon freshly ground black pepper
½ teaspoon ground cloves
¼ to ⅓ cup dark rum, preferably Jamaican

Makes about 7 cups

1. Combine the raisins, onion, garlic, and tomato paste in a blender (which does the best job of pureeing) or food processor and puree them until smooth, adding some of the vinegar, as necessary, to help the job along. Scrape the puree into a preserving pan.

2. Peel the bananas, cut them into chunks, and puree them in turn, adding some of the vinegar to help. Add the puree to the mixture in the pan. Add the remaining vinegar, 4 cups of the water, the brown sugar, salt, and ground hot red pepper.

3. Bring the mixture to a boil over medium-high heat, stirring it frequently. Lower the heat to medium-low and cook the ketchup, uncovered, for 1¼ hours, stirring it often. If there is a threat of sticking at any point, add some of the remaining water as needed, up to 2 cups.

4. Add the corn syrup, allspice, cinnamon, nutmeg, black pepper, and cloves. Continue to cook the ketchup, stirring frequently, for 15 minutes longer, or until it is thick enough to coat a metal spoon. To test its consistency further, remove the pan from the heat and spoon a little ketchup onto a saucer. Let it cool; if very little or no liquid emerges around the sample, the ketchup is thick enough. If it does not

Yes, We Have Some Bananas

In the market season for well-priced bananas—around here it seems to be late spring—I like to gather a few promising "hands" and keep them around to become really ripe, fragrant, and well-freckled. When they have gained lots of flavor they go into a batch of this condiment, one of my great favorites.

pass this test, resume cooking for as long as necessary. Let the panful of ketchup cool for a few minutes.

5. Puree the ketchup again in the blender or food processor until it is satin smooth, or force it through a fine-meshed sieve or food mill. Rinse out the preserving pan and return the ketchup to it. Taste it for hotness and sharpness and add more red or black pepper, or more vinegar, or more sugar, as needed. Be cautious about adding more allspice, cinnamon, nutmeg, or cloves, because their flavors will strengthen later; they shouldn't dominate the fruit.

6. Bring the ketchup to a boil again over medium heat, stirring constantly. Add the rum and remove the pan from the heat. Ladle the boiling-hot ketchup into hot, clean half-pint or pint canning jars, leaving ¼ inch of headspace. Seal the jars with new two-piece canning lids according to manufacturer's directions and process the jars in a boiling-water bath for 15 minutes for half-pints, 20 minutes for pints (page 283). Cool, label, and store the jars. The ketchup will be ready to serve after 2 weeks, but it continues to improve in the jar for a month or so and will keep in a cool spot for at least a year.

Mushroom Ketchup

Culinary literature records any number of delectable-sounding condiments based on mushrooms. Some are liquid essences—see my version, on page 206—others are thick table sauces, and like a variety of other such sauces, are called "ketchups" or "catsups." Here is one such mushroom ketchup, an asset to keep on hand.

Most of the old ketchup formulas were created for wild mushrooms, which are in the quantities required for a decent-sized batch of sauce. Therefore this recipe has been devised for cultivated mushrooms, whose flavor unfortunately doesn't come up to their looks, plus a flavor kick supplied by dried boletus mushrooms. These fungi, almost always imported, are stocked by specialty food stores; they may be labeled *cèpes secs, funghi secchi porcini, boletus, boletes, Steinpilze,* or, sometimes, just "dried mushrooms." If the last is the only designation on the label, try to make sure you're getting boletus mushrooms (boletes) and not a lesser mushroom. (The undersurface of boletus pieces show a layer of pores, not gills.)

This condiment does good things for steaks, lamb chops, the lowly hamburger, and seafood. It's also a transforming seasoning for gravies, savory sauces, and dressings for hearty salads.

Ketchup De Luxe

Not meant to be a soulmate, exactly, for lunch-counter food, this velvety mushroom ketchup rates the choicest of table companions. It's also an estimable seasoning for pan sauces and sautés and is especially good with seafood dishes.

1½ pounds firm, fresh cultivated mushrooms, preferably with unopened caps
1½ tablespoons pickling or other fine noniodized salt (increase by 1½ teaspoons if coarse salt, such as kosher salt, is used)
1 ounce dried boletus mushrooms (*cèpes, porcini,* etc.)
3 cups hot water
2 cups white wine vinegar or 1⅔ cups distilled white vinegar plus ⅓ cup water
3 large shallots or 1 small onion, peeled
1 clove garlic, peeled
10 whole allspice or ¼ teaspoon ground allspice
4 whole cloves
3 large blades mace (whole mace)
2 bay leaves
½ teaspoon ground ginger
½ teaspoon freshly ground pepper, black or white
¼ cup medium or dry sherry

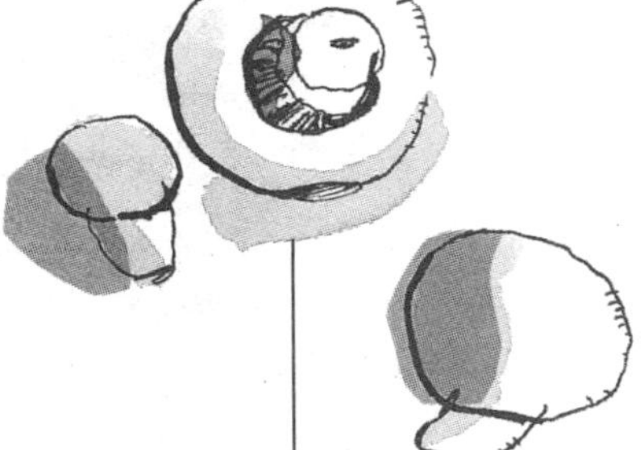

Makes about 4 cups

1. Wipe the mushrooms clean with a damp cloth, or brush them clean. Avoid washing them if possible; if it is necessary, swish them rapidly through a bowl of water and lift and drain them promptly. Trim off any discolored stem ends or damaged portions. Slice the mushrooms thin (a food processor fitted with the thin-slicing disc makes short work of this task) and mix them thoroughly with the salt in a ceramic or glass bowl. Cover the bowl with a cloth and let the mushrooms stand 24 hours, stirring them occasionally. They will become dark (the finished ketchup will be approximately the color of black bean soup).

2. At least an hour before the end of the salting period, soak the dried mushrooms in the 3 cups hot water until completely soft.

3. Lift the soaked mushrooms from their liquid with a slotted spoon (this is to avoid any grit that may be in the liquid) and place them in a blender or food processor. Let the soaking liquid settle for a minute or two, then carefully pour it back over the mushrooms, stopping before any grit is poured out. Puree the soaked mushrooms, then pour the puree into a preserving pan. Without rinsing the blender container, puree the salted mushrooms, add this puree to that in the pan.

4. Place about ½ cup of the vinegar in the blender and add the shallots and garlic; process them to a puree. Add this puree to the mushroom puree in the pan, together with the rest of the vinegar, the allspice, cloves, mace, bay leaves, ginger, and pepper. Bring the mixture to a boil over medium-high heat, then lower the heat and simmer the ketchup, uncovered, stirring it often, for 1 to 1½ hours, or until the tiny fragments of mushroom are very soft, almost jellylike, and the ketchup is thick. To test for correct consistency, pour a spoonful onto a saucer and let it stand 10 minutes, with the pot off the heat; if very little or no liquid seeps from the solids, the ketchup has thickened enough. If it does not pass this test, resume the cooking for as long as necessary.

5. Press the ketchup through a sieve to remove the bay leaves and whole spices, then puree the ketchup, in batches if necessary, in a blender or food processor until velvety smooth.

6. Return the ketchup to the rinsed-out pan and bring it to a full boil again over medium-high heat, stirring it constantly. Stir in the sherry. Ladle the boiling-hot ketchup into hot, clean half-pint or pint canning jars, leaving ¼ inch of headspace. Seal the jars with new two-piece canning lids according to manufacturer's directions and process for 15 minutes (for either size jar) in a boiling-water bath (page 283). Cool, label, and store the jars. Let the ketchup mellow for a few weeks before serving it. It will keep for at least a year in a cool cupboard.

Piquant Golden Raisin Chutney

A terrific keeper and simple to make, this chutney gets better by the week as it mellows. Serve it with all the usual suspects—including curries—but keep in mind its affinity for sandwiches, cheeses, and cold meats. I whisk a spoonful or two into the dressing for chicken, turkey, potato, or pasta salad, where its sweet-hot character enlivens those fundamentally bashful dishes.

1½ cups (packed) golden raisins
1 cup diced red or sweet white onion
½ cup water, or more as necessary
1½ teaspoons finely minced garlic
¼ cup mild red wine vinegar, or more to taste
3 tablespoons granulated sugar, or more if needed
1 cup diced sweet red (bell) pepper
1½ teaspoons mustard seed
1 teaspoon curry powder, or more if needed (see page 193 to make your own)
½ teaspoon salt, or to taste
Pinch of hot red pepper flakes, optional

Makes about 2 cups

Beginner's Chutney

Start with golden raisins and in short order you can whip up a scrumptious relish. Notice that this is stored in the refrigerator or freezer—no special preserving steps are called for.

1. In a small bowl, cover the raisins with warm water and soak them for 1 hour.

2. Spray a medium-size nonstick skillet or heavy-bottomed saucepan with cooking spray and set over medium heat. Add the onion and cook, stirring often, until hot and fragrant but not at all browned. Add ½ cup water, cover partially, and simmer until the onion pieces are tender-crisp and the liquid has evaporated.

3. Add the raisins and their soaking water, the garlic, vinegar, sugar, sweet red pepper, mustard seed, curry powder, ½ teaspoon salt, and the hot red pepper flakes (if used). If needed, add water; the liquid should just reach the top layer of ingredients. Bring to a boil, then lower the heat and simmer, uncovered, stirring occasionally, until the spicy syrup has thickened slightly, about 20 minutes. Taste and decide whether to add more sugar, vinegar, curry, salt, or hot red pepper flakes, keeping in mind that the flavor of the chutney will "bloom" in the jar.

4. Remove about half a cup of the chutney to the blender or food processor and pulse the machine until you have a coarse puree. Mix the puree with the unchopped chutney, scrape the mixture into a clean, dry jar or jars, cool, cover, and refrigerate to mellow for a few days before it's served. For longer storage, it may be frozen for several months. Let it return to room temperature before serving.

Mango & Tamarind Chutney

Most mangoes come to market from May until late fall, and most of them arrive in a state of rock-hard unripeness that can be discouraging if you're looking for fragrant, melting fruit to eat out of hand. (They will ripen in time, if handled gently and left in an airy spot out of the sun.) Meanwhile, you can use green fruit to make a luxurious chutney given additional zing by tamarind. (Fresh lime juice can be substituted for tamarind, as described in step 1.) You can also make a chutney of softer texture by including part (or all) almost-ripe fruit.

If you like jammy chutney, cut the fruit into small bits; for a chunky product, use half-inch or larger cubes and stop cooking the mixture as soon as the fruit pieces are translucent. This chutney is only moderately hot and spicy. If you'd like more heat, increase the ginger by as much as 2 tablespoons and increase the hot pepper to taste.

TAMARIND

Dealers in Asian foods can supply tamarind for use in this recipe. A seedy, stringy, sour fruit pod of a tree native to East Africa, tamarind is most often used in Indian cooking, especially chutneys and curries. It is usually sold dried and compressed into bricks, which last almost forever on the pantry shelf, but in some places the pulp is available in jars or in powdered form.

½ cup (packed) dried tamarind pulp
2½ cups water
3 pounds unripe, half-ripe, or part unripe and part ripe mangoes
1 cup diced onions
1 cup golden raisins
1 cup dried currants
¼ cup minced fresh ginger
3 large cloves garlic, peeled and minced fine
Grated zest (outer peel only, no white pith) of 1 lemon
2 cups (packed) light brown sugar
¾ cup granulated sugar
2 tablespoons mustard seed
1 tablespoon salt
2 teaspoons hot red pepper flakes; or 2 dried hot red peppers (2½ to 3 inches long), seeded, then crumbled; or 1 tablespoon finely minced fresh hot peppers, red or green (increase any to taste)
2 teaspoons ground cinnamon
½ teaspoon ground turmeric
¼ teaspoon ground cloves
¼ teaspoon ground hot red (cayenne) pepper
1½ cups distilled white vinegar

Makes 6 to 7 cups

1. Crumble the tamarind into a small bowl and stir in 1½ cups of the water; let the tamarind soak for at least an hour. (If tamarind isn't easily obtainable, substitute ½ cup strained fresh lime juice plus ½ cup water for the prepared tamarind.)

2. Meanwhile, prepare the remaining ingredients. Peel and dice the mangoes, cutting them into small pieces for a jamlike chutney, into ½-inch or larger dice for a chunky mixture. Place the pieces in a preserving pan. Add the onion, raisins, currants, ginger, garlic, lemon zest, brown and granulated sugars, mustard seed, salt, hot red pepper flakes, cinnamon, turmeric, cloves, ground red pepper, vinegar, and the remaining 1 cup water; stir the mixture and let it rest until the tamarind is ready, or for up to several hours if that is convenient.

3. When the tamarind pulp is very soft, pour pulp and liquid into a sieve set over a bowl. Press the tamarind to force through all possible pulp; discard the debris in the strainer. Add the strained tamarind to the chutney ingredients.

4. Set the pan over medium heat and bring the ingredients to a boil. Lower the heat so the mixture simmers and cook it, stirring often, until the mango and onion pieces are translucent and the chutney has thickened to the consistency of preserves, 1 to 2 hours depending on the firmness of the fruit. (The chutney will thicken further in the jar, so don't reduce it too much.) If the chutney threatens to stick before the mango pieces are translucent, add a little water.

5. Remove the chutney from the heat, cool a sample, and taste it for tartness, sweetness, and hotness. (The overall flavor will be elusive at this point, but these three factors can be judged.) If you wish, add a little more vinegar, sugar, or ground hot red pepper.

6. Reheat the chutney to boiling and ladle it into hot, clean pint or half-pint canning jars, leaving ¼ inch of headspace Seal the jars with new two-piece canning lids according to manufacturer's directions and process the jars 15 minutes (for either size) in a boiling-water bath (page 283). Cool, label, and store the jars for a few weeks before serving the chutney. It will keep for at least a year in a cool cupboard.

Gingery Rhubarb Chutney

Tender pink rhubarb plus fresh ginger, spices, and seasonings add up to a lively (and simply made) condiment that adds zest to any curried dish or to hot or cold roasted meat or poultry.

If green-stalked rhubarb is what you have, just strip off any truly tough skin and proceed. The flavor will be just as good.

2 pounds rhubarb (trimmed weight), preferably red-skinned, washed, drained, and cut into ½-inch dice (6 to 7 cups)
1½ cups coarsely chopped onion
1½ cups golden raisins
1½ cups sugar
4 large cloves garlic, or more to taste, peeled and minced
2 tablespoons finely minced fresh ginger
1 tablespoon pickling or other fine noniodized salt (increase by 1 teaspoon if coarse salt, such as kosher salt, is used)
2 teaspoons mustard seed
1 teaspoon ground allspice
1 teaspoon ground coriander, preferably freshly ground
½ teaspoon hot red pepper flakes, or to taste
¼ teaspoon ground cinnamon
¼ teaspoon ground cloves
2 cups cider vinegar
¼ cup light corn syrup

Makes about 7 cups

Springtime Chutney

When spring rhubarb is matched with glossy, juicy-fleshed fresh ginger in this sweet-savory, somewhat piquant condiment, rhubarb skeptics just may be converted into rhubarb fans.

1. Combine all the ingredients except the vinegar and corn syrup in a preserving pan and mix well. Bring to a boil over medium heat, then lower the heat, partially cover the pan, and simmer the mixture, stirring it occasionally, until the onion pieces are translucent, about 30 minutes.

2. Add the vinegar and corn syrup and cook, uncovered, over medium-high heat, stirring almost constantly, until the chutney is thick enough to mound up slightly in a spoon, 20 to 30 minutes.

3. Ladle the boiling-hot chutney into hot, clean half-pint or pint canning jars, leaving ¼ inch of headspace. Seal the jars with new two-piece canning lids according to manufacturer's directions and process them for 10 minutes (for either size) in a boiling-water bath (page 283). Cool, label, and store the jars for 3 weeks before opening. The chutney will keep for at least a year in a cool cupboard. Refrigerate after opening.

Glorious Garlic & Hot Pepper Jelly

Creamy-looking thanks to its rich burden of garlic pulp plus a little hot red pepper, this relish doesn't look like most jellies and goodness knows it doesn't taste like them either: it's for real garlic lovers only. As we're unreconstructed members of that crowd, we find it delectable on crackers or Melba toast and with cold ham or sausage or cheese. As an accompaniment for corn fritters, it's light years ahead of the traditional maple syrup.

For Glorious Jelly

The wonderful wallop of this garlicky condiment depends on using great raw material. Which means that this jelly should be made when you can get crisp, juice-filled garlic heads bursting with flavor. Old garlic just won't do as well.

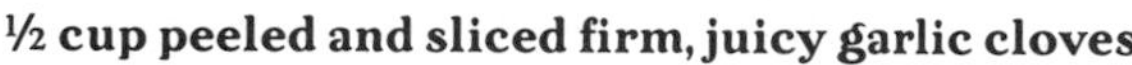

½ cup peeled and sliced firm, juicy garlic cloves
2 cups water
4 cups sugar
¼ cup white wine vinegar or Japanese rice vinegar
½ teaspoon salt
⅛ to ¼ teaspoon ground hot red (cayenne) pepper, or to taste
One 3-ounce pouch liquid pectin, or half a 6-ounce bottle

Makes about 4 cups

1. Puree the garlic with half of the water in a blender or food processor, running the machine until the texture is fine (the puree will be foamy). Pour into a large saucepan and add the second cup of water. Set over medium heat and bring to a simmer; simmer, stirring, for 2 minutes, then remove from the heat and skim. Measure out 1¾ cups of the puree, discarding any surplus, and return it to the pan.

2. Stir in the sugar, vinegar, salt, and hot red pepper. Set over medium-high heat and heat, stirring, until the mixture boils hard (a rolling boil that cannot be stirred down). At once add the pectin, stirring, and bring again to a hard rolling boil. Start timing and boil for exactly 1 minute. Remove from the heat.

3. Skim off any foam, then ladle the jelly into sterilized (page 282) jelly glasses or half-pint canning jars, leaving ½ inch of headspace in glasses and ⅛ inch in jars. Seal the jelly in glasses with a film of melted paraffin; cover jars with sterilized two-piece canning lids following the manufacturer's directions. Cool the jelly completely, then cover jelly glasses with their lids. This jelly takes a few days to set, so don't plan on using it at once. Stored in a cool cupboard, it will keep for a year.

Red Rosemary Jelly

A distinguished herbal relish is created when oranges, cranberries, and a seasoning of resinous, pungent rosemary are compounded into a substantial crimson jelly. The rosemary, though not assertive, makes the jelly a highly compatible relish with pork, venison, game birds, or turkey.

2 medium oranges
3½ cups water
2 cups cranberries, fresh (picked over and rinsed) or frozen (thawed)
¼ cup (lightly packed) fresh rosemary leaves (tender tips of the branches may be included)
4 whole cloves
Sugar

Makes about 3 cups

1. Wash the oranges and slice them paper-thin; quarter the slices. Combine the slices with the water in a medium-size glass, plastic, or pottery bowl, cover the bowl, and let the oranges stand at least 8 hours or, even better, overnight.

2. Place the oranges and their liquid in a nonreactive saucepan, bring to a boil, then lower the heat, cover, and simmer 15 minutes. Uncover and mash the oranges slightly with a spoon or whisk. Add the cranberries, rosemary, and cloves, re-cover the pan, and simmer the mélange until the oranges and cranberries are very soft, 15 to 20 minutes.

Autumn Strategy

If, like me, you cherish a pot or two of rosemary, which is sensitive to cold weather and must be wintered indoors in most places, it's a good strategy to postpone the autumn pruning of your plants until fresh cranberries have come to market so you can use fresh leaves in this jelly. Dried rosemary can be substituted: use about one-half the quantity listed for fresh leaves. Cranberries from the freezer will also work well, so there is some seasonal flexibility here.

3. Ladle the mixture into a jelly bag (page 281) placed over a bowl and allow the juice to drip until the pulp yields no more liquid, 2 or 3 hours. When the drip has slowed down, it's permissible to press the sides of the bag lightly to encourage the last drops to drip, but don't actually squeeze the bag—that would cause pulp to pass through and make the jelly cloudy.

4. Measure the juice—there should be 2½ to 3 cups. Place it in a preserving pan or large saucepan and bring it to a boil. Stir in 1 cup of sugar for each cup of juice and boil the mixture hard until it passes the jelly test (page 282). Remove the jelly from the heat, skim it if there is any foam or scum, and ladle at once into hot, sterilized (page 282) jelly glasses or half-pint canning jars, leaving ½ inch of headspace in glasses, ⅛ inch in jars. Seal the glasses with melted paraffin wax; seal the jars with sterilized new two-piece canning lids according to manufacturer's directions. Cool, label, and store the jars. The jelly keeps well in a cool cupboard for at least a year.

RED-HOT & SWEET RED PEPPER "JELLY"

Red pepper "jelly," which is what everyone seems to call a piquant jam or relish based on sweet and/or hot peppers, has become an American classic, especially in the South. Those who seize every chance to obtain a jar from the fancy-food shelves or specialty catalogs don't need advice about how to serve it. Pepper jelly is perfect, with its sweet-hot piquancy, on crackers spread with cream cheese. For fancier occasions, it might be spooned into tiny tartlet shells made with cream-cheese pastry (see a good general cookbook for this). At mealtime, it's a lively relish alongside meat, poultry, or even fish.

Increase the fieriness of this jelly, if you wish, by upping the proportion of hot peppers, being sure to keep the total quantity of all peppers about the same. You can also heat it up further by adding drops of Tabasco or other bottled pepper sauce, or your own home-crafted hot stuff (see the Index). If you want to stay on the mild side of the heat gauge, use only 1 to 2 tablespoons of chopped hot peppers in place of the ¼ cup listed in the recipe. Or make a completely mild jelly by omitting the hot peppers and increasing the sweet red peppers by ¼ cup.

2 cups stemmed, seeded, deribbed, and coarsely chopped sweet red (bell) peppers
¼ cup stemmed, seeded, deribbed, and coarsely chopped fresh hot red peppers or drained and chopped canned whole jalapeño peppers (see the note on handling hot peppers, page 161)
1½ cups cider vinegar
1 teaspoon salt
6½ cups sugar
1 bottle (or 2 pouches) liquid pectin (6 ounces total)
Tabasco or other hot pepper sauce, optional

Makes about 7 cups

1. In two or more batches, chop the sweet and hot peppers to a coarse puree in a blender or food processor, using some of the vinegar as liquid. Scrape the peppers into a preserving pan. Add the remaining vinegar and the salt.

2. Bring the mixture to a boil over medium heat; lower the heat and simmer it, uncovered, stirring occasionally, for 5 minutes. Remove from the heat. Measure the mixture and return 3 cups to the pan. If you have less than 3 cups, add water to make up the difference. Stir in the sugar.

3. Stirring constantly, bring the mixture to a full rolling boil (a boil that cannot be stirred down) over high heat and boil it for exactly 1 minute. Remove from the heat.

4. Stir in the pectin thoroughly. Taste for hotness and add drops of Tabasco or other hot pepper sauce if desired. Skim off any foam. Cool for 3 minutes, stirring occasionally to prevent the peppers from floating after the jelly is in the jars.

5. Ladle the jelly into hot, sterilized (page 282) half-pint canning jars, leaving ¼ inch of headspace. Seal the jars with sterilized new two-piece canning lids according to manufacturer's directions. Cool, label, and store the jars. The jelly will keep for a year in a cool cupboard.

It Isn't Jelly, But Is It Jam?

Usage has gotten ahead of accuracy in the common name—"pepper jelly"—of this relish, but never mind. By any name, it's an all-American invention beloved from sea to sea. Note that the recipe provides for various degrees of fieriness, so you can suit yourself on that point.

Sherried Onion Marmalade

Onions are here mellowed by the sweet ancestral grape flavor that lingers in sherry, plus a touch of honey and a little wine vinegar, then aromatized with crumbles of rosemary and slow-cooked into a savory jam. This delicious amber-colored condi-

SHERRY & GOOD FOOD

It's perfectly feasible to keep a bottle of sherry on hand for cooking, as this fortified wine keeps much better after opening than do table wines. (Just store it, well corked, in a cool, dark spot.) Don't, please, purchase—much less use—the "cooking wines" sold in supermarkets, because those wines have been salted to make them theoretically undrinkable and so eligible for stocking in food stores. (Some states are enlightened enough to make possible one-stop shopping for food and real wine in supermarkets, and I'm all for it.) Wherever you get it, buy a decent bottle of sherry, the degree of dryness or sweetness being up to you. Sherry needn't cost a lot, but even the lowest-priced bottle at the wine merchant's will be kinder to your food than "cooking sherry" could possibly be.

ment, by courtesy a "marmalade," is an enlivenment for broiled or sautéed chicken, pork chops cooked any which way, grilled, roasted, or pot-roasted beef, or most especially with sautéed calf's liver. The marmalade is also great on a burger, either meaty or soy, or a cold meat or cheese sandwich.

2 pounds (7 or 8 medium, for about 6 cups sliced) mild onions, peeled and sliced paper-thin (a good job for a food processor)
3 tablespoons olive oil
4 large cloves garlic, peeled and minced fine or pushed through a garlic press
2 to 3 tablespoons medium or sweet sherry combined with 2 to 3 tablespoons red or white wine vinegar, or substitute ¼ to ⅓ cup sherry vinegar
3 tablespoons honey or 2 tablespoons (packed) light brown sugar
2 teaspoons well-crushed dried rosemary
½ teaspoon salt or to taste
Pinch (or more) of ground hot red (cayenne) pepper, optional

Makes about 2 cups

1. Stir together the onions and olive oil in a nonreactive heavy wide skillet and cook, stirring often, over medium heat until well wilted and lightly colored; the onions should be pale gold, no more.

2. Stir in the garlic, ¼ cup of the mixed sherry and vinegar (or the sherry vinegar), the honey, and rosemary and cook over low heat, stirring often, until the mixture has deepened in color and is almost dry. Add enough water to reach the top layer of onions, cover partially, and continue cooking over low heat, stirring occasionally, until the liquid has evaporated again. Test a strand or two; the onions should be very soft, with just a ghost of crunch. If necessary, add water and reduce the liquid again until the marmalade is light caramel in color and jamlike in texture. (The cooking may be done in more than one episode, if more convenient.)

3. Off the heat, season with the salt and, if you like, the optional hot red pepper. Let the marmalade cool. Taste for seasoning and add more of the sherry plus vinegar (or sherry vinegar) if more tartness is needed, plus more honey, salt, and/or cayenne as required. Scrape the marmalade into a clean, dry jar, cap snugly, and store in the refrigerator.

4. The marmalade will keep for a few weeks, refrigerated. Frozen, it will hold its quality for at least 2 months. Let it return to room temperature (or warm it slightly in a microwave) before serving it.

MARINADES, SPICE & HERB BLENDS, DRY RUBS, SEASONING MIXES FOR CHILI, CURRY, GUMBO, JERK MEATS, & ADOBO, & MORE BESIDES

SEASONINGS SUBTLE AND SMASHING

Blending some of your own seasonings is a bit of foodcraft worth acquiring for a couple of reasons. First, there's quality—if you start with the freshest possible spices and dried herbs (I buy most of ours from mail-order specialists), you can create seasonings that sparkle with flavor instead of smoldering with exhaustion from being too long on the shelf. Then there's wise frugality, an idea not yet out of fashion.

When you reckon grocery-shelf prices for, say, an Italian herb blend against your do-it-yourself cost—assuming you've bought your ingredients in good-sized batches instead of tiny jars—a pretty penny is saved for your personal truffle (or champagne) fund.

Equipment for grinding and blending seasonings is already on hand in most kitchens. If you don't possess a small coffee (or spice) mill—an appliance I value highly—but do have a blender, you're in business. If you find your blender is spinning its wheels instead of dealing vigorously with a given quantity of ingredients, the problem can be solved by doubling the recipe. If you lack either a spice or coffee mill or a blender, the grinding can be done with a mortar and pestle plus some muscle power.

A Short Cruise Through Schools of Marination

Liquid marinades are usually described in detail in the cookbook recipes for which they're needed, but the basic patterns are useful to creative types who like to wing it on the grill. Changes of ingredients are at the cook's pleasure.

When using these patterns, exact measurements aren't as important as the cook's eye. In general, in non-Asian marinades the emollient (oil) is more plentiful than the acid (lemon, wine, yogurt), but again that will depend: fatty fish or meat to be marinated obviously requires less oil than lean. The overall quantity of liquid isn't crucial so long as there's enough to keep the food moist; the marinade should come to about half the thickness of the food when it is fitted into a flat-bottomed china or plastic (not reactive metal) dish. (An easy alternative way to marinate food: Put everything in a sturdy plastic bag, then zip it shut or close it with a wire twist.) Turn the food in the dish (or turn the whole bag) occasionally during marination.

At cooking time, strain any coarse bits of seasoning from the marinade and use the liquid as a baste for the food. If you're broiling, the pan drippings at the end will beg to be made into a little sauce, into which any remaining marinade should be stirred as it cooks.

To salt or not to salt the marinade: Except for marinades using soy sauce, in which saltiness can't be avoided (it can be reduced by choosing reduced-salt soy), I prefer to omit salt from most marinades, as it tends to draw the juice from flesh. Instead, I salt the food during cooking (after it's had a chance to brown a bit), or I leave it to the diners to add salt after tasting. However, some fine cooks salt and pepper meat, fish and fowl before marination, so you'll be in respectable company if you put a little salt into non-soy marinades.

Italian-Style Marinating

For chicken, beef, or grilled vegetables: Blend olive oil, a little less red wine or dry vermouth than oil, chopped or pressed garlic, a few drops of orange oil or a scattering of grated orange zest, chopped fresh rosemary leaves (or soaked and chopped dried rosemary), coarsely ground black pepper. Optional: A little chopped sage. Marinate flattened or cross-slashed chicken breasts (2 to 4 hours) or well-scored and trimmed flank steak (up to 8 hours), or lamb chops or steaks (up to 8 hours).

Cooling It

Foods can be safely marinated at room temperature for an hour or so at any season, even in summer, or for up to 3 hours if the room is quite cool. For longer periods, play it safe and do the job in the refrigerator. It's a good idea to remove the marinating food from the fridge an hour or so before you'll be cooking it to let the chill dissipate.

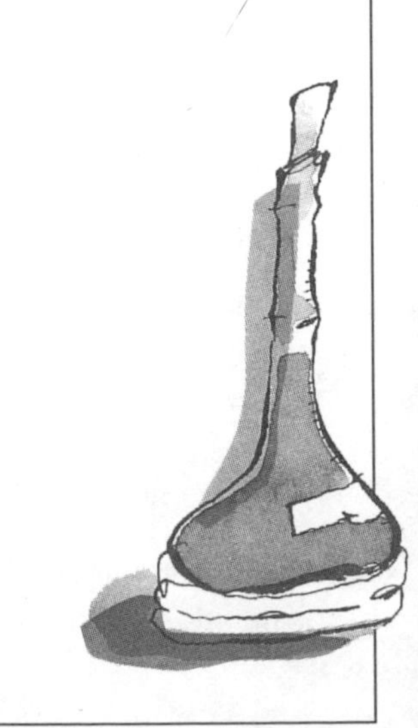

THE OREGANO TRAIL

Not even herbalists are very clear about the world's many kinds of oregano, especially the differences between oregano and sweet marjoram, both members of the mint family. (Oregano is sometimes called "wild marjoram.") Oregano came into its own in the U.S. after the Second World War, and we now consume it by the ton, mostly on pizza. For Old World dishes, Italian and Greek oregano are most authentic. Experts on Mexican food say that there are at least a dozen kinds of Mexican oregano, another valuable herb, which is not at all closely related to the European kinds; it has a strong, dry pungency that's sniffably different from the aroma of the Old World herb. For both sorts, as well as good-quality sweet marjoram—a lovely, delicate herb that should be better known—a specialist spice merchant is your best bet.

For vegetables: The same mixture as above is also good for thick slices of eggplant, zucchini, onions, or tomatoes, too. Marinate vegetables for several hours and grill quickly and briefly.

For fish: Flavorful olive oil, a little fresh lemon juice, a generous amount of one or more chopped fresh herbs (such as basil—first choice—tarragon, thyme or oregano, and a little rosemary), plus freshly ground pepper and, optionally, salt. Marinate fish for an hour or so at room temperature, up to 3 or 4 hours if refrigerated.

GREEK-STYLE MARINATING

For lamb: Blend olive oil, half as much fresh lemon juice or red wine, bay leaves, herbs of choice (oregano, thyme, and/or rosemary), black pepper. Marinate lamb chops or boned and butterflied leg of lamb 4 hours in a cool spot, or for up to 8 hours in the fridge. Grill, basting with any remaining marinade during grilling. This mixture is also good for grilled vegetables (see Italian-style marination above).

For fish: Fresh lemon juice plus red wine vinegar, two or three times as much olive oil as acid, fresh pepper, a little salt. Optional: chopped or sliced mild onion or shallots, a pinch of fresh thyme and/or Powdered Bay Leaves (see Index). Marinate substantial fish steaks or fillets about 1 hour, then drain, brush with oil, and grill.

For chicken: Fresh lemon juice, twice as much oil, minced parsley or crumbled Greek oregano, fresh pepper, a little salt added while the bird is grilling. Marinate for at least 1 hour, better 2 or 3. Thyme may replace the oregano.

TERIYAKI-STYLE MARINADES

For chicken, thin-sliced beef, or fish: Genuine teriyaki sauce isn't a marinade; it's brushed on during broiling or pan-frying food and usually contains Japanese soy sauce, mirin (sweetened rice wine), sake (rice wine for drinking), and sugar. Oil, minced garlic, and/or minced ginger are sometimes added.

To adopt the teriyaki flavors for a marinade and a different cooking method, blend Japanese soy sauce, a little vegetable (not olive) oil, a little dry sherry, grated or minced fresh ginger, pressed or grated garlic, and a generous sprinkle of sugar (important for flavor balance). Marinate the food for 20 to 30 minutes, then broil or grill it not too close to the heat, basting it several times with the marinade, which will create a moist, almost syrupy glaze.

For poultry, pork, or red meat: Another teriyaki knockoff, this represents a little hands-across-the-sea interplay between East and West. Mix Japanese soy sauce, white wine or dry vermouth, a good dollop of honey, minced fresh ginger, and minced garlic. Marinate the meat for at least 2 hours, or for up to 8 hours in the refrigerator, then broil, basting with pan juices and any remaining marinade; or grill, basting with remaining marinade. The surface should be glazed, not crusty, so don't overcook the meat or poultry.

French-Style Marinating

For lean fish: Fresh lemon juice and three times as much olive oil, seasoned with crumbled dried thyme or chopped fresh thyme plus a torn-up bay leaf or two (or use ground bay leaves); add a little freshly ground pepper if you wish. Marinate for 30 minutes to 1 hour, or a bit longer for thicker cuts of fish. *For fatty fish,* reduce the proportion of oil in relation to lemon juice.

For poultry and steaks or chops: Plenty of olive oil, about a quarter as much fresh lemon juice or red wine, freshly ground pepper, chopped shallots or mild onion, crumbled or chopped thyme, a torn-up bay leaf or a pinch or two of Powdered Bay Leaves (page 195), a little minced garlic.

Middle Eastern Marinating

For shish kebab—skewered and grilled lamb or beef: The basic marinade is olive oil, fresh lemon juice (proportions vary—try equal parts to start), a generous helping of very finely chopped onion (or onion pushed through a garlic press), crumbled Greek oregano (sometimes thyme) and torn-up bay leaf (or use Powdered Bay Leaves, page 195), plus fresh-ground pepper. Salt is usually added, but you decide for yourself. At least 3 hours' marination is in order before the meat is skewered, with or without chunks of vegetable punctuation (peppers, onion, tomato), and grilled over hot coals with bastings of the remaining marinade.

Some versions of shish kebab are prepared with yogurt in place of the lemon juice.

Custom-Made Chili Seasoning

Fancy-food shelves are aromatic with chili powders, most of them containing a lot of ingredients besides chile peppers. They range from jars of reddish-black compounds to kits containing an array of separate seasonings for making hot, hotter, or hottest chili con carne. Some are good, some not so good. Any chilihead, whether casual

Measuring Herbs

For accuracy, crumble leaf herbs before scooping up the measuring spoonful. The easiest way to crumble a moderate quantity is in the palm of one hand, which serves as the mortar while the fingers of the other hand function as the pestle.

or dedicated, can do better by making a custom blend, starting with either dried whole chiles or ground dried chiles and adding a few other items to compound a vibrant seasoning suited to the maker's taste.

More of any element can be added to the formula here. Put in some extra-hot chiles of your choice (such as caribe or other scorchers) if you're sure about your heat tolerance. Or you can add a couple of teaspoons of salt (I don't). The powdered garlic, too, is optional—I think it pulls together the flavors, though.

Besides being the soul of a delectable pot of chili (see Chili Bricks, page 24), this seasoning, sprinkled over a buttered ear of corn, is a great enlivener. A smidgen of chili seasoning is also a great addition to the dressing for a salad of chicken and celery (or chicken and slivered jicama), or the dressing for a halved avocado.

If you use whole dried chiles in place of the ground pure chile called for: Use 4 to 5 ounces of dried ancho, pasilla, New Mexico red, or other mild chiles. As described in step 1, toast, stem, and seed them before proceeding to grind the ingredients.

For a smoky seasoning: Include 1 to 2 tablespoons ground chipotle chiles, which are smoke-dried ripe (red) jalapeños with a character all their own.

For more hotness: Increase the share of hot chiles, but don't overbalance in the direction of heat or you'll swamp the flavors of the milder ingredients. Good chili should have taste, not just heat.

2 to 4 dried long hot chile peppers such as cayenne, optional
2/3 cup (4 ounces) pure ground mild dried ancho chiles or other mild chiles
2 tablespoons crumbled dried oregano, preferably Mexican
2 tablespoons sweet, medium, or hot imported Hungarian paprika
2 tablespoons cumin seed
1 tablespoon coriander seed
2 teaspoons granulated dried garlic or garlic powder (not garlic salt)
4 whole cloves

Makes about 1 cup

1. If the hot peppers are used, toast them, turning often, in a heavy skillet over medium heat until they are fragrant and slightly crisp and only slightly darkened, not blackened. Remove stems and seeds and break the peppers into bits.

2. Combine the hot pepper pieces, if used, the ground ancho chiles, oregano, paprika, cumin, coriander, garlic, and cloves in the container of a blender or in a spice mill. Grind to a fine powder.

CUMIN—NOT JUST FOR CHILI POWDER

Especially hard to describe, the flavor of cumin is . . . strong, even "raucous," and warm; a little strange when first experienced—"Do I really like this?" the tastebuds may ask. Related to caraway (with which it is often confused when popular names in various languages are used), cumin is not at all similar to caraway either in taste or culinary uses. It is indispensable in the cooking of India, the Middle East, North Africa, Mexico, and Latin America, as well as Asia. The seeds, whole or ground, are interesting to experiment with; I like to sprinkle a little cumin into the pot when I make ratatouille, for instance.

3. Pack the chili seasoning into a jar, cap, and refrigerate, freeze, or store in a cool dark cupboard. It will keep longest if kept cold, but it will be okay at room temperature for a few months. I've kept a frozen test supply for years and it's still good whenever dipped into.

Filé Powder (Filé Gumbo)

Wherever sassafras trees grow wild in the eastern part of the nation, it's the work of a few moments (plus drying time for the sassafras leaves) to prepare your own filé powder, also called filé gumbo. You can choose to make it plain and classic, or add dried thyme as some Louisianans like to do.

This is a subtle seasoning, introduced to settlers by the Native Americans in the present U.S. Southeast, and its use still thrives in the glorious gumbos of that region. It functions mainly as a thickener for almost any highly seasoned soup or stew, with or without meat or seafood or poultry, but it has a delicate herbal quality all its own.

To prepare filé powder: Gather tender leaves from a wild sassafras tree in early summer. Dry the leaves as outlined for all herbs (Drying Fresh Herbs, page 188), then strip off any stems. Grind the sassafras leaves to powder in a spice mill, a small coffee mill dedicated to spices, a blender, or a food processor. (The latter two will work well only with a lot of dried material.) Pack the filé powder snugly into a small jar or bottle, cap, and store in a cool dark cupboard. I've kept this seasoning for more than a year in the cupboard and for more than 3 years in the freezer.

To use filé powder: Remove from the heat the pot of gumbo or whatever it is you're cooking and stir in from ½ to 1 teaspoon of the powder per portion. If reheating should be necessary, don't let the dish reach anywhere near boiling point or its texture will become stringy.

Filé Powder with Thyme

To each ½ cup of powdered dried sassafras, add about a tablespoonful of dried thyme leaves and grind the two together. More thyme can be added later, if you like, after your blend has been kitchen-tested in a gumbo.

Finding the Mitten Tree

To identify a sassafras tree, look for a smallish tree or even smaller seedling with medium-green leaves, about the size of a human hand, that rejoice in three shapes, all found on the same plant. Some leaves are long ovals, some have three lobes, and some resemble a mitten. To check the identity of what you've found, break a twig and sniff: Sassafras aroma is spicy and sweet, rather like that of root beer. (Sassafras tea, made from the plant's roots, is an old American beverage.)

THE PRICE IS RIGHT

And so is the quality, when you put together pepper mixes like this for yourself. Last time I checked, a blend of four kinds of peppercorns was priced by one spice merchant at about 20 bucks for a mere 4 ounces.

FIVE-PEPPERCORN MIX FOR THE MILL

Some of the "peppercorns" in this fragrant seasoning are true peppers—specifically, the black, white, and green peppercorns, all alike in being the berries of *Piper nigrum,* native to India, which look and taste different from each other because of differences in ripeness at harvest and the different ways they're processed. So-called pink peppercorns, mostly from Madagascar, are the mildly spicy, somewhat sweet berries of an ornamental plant of the *Schinus* genus that came to popularity in America with the nouvelle cuisine of the 1970s. The allspice in this mix used to be called "Jamaica pepper" and is still often called "pimento." It is most widely used as a sweet spice in baking and pickling and is a pepper only by courtesy. Its touch of fragrance in the blend is a delicious note in a multipepper mix like this, whose tingling subtlety is far removed from the ho-hum hotness of ground pepper from a tin or the monotone of fresh-ground pepper of any single sort.

The sensibly frugal may note that this specialty mixture would cost several times the price of all its ingredients if purchased in small jars from a "gourmet" source. Gift-givers may want to consider doubling or tripling the ingredients and packing the pretty blend in decorative jars. All will be wise to buy peppercorns in quantity from a spice merchant (see Mail-Order Sources, page 390).

¾ cup (4 ounces) fine black peppercorns, for example Tellicherry
⅓ cup (2 ounces) white peppercorns such as Muntok
2½ tablespoons (¼ ounce) dried green peppercorns
2 tablespoons (⅜ ounce) pink peppercorns
1 rounded tablespoon (about ¼ ounce) whole allspice, preferably small berries

Makes 1½ cups (about 7 ounces)

1. Stir all the spices together, or shake in a jar to mix. Store the blend in a covered jar airtight in a cool spot out of the light, or refrigerate for the best preservation of flavor. The blend keeps indefinitely if not assaulted by heat, light, or damp.

2. When filling the peppermill, leave a little space to permit shaking occasionally to remix the elements, as the lighter-weight pink and green peppercorns tend to "float" toward the top of the mill.

Herbs: Stretching the Summer

Perhaps because we try to have herb plants at all seasons, outdoors in summer, indoors in winter, I feel the flavor of our own harvest, put away carefully for off-season use, is hard to match by supermarket supplies. For others who feel the same and have a garden patch and/or access to locally grown herbs, here are some tips on extending the season. (See the Index for herbal blends, vinegars, jellies, and mustards, too.)

Drying Fresh Herbs

Dried and stored under good conditions (coolness, darkness, no damp), herbs will keep for up to a year.

Herbs suitable for drying are listed below. Some, you'll notice, are also listed among the good candidates for freezing a bit farther along.

Basil
(but freezing preserves truer flavor)

Bay leaves
(true bay, *Laurus nobilis;* can be ground after drying—see the Index)

Fennel leaves

Horseradish root
(scrape and slice thin; dry in low oven)

Marjoram
(sweet marjoram)

Mint

Oregano

Rosemary

Sage

Sweet woodruff
(a pretty ground-cover plant that is the soul of May wine and similar punches)

Tarragon

Thyme

Harvesting herbs and preparing them for drying: If the herb is a flowering one, cut the branches or sprigs before the flowers open. Harvest all herbs before the heat of the day comes on. Only if the plants are dusty should the herbs be rinsed; after rinsing them, shake off all possible moisture, then roll them in a terry towel to blot them further.

Drying in bunches: This is suitable for long branches (oregano, mint, sage, sassafras, prunings of bay trees, etc.). Gather a few branches together, tie the stems loosely, and place them, head down, in a large paper bag. Tie the neck of the bag around the stems; hang the bag up-

If You'd Like to Grow Herbs . . .

For suppliers of plants, seeds, and know-how, see Mail-Order Sources, page 390.

Herbs easily grown from seed: *These include parsley, basil, sweet marjoram, oregano, fennel, cilantro (fresh coriander), summer savory, chives, Chinese chives, anise, caraway, dill, and many more.* Don't *buy tarragon seed; it produces a tasteless relative of the real thing, which does not produce seed. However, there is a tarragon taste-alike to try in addition to true tarragon—look for seed of* Tagetes lucida. *The flavorful leaves can fool you nicely, and they dry well.*

For quicker garden results: *Start with plants of*

such perennials as sage, thyme, French tarragon, mint, and others you find available. Many garden centers sell started plants of annual herbs, too.

Pot plants: *Buy a plant or two each of bay and rosemary and plan to winter them indoors unless you live on a balmy fringe of the continent. Bay plants become quite large but are kept in bounds by harvesting the tips of the branches for drying. (Try using the leaves fresh, too).*

Horseradish: *This is started from a purchased root or one begged or borrowed from a gardening friend. It goes on forever, once established.*

side down in a warm, dry, airy spot—an attic, a shed, or a shady spot outdoors. If the herbs are dried outdoors, which is fine when the weather is hot and dry, they must be taken inside before nightfall, then returned to the open air for as many days as needed. If wet weather interferes, switch to oven drying (below).

When the herbs are brittle, strip the leaves from the stems and pack them into screw-topped jars without crushing them too much. Store the jars out of the light and away from dampness or heat. Putting the jars in the freezer extends the shelf life of dried herbs considerably. Crumble or crush the herb when you're ready to use it.

Oven drying: Divide herbs into small sprigs, or strip large, thick leaves (as of bay trees) from their branches—this makes for uniform drying. Arrange the herbs on wire cake racks or mesh drying shelves if you have them and dry them at a low oven temperature (around 100°F is ideal, but up to 140°F is acceptable) with the oven door propped slightly open. When the herbs are crisp-dry (which may take only a couple of hours for delicate leaves or sprigs), let them cool and pack them as described above.

Microwave drying: With care, this works beautifully, especially if your microwave has a turntable. (I do bay leaves, tarragon, mint, oregano, and thyme, among others, this way.) Spread a double layer of *microwavable* paper towels (read the label) on the turntable or oven bottom, scatter a generous handful of herbs (not too many) over the towels, and dry them for 1 minute at full power. Rearrange the herbs and continue to dry, if necessary, in 30-second or shorter increments, checking after each power period and rearranging the herbs as necessary, until the leaves are crisp. For most kinds, about 3 minutes usually does the job. When the leaves are just right, you may find that any thick stems will not have dried, so strip off the leaves at once if this is the case. Cool and store as described.

Herbs & How-To's for Freezing

The flavor of certain herbs can be preserved better by freezing than drying. (It's assumed that a true freezer—kept near 0°F—is used, not a refrigerator's freezing compartment.) Expect frozen herbs to keep for up to 9 months. Here are some candidates for freezing and a roundup of methods to use, as well as a few alternatives to freezing.

Basil: Blanch sprigs a few seconds in boiling water, then chill them well in ice water. Pat the sprigs dry, then pack them flat in small plastic freezer bags, expel all air, and freeze them.

Alternatively, place unblanched basil leaves in a clean, dry jar, cover them with olive oil, and cover and refrigerate the jar. (The flavored oil is a bonus, used for salads.)

Or make a paste of unblanched basil leaves plus olive oil (¼ cup to each packed cup of leaves), using a blender or food processor; pack the puree in a clean, dry container with an airtight lid, leaving ½ inch of headspace; freeze. Or make and freeze Pesto (see the Index).

Chives and Chinese (garlic) chives: Bunch the spears, then slice them fine with a very sharp knife. Freeze the bits loose on a baking sheet. When they are frozen hard, pack them tightly into a clean, dry jar with an airtight lid and place it at once in the freezer. To use, scoop out the amount you want without allowing the remaining chives to begin thawing.

Cilantro (fresh coriander): Pick the leaves from the stems, then puree them in a blender with a very little water. Freeze the puree in an ice-cube tray. Unmold the cubes, pack them in a freezer-weight plastic bag, expel all possible air, seal the bag, and store it in the freezer. Average-size ice trays will make coriander cubes equivalent to about 2 tablespoons of the puree.

Dill: Mince the leaves fine, freeze them loose on a baking pan, pack quickly and firmly into a clean, dry jar with an airtight lid, and pop the jar into the freezer at once. To use, scoop out the amount wanted and replace the jar in the freezer before its contents can soften.

Fennel leaves: Same as dill.

Horseradish: Scrape fresh roots clean; wrap them airtight in plastic or foil freezer wrap, and freeze them. Grate a portion of the unthawed root as needed.

Mint: As for blanched basil.

Parsley: As for dill.

Sage: As for blanched basil.

Summer savory: As for blanched basil.

Sweet marjoram: Blanch, chill, and pack small sprigs in the same way as blanched basil.

Tarragon: As for blanched basil; or strip the leaves from the stems, freeze them loose on a baking pan, pack them quickly into a clean, dry jar with an airtight lid, and store it in the freezer.

SEED HERBS

Herbs grown for their flavorful seeds—anise, caraway, cilantro (fresh coriander), cumin, dill, and fennel, among others—should be watched like a hawk after the seeds have formed: Let the seed heads dry on the plants, but don't leave them so long that the seeds drop and scatter. It's a good idea to check daily to see which heads are ready to harvest. Stored in a cool, dark cupboard, seeds will keep for at least a year.

When the heads are ripe, clip them into a paper bag. Spread them on a tray and let them dry thoroughly in a warm airy spot out of the

JUNIPER BERRIES—WILD STUFF FOR THE HERB SHELF

In autumn, check in your garden, if you grow junipers, or look along sunny roadsides for heavily berried bushes. Pick only fat, dark-blue berries (the others are immature—juniper berries take three years to reach full flavor). Spread them on a screen or in a pan in a shady spot to dry for a few days, until they seem leathery (they will not dry completely). Store them in a capped clean, dry jar away from light and heat.

Sage Decisions

Sage suffers from a bum rap and consequent neglect in much American cookery. It is mostly associated with breakfast sausage and poultry stuffing, not with its good effect on a pork roast (rub it on before cooking, using either crumbled dried sage leaves or bottled rubbed sage), or on veal (and not just in saltimbocca), or stuffed or creamed onions, or any sauce involving tomatoes in a major way. This Italian-Style Herb Blend would be a lesser seasoning if the sage were omitted, a proposition that's easily put to the test by sampling it both with and without. Two caveats: Store sage carefully (airtight, cool, and dry) to preserve its flavor, which deteriorates easily, and use it with respect for its strong character. Fresh sage is less powerful than dried and can be used more freely; young leaves make a delicious seasoning when threaded onto the skewers with meat for kebabs, for instance.

sun, or in an oven set very low, about 100°F. When the material is thoroughly dry, fan away any loose bits of stem or leaf, then pack the seeds in clean, dry jars with airtight lids. If any sign of dampness appears on the inside of the jars after a day or two, remove the seeds and dry them further, then check the jars for dampness after repackaging them.

Italian-Style Herb Blend

As a many-flavored herbal sprinkle for finished food, this little mixture perks up dishes that need a lift, and it has unlimited uses as an ingredient, too, so it is a pantry treasure. According to my palate, it's an improvement on commercial Italian seasoning blends, which tend to lean too heavily on oregano while neglecting the more delicate herbs. It's used a lot at our house, in tomato, vegetable, meat, or seafood sauces for pasta, on hot vegetables, in salads hearty and plain green, and as a table sprinkle, where it's a godsend for anyone whose food must be prepared with no salt or with less salt than usual.

Fresh, bright-flavored dried herbs are the only kind worth using in this or any other custom blend. After you've assembled it, you can make additions at any point: For more earthiness, add more thyme, oregano, or sage; to add more aromatic character, more basil and/or mint, or sweet marjoram, would be the way to go.

¼ cup crumbled dried thyme leaves
¼ cup crumbled dried basil leaves
¼ cup crumbled dried sweet marjoram leaves
2 tablespoons crumbled dried savory leaves, optional
2 tablespoons crumbled dried oregano leaves
4 teaspoons crumbled dried rosemary leaves
3 to 5 teaspoons crumbled dried mint leaves, to taste
2 teaspoons crumbled dried leaf sage or rubbed sage
1 teaspoon Powdered Bay Leaves (page 195), optional
¼ to 1 teaspoon best-quality granulated garlic or garlic powder (not garlic salt), to taste (optional)

Makes about 1 cup

1. Combine all the ingredients and crumble them further—but don't powder them—by processing the mixture *briefly* in a blender, a mini food processor, or an electric spice mill (or a coffee mill reserved for use with herbs and spices).

2. Pack the herbs down well in a small clean, dry jar or jars. Cap tightly and store in a cool cupboard for a few weeks or, even better, in the refrigerator or freezer for months.

Many-Herbed Seasoning Salt

Salting and drying herbs works like a charm if you want to preserve the flavors of summer in a convenient seasoning mixture. This recipe, which I devised in a summer of great harvests, can be adapted to your own preferences or to the availability of the raw materials, a flexible list.

The essential elements are parsley, chives, and thyme. In addition, garlic, tarragon, and/or chervil are highly desirable, as is the touch of celery, but you may increase the basil to replace the tarragon and chervil, depending on what you like and what you have. The other ingredients are the cook's choice. You can add sweet marjoram, which is especially good with beef, if you have it. If any herb isn't available fresh, the dried herb (except for parsley and chervil) may be substituted; use one third the quantity listed.

When using this salt-based seasoning, don't add extra salt until you have tasted the food. You may find that the level of seasoning is fine without more NaCl.

½ cup coarse (kosher) salt
1 or 2 large cloves garlic, or to taste, minced or pushed through a press
1 cup (lightly packed) fresh parsley leaves (no stems)
½ cup (lightly packed) coarsely snipped fresh chives
1 to 2 tablespoons (lightly packed) fresh thyme leaves (no stems), to taste
½ cup (lightly packed) fresh chervil leaves (no stems), or replace with tarragon, or combine the two
¼ cup (lightly packed) tender celery leaves
2 tablespoons (packed) coarsely cut or torn fresh basil leaves
4 to 6 drops lemon oil or 1½ teaspoons finely grated lemon zest (outer peel only, no white pith)
¼ to ½ teaspoon freshly ground white pepper, to taste
Small pinch ground hot red (cayenne) pepper, optional

Makes about ¾ cup

One-Stop Seasoning

When herbs are plentiful, this bit of kitchencraft is an amusing project that pays off later in convenience. Both spicy and herbal, the seasoning salt can be hotted up (add more garlic and/or pepper) or given a sweeter edge by including more tarragon, chervil, or basil, or more of all three.

1. Measure the salt, garlic, parsley, chives, and thyme into the workbowl of a food processor. Chop everything rapidly with on-off pulses of the machine until the herbs are in fine bits. Add the remaining herbs and lemon oil or zest, being careful to pour the lemon oil, if used, onto the ingredients rather than the surface of the bowl. Pulse the machine again, scraping down the sides of the bowl once or twice, until the herb bits are tiny. The mixture will be green and damp.

2. *If you have a food dehydrator:* Smooth the paste onto one or more of the plastic sheets used for drying fruit leathers. Dry in the machine, beginning with a temperature of 135° to 140°F. Check after an hour, stir the paste if it is drying unevenly, and continue drying at a slightly lower temperature until it is bone-dry.

To dry the paste in an oven: Cover a cake rack with tightly pinned fine-woven cheesecloth or muslin. Spread the paste on the cloth and dry it in an oven set at 140°F (or its "keep-warm" temperature) and leave it until it passes the dryness test.

3. Place the dried mixture in the workbowl of a food processor. (Or a mortar and pestle can be used for this step.) Add the pepper and the optional hot pepper. Pulse the machine (or pound the mixture in the mortar) until the texture is uniform.

4. Store in a tightly covered clean, dry jar in a cool cupboard or, even better, in the freezer. The seasoned salt keeps for months if not allowed to become damp. Use in soups, salad dressings, stews, and casseroles whenever fresh herbs are unavailable.

Fenugreek, Obscure but Versatile Herb

With its odd name meaning "Greek hay," this Asian and Mediterranean plant yields spicy seeds, tender young sprouts, and leaves used in cookery, and it is also grown as animal fodder. The seed of fenugreek (methi) *is an indispensable seasoning in India and the Mideast, and it is often included in commercial curry powders. Fenugreek seeds should be toasted* lightly *before grinding—overtoasting makes them bitter. Plain or toasted, good-quality fenugreek has a fragrance that indicates another and surprising culinary use—the seeds are the source of imitation maple flavoring.*

Mild Curry Powder & Variations

On the Indian subcontinent most cooks have never heard of the commercial "curry powder" blends so popular in the West. Their way is to compound from scratch the medley of spices, herbs, and other seasonings suitable to each dish. However, North Indian cooks sometimes keep on hand spice mixtures of their own devising, no two alike, called *masalas;* these are often sprinkled over finished dishes. The "curry powder" below, which is more fragrant and "sweet" than hot, is modeled on *garam masalas* and is used as Western cooks are accustomed to use curry powder. (I may get in trouble over this!) It has been worked out to please our household, which has not been blessed with palates that can tolerate very hot seasoning. It's easily modified to other tastes.

To increase piquancy: Add ground hot red (cayenne) pepper, starting with ½ teaspoon or so, and/or increase the black pepper. Or remove the seeds from a few small dried hot red peppers (some kinds of these are ferociously hot) and toast the peppers with the whole spices in step 1 below. Other "hot" additions: 2 teaspoons of mustard seed (toast it with the whole spices); additional ground ginger. The sky is theoretically the limit.

To emphasize fragrance and flavor: Add more of the "sweet" spices—cinnamon, coriander, cardamom, allspice, and/or cloves—or add a little mace.

For color: If a brighter golden tint appeals, increase the turmeric, whose main function is to add color. Turmeric may be omitted if you choose.

Other wrinkles: Include 2 or 3 bay leaves when grinding the spices; include a tablespoonful of fenugreek seed in the toasting step; include a tablespoonful of sweet or hot Hungarian paprika (or more, to taste) in the final mixture. In other words, suit yourself.

For preparing the seasoning, a spice mill (or a small coffee mill, kept just for spices) will achieve the finest grind, but a blender can be used; it will be necessary to scrape down the sides of the container repeatedly to promote a uniform grind.

6 tablespoons (about 1 ounce) whole coriander seed
4 tablespoons (about 1 ounce) cumin seed
6 (about 1 ounce) 2½- to 3-inch sticks of cinnamon
1 tablespoon (about ¼ ounce) whole black peppercorns
1 rounded tablespoon (about ¼ ounce) whole green or white cardamom pods
1½ teaspoons whole cloves
1 tablespoon ground turmeric, or to taste
⅜ teaspoon ground ginger
2 big pinches (about ⅛ teaspoon) ground allspice

Makes about 1 cup

1. Toast the whole spices (coriander seed, cumin seed, cinnamon, peppercorns, cardamom, and cloves, plus any such extras as dried hot peppers, mustard seed, or fenugreek seed) in a small heavy skillet over medium heat, stirring, until the spices are hot and fragrant and *lightly* toasted, perhaps 3 or 4 minutes; avoid overdoing this. Remove and cool.

2. Grind the whole spices in small batches in a spice mill, trying for fine texture.

3. Stir the batches of freshly ground spices together with the turmeric, ginger, and allspice. If the texture is uneven, sift through a medium-fine sieve, or grind everything together again.

CARDAMOM

Not to be found on every kitchen shelf, cardamom is one of the most seductive of spices, once tasted never again neglected. It nestles at the heart of Indian cooking, but its usefulness extends to countless Middle Eastern, North African, and European dishes, especially northern European and Scandinavian baked goods. An ancient spice, it is wonderful in fruit dishes (it flavors both Holiday Keeping Cake and Cranberry Preserves with Orange & Cardamom; see the Index), and a few of the seeds, crushed or ground, will put new interest into slow-baked rice pudding. Ground cardamom is convenient to use but it quickly loses flavor, so it's better to buy the green pods (for most cooking uses) or white pods (preferred for baking by some experts). Store them in a capped jar and shell out and crush or grind the intensely fragrant seeds just before they're needed.

4. Pack tightly into a clean, dry 1-cup jar, cover tightly, and store in a cool, dry cupboard for 3 months or for 6 months in the refrigerator. Like all spices, the mixture will keep its liveliness longer if it is kept in the refrigerator.

Powdered Bay Leaves

Spice packers used to offer jars of ground bay leaves, but it's been a long time since I've spotted this useful preparation in a shop. So I grind my own, a simple job for the little electric spice mill I use for many other seasonings as well. (Equally effective is a small coffee mill that has a horizontal, or "windmill," grinding apparatus. A blender will also do.) Be aware that a huge pile of dried bay leaves will reduce to a small jar of powder, so this project is most feasible if you have bay plants or if you buy leaves in bulk from a spice specialist.

Tips: Remove any stems, which are hard to reduce to powder, and crumble the leaves roughly before starting to grind them. Grind enough bay leaves for a tiny jarful at a time, as the powder doesn't hold onto its flavor as long as whole leaves.

Pack the powder firmly into a small clean, dry jar, cover tightly, and store away from heat and light for a few months.

Weights & Measures

The curry powder recipe opposite gives both measures and weights, the latter for the convenience of cooks who have a small kitchen scale. Those who don't use a scale might consider investing a few dollars in one—it's much easier to weigh out 4 ounces of solid vegetable shortening onto a scrap of waxed paper placed on a scale, for instance, than to pack ½ cup of shortening into a measuring cup, scrape it out, and wash the cup.

Provençal Herb Blend

(Herbes de Provence)

Here's a quickly made but luxurious seasoning that's the work of mere minutes if you have on hand a supply of good, fresh basic herbs plus lavender (if you want to include it, which I do). *Herbes de Provence* is one of the most distinctive classic blends, called for in many recipes originating in the south of France.

This version of the blend has been worked out for my own tastebuds. Looking into other cooks' preferences, I have found formulas that differ wildly, some including tarragon, chervil, mint, and/or orange peel and some including sweet spices (nutmeg, cloves) and pepper, but all are basically faithful to the warm, sunny herbal flavors of southern France. All demonstrating, yet again, that no blend will be perfect to all palates. Pleasing yourself, after trying the recipe as written, is the way to go.

1 tablespoon whole coriander seed
1 teaspoon fennel seed
1½ tablespoons crumbled dried thyme leaves
1½ tablespoons crumbled dried rosemary leaves
1 tablespoon Powdered Bay Leaves (page 195)
1½ tablespoons crumbled dried basil leaves
1 tablespoon crumbled dried savory leaves
2 teaspoons dried lavender flowers, optional but recommended
1 teaspoon crumbled dried oregano leaves, preferably Greek

Makes about ½ cup

1. Using a mortar, a spice grinder, or a mini food processor, crush or grind coarsely the coriander and fennel seed; reserve.

2. Combine the remaining ingredients and crush or process them *briefly*, just to reduce any coarse pieces a bit; don't grind the mixture to a powder. Add the coriander and fennel and stir well to mix.

3. Pack the seasoning into a clean, dry jar and cap it tightly. It will keep for several months in a cool cupboard, or even longer in the refrigerator or freezer.

Some Uses for Herbes de Provence

In Provence, this mixture (in any of its uncounted versions) is rubbed onto chicken and other poultry, fish, rabbit (an estimable and neglected edible in the U.S.), lamb, beef, and pork and left for a while to lend flavor before grilling, baking, or roasting. The herbs are also used in sauces and stews and in the filling for stuffed and baked summer squash or zucchini, tomatoes, and eggplant.

Quatre Epices

"Who's counting?" is the question when making this classic (but very varied) spice mixture. Blends such as the two that follow, usually called *quatre épices* regardless of how many spices (and herbs) they contain, are golden spoonfuls for seasoning meaty preparations such as pâtés, meat loaves, sausage mixtures, sauces, and stews. Once you have made a supply of either seasoning (or better yet, both), you'll take them from the shelf very often.

Quatre Epices, Basic

⅓ cup whole peppercorns (all white, or half white, half black)
4 teaspoons ground ginger
4 teaspoons (lightly packed) freshly ground nutmeg
1 teaspoon whole cloves

Makes about ½ cup

Place the spices in a spice mill (or a small coffee grinder dedicated to spices only) and grind them to a fine powder. (If you must use a blender, double the recipe so the blade will have enough volume to work well.) Sift the mixture through a fine sieve. Pack it tightly into a

small clean, dry jar and cover tightly. Stored away from heat and light in a cool cupboard or pantry, this mix will keep its zip for 6 months.

Quatre Epices, Enhanced

The ingredients for Quatre Epices, Basic, above
2 average-size (about 2 inches each) sticks of whole cinnamon, broken up
4 medium-large bay leaves, crumbled
1½ tablespoons crumbled dried thyme leaves
1 teaspoon mace blades (whole mace), crumbled before measuring
½ teaspoon whole allspice

Makes about ⅔ cup

Combine all the ingredients and grind them fine in a spice mill (or a coffee mill kept for spices); if necessary, work in batches. (Or use a blender, which will work well with this volume of ingredients.) Sift the spices through a fine sieve and pack the mixture tightly into a clean, dry jar or jars. Cover tightly and store away from heat and light. The blend will keep for 6 months in a cool cupboard.

What's In a Name?

The word "spice" has lately come to mean almost any seasoning put into a dish except, possibly, salt. "Spices" originally meant the exotic seasonings shipped to Europe from the Orient and did not apply to domestically available green herbs and herb seeds. Careful writers and cooks still observe the difference, although the line must have become blurred quite a while back, at least in the case of Quatre Épices. That name is accurate when only spices are used (as in the basic recipe here), but when an enhanced version contains herbal material, the totality is still called épices. *I can live with that, but surely there is little excuse for a TV chef who announces that she/he is putting "onions and other spices" into a dish.*

The Bouquet Garni

Ready-to-use herb bundles for seasoning stocks, sauces, stews, and soups can be purchased, but it's a simple proposition to prepare a supply for your own use or for gift giving. You'll notice that parsley isn't included in these bundles, although it is one of the three classic elements of the basic bouquet garni (or "faggot of herbs"), together with thyme and bay leaf. That's because dried parsley is sadly lacking in flavor, so it's much better to add fresh sprigs, preferably of flat-leafed or Italian parsley, when the bouquet goes into the pot. You can tie the parsley to your basic bouquet or leave it loose to be fished out at the end.

Bundling the bouquets: Use soft string to tie firmly together a big sprig of dried thyme and a bay leaf (or two or more of either, if they're small). Leave generous ends of string so parsley can be added to the bouquet when you're ready to use it.

More handily: Bundle thyme leaves and crumbled bay leaf, plus any additions (see those suggested below) into squares of cheesecloth and tie into a little bag shape with string. Leave ends of string long enough to secure other seasonings—parsley, a celery top, or a sprig of any other fresh herb you want to add at the moment of use.

Alternatives to cheesecloth: Purchased cloth bags with drawstrings, made just for this purpose, are reusable and convenient. Also convenient, but not reusable, are the bags made of filter paper sold for filling with your own choice of tea. Both are kitchen-shop items not likely to be found at the supermarket.

Some Herb Combinations

Each bouquet starts with bay leaf and dried thyme. Fresh parsley is added at the time of use. To add garlic, impale a whole clove or cloves on a toothpick, which makes it easy to retrieve before serving.

For beef: Add a sprig or two of dried celery leaves (to dry, leave celery tops in an oven at "keep-warm" temperature until they're crisp), plus dried sweet marjoram and/or dried savory and a *tiny* bit of rosemary if you like it. A single clove is a good inclusion for meats, and a scrap of dried orange or tangerine peel is a traditional Provençal addition.

For fish stock or fish soup: Add a dried fennel branch or a little fennel seed, plus dried celery leaves.

For poultry: Add dried tarragon. If you grow lemon thyme, use a little in bouquets for poultry.

For pork: Add sage or fennel. Other possibilities: sweet marjoram or rosemary.

For tomato sauces: Omit the bay leaf and add basil and/or oregano. Dried celery leaves are good too.

Other possibilities for other dishes: Consider peppercorns, dried onion, a little hot red (cayenne) pepper, or any other appropriate herb or spice all easily added to a bagged bouquet.

Dried Seasonings to Avoid

Most commercially dried herbs are satisfactory to use if they haven't been shelved too long, but some aren't worth the trouble of bottling, much less the price they're sold for. High on the no-no list of near-tasteless dried seasonings: parsley, chervil, bell peppers (a personal prejudice), coriander (cilantro), and fines herbes *(because the aforementioned tasteless parsley and chervil are the mainstays of this mixture). Dried chives would formerly have made the condemned list, but nowadays dried chives are usually freeze-dried and excellent.* A hedge-note: *If any of the seasonings denounced above should turn up in freeze-dried form, they'd be worth trying.*

Toasted Sesame Salt

The simple Japanese seasoning called *goma shio* adds both saltiness and nuanced nuttiness to stir-fried or steamed vegetables, rice, and even small pasta shapes (orzo and thin noodles come to mind). It's a good sprinkle for salads or raw vegetables, too, as a replacement for plain salt, and we like it as a subtle seasoning for baked or gently broiled chicken halves. It really shines as the topping of your own Sesame Crackers (see the Index).

Either hulled white sesame seed or black sesame seed, which is harder to find and more assertive in flavor, can be used. Proportions of sesame and salt in the mixture depend on the maker's taste. Formulas range from 24 parts sesame seed (8 tablespoons) to 1 part (1 teaspoon) salt, at one end of the scale, to 3 tablespoons sesame seed to 1 tablespoon salt at the other. Made in the 6-to-1 proportions given here, the *goma shio* seems just right, but you can suit yourself about the degree of sesame savor you prefer.

1 tablespoon coarse (sea or kosher) salt
6 tablespoons hulled sesame seed, either white or black

Makes about ⅓ cup

1. Heat a heavy skillet until medium-hot. (Use a deep pan if you have a choice, as the seeds hop about while toasting.) Add the salt and stir it until hot, about 1 minute. Add the sesame seeds and stir constantly until they are golden and fragrant. Remove from the pan at once and cool.

2. Grind the mixture in a Japanese mortar (*suribachi*) if you have one, or in a spotlessly clean spice grinder or coffee mill. Spoon the *goma shio* into a clean, dry jar and store it in a cool spot for up to a few weeks or, even better, in the refrigerator or freezer for up to several months.

The Colors of Sesame

White, brown, or black, sesame seeds are about half oil (important to the world's cooking), and after they have been toasted lightly, they're packed with nutlike flavor. Sesame, said to be native to India, has been known to all major cuisines and some minor ones since antiquity; it's especially treasured in the Orient (roasted sesame oil is a flavoring staple) and the Middle East (think of hummus *and* tahini, *or* tahina*). Experts consider that flavor differences exist between seeds of various colors, and tasting could be helpful in deciding if the experts are right. White seed—be sure it is labeled "hulled"—is more widely available than the black, which is most likely to be found in Asian and Middle Eastern groceries.*

Two Salt-Free Seasonings—A Versatile Herb Blend & A Rub for Roasts

Salt-free herbal seasonings that would cost a pretty penny at a shop are a snap to stir together, using a spoonful of this herb and that spice from a reasonably well-supplied kitchen shelf.

When you're adding zest to low-salt meals or seasoning sauces, salads, vegetables, and casseroles with the herb blend, remember the value of adding a few drops of lemon juice. Use the rub for roasts of beef or pork. (See the Index for other rubs, which can be prepared without salt if you wish.)

These mixtures may be varied endlessly to suit individual liking, so the experimental cook may want to try adding other herbs or substituting one for another.

Salt-Free Herbal Blend

1 teaspoon crumbled dried oregano leaves
1 teaspoon crumbled dried sweet marjoram leaves
1 teaspoon crumbled dried thyme leaves
1 teaspoon crumbled dried savory
1 teaspoon finely crumbled dried leaf sage or rubbed sage
½ teaspoon crumbled dried tarragon leaves
1 tablespoon freeze-dried chives or dried onion bits, optional
1 tablespoon best-quality granulated garlic or garlic powder (not garlic salt)
1 teaspoon freshly ground black or white pepper, or to taste
½ teaspoon freshly grated nutmeg or ground mace
¼ teaspoon ground hot red (cayenne) pepper, or to taste

Makes about ¼ cup

Mix the herbs and spices thoroughly, then pack the mixture into a small clean, dry jar and cap airtight. Store out of direct light at room temperature for up to a few weeks, or keep the jar in the freezer to retain the flavors almost indefinitely.

Salt-Free Seasoning Rub

Rub this blend generously into all surfaces of a cut of pork or beef up to 12 hours before it's due to be roasted, enclose the meat in a plastic bag, and let it rest in the refrigerator. If time permits, let the meat return to room temperature before it is cooked.

3 tablespoons freshly ground black pepper
3 tablespoons crumbled dried oregano leaves
1 tablespoon high-quality granulated garlic or garlic powder (not garlic salt)
1 tablespoon sweet Hungarian paprika
2 teaspoons ground turmeric
1 teaspoon crumbled dried leaf sage or rubbed sage
¼ to ½ teaspoon ground hot red (cayenne) pepper, to taste, optional

Makes about ½ cup

Grind all the ingredients together in a mortar with a pestle, or place them in a heavy bowl and rub them together with a spoon. Pack the mixture in a clean, dry jar, cover it airtight, and store it in a cool cupboard for a few weeks, or in the freezer for several months.

Salt Philosophy

Unless it's indicated for reasons of health, leaving salt out of food is not something I'd normally advocate. However, there are many people for whom a lower-salt diet is a good idea or even essential and, for them, seasonings like the two on this page are helpful.

Savory Rubs for Meats, Poultry, & Fish

Whether they're called rubs or dry marinades, these mixtures of spices and herbs do good things for a whole lineup of grilled, broiled, barbecued, roasted, sautéed, or pot-roasted viands. Choose to enliven beef (steaks, kebabs, ribs, thick hamburgers, pot-roasted or slow-barbecued brisket); pork (any cut of ribs, slow-cooked butt, loin roasts, chops), lamb (butterflied and grilled leg, baked or grilled riblets); broiled, baked, or grilled sections of young turkey; and grilled, broiled, or baked split broiler-fryer chickens or Rock Cornish game hens. Then there are all the fish suitable for broiling or grilling: for seasoning these finny creatures, consider especially the chicken, jerk, and adobo rubs.

To give flavors a chance to shine, rub the dry marinade into all surfaces of the food, then refrigerate it for several hours or even overnight (for meats and poultry) or a couple of hours (fish). In a rush, an hour or two at (cool) room temperature is better than no marination at all. Just before cooking, a spritz or brushing of olive or vegetable oil (or butter, if you like) is a good idea. If your well-seasoned bird or beast is roasted in a pot, add a little more rub mixture to the gravy at the end.

Old Idea, New Name

Dry marinades have been around kitchens since roasting came indoors from the campfire, but calling them rubs is quite recent. The term is a good one, indicating, in only three letters, how to use the mixture. Choose here from generic rubs, variously compounded according to the bird, beast, or fish they're intended to season, or sample the flavors of Jamaican jerk seasoning or Mexican adobo.

Rub for Chicken, Sections of Young Turkey, Game Hens, Pork, or Fish

If you're dealing with a pork loin or some other thickish roast, be sure to prick the surface deeply after massaging it with the rub, then add more rub and work it in a bit. I like to lard such a roast with plenty of garlic slivers poked into holes a couple of inches apart. A largish piece of meat like this should be marinated overnight in the refrigerator.

¼ cup coarse (kosher) salt
3 tablespoons medium or sweet Hungarian paprika
4 to 5 teaspoons freshly ground white pepper, or half white and half black pepper, to taste
4 teaspoons dry mustard, preferably imported (Colman's, for choice)
2 teaspoons Powdered Bay Leaves (page 195)
2 teaspoons high-quality granulated garlic or garlic powder (not garlic salt)
2 teaspoons ground ginger

Makes about ⅔ cup

1. Combine everything in a blender or spice mill and whirl briefly to a uniform texture. Stored in a covered clean, dry jar in a cool cupboard, the seasoning will keep for months.

2. *To use:* Rub the mixture into the food to make a generous coating and let stand 1 to 2 hours at room temperature or for several hours, as discussed above, in the refrigerator. Spray or brush the surface lightly with olive or vegetable oil (or with melted butter, if it's more compatible with the food) before cooking.

VARIATIONS:

Rub pork chops, chicken, or ribs with soy sauce before applying the rub as described.

Fans of MSG (monosodium glutamate) may want to include a teaspoonful or two of that "flavor powder." I don't think it's needed, myself.

ABOUT DRIED GARLIC

Mass-market garlic powder can be pretty awful (as garlic salt nearly always is), but good herb and spice specialists can supply granulated garlic of superior quality. It's quite true in flavor and very useful in mixtures like these salt-free blends. In a pinch (such as a lack of fresh garlic), it's okay for general cooking too.

RUB FOR BEEF, PORK ROAST, PORK RIBS, OR BUTTERFLIED LEG OF LAMB

3 tablespoons coarse (kosher) salt
3 tablespoons medium or sweet Hungarian paprika
2 tablespoons (or more, for more pepperiness) whole black or white peppercorns, or half and half
2 tablespoons crumbled dried thyme leaves
1 tablespoon whole coriander seed
1 tablespoon high-quality granulated garlic, or slightly less garlic powder (not garlic salt)
1 tablespoon (packed) brown sugar, dark or light
2 teaspoons Powdered Bay Leaves (page 195)
2 teaspoons caraway seed
¼ to ½ teaspoon ground hot red (cayenne) pepper, to taste, optional
8 to 10 drops lemon oil or 2 teaspoons finely grated fresh lemon zest or 1 teaspoon dried lemon zest

1. Combine everything in a blender or spice grinder, carefully dripping the lemon oil, if you're using it, onto the other ingredients, not down the side of the blender jar. Whirl briefly to a uniform fine texture and store, tightly covered, in a clean, dry jar in a cool cupboard. The mixture keeps for months.

2. *To use:* Rub a generous coating onto the meat and let stand at least 1 hour at room temperature or for several hours (or overnight) in the refrigerator. Spray or brush the food lightly with oil before broiling, grilling, or baking.

When seasoning a thick chunk of meat, such as a pot roast, or a brisket to be oven-baked in foil or a covered pan, apply a coating of the rub, then pierce the meat deeply with a sharp fork and massage in more of the mixture. Refrigerate for several hours or overnight.

VARIATIONS:

You may be inspired to add a little dry mustard, dried onion, celery seed, cumin, sweet marjoram, or savory to the rub after you've tried it as written. One school of thought adds MSG (monosodium glutamate) to rubs for meat and poultry; I don't.

JAMAICAN JERK RUB FOR PORK, LAMB, BEEF, CHICKEN, OR FISH

Genuine Jamaican "jerk" barbecue really can't be carbon-copied in any place other than that lovely island, where the meat, fish, or fowl is slow-cooked over the smoldering wood of the pimento (allspice) tree. Nevertheless, because allspice berries and hot peppers are freely available here, we can enjoy good versions of jerk to celebrate the coming of Jamaican cooking to the U.S.

I first tasted jerk pork some years ago at Jamaica's Boston Bay, at a locally famous barbecue pit on a beach where we'd stopped for a swim on the way from Kingston to Port Antonio. The peppery and spicy succulence of the meat and the marvelous fragrance of allspice smoke have lingered in my memory of good food experiences.

The formula that follows draws on recollections of that and later "jerk" feasts, but it's mainly indebted to the recipes of Jamaican barbecue professionals. Besides allspice, fresh thyme is a typical ingredient in jerk seasoning, as are the especially pungent scallions and the small Jamaican peppers that are among the world's hottest. But away from Jamaica, dried thyme will do, as will supermarket scallions and hot peppers, on the theory that pretty good jerk is better than no jerk at all.

VARIATION—A TRUE MARINADE:

If you prefer a wet marinade, make the jerk paste as described, then add 2 tablespoons vegetable oil and 6 tablespoons red wine or water (or 3 tablespoons red wine or water and 3 tablespoons soy sauce). Pour over the meat or poultry and marinate for several hours in the refrigerator, turning several times. Fish should be marinated for about 1 hour. Baste the food as it cooks, using any remaining marinade.

DRY INGREDIENTS:
2 tablespoons whole allspice
2 teaspoons coarse (kosher) salt
2½ teaspoons whole black peppercorns
1½ teaspoons whole dried thyme leaves (or 3 to 4 teaspoons fresh thyme leaves, if available)
½ whole nutmeg, cracked (use a nutcracker)
½ teaspoon ground cinnamon, or a heaped teaspoon broken-up stick cinnamon

WET INGREDIENTS:
1 medium-large onion (about 6 ounces), peeled and chopped
3 large scallions, both white and pale-green parts, chopped
1 or 2 cloves garlic, peeled and sliced
1 teaspoon cider vinegar
1 teaspoon sugar
Hot peppers, to taste: Use up to 6 small hot Caribbean peppers (such as Scotch bonnet) or fresh jalapeño peppers, stemmed and seeded, veins removed (in a pinch, rinsed, seeded, and deveined pickled or canned jalapeños can be used in place of fresh peppers; use only ½ teaspoon of vinegar if pickled peppers are substituted)
A little water, if needed for pureeing

Makes enough rub for a dozen or more servings of jerk pork, beef, fish, or chicken

1. For the spice base, combine all the dry ingredients in a blender or spice mill and run the machine until the texture is uniform. Store in a clean, dry jar in the cupboard, or complete the recipe and refrigerate the paste.

2. To complete the paste for use, puree the onion, scallions, garlic, vinegar, sugar, and prepared hot peppers in a blender or food processor until smooth, adding a little water as necessary to chop the ingredients to a smooth paste. Add the dry ingredients and pulse the machine to mix. After combining, the jerk paste may be kept, refrigerated, for up to 2 weeks.

3. *To use the rub:* Rub the paste into chicken halves or sections prepared for grilling, or season chops or other pieces of pork, lamb, or beef cut no more than 1½ inches thick, or fish steaks or fillets about 1 inch thick. Allow meat or poultry to marinate for at least 4 hours in the refrigerator; 1 hour is long enough for fish. Let the food come to room temperature and grill it about a foot above a bed of ash-covered charcoal to which soaked hickory or other "barbecue" wood is added at intervals to create a light smoke. (Allspice wood is a key source of the authentic flavor in Jamaica.) Cook the food very slowly and turn it every 10 minutes or so, allowing 1½ to 2 hours for a big broiler-fryer, longer for most cuts of meat, less time for fish (keep an eye on it). All jerk should be succulent, not dry, and permeated with spices and smoke.

Oven-Baked Jerk Lamb or Chicken (Cheatin' on Some Barbecue)

This caper is for use when the weather decrees that outdoor cooking is *out.* Trim ¾-inch-thick shoulder lamb chops, removing all possible surplus fat, or cut smallish chickens into serving pieces. Smear the pieces thickly with the jerk paste, covering all surfaces. Leave to marinate, covered, for 4 hours or more in the refrigerator or 2 hours at room temperature.

Arrange the chops or chicken on a rack in a baking pan. Cover tightly with aluminum foil and bake in a preheated 350°F oven for 30 minutes, then reduce the setting to 300°F and continue to bake until the pieces are very tender, about 1¼ hours for chops or about an hour (depending on their size) for chicken parts. Baste at intervals with the juices that collect in the pan. Bake, uncovered, for a few minutes at the end.

If you possess a stovetop smoker large enough to deal with the batch, try finishing the cooking with a brief smoking over hickory or other "smoke dust" that has been sprinkled with a tablespoonful of allspice berries previously soaked in warm water during the oven-cooking phase.

Adobo-Style Seasoning Rub

For those with a soft spot for south-of-the-border flavors, this oniony, peppery blend is a natural. Its elements reflect the seasonings of the many sauced and simmered Mexican dishes made in the style called adobo, but this mixture is for grilled, broiled, or sautéed pork, chicken, or fish, not for the juicy adobos made with meat, eggs, fish, poultry, or vegetables. When using this rub, the requisite touch of tartness is provided by rubbing the food with a little lime or lemon juice before the seasoning is applied. Key lime juice is especially good (and it's available bottled, without sweetening).

Salt-Watcher's Note

I've experimented with a commercial no-salt rub containing some of the same seasonings I've used in Adobo-Style Rub and found it a great help when preparing certain dishes for people who enjoy vibrant flavors but must avoid the salt shaker. If that notion is useful, just omit the salt from this recipe.

This seasoning is also a great finishing sprinkle for beans, rice, or soup, and it's especially good worked into butter, along with a generous squeeze of lime juice, for spreading on hot corn on the cob. It's a delicious seasoning, too, on slices of eggplant brushed with oil and baked on a cookie sheet in a 400°F oven.

¼ cup high-quality dried onion bits
¼ cup crumbled dried oregano leaves, preferably Mexican
1½ tablespoons whole black peppercorns
1½ tablespoons cumin seed
1 tablespoon coarse (kosher) salt, optional
2 teaspoons high-quality granulated garlic or garlic powder (not garlic salt)
2 teaspoons whole coriander seed
½ to 1 teaspoon pure ground chile (such as ancho), or to taste

Makes about ⅔ cup

1. Combine the ingredients in a blender, food processor, or spice mill and run the machine until you have a uniform mixture. Stored airtight in a clean, dry jar in a cool cupboard, the seasoning will keep well for a couple of months or more

2. *To use:* Rub the chicken, pork, beef, or fish with freshly squeezed lime juice, then with the adobo seasoning. Let the food marinate in the refrigerator for 2 hours, then brush with oil or melted butter and grill or broil, or sauté in oil or butter.

Mushroom Essence

Designed for the freezer, this preparation came about as first aid for the terminal blandness of most cultivated mushrooms, but it also enhances greatly any dish or sauce compatible with that of wild mushrooms. Toss a cube or two into the liquid in which pot roast is braising; the gravy will be exceptional.

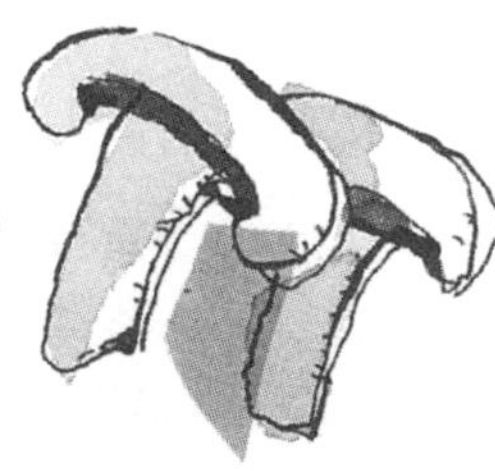

To impart extra flavor to tame mushrooms, add a cube of the essence to a half pound of mushrooms as they sauté; cover the pan and let the whole business simmer a few minutes. After that, either uncover the pan and cook the mixture longer to evaporate the liquid or use the liquid together with the mushrooms if that better suits the requirements of the dish you're preparing.

Cosseting Dried Mushrooms

These pantry treasures keep well in a closed canister on a cool shelf out of the light, but they keep even better sealed within two or three layers of sturdy plastic bags and frozen. Expel all possible air from each bag as it's closed. The mushrooms are ready to soak and use as they come from the freezer—no thawing is needed.

Hunting Dried Mushrooms

The cream of the crop of dried fungi? Boletus mushrooms, variously called boletes, cèpes, ceps, porcini, funghi secchi porcini, Steinpilze, *just "dried mushrooms," sometimes "Chilean dried mushrooms" (these last are cheaper than choicer kinds). To tell whether you've bagged true boletes, look for pores, not gills, on the undersurface of the pieces of cap. Good boletes have a rich aroma and are best preserved by bone-dry storage in a closed canister, where they'll keep for a long time.*

1 ounce (⅔ cup) high-quality dried mushrooms, preferably boletes (*cèpes, porcini, Steinpilze*, etc., also boletes marketed as "Chilean dried mushrooms")
4 cups very warm water
2 cups cold water
2 medium shallots, peeled and chopped
6 peppercorns
1 mace blade (whole mace) or pinch of ground mace
½ small bay leaf

Makes 16 cubes, about 2 tablespoons each

1. Combine the mushrooms in a bowl with the 4 cups very warm water. Push them under the surface, weight them with a saucer, and let them soak at room temperature overnight or for at least 6 hours, until they are very soft.

2. Lift the mushrooms from the liquid with a slotted spoon (save the liquid) and chop them fine, saving as much juice as possible. Combine them with the 2 cups cold water in a saucepan, bring them to a simmer, and simmer, covered, for 20 minutes, or until the bits are completely soft, almost a mush.

3. Meanwhile, to clear the soaking liquid of grit, pour it carefully into a bowl, leaving behind the sediment—this is certain to be sandy. Let the liquid settle again and again pour it off; repeat, if necessary, to be sure all possible grit has been left behind.

4. Pour the simmered mushrooms and their liquid into a sieve set over a bowl and lined with cheesecloth or fine nylon net. Press on the mushrooms to extract all possible liquid; discard the debris in the sieve. Let this second batch of liquid settle, then decant it as described for the soaking liquid; repeat if there's fingertip evidence of any remaining grit. To be doubly sure, the liquid may be finally poured through a sieve lined with dampened fine cheesecloth.

5. Combine the two batches of liquid with the shallots, peppercorns, mace, and bay leaf in a saucepan. Bring the liquid to a boil over medium-high heat and simmer it briskly, uncovered, until it has reduced to 2 cups.

6. Strain out the solids and let the concentrated liquid settle for one last time—we're still on the track of any sand that may remain despite all the valiant efforts that have gone before. Decant the cooled essence, then freeze it in an ice-cube tray. Remove the cubes from the tray and store them in an airtight freezer container or two sealed freezer bags, one inside the other. They will keep for up to a year.

Home Dairying

DAIRYING

A FEW SIMPLE DELICACIES

The word "dairying" conjures up a bucolic image of a lass milking a cow in a meadow, then trudging to the farmhouse to turn Bossie's creamy milk into butter-yellow Cheddar, but that's the wrong movie for this day and age. Our little venture into dairying is more modest, leaving the making of ripened cheeses to those with the workspace, equipment, and time for such projects; we stay with the how-to's of a few milk-based specialties that are simple enough for a novice to tackle in an ordinary kitchen.

If you play with all the recipes, you'll need no more than good milk, which should be as fresh as possible; cultured buttermilk (for some recipes), which could also be very fresh; dried milk powder (to put extra oomph into homemade yogurt and yogurt cheeses); good Cheddar or Monterey Jack to turn into potted cheese; and a gamut of seasonings, such as black walnuts, beer, herbs, spices, Worcestershire, blue cheese, olives, garlic, and capers. You'll finish up with a cluster of potted cheeses to use as spreads; yogurt both "straight" and turned into a collection of yogurt cheeses and dips; and little rounds of white cheese stored in olive oil with herbs.

For those lucky enough to be able to buy *real* whipping (or heavy) cream, not the ubiquitous ultrapasteurized kind, there is a little recipe here for crème fraîche. That slightly ripened cream keeps beautifully, making it possible to top a dessert with heavy cream or use it as an ingredient when you feel like it, without last-minute shopping or concern about the quick spoilage that plagues fresh cream unless its flavor has been massacred by ultrapasteurization.

Cheese Potted with Black Walnuts

Potted cheese—which is the old and appropriate name for a custom-made cheese mixture stored in a crock, not for "pot cheese"—is a pleasure to have on hand, especially in this version, which becomes even better as it mellows. The deep, almost gamy flavor of the black walnuts is highly compatible with the types of cheese suggested for the recipe.

The formula is flexible—the combination of Cheddar and a good Monterey Jack is especially good, but all Cheddar or all Jack would be fine, too. You could use many other firm, moderately rich cheeses such as Edam, Gouda, Colby, Jarlsberg, or mild Munster. If black walnuts aren't available, use another nut of assertive character; English walnuts, hazelnuts, or pistachios are good, but almonds are too mild.

Potted cheese will taste best if it is allowed to soften slightly at room temperature before it is served. Enjoy it on crackers or, even better, on Oatcakes (see the Index). Shave curls of the chilled cheese onto hot vegetables—broccoli or snap beans come to mind; and, for cheeseburger fans, top the cooked meat patties with a thin slice of the mixture for a snappy sauce.

¼ pound sharp natural (not processed) Cheddar, shredded (about 1⅓ cups, lightly packed)
¼ pound mild Monterey Jack cheese, shredded (about 1⅓ cups, lightly packed)
6 tablespoons sweet (unsalted) butter, slightly softened, at room temperature
2 tablespoons dry vermouth, dry sherry, or dry white wine, or more as needed
Small pinch of ground mace
½ cup black walnut meats, chopped medium-fine (English walnuts, hazelnuts, or pistachios may be substituted)
Clarified Butter (page 35) for sealing

Makes about 2½ cups

1. Beat the cheeses and butter together until the mixture is creamy and almost smooth (don't try to eliminate all texture); this is most expeditiously done in a food processor or in an electric mixer fitted with a paddle beater. Beat in the vermouth and mace. Use a little more vermouth if necessary to make the mixture slightly soft (it will become firmer with keeping). Stir in the black walnuts.

Spreading Pleasure

Using Cheese Potted with Black Walnuts as a pattern, experiment with other potted cheeses seasoned to your own taste. For example: To the cheese, butter, and liquid listed in the recipe, for a rosy paprika-seasoned spread add a little minced shallot, a minced small clove of garlic, and a good strewing of sweet, medium, or hot Hungarian paprika.

2. Pack the potted cheese tightly into small crocks or pottery custard cups. Smooth the tops and seal the cheese with a ¼-inch layer of melted clarified butter, making sure it seals to the sides of the containers. (The butter covering may be omitted if the cheese will be used within a couple of weeks.) Cover or overwrap the containers and refrigerate the cheese for up to 3 weeks. For longer storage, wrap it for the freezer and freeze for up to 2 months.

3. Thaw frozen cheese in its wrappings. Serve at room temperature. Smooth a piece of plastic wrap onto the surface of leftover cheese before covering the container and refrigerating it again.

FRESH WHITE CHEESE
(FROMAGE BLANC)

Deliciously fresh and sweet homemade white cheese, which has different names in various cuisines, is a versatile product of simple dairying, easy enough for absolute beginners. Just use the freshest available milk and buttermilk, and pay attention to your thermometer readings.

2 quarts whole milk, as fresh as possible (include ½ pint cream, if you want especially rich cheese)
2 cups very fresh cultured buttermilk
2 tablespoons strained fresh lemon juice
Salt, if desired (¼ to ½ teaspoon)
Cream, optional

Makes about 1 pound (2 cups)

1. Measure the milk into a heavy saucepan or pot, the heavier the better. Stir the buttermilk and lemon juice together thoroughly, then stir the mixture into the milk.

2. Set the pan over very low heat (it is desirable to use a heat-tamer mat under even a very thick pot) and begin to heat the milk. If you have a candy/jelly thermometer, attach it to the pan, otherwise, have at hand an instant-reading thermometer for frequent checks on the temperature. Heat the mixture slowly to a thermometer reading of 175°F. Stir the milk very gently with a pancake turner or similar flat-ended implement once or twice after it begins to thicken, stirring only two or three strokes. Once a thermometer reading of 175°F has been reached, turn off the heat and let the milk stand for 10 minutes undisturbed. Masses of white curd suspended in yellowish liquid (the whey) will appear.

OTHER LANDS, OTHER NAMES

Fresh cheeses to sample are the familiar cottage, cream, farmer's, and pot cheeses, all in many versions; Indian panir *or* paneer; *various buttermilk cheeses, which resemble cottage cheese; French Gervais (or Petit-suisse) and Neufchâtel, both cream cheeses; kefir cheese, similar to Yogurt Cheese (page 216), rich Italian mascarpone; European quark, either low-fat or somewhat richer, similar to cottage cheese; and ricotta, now in every U.S. dairy case in various degrees of richness.*

3. Line a sieve with two layers of dampened fine cheesecloth or nylon net and set it over a large bowl. Ladle the curds and whey gently into it and drain off the whey until the drip slows after a few minutes. Tie the corners of the cloth to make a loose bag and hang it over the bowl from a cupboard handle or hook. Drain the cheese for about an hour or until the consistency suits you, from creamy to somewhat firm. (Whey is great for breadmaking—I freeze it for future use.) Scrape the cheese into a bowl, cover, and refrigerate it for use within about 5 days.

4. *For soft, light cheese to serve as is* (or perhaps with preserves for dessert): Turn the drained cheese into a bowl and stir in a little salt and/or a little cream, if you wish. If a smooth texture is wanted, beat the cheese briefly with an electric mixer.

5. *To mold the cheese:* Pack the drained cheese firmly into a 2-cup bowl lined with cheesecloth. Fold over the ends of the cloth and invert the bowl onto a plate. Refrigerate to drain further for several hours or up to a day. To serve, unmold onto a dish and strip off the cloth.

Some Ways to Use the Finished Cheese

Pepper-Coated Cheese: Sprinkle the molded cheese thickly with fresh, very coarsely ground black pepper. Serve with crackers.

Herbed Cheese: Mix the freshly drained cheese with salt and pepper, plus a little mashed garlic and a handful of minced fresh herbs. A good combination is parsley, chives, and thyme and/or tarragon or basil. When most fresh herbs are out of season, the cheese will still be good if you settle for fresh parsley, frozen chives, and dried thyme, tarragon, or basil (use about a third as much dried herb as you would if it were fresh). Mold the cheese as described above and refrigerate it for several hours or overnight before serving.

Small White Cheeses in Olive Oil & Herbs: See recipe opposite.

White Cheese Spreads & Dips: For these, choose from the flavorings suggested for Yogurt Cheese Spreads & Dips (page 217).

Cheese Potted with Beer

This mellow but zippy cheese spread shares some of the character of a Welsh rabbit, thanks to its seasoning with beer and other oddments. It's quite addictive with or without a cool glass of beer, and as a good keeper, it's an excellent thing to keep on hand.

Potted beer cheese has been known to appear at breakfast at our house (delicious on toast) as well as at cocktail or snack time.

A BRANDY UPGRADE FOR POTTED CHEESE

For a variant of beer cheese, omit the mustard, beer, and Worcestershire; for the beer, substitute ¼ cup white wine, 2 tablespoons good brandy, and a little water if it's needed for good consistency. Optionally, add a pinch or two of fresh garlic minced to a paste. If you'd like to use more brandy, reduce the wine accordingly, but don't let the alcohol dominate the cheese—it's there as a complement, not a competitor.

¾ pound fine-quality natural (not process) Cheddar (choose mellow, sharp, or extra-sharp, or combine kinds to taste)
1 teaspoon dry mustard powder
⅔ cup excellent beer (it must be smooth and flavorful)
½ cup (1 stick) sweet (unsalted) butter, at room temperature
1 teaspoon Worcestershire sauce
Generous grinding of fresh white pepper
Pinch or two of ground hot red (cayenne) pepper, or a few drops of Tabasco or other hot pepper sauce
Salt, only if needed
Clarified Butter (page 35) for sealing

Makes about 2⅔ cups

1. Grate the cheese. Place it in a bowl and add the dry mustard and the beer. Stir the mixture, press the cheese down until it is covered by the beer, cover the bowl, and let it stand at room temperature for a few hours to soften (it can rest as long as overnight, if that is most convenient).

2. Place the butter in the container of a food processor or blender and beat it briefly until it is creamy. Add the beer and cheese mixture, the Worcestershire sauce, freshly ground white pepper, and red pepper or Tabasco. Process the whole business until the mixture is smooth, scraping down the bowl once or twice. Taste the "rabbit" and add more seasonings if they are needed. Whether more salt is needed will depend on the cheese. The mixture should be highly seasoned.

3. Pack the cheese firmly into one or more crocks or small bowls, smooth the top(s), cover airtight with plastic wrap or foil, and refrigerate. The spread can be stored without further covering if it will be used within 2 weeks or so. For longer storage, melt enough clarified butter to cover the potted cheese by ¼ inch and pour it over the chilled cheese, making sure it seals to the sides of the container(s). Cover snugly and refrigerate again.

4. Serve the potted cheese at room temperature for the best flavor and easiest spreading.

SMALL WHITE CHEESES IN OLIVE OIL & HERBS

These little cheese balls keep for several weeks in their bath of olive oil and herbs, gradually becoming stronger in flavor. Well drained, they are a savory addition to a cheese tray, and they are especially good on the plate beside a mixed green salad. Save the flavorful oil for making a vinaigrette or another kind of salad dressing when the cheese balls are all gone.

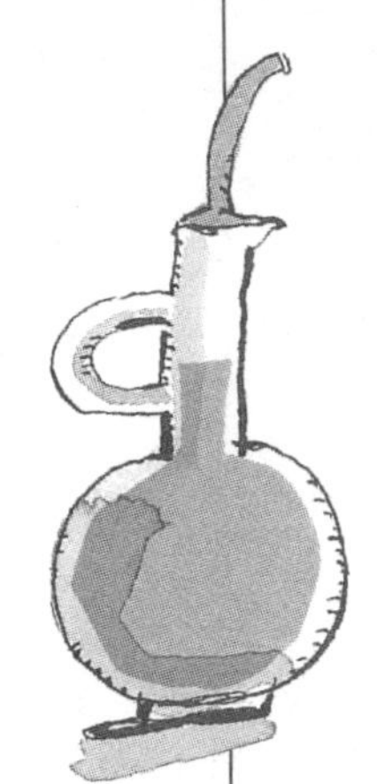

Fresh White Cheese (page 211), drained as described in step 3 of that recipe
½ teaspoon salt, or to taste
2 medium cloves garlic, slightly flattened
4 teaspoons crumbled dried rosemary
4 teaspoons crumbled dried thyme
3 medium bay leaves, torn into quarters (or use ⅛ teaspoon Powdered Bay Leaves, page 195)
2 to 4 small dried hot red peppers, crumbled (or substitute ½ teaspoon, or to taste, dried red pepper flakes)
12 to 15 whole black peppercorns, depending on size, slightly crushed
About 1½ cups olive oil
1 tablespoon white wine vinegar

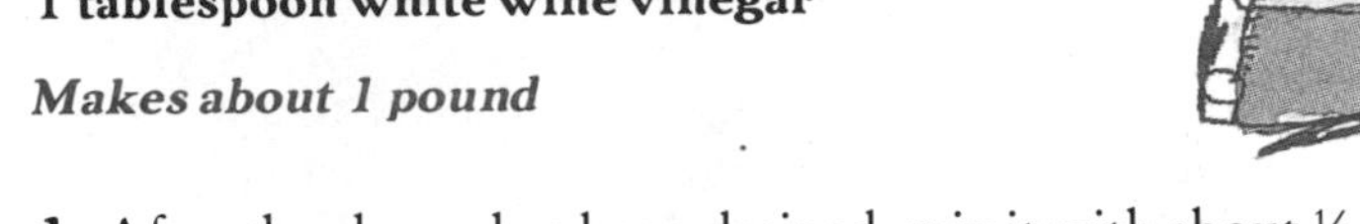

Makes about 1 pound

1. After the cheese has been drained, mix it with about ½ teaspoon salt, then drain it again in the cloth bag until it is quite firm, perhaps 3 hours.

2. Form the cheese into a flat oblong about an inch thick, wrap it in the cheesecloth, set it on a plate, cover it with a flat dish or a pie plate, and weight it with a 1-pound can of food or another object of about the same weight. Let the cheese remain under the weight for an hour or two (or it may remain in the refrigerator, under its weight, for as long as overnight).

3. Unwrap the pressed cheese and cut it into one-inch cubes; with your fingers, form the cubes into balls (don't labor over making them absolutely spherical: a little roughness is more attractive). Place the little cheeses in a clean, dry wide-mouthed quart jar as they are shaped, then drop in the garlic, rosemary, thyme, bay leaves, red pepper, and peppercorns. Pour in enough olive oil to cover the cheeses completely, then add the wine vinegar. Cover the jar with a tight lid and invert it or shake it gently two or three times to distribute the seasonings among the miniature cheeses.

4. Marinate the cheeses at cool room temperature for at least 2 days before serving them; they will keep for at least a month under such moderate conditions, but if the weather is hot, you may wish to refrigerate them. Shake the jar gently or invert it once or twice every few days to distribute the seasonings.

SMALL FRESH GOAT CHEESES, MARINATED

This marinade is also a dandy treatment for small fresh goat cheeses. The flavor of even the freshest goat cheese is more assertive than that of your own simple cheese, so you may want to increase the quantify of herbs in the marinade by half.

Controlling the Acidity of Yogurt

As remarked in the Yogurt recipe, the cook is in charge of the mildness or tartness of the finished yogurt. Beginning yogurt makers will want to keep a close eye on proceedings after the yogurt has incubated for no more than 4 hours. Refrigerate it as soon as it has "jelled" sufficiently (see the recipe directions) if sweet, mild yogurt is what you like.

Yogurt–Making It & Using It

The formula for homemade (meaning sweet and smooth) yogurt that follows gives you a choice of yogurt based on skim milk that is as low as possible in fat and cholesterol, or yogurt made with either low-fat (1% milkfat) or middling-fat (2%) or whole (4% milkfat) milk. All versions contain added dry milk powder, which improves the texture as well as the nutritiousness of the batch. All versions can be drained a longer or shorter time to any stage from creamy thickness, to near-firm creaminess, to the cream cheese–like texture of Yogurt Cheese, for which directions follow the main recipe.

Yogurt

6 cups skim milk, 1% or 2% milkfat milk, or whole milk, as preferred
6 tablespoons high-quality nonfat dry milk powder
½ cup fresh plain active-culture yogurt without additives

Makes about 6 cups

1. Whisk together the milk and dry milk powder in a large saucepan and heat the mixture slowly to simmering, stirring it almost constantly; it should reach a temperature of at least 180°F. Set aside, covered, to cool to 110°F, or until a drop feels only faintly warm when dribbled on the inside of the wrist. Remove any skin that has formed on the top of the milk.

2. Whisk the yogurt smooth in a bowl that has just been rinsed out with boiling water, then whisk in the lukewarm milk.

3. Cover the bowl and keep the contents warm: Either wrap the bowl in several layers of heavy towels; or set the bowl in an oven warmed only by a pilot light (the oven temperature should be around 100°F); or set the bowl in a pan of warm (100°F) water, overwrap the whole works in terry towels or other thick cloth to retain warmth, and replace the water from time to time to maintain its temperature; or, finally, decant the mixture into the warmed, clean containers of a yogurt-making appliance and follow the manufacturer's directions for the incubation period.

4. The yogurt may reach a custardlike consistency in as little as 4 hours, so begin to check it at that point. For the mildest flavor, refrigerate the yogurt as soon as it has coagulated softly (it will be jiggly when the container is shaken a little); it will become firmer after chilling. Letting the yogurt incubate in the warmth longer will increase its tartness.

5. Refrigerate the yogurt, closely covered and without disturbing the curd, for several hours or overnight before serving it or making Yogurt Cheese as described below. It keeps well for at least 2 weeks in the refrigerator.

YOGURT CHEESE

Even fat-free yogurt becomes creamy in texture when given this easy treatment. You can control the consistency of yogurt cheese by draining your custom-made yogurt a shorter or longer time, so you can choose any texture from that of thick sour cream to the firmness of cream cheese. Yogurt drained to the texture of sour cream makes a refreshing simple dessert when paired with fresh or poached fruit or preserves.

Yogurt Cheese can be the base of spreads and dips without number; some ideas are outlined beginning on the next page.

½ batch (3 cups) Yogurt, above, chilled overnight or longer
¼ teaspoon salt, optional

Makes about 1½ cups

1. Line a colander or sieve with a double layer of fine cheesecloth or a single layer of very fine nylon net, with a generous overhang all around. Set the strainer over a bowl.

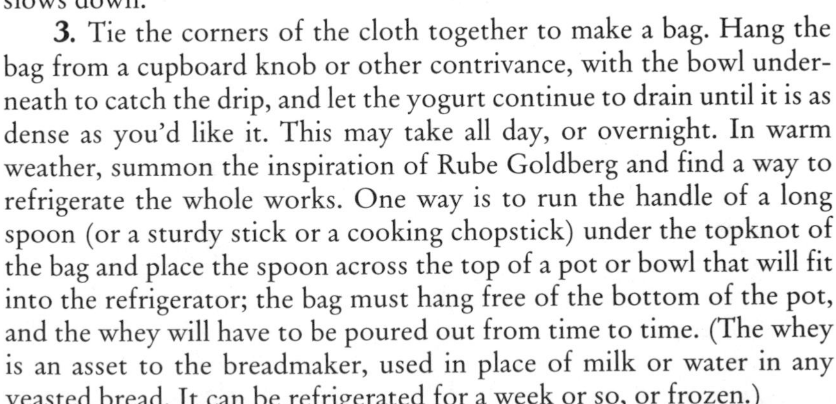

2. Stir the salt, if used, into the yogurt. Scrape the yogurt into the lined colander and let it drain for 1 to 2 hours, until the drip of liquid slows down.

3. Tie the corners of the cloth together to make a bag. Hang the bag from a cupboard knob or other contrivance, with the bowl underneath to catch the drip, and let the yogurt continue to drain until it is as dense as you'd like it. This may take all day, or overnight. In warm weather, summon the inspiration of Rube Goldberg and find a way to refrigerate the whole works. One way is to run the handle of a long spoon (or a sturdy stick or a cooking chopstick) under the topknot of the bag and place the spoon across the top of a pot or bowl that will fit into the refrigerator; the bag must hang free of the bottom of the pot, and the whey will have to be poured out from time to time. (The whey is an asset to the breadmaker, used in place of milk or water in any yeasted bread. It can be refrigerated for a week or so, or frozen.)

4. When the yogurt suits you, transfer it to a bowl and refrigerate it, covered. It will keep for at least 2 weeks in the refrigerator.

MOVE OVER, CALORIFIC CREAM

If you're keeping an eye on your family's (or your own) intake of fat, you are likely to become a fan of yogurt cheese, if you aren't already. Because the yogurt whey, which can be quite tart, has been removed, the cheese tends to be sweeter and milder than the yogurt it was made from. Whisked with a little milk, drops of vanilla, and some sugar or noncaloric sweetener, it makes a delicious "pouring cream" for desserts. Or simply sweeten the yogurt cheese lightly, add vanilla if you like, and spoon dollops onto any dessert, plain or fancy, that you'd ordinarily top with whipped cream.

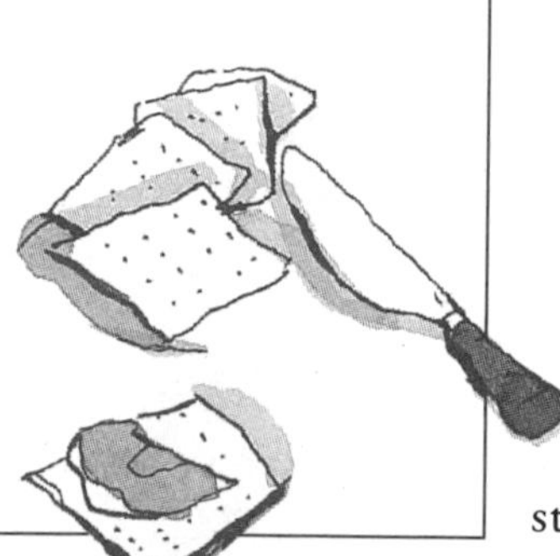

YOGURT CHEESE SPREADS & DIPS

To make spreads, add to a cupful of firm drained mild yogurt your choice of the sets of ingredients that follow, or invent a few of your own. To turn a spread into a dip, soften the mixture with a little milk or cream and increase the seasonings to taste. These mixtures keep well, refrigerated, for up to 2 weeks.

CARAWAY CHEESE SPREAD

1 cup firm Yogurt Cheese (see opposite)
4 tablespoons (½ stick) sweet (unsalted) butter, at room temperature
2 teaspoons caraway seed, crushed slightly in a mortar
A little salt, if desired
Freshly ground white pepper, to taste

Makes about 1¼ cups

Cream everything together by beating with a wooden spoon or in an electric mixer. Cover, refrigerate, and allow to mellow for a few hours, if possible, before serving.

Low-cholesterol version: Use Yogurt Cheese made with skim or 1% milkfat milk. Substitute low-cholesterol corn-oil margarine for the butter.

HERBED YOGURT CHEESE

Dried herbs can be substituted for the fresh kind in this formula (except for parsley, which must be fresh). Use about a third as much, by measure, of any dried herb as fresh, and revive its flavor by soaking in a little white wine or dry vermouth for a few minutes before using.

1 cup firm, mild Yogurt Cheese (see opposite)
2 tablespoons sweet (unsalted) butter, softened
3 tablespoons (or more) minced fresh herbs: parsley plus thyme, chives, and tarragon; or parsley plus chives and oregano or basil; or parsley and dill leaves; or any favorite combination of herbs
1 small to medium clove garlic, minced to a fine pulp
Salt, to taste
Freshly ground white pepper, to taste
Drops of fresh lemon juice, to taste
Drops of Tabasco or other hot pepper sauce, optional

Makes about 1¼ cups

Beat the yogurt with the butter until amalgamated to a cream, then stir in the remaining ingredients. Taste and add more of anything that seems like a good idea. Let the spread mellow and develop flavor for an hour or two at room temperature before serving. Refrigerate leftovers for up to 2 days.

Yogurt Cheese with Three Peppers & Garlic

1 cup firm Yogurt Cheese (page 216), mild or tart as preferred
2 tablespoons sweet (unsalted) butter, softened
Salt, to taste
1 small or medium clove garlic, minced to a fine pulp, optional
Medium or sweet Hungarian paprika, to taste (start with 1 teaspoon)
Freshly ground white pepper, to taste
2 to 3 tablespoons chopped, well-drained bottled pimientos or roasted red peppers (for a mild spread); or 1 tablespoon, or more to taste, chopped, well-drained canned or pickled jalapeño peppers (for a hot spread)

Makes about 1⅓ cups

Beat the yogurt with the butter, a little salt, the optional garlic, the paprika, and white pepper until amalgamated to a cream. Fold in the pimientos or the jalapeños (or use both for a double whammy). Let all this mellow for a while at room temperature before serving and adjust the seasonings after the mellowing period. Refrigerate leftovers for up to 2 days.

Yogurt Cheese with Two Kinds of Olives

1 cup firm Yogurt Cheese (page 216), mild or tart as preferred
2 tablespoons sweet (unsalted) butter, softened, or 1 tablespoon full-bodied olive oil
2 tablespoons chopped, pitted oil-cured black olives
2 tablespoons chopped, pitted green olives
1 to 2 teaspoons chopped drained capers, optional
Freshly ground white pepper, to taste
Few drops of fresh lemon juice, if needed

Makes about 1⅓ cups

Beat the yogurt with the butter until amalgamated to a cream, then fold in the olives, the capers, if used, and the pepper. Taste and add a few drops of lemon juice if you think the added tartness would be good. You won't need salt, thanks to the olives. Let the spread mellow for an hour or two at room temperature before serving. Refrigerate leftovers for up to 2 or 3 days.

Blue Cheese Spread

1 cup firm, mild Yogurt Cheese (page 216)
¼ to ⅓ cup crumbled blue-veined cheese (*bleu,* Roquefort, Saga, Gorgonzola, etc.)
1 medium clove garlic, minced to a fine pulp
¼ teaspoon Italian-Style Herb Blend (page 191), optional

Makes about 1⅓ cups

Beat the yogurt with the blue cheese, garlic, and herbs until amalgamated to a cream. You won't need salt because of the cheese. Let mellow for an hour or two at room temperature before serving. Leftovers will keep, refrigerated, for 2 or 3 days.

Crème Fraîche

Here's a reprise, for anyone who needs a reminder, of the best way to keep a supply of heavy cream on hand for cooking or for serving with desserts.

Fresh, pasteurized heavy cream has a short life, once brought home; "ultrapasteurized" cream keeps well, but it tastes so awful that there is little temptation to use it. That leaves the field open to this mildly tart approximation of the French original, which is heavy cream ripened by letting it stand after adding a culture.

Crème fraîche, used in place of heavy cream in cooking, resists curdling better than uncultured cream, and it can also be whipped.

1 pint (2 cups) heavy (whipping) cream, *not* ultrapasteurized
¼ cup cultured (dairy) sour cream from a fresh batch

Makes a little more than 2 cups

1. Warm the heavy cream over low heat in a thick-bottomed saucepan, stirring, until it is just blood-warm (a drop on the inside of your wrist will feel neither warm nor cold), 90° to 95°F on an instant-reading thermometer.

2. Whisk in the sour cream thoroughly. Pour the mixture into a jar has been rinsed out with boiling water. Cover the jar and let it stand until the cream has ripened enough to thicken lightly, which will take 8 to 12 hours at moderate room temperature, longer in a cold room.

3. Stir the cream and refrigerate it, covered, for 8 hours or more before using it. It will thicken further as it chills. Refrigerated, it keeps for 2 weeks or more.

Calling All Cows

Why, oh why, has real cream vanished from our ken? Is there nowhere *in the nation where good, thick, sweet cream has survived, cream that has been spared the flavor-destroying process of ultrapasteurization? At the time of writing, in an area where there are as many upscale food shops as supermarkets, I'm unable to find such cream.* Help.

PICKLE PICKS

PICKLING

SWEET & TART, SALTY, PUNGENT, & SPICY TIDBITS

Any student of food history or culture who knows his/her (pickled) onions is bound to agree that a pickle barrel would be a great vessel for a metaphorical voyage around the world of food: There seems to be no country without a passion for some sort of pickles—broadly defined as vinegared, fermented, and otherwise emphatically soured edibles. (Even the Inuit of the Arctic regions contrive to ferment certain viands to a state that could be called pickled.) Thus we find that the United States, with its spaghettilike tangle of food traditions from scores of countries, is correspondingly rich in pickles.

To offer a reasonably broad sampling in this brief chapter, new items have been added to some cherished recipes republished from *Fancy Pantry* to create something like a pickle potpourri. Besides the melting-pot American entries, some of whose origins have grown rather dim (crisp green beans pickled with dill, or Very Hot Pickled Green Peppers, or pickled mushrooms or celery or carrots), there are a couple of fully French contributions, Tart Pickled Cherries in the French Style and Cold-Pickled Cornichons. The countries of North Africa inspired Translucent Salt-Cured Lemons; the British Isles contributed the notion of Pub-Style Pickled Shallots or Baby Onions (at home, bigger onions are often pickled); and for those who like the zesty impact of ginger, there is the Japanese specialty of pickled young ginger (*beni-shōga*), wonderful with many foods besides sushi and sashimi, alongside which most adventurous eaters first meet this vinegary delight.

With these and other destinations in mind, it's time to hoist sail and launch onto the briny deep of the pickling crock, a *bon voyage* guaranteed.

Tarragon-Pickled Flame Grapes

Seedless red grapes of the Flame variety are notable for their crisp sweetness. Delicious to eat from the bunch, they are equally delectable when preserved in the form of this delicate and unusual little relish.

Serve the firm pickled grapes as you would cornichons, alongside pâtés or other charcuterie or simple cold meats, with ham or chicken sandwiches, and with hearty salads. I like to nest them in clumps of watercress as a garnish for roast pork or roast chicken. They're also compatible with baked or broiled fish.

This recipe also works for the green-white Thompson seedless grapes that are more readily found in markets than Flame. If you pickle white grapes, be sure they are ripe enough to be sweet but not overripe to the point of softening.

At the end of the jarful of grapes, the pickling liquid can be used in place of tarragon vinegar in salad dressings. Just allow for the salt and sugar in the liquid.

3½ cups firm-ripe Flame variety or other seedless grapes, stemmed
8 sprigs (about 4 inches long) fresh tarragon (or substitute tarragon vinegar for the white wine vinegar listed below)
1½ cups white wine vinegar (substitute tarragon vinegar if you are not using the fresh tarragon listed above)
3 tablespoons sugar
1½ teaspoons pickling salt or other fine pure salt (no additives)

Makes 1 quart

1. Rinse the grapes and drain them, then roll them in a towel until they are well dried.

2. Rinse the tarragon and pat the sprigs completely dry on a towel. Place the tarragon in a sterilized (page 282), dry quart jar. Add the grapes, which should come just to the shoulder of the jar, leaving the neck clear.

3. In a bowl, stir together the vinegar, sugar, and salt until the sugar and salt have dissolved. Pour the solution over the grapes, which should be covered by at least 1 inch so they can "swim" freely. (If necessary, add a little more vinegar.) Remove any air bubbles by running a long thin knife blade or a cooking chopstick around the inside walls of the jar. Cap the jar with a sterilized new two-piece canning lid, according to manufacturer's directions.

4. Store the grapes in a cool, dark cupboard for at least a month before serving them. They will keep for up to a year.

Year-Round Tarragon

Tarragon is seldom sold fresh in markets, but it's not difficult to grow; so here's a plug for planting a few clumps of this incomparable herb. I like Tarragon-Pickled Flame Grapes best when they're prepared with fresh tarragon, but if you have tarragon vinegar on hand (see the Index) you can use some of that to pickle the grapes any time they're in season (much of the year, seemingly).

You can also preserve tarragon sprigs in vinegar for use as an herb: Just place the clean branches in a jar, filling it loosely but putting in more than you'd need for flavoring tarragon vinegar. (If the tarragon must be rinsed, pat or spin off all possible moisture). Fill the jar with white wine or plain white vinegar, cap it, and store it out of the light in a cupboard. Drained, the tarragon is ready to strip from the stem and use in sauces and dressings in the same way as the fresh herb. As long as its texture is good, it's usable.

Translucent Salt-Cured Lemons

(Preserved Lemons Moroccan Style)

So what does the questing cook do with preserved lemons? Not being especially qualified to turn out North African dishes, I use this delightful zesty condiment in ways that would be unrecognizable in Morocco, but never mind—just taste, you'll like. Almost anywhere a (sharp) fresh lemon or its peel can go, these mellow (nonsharp) wedges can go better.

Most often the translucent peel alone is used after lemons have been transformed by the salting process, but perhaps you'll want to experiment with using the pulp as well, as it is also rich in flavor. In general, use some of the lemon, chopped, in any sauce or dressing that would be all the better for the blessing of lemoniness without the sharpness of the fresh fruit. I especially like chicken baked with a scattering of preserved lemon, but it's also great in other sauced meat dishes and in salads of almost any description, especially those involving a starch (pasta, rice, tiny potatoes), or in coleslaw based on any kind of cabbage, including Chinese. Before grilling fish or poultry, try rubbing chopped peel into the flesh; leave to marinate for at least half an hour before wiping the surface, brushing with oil, and broiling.

Wherewith Shall It Be Salted?

The savor of salt is something people crave, but all salts aren't the same—it's intriguing to taste the very real differences between them. To investigate the many kinds of salt, a curious cook might sample sea salt (many kinds and grades), rock salt, kosher salt, coarse French common salt, fine plain and iodized common table salt, and pickling salt. The recipes in these pages expect you'll use table salt when no type is specified; but if a recipe says "pickling salt" (which is free of the additives that would make pickles cloudy), that salt should be used. When substituting kosher salt for table salt, increase the measurement by one-third.

3 or 4 fully ripe, juicy medium lemons
About 4 tablespoons coarse (kosher or sea) salt
Juice of about 3 additional lemons, or more if needed
Oil for topping the jar, optional

Makes about 1 pint

1. Scrub the lemons well, rinse, and wipe dry. Cut a thin slice off the stem end, using a fine serrated "tomato" knife if you have one. Stand the lemon upright and cut it into 4 wedges, stopping short of the base so the segments remain attached. Spread the wedges open gently and cut each lengthwise in half, again leaving the slices attached at the base. Sprinkle the flesh generously with salt, close the segments, and place the lemon in a clean, dry pint jar, preferably of a roundish rather than tall shape. Repeat with the rest of the lemons, stopping when the jar is almost full when the fruit is pressed down firmly. Pour in enough lemon juice to cover by half an inch or so. Cap the jar and place it on the counter where you'll remember to shake it daily. If the level of juice drops below the top of the fruit, add more lemon juice.

2. The lemons are ready to use when the peel has become translucent, which will take at least a week; they're even better if left to mellow longer. Refrigerated, the lemons keep for months. If you wish, float a layer of olive or other oil on top of the jarful to exclude air during storage—I usually don't bother. If in time the flavor and color change noticeably, toss the contents of the jar and start again.

3. To use, scrape the salty pulp from the lemon segments, if you wish (but try using some along with the peel), rinse the pieces, and chop.

Tart-Pickled Cherries in the French Style

Preserved in vinegar with only a touch of added sugar and salt, these cherries (*griottes* to the French) are, like cornichons, a perfect accompaniment for pâtés and other forms of charcuterie. (Interestingly enough, American cooks long ago had their own version of pickled cherries, prepared without tarragon and called "cherry olives." A French connection?)

If fresh tarragon is not at hand, simply replace the white wine vinegar with tarragon-flavored white wine vinegar. Beware of any commercial brand that begins with distilled white vinegar. These can be harsh.

1 pound ripe but firm Bing, Lambert, or other sweet cherries (sour cherries may also be used)
5 or 6 sprigs of fresh tarragon, each at least 4 inches long
2 cups high-quality white wine vinegar
¼ cup sugar
2 teaspoons fine pickling or other pure salt (no additives)

Makes 1 quart

1. Sort the cherries, discarding any with soft spots or blemishes, then rinse and drain. Clip the stems to ½ inch. Roll the cherries in a towel to remove all possible moisture.

2. Rinse the tarragon sprigs and pat them dry. Drop them into a sterilized (page 282), dry 1-quart canning jar. Add the cherries, which will not quite fill the jar.

3. Stir together the vinegar, sugar, and salt in a stainless-steel or other nonreactive saucepan. Heat to simmering, stirring until the sugar and salt have dissolved. Remove from the heat and cool completely.

4. Pour the cooled liquid over the cherries, being sure to cover them completely. Remove any air bubbles by running a long thin knife

Griotte Idea

Spending a few minutes pickling cherries this way pays off when an unusual tracklement is needed to accompany special dishes. Drain enough cherries to garnish the platter bearing a Mousse of Chicken Livers or perhaps Country-Style Pâté with Black Walnuts (see the Index), and have some more on the side for second tastings.

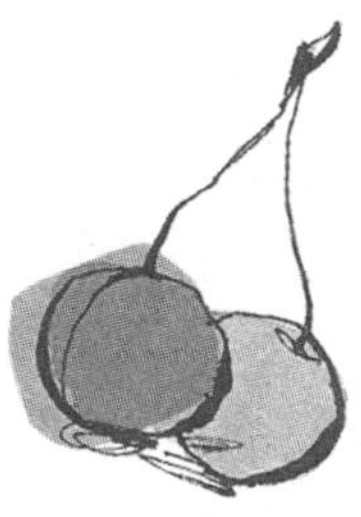

blade or a cooking chopstick around the inside walls of the jar. Add more liquid if necessary, leaving ½ inch of headspace. Seal the jar with a sterilized new two-piece canning lid according to manufacturer's directions. Store the cherries in a cool cupboard for at least a week (even longer is better) before serving them. They will keep for a year or so.

Very Hot Pickled Green Peppers

The natural ferocity of crackling-hot small green peppers is only slightly tamed by pickling, even with the further benison of olive oil in this recipe, so . . . fair warning. These are *hot.* For those who can take it, they are fine companions for everything from a deli corned-beef sandwich to Tex-Mex, Cal-Mex, or other Southwestern specialties. Use these as an ingredient, too, when a recipe calls for pickled jalapeños.

Let these little peppers mellow (if that's the word) in the jar for a month or more before sampling them.

2 pounds small fresh hot green peppers, preferably oval-shaped
4 cloves garlic (or more, if you like), peeled
8 whole allspice
24 whole black peppercorns
1 large bay leaf, torn into quarters
2 cups white (distilled white) vinegar
2 cups water
2 teaspoons salt
4 tablespoons olive oil, or as needed

Makes 4 pints

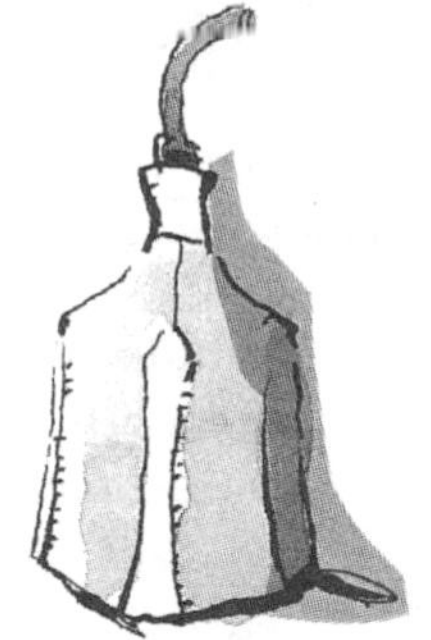

1. Rinse and drain the peppers; trim stems to a stub. Pack the peppers into 4 clean, dry wide-mouthed pint canning jars, dividing them equally. As the peppers are packed, scatter among them a share of the seasonings: In each jar place 1 garlic clove, split; 2 allspice berries; 6 peppercorns; and a quarter of a large bay leaf.

2. Combine the vinegar, water, and salt in a stainless-steel or other nonreactive saucepan and heat the mixture to simmering. Pour the hot solution over the peppers, covering them completely and leaving 1 inch of headspace. Remove any air bubbles by running a long thin knife blade or a cooking chopstick around the inside walls of the jars and add liquid

THE PEPPERS TO PICKLE

The world is full of hot peppers, whether they're called chiles, chili peppers, or another name, and what kinds will come to any given market (and almost certainly be offered sans *identifying labels) is a toss-up. Fortunately, it isn't important to use only one kind of hot green pepper (or* chile*) for pickling as described in this recipe. If you have the chance to choose among peppers, look first for jalapeños, then caribes (most often golden, not green), serranos (thin, small, extremely hot), or Fresnos. Pass up peppers that aren't shiny-skinned and firm.*

if necessary to maintain the inch of headspace. (If there isn't enough pickling solution to cover the peppers, make more in the same proportions; no harm will be done timewise for this.) Pour enough olive oil into each jar to cover the surface of the liquid, about 1 tablespoon.

3. Seal the jars with new two-piece canning lids according to manufacturer's directions and process for 15 minutes in a boiling-water bath (page 283). Cool, label, and store. The peppers are good to eat after 2 weeks, but they will be better after a month's rest. They will keep for months in a cool pantry. Refrigerate after opening.

Crunchy Pickled Onion Rings

Flavor, crunch, and color are what these onion rings have going for them: Their oniony flavor is spiced up just a bit, their crunch is preserved by minimal processing, and their bright gold color comes from a touch of turmeric.

• Serve these well chilled, with (or in) sandwiches, with cold cuts, pâté, or just cold meat loaf or sliced chicken or roast meat, and with any hearty salad, whether it involves seafood, meat, poultry, cheese, vegetables, rice, or pasta.

• When the rings have been consumed, save the pickling syrup to add pizzazz to dressing for potato salad or any other vegetable salad. The syrup also makes a splendid glaze for freshly cooked corned beef (poached, not boiled). See the sidebar for how-to's.

1½ pounds small to medium mild onions
18 whole cloves
18 whole black peppercorns
3 teaspoons mustard seed
1½ teaspoons celery seed
2 cups white (distilled white) vinegar or cider vinegar
½ cup water
1 cup sugar
2 teaspoons salt
1½ teaspoons ground turmeric
⅛ teaspoon ground cinnamon

Makes 3 pints

1. Peel the onions and slice them ¼ inch thick; separate the slices into rings. Divide the onion rings among 3 clean, dry pint canning jars.

Glazed Corned Beef

Place hot, fully cooked corned beef in a baking dish with fat side up. Drizzle it generously with syrup left over from Crunchy Pickled Onion Rings, then sprinkle it with brown sugar. Bake at 425° to 450°F, basting occasionally with more pickling syrup, until the coating has bubbled into a crust, about 15 minutes. Let the beef rest for 20 minutes before slicing it. Good hot or cold.

2. To the onions in each jar add 6 whole cloves, 6 peppercorns, 1 teaspoon mustard seed, and ½ teaspoon celery seed.

3. Combine the vinegar, water, sugar, salt, turmeric, and cinnamon in a stainless-steel or other nonreactive saucepan. Heat to boiling, then simmer 2 minutes.

4. Fill the jars with the hot liquid, leaving ¼ inch of headspace. Remove any air bubbles by running a long thin knife blade or a cooking chopstick around the inside walls of the jars and add liquid if necessary to maintain the ¼ inch of headspace.

5. For refrigerator storage: Let the jar(s) cool uncovered, then cover with a doubled sheet of plastic wrap and a cap, any kind, that fits the jar. Refrigerate for at least 2 weeks before serving. The pickles keep (and improve) for many months in the refrigerator.

For sealed storage in a cupboard: After step 4, seal the jars with new two-piece canning lids following manufacturer's directions. Process for 10 minutes in a boiling-water bath (page 283). Cool, label, and store the jars. Let the pickles mellow for about a month before serving them. They will keep for a year or more in a cool cupboard.

Noticing Peppercorns

When a recipe doesn't specify either black or white peppercorns, you can suit yourself. Experts consider white peppercorns, which are prepared by soaking and hulling mature black peppercorns, to be somewhat "hotter" in character and richer in flavor than peppercorns with the dark outer layer in place. Among black peppers, larger-berried sorts (such as Tellicherry) have been allowed to ripen longer than other widely marketed kinds. (Peppercorns are picked green and dried in the sun.) Common agreement seems to put Malabar pepper at the top of the list for flavor. Peppercorns keep well, so it pays to order a generous supply from a spice specialist and store them in a jar.

Ground pepper from the supermarket? It has more heat than flavor, is often stale, and may contain stems, dust, and other debris.

Pickled Celery Sticks

The ivory-colored inside ribs of celery look most elegant done this way, but the fleshier green outside ribs have more intense flavor going for them and make more substantial sticks.

Besides snacking on these or serving them with drinks, add them to an antipasto plate, or chop a few into a seafood or potato salad.

Crisp fresh celery (you'll need most of a big bunch)
6 cups water
1 or 2 bay leaves
½ lemon, sliced
Salt, as needed
2 tablespoons sugar
2 large cloves garlic, peeled
1 teaspoon mustard seed
¼ teaspoon hot red pepper flakes, or more to taste
Whole black peppercorns, about 12
2 whole cloves
1½ cups white (distilled white) vinegar plus ¾ cup water, or 2¼ cups white wine vinegar or Japanese rice vinegar

Makes 2 pints

1. Trim ribs of celery into lengths (about 3 inches) that will fit into wide-mouthed pint canning jars. (If you're using the fat-bellied type of short jar with a clamp closure, trim the celery accordingly.) Using a paring knife and a swivel peeler, remove all possible strings from the celery. Cut the lengths into strips about ½ inch wide. Using a jar as a measure, prepare enough celery to fill both very snugly (the celery will shrink during blanching).

2. Heat the water to a boil in a nonreactive saucepan and add the bay leaves, lemon slices, and 1 teaspoon salt. Boil the liquid for 2 minutes, then add the celery and return to a boil. Begin timing and boil for 2 minutes, no more. Drain the celery in a colander, then spread it out to cool until it is comfortable to handle.

3. Place in each of 2 clean, dry wide-mouthed pint canning jars ½ teaspoon salt, 1 tablespoon sugar, 1 clove garlic, sliced, ½ teaspoon mustard seed, ⅛ teaspoon hot red pepper flakes, half a dozen black peppercorns, and 1 whole clove. Arrange half of the celery sticks in each jar and pour in enough of the mixed vinegar and water to submerge the celery. Cap the jars and shake and rotate them to distribute the seasonings.

4. Refrigerate the celery and allow it to mellow for a few days before serving, shaking and rotating the jars when you think of it. The celery keeps indefinitely under refrigeration.

Pub-Style Pickled Shallots or Baby Onions

The pickled onions so beloved by our British cousins are a sturdy item, traditionally preserved in strong malt vinegar with or without spicing and served with the pub meal of crusty bread and cheese called a ploughman's lunch.

For some tastes, malt vinegar is a bit harsh, so my pickled shallots (a departure from the pattern) or small onions are put up in a combination of vinegars, cider and white wine (or rice). Let these mellow in the jar for a good while (I'd say 3 months) before serving them.

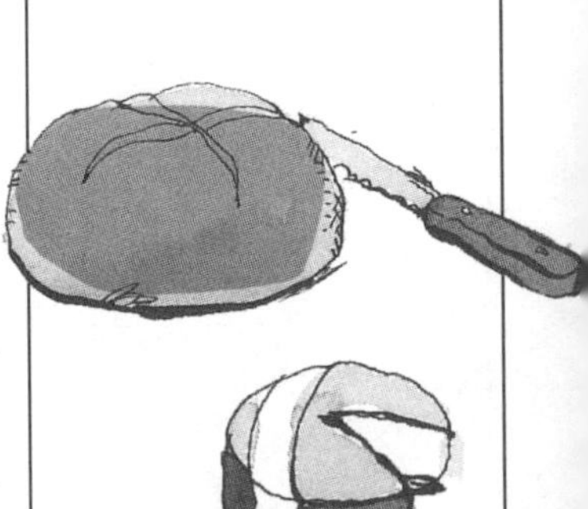

If you'd like to try malt vinegar, which used to be a curiosity to be read about in cookbooks, it can be found among other special vinegars in good groceries. Invented in Great Britain and made from a kind of beer or ale or from malted barley, it's popular in its homeland for pickling. However, it really comes into its own as a condiment—sprinkled on fish and chips, it's a national institution. Try it, if you buy it, on all-American cooked greens, too, in place of the traditional cider vinegar.

2 pounds firm, juicy shallots, preferably of uniform size, or small (up to 1 inch) white-skinned onions
Salt: 2 tablespoons pickling salt or other fine pure salt (no additives) for step 1, plus 1 to 2 teaspoons for the pickling solution
3 bay leaves, coarsely crumbled
2 teaspoons whole black peppercorns
1½ teaspoons whole allspice
1 teaspoon mustard seed
½ teaspoon hot red pepper flakes, or 3 or 4 tiny dried hot peppers
3 cups cider vinegar
1½ cups white wine vinegar or Japanese rice vinegar

Makes 3 pints

1. Place the shallots in a heatproof bowl and pour enough boiling water over them to cover them well; let stand for 2 to 3 minutes. Pour off the water and run cold water into the bowl to cool them quickly, then drain in a colander. Trim away the base and slip off the papery skin and any leathery layers inside the skin.

2. Return the shallots to the bowl and mix them well with the 2 tablespoons salt. Cover and let stand at room temperature overnight or for about 8 hours, stirring them once or twice if you think of it.

3. At the same time, combine 1 to 2 teaspoons additional salt with the bay leaves, peppercorns, allspice, mustard seed, hot red pepper flakes, and the two vinegars in a stainless-steel or other nonreactive saucepan. Heat the pickling solution to simmering and simmer for 2 minutes, then remove from the heat and let stand, covered, until you are ready to finish the pickling.

4. Strain the pickling solution into a preserving pan and set it over low heat. Meanwhile, rinse the shallots repeatedly with cold water, then roll them in a spanking-clean towel until well dried. When the pickling solution simmers, add the shallots and raise the heat until the mixture boils. Cover the pan, lower the heat, and simmer until the shallots are about half-cooked, with a firm core and translucent outside (test samples with a sharp fork or knife tip), about 5 minutes

5. Divide the shallots among 3 hot, clean pint canning jars and fill with the pickling solution, leaving ¼ inch of headspace. Cover with new two-piece canning lids according to manufacturer's directions and process for 10 minutes in a boiling-water bath (page 283). Cool, label, and store the jars. Let the shallots mellow in a cool cupboard for about 3 months before serving them. They will keep for at least a year.

Alternative Storage

Use jars sterilized by boiling in water to cover (see page 282). Fill as described in step 5, removing any air bubbles by running a long thin knife blade or a cooking chopstick around the sides of the jar, then seal with sterilized lids according to manufacturer's directions, without further processing. Store in a cool cupboard for about 3 months before serving. They will keep for at least a year.

Second Alternative

If refrigerator space is available, pickled shallots in sterilized jars, covered with sterilized lids (or 2 sheets of plastic wrap, then a clean lid) may be kept in the refrigerator to mellow for the requisite period before serving. The storage expectancy is the same.

Quick-Pickled Green Beans with Dill & Hot Pepper

Tart and spicy, a refrigerator pickle that's quickly prepared and soon ready to enjoy, these nibbling beans can be served within a couple of days of being arranged in their jars. They repay patience, though, rewarding you with more dilly flavor and pepperiness as time goes by.

1½ pounds firm, fresh medium or small snap beans
3 large cloves garlic, peeled
3 bay leaves
3 small dried hot red peppers, or 1½ teaspoons hot red pepper flakes, or more to taste
1½ teaspoons dill seed
1½ teaspoons dried dill weed
2 cups Japanese rice vinegar or high-quality white (distilled white) vinegar
2 cups water
2 tablespoons pickling or other pure salt (no additives), or less if desired
1½ tablespoons sugar

Makes 3 pints

1. Trim the ends from the beans, rinse, and drain them. If any beans are too long to fit into the jars, halve them. Steam the beans just until crisp-tender, testing often after 5 minutes' cooking; the time required will depend on their age and size. Rinse copiously with cold water to stop the cooking; drain.

2. Into each of 2 clean, dry straight-sided pint canning jars slice a clove of garlic and add a bay leaf, a hot pepper, or one-third of the hot pepper flakes, ½ teaspoon dill seed, and ½ teaspoon dill weed. Arrange the beans vertically in the jars, packing them lightly.

3. In a bowl, stir the vinegar and water with the salt and sugar until dissolved. Pour over the beans to cover them completely, almost to the jar rims. Cap the jars and shake to distribute the seasonings. Refrigerate until wanted. The pickled beans will be ready in 2 days or so but develop fuller flavor over time. They'll keep for many weeks in the refrigerator.

To Stir a Martini

Back when the Martini cocktail was the number-one drink at parties, it was chic for a while to garnish the glass with a pickled green bean, often from a jar labeled "dilly beans." The beans and the drink got along fine, as I recall, and if cocktails continue to make a comeback against the tide of white wine and mineral water, perhaps the pickled bean will rise again.

Carrot Sticks Pickled with Dill & Hot Pepper

For these spicy bites, use the ingredients and follow the directions for Quick-Pickled Green Beans with Dill & Hot Pepper, substituting 2 pounds of sweet, firm carrots for the beans. For this project I'd use short, fat, clamp-top pint jars (for looks), but wide-mouthed straight-sided pints are okay if that is what you have.

Scrape or pare and trim the carrots and cut them into ¼-inch sticks about 3 inches long. When you steam the carrots, be sure to undercook them: they should give up only a bit of their hard-heartedness without actually softening, so test them often with the tip of a sharp knife after they have steamed for a few minutes.

The carrot sticks are ready to eat in 2 days or so but, like the beans, they will develop more flavor as they rest in the jar, and they will keep for many weeks in the refrigerator.

Makes 3 pints

Two Kinds of Mushrooms, Pickled

Little button mushrooms make a pretty pickle, but their flavor is not in the same league with that of *porcini,* the best of the (expensive) boletus mushrooms. So here we persuade dried *porcini* to lend their fine taste and earthy color to an agglomeration of formerly bland buttons that's fit to grace the finest antipasto platter.

For the flavoring element, look for dried mushrooms labeled *cèpes, porcini, boletus,* or *boletes.* They are sometimes to be found marked "dried European mushrooms," and those imported from Chile can be quite good, too.

There is a bonus from this creative pickling—the flavorful cooking liquid makes a fine base for a soup or a sauce. If you don't choose to pickle the pieces of porcini, save them for recycling in soup.

2 pounds small, firm white button mushrooms
1 ounce (about 2/3 cup) dried *porcini* or other boletus mushrooms
4 cups water
3 teaspoons salt
1½ cups red wine vinegar
1½ cups white (distilled white) vinegar
3 large cloves garlic, peeled and halved
2 dozen whole peppercorns, black or white
6 medium bay leaves
9 whole cloves
3 large mace blades (whole mace)

Makes about 3 pints

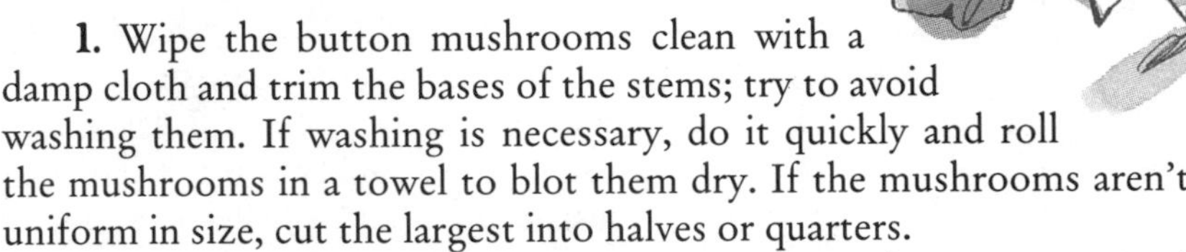

1. Wipe the button mushrooms clean with a damp cloth and trim the bases of the stems; try to avoid washing them. If washing is necessary, do it quickly and roll the mushrooms in a towel to blot them dry. If the mushrooms aren't uniform in size, cut the largest into halves or quarters.

2. Combine the mushrooms, *porcini,* water, and 1½ teaspoons of the salt in a large saucepan. Bring the liquid slowly to a boil and simmer the mushrooms uncovered until the buttons are tender, 10 to 15 minutes. Pour the whole business into a bowl, let the mushrooms cool, then cover and refrigerate overnight.

3. Drain the mushrooms in a colander set over a bowl (be sure to save the delicious liquid). Either remove the pieces of boletus and add them to the reserved liquid (puree this for a superb soup), or leave them mixed with the buttons; although not handsome, the pieces of boletus are delicious.

4. Combine the remaining salt with the two vinegars, the garlic, peppercorns, bay leaves, cloves, and mace in a stainless-steel or other nonreactive saucepan and bring to a boil. Cover the pan and simmer for 5 minutes.

5. Meanwhile, divide the drained mushrooms among three pint canning jars. Divide the seasonings from the boiling-hot pickling liquid equally among the jars, then pour the spiced vinegar over the mushrooms. The liquid should cover them well; if not, add a little more vinegar (either kind) or water as required. Let the mushrooms cool, cover the jars, and refrigerate them to mellow for at least 3 days before serving them. They keep well for up to 6 months in the refrigerator.

6. At serving time, drain the mushrooms and, if you like, toss them with a little good olive oil and garnish them with a sprinkling of minced parsley.

Young Ginger Pickled in the Japanese Fashion

If you enjoy the pungent ribbons of vinegar-pickled ginger that accompany sushi in Japanese restaurants, you don't need to dine out to taste this relish, now that fresh ginger is stocked almost everywhere, not just in specialist greengrocers' shops.

Try to obtain the tender young ginger rhizomes called "stem ginger," usually available for only a few weeks after midsummer and most likely to be found in communities where Asian cuisines are flourishing. Stem ginger has skin that is barely a skin at all—it is as baby-tender as that of a new potato—and the juicy rhizomes are further identifiable by the pink-tinted bases of the leaf sheaths that show where the stems of the ginger plant have been trimmed off.

If stem ginger is not to be had, shop for very fresh ginger "hands" with smooth, silky skin and no sign of withering or mold. The fibrous cores of older ginger, left when the tender outer flesh has been prepared for pickling, can be used to make Fresh Ginger Jelly (see the Index).

The method of preparation in the following recipe is hybridized from Shizuo Tsuji's recommendations in his fine book *Japanese Cooking: A Simple Art* and the directions for Chinese-style pickling in *A Popular Guide to Chinese Vegetables*, by Martha Dahlen and Karen Phillipps. The technique for dealing with elderly ginger is my own. I prefer Japanese rice vinegar for pickling ginger, but ordinary supermarket white vinegar will do.

Not Just for Japanese Food

Rosy-pink shavings of picked ginger go well with all manner of foods in addition to sushi and sashimi. For a start, try pickled ginger with cold meats, alongside sandwiches or hearty salads of potatoes, pasta, or rice, and with cooked or briny raw seafood—try nibbling a bit of ginger after swallowing each icy-cold oyster or clam on the half-shell. You may want to save the pickling liquid from the ginger to add zing to fruit salad dressings.

1 pound tender young ginger (stem ginger), or at least twice as much mature ginger
1½ tablespoons pickling salt or other fine pure salt (no additives)
1½ cups Japanese rice vinegar or white (distilled white) vinegar
6 tablespoons water
6 tablespoons sugar

Makes about 1 quart

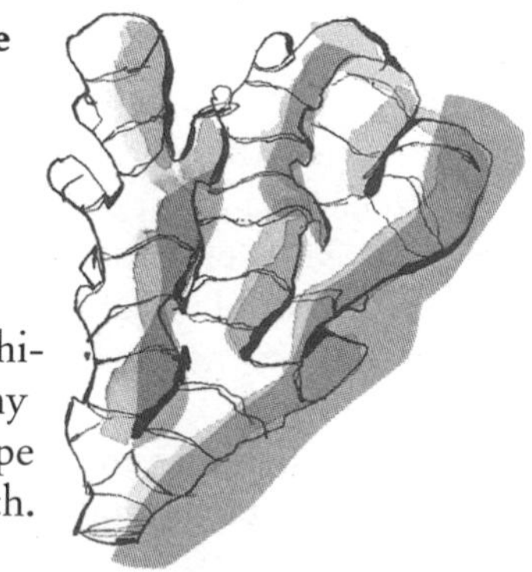

1. *To prepare stem ginger:* Break the rhizomes apart at the joints and trim off any bruised, withered, or callused portions. Scrape off the skin and papery bits of leaf sheath. Rinse the pieces and pat them dry.

To prepare mature ginger: If the ginger is the mature and fibrous kind, peel it, using a swivel-bladed peeler, or scrape off the skin. Shave the tender outer layer into thin lengthwise strips, using the peeler; stop making strips and move to another area when the blade begins to encounter tough fiber.

2. Combine the stem ginger sections or strips of mature ginger with the salt in a ceramic, glass, or stainless-steel bowl; turn the pieces to coat them with salt. Cover and set aside for 24 hours, turning the ginger in the liquid a few times when you think of it.

3. Drain the ginger; discard the liquid. Dry the pieces thoroughly with paper towels. Place the ginger in a clean, dry quart jar or 2 pint jars (it isn't necessary to use canning jars).

4. In a bowl, stir together the vinegar, water, and sugar until the sugar has dissolved. Pour the liquid over the ginger, covering the pieces by at least ½ inch. Cover with a lid and refrigerate. The ginger strips will be ready to eat in 2 or 3 days; the knobs, depending on their size, will require at least a week to pickle. The ginger will keep, refrigerated, for at least a year.

5. To serve the strips, simply drain them. To serve pickled ginger knobs, shave the thinnest possible lengthwise slices from them, using a swivel-bladed peeler. If a fine white sediment appears in the liquid at any point, disregard it—it is harmless starch precipitated from the ginger, not a sign of spoilage.

COLD-PICKLED CORNICHONS

The French cucumber pickles called *cornichons* are a longer-running favorite than ever at our house, a decade's worth of cucumber crops having passed since this recipe made its debut.

For cornichons you need to get your hands on tiny cucumbers, and that is not always easy. Grow your own, if you have a sunny garden spot, planting the seeds of gherkins (which are small and prickly) or of a more easily available cucumber variety meant for pickling. Pick the fruits when they're no more than a couple of inches long; one-inch specimens make especially fetching pickles. If your neighborhood has farmers who sell fresh vegetables, ask at a farm stand about ordering a batch of specially picked small cukes in early summer. Or offer to pick your own, if the farmer will allow it. The tiny cucumbers are worth working for.

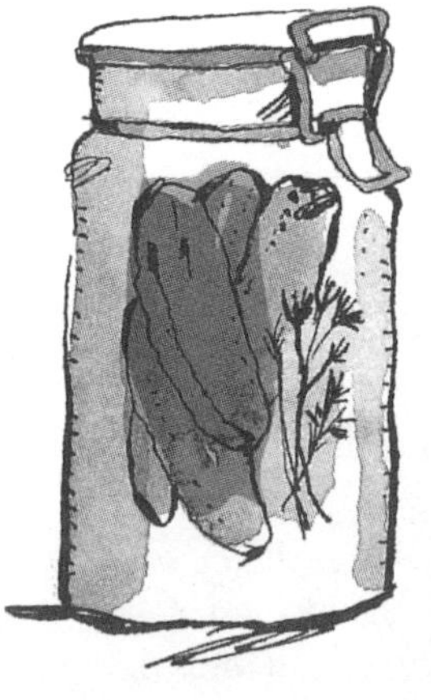

Begin pickling the cucumbers the day they're picked, if possible; don't delay starting more than 24 hours, for the crispest pickles. After that, enzyme action begins working against you.

CUTTING CUCUMBERS DOWN TO SIZE

This is a desperate measure to use when tiny cucumbers, the best kind to prepare as cornichons, aren't to be had for love or money. Buy the freshest, firmest, and smallest cucumbers you can find of the Kirby variety—they're sold widely, unwaxed—and do as follows: Trim off the stem and blossom ends after scrubbing the cucumbers. Cut each lengthwise into quarters or sixths, depending on how thick they are, and proceed to treat them as the recipe directs. A shorter period of salting will be sufficient, as the strips are less protected by skin and lose their surplus liquid quite readily. The pickles are softer than classic cornichons. I store them in the refrigerator, not the cupboard.

2 to 2½ quarts (about 3 pounds) freshly picked tiny cucumbers or gherkins, as small as possible
¾ cups coarse (kosher) salt or a generous ½ cup pickling salt (or other fine pure salt, no additives)
3 tablespoons white (distilled white) vinegar
About 10 bushy sprigs (4 to 6 inches long) fresh tarragon
3 large or 5 medium shallots, peeled and sliced
1½ teaspoons mustard seed
1½ teaspoons whole peppercorns, black or white
½ teaspoon whole allspice, optional
3 whole cloves, optional
4 cups white wine vinegar, or more if needed

Makes about 2 quarts

1. Cover the cucumbers with cold water and wash each with a soft cloth, being careful to remove any remnants of blossoms; do not scrub them roughly. Rinse and drain. Mix the cucumbers gently with the salt in a ceramic, glass, or stainless-steel bowl. Cover with a cloth and leave them for 24 hours at room temperature, turning them occasionally in the brine that will form.

2. Drain the cucumbers, then swish them through 2 quarts of cold water mixed with the distilled white vinegar. Drain the cucumbers again, then wipe each gently dry with a soft cloth.

3. Scald and drain 2 hot, clean quart jars or a half-gallon jar or crock. Dividing the ingredients equally, layer the cucumbers and seasonings in the containers, starting with a few tarragon sprigs in the bottom. Pour in enough white wine vinegar to cover the pickles by at least an inch—2 inches if possible. (The amount of vinegar needed will depend on the shape of the containers and the size of the vegetables.) Cover the containers with their caps or with two layers of plastic wrap, held in place with rubber bands.

4. Leave the pickles in a cool, dark spot for a month. They are then ready to use. At that point they may be packed into smaller jars, together with the seasonings, if you wish. Sealing isn't necessary, but the jars should be covered snugly and stored in a cool, dark cupboard. With care and luck, cornichons will keep for a year; if assaulted by light and/or heat, they will tend to soften after a shorter time.

Fruit, Herb, & Wine Vinegars, Many Mustards, & Infused Oils

BIG FLAVORS~

SPECIAL VINEGARS, MUSTARDS, & OILS

Customizing a cupboardful of great flavors is what you're doing when you make the condiments and seasonings gathered here. If you haven't explored this particular byway of kitchencraft, try a recipe or two—perhaps one of the many Fruit- & Berry-Flavored Vinegars, or Roasted Garlic Paste—and you'll find the processes simple and the results rewarding.

Then, perhaps, on to the mustards either smooth or grainy, the many herbal vinegars, the seasoned oils and oils for seasoning, including Three-Flavor Oil for Stir-Frying, and even your own wine vinegar, simpler to make at home than might be thought. . . .

The special things you've put up in your bottles and jars will add palatal pleasure to your cookery clear across the board: salads, sandwiches, casseroles, soups, stews, roasts, and most especially those in-between dishes that are the fruits of sheer invention. Your seasonings will be doubly helpful if you're an enlightened cook who relies less than you used to on the richness of fats, butter, and cream to give interest to food.

Store-bought specialties in the categories covered by this chapter—some of them excellent, a few slightly gimmicky—have been crowding onto fancy-food shelves in response to a growing appreciation of tastier (but lighter and more healthful) food. Like the handsomely packaged commercial versions, your "big flavors" will not only add zip to your table, they'll make dandy gifts for food-loving friends, especially if you choose those that keep well. (Each recipe indicates shelf life.) And there's a bonus, not to be sniffed at by the sensibly frugal: The cost per gift will be a pittance compared with the price tag on the competition.

FRUIT- & BERRY-FLAVORED VINEGARS

Creating bright and pretty custom-made vinegars flavored with berries or fruits is one of the more delightful kitchen capers, one that's especially rewarding because little time and no experience is required. Success is almost unavoidable if these simple suggestions are followed for creating irresistible additions to your seasoning shelf.

The vinegars to use: My own first choice is a vinegar based on white wine, Champagne (for a splurge), or rice (Japanese rice vinegar, also called rice wine vinegar). The vinegar should have at least 5% acidity (check the label). Distilled white vinegar is satisfactory; mild red wine vinegar is highly compatible with raspberries or other berries of decided character (strawberries are too delicate). To my taste cider vinegar has too much flavor of its own to be used with most fruits, but it works quite well with citrus, as noted below.

The fruits and berries to use: Almost all berries will flavor vinegar deliciously. Red raspberries come first to mind, but don't ignore blackberries, blueberries (especially wild ones, which can be purchased frozen), huckleberries, strawberries, cranberries, red currants (or the rare black currants), and gooseberries. And then there are the less common berries—loganberries, dewberries, boysenberries, tayberries, and marionberries, if you're fortunate enough to obtain them.

Among everyday fruits, consider, for openers, apricots, peaches, nectarines, pineapple, tart plums of any color, and sour cherries. And don't neglect the citrus bins: Vinegars flavored with oranges, tangerines, limes, or lemons are especially simple to prepare (see Citrus Vinegar on page 240).

Using exotic fruits to flavor a set of vinegars is still on my list of things to try. I do believe that such no-longer-uncommon fruits as mangoes, papayas, and well-ripened kiwi fruit (beware tasteless kiwis) would be wonderful in vinegars to sprinkle over mixed-fruit desserts and fruit salad plates.

Getting ready: Neatness (meaning cleanliness) counts when working with fruits, which are spoilage prone. Equipment such as bowls, jars, or crocks for steeping or storing the vinegar should be made of nonreactive material such as glass, china, or plastic (stainless steel is fine for brief use—for mixing, for example, but not for storage). Wash, rinse, and air-dry such items, or dry them with a fresh towel. Prepare jar lids the same way. When you reach the stage of decanting the vine-

TO SWEETEN OR NOT TO SWEETEN

Old-time directions for making fruit vinegars call for a lot of sugar (and so do some modern recipes). Omitting all but a touch of the sweetening, as recommended in the pattern recipe here, makes the vinegar much more versatile—it can be used for saucing nonsweet dishes, for instance—and it's simple enough to add sweetening separately to any vinegar-enhanced dish that requires it.

gar for storage, it's a good idea to sterilize bottles or jars and their tops (including corks, which should be brand-new; see page 283).

Preparing the fruit: Sort out any oversoft or moldy or damaged specimens. If berries are very clean (raspberries usually are), try to avoid rinsing them. If fruits or berries are dusty or sandy or sticky from touching crushed neighbors, rinse them well and dry them by rolling gently on paper towels or tea towels. Small blemishes may be cut out of peaches or other large fruits. Peel fruit if you wish and stone when necessary. Crush berries in a bowl with a potato masher, or chop either fruit or berries by pulsing a food processor on and off a few times—avoid making a puree, though.

Making Fruit Vinegars: A Pattern

The single-steeping method: As a general rule, allow 2 cups of your chosen basic vinegar to a pound (about 2 cups, measured after crushing) of prepared fruit (hereafter meaning either fruits or berries).

Combine the vinegar and fruit in a squeaky-clean, dry nonreactive container such as a jar or crock and cover it tightly with a lid. If the cover is metal, interpose a double layer of plastic wrap between container and lid.

Leave the mixture in a cool spot out of the light for a week, then taste it. (It speeds up the mingling of flavors if you shake or swirl the jar once a day, or when you think of it.) For stronger flavor, leave the mixture in peace for up to a month, tasting it occasionally to check progress.

When you decide you like the flavor (if you want more oomph, see the double-steeping method on the next page), strain the vinegar through a plastic or stainless-steel sieve lined with two layers of scalded and wrung-out cheesecloth. Press only lightly if at all on the pulp when all the liquid has run through (this is to prevent cloudiness).

Decide at this point how much sugar to add, remembering that lightly sweetened vinegar is versatile but a very sweet mixture isn't. About 1 tablespoon per cup of liquid, to a maximum of 2 tablespoons, suits my palate, but cooks should suit themselves. Combine the vinegar and sugar in a nonreactive saucepan (stainless steel, glass, or enamel). Heat it just to a simmer and barely simmer it for 3 minutes, watching to prevent any approach to boiling. Skim any foam from the vinegar,

A Pocketful of Vinegar

Presumably for the convenience of travelers devoted to the tang of vinegar with their viands, the author of Country Contentments, or The English Huswife, *writing in 1623, describes how to prepare an item possibly as useful as the "portable soup" that foreshadowed today's bouillon cubes. Gervase Markham directs that wheat or rye kernels be pounded to a paste with strong vinegar, shaped into balls, and dried. The Dry Vinegar could then be cut or shaved into wine to make an instant condiment.*

let it cool uncovered, then funnel it into sterilized, dry bottles. Cap or cork it (using sterilized lids or sterilized new corks) and let it mellow in a cool cupboard for a few weeks before using it. The vinegar keeps almost indefinitely, but it is at its best within a year of making.

If sediment forms as the vinegar stands and the sight of it bothers you, carefully filter the liquid into a freshly sterilized jar or bottle, using coffee filter paper and a funnel. Alternatively, just ignore the sediment, but decant the vinegar carefully when you use it.

The double-steeping method: For extra character, this method flavors the vinegar with two separate batches of fruit. Allow up to twice as much fruit, overall, as for the single-steeping method. (The second lot of fruit may be stored in the freezer, cleaned and ready to chop, when you begin to steep the first batch, a good idea if you're using a seasonal item that might be hard to get in a few weeks.)

Prepare the vinegar as directed through the step of straining out the pulp. Add the liquid to the second installment of chopped fruit. Steep the vinegar again as before, then strain, sweeten, pasteurize, and bottle it as described.

Yield: Usually about 20% greater than the quantity of vinegar first added to the fruit

Citrus Vinegar

Using a swivel-bladed peeler (or the handy gadget called a zester), strip about half of the colored outer layer (the zest) from one or two scrubbed and dried oranges, tangerines, limes, or lemons. (I like using one lemon plus one orange.) Reserve the zest. Using a sharp knife, cut away all the white pith from the fruit. Slice or dice the flesh, saving all the juice.

Put the zest, fruit, and juice into a clean, dry jar and add enough of your selected vinegar to cover them by an inch or so. (White wine, Champagne, or rice vinegar would be my choice, although the more assertive cider vinegar works satisfactorily in the presence of the equally assertive citrus flavors.) Cover the jar closely and set it in a convenient spot so you'll remember to shake or swirl it daily.

The citrus vinegar will be ready to use in a week or so. Strain out the debris, sweeten it slightly if you wish (but don't heat it), and bottle the vinegar as described in the pattern recipe. Or simply leave the vinegar and fruit in the jar and pour off the liquid as it's needed.

This vinegar will keep in a cool cupboard for a few months. As it mellows it will produce a good deal of sediment, which can either be ignored or filtered out, as described in the master recipe above.

NOT EXACTLY YOUR BASIC VINEGARS

Just as wine has been made for millennia from almost anything edible, including parsnips and primroses, vinegar (which probably came into being as wine gone sour) has been concocted from maple or birch sap, honey, molasses, sugar cane, corncobs, berries, pears, stone fruits, pineapple, the residue of winemaking, raisins, and—yes, again—primroses.

USING FRUIT VINEGARS

• The first and perhaps highest use of these condiments is in vinaigrettes for great green salads. Combine any fruit vinegar with a light salad oil (such as walnut oil) or excellent olive oil in a simple dressing, starting with twice as much oil as vinegar then adjusting the proportions to taste. Season the dressing with the usual salt and pepper.

• Stir berry vinegar into lightly salted sour cream as a dressing for finely shredded tender cabbage (such as Savoy). Let this delicate slaw marinate for several hours or overnight.

• Use fruit vinegars instead of lemon juice or wine vinegar in dressings for fruit and vegetable salads, and in sauces hot or cold that require a touch of tartness plus fruit. For instance, use fruit or berry vinegar (especially blueberry) in place of lemon juice in the pan sauce when preparing a sauté of veal scallops, calf's liver, or breast of chicken.

• Sprinkle fruit vinegar over sugared fresh berries for a subliminal lift, particularly if the berries are underripe or on the bland side (as early strawberries often are). Do the same favor for other sliced fruits that need a pick-me-up (especially less-than-perfect peaches or nectarines) and for any combination of mixed fruits for dessert.

• Replace the lemon juice with a little fruit or berry vinegar when you're poaching fresh or dried fruit or making fruit preserves. This also does good things for the fruit for a pie.

• To update the traditional beverage called shrub, stir blackberry or raspberry vinegar into chilled club soda with sugar or honey to suit, plus ice. Very refreshing.

MAKING HERBAL VINEGARS: A PATTERN

To the creating of herbal vinegars there need be no limit if you like to perk up your cuisine with such condiments. You'll find it's a delightful occasional pastime to transform basic vinegars into flavorful seasonings, or even to make your own basic wine vinegars, using the pointers beginning on page 245. (For vinegar-based pepper sauces, see the Index.)

THE VINEGARS TO USE

Any vinegar you plan to infuse with herbal flavor should be of excellent quality—adding the best of herbs won't disguise harshness or off-flavors.

• Red wine vinegars vary a lot. They may be deeply flavored and colored because they're made from "big" wines, or they may be mild. Both kinds have their uses, according to individual taste.

• Full-bodied red wine vinegar is the best kind to use with such pungent seasonings as garlic, shallots, and the more assertive garden herbs, singly or in such combinations as thyme plus rosemary, basil, and oregano, with or without garlic. I use a full-bodied red vinegar with purple-leaved basil because of the stunning color of the finished condiment, but I like white wine or rice vinegar with green and violet basils. The milder kinds of red wine vinegar match well with most herbs, if you happen to prefer red vinegar to white.

• White wine vinegar, rice vinegar (also called rice wine vinegar), or champagne vinegar are my choices for pairing with most mild and middling herbs, chervil, tarragon, chives, garlic chives (Chinese chives), dill, lemon thyme, lemon balm, and, as noted, green- or violet-leaved basils.

• Cider vinegar, because of its strong apple scent and outspoken acidity, is more limited in usefulness than wine vinegars. Try steeping mint, basil, or dill (young fresh seed heads or the dried seed from market or garden) in this vinegar, which is also satisfactory for a combination of garlic or shallots with dill, basil, lemon thyme, or lemon balm.

• Sherry vinegar, which is full of its own flavor, is a good bet for chervil, garlic chives, tarragon, basil, and dill.

• Ordinary white vinegar, usually made from acetic acid plus water and often labeled "distilled white vinegar," tends to be harsh. Fruits and berries work better than herbs with this vinegar, if it is the only kind available.

Broadening Herbal Horizons

Browsing in the catalogs of culinary herb specialists—whether they sell plants or the harvested leaves, roots, or seeds—is one of the most enjoyable routes to herbal knowledge. You needn't actually grow your own herbs (although anyone who has space and likes light gardening will enjoy doing so) in order to benefit from the encyclopedic lore found in growers' and merchants' catalogs. *(See Mail-Order Sources, page 390.)*

The Herbs to Use

Herbs fresh from the garden or the farmer's market are first choice, but in the off-season greenhouse herbs from the supermarket, dried herbs, and such kitchen staples as garlic and shallots are excellent fallback supplies.

Among the hundreds of culinary herbs, those listed below are recommended for flavoring vinegars. Some are good "straight," as indicated, whereas others are best combined with other herbs (here's where the creative palate comes in) or combined with such enhancements as sweet or pungent spices (cinnamon, cloves, nutmeg, cumin, cardamom, coriander), hot peppers or pepper flakes, horseradish, garlic, mustard seed, peppercorns, citrus peel, ginger root, and so on.

Single Herbs

• Basil, in its countless varieties. Try first the tiny-leaved green basils, which are especially intense in flavor, and the violet and purple-leaved basils, the darkest of which is the variety called Opal or Dark Opal.

• Bay leaves, in combination with other herbs.

• Burnet, its cucumber-like flavor good combined with dill. So is borage, which is similar in taste.

• Chervil, its delicate flavor reminiscent of tarragon making one of the most delightful herbal vinegars of all.

• Chives (and chive blossoms, for garnishing bottles of finished vinegar).

• Dill, both leaves and immature seed heads, or dried dill seed alone or with dill leaves.

• Fennel seed heads and leaves, both solo and in herbal combinations.

• Garlic, making one of the best flavored and generally useful vinegars of all. (For how-to's, see the sidebar on page 244.) Garlic may also be combined with dill, basil, mint, tarragon, bay, or thyme, singly or in combinations.

• Garlic chives (Chinese chives), distinguished by both oniony and garlicky flavor notes. Their fragrant white flower heads make a pretty garnish in the finished bottle.

• Juniper berries, steeped in red wine vinegar, for use in meat marinades.

• Lemon balm, whose delicate citrus character is best served by pairing with white wine or rice vinegar. This is also true of lemon thyme and lemon grass. (If you have more than one kind of lemony herb, by all means try combining them in a vinegar.)

• Lovage, with its celery-like flavor, especially good in combination with garlic or shallots.

• Mint, especially spearmint, as a solo flavoring or in combination with other herbs.

• Oregano, most useful in combination with other herbs.

• Rosemary, like oregano, a powerful herb and best used in combinations.

• Sage, used sparingly in combinations.

• Savory, either summer or winter, in combinations.

• Shallots, second only to garlic as a pungent flavoring either solo or as a backup for more aromatic flavorings. For shallot vinegar, proceed as for garlic (see the sidebar on page 245).

• Sweet marjoram, in combinations.

• Tarragon, far the best known of herbal vinegars, both red and white; it's impossible to have too much of this condiment on hand.

Non-Herbal Victorians?

A nineteenth-century household manual whose fascinating recipes (such as Wow-Wow Sauce) are tossed in higgledy-piggledy with moral, medical, legal, and housekeeping advice gives short shrift to herbs when vinegars are discussed. (Mustard fares even worse, being mentioned mostly for medical uses.) The author does advise infusing vinegar with mint or raspberries, but beyond that, the only suggestions offered are for steeping celery or cress seeds or horseradish in vinegar—kind not specified—to make condiments for meat.

• Thyme, lacking subtlety on its own but good in combinations. Lemon thyme, with its citrus overtones, is fine on its own, but it can be combined to advantage with tarragon or rosemary.

Herb Combinations

Here are a few herb combinations to get ideas for vinegar flowing. Try tarragon and rosemary; basil and chervil; thyme and sweet marjoram; oregano and sweet marjoram; bay leaf, bruised peppercorns, thyme, and rosemary; savory and thyme; thyme plus tarragon and a little rosemary; and for vinegar earmarked for use in marinades, combine crumbled bay leaves, bruised juniper berries and black peppercorns, and a good share of dried thyme.

To any of these combinations (or others you're sure to create), I'd add sliced garlic or shallot (at least the equivalent of a large clove of garlic to 2 cups of vinegar), or a handful of cut-up garlic chives or garden chives.

Preparing the Equipment

Use only nonreactive glass, china, or plastic vessels. Wash, rinse, and air-dry (or dry in the dishwasher) the jars or crocks you'll be using to steep the vinegar. Store finished vinegar in bottles or jars sterilized by 10 minutes' boiling, then drained until dry; for covering bottles or jars, use caps, corks (new corks only), or lids that have been sterilized by boiling (see page 283).

Preparing the Herbs

Allow a cupful of fresh herbs, loosely packed, to 2 cups of vinegar. (If you're working with dried herbs, ⅓ to ½ cup should be sufficient.)

The fresher the herbs, the better. Rinse them well, unless you're sure there are no bugs or dust. Roll the sprigs in towels and pat off all possible moisture. Either pull the leaves from the stems (if they're large, like those of some basils) or break or cut the sprigs into manageable pieces (tarragon, thyme, and other small-leaved herbs).

Putting It Together

For vinegar flavored with garlic or shallots, see the directions in the sidebars.

For leafy material, proceed by first measuring the herbs. Place them in the prepared jar or crock; with a wooden spoon, mash them a bit to begin the release of flavor. Add the chosen vinegar, which may be warmed to barely hot (not simmering) if you wish (I don't bother). Be sure there's enough vinegar to cover the herbs well. Let cool, uncovered, if you have warmed the vinegar.

Cover the jar and leave the vinegar somewhere handy but out of strong light. Shake the jar every day or two and begin tasting the com-

Making Garlic Vinegar

Peel a big handful of juicy garlic cloves (preferably of new-crop garlic, which appears around July) and flatten them slightly. Combine with about 3 cups of red or white wine vinegar, cover the bottle or jar, and set it aside out of the light for at least 10 days, or until you like the flavor, shaking or swirling the contents occasionally. As the vinegar is used, keep the garlic covered with added vinegar, continuing as long as the flavor is good.

MAKING SHALLOT VINEGAR

The garlic method is used for shallots, which should be sliced if you're using a large variety.

pound after a week. Let the vinegar steep for up to a month, if the flavor isn't strong enough before that. When the flavor suits you, either bottle the vinegar at once (see below) or add it to a fresh batch of prepared herbs for a second steeping if you want a more emphatic flavor. Set the second-round bottle or jar aside in a cool dark spot as before, shaking it regularly at intervals until you can pronounce the flavor satisfactory.

BOTTLING

When the vinegar is ready, strain out the debris through a sieve lined with cheesecloth. Funnel the liquid into sterilized bottles or jars and cap or cork with sterilized tops (see page 283) and label the containers. Store out of the light and away from heat for the greatest longevity. Shelf life of a year is a reasonable expectation.

If the vinegar begins to cast a sediment, you can either filter it through a dampened coffee filter into a freshly prepared container, or simply ignore the harmless deposit.

FINISHING TOUCHES

If you're bottling vinegar with an eye to gift giving, choose a handsome bottle (which may be a recycled one, if you have an eye for shape) and push a fresh sprig or two of the flavoring herb into the bottle. If the herb is a flowering kind (chives or Chinese chives, for instance), a blossom or two, plus a spear or two of leaves, makes a pretty decoration. Spear a peeled fresh clove or two of garlic on a toothpick to bottle with garlic vinegar.

For bottles sealed with corks, you can achieve a handsome airtight seal by dipping the top of the corked bottle repeatedly into melted paraffin. If you'd like to tint the wax, melt with the paraffin some recycled candle ends left from festive occasions. Red wax is especially handsome used this way.

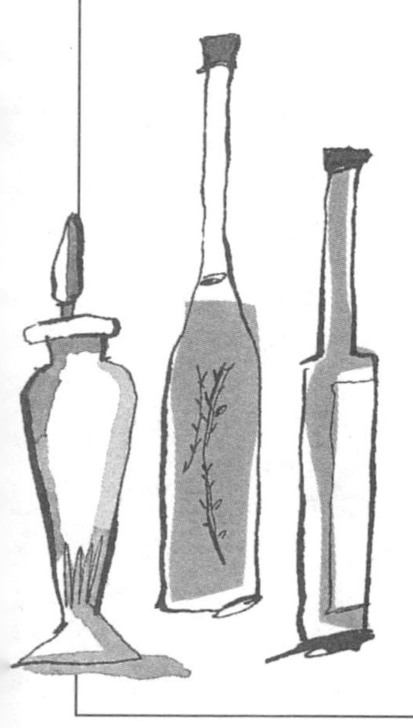

WINE VINEGAR: HOW TO MAKE THREE KINDS

Down cellar at our house, shelved with other culinary equipment too good to part with, there's a two-gallon barrel that we once used for making red wine vinegar. It worked very well, but it took a lot of wine to get it up to speed, and evaporation from the large surface area of the liquid caused the yield of vinegar to be relatively low. Our wine vinegar is now produced in a set of half-gallon jugs kept right in the kitchen. Here's how we do it.

The raw material: It's essential to start with wine that hasn't been pasteurized; further, the fewer chemicals that have been used in its making, the better. Read the label and check with your wine merchant for as much information as you can get. Wine of decent quality will produce better-tasting vinegar than nondescript "plonk," so purchase accordingly.

Don't let the wine become sour or stale before using it. Some carefully kept leftover wine can be used as part of the total, but for good results rely mainly on freshly opened wine.

Red Wine Vinegar

For making this, you need some good, unpasteurized red wine vinegar, preferably from France, to use as a starter. Or, if it is available, use a small handful of "mother," the gelatinous matter, full of lively yeast cells and helpful bacteria, that grows in all kinds of vinegar and is responsible for converting the raw material (wine, apple juice, or whatever) into its final state. If you can't get some mother from a friend or from a dealer in winemaking supplies (see Mail-Order Sources, page 390), check for its presence in a bottle of unpasteurized wine vinegar that has been open for a while. To obtain it, just strain it out with a fine-mesh sieve.

Combine the wine with the mother, or with about one fourth of its volume of "starter" wine vinegar, in a half-gallon or gallon jug; don't fill the jug above its widest point, as you want as much surface exposure to air as possible. Fasten a double layer of cheesecloth or a piece of muslin over the top (to keep out fruit flies and their ilk) and set the jug in a spot where you will remember to look at it once in a while. Leave it in peace for several weeks, or until a sniff and a taste indicate that you have created vinegar. (The flavor intensifies with more time.)

Strain the vinegar into a sterilized, dry bottle and cap or cork it (see page 282). Return to the jug the "mother" that will be present even if you started with none. If you don't want to start more vinegar just yet, add enough wine (or enough of the vinegar you have just decanted) to keep the mother well covered. Cap the jug until you're ready to make another batch of vinegar, then start the cycle again. If the mother is kept for a lengthy time, I feed it more wine occasionally.

Pasteurizing the vinegar is optional, but pasteurized vinegar keeps better than untreated vinegar. To pasteurize, heat the vinegar to the simmering point and simmer it, without boiling, for 5 minutes. Cool, bottle, and cap or cork it. It keeps indefinitely in cupboard storage.

The Many-Branched Vinegar Tree

Vinegar has been a culinary staple since a possibly Paleolithic cook twigged to the fact that spoiled (fermented) fruit would turn into an agreeable, buzz-producing (alcoholic) drink that would in turn, if left standing, become a pleasantly sour substance good for seasoning, pickling, and preserving food.

Vinegar achieves these things because of its acetic acid content, usually between 4 and 6%, but in vinegars for special uses—some distilled vinegars and the slightly alcoholic spirit vinegar—it can be higher. Acidity can be lower, too, as in homemade vinegars and almost all balsamic vinegars, the finest of which are made from unfermented grape juice mellowed to liqueur-like richness in special casks.

Market Report

Today's most popular salad vinegars are made from wine—red, white, sherry, and others, as indicated on labels—but other big sellers begin with apples or apple cider or pulp (cider vinegar) or with specially treated ordinary vinegar, or sometimes acetic acid plus water (white or distilled white vinegar), mostly used for pickling. Other vinegars to be found on well-stocked shelves are made from rice or rice wine (Japanese rice or rice wine vinegar) or from malted barley or unhopped beer (malt vinegar). Recipes indicate the type of vinegar best for the purpose at hand.

White Wine Vinegar

Before you tackle this, please read the general discussion of wine vinegar as well as the directions for Red Wine Vinegar.

For reasons related to the high acidity of white wines, this is trickier to produce than red wine vinegar. The best bet is to dilute freshly opened white wine half and half with water; then add mother, as for red wine vinegar, and proceed as described. (Mother produced in red wine vinegar is okay to use. However, appropriate mother for several vinegars is available from dealers in wine-making supplies. See Mail-Order Sources, page 390.) Allow plenty of time for the vinegar to develop; it can take months. Strain, bottle, and store it as directed, pasteurizing it or not as you wish.

Sherry Vinegar

First, digest all the preceding information. Sherry is tricky to use because of its level of alcohol, which is higher than that of red or white wine. I've found the 50% dilution used for making white wine vinegar, when applied to a medium or medium-dry sherry of a respectable brand, will produce, very slowly, an exceptionally mellow product. It's worth waiting for, though, if you'd like to try your hand at a moderately challenging project.

Once you have achieved sherry vinegar, strain, bottle, and store it as described for the other wine vinegars. Pasteurize it or not, as you prefer; I think it's a good idea, as this vinegar is most prolific of "mother," which tends to devour the vinegar if left too long.

Great Grainy Mustards

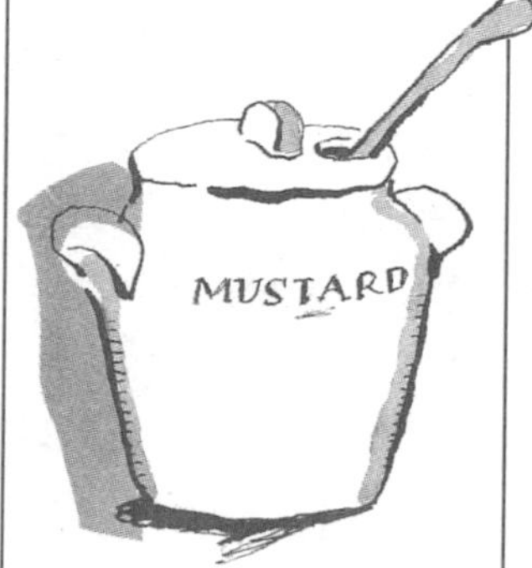

As a base for these flavorful coarse mustards, it's easiest to use crushed brown mustard seed, which is available from spice specialists, but it's equally feasible to crunch up whole brown mustard seed in a spice mill or a small coffee grinder reserved for spices. Adding a little mustard powder, such as Colman's, is optional when grinding the seeds.

For a paler and somewhat milder base, use ordinary white mustard seed, which is widely available on spice racks and, of course, from specialist suppliers of herbs and spices. (For names and addresses of some merchants, see Mail-Order Sources, page 390.)

Base for Grainy Mustards

FOR DARK MUSTARD:
1 cup crushed brown mustard seed, or ⅔ cup brown mustard seed briefly ground in a spice mill with 1 to 2 tablespoons dry mustard powder (the more powder, the hotter the finished mustard will be)
1 cup water

FOR LIGHT MUSTARD:
⅔ cup white (light) mustard seed, briefly ground in a spice mill with 1 to 2 tablespoons dry mustard powder
1 cup water

Makes about 1½ cups

Stir the crushed mustard with the water in a wide ceramic or glass bowl and leave it, at room temperature, covered lightly with a cloth or uncovered, for several hours or for as long as 24 hours. Give it a stir when you think of it, the oftener the better. (This helps disperse the fire.)

Grainy Mustard with Honey & Tarragon

Aromatic and well balanced, this condiment is especially good with picnicky foods, whether they are enjoyed indoors or out. If possible, flavor it with summer's fragrant fresh tarragon.

Like the other mustard formulas offered here, this is a guide, not a blueprint. After any of these mustards have mellowed for a day or two, taste the jarful again and decide whether to add more of any of the flavorings, or more acid, sweetening, or salt.

Base for Grainy Mustards, above, using brown mustard seed
2 tablespoons whole-wheat flour
½ cup vinegar (white wine, champagne, or rice)
3 tablespoons honey, preferably a mild kind (sugar may be substituted)
2 to 4 tablespoons minced fresh tarragon leaves, or more to taste (2 to 4 teaspoons thoroughly crumbled dried tarragon may be substituted)
2 teaspoons salt, or to taste
Pinch of ground mace or freshly grated nutmeg, optional
Pinch of ground cinnamon, optional

Makes about 2 cups

1. Into the mustard base whisk the whole-wheat flour, then whisk in the vinegar, honey, tarragon, salt, and the optional mace and cinna-

Mustard Seed

It may be useful to know that dark mustard seed (black or brown—few dealers distinguish between the terms) is more pungent than the white or yellow seed that is a supermarket staple. However, the difference isn't great enough to justify a safari around town in search of the dark seed; either light or dark seed may be used in the recipes for coarse-ground mustards. (You might also like to try the crushed brown mustard seed that's available from spice specialists.) Like almost all spices and herbs, mustard seed is most economically purchased in bulk from a spice merchant rather than a supermarket, where the per-ounce price is very high.

mon. Taste and adjust the flavorings if more of anything seems to be needed. (Repeat the tasting after a few days' mellowing and adjust again, if you wish.)

2. Whiz part or all of the mustard briefly in a blender or a food processor if you wish to smooth out the texture somewhat.

3. Store the mustard in a clean, dry jar, tightly capped, at room temperature if you would like it to mellow fast. To preserve more of its hotness, refrigerate the mustard. It may be served immediately, but a few days' rest in the jar will allow the flavor to bloom. However stored, the mustard will keep a long time if not allowed to dry up.

LIME OR LEMON GRAINY MUSTARD WITH CORIANDER

When fresh limes are at their best—from midsummer to early fall—I prefer them to lemons as flavoring for this balanced, mild, rather dark mustard with an additional citruslike note contributed by coriander seed. Make sure the limes you use are strongly aromatic—scratch the skin of one and sniff. (It's also a good idea to check lemons this way.)

Base for Grainy Mustards, above, made with white mustard seed
2 tablespoons whole-wheat flour
½ cup berry- or fruit-flavored vinegar, or white wine, champagne, or rice vinegar
3 tablespoons mild honey, or substitute light corn syrup
2 to 3 tablespoons sugar, to taste
2 teaspoons salt, or to taste
2 teaspoons ground coriander seed, preferably freshly ground
2 teaspoons (packed) very finely chopped fresh lime or lemon zest (outer peel only, no white pith), or ⅛ teaspoon, or to taste, lime or lemon oil (measure this carefully, as it's powerful)
About 2 tablespoons strained fresh lime or lemon juice

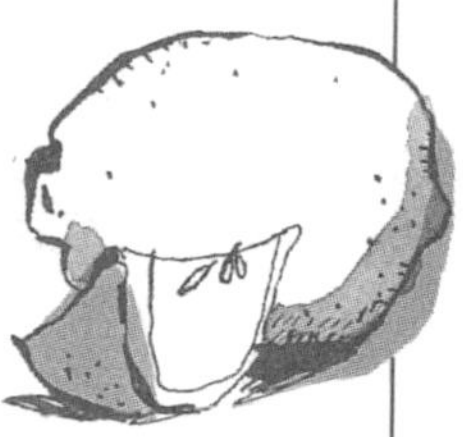

Makes about 2 cups

1. In a bowl, whisk together all the ingredients except the lime or lemon juice and taste carefully, bearing in mind that the various flavors will become more harmonious with time. Add more salt and/or sweetening if needed, and blend in lime or lemon juice to taste.

2. If you'd like to smooth out the texture somewhat, scrape all or half of the mustard into the container of a blender or food processor and pulse the machine on and off until you like the consistency. Recombine with the rest of the batch.

3. Scrape the mustard into a clean, dry jar, cover tightly, and store at room temperature (for faster mellowing) or in the refrigerator (to preserve its mild hotness longer). It can be used at once, but it is better after a few days' rest has allowed the flavorings to become better acquainted. It keeps indefinitely.

Grainy Balsamic Mustard with Roasted Garlic

Mellowness is the chief charm of balsamic vinegar, once rare and now a widely available standby of knowledgeable home cooks, so this balsamic mustard is indeed mellow, with a touch of pungency provided by Roasted Garlic Paste. If you don't have a supply of that gorgeous stuff, fresh garlic may be substituted, but the impact will be sharper.

Base for Grainy Mustards, above, using either brown or white mustard seed
2 tablespoons whole-wheat flour
⅓ cup imported balsamic vinegar
2 to 3 tablespoons vinegar (white wine, champagne, or rice), as needed
2 tablespoons sugar
2 teaspoons salt, or to taste
2 to 3 teaspoons, or to taste, Roasted Garlic Paste (page 260), or 1 to 2 large cloves fresh garlic, minced to a paste or passed through a press

Makes about 2 cups

1. Whisk together the mustard base, flour, balsamic vinegar, 2 tablespoons of the other vinegar, the sugar, salt, and 2 teaspoons garlic paste.

2. Taste the mustard, remembering that the flavors will come together and mellow, and decide whether to add the remaining tablespoon of the other vinegar (it may be needed if the balsamic vinegar is especially low in acidity). Check also for sugar, salt, and garlic, and add more if your tastebuds vote in favor. If you prefer a smoother texture, whiz all or part of the mustard in a food processor or blender, pulsing the machine on and off until the texture suits you.

3. Store the mustard in a tightly covered clean, dry jar at room temperature (for faster mellowing) or in the refrigerator (to preserve more hotness). Ready to use in a few days, it keeps indefinitely.

. . . And Yet More Grainy Mustards

Grainy Horseradish Mustard: To ¾ cup (half of the recipe) of the Base for Grainy Mustards above, add 1 tablespoon whole-wheat flour;

Mixing Up the Mustard

Some notion of the room for experiment that's possible when making your own mustard comes from books dealing with foodcraft in times gone by. For turning mustard powder into a condiment for the table, some of the suggested mixers are stale beer, onion juice, verjuice (the sour juice of unripe grapes or apples), white wine, honey (those two sound familiar), cherry juice, and butter.

2 tablespoons (or more for horseradish fiends) well-drained prepared horseradish; 1 tablespoon distilled white vinegar, white wine vinegar, or rice vinegar; a medium-large clove garlic, finely minced, or ¼ teaspoon granulated dried garlic; ½ to 1 teaspoon salt, to taste; 1 teaspoon sugar; and, optionally, a good pinch of ground allspice. Taste and adjust seasonings. Store as described for the other grainy mustards.
Makes about 1 cup

Grainy Sweet & Hot Orange Mustard: To ¾ cup (half of the recipe) of the Base for Grainy Mustards above, whisk in 1 tablespoon whole-wheat flour; ⅓ cup chopped-up bitter orange marmalade (or Temple Orange Marmalade, page 304); 2 tablespoons white wine or champagne vinegar; 2 to 3 teaspoons, or to taste, well-drained prepared horseradish; the finely shredded zest (outer peel only, no white pith) of a large orange, boiled 5 minutes in plenty of water and drained (or substitute about 10 drops of orange oil); 1 teaspoon salt, or to taste; a few drops of hot pepper sauce (optional). Blend everything and adjust the seasonings. Store as described for the other grainy mustards.
Makes about 1¼ cups

Herbed Grainy Mustard: To ¾ cup (half of the recipe) of the Base for Grainy Mustards above, add 1 tablespoon whole-wheat flour; 2½ tablespoons, or more if needed, white wine or champagne vinegar; 1 teaspoon finely crumbled dried tarragon (or up to 3 teaspoons finely chopped fresh tarragon leaves); ½ teaspoon finely crumbled dried thyme (or 1½ teaspoons minced fresh thyme leaves); 2 teaspoons snipped fresh chives or 1 teaspoon freeze-dried chives; ¼ teaspoon finely crumbled dried sweet marjoram; 1 medium clove garlic, minced to a paste, or ¼ teaspoon granulated dried garlic; 2 teaspoons (packed) brown sugar, light or dark; 1 teaspoon salt, or to taste; a big pinch of ground allspice; a big pinch of freshly ground pepper; a pinch of ground cinnamon. *Makes about 1 cup*

A Suave Set of Smooth Mustards

To make first-rate mustard of any type, from basic to elaborate, it's necessary to get rid of some of the fieriness of the mustard powder you begin with—which is unbearably hot, or sharp, edgy, bitter, burning, or pungent, according to tastebuds and vocabulary—without making it cease to be *mustard.*

Skirting around the food chemistry involved, it can be said that first soaking mustard powder (or cracked mustard seed, as for Great Grainy Mustards, page 247) makes your condiment considerably more palatable for anyone but a fire-eating dragon. The problem is that soaking can make for a runny consistency when wine, vinegar, fruit juice, honey or other liquid is added to the base.

Therefore, adding a little wheat flour to the raw material (as is done to stocks of mustard powder in Britain, the condiment's spiritual home), I've concocted the Base for Smooth Mustards that follows. (Flour is also used in some of the grainy mustards, too.) This base is cooked to a substantial thickness, which prevents added liquid ingredients from producing a drippy condiment. (Honey has an especially liquefying effect.)

Following the recipe for the base, you'll find formulas for several flavored mustards. For additions, see the set of grainy mustards beginning on page 248.)

Base for Smooth Mustards

1 cup (4-ounce container) imported English mustard powder, preferably Colman's
3 tablespoons all-purpose flour
1¾ cups water

Makes about 2 cups

1. Stir together the mustard powder, flour, and water in a large glass or ceramic bowl. Leave at room temperature, covered with a cloth, for at least 3 hours or for as long as overnight. Stir occasionally, the oftener the better—this helps disperse the fieriness of the raw material.

2. Scrape the mixture into the top of a double boiler or a heatproof glass bowl. Cook over simmering water, whisking almost constantly, until thickening is complete, then whisk and cook for 2 minutes longer, a total of about 8 to 10 minutes. (Relentless whisking creates a velvety texture.) Remove from the heat, cover (to prevent a skin from forming), and cool. Use to make Real Honey Mustard and Basic Smooth Mustard, below.

Real Honey Mustard

Here's a honey mustard, based on the preceding base recipe, that's actually made with the product of the beehive, unlike commercial products dubbed "honey mustard" but sweetened with sugar.

Honey contributes flavor as well as sweetness to this delicious condiment, so be sure to choose an assertive kind, not a dainty teatime honey such as orange blossom or clover.

Powder Power

Dry mustards aren't all alike. Some domestic brands are virtually without flavor, having only hotness to offer. Imported mustard powder is better, and a widely distributed brand—Colman's—must be mentioned. All Colman's mustard powders are hot; Colman's Special Mild Blend, for example, is mild only in comparison to their other blends, which are Genuine Double Superfine (hottest) and Double Superfine (quite hot). For export to the U.S., the English makers pack these at full strength; back home in Britain, the powders are toned down by the inclusion of a little wheat flour.

Besides serving honey mustard as a condiment with hot or cold meats (especially those of a sausagey nature), in sandwiches, and as an ingredient in vinaigrettes and other dressings and sauces, try it as a generous brushed-on coating for skinned chicken parts, which you then oven-bake at around 375°F for 30 to 40 minutes or so, with an added brushing of mustard midway. Honey mustard is also a dandy finish for a skinned and scored baked ham: Spread it over the ham, add a nice old-fashioned decorative pattern of whole cloves if you wish, and return the ham to a moderately hot oven for 20 to 30 minutes to acquire a handsome glaze.

½ recipe (⅞ cup) Base for Smooth Mustards, above
¼ cup full-flavored honey, either liquid (regular) or creamed
1½ tablespoons vinegar (white wine, champagne, or rice)
1 teaspoon salt
Small pinch of ground allspice or cinnamon, or a little of each

Makes about 1¼ cups

1. Whisk together the mustard base, honey, vinegar, salt, and optional allspice and/or cinnamon (if used). Taste carefully and adjust the flavorings, adding more acid, salt, and/or cinnamon if needed. If you'd like the mustard to be sweeter, add a little more honey.

2. If any lumps should have eluded your whisk, press the mustard through a sieve. Scrape it into a clean, dry jar, cap it snugly, and store it at room temperature (where it will mellow more rapidly than in cold storage) or in the refrigerator (where it will keep more hotness longer). The mustard keeps indefinitely.

Variations on Honey Mustard

Honey plus Tarragon: Crumbled or chopped tarragon is highly compatible with the honey flavor; add 2 tablespoons or more finely chopped fresh tarragon leaves, or 2 teaspoons or more crumbled dried tarragon.

Honey plus Orange: Add ½ teaspoon or more grated orange zest or a few drops of orange oil (not extract).

Basic Smooth Mustard

Serve this straight, or use it as the base for the fancier condiments for which recipes follow. Those are far from the end of the line for variations, however, as a glance at the mustard shelf at any fancy-food shop will show; so this mustard can be varied almost endlessly. Best bets for improvisations: things fruity, tomatoey, peppery, herbal, spicy (but always spice with a light hand). Which means no hot fudge, or none of the other ridiculous additives that can be spotted on labels.

Citric Acid Powder (Sour Salt)

This tangy stuff is what makes citrus fruits sour, and, like citrus, it has many uses. Sour salt is a classic ingredient in some versions of borscht and is a good all-around pinch hitter for lemon juice. Dissolved in water, it prevents cut-up apples or pears from turning brown while waiting for the pot, and nowadays a pinch is often added to tomatoes being canned at home to replace the natural acid bred out of modern varieties. I sometimes use it in mustard, where it replaces the acid called for. If you can't find sour salt at your grocer's (check the spice section), you'll find it in The Baker's Catalog (Mail-Order Sources, page 390).

½ recipe (⅞ cup) Base for Smooth Mustards (page 252)
2 tablespoons dry white wine or white vermouth
1 tablespoon vinegar (distilled white, white wine, champagne, or rice vinegar)
2 teaspoons sugar
1 teaspoon salt, or more
Small pinch each of allspice and cinnamon
Tiny pinch of citric acid powder (sour salt), if available

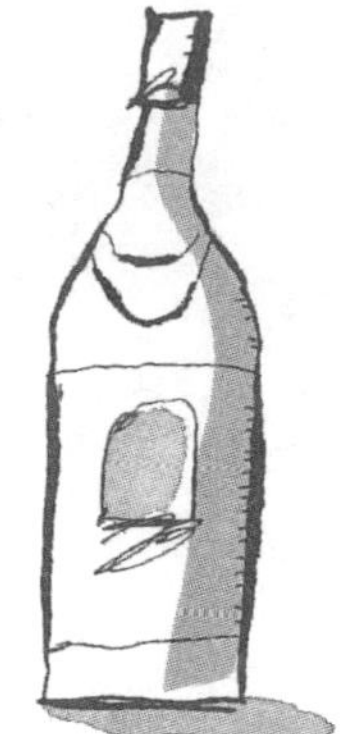

Makes about 1 cup

1. Whisk together all the ingredients and taste carefully. Adjust the seasonings, bearing in mind that the mustard will mellow and gain balance with time.

2. Press through a sieve to remove any lumps. Scrape into a clean, dry jar, cap it tightly, and store either at room temperature (where it will become milder more rapidly than if refrigerated) or in the refrigerator. It will be ready for use after resting for a week or so, and it keeps indefinitely.

The mustard base needn't be given a rest before being made into any of the mustards that follow; the whole business will mellow at the end of the second step.

Smooth Tarragon Mustard

Basic Smooth Mustard, above, preferably made with champagne vinegar
1½ tablespoons finely minced fresh tarragon leaves, or 1½ to 2 teaspoons crumbled dried tarragon
1 teaspoon finely snipped fresh chives or ½ teaspoon freeze-dried snipped chives
2 teaspoons honey, either liquid (regular) or creamed
Pinch of ground cinnamon
Salt, if needed

Makes about 1 cup

1. In a bowl, whisk together the mustard base, tarragon, chives, honey, and cinnamon. Taste for salt and add a little if needed. (Mustard made without any salt at all can be an asset to a low-sodium regimen.)

2. Transfer the mustard to a clean, dry jar, cover, and let mellow overnight at room temperature. Taste again and add more herbs, honey, cinnamon, and/or salt if needed, then let it rest again, refrigerated, for about a week before serving it. It keeps indefinitely either on the shelf, for faster mellowing, or in the refrigerator, to maintain its heat level longer.

THE GREENING OF PEPPERCORNS

Only a few food fads ago, green peppercorns, poivre vert, *were the culinary wrinkle of the year, folded into every imaginable dish, possibly even ice cream. Now they're rightly valued for their fragrant, peppery character, quite different from that of the black peppercorns they would have become if dried in the traditional way (for both preparations, the berries are picked underripe).* Piper nigrum *berries bound for green peppercornhood are promptly freeze-dried or packed in brine or vinegar. Dried green peppercorns will keep for 6 months or so; brined or vinegared peppercorns, refrigerated after opening, keep for about 6 weeks. Not the least attraction of green peppercorns is their tenderness: Crunched lightly, they release gentle warmth that's most pleasant on the palate.*

GREEN PEPPERCORN MUSTARD

Basic Smooth Mustard (page 253)
1 tablespoon drained and mashed green peppercorns packed in brine
1 teaspoon Cognac or other brandy, optional
½ teaspoon finely crumbled dried tarragon, or 1 to 1½ teaspoons finely chopped fresh tarragon leaves
Salt, if needed
Pinch of sugar, optional
Few drops of strained fresh lemon juice or mild vinegar, if needed

Makes about 1 cup

1. In a bowl, combine all the ingredients except the salt, lemon juice, and sugar, then taste carefully. Remembering that the peppercorns will become more assertive as the mustard rests, check the seasonings and add salt and more of anything else that seems to be needed, including a little lemon juice or vinegar and the sugar, which serves here to harmonize and smooth out the pungent elements, not to sweeten.

2. Store the mustard, tightly covered, in a clean, dry jar at room temperature or in the refrigerator for a week or so before using. (It will mellow more rapidly if not chilled.) It keeps indefinitely in either cupboard or fridge, but like all mustards it retains more friskiness of flavor in cold storage.

HORSERADISH MUSTARD

Basic Smooth Mustard (page 253)
1½ tablespoons well-drained prepared horseradish
1 medium clove garlic, peeled and minced to a paste or pushed through a garlic press, or ⅛ teaspoon granulated dried garlic
½ teaspoon sugar
Pinch of ground allspice
Salt, if needed
Few drops of strained fresh lemon juice or mild vinegar, if needed

Makes about 1 cup

1. In a bowl, combine all the ingredients except the salt and vinegar, taste, and add salt, drops of lemon juice or vinegar, and more horseradish or any other flavoring if you wish.

2. Stored, tightly covered, in a clean, dry jar in the refrigerator, the mustard is ready to use after 24 hours, but it continues to mellow with keeping. It keeps indefinitely.

Mixed Herb Mustard

Basic Smooth Mustard (page 253)
1 medium clove garlic, peeled and minced to a paste, or 1/8 teaspoon granulated dried garlic
1½ teaspoons very finely crumbled dried herbs, a mixture of tarragon, thyme, sweet marjoram or basil, and a pinch only of oregano (or substitute Italian-Style Herb Blend, page 191)
2 teaspoons finely minced fresh parsley leaves
1 teaspoon finely snipped fresh chives or freeze-dried chives
½ teaspoon finely crumbled dried tarragon
Few drops of lemon juice
Pinch or two of sugar
A few grinds of fresh pepper, black or white
Salt, if needed
Ground hot red (cayenne) pepper, optional

Makes about 1 cup

1. In a bowl, whisk together all the ingredients except the salt and ground hot red pepper. Scrape into a clean, dry jar, cover, and refrigerate for a few hours or overnight.

2. Taste the mustard and adjust the seasonings to suit, adding more herbs, lemon juice, and/or salt and pepper as needed, plus a little ground hot red pepper if you like it. (How much of any single herb is "enough" will depend on the quality of the herb itself.)

3. Refrigerate for storage, preferably allowing the mustard to mellow for a few days before serving. It keeps indefinitely.

Shallot Mustard

2 tablespoons minced fresh shallots
1 cup boiling water
Basic Smooth Mustard, (page 253)
1 tablespoon strained fresh lemon juice
2 or 3 drops of lemon oil, optional
Freshly ground white pepper, to taste
Salt, if needed

Makes about 1 cup

1. Cover the shallots with the boiling water and blanch for 1 minute. Drain them thoroughly.

2. Stir together the shallots, mustard, lemon juice, lemon oil (if used), and pepper. Taste and add salt, and/or more lemon juice and pepper, if it seems to be needed.

Ways to Use Olive Oil Flavored with Mixed Herbs

- *Drizzle herbed oil, whisked with lemon juice, over a salad plate of sliced oranges, oil-cured black olives, and rings of sweet red onion.*
- *Toss mixed-herb oil with hot pasta, adding finely minced garlic, fresh-ground black pepper, and grated Parmesan.*
- *Rub the oil into beef or lamb steaks, duck breasts, or chicken halves, then broil or bake them, basting with more oil now and then.*

3. Scrape into a clean, dry jar, cover, and refrigerate. Let the mustard mellow for a few days before serving it, then check and adjust the seasonings again. Stored in the refrigerator, it will keep indefinitely.

. . . Making More Smooth Mustards

Peppery Mustard: Season Basic Smooth Mustard with finely chopped fresh or drained pickled jalapeño peppers, minced Roasted Red Antipasto Peppers (page 60) or store-bought roasted peppers from a jar, a little sherry vinegar (or substitute balsamic vinegar), a touch of Roasted Garlic Paste (page 260) or granulated dried garlic or garlic powder, and a pinch of ground cumin. Refrigerate for storage. The mustard keeps indefinitely.

Many-Fruited Mustard: To a batch of Basic Smooth Mustard add a tablespoon or more of strained fresh lemon juice and about ¼ cup, in all, of a selection of finely chopped dried or candied fruits—dried or candied cranberries, dried or candied cherries, dried pineapple, apricots, and peaches, or dried figs or raisins, in whatever combination you like. Add 1 to 2 teaspoons of finely grated orange zest (outer peel only, no white pith), or substitute 6 to 8 drops of orange oil, plus a little sugar. Add salt and more lemon juice if indicated.

. . . Making Do with Store-Bought

Using store-bought mustard as a base for the collection of flavored mustards in this group is a respectable caper, in my opinion, whenever starting from scratch with mustard powder isn't a practical option.

In any of the preceding recipes that start with Basic Smooth Mustard, substitute the same quantity of smooth Dijon-style mustard, preferably Grey Poupon or mustard of comparable quality, and add the other ingredients as directed.

Olive Oil

Good olive oil is available at moderate cost (as well as at carriage-trade prices), but to find oil of the character you prefer, in any price category, it's wise to taste and judge various brands from various regions. Look for extra virgin on the label; ignore lesser grades, especially those labeled as light, which are light in flavor, not calories.

Herb-Flavored Olive Oils

Flavors redolent of . . . Provence? . . . make olive oil slowly infused with mixed herbs (the first recipe below) a luxurious standby to use whenever you would use fine, plain olive oil plus herbal flavorings of similar character to those added to the oil. For introducing the flavor of a single herb, I like to flavor oil with the pureed fresh leaves, as described in the second recipe. These fresh herbal oils are ready to use within hours, and may be kept for a week or so.

Olive Oil Flavored with Mixed Herbs

A bushy 6-inch branch of fresh rosemary that can be fitted into a decorative quart or liter bottle (or use a recycled wine bottle)
A 4-inch sprig of fresh basil, either green, violet, or purple
A handful of sprigs of dried thyme, the most flavorful available
3 large bay leaves
2 cloves garlic, peeled and split
1 teaspoon freeze-dried green peppercorns or whole black or white peppercorns
Piece (about 1 inch square) of dried orange or tangerine peel (see page 152), or about 2 square inches of fresh orange zest (outer peel only, no white pith)

OPTIONAL (USE ANY OR ALL):
Two or three sprigs of dried oregano; a pinch of dried lavender flowers; a small sprig or two of fresh or dried sweet marjoram
Olive oil of good quality (it needn't be extra-virgin)

Makes about 3½ cups

1. Rinse the fresh herbs well, shake off clinging water (or spin them in a salad drier), then roll them in a towel to remove every possible bit of remaining moisture.

2. Push the herbs, beginning with the biggest items, into a completely dry and squeaky-clean quart or liter bottle. Drop the garlic, peppercorns, dried citrus peel, and any optional additions into the bottle, arranging them with the help of a thin chopstick if you are interested in good looks. Funnel in enough olive oil to fill the bottle almost to the brim. Cork or cap tightly (use a new cork only) and store the oil for a month in a cool cupboard to allow flavor to develop. Be sure the oil covers the herbs at all times; add more if the level should drop.

3. As the oil is used, it's permissible to add more to keep the herbs covered, but this can't go on forever. When you judge the flavor is fading, strain the oil into a smaller bottle or jar, cap it tightly, and store it in a cool dark spot as before. (It may be refrigerated if that's the only way to keep it cool. This will make it cloudy, but it will clear when returned to room temperature.) This oil is best if used within a few months.

Olive Oil Flavored with Single Herbs

Good herbs to begin with are fresh basil (my favorite), chives and garlic (Chinese) chives, thyme, rosemary, sage, parsley, and, if you're fond of its special flavor, cilantro (fresh coriander). Is it needless to say

Using Herb-Infused Olive Oils

Oil flavored with basil, as described in Olive Oil Flavored with Single Herbs, is wonderful on tomato salad or in a vinaigrette for a mixed salad. Like oil infused with thyme, rosemary, or sage, it's a great pre-grilling rub for meat or poultry or fish, too. Experimenting with infused oils pays off in flavor, and you're likely to branch out by using other herbs as time goes by.

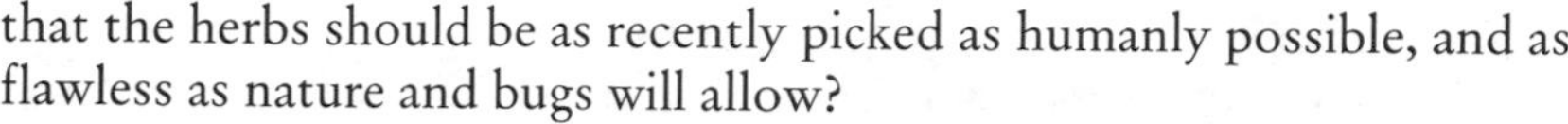

that the herbs should be as recently picked as humanly possible, and as flawless as nature and bugs will allow?

A pinch or two of grated lemon zest is an optional (and very good) addition to oils flavored with thyme, chives, garlic chives, parsley, or rosemary. For some other infused oils, see below and later in this chapter for Three-Flavored Oil for Stir-Frying, Red-Hot Pepper Oil, and Garlic-Infused Olive Oil.

Don't plan on making more oil flavored with fresh herbs than you will use within a week or so, because longer storage carries risks of spoilage that may be hard to detect by appearance or odor.

Freshly harvested (if possible) basil, chives, garlic (Chinese) chives, thyme, parsley, rosemary, sage, tarragon, or another kind of fresh herb

Good-quality mild-flavored olive oil (or vegetable oil, if preferred)

Yield is about equal to the amount of oil added to the herbs

1. Sort the herbs, removing any damaged or wilted parts. Rinse very thoroughly in two batches of fresh water, then spin in a salad spinner (or drain and pat dry with towels) to remove all possible moisture.

2. Remove any woody stems and measure the herbs, packing them down lightly. Place in a blender or food processor with twice as much oil as the measure of herbs. Process the herbs just until well chopped—don't overdo this.

3. Decant the mixture into a jar or bowl and leave it, covered, at room temperature for 3 to 6 hours. Strain the oil through a very fine sieve, pressing lightly on the debris to extract all possible oil. If you like, filter the oil through coffee filter paper after it has settled a bit (but this isn't necessary).

4. If you're not planning to use the oil immediately, store it in a covered bottle or jar in the refrigerator. It may be kept for several days, but I wouldn't recommend keeping it for more than a week.

Adding Nuance to Hotness

The touch of sweetness in paprika and the nutty fragrance of roasted sesame oil add extra dimensions of flavor to this condiment, although those ingredients aren't traditional in Chinese versions of hot pepper oil.

Red-Hot Pepper Oil

Not for Chinese cooking only, this flame-red seasoning is a kitchen and table condiment that adds just enough heat to foods ranging from a quick dish of buttered pasta to cooked greens to Sichuan-style specialties. You'll find it a zesty alternative to vinegar-based hot sauces.

1 cup high-quality peanut or corn oil
¼ cup stemmed and coarsely broken small dried hot red peppers
1 tablespoon medium or hot Hungarian paprika, optional
1 tablespoon roasted (dark) sesame oil

Makes about 1 cup

1. Combine the peanut oil and peppers in a heavy saucepan and heat them slowly over low heat for about 10 minutes, until the oil is hot but not smoking and the peppers have darkened *slightly* (they should not blacken). Remove from the heat.

2. Let the oil and peppers cool slightly (about 5 minutes), then stir in the paprika if you are using it. Let the mixture stand for a few hours (for the mildest oil), then strain off the oil through a fine sieve or an ordinary sieve lined with fine-meshed nylon net. (For more hotness you can leave the peppers in the oil for up to 3 days—the longer, the hotter.) Add the sesame oil.

3. Funnel the oil into a clean, dry bottle and cap it tightly. Stored in a cool cupboard, the hot oil keeps for many months, or it may be refrigerated almost indefinitely. Chilling may cause harmless cloudiness, which will disappear as the oil returns to room temperature.

ROASTED GARLIC PASTE

Even if garlic in any form were not said to be outstandingly good for us, who could resist its gustatory charms both subtle and otherwise? Certainly not someone (like me) who had a garlic-deprived upbringing but who has been lucky enough to sample a world of robust garlicky dishes since then.

With its propensity to overpower, garlic needs to be tamed a bit unless it's to be reduced to a demure whisper (rubbed around a salad bowl, then discarded, as people used to do and may still do, but not at my house). Baking a lot of fine *fresh* garlic with olive oil is the start of a supply of mellow garlic paste to be kept on hand and ready to go into creations ranging from Pasta for Garlic-Lovers (see the Index) to a supply of garlic-infused oil (directions are below).

The paste is a seasoning to reach for when you're correcting the lack of oomph in a salad or sauce or soup, and it's a splendid shortcut to hot garlic bread or bruschetta.

And while we're on the subject: For other characterful uses of (unroasted) garlic, see the Index for Garlic & Hot Pepper Jelly and page 244 for garlic vinegar.

WHEN TO DO A GARLIC ROAST

Watch the harvest calendar for late summer's fresh garlic crop, which will be a delight if you have tasted only tired, rubbery garlic with the internal sprouts that show it's ready to plant, not to be eaten if you can help it. At other seasons than summer, garlic shipped in from other growing regions may be well above the (low) market average. If you ask the greengrocer for good garlic, you may help to eliminate the scourge of withered garlic huddling in tiny boxes in a far corner of the salad display.

¾ pound (4 to 6 large heads) firm, fresh, juicy garlic, with no green sprouts inside the cloves
4 to 6 tablespoons good olive oil, plus more for topping the jar of finished paste
A little salt, optional

Makes about ¾ cup

1. Preheat the oven to 350°F.

2. Dismantle the heads of garlic and discard the root disks of the heads, any loose papery skin, and the central stems. (To break open a head easily, lay it on its side on a work surface, lay a cleaver or heavy knife blade against it, and lean a heavy hand on the blade, exerting force downward in a diagonal direction. If this doesn't break the cloves apart—it takes a powerful push—just do the job by hand.) Using a small, very sharp knife, cut off and discard the root platelets.

3. Tear off a large square of heavy-duty aluminum foil. Dump the garlic cloves onto the foil and drizzle 2 to 3 tablespoons of the oil over them; stir them until well coated, then gather the foil into a loose bundle. Set it on a baking pan.

4. Bake the garlic in the preheated oven for about 1 hour, opening the bundle once or twice to stir the cloves and check on progress. If the garlic begins to brown at all before the cloves are tender (a golden color only is what you want), lower the oven heat to 300°F, re-close the packet, and continue baking until the cloves are golden and feel soft when squeezed. Remove the package from the oven, open it, and let the garlic cool enough to be handled.

5. Pour any oil in the foil packet into a bowl and set it at hand. Working on a cutting board, use a small knife to press garlic pulp from each clove, pushing from tip to base. Add the pulp to the oil.

6. Press the pulp and oil through a medium-meshed sieve. Add, if you wish, a pinch or two of salt, then stir in the rest of the olive oil. Pack the garlic paste into a clean, dry jar. Cover the paste with a layer of additional olive oil, cap it tightly, and store it in the refrigerator. For freezer storage for up to 2 months, omit the oil topping and freeze the paste in a small capped glass jar. (I keep some for everyday use in the fridge and a backup supply in the freezer.) Plan to use the refrigerated supply within a few weeks.

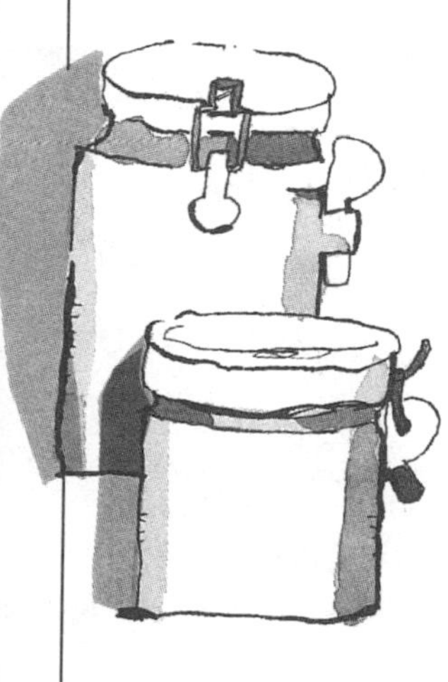

Chicken Baked with Roasted Garlic

Remove the skin and surplus fat from the separated legs and thighs of broiler-size chicken(s). Rub the pieces generously with Roasted Garlic Paste, sprinkle them with salt and pepper, and leave them at room temperature for 30 minutes. Bake the chicken for about half an hour in a shallow pan in a preheated 375°F oven, turning the pieces now and then. They're done when an instant-reading thermometer registers from 175° to 180°F.

Three-Flavor Oil for Stir-Frying

For the increasing crowd of cooks who like to prepare fast Chinese-style stir-fries of vegetables, or meat, or tofu, or seafood plus vegetables, a bottle of preseasoned peanut oil is a great time-saver.

Without this flavored oil, the razor-edged cleaver must move to the cutting board, garlic must be minced, fresh scallions must be dug from the refrigerator and trimmed and sliced, fresh ginger must be peeled and minced, all for the seasoning of ingredients that will otherwise take only a few minutes to prepare for cooking. With Three-Flavor Oil on hand, you set the wok over the heat, add your flavored oil, and proceed to cook any Chinese dish that calls for oil plus the usual aromatics (garlic, ginger, and scallions).

2 cups peanut oil (preferable) or corn oil
8 quarter-sized slices fresh ginger root, 1/8 inch thick (no need to peel it)
6 medium or large scallions
4 large cloves garlic

Makes about 2 cups

1. Pour the oil into a heavy saucepan.

2. Smash the slices of ginger slightly on a cutting board, using the flat side of a large knife or cleaver. Drop the slices into the oil. Trim the scallions of their roots, loose skin, and all but an inch or so of their green tops. If you must rinse them, pat them dry. Slice them crosswise into thin rounds and add them to the oil. Flatten and peel the garlic cloves by laying the flat of your knife or cleaver on each in turn, then hitting the metal a sharp blow with your fist: pull off the loosened skin. Drop the garlic into the oil.

3. Set the pan over low heat and warm the contents gradually; a gentle sizzling will begin as the moisture begins to emerge from the seasonings. Keep the heat low and cook the oil very slowly for about 10 minutes after the bubbling begins, or until the pieces of scallion begin

A Stir-Fry Facilitator

Because the aromatic elements are cooked with the oil before it's bottled, this flavorful stir-fry oil keeps very well in the refrigerator or, for a shorter time, in a cool cupboard. Oils infused with fresh, juicy herbs have a shorter storage life, as their recipes indicate.

to appear translucent and the oil smells delicious. Do not let the flavorings brown at all. Remove from the heat.

4. Let the oil and flavorings stand overnight at room temperature, then strain off the oil through a fine sieve and funnel it into a clean, dry bottle and cap or cork it. Discard the seasonings. Store the oil in the refrigerator for indefinite storage, or in a cool cupboard for a month or so. Refrigerated oil is likely to become (harmlessly) cloudy. The cloudiness clears when the oil returns to room temperature.

Garlic-Infused Olive Oil

It may not look like an advertiser's dream—it's murky, to put it politely—but olive oil blended with mellow roasted garlic tastes pretty splendid. It's virtually a pasta sauce all by itself (fresh black pepper and some freshly grated Parmigiano-Reggiano complete the dish), and no *au courant* cook needs to be told what else to do with garlic-flavored oil, though it's a relative newcomer to the fancy-grocery shelf. It's for sautéing chicken, meat, or seafood, or dressing salads, or making sauces, or drizzling over hot vegetables, just for starters.

Keep this oil in the refrigerator in a quantity that will be used up within a couple of weeks, just to be on the food-safety side of the equation. (Store-bought infused oils have longer shelf life than your custom-made supply because of the special methods of preservation available to the packers but not to home cooks.) When you need to refill the oil bottle, just draw on your frozen stash of Roasted Garlic Paste.

Double Whammy

Garlic-infused oil and herb-flavored oils (see page 257) may be combined in more or less equal proportions in salad dressings, sauces, and pre-grilling rubs for meat, fowl, and fish.

2 tablespoons Roasted Garlic Paste (see the preceding recipe), or more to taste
Pinch of salt, if the paste has not been salted
1 cup full-flavored (fruity) olive oil

Makes about 1 cup

1. Measure the garlic paste into a small bowl, sprinkle the salt over it, then stir in the olive oil until completely blended. (A mortar and pestle are ideal for this job.)

2. Pour the oil into a clean, dry jar or bottle and store, tightly capped, in the refrigerator for up to 2 weeks. The oil is ready to use at once, but the ingredients continue to get better acquainted for a day or two after it's made. If necessary, shake gently before using.

PASTAS: A MASTER RECIPE & SOME OFFBEAT NOODLING

The Pleasures of Pasta Making

The enthusiastic making of fresh pasta at home was well under way when the writing of *Fancy Pantry* began back in the '80s. Enthusiasm was bubbling partly because dandy little machines for rolling and cutting the dough were being sold everywhere, but mostly because pasta dishes had become all-time American favorites. That book therefore included the how-to's of making, storing, and cooking fine, basic semolina pasta plus some flavorful variations. That lore is republished here with the addition of recipes for noodles redolent of garlic or saffron.

In devising the recipes for flavored noodles I've been conservative, sticking with enhancements that work and also suit me, but that doesn't mean you shouldn't experiment, using the recipes as patterns. Just be aware, before tinting dough with beets or tomatoes or carrots or artichokes, that your effort is likely to exceed your reward in flavor when mild-tasting vegetables are used.

Machines can make noodling a quick as well as satisfying project, but don't be put off by the lack of either a food processor or a pasta machine. All you really need for pasta projects is a board for mixing, kneading, and rolling the dough, a rolling pin, and a sharp knife, plus the pointers included in the master recipe for Semolina Pasta.

Semolina Pasta:

A Master Recipe & An Outline of Noodle Making

Fine-ground semolina flour, often labeled "pasta flour" or "durum flour" and not to be confused with the coarser grades of semolina (more like farina in texture), makes the best commercial as well as homemade pasta. Cooked semolina pasta is pleasantly resistant to the tooth, not mushy, because of the high gluten content of the flour.

Don't be discouraged by the occasional cookbook warning that semolina flour is too difficult to use at home. That's true only if you use coarse semolina, which can be made into a coherent pasta dough with superhuman effort alone. Fine semolina makes a firm, satiny dough after normal kneading.

Pasta flour isn't a corner-grocery item, but it is to be found in markets that are more super than most and in health-food stores and specialty food shops; mail order is another good bet. All-purpose flour can be substituted for semolina, but the cooked pasta will be softer and will tend to stick together somewhat after cooking, particularly if it is cooked fresh, not dried.

This recipe tells how to make egg pasta (or noodles, among friends) entirely by hand; partly by hand, with a pasta machine used for rolling and cutting the dough; and with a food processor for making dough to be rolled and cut either by hand or pasta machine.

3½ cups fine semolina (pasta) flour (or substitute all-purpose flour for half or all of the semolina flour)
1½ teaspoons salt, or to taste
3 large eggs
2 tablespoons olive oil
2 to 4 tablespoons water, as required
Additional flour for kneading and cutting the dough (all-purpose flour is fine)

Makes about 2 pounds, fresh weight

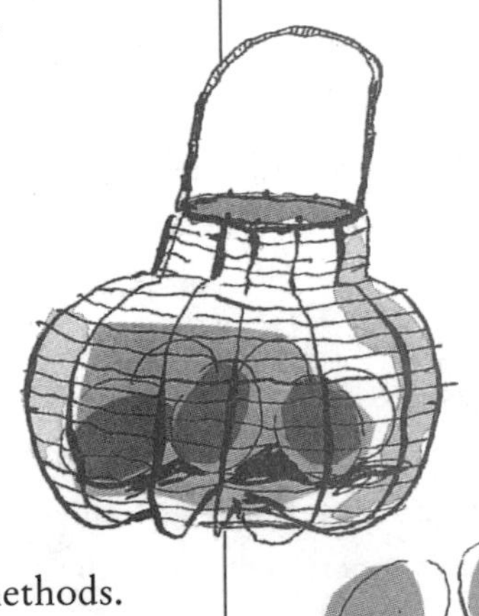

1. Mix and knead the dough by one of the following methods.

To mix pasta dough by hand: Heap the flour in a bowl or on a kneading surface and make a hollow in the center of the heap. Place the salt, eggs, oil, and 2 tablespoons of the water in the hollow. Stirring with your fingers, mix the salt, eggs, oil, and water with a little of the immediately surrounding flour, moving gradually outward as you draw

Making a Pasta Pin

Here's how Margery Tippie, longtime food-friend and one of the editors of this book, suggests making your own rolling pin for handmade pasta. From the hardware store (or lumberyard, if handier) obtain a length of dowel 1 inch or so in diameter; 2 feet is long enough unless you have a lot of work space. Sand the cut ends smooth and sand any rough spots, and there you have it.

the remaining flour into the dough. When all the flour has been roughly incorporated (you will have a collection of clumps), sprinkle on and work in as much of the remaining water as needed to make a firm dough. Try not to add too much water—the less you use, the better—but if your dough becomes too wet, the consistency can be corrected by working in additional flour at the kneading stage.

Kneading by hand: Gather the dough into a ball, scrape the board clean, dust it with flour, and knead the dough vigorously in the same fashion as bread dough (push the dough away from you, fold it over, give it a quarter-turn, push again, and so on), using more flour on the board as necessary to prevent sticking. Keep kneading until the dough is smooth and elastic; it's better to overdo the kneading than to skimp. Wrap the dough in plastic and let it rest for 30 minutes.

Kneading with a pasta machine: Mix the dough by hand as described in step 1; gather it into a ball. Set the rollers of your pasta machine at their widest setting. Divide the dough into three or more parts for convenience in handling; cover all but one piece with plastic wrap or foil. Flatten the remaining portion of dough into a rough strip that will pass through the rollers, dust it lightly with flour, and sweep with a dry pastry brush to remove excess flour. Pass the dough through the rollers repeatedly to knead it, folding the edges to the center after each rolling. As you knead, dust the dough with more flour only if necessary to prevent sticking. When the strip is satiny, it has been kneaded enough and is ready for final rolling and cutting (step 2). Lay it aside for the moment and knead the reserved portions of dough.

Mixing and kneading the dough in a food processor: Place the flour and salt in the workbowl of a food processor fitted with the steel knife and flick the motor on and off to mix them. Break the eggs into a cup, beat them a little with a fork, add the oil and half of the water, start the machine, and add the liquid ingredients gradually through the feed tube. Continue to run the machine for 30 seconds; if the dough is still crumbly, very gradually add a little of the remaining water as the machine runs; you need to add just enough to make a dough ball that whirls around on top of the blade, so give the machine a chance to pull the dough together before deciding to add more water. When the dough ball has formed, let it whirl for about 15 seconds. Wrap the dough in plastic and let it rest for 30 minutes.

2. Proceed to roll and cut the dough:

Rolling and cutting pasta dough by machine: Pass each strip of dough that has been kneaded with the pasta machine through successively closer settings of the rollers until you have dough of the desired thickness (the #5 setting of most machines is neither too thick nor too thin). Dust with flour only if necessary to prevent sticking, and brush off excess flour with the dry pastry brush. Hang each rolled-out dough

Cooking Custom-Made Pasta

Whether it's to be cooked fresh or after partial or complete drying, boil your semolina pasta in a large quantity of boiling water—ideally, 5 quarts to a pound of noodles. Add salt to taste, if you wish, after the water boils, then drop in a few noodles at a time, with the water boiling hard, to keep the strands from sticking together. Fresh noodles are done almost as soon as they float to the top, in about 2 to 3 minutes. Dried noodles take a bit longer; test by biting a strand, as you don't want to overcook these delicate morsels. Drain noodles promptly by lifting them with tongs or by pouring them into a colander. Fresh noodles, softer and stickier than the dry form, are best drained in a colander and rinsed with boiling water to discourage clumping. Sauce your drained noodles promptly in a warmed bowl, tossing them with two forks.

strip on a pasta rack or lay it on a lightly floured cloth to dry slightly. Let the strips dry for a short time (how long "a short time" turns out to be will depend on the humidity of the room), until the surface has dried a bit but the strips are still pliable. (If overdried, they will be too brittle to cut into recognizable noodles. If that happens, the best recourse is to let the sheets dry completely, then break them into bits to use in soup or as small irregular pasta shapes.)

Cutting: Using the cutter attachment of the pasta machine, cut wide or narrow noodles, as preferred. If you will be cooking the pasta within 2 or 3 hours, form small handfuls of the cut noodles into loose coils on a tray or wire rack and leave them until they are wanted.

Rolling and cutting pasta dough by hand: Cut the kneaded and rested dough into 4 portions (or more if your rolling surface is small) and wrap all but one piece in plastic. On a floured surface, roll the piece of dough out until it is uniformly very thin, stretching it as you roll. (Experienced makers of hand-crafted pasta use a thin, straight rolling pin that is rather like a broomstick—see page 266—and roll the dough around the pin as they work, frequently stretching the layers toward the ends of the roller with outward smoothing motions of the hands. This is fun after the knack is acquired and it makes beautiful noodles. You must keep the dough dusted with just enough flour to keep the layers from sticking together as the roller does its work of thinning and enlarging the sheet rolled around it.) Set the piece aside on a floured cloth or hang it up to dry until it is firm but still pliable, meanwhile rolling out the remaining pieces.

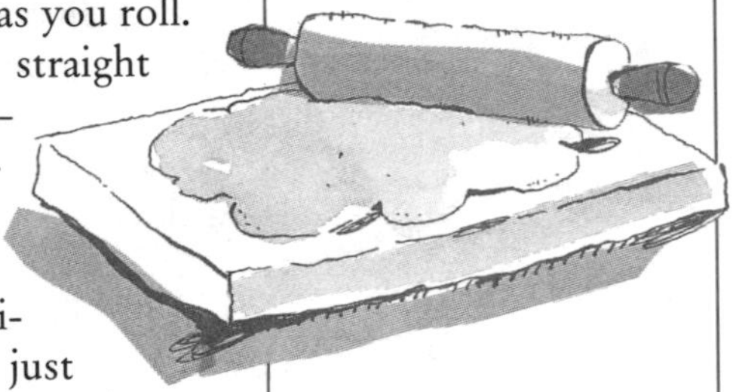

Cutting: However you have rolled them, let the sheets of dough dry slightly as described; then carefully fold up or roll the partially dried sheet of dough and cut crosswise slices of the desired width, using a very sharp serrated knife. Unroll the noodles, toss them to separate the strands, and leave them in loose tangles if they will be cooked within an hour or two; otherwise dry them (step 3). For special shapes, use a sharp knife, a pastry wheel, or a cookie cutter to cut the rolled-out dough.

3. ***Drying and storing the noodles:*** Fresh noodles can be bagged in plastic and refrigerated for 2 or 3 days. To dry noodles for longer keeping, drape them over a pasta rack, the cloth-covered back of a chair, or other improvised arrangement, or spread them in loose tangles on wire cake racks and turn them occasionally until they have reached the dryness wanted. If you have a food dehydrator, noodles can be dried quickly, using very low heat.

Half-drying: For refrigerator or freezer storage, you can dry the noodles just until they bend instead of breaking when a strand is tested. Then gather them into plastic bags (or plastic boxes, for less risk of breakage), close the container, expelling as much air as possible, and refrigerate them for a week or two, or double-bag them and freeze them for a month, maybe two.

Complete drying: For cool pantry (or long-term refrigerator) storage, dry noodles until they are brittle, then package them airtight for storage in a cool cupboard for a month or so, or in the refrigerator for up to 3 months, or in the freezer for a longer period.

Herbed Green Noodles

Outshining the now-familiar spinach pastas, these are among the tastiest of all possible green noodles. Made with fresh herbs (dried herbs won't do), they can wander from the specifics of this recipe, which is more pattern than prescription, if you can lay hands on other kinds of fresh herbs. Chinese (or garlic) chives plus parsley are a good bet, and a combination of scallions, thyme, a few leaves of sage, a little fresh rosemary, and a good amount of parsley makes marvelous noodles to go with hearty roasts of pork or veal.

For anyone who needs to be reminded how to make spinach pasta, a reprise of that recipe follows the main event below.

1 cup (packed) fresh basil or sweet marjoram leaves, or a combination of basil, marjoram, thyme, and snipped fresh chives
1 cup (packed) flat-leaf (Italian) parsley, leaves only
2 medium scallions, including part of the green tops, sliced
3 large eggs
1 to 2 tablespoons olive oil, optional
2 teaspoons salt, or to taste
¼ teaspoon freshly ground white pepper
4 cups fine semolina (pasta) flour, or 2 cups each semolina and all-purpose flour (use more if more is needed)
Additional flour for kneading and dusting the dough (all-purpose flour is fine)

Makes about 2½ pounds, fresh weight

1. Puree the herbs, including the parsley and scallions, in a blender or food processor until very smooth. If the puree seems watery, drain surplus liquid in a sieve lined with cheesecloth.

2. Following the general instructions in the master recipe (Semolina Pasta, page 266), combine the puree, eggs, oil (if used), salt, pepper,

"I Say It's Spinach, and I Say to Hell with It"

—Cartoon caption

Herbed Green Noodles may look as if they're made with the spinach denounced in the classic New Yorker *cartoon, but one taste will disabuse the skeptical—spinach, noble though it is, never tasted like this. For those who like spinach very much (as I do, possibly thanks to Popeye comics in my youth, not the* New Yorker*), the main recipe is followed by a reminder of how to make spinach pasta.*

and flour. Knead, rest, roll, and cut the dough as described. Dry the noodles slightly before you either cook them or store them as described for fresh noodles.

3. The fresh noodles may be kept for 2 or 3 days in the refrigerator or for up to 1 month, double-bagged or freezer-wrapped, in the freezer.

Spinach Pasta–A Reprise

Substitute 1 pound of spinach, trimmed of roots, washed, and drained, for the herbs in the preceding recipe. Blanch the spinach in a large pot of boiling water until tender, about 3 minutes, then drain it well in a colander, pressing the leaves hard to remove as much water as possible. Puree the spinach in a food processor or blender. If the pulp is watery, drain it again as described in step 1 of the main recipe above. Then proceed with the recipe.

The moisture content of the spinach is a variable, so more semolina flour may be needed if the dough is sticky at any point.

Peanut Pasta

Thin-cut noodles based on fresh-ground peanuts make an especially good cold dish when tossed with a Far Eastern sauce involving more peanuts plus sesame and soy. (See the recipe opposite.) Cut wider, peanut noodles are a delicious side dish served hot with a drizzle of lightly browned or melted butter, good with fish or fowl.

For superb, silky but firm pasta, use semolina flour if you can. All-purpose flour can be substituted, but the noodles will be softer.

1 cup high-quality roasted unsalted peanuts (or substitute ½ cup excellent creamy-style peanut butter)
1½ to 2 teaspoons salt, to taste
2 large eggs
4 to 5 tablespoons water, as needed
3 cups fine semolina (pasta) flour (or substitute all-purpose flour)
Additional flour for kneading and dusting the dough (all-purpose flour is fine)

Makes about 2 pounds, fresh weight

BETTER PEANUT BUTTER

The first step of this recipe also indicates how you can make your own fresh peanut butter. In the way described, just grind any desired quantity of roasted, unsalted peanuts with a little salt (optional), a little sugar (also optional), and a few drops of peanut oil, if you like—it helps to create a spreadable consistency. For 1 pound of nuts, start with ½ teaspoon each of salt and sugar and adjust after final sampling.

If chunky peanut butter is your pleasure, chop some additional peanuts separately (use on-off bursts of the food processor, or a big sharp knife on a cutting board) and blend them in.

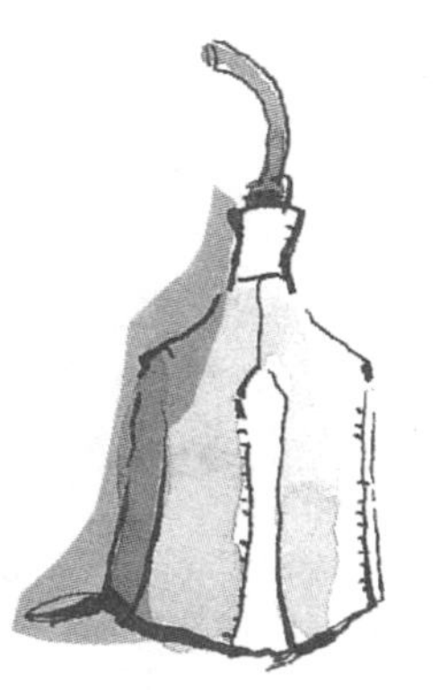

1. Using a food processor or blender, grind the peanuts to a slightly grainy paste, scraping down the sides of the bowl once or twice. Measure out ½ cup.

2. Following the general directions in the master recipe (Semolina Pasta, page 266), combine the nut paste with the salt, eggs, and 5 tablespoons of water, if you're using pasta flour; if you're using all-purpose flour, use only 4 tablespoons initially. Mix, rest, knead, roll, and cut the dough as described, using a little more water (or flour) in the mixing if necessary to make a cohesive dough. For cold noodle dishes, cut the dough into narrow noodles; for hot dishes, they may be narrow or wide.

3. Let the cut noodles dry slightly, until they are firm but still pliable; this pasta isn't suitable for complete drying and shelf storage. Use the pasta at once, or bag the noodles and refrigerate them for up to 3 days; or double-bag and freeze them for up to 1 month.

4. *To cook peanut pasta:* Don't thaw the noodles if frozen. Drop them by handfuls into at least 5 quarts of boiling, salted water. Stir them, let the water return to a boil, turn off the heat, cover the pot, and let the noodles poach just until they are tender, about 2 or 3 minutes (for wide noodles) or 1 to 2 minutes for very thin pasta. Drain them at once and serve them promptly if you're eating them hot. If they're intended for a cold dish, drain them promptly, drop them into a big bowl of cold water and ice, leave them until chilled, then drain again. They may be refrigerated for a few hours before they are served.

CHILLED PEANUT NOODLES IN A FAR EASTERN SAUCE

For 1 pound (½ recipe above) of fresh peanut noodles, cooked, chilled, and drained as described:

¼ cup imported soy sauce
¼ cup dark (roasted) sesame oil
3 tablespoons dark Chinese vinegar (or half balsamic vinegar, half red wine vinegar)
3 tablespoons smooth peanut butter or roasted unsalted peanuts ground to a paste
2 teaspoons sugar
Salt, if needed
About ¼ teaspoon Red-Hot Pepper Oil (page 259)
1 medium clove garlic, minced to a paste, optional
½ to ¾ cup crisp fresh rings of scallion, including part of the green tops

Whisk everything except the scallions together to make a smooth dressing. Taste and adjust the seasonings, adding more of any ingredient to suit yourself. Toss the dressing and scallions with the cooked, chilled, and drained noodles. Serve the noodles promptly, within half an hour or so for the best texture.

Hazelnut or Black Walnut Pasta

Made with either hazelnuts (filberts) or black walnuts, these nutted noodles are richly flavored, an excellent dish on their own and equally excellent companions for sauced meat or game dishes or any sort of poultry.

To make about 2 pounds of noodles (fresh weight), follow the recipe for Peanut Pasta, above, substituting ½ cup of hazelnut or black walnut paste (below) for the peanut paste or peanut butter.

Cook the noodles in exactly the same way and serve them hot, either with melted butter, browned butter, a mushroom sauce, or a spoonful of the sauce of the meat or poultry they are served with.

Like peanut noodles, these aren't suitable for dry storage. Plan on drying them partially and keeping them for 3 days, refrigerated, or for up to 1 month in the freezer.

Preparing the Nut Paste

For hazelnut noodles: Toast about 1¼ cups of hazelnuts on a baking sheet in a 350°F oven, stirring them occasionally, until their skins are crisp and the nuts smell rich and toasty, about 8 to 10 minutes. Rub the hazelnuts in a towel to remove as much of the brown skin as possible (it doesn't matter if patches remain), then grind them to a grainy paste in a food processor or blender and measure out the needed ½ cup.

For black walnut noodles: Be sure to use absolutely fresh nutmeats (the distinctive flavor of these rich native nuts vanishes quickly once the nuts have been shelled unless they are frozen or at least refrigerated). To make the paste, use a food processor or a blender to grind about 1¼ cups of the nuts, scraping down the sides of the container once or twice. Stop while the texture is still a little grainy and measure out ½ cup of the paste.

A Treasure to Look For

Our native black walnuts are much scarcer and therefore known to fewer cooks than they used to be, mostly because so many of the great trees (they can reach a hundred feet) have been cut down for their valuable timber. (Their range includes almost half of the fifty states, so foraging is an option for many—we're lucky enough to go walnutting every October.) Black walnuts were long ago replaced in general use by the "English" walnuts (thet're actually European and Asian) shipped by the ton from the West Coast, but cognoscenti who rejoice in the dusky, rich nutmeats can get the native nuts from a specialist. One such supplier is Missouri Dandy Pantry—see Mail-Order Sources, page 390, for the address.

You may have a small surplus of nut paste of either kind. It's a delicious snack for the cook, spread on a cracker and dusted with salt, or it can be tossed with the cooked noodles.

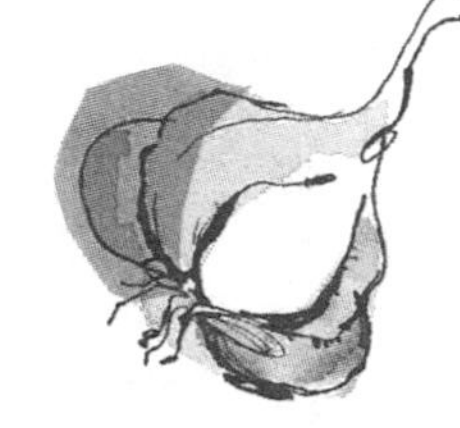

PASTA FOR GARLIC LOVERS

Heady stuff, these noodles, especially if you add roasted garlic with a generous hand (recommended), but the flavor is mellow, not acrid as it would be if raw garlic were used. The recipe gives you the choice of preparing the garlic just before use, or using Roasted Garlic Paste you've kept on hand.

Garlic noodles are admirably matched to sturdy marinara or meat sauces, or pesto (see the Index), or a simple tossing with good olive oil (or browned butter), good cheese (meaning real Parmesan) and some fresh-ground pepper. Another quick no-cooking possibility: Caponata (see the Index), chopped up a bit, warmed, and tossed with the noodles and a little olive oil—unorthodox but good.

A whole head of firm, juicy garlic (about 3 ounces) for mild flavor, twice as much for real garlic lovers; or use 2 to 4 tablespoons of Roasted Garlic Paste (page 260)
1 to 2 tablespoons olive oil
2 large eggs
1½ teaspoons salt, or to taste
3 cups fine semolina (pasta) flour (or substitute all-purpose flour)
2 to 4 tablespoons water
Additional flour for kneading and dusting the dough (all-purpose flour is fine)

Makes about 1¼ pounds fresh weight, 1 pound dried

1. If you're starting from scratch with fresh garlic, pull the head apart and remove any loose bits of skin from the cloves. Lay the cloves on a square of foil and dribble 1 tablespoon oil over them. Wrap loosely in the foil and bake, in a preheated 350°F oven, for 45 minutes to 1 hour, or until soft and somewhat golden. Cool. A clove at a time, cut off the root end and squeeze out the pulp; or press the pulp through a fine sieve. A whole head of garlic should yield about 2 tablespoons

2. Following the general directions in the master recipe (Semolina Pasta, page 266), combine the garlic pulp, 1 tablespoon olive oil, the eggs, salt, and semolina flour to make a dough, adding 2 tablespoons of water at the beginning and more water, 2 tablespoons maximum, added cautiously during mixing if needed to make a barely cohesive dough. The dough should not be wet, or you'll have to knead in a good deal of flour later to correct matters. Rest, knead, roll, and cut the dough as described.

3. Cook the noodles from their fresh-cut state, or refrigerate them for up to 3 days or freeze them, partially dried, for a month or two.

Porcini Pasta

Pure manna for mushroom lovers describes these noodles made with dried *porcini,* the boletus mushrooms imported in dried form from Italy and France as *porcini, funghi secchi porcini, cèpes,* and so on. (Certain dried mushrooms imported from Chile are closely related to European boletes; they may also be used, as can any dried American boletes you're lucky enough to acquire.)

These noodles are good enough to be a main dish on their own, simply sauced with butter or olive oil and imported Parmesan (Parmigiano-Reggiano) or combined Parmesan and pecorino. Or have an opulent bowlful tossed with sliced fresh mushrooms (any kind, wild or tame) sautéed in olive oil or butter and a little garlic, plus fresh-ground pepper. If a sauce appeals, thicken heavy cream by simmering it and add fresh-snipped chives or a combination of any favorite fresh herbs and add to the pasta with or without grated cheese. To complement roasted meat or poultry, toss the hot noodles lightly with a bit of butter and a spoonful of the pan sauce from the roast.

Upping the Ante

The quantity of porcini listed for this pasta imparts a good mushroomy savor. If you are lucky enough to have a whole bagful of dried mushrooms (most likely if you live in good mushroom country), feel free to increase the measurement when you're making special pasta for a special occasion.

1 ounce (¾ to 1 cup) dried *porcini* or other high-quality dried boletus mushrooms
1½ cups very hot water
2 large eggs
2 tablespoons olive oil, optional
1½ to 2 teaspoons salt, to taste
3 to 3½ cups fine semolina (pasta) flour (or substitute all-purpose flour)
Water, if necessary
Additional flour for kneading and dusting the dough (all-purpose flour is fine)

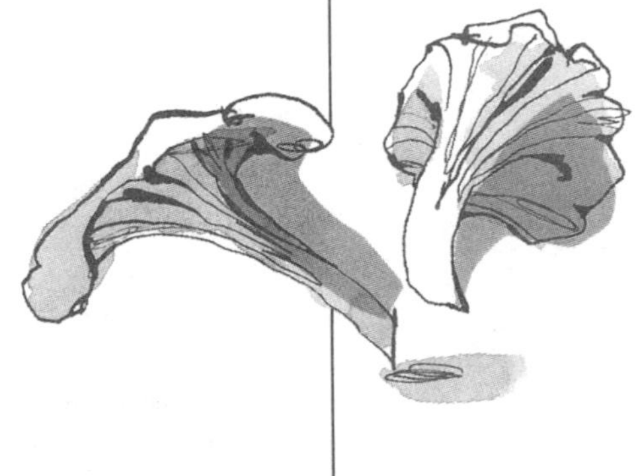

Makes 1¾ to 2 pounds, fresh weight, or 1¼ pounds dried

1. Combine the *porcini* and the hot water in a small bowl. Cover the bowl and soak the mushrooms for about 30 minutes.

2. Lift the mushrooms from the liquid into a saucepan, using a slotted spoon. Carefully pour the soaking liquid into the pan, leaving behind any grit they have released. (Or strain the liquid into the pan through a fine-meshed sieve lined with cheesecloth).

3. Cook the mushrooms, covered, over low heat until they are soft, about 20 minutes. Lift the pieces with a slotted spoon into a sieve over a bowl; press out all possible liquid and return it to the pan. Place the mushrooms in a blender or food processor. Simmer the liquid until it has reduced to 2 or 3 tablespoons and add it to the mushroom pieces, again being careful to leave behind any grit. Process the mushrooms with the liquid to a smooth paste. Let cool.

4. Following the general instructions in the master recipe (Semolina Pasta, page 266), combine the mushroom puree, eggs, oil (if used), salt, and semolina flour to make a dough; if necessary, add a little more liquid (a few drops of water) or a little more flour to make a dough that is neither too dry nor too sticky. Rest, knead, roll, and cut the dough as described in the master recipe.

5. Use the pasta fresh, cooking it in the way described, or prepare it for storage, fresh or dried, and store it as outlined in the master recipe.

Red Pepper Noodles, Mild or Hot

In their mildest version, these noodles take their sumptuous flavor from sweet red peppers or, at a pinch, bottled pimientos. From that baseline you can add hotness to taste: Add fresh red chilies or fresh hot peppers to the sweet peppers before they're steamed and pureed; or stir into the sweet-pepper puree some ground, dried red chiles (not multi-ingredient commercial chili powder), or a little ground hot red (cayenne) pepper, or hot Hungarian paprika. The ultimate degree of piquancy is up to you.

Serve any version of these pepper-pink noodles with chicken simmered in sour cream, or with a straightforward veal stew, or with any fish, fowl, or meat dish that can use a zippy accompaniment. Try ladling some *good* chili con carne (the real thing, with no beans—see the Index) over a nest of red pepper noodles and gild the composition, if you like, with a grating of good yellow "store" cheese.

Preparing the Pepper Puree

Steam 6 very large or 8 large sweet red (bell) peppers, stemmed, seeded, cored, and cut up, until very soft. Press the pulp through a food mill, or puree the peppers in a blender or a food processor. Or drain and puree three 4-ounce jars of pimientos.

1 cup pureed steamed sweet red (bell) peppers (see sidebar page 275) or canned pimientos, plus (optional) any or a combination of the following, for "hot" noodles:
- **From a pinch to ½ teaspoon ground hot red (cayenne) pepper**
- **Up to 4 tablespoons hot Hungarian paprika (or medium paprika, for less piquancy)**
- **Up to 4 tablespoons pure ground dried chiles**
- **Or include 1 or 2 fresh red chili peppers or a few small fresh hot peppers when preparing the sweet pepper puree**

3 large egg yolks
2 tablespoons olive oil, optional
2 teaspoons salt, or to taste
4 cups fine semolina (pasta) flour, or 2 cups each semolina flour and all-purpose flour
Additional flour for kneading and dusting the dough (all-purpose flour is fine)

Makes about 2½ pounds, fresh weight

1. Place the pepper puree in a sieve lined with two layers of *dry* cheesecloth and set over a bowl. Let the puree drain for as long as convenient, an hour or longer. You should have 1 cup, give or take, of firm puree.

2. Add to the puree any of the hot-pepper enhancements, if you wish. Following the instructions in the master recipe (Semolina Pasta, page 266, combine the puree, egg yolks, oil (if used), salt, and flour. Mix, knead, rest, roll, and cut the dough as described.

3. Cook the pasta at once, or store it fresh. Or dry it partly or completely. Fresh noodles will keep for up to 3 days in the refrigerator or for 1 month in the freezer. If they're partly dried (until leathery), count on up to 2 weeks in the refrigerator, 1 month in the freezer. Fully dried noodles are keepable for 3 months in either the refrigerator or freezer.

A Dried Chile with a Difference

If you plan to add ground hot chile to the dough for these noodles, consider chipotle chiles, which are ripe jalapeños dried over smoke. They are available whole, ground (the handiest form), or pickled, or put up in adobo sauce. Ground chipotles work best here.

Saffron Noodles

Unique in flavor and priced accordingly, saffron is too precious to strew around with abandon. Using saffron in these deep-golden noodles, though, is a worthwhile splurge if you'd like to serve a distinctive accompaniment for delicately (meaning creamily) sauced chicken, veal, or seafood.

Golden Luxury

Not your everyday plain-Jane pasta, Saffron Noodles are meant to accompany main dishes that complement instead of overpowering their delicate flavor. How about exotic mushrooms in cream? Buttered and lemon-sprinkled hot crabmeat, or shelled-out and butter-warmed lobster? Lemon-piqued chicken? Or a creamily sauced sauté of veal, sweetbreads, or bay scallops?

Be sure to use high-quality saffron threads, not powdered saffron, which may or may not be the genuine article. A loosely filled teaspoonful of the filaments will create noodles of delicate flavor and aroma; use up to twice as much if you like saffron a lot.

1 to 2 teaspoons saffron threads
¼ cup hot water
1½ teaspoons salt, or to taste
2 large eggs
1 to 2 tablespoons olive oil, to taste
3 cups fine semolina (pasta) flour or all-purpose flour
Additional water as needed for making the dough
Additional flour for kneading and dusting the dough (all-purpose flour is fine)

Makes about 1¾ pounds, fresh weight

1. Soak the saffron in the warm water until softened, then process the mixture in a blender until the threads are well chopped.

2. Following the general directions in the master recipe (Semolina Pasta, page 266), combine the saffron mixture, salt, eggs, olive oil, and flour to make a firm dough, adding a little water as necessary to make the ingredients cohere. Rest, knead, roll, and cut the dough as described.

3. Cook the fresh pasta at once, or dry it for storage as described in the master recipe.

Fruit Preserves & Butters, Jams, Jellies, Conserves, & Marmalades

PRESERVING

SWEET STUFF IN NEAT JARS

Summer is high season for fruits, so creating some of the jellies, conserves, butters, marmalades, jams, and classic preserves in this chapter usually requires warm-weather effort that pays off later. However, if a hammock is more inviting than cookery when the cherries are ripe, you can always freeze fruit and preserve it later, or you can plan to use the recipes for all seasons—for example, those based on apples, honey, wine, ginger, or dried apricots—or those recipes meant for winter use, such as Temple Orange Marmalade and Cranberry Preserves with Orange & Cardamom.

With missionary zeal, I'd love to convert the inexperienced to the joys of preserving, which I discovered early in my California childhood, helping my mother make strawberry, apricot, and peach jams, plus loquat and guava jellies. So we have here some easy recipes for novices as well as classics and a sprinkling of exotica. For beginners, the butters (spreads) made with apples, Bartlett pears, or pumpkin puree plus nuts are excellent start-up projects. (Preserving pointers begin on the next page.)

Seasoned preservers may ignore the preceding sentences and go directly to such devisings as Ginger Marmalade, Tomato Jam with Ginger & Coriander, and the set of intriguing wine jellies. If you invite me, I'll be over for tea, hoping for scones and *lots* of jam.

The Delightful Differences– "Preserves" Defined

To most of us, "preserves" means almost anything fruity and sweet and meant for spreading on bread, but the term formerly referred to any food specially prepared for long keeping—even pickles and smoked meats and liqueurs and dried vegetables. Here are definitions of the spreads in this chapter, most of them based on fruit (loosely including berries):

• **Butters** are usually but not always based on fruit and are smooth (buttery) in their basic texture (Apple Butter), or their smoothness may be punctuated with nut bits (Spiced Pumpkin & Pecan Butter). They are usually less sweet than jams, marmalades, conserves, jellies, and the chunky fruit preparations, neither jam nor jelly, called just "preserves."

• **Preserves**—meaning here a specific kind of "preserves," not the whole gamut of sweet spreads broadly defined by this term—are small chunks of translucent fruit or more or less whole berries suspended in syrup, which is often lightly jellied.

• **Jellies** are translucent, ideally as clear as possible, with no cloudiness from fruit pulp. A jelly holds its (jellied) shape when turned out of its container or when served with a spoon. Jellies may be made from fruit juice or may be based on such flavorful ingredients as wine, ginger, honey, or essences extracted from herbs or seeds, as you will see as you browse along. Some jellies require the help of pectin (see Jams, below).

• **Jams** are dense, usually somewhat jellied masses of mashed and sweetened fruit (or sometimes the pulp of an unusual one, such as tomato). Often lemon juice and/or pectin, a natural substance extracted from apples or citrus, is added to both jellies and jams to help the jellying process. *Pectins* include regular fruit pectin, either liquid or powdered, and "light" or "low sugar" powdered pectins used with the help of special recipes to make no-sugar or low-sugar jams and jellies. (This kind can't be used with the recipes here.)

• **Conserves** can be chunky or jammy in texture, and by definition they include extra elements, such as nuts, raisins, a touch of liqueur or brandy, or sometimes all of the above.

• **Marmalades** are traditionally made from citrus fruit (see Temple Orange Marmalade), but the name isn't restricted to citrus-based preserves, as Ginger Marmalade illustrates. Typical citrus and pulp marmalades contain thin shreds of peel in a softly jellied syrup.

• **And more besides** . . . For the curious cook, other kinds of sweet preserves include fruit curds (lemon is the most famous), pastes or cheeses (quince, guava, and so on), syrups (see the Index), and spiced (often called "pickled") fruits.

PRESERVING NOTES

There is no need to invest in special equipment (such as a pressure canner) or a cupboardful of gadgets for the preserving projects in this book. Here are notes on basic equipment and procedures called for in the recipes.

CANNING EQUIPMENT

Canning jars: Jars for preserving come in sizes that hold from half a pint to a quart. (Half-gallon jars are also available, but aren't recommended for general preserving, although they're great for storage and for certain unsealed pickles.) Cases of jars are sold in groceries and housewares and hardware stores; yard sales often yield bargains. Canning jars are made of tempered glass that can withstand heat processing and a certain amount of hard usage. This isn't true of recycled mayonnaise jars and the like, which should not be used for preserving, because the glass is not tough enough.

Both old and new types of canning jars are on the market, some of them quite exotic (the fat little round-bellied jars are especially pretty containers for preserves you want to show off). If you have anything other than the standard "Mason" jars (named for their nineteenth-century inventor), follow the manufacturer's instructions for using them. Mason jars are sold with a supply of two-piece "dome" or vacuum lids, which can also be bought separately. The jars and the ring portion of the lids can be recycled indefinitely, but the flat disks that bear the sealing material cannot be reused for canning; however, the disks may be recycled for unsealed cupboard storage of dry groceries and the like.

Jelly glasses are made of tempered glass, but their tops are not threaded to accept screw-on lids, so they must be sealed by other means, most often by a layer of paraffin wax (see page 283 for how-to's on this). The glasses are then covered with unthreaded metal or plastic lids.

Using jars for jelly: It's feasible to use straight-sided half-pint or pint canning jars and two-piece dome lids for jelly as well as jam and miscellaneous preserves. Special designs in patterned glass, with decorated lids, are available in the half-pint size.

Other equipment: Everyday spoons, ladles, bowls, sieves, and pots are fine, so long as the pots are made of nonreactive material that won't respond undesirably to the presence of acids—stainless steel, heatproof glass, or porcelain-clad or enameled metal are all satisfactory. A few special gadgets are worth acquiring, notably a wide-mouthed funnel for filling jars neatly and a jar lifter—an improvement on the usual tongs—for handling hot jars by grasping them from above. A rodlike plastic spatula for releasing bubbles from filled but not yet capped jars is useful but not essential—a long bamboo cooking chopstick, thin wooden rod, or long thin knife will do very well instead. You'll need some means of straining juice from fruit if you're planning to make jelly; see the next paragraph.

To improvise a jelly bag: Here's how to extract fruit juice for jelly without investing in a special jelly-bag setup.

Set a sieve or colander over a large bowl and line it with a large square of dampened cheesecloth, doubled if the cheesecloth is the common coarsely woven kind. (A great alternative is a piece of fine-woven nylon curtain material, which filters the juice like a charm and which can be laundered and reused for years.)

Pour the prepared fruit into the lined sieve, tie the corners of the cloth to make a bag, and hang it over the bowl from a cupboard knob or a handy hook. For the clearest possible jelly, let the juice drip on its own without putting any pressure upon the pulp. If jelly that is clear enough to win the blue ribbon isn't important to you, a little gentle pressure on the sides of the bag may be applied toward the end of draining in order to obtain more juice. How long draining will require depends on the consistency of the fruit mixture you're working with but a few hours should be allowed.

The Jelly Test

To determine whether a jelly or jam has reached the point where it will set to the correct jellied or jammy texture after cooling, dip up a small amount of the boiling mixture with a cold metal spoon and immediately pour it back into the pan from a height of about 18 inches. If the last few drops join together and shear cleanly from the spoon to drop in a small sheet, the mixture has passed the jelly test (also called the sheet test). If the sample falls in a stream or in separate drops, continue cooking and retest frequently. While testing, it's a good idea to remove the jelly/jam from the heat so it won't overcook while you test. Between tests, rinse and dry the spoon; a coating of jelly or jam from a previous test can cause a false "done" reading.

Using a candy/jelly thermometer for testing: This is the most precise way to judge the stage jelly/jam has reached. Follow the manufacturer's instructions for using your brand of thermometer; placement in the pot is important, and so is the elevation above sea level if you live above 1,000 feet. Fortunately, all the cook needs to remember is that the jellying point of a preserve is 8 degrees above the boiling point of water at a given elevation. Between sea level and just under 1,000 feet, the boiling point of water is 212°F, so the reading for jelly or jam is 220°F. At higher elevations than 1,000 feet, first use your candy/jelly thermometer to establish the temperature at which water boils vigorously, then add 8 degrees to that reading to establish the "done" temperature for jellied preserves.

Timing the boiling is used for determining the doneness of preserves only when pectin is being used; follow the recipe exactly for boiling times.

Other tests: Recipes sometimes indicate other ways of judging a mixture—for example, by chilling a sample on a cold saucer. This is suitable for some preserves that aren't meant to set firmly; the recipe will tell how the food should look if it has cooked enough.

How to Sterilize Jars & Lids

When sterilized canning jars or jelly glasses are called for, boil the clean containers for 10 minutes in enough water to cover them completely. Leave them in the hot water until they're needed, then lift them out with tongs and drain them briefly on a rack or a folded tea towel; they should be hot when they're filled.

When the jars and their contents are to be processed in a boiling-water bath, the jars needn't be sterilized, as the final processing will do the job. Jars should be spanking clean and scalded in hot water just before use; running them through a brief rinse and dry in the dishwasher is a handy ploy.

Lids: If you're using two-piece ("dome") lids, scald the flat disks (which must be new) and the clean rings (which are reusable) by immersing them in boiling water; leave them in the water, off heat, until they're needed. If another type of lid is used, consult the manufacturer's directions.

Corks used to seal vinegars or syrups should be new, not recycled. Boil them for 10 minutes, then drain them until cool and dry.

How to Fill & Seal Jars

When filling jars or jelly glasses, use a funnel to keep the rims clean. Fill them to the level specified in the recipe, which will indicate the level as "headspace." (Headspace varies according to the type of food being dealt with.) Wipe the rim of the filled jar with a folded cloth or paper towel dipped into boiling water, lay the disk portion of the two-piece dome lid in place, then screw on the ring with only moderate firmness—don't overtighten it. Don't assemble the two pieces and then apply the lid to the jar—this can prevent sealing.

If you use another type of lid or jar closure, follow the manufacturer's sealing instructions. For sealing jellies with paraffin, see "Sealing with Paraffin." If the recipe calls for processing jars in a boiling-water bath, proceed as described in "How to Process Jars in a Boiling-Water Bath."

Removing air bubbles: This is necessary when largish pieces of food are involved (for some pickles, for instance); it's not necessary for jams and such. A plastic or wooden implement is run down inside the jar to release any air bubbles. I use a long bamboo chopstick that does double duty as part of a set for Chinese cooking; a special rod for the purpose is sold by vendors of canning supplies.

Cooling: When the sealing or processing is complete, set the jars or glasses to cool on a wooden, plastic, or cloth-covered surface; if set directly on cold tile, metal, or marble, it's possible (if uncommon) for hot jars to crack. Do not attempt to tighten the rings of two-piece lids even if they seem loose after processing; this may break the seal on the disk.

Testing the seal: After cooling is complete (allow at least 12 hours), tap the center of dome lids with a teaspoon. A clear "ping" indicates a complete seal; a dull sound indicates an incomplete seal. Either replace the cap with a new one and redo the entire processing (the time will be the same as before), or store the jar in the refrigerator and use the food within its normal refrigerator lifespan.

If you have used another type of lid or closure, check the seal in the way directed by the manufacturer.

To Process Jars in a Boiling-Water Bath

After each jar is filled and capped, set it on a rack or a folded tea towel in a deep pot set on a stove burner and half filled with hot water. Use a canning kettle with a rack if you have one; otherwise, improvise with a stock pot or other vessel at least 4 or 5 inches deeper than the height of the rack plus jars. The jars should not touch each other or the side of the pot. When all the jars are in place, add boiling water to cover the lids by at least 2 inches.

Timing: Raise the heat and bring the water to a tumultuous boil, then start timing the processing; maintain a steady boil for the time specified in the recipe. (See below for adjusting the timing for higher elevations.) Remove the jars from the water and set them well apart on wire racks or on a layer of folded towels to cool. After leaving them overnight or for up to 24 hours, test the seal (page 283).

Adjusting the processing time for higher elevations: When a recipe says to process jars for 20 minutes or less, that timing is correct for elevations of less than 1,000 feet. At 1,000 feet, add 1 minute of processing time, and add 1 minute for each additional 1,000 feet or fraction of 1,000 feet.

When using a recipe calling for more than 20 minutes of processing time, add 2 minutes at 1,000 feet; add 2 minutes more for each 1,000 feet or fraction.

Sealing with Paraffin

Sealing jelly or certain other preserves (by no means *all* sweet preserves) into glasses or straight-sided jars with paraffin wax is a time-honored and handy way to protect them from deterioration. Don't seal with paraffin unless the recipe so directs.

Cut new paraffin wax (old wax should not be reused, as it can cause spoilage) into chunks and melt it in a clean, dry metal container set in a pan of simmering water. (You can improvise a container from a washed and dried food can, with the edge pinched to form a lip for pouring.) Set aside in the hot water.

After filling the jelly glasses or jars, wipe any splashes of jelly from the headspace area with a spotless cloth dipped into hot water. Pour a thin layer of wax—about ⅛ inch—over the hot jelly, making sure it touches the glass all around. If any bubbles appear, prick them. Let the wax set, then remelt the remaining wax and add a second thin layer, tilting the glass to seal the edges of the second coat to the glass. When the wax and jelly are completely cool, cover the glasses with their plastic or metal lids, or improvise snug covers with foil or plastic wrap and rubber bands.

Store the container of leftover wax in a closed plastic bag in the cupboard.

Labeling for the Sake of Sanity

Here speaks the voice of experience: Don't assume that you'll remember next December exactly what's in the jars you lovingly filled in June. Invest in a package of self-stick labels from the office-supplies counter and label each and every jar as soon as it has cooled (if it was hot to begin with). Include the date and, if you're likely to need the reminder, a "use-by" date, to be sure the contents are enjoyed at their best.

Storing Preserves

A dark, dry, cool cupboard is the best place to keep all preserves, pickles, condiments, and relishes. If finding the perfect spot is impossible, at least avoid putting your goodies in a strongly lighted, hot, or damp location. I've tried keeping preserves for as long as a decade and found many, especially marmalades, to be perfectly fine after their Rip van Winkle nap, but quality does tend to head downhill after a year or two.

Alternative Storage

Storing a small batch of preserves in the refrigerator (for a few weeks) or the freezer (for considerably longer, but not forever) can be convenient. (Jellies don't freeze well, however.) No need to seal and process jars for either storage mode, but be sure to allow an inch of headspace in jars bound for the deep-freeze, as the contents will expand.

APPLES FOR EXCELLENCE, NOT JUST LOOKS

Orchardists who grow the apples they find most delectable and best adapted to their area, leaving the mass market to agribusiness, are thriving here and there, much to the benefit of neighboring consumers. (An example: John Halsey, of a family that has farmed here on eastern Long Island for eleven generations, now grows twenty or more kinds of apples and has plans for adding more in coming seasons.) Each October, we're able to buy Mutsu (or Crispin), Braeburn, Gala, Paulared, Granny Smith, Jonamac, Jonagold, Macoun, Cortland, Golden Delicious, Empire, Winesap, Stayman, Idared, Ginger Gold, Golden Russet, Baldwin, McIntosh, Fuji, Pink Lady, Honey Crisp, and more besides. Some varieties of our local apples are available for about nine months of the year, thanks to modern storage. Past fall, choosing a few of each kind of local apples we'd bought

(cont.)

APPLE BUTTER WITH (ALMOST) NOTHING ADDED

Wonderful apples of unusual varieties are such an October luxury that I can't resist making old-fashioned apple butter from local fruit plus (supermarket) apple juice, throwing in a sprinkling of spice if I'm feeling expansive. For our taste no sugar is needed in a really great batch, but that will depend on the choice of fruit and the cook's opinion of the final sweetness of the potful.

Choose the winiest, crispest apples you can get, plus a few of a fragrant, sweet kind for balance; you can mix apple varieties endlessly, depending on what's available to you. It's a good thing to make your apple butter while the new crop is still new, before the season of stored apples sets in.

A big (5-quart) slow-cooker is the utensil to use unless you are going to be free to check and stir a stovetop pot very often. Either way, the cooking may be done in more than one "spell," as described below, if your schedule is fragmented. If you would like to double the batch, bring the apples and liquid to a boil on the stovetop and cook, stirring occasionally, until the apples have collapsed to a manageable measure, then switch to the cooker.

6 pounds of really fresh apples, pared, cored, and sliced
1 can (12 ounces) frozen apple juice concentrate, thawed, or 1½ cups water
Optional spices: 2 or 3 whole cloves, 2 or 3 whole allspice berries, about 2 inches of stick cinnamon, broken up
Sugar or sugar substitute, optional (use a sugar substitute that is heat stable)
Strained fresh lemon juice, optional

Makes about 4 half-pint jars

1. Combine the apples and concentrated apple juice or water in a slow-cooker, stirring to moisten the pieces. Cover and cook on high until boiling; lower the setting to low, or maintain high heat throughout the cooking as preferred. Uncover the cooker, wipe accumulated moisture from the underside of the cover, and stir the mixture every hour or so. (Optionally, jump-start the job by cooking the mixture over direct stovetop heat until the apple pieces have begun to soften, then continue with the slow cooker. This reduces the overall cooking time.) Lacking a slow cooker, use a heavy nonreactive pot and a protective mat over the stove burner; cook the apple butter uncovered, stirring it very often and taking care not to allow it to scorch.

2. Cook the apple butter until it is thick and prune-colored. If you decide to use the spices, add them about midway. The spread is done when it is thick enough to mound up in a spoon when a sample is lifted. (Or test by spooning some onto a plate and leaving it for a few minutes; very little liquid should seep out.) Depending on the level of heat chosen, slow-cooked apple butter will be done in 8 to 10 hours. Cooking may be done in two or more sessions if more convenient; cool the apple butter, uncovered, between sessions, or refrigerate if it must wait more than a few hours.

3. When done, press the apple butter through a sieve or a food mill, using the fine disk, or puree it in a blender, then sieve it for super silkiness if you wish. Taste for sweetness and decide whether to add a little sugar or sugar substitute. If the spread needs a touch of tartness (this will depend on the raw material), add a little fresh lemon juice.

4. *For refrigerator or freezer storage:* Reheat the apple butter and ladle it into sterilized jars (page 282), leaving an inch of headspace if it's to be frozen, and cover with sterilized lids. It keeps well for a month or two in the fridge, indefinitely in the freezer.

For pantry storage: Reheat it to boiling and ladle it into hot, clean half-pint or pint canning jars, leaving ¼ inch headspace. Fit new two-piece canning lids in place according to manufacturer's directions and process the jars for 10 minutes in a boiling-water bath (page 283). Cool, label, and store in a cool, dry cupboard for up to a year.

APRICOT PRESERVES

When all's said and done, this may be the best fruit preserve of all, with the possible exception of . . . well, let's not play favorites. Certainly ripe, fragrant apricots make a peerless sweet spread to enjoy with toast, or croissants, or muffins. It's the pastry chef's choice for glazing the top of a fruit tart, or for filling tartlets. Stirred with a few drops of Amaretto or other liqueur, apricot preserves top off a scoop of basic vanilla ice cream in great style.

To avoid disappointment, buy only those apricots that look as if they might come to full ripeness—it is too much to hope, except perhaps in a California backyard, to find tree-ripened fruit. Very green or oversoft specimens will not give good results. If your apricots for preserving are a mixed bag, in order to have the whole batch ready for use at the same time, you might refrigerate the fruits as they become firm-ripe and let the rest catch up at room temperature.

Another possibility for apricot fans: Dried Apricot & Amaretto Conserve (see the Index).

(cont.)

(including Orange Pippins we scooped up at one farm), we made several batches of apple butter sans *sugar, some piqued with the smallest touch of spicing, and enjoyed the relatively low-calorie spread all winter (and it hasn't all been eaten up yet).*

If you must rely on store-bought apples, make apple butter while the crop is still fresh, and try to find varieties with tartness and character. Only sampling will tell you which of the commercial varieties have good looks but little flavor. My own nomination for a disappointing apple is the good-looking Red Delicious.

Apricots—The Gardener's Hope

Writing recipes for fresh apricots requires a hopeful spirit—for complicated reasons, this earliest and most delectable of the summer fruits is rarely found to be of good quality (meaning ripe and fragrant) in markets. Try to find apricots that are well colored but still firm; mushy and green fruit are both pretty useless. The best-flavored varieties—like Blenheim—are seldom if ever found in commerce, so anyone having space and inclination to grow a few trees might consult nurserymen's catalogs for apricots suitable for their region. Our own tree blossoms without fail—a lovely spectacle, especially in a late snowfall—and some years it even produces apricots. We appreciate the fruit when it does appear, watching sharply to harvest it before the squirrels do.

3 pounds ripe apricots, preferably large ones
6 to 8 apricot kernels, optional (see steps 1 and 2)
⅓ cup strained fresh lemon juice
6 cups sugar

Makes about 7 cups

1. Scald the apricots in batches by placing them in a sieve and plunging them into boiling water for about 15 seconds; then drop them into a bowl of cold water and ice. Drain the apricots, strip off their skins, quarter them, and save the pits, if you wish to include a few of the kernels in the preserves—they contribute a delicate touch of almondlike flavor.

2. If you are using the kernels, crack 6 to 8 pits (a sledgehammer or a heavy-duty nutcracker, such as one designed for black walnuts, makes short work of this) and remove the kernels. Blanch them for a moment or two in boiling water, then drain them and slip off the skins of the kernels, which look very much like almonds.

3. Combine the apricots, kernels (if used), and the lemon juice in a ceramic, glass, or stainless-steel bowl and mix them gently with a rubber spatula. Add the sugar and mix again. Set the mixture aside for a few hours (or for as long as overnight, in this case in the refrigerator), stirring it gently a few times.

4. When almost all of the sugar has dissolved, transfer the mixture to a preserving pan and set the pan over medium heat. Bring the mixture to a boil, then adjust the heat and simmer for 10 minutes, stirring a few times with a straight-edged spatula. Skim off any foam, then cook the preserve for 20 minutes more, or until the fruit is translucent. (The actual time will depend on the variety and ripeness of the fruit. Don't cook too fast or too long or the fruit may turn to mush.)

5. Pour the mixture into a bowl and let it cool, then cover with a cloth and leave at room temperature overnight or for at least 6 hours.

6. Lift the fruit with a slotted spoon into a sieve set over a bowl. Let the juice drain from the fruit for a few minutes. Return all the juice to the preserving pan and bring it to a boil over medium-high heat; boil it rapidly until it passes the jelly test (page 282). Return the fruit to the boiling syrup, together with any additional syrup it may have released, and bring everything to a boil; boil hard for 1 minute. Remove from the heat.

7. Cool the preserves for 5 minutes, stirring occasionally, then ladle into hot, clean half-pint canning jars, leaving ¼ inch of headspace. Seal the jars with new two-piece canning lids according to manufacturer's directions and process for 15 minutes in a boiling-water bath (page 283). Cool, label, and store the jars. The preserves keep for at least a year in a cool cupboard.

Bartlett Butter~A Fruit Spread

No special talent for preserving is needed for creating this fragrant, just-sweet-enough spread made from Bartlett pears, which seem to be available in the market almost the year around. (But their fragrance and flavor are best in their harvest season, late summer and fall.) The pear butter may be refrigerated for storage (or frozen for future reference) if you prefer not to seal it for the cupboard shelf.

The touch of pear brandy (eau de vie) adds an extra dimension, but it may be omitted. It's fine to double this recipe, and a slow-cooker works very well with it. Slow-cooked pear butter will be ruddy in color; stovetop cooking preserves more of the greenish-gold of fresh pears.

4 pounds fully golden-ripe but not spotted or mushy Bartlett pears (they are ripe when they yield to light pressure near the stem)
1 cup water
6 tablespoons fresh lemon juice (juice of 2 lemons)
2 teaspoons finely grated or minced lemon zest, outer peel only, no white pith (or substitute ¼ teaspoon lemon oil—*not* lemon extract)
¼ teaspoon salt, optional (but it rounds the flavor)
½ vanilla bean, split, or ⅛ teaspoon ground vanilla from a specialist supplier)
1 cup sugar, or more to taste
1 to 2 tablespoons pear eau-de-vie (pear brandy) or pear schnapps, optional

Makes about 3 cups

1. Peel, core, and chop the pears roughly to make 8 cups fruit.

2. Combine the pears in a large stainless-steel or other nonreactive pot with the water, lemon juice, zest, salt, and vanilla. Bring the mixture to a boil, stirring, then regulate the heat to maintain a gentle boil and cook, uncovered, stirring often to prevent sticking, until the pears are very soft.

3. Remove the vanilla bean, if used, and press the pears through the fine disk of a food mill or a medium-fine sieve and return the pulp to the pan. Add 1 cup of sugar and cook, stirring almost constantly, until the butter is dense enough to mound in a spoon when a sample is lifted. (Or test by spooning a sample onto a saucer and setting it aside

To Microwave Fruit Butter

A large microwave oven plus a large glass or ceramic casserole, and you're in business with fruit butter–making with no watching and only occasional stirring. The trick is dividing cooking time into periods after the pears (or apples, for apple butter) have come to a boil at full power. At that point, reduce the power and cook the fruit gently, partly covered, until soft, for a few minutes at a time, stirring in between. After the fruit has been pureed and sweetened, again cook the butter, now uncovered, for a few minutes at a time, stirring and checking its consistency after each period. Total cooking time will depend on the power of the microwave and the size of the batch.

for a few minutes—very little liquid should seep out.) Taste for sweetness and a desirable small touch of tartness. If necessary, add more sugar and/or drops of lemon juice. Stir in the pear eau de vie (if used).

4. *For refrigerator or freezer storage:* Spoon the spread into jars that have been sterilized (page 282), leaving ½ inch of headspace (1 inch if you're going to freeze the butter). Cover with sterilized lids and cool. Refrigerate for several weeks' storage, or freeze almost indefinitely.

5. *For pantry storage:* Ladle the spread into hot, clean half-pint canning jars, leaving ¼ inch of headspace. Cover with two-piece canning lids according to the manufacturer's directions and process for 10 minutes in a boiling-water bath (page 283). Cool, label, and store in a cupboard for up to a year.

Blueberry & Orange Preserves

A soft preserve of the classic type, this spread has chunky blueberries and shreds of orange zest suspended in a rich syrup. For the proper delicate texture, be careful not to cook the preserves to the jam stage, which is considerably stiffer and can be rather boring if the fruit flavors are subtle, as here.

The light spicing prescribed by the recipe is optional if you are using wild blueberries, which are more flavorful than the tame kind.

2 large, clear-skinned oranges, preferably seedless
1 cup water
3 pint baskets (about 9 cups) fresh blueberries, cultivated or wild
7 cups sugar
¾ cup strained fresh lemon juice
1 teaspoon freshly ground coriander or ground cinnamon, optional
½ teaspoon ground allspice, optional

Makes about 8 cups

1. Remove the zest (outer peel only, no white pith) from the oranges with a coarse grater or a citrus zester and combine it with the water in a small heavy saucepan. Cook the zest, covered, over medium heat for 15 minutes; uncover the pan and continue to cook until most of the liquid has evaporated. Reserve. Meanwhile, squeeze, strain, and reserve the juice of the oranges.

Winter Preserving

Fresh blueberries freeze beautifully, as noted elsewhere, so making this sweet spread in the dead of winter is perfectly feasible. If you haven't wrapped and frozen pints of the berries in midsummer, berries frozen commercially without sugar are usually excellent. Try to find wild blueberries, which have a special fragrance of their own.

2. Pick over the blueberries; rinse and drain them, then crush them slightly, a layer at a time, in a preserving pan. (Easiest to do with a pestle-type potato masher or the bottom of a heavy bottle.) Add the orange juice. Bring the mixture to a boil, cover the pan, lower the heat, and simmer the fruit 10 minutes, stirring it often.

3. Add the orange zest and its liquid, the sugar, lemon juice, and the spices (if used). Stir the mixture and bring it to a boil over medium-high heat. Cook the preserves, stirring often, until the fruit pieces no longer float and the syrup passes the jelly test (page 282). Remove the pan from the heat and let stand, stirring the preserves occasionally, for 5 minutes.

4. Ladle the hot preserves into hot, clean pint or half-pint jars, leaving ¼ inch of headspace. Seal the jars with new two-piece canning lids according to manufacturer's directions and process for 10 minutes (either size jar) in a boiling-water bath (page 283). Cool, label, and store the jars. The preserves keep for at least a year in a cool cupboard.

Classic Strawberry Preserves

The way I make classic pure strawberry preserves—whole berries suspended in a not-quite-jellied syrup made without added pectin—may need explanation for strawberry fans expecting to find a jam-making method.

Several steps are involved, but not much working time. Don't be tempted to double the size of a batch being cooked, as the briefest possible cooking is essential. However, doubling or tripling the ingredients is feasible—just divide the large batch of macerated fruit and syrup into halves or thirds, as appropriate, and cook one batch at a time. All the jars from the batches can be processed together—just set the first batch(es) of filled and capped jars aside until the rest are ready, then proceed with the boiling-water processing of all the jars at once.

You'll notice that the berries and sugar produce a frightful amount of syrup in step 1 and the berries look shriveled, not to say puny. All is as it should be; the remainder of the process plumps up the berries remarkably, and by the time they reach the jars they are perfect.

2 quart baskets small firm-ripe strawberries, the finest-flavored you can find
6 cups sugar
Strained juice of 1½ large lemons, or more if needed

Makes about 5 cups

Strawberry Fields Less Than Forever

My way of making strawberry preserves stems from the teachings of a Long Island lady whose family cultivated broad fields of berries within fog-reach of the ocean beaches, here where I used to live in the summer and now live all year. Sadly, fewer strawberry fields remain each season—big handsome vacation houses are being planted where big, handsome berries used to thrive in summer sun and mist.

1. Sort, hull, rinse, and drain the berries; discard any with either soft or unripe areas. Layer the berries with the sugar in a ceramic, glass, or stainless-steel bowl, then fold the fruit and sugar together with a rubber spatula. Let the berries stand overnight at room temperature, covered, stirring them gently a few times when you think of it; the idea is to dissolve all the sugar before proceeding.

2. Scrape the berries and syrup into a preserving pan or a large (12-inch) sauté pan or nonstick skillet. Add the juice of 1½ lemons. Bring the mixture to a boil, stirring it occasionally, and boil it briskly for 3 minutes, giving it a stir from time to time. Pour the berries and syrup into a bowl and cool uncovered. Cover with a cloth and leave undisturbed at room temperature for at least 6 hours or for as long as overnight.

3. Drain off all the syrup through a colander or sieve and return it to the pan. Bring it to a boil over medium-high heat, then boil hard until the syrup passes the jelly test (page 282). Add the berries and any syrup they have accumulated to the pan of syrup, bring everything to a boil again, stirring gently once or twice to prevent sticking (be careful not to break the fruit). Boil the preserves until the berries are translucent and the syrup again passes the jelly test. Depending on the original juiciness of the fruit, this will take only 2 to 4 minutes. Remove from the heat. Taste the syrup; if a little more tartness is needed (berries vary a lot in acidity), add a little more strained fresh lemon juice.

4. Skim off any foam and stir the preserves gently from time to time for 5 minutes, to prevent the fruit from floating in the jars. Ladle the preserves into hot, clean half-pint canning jars, leaving ¼ inch of headspace. Seal the jars with new two-piece canning lids according to manufacturer's directions and process for 15 minutes in a boiling-water bath (page 283). Cool, label, and store the jars. The preserves will keep for at least a year in a cool cupboard.

Preserves Made with Frozen Strawberries

Strawberries frozen whole, without sugar, make good preserves if they haven't been frozen too long; 6 months is the limit of freezer life if you expect good flavor, and it's preferable to use the berries much sooner.

Use 2 cups of sugar for each pound (about 3 cups) of frozen berries, plus the strained juice of a small lemon or half of a very large lemon. Add more lemon juice at the end of cooking if needed for sweet-tart balance. There is no need to thaw the berries before macerating them with the sugar; dissolving the sugar will take considerably longer, and the mixture will require occasional stirring.

Coriander Seed & Honey Jelly

The subtle perfume of honey and the citrus-like flavor of coriander seeds make this jelly a favorite at our house. Golden-amber in color, it is delicately spicy and only slightly tart, lovely on buttered toast, English muffins, or all-American hot breads. A few spoonfuls, melted with a little water, make a glistening glaze for a tart made with any fruit.

Coriander seed, for any who may not know it, has a flavor and aroma reminiscent of a ripe orange, both a world away from the brash pungency of fresh coriander (cilantro) leaves. The leaves, which are much used in Asian and Mexican cuisines, take some getting used to, but the delicate and delightful seed is another matter entirely.

⅓ cup coriander seed
3 cups water
¼ cup strained fresh lemon juice
¼ cup mild-flavored honey
1 package (1¾ ounces) regular powdered pectin (not the kind meant for making low-sugar preserves)
3 cups sugar

Makes about 4 cups

1. Crush the coriander seed in a mortar, or whirl it briefly in a blender, or spread between sheets of plastic or waxed paper and crack with a rolling pin.

2. Combine the seed and water in a saucepan. Bring the mixture just to a boil over low heat. Remove the pan from the heat, cover, and let stand for 3 to 6 hours.

3. Strain the liquid through a sieve lined with two layers of cheesecloth or a layer of very fine nylon net. Measure 2½ cups of the liquid into a preserving pan.

4. Add the lemon juice, honey, and pectin to the liquid and stir them together thoroughly. Set the pan over medium-high heat and bring the mixture to a hard boil (a boil that can't be stirred down). Stir in the sugar and again bring the mixture to a boil; when it reaches a full rolling boil that can't be stirred down, begin timing and boil the mixture exactly 1 minute. Remove from the heat.

5. Skim off any foam and pour the jelly at once into hot, sterilized (page 282) jelly glasses or straight-sided half-pint canning jars, leaving ½ inch of headspace in the glasses or ⅛ inch in the jars. Seal the jelly in

Coriander Seed from the Garden

Coriander is easy to grow—simply sow some of your kitchen supply of seed in a sunny outdoor spot in spring, or buy a packet of seed from a garden center. To assure a seed crop, don't harvest the foliage, or do so very lightly. Gather the seed in late summer as soon as it has dried a bit but has not begun to drop to the ground. Let it dry thoroughly out of the sun, then store in a stoppered bottle in a cool cupboard.

glasses with melted paraffin; seal the canning jars with sterilized new two-piece lids according to the manufacturer's directions. Cool, label, and store. The jelly will keep for a year in a cool cupboard.

Cranberry Preserves with Orange & Cardamom

Cardamom, one of the most delightful of spices but too little used, here subtly emphasizes the flavors of both cranberry and orange in a versatile compound that's both a table relish (we're thinking here of cranberry sauce with a big difference) and a chunky, sweet-tart spread for toast and such. The cranberries are translucent and almost whole because they're baked, not boiled, a process that happily requires little attention.

If you have a spice mill, by all means grind the fragrant cardamom yourself instead of buying it ready ground; it tends to lose flavor quickly after grinding. For a double batch of preserves, use a large, shallow nonaluminum roasting pan. The timing will be the same.

4 cups firm fresh cranberries, picked over and rinsed (if they are frozen, it is not necessary to thaw them)
1 medium-size seedless orange
3 cups sugar
1/8 teaspoon ground cardamom, freshly ground if possible
1/4 cup water

Makes about 3 cups

1. Spread the cranberries in an 8-inch square glass baking dish or other shallow nonaluminum pan of about the same overall area.

2. Remove the skin from the orange in strips and scrape the white pith from the inside; discard the pith. Chop the outer peel and the pulp of the orange very fine (a food processor will do this quickly); remove any large bits of membrane that survive the chopping.

3. Stir the chopped orange, sugar, and cardamom into the cranberries, mixing them thoroughly. Sprinkle the water over the mixture, then cover the dish tightly with aluminum foil.

4. Bake the mixture in the center of a preheated 350°F oven for 30 minutes. Then lower the oven heat to 325°F, uncover the dish, and stir

Exploring Cranberries

They're not for relishes only, these brilliant, tart berries—anyone devoted to their zesty character will dote on this cardamom-scented cranberry preserve. Spread it on whole-grain toast for a different breakfast bite.

the fruit in the syrup that has formed, using a flat spatula; then continue to bake the preserves, uncovered, until the berries are translucent and the syrup has thickened, about 45 minutes, stirring the mixture gently every 10 or 15 minutes.

5. Spoon the hot preserves into hot, clean half-pint or pint canning jars, leaving ¼ inch of headspace; seal with new two-part canning lids according to manufacturer's directions and process for 10 minutes (for either size jar) in a boiling-water bath (page 283). Cool, label, and store the jars. The preserves will keep for a year in a cool cupboard. Alternatively, you can refrigerate the preserves, unsealed, in a sterilized jar (page 282) for several months.

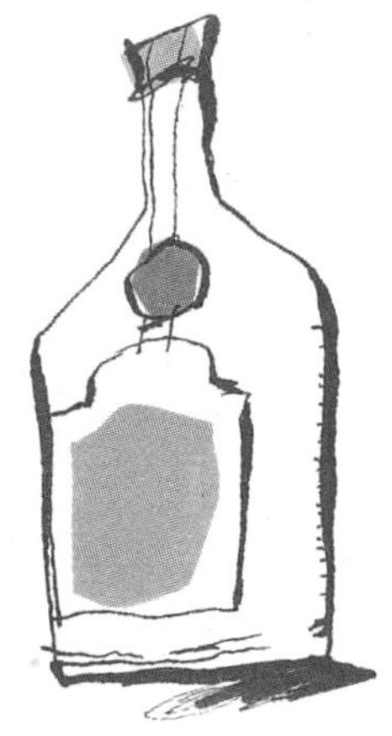

Dried Apricot & Amaretto Conserve

Not to worry if you'd like to give distinctive Christmas presents when your stock of choice preserves is running low or running on empty: this golden, almond-studded conserve can be made at any season. Dried apricots are always to be had, as is Amaretto liqueur, the almond-flavored liaison between fruit and nuts.

Taste the fruit before buying it; high-quality dried apricots positively shimmer with flavor, but lesser grades have mostly tartness to recommend them.

½ pound high-quality dried apricot halves, about 1½ cups
1 cup golden raisins
3 cups water, more if needed
1½ teaspoons finely grated orange zest (outer peel only, no white pith)
1 cup strained fresh orange juice
2 tablespoons strained fresh lemon juice
2½ cups sugar
½ cup slivered blanched almonds (see sidebar opposite)
3 tablespoons Amaretto liqueur

Makes about 4 cups

1. Snip the apricots into thin strips, using scissors. Combine them with the raisins in a bowl, add the water, and let the fruit soak until it is very soft, several hours (or overnight, refrigerated).

An Apricot Hedge

Elsewhere in these pages the scarcity of good fresh apricots has been bewailed. This conserve of dried fruit will make apricot aficionados quite happy when obtaining fresh fruit is out of the question. It pays to shop around for dried fruit—(don't overlook mail order). Your enjoyable researches will uncover apricots imported from Turkey, France, Pakistan (the famous Hunza fruit), Iran, and Australia, as well as domestically grown and dried kinds.

To Blanch Almonds

Drop them into a panful of simmering water, then remove the pan from the heat. After a minute or two, when the skin slips easily from a sample, drain the almonds and skin them. Spread them on a baking pan in a warm (200°F) oven to dry for about 15 minutes, then sliver them with a heavy knife on a cutting board.

2. Tip the fruit and liquid into a stainless-steel or other nonreactive heavy saucepan; if there is not enough liquid to come halfway to the top of the fruit, add up to another cup of water. Add the grated orange zest. Heat the mixture to simmering and cook it, stirring once or twice, until the fruit is very tender, about 15 minutes.

3. Stir in the orange and lemon juice and return the mixture to a boil. Add the sugar and cook the conserve over medium heat, stirring it almost constantly with a wooden spatula or other straight-ended implement, until it is thick, 20 to 30 minutes. To test, remove the pan from the heat, spoon a sample onto a chilled saucer, and let it cool; when the saucer is held on edge, the conserve should cling and its surface should wrinkle. Add the almonds and cook, stirring, 5 minutes longer. Remove from the heat.

4. Stir in the Amaretto. Ladle the conserve into hot, clean half-pint canning jars, leaving ¼ inch of headspace. Seal the jars with new two-piece canning lids according to manufacturer's directions and process them 10 minutes in a boiling-water bath (page 283). Cool, label, and store the jars. The conserve is all the better for mellowing in the jars for a week or two before it is served. It will keep for at least a year in a cool cupboard.

Fresh Ginger Jelly

Sweet-hot ginger jelly rejoices in a delicate peach-amber color and a take-charge flavor that makes it quite addictive once tasted. Fortunately, it can be made at any time of the year, not just the brief summer season of the very young, tender crop of stem ginger preferred for Ginger Marmalade and Ginger Pickled in the Japanese Fashion (see the Index). The ginger you use for this jelly, if it's mature (most is), should be plump and silky-skinned, not withered and weary.

If, like me, you hate to waste bits and pieces of good stuff, you'll welcome the tidings that this jelly can be made satisfactorily from the fibrous cores of mature ginger set aside when making either the pickled ginger or the marmalade.

Ginger jelly is especially good on toast, muffins, or biscuits when ham, bacon, sausage, or other meaty items are on the breakfast or brunch table. It's a lively topping for crackers spread with cream cheese (or low-fat Yogurt Cheese; see the Index). It highly complements to cold meats, especially roasted or smoked chicken and cold roast pork, the latter an unjustly neglected cold viand that makes fine eating on a hot day.

A Gingery Invention

Ginger marmalade (see page 296 for a recipe) has been around in fancy-food circles for a while, but I meet Ginger Jelly only after I've made a batch at home. Doing likewise is most cordially urged upon anyone who likes both ginger and unusual spreads.

¼ pound fresh, juicy ginger (for about 1 cup, sliced)
1 cup water, or more as needed
6 tablespoons strained fresh lemon juice
3½ cups sugar
1 pouch (3 ounces) or one-half 6-ounce bottle liquid pectin

Makes about 3 cups

1. Scrub the ginger; it is not necessary to peel it. Trim away any bruised, soft, or callused parts; slice roughly.

2. Combine the ginger pieces with the 1 cup water in the container of a food processor or blender and run the machine in on-off bursts just until the ginger has been chopped fine—don't puree it.

3. Pour the chopped ginger and its liquid into a fine-meshed sieve set over a bowl and press as much liquid as possible out of the pulp. Discard the pulp. Let the liquid stand at least 1 hour to settle.

4. Carefully pour the liquid off the starchy-looking sediment into a 2-cup measure. You should have 1¼ cups; if not, add enough water to make up the amount.

5. Combine the ginger liquid with the lemon juice in a preserving pan. Heat to simmering over medium-high heat, then add the sugar and stir until it has dissolved completely. When the mixture reaches a hard boil (a boil that cannot be stirred down), stir in the pectin. When the mixture returns to a full rolling boil, start timing and boil for exactly 1 minute. Remove the pan from the heat.

6. Skim off any foam and pour the jelly at once into hot, sterilized (page 282) jelly glasses or straight-sided half-pint canning jars, leaving ⅛ inch of headspace in the jars and ½ inch in the glasses. Seal the jelly in glasses with melted paraffin; seal canning jars with new two-part lids according to manufacturer's directions. Cool, label, and store the jars. The jelly keeps for at least a year in a cool cupboard.

GINGER MARMALADE

One of the best of all possible marmalades is this tender jelly studded with shreds of ginger—a connoisseur's choice, when it can be found in shops.

Ginger marmalade is ideally made with stem ginger—young, tender-skinned, juicy ginger—which isn't available always, much less everywhere. However, wherever there is a Chinatown, it can be found in its short season, the few weeks after midsummer. At other times and in

Big-City Advantage

For wonderfully fresh fruits and vegetables, farm-stand country more than holds its own, at least in summer, against the big city. But when you're looking for special ingredients needed for the ethnic cuisines that survive best in urban centers, the cities win. For stem ginger, for instance, you need a city greengrocer with an Asian clientele. However, as noted in the recipe, mature ginger can be used for Ginger Marmalade, and fortunately it is now sold everywhere in supermarkets.

other places, the tender layer of flesh just under the skin of regular (mature) ginger can be used; the modifications of method are noted in the recipe. Be careful to choose only plump, unwithered "hands" if you are using mature ginger.

½ pound unblemished stem ginger (young, pink-tinged ginger) or 1 to 1¼ pounds mature ginger
6 cups water
½ cup strained fresh lemon juice
4 cups sugar
Pinch of salt, optional
1 pouch (3 ounces) or one-half 6-ounce bottle liquid pectin

Makes about 5 cups

1. *Using stem ginger:* Scrape the skin of stem ginger lightly with a small sharp knife, removing any blemishes as well as the papery bits of leaf sheath that are attached here and there. Trim off any dried ends. Rinse the pieces, pat them dry, and break them apart at the joints. Using a citrus zester or a grater with small sharp teeth, shred the ginger into threads, working over a bowl to catch all the juice. You should have 1⅓ to 1½ cups, lightly packed.

Using mature ginger: Pare or scrape off the skin and grate the tender outer layer only (save the fibrous cores to make Fresh Ginger Jelly, page 295); grate enough to obtain 1⅓ to 1½ cups, lightly packed. Combine the grated ginger with a quart of water, bring to a boil, and boil 5 minutes. Drain; add fresh cold water, then repeat the boiling and draining twice. Drain well.

2. Combine the grated ginger, its juice (if you are using stem ginger), and 6 cups water in a preserving pan; bring the mixture to a boil, cover, lower the heat, and simmer the ginger gently until the shreds are very tender and almost translucent, about 1¼ hours. Remove from the heat.

3. Measure the ginger and liquid. If you have more than 3 cups, spoon off the surplus liquid. (Save it—add sugar and mix the resulting syrup with chilled club soda for a pleasant refreshment while you make the marmalade.)

4. Combine the measured ginger and liquid, the lemon juice, sugar, and salt in the rinsed-out preserving pan. Bring the mixture to a hard boil (a boil that cannot be stirred down) over medium-high heat and boil it exactly 1 minute. Stir in the liquid pectin and return to another full, rolling boil that cannot be stirred down; boil exactly 1 minute. Remove from the heat.

5. Stir the marmalade for 5 minutes to prevent the bits of ginger from floating, then ladle it into hot, clean half-pint canning jars, leaving

¼ inch of headspace. Seal the jars with new two-piece canning lids according to manufacturer's directions and process the jars for 15 minutes in a boiling-water bath (page 283). Cool, label, and store the jars. The marmalade will keep for at least a year in a cool cupboard.

HONEY JELLY

Unless you happen to be Winnie-the-Pooh or an equally accomplished bare-paws honey eater, there is always the little problem of keeping honey on the toast and off the chin, fingers, and tablecloth. Well, Honey Jelly (or should it be called Jellied Honey?) solves that problem; besides tasting good, Honey Jelly is certain to stay where you put it, even on hot biscuits (highly recommended).

If you should have on hand some honey that has crystallized in the jar, it can be used for making jelly so long as its flavor is intact; taste to be sure.

2 cups honey, preferably of delicate flavor
1 cup light corn syrup (or substitute another cup of honey, if it is a mild kind)
¾ cup water
3 tablespoons strained fresh lemon juice
1 pouch (3 ounces) or one-half 6-ounce bottle liquid pectin

Makes about 4 cups

1. Stir the honey, corn syrup, water, and lemon juice together thoroughly in a preserving pan. Set it over medium-high heat and bring to a boil. As soon as there are vigorous bubbles all over the surface, stir in the pectin. Start timing when the mixture begins to boil hard (a boil that cannot be stirred down); boil the jelly for exactly 1 minute. Remove from the heat.

2. Set the jelly aside for 1 minute, or just until the foam on top coalesces into a film. Quickly skim off the film and pour the hot jelly into hot, sterilized (page 282) jelly glasses or straight-sided half-pint canning jars, leaving ⅛ inch of headspace in the jars or ½ inch in the glasses. Seal the jelly in glasses with melted paraffin; seal canning jars with sterilized new two-piece lids according to the manufacturer's directions. Cool, label, and store the jars. The honey jelly will keep for at least a year in a cool cupboard.

WHY PECTIN?

Pectin—which causes jelly to jell and jam to jam—occurs naturally in fruits, more abundantly in some fruits than others. When there's enough pectin present and you add sugar plus a little acid (if more acid is needed) to the fruit, jelling follows as the night the day if the recipe has been followed correctly. To fruits low in pectin, commercial pectin (see page 280), which is extracted from apples or citrus fruit, must be added to ensure jelling. (Grandmother would have added apples to the basic fruit and gotten a similar result.) Adding pectin also permits the making of nonfruit jams and jellies—spreads or relishes that begin with such unlikely makings as red peppers (Red-Hot & Sweet Red Pepper "Jelly"), garlic (Glorious Garlic & Red Pepper Jelly), and honey (Honey Jelly and Coriander-Seed & Honey Jelly).

Peach or Nectarine Jam with Brown Sugar & Rum

The blended flavors here are reminiscent of Philadelphia's famous Fish House Punch, a notably smooth and delicious potable in which dark rum, peach brandy, and lemon juice all play a role. (However, note that the jam is not alcoholic, as its tot of rum loses its alcohol during cooking.)

Made as described, the jam is a rich deep gold in color. If you'd like a deeper color and a more pronounced brown-sugar flavor, use dark brown sugar instead of light brown. For more rumminess, the liquor may be increased by 2 tablespoons.

6 cups coarsely chopped peeled firm-ripe peaches or nectarines (about 4 pounds)
2 cups (packed) light brown sugar
6 tablespoons strained fresh lemon juice
¾ cup dark rum, preferably Jamaican
2 cups granulated sugar

Makes about 6 cups

1. Stir the peaches with the brown sugar and lemon juice and about half of the rum in a large bowl. Cover the mixture and let it stand overnight at room temperature.

2. Pour the fruit mixture into a preserving pan. Bring it to a boil over medium-high heat. Cover the pan, reduce the heat, and cook the mixture until the peach chunks begin to look translucent, 15 to 20 minutes; stir it occasionally to prevent sticking. If the jam becomes too thick and threatens to scorch before the fruit clarifies, add 2 or 3 tablespoons of water. Add the granulated sugar and cook the jam rapidly, stirring almost constantly, until a spoonful placed on a chilled saucer and refrigerated for a few minutes wrinkles all over instead of running when the saucer is tilted. (Take the jam off the heat while doing this.) Add the remaining rum and stir the jam for 2 minutes over the heat.

3. Ladle the boiling-hot jam into hot, clean half-pint canning jars, leaving ¼ inch of headspace. Seal the jars with new two-part canning lids according to manufacturer's directions and process for 15 minutes in a boiling-water bath (page 283). Cool, label, and store the jars. The jam is ready to use immediately. It will keep for at least a year in a cool cupboard.

Purple Plum Jam with Orange Liqueur

This happy pairing of fruit and liqueur points up the purple plum's distinctive flavor without letting the spirits dominate. A subtle added taste teases the palate—there's something more than just plain plum going on here, but what?

This is a soft jam, dark in color and rich in flavor; it's one of the highest and best uses for the purple (or blue, or prune, or Italian) plums that round off the season of summer fruits when fall is on the next leaf of the calendar.

The blue or Italian plums most usually dried to become prunes are less commonly sold as fresh fruit, but they do turn up at the greengrocer's in the fall, oval, dusty-blue, and juicy. They aren't especially good to eat as is, but they make, besides Purple Plum Jam, a delicious dish for dessert you'll find in the Index—Prune Plums Poached in Wine.

4 pounds firm-ripe blue (Italian or prune) plums
2 cups water
¼ cup strained fresh lemon juice
4 cups sugar
½ cup Cointreau or other orange-flavored liqueur

Makes about 6 cups

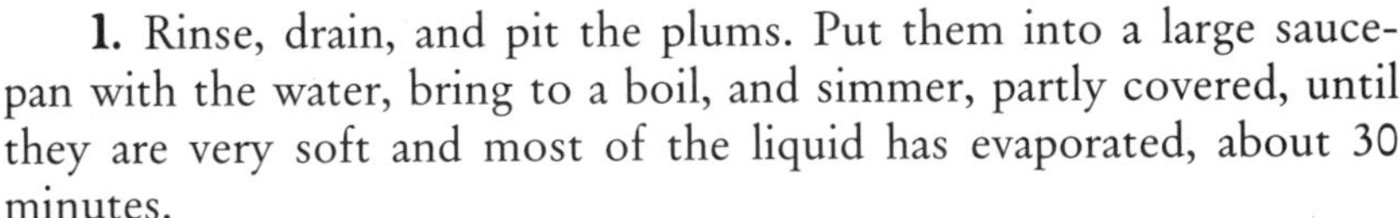

1. Rinse, drain, and pit the plums. Put them into a large saucepan with the water, bring to a boil, and simmer, partly covered, until they are very soft and most of the liquid has evaporated, about 30 minutes.

2. Press the plums and their liquid through a food mill or a coarse sieve. Combine the pulp, lemon juice, and sugar in a preserving pan and stir the mixture over medium-high heat until the sugar has dissolved. Cook the jam at a brisk boil, stirring it often, until it passes the jelly test (page 282), about 10 minutes. Add the orange liqueur and cook the jam for another minute or two.

3. Ladle the hot jam into hot, clean half-pint canning jars, leaving ¼ inch of headspace. Seal the jars with new two-part canning lids according to manufacturer's directions and process for 15 minutes in a boiling-water bath (page 283). Cool, label, and store the jars. The jam will keep for at least a year in a cool cupboard.

Waste Not, Want Not

Much flavor remains in the seedy residue after the berry pulp has been passed through the sieve. Stir the raspberry residue into a cupful of white wine vinegar or Asian rice vinegar and let the mixture stand in a capped jar for a week or two. Strain off the resulting raspberry-flavored vinegar, then scald it to simmering and bottle it for shelf storage.

Red Raspberry Preserves

Not many classic preserves made the final cut for inclusion in these pages, but this soft raspberry delectability just can't be left out.

The secret of making brilliantly colored and fresh-tasting preserves from red raspberries is brief, fast cooking in small batches. So you'll need to use a wide, shallow pan; a 12-inch (or larger) sauté pan or skillet is perfect. Don't try to cook a double batch; you'll slow down the process of evaporation too much and end up with a dark or gummy result.

Directions for a seedless jam follow the main recipe.

4 cups red raspberries, fresh or frozen without sugar
3 cups sugar
¼ cup strained fresh lemon juice

Makes about 3 cups

1. Sort fresh raspberries, discarding any that are soft, moldy, or otherwise dubious looking. Rinse and drain them well. Thaw frozen raspberries, saving all their juice.

2. Stir the raspberries (including the juice from thawed berries), the sugar, and lemon juice together in a bowl, using a rubber spatula. Let the mixture stand, stirring gently once or twice, until the sugar has dissolved, about 2 hours.

3. Scrape the mixture into a stainless-steel or other nonreactive large skillet or sauté pan. Bring it to a boil, stirring constantly with a straight-ended wooden or nylon spatula, and boil it rapidly, stirring often, until it passes the jelly test (page 282); this will take from 3 to 5 minutes, depending on the juiciness of the berries. Remove from the heat.

4. Skim off any foam and ladle the boiling-hot preserves into hot, clean half-pint canning jars, leaving ¼ inch of headspace. Seal the jars with new two-piece canning lids according to manufacturer's directions and process for 10 minutes in a boiling-water bath (page 283). Cool, label, and store the jars. The preserves will keep for at least a year in a cool cupboard.

Seedless Raspberry Jam

Use the preceding recipe, but begin with 5 to 6 cups of raspberries. Mash the berries to a pulp or puree them, then press them through a fine sieve to remove the seeds. Combine the pulp (which will be very liquid), sugar, and lemon juice in a stainless-steel or other nonreactive wide skillet or sauté pan and proceed to cook over high heat, stirring it constantly until it passes the jelly test (page 282). Skim, seal, process, and store as described.

Spiced Pumpkin & Pecan Butter

Pumpkin is one of the few things put up in cans that can be commended to even the fussiest cook, and it's hereby recommended as a great time-saver when making this spicy spread enlivened with citrus and chopped nuts. The butter is delectable on toast or any hot bread, or on pancakes, waffles, or French toast in place of syrup. According to me, it's also delicious over ice cream or frozen yogurt, but then I like pumpkin a lot.

If you have a fresh "pie" or sugar pumpkin—not a jack o' lantern variety, which will be both watery and stringy after cooking—prepare it by paring, cubing, and steaming until very tender (this can be done in a covered casserole in the oven), then pushing the flesh through a sieve or the fine disk of a food mill. If the pureed pumpkin is too moist—which it is if liquid quickly seeps from a sample spooned onto a plate—line a colander with cheesecloth and drain the puree for an hour or so. To make enough puree for this recipe, start with a good-sized pumpkin, say 5 pounds.

Hard-fleshed winter squash (Hubbard, etc.) can be used instead of pumpkin; prepare it in the same way.

Zest (outer peel only, no white pith) of 1 orange, or zest of ½ orange and ½ lemon, removed in wide strips with a swivel peeler
1 large can (29 ounces) solid-pack pumpkin plus ½ cup water, or 3½ to 4 cups pumpkin puree prepared from scratch (see the headnote)
2 cups (packed) light brown sugar or 1½ cups (packed) light brown sugar plus ½ cup mild honey or light corn syrup
3 tablespoons strained fresh orange juice
3 tablespoons strained fresh lemon juice
1½ teaspoons ground cinnamon
½ teaspoon salt
¼ teaspoon ground allspice
¼ teaspoon ground ginger
Pinch of ground cloves
⅓ cup pecans or walnuts, lightly toasted (see sidebar) and grated or very finely chopped

Makes about 5 cups

To Toast Pecans or Walnuts

Spread shelled nuts in a baking pan and bake them for about 5 minutes in a 350°F oven, stirring them several times (they scorch easily). Bake them just until they are slightly toasted and fragrant, not actually browned. Cool the nuts (to regain crispness) before using them.

1. Simmer the orange zest in 2 cups water in a saucepan for 10 minutes, then drain it and mince it to a fine pulp. Measure out 1 tablespoon and reserve.

2. Combine in a heavy-bottomed stainless-steel or other nonreactive saucepan the pumpkin (and water, if canned pumpkin is used), orange zest, sugar, orange juice, lemon juice, cinnamon, salt, allspice, ginger, and cloves. Bring to a boil over medium-high heat, stirring constantly; lower the heat and simmer the mixture, stirring it very often with a wooden spatula, until it has become very thick, about 15 minutes. Sample the butter and add a little more of any or all of the spices, if you like (remember, the flavors will blossom in storage). Add more sweetening if your tastebuds request it.

3. Stir in the nuts and continue to cook for another 2 or 3 minutes. Ladle the boiling-hot pumpkin butter into clean, hot half-pint canning jars, leaving ¼ inch of headspace. Seal the jars with new 2-piece canning lids according to manufacturer's instructions. Process the jars for 10 minutes in a boiling-water bath (page 283). Cool, label, and store for up to a year in a cool cupboard.

4. For refrigerator storage, see page 284.

Sour Cherry Preserves with Cherry Brandy or Amaretto

One of the nicest things to do with sour cherries is to make this delicately brandied sweet, especially if fresh sour cherries are available. Where I live, only frozen specimens are to be had for love or money, but they make a delectable preserve all the same.

Cherry brandy or eau de vie—kirsch or another variety—is naturally most harmonious with the fruit here, but don't overlook the charms of Amaretto, whose almond flavor is highly complementary.

4 pounds fresh sour cherries (about 2⅓ quarts after pitting) or the same measure of frozen pitted sour cherries, thawed
½ cup water
¼ cup strained fresh lemon juice
5½ cups sugar
8 to 10 tablespoons kirsch, other cherry brandy, or Amaretto liqueur, optional

Makes about 6 cups

A Small but Stretched-Out Effort

Sour Cherry Preserves illustrates a good way to concentrate the flavor in fruit without boiling it to death. The long rests between short spells of cooking allow the flesh to imbibe syrup and become succulent in a syrup that is limpid, not gummy.

1. Rinse, stem, and pit fresh cherries, saving all the juice. Thaw frozen cherries. Combine the cherries, their juice, and the water in a preserving pan.

2. Cook the cherries over medium heat until tender, 15 to 20 minutes; stir the cherries or shake the pan occasionally. Pour the cherries and juice into a colander set over a bowl. Drain off all possible juice and return it to the preserving pan (no need to rinse the pan first).

3. Add the lemon juice and the sugar to the juice, stir it over medium heat until it boils, and boil the syrup for 5 minutes. Add the cherries; remove from the heat. Pour the cherries and syrup into a bowl and set the bowl aside at room temperature, covered with a cloth, overnight or for as long as 24 hours.

4. Return the cherries and syrup to the preserving pan. Bring the mixture to a boil over medium-high heat, shaking the pan often or stirring the preserves gently with a straight-ended spatula. Boil the mixture 4 minutes, then set it aside again in a bowl, letting it rest overnight or for as long as 24 hours.

5. Once again bring the preserves to a boil, boiling the mixture only about 3 minutes, until the syrup has thickened slightly—it won't pass a jelly test. Remove from the heat. Skim any foam from the preserves and add the kirsch or Amaretto.

6. Ladle the preserves into hot, clean half-pint or pint canning jars, leaving ¼ inch of headspace. Seal the jars with new two-piece canning lids according to manufacturer's directions and process them for 15 minutes (for either size jar) in a boiling-water bath (page 283). Cool, label, and store the jars. The preserves will keep for at least a year in a cool cupboard. (For alternate storage, see page 284.)

Temple Orange Marmalade

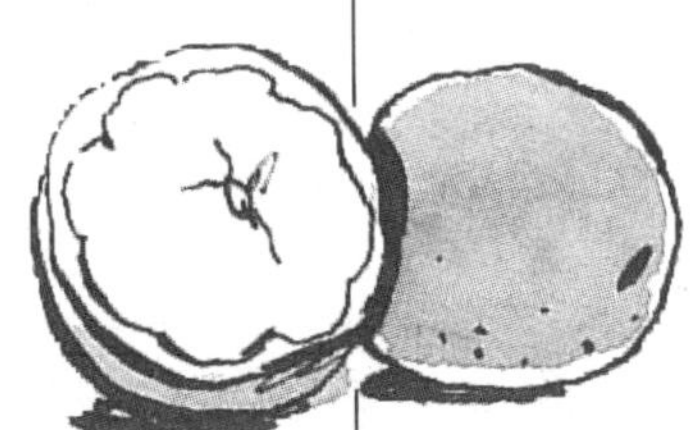

A delicately bittersweet marmalade made with Temple oranges (which are named for a person, not a place of worship), this celebrates one of the most delicious of winter citrus fruits. Temples are much like tangerines, especially in their "kid-glove" skins, but they're larger and sweeter. Temples make an exceptional marmalade, closer to the bitter orange classic model than to the relatively insipid spread made from most kinds of "eating" oranges. Gild the lily, if you like, by adding orange-flavored liqueur or a touch of Scotch whisky at the finish.

Is Bitter Better?

Bitter (or Seville) oranges are the royalty of marmalade makings as well as the classic orange for use in savory dishes (bigarade sauce for duckling and so on). They're hard to get, which is why this recipe was worked out for Temple oranges. If you can persuade a fruitseller to order you some bitter oranges around January, check a comprehensive preserving book for a recipe designed for them. (My own method is included in my book Better Than Store-Bought, *written with Elizabeth Colchie.)*

6 medium-large Temple oranges, about 3 pounds
Water, as needed
4 medium lemons
8 cups sugar
3 tablespoons Cointreau or other orange-flavored liqueur, or Scotch whisky, optional

Makes 7 to 8 cups

1. Scrub, rinse, and drain the oranges. Cut and discard a slice of skin from both stem and blossom ends, then remove the remaining peel, with its attached pith, in quarters. (Cut through the skin, then pry it off with a teaspoon, the bowl facing the fruit.) Reserve the orange flesh.

2. Place the peel in a saucepan with 2 quarts of water, bring it to a boil, and boil it 10 minutes. Drain the peel, add 2 quarts of fresh water, boil it again for 10 minutes, and drain it. Add the same amount of fresh water and bring to a boil for the third time; simmer the peel, partly covered, until it is very soft and the liquid is reduced to 2 cups, about an hour. Reserve the peel and liquid, covered, at room temperature.

3. Chop the pulp of the oranges (quickly done in a food processor) and place it in a large ceramic, glass, or stainless-steel bowl.

4. Pare the peel and not quite all the white pith from the lemons and discard it. Chop the lemon pulp, disregarding the seeds, and add it to the orange pulp. Add 2 cups of cold water, cover, and let stand overnight at room temperature.

5. Press the fruit pulp through the coarse disk of a food mill or a coarse sieve; continue until you've obtained all possible pulp and juice. Discarding the debris, place the pulp in a preserving pan. Drain off the liquid from the reserved peel and add it to the pan.

6. Cut the peel into fine shreds, using kitchen shears or a sharp knife on a cutting board. (To speed up hand cutting, slice several stacked peel sections at a time.) Add the peel to the mixture in the pan.

7. Bring the mixture to a boil over medium-high heat and boil it, uncovered, 10 minutes. Gradually stir in the sugar and boil the marmalade over medium-high heat, stirring often, until it passes the jelly test (page 282), 20 to 30 minutes. Remove the pot from the heat and stir in the orange liqueur or the whisky, if you are adding either. Cool the marmalade 5 minutes, stirring it several times, to prevent the peel from floating.

8. Ladle the hot marmalade into hot, clean half-pint or pint canning jars, leaving ¼ inch of headspace. Seal the jars with new two-piece canning lids according to manufacturer's directions and process for 20 minutes (for either size jar) in a boiling-water bath (page 283). Cool, label, and store the jars. Like other fine marmalades, this improves with time and will keep almost indefinitely in a cool cupboard.

Tomato Jam with Ginger & Coriander

A soft, fragrant jam with a delicate flavor and a rosy-apricot color, this preserve is one of the best of good things to make from "love apples." If you have yellow tomatoes, they make a paler but very pretty jam. Both versions seem exotic, and it's always hard to convince tasters that they began with tomatoes.

5 pounds firm but fully ripe fleshy tomatoes
2 large lemons
1 tablespoon very finely minced fresh ginger or 2 tablespoons chopped Crystallized Ginger or Ginger Preserved in Syrup (page 315 or 317)
½ teaspoon salt
5 cups sugar
1 tablespoon ground coriander, preferably freshly ground

Makes about 4 cups

1. Dip the tomatoes a few at a time into boiling water for 10 seconds, then drop them into cold water. Skin the tomatoes, cut out the stem ends and hard cores, halve them crosswise, and squeeze the seeds into a sieve set over a bowl. Discard the seeds; reserve the juice. Chop the tomatoes coarsely and put them, with the juice, in a preserving pan.

2. Grate the zest (outer peel only, no white pith) from the lemons and add 2 packed teaspoons of the zest to the tomatoes. Squeeze the lemons, strain the juice, and add 6 tablespoons of the juice to the tomatoes. Add the ginger and salt.

3. Bring the mixture to a boil over medium-high heat, stirring occasionally, then lower the heat and simmer the jam, uncovered, stirring from time to time, until the tomato pieces are soft, about 15 minutes. Stir in the sugar. Raise the heat to medium high and cook the jam, stirring almost constantly, until a candy/jelly thermometer reads 219°F (slightly under the usual "done" temperature for jam), or until a small amount spooned onto a saucer congeals quickly when chilled and does not run when the saucer is tilted. (Take the pan from the fire while testing.) When the jam is done, stir in the coriander.

4. Ladle the boiling-hot jam into hot, clean half-pint canning jars, leaving ¼ inch of headspace. Cover with new two-piece canning lids according to manufacturer's directions and process for 15 minutes in a boiling-water bath (page 283). Cool, label, and store the jars. The jam will keep for at least a year in a cool cupboard.

Now That's a Tomato

For great tomato jam, hand-pick the tomatoes from among those available, using either slicing tomatoes or the fleshier and less seedy Italian-type tomatoes. Squeeze each gently in the palm (don't pinch) to be sure the flesh is willing to yield a bit but isn't mushy. If the fruit is squishy, make a soup; if it's rigid, leave it to ripen for another day.

Glazing a Tart

Brush on a shining coat of wine jelly to enhance the looks and taste of a fruit tart made with uncooked fruit (berries, peaches, and so on) or fruit baked in the crust. Try a Sherry Jelly glaze on peaches, apples, or apricots, or brush a jelly made from red wine, fortified or otherwise, over a blueberry or plum tart. To do: *Melt a generous ½ cup of wine jelly over low heat, stirring in about a tablespoonful of water. Brush the warm jelly over the fruit and let the glaze set before serving the tart at room temperature, never chilled.*

Wine Jellies

Having written about preserving quite a bit, I've been asked any number of times how to make wine jellies—preserves, that is, not desserts—which are delicious and expensive specialty-shop items. Here, therefore, are some tips and recipes.

In a nutshell, wine jellies require the addition of fruit pectin, as wine lacks this substance essential to jelling. Wine *does* supply the necessary acid, which is, together with sugar, also essential. For these jellies I prefer powdered pectin to the liquid kind, as it can be used without boiling the wine and dissipating its flavor.

Jelly made from any decent table wine will be good, but you'll get a reward in flavor if you use wine of emphatic character and good quality. Red wine should be full-bodied and fruity; a white should be fragrant and not too dry (I like whites that are amber-tinged or golden); a rosé should taste good, not just look pretty. Jellies made from premium-quality fortified wines—sherry, Marsala, Madeira, port, and so on—are expectably more complex in flavor than table-wine jellies. Adding the flavors of spice and a roasted whole orange to a fortified wine produces Mulled Port Wine Jelly, below (warmly recommended).

At our house we like wine jellies with toast when breakfast includes an occasional indulgence of ham or sausage, and at snack time they're commendable on crackers spread with cream cheese. They also glaze fruit tarts beautifully (see the sidebar).

Red, White, Pink, Golden, or Amber Wine Jelly

¾ cup water
¼ cup strained fresh lemon juice
1 package (1¾ ounces) regular powdered pectin (not the kind meant for making low-sugar preserves)
3 cups full-flavored wine of your choice—red, white, amber, or rosé
4½ cups sugar

Makes about 6 cups

1. Measure the water and lemon juice into a preserving pan. Stir in the pectin. Set the pan over medium-high heat and stir the mixture constantly until any lumps of pectin are gone, then boil it hard (at a boil that can't be stirred down) for exactly 1 minute.

2. At once add the wine and the sugar. Lower the heat and stir the mixture until the sugar has dissolved, 2 or 3 minutes; do not let it boil or even approach a simmer. Remove from the heat.

3. Skim off any foam and ladle the jelly into hot, sterilized (page 282) jelly glasses or straight-sided half-pint canning jars, leaving ½ inch of headspace in jelly glasses or ⅛ inch in the jars. Seal jelly in glasses with a thin layer of melted paraffin wax; seal jars with sterilized new two-piece canning lids according to manufacturer's directions. Cool, label, and store the jars. The jelly will keep for a year in a cool cupboard.

Madeira, Marsala, Port, or Sherry Jelly

Any type of Madeira, Marsala, port, or sherry can be used, but dry Marsala, red ports, and cream sherries are recommended.

¾ cup water
⅓ cup strained fresh lemon juice
1 package (1¾ ounces) regular powdered pectin (not the kind meant for making low-sugar preserves)
2½ cups premium-quality Madeira, Marsala, port, or sherry
4½ cups sugar

Makes about 6 cups

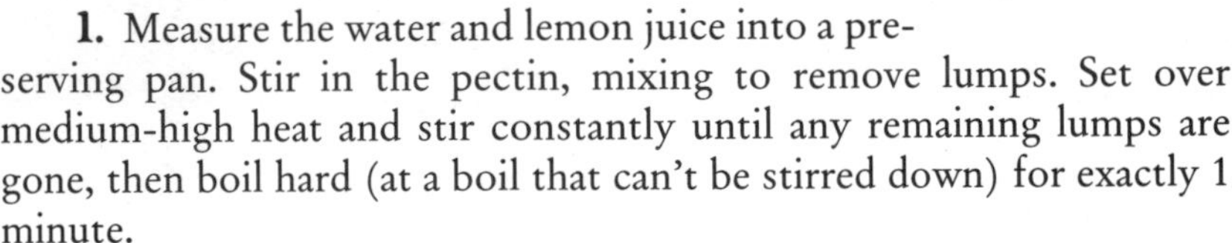

1. Measure the water and lemon juice into a preserving pan. Stir in the pectin, mixing to remove lumps. Set over medium-high heat and stir constantly until any remaining lumps are gone, then boil hard (at a boil that can't be stirred down) for exactly 1 minute.

2. At once add the wine and the sugar. Lower the heat and stir the jelly mixture just until the sugar has dissolved, a matter of 2 or 3 minutes at most; do not let it boil or even simmer. Remove from the heat.

3. Skim off any foam and ladle the jelly into hot, sterilized jelly glasses or straight-sided half-pint canning jars, leaving ½ inch of headspace in jelly glasses or ⅛ inch in the jars. Seal jelly in glasses with melted paraffin wax, seal jars with sterilized new two-piece canning lids according to manufacturer's directions. Cool, label, and store the jars.

Mulled Port Wine Jelly

Flavored with an orange that has been stuck with cloves and roasted, plus whole cinnamon and allspice, this is a rich, deep, dark-

It Must Be Jelly, 'Cause Jam Don't Shake Like That. . . .

Jellies may all quiver delightfully, but no, they aren't all sweet. In fact, fruit-flavored sweet jellies weren't invented until the seventeenth century and didn't become well known for another century or so; meanwhile, jellies were meat-based affairs, congealed by the gelatinous substances in such ingredients as calves' feet. (Those early jellies survive today as aspics.) Something of a hybrid between those savory jellies and today's delicate sweet spreads are the tart-and-sweet, spiced, herbal, pungent, or piquant jelly-relishes meant to be served with meat, fowl, and fish; you'll find several in these pages. The neighboring recipes, beginning on page 307, present Wine Jellies in variety; see the Index to locate recipes for Glorious Garlic & Hot Pepper Jelly, Red Hot & Sweet Red Pepper "Jelly" (or call it a jam), and resinously herbal Red Rosemary Jelly, based on cranberries.

flavored wine jelly, superb as a relish with venison and other game, poultry, or cold meat.

For making this, a premium-quality California red port is fine; you do not need to buy an imported bottle. The jelly is also excellent when made with a decidedly full-bodied red wine—Rhône, Burgundy, Zinfandel, or whatever hearty sort you prefer.

1 unblemished medium eating orange
8 whole cloves
1 stick (about 2½ inches) cinnamon, broken
6 whole allspice, slightly bruised
1½ cups boiling water
1 (1¾ ounces) regular powdered pectin (not the kind meant for making low-sugar preserves)
2½ cups good-quality red port (or substitute Madeira, Marsala, or a full-flavored red table wine
4½ cups sugar

Makes about 6 cups

1. One day (or at least several hours) before you make the jelly, preheat the oven to 350°F. Scrub the orange, stick the cloves into it, wrap it loosely in foil, and bake it, set on the oven shelf, for 1 hour. Unwrap and check the orange; if it is very soft and the juices have begun to caramelize, it is ready. If not, continue baking for up to another 30 minutes.

2. Drop the orange, *sans* foil, into a bowl. Add the cinnamon and allspice and mash everything well. Add the boiling water, cover, and let stand for 6 hours, preferably as long as overnight.

3. Pour everything into a sieve set over a bowl and strain off the liquid, pressing on the solids to extract the last drops. Discard the debris. Strain the liquid again through a fine sieve or a sieve lined with cheesecloth. Measure the liquid; if you don't have 1½ cups, add water.

4. Pour the liquid into a preserving pan, add the pectin, and stir well. Set over medium-high heat and bring to a boil, stirring constantly until any lumps of pectin have melted. Raise the heat and boil the mixture hard (at a boil that can't be stirred down) for exactly 1 minute. At once add the wine and the sugar, lower the heat, and stir the mixture just until the sugar has dissolved, 2 or 3 minutes; it should not even simmer, much less boil. Remove from the heat.

5. Skim the jelly and ladle it into hot, sterilized (page 282) jelly glasses or straight-sided half-pint canning jars, leaving ½ inch of headspace in glasses or ⅛ inch in jars. Seal jelly glasses with melted paraffin; seal canning jars with sterilized new two-piece canning lids, following the manufacturer's directions. Cool, label, and store the jars for up to a year in a cool cupboard.

Confections

CONFECTIONERY~
A SMALL BANQUET OF SWEETMEATS

If they were all to be served forth together, the confections and other sweet temptations in this chapter and the next two would make a dessert banquet opulent enough for the first Queen Elizabeth, who loved sweets and most especially *marchpane,* ancestor of the marzipan that comes first below. Elizabeth didn't reign long enough to taste confections made of chocolate, as that food of the gods was only barely known as a drink in England in her time. If she *had* met up with solid chocolate, marzipan might have given place in her affections to some Elizabethan version of the delectable truffles that round off this chapter.

Sweet nibbles, not major productions, are what we have here—confections that are simple to make at home without special equipment or expertise. Some recipes come from *Fancy Pantry,* notably those for crystallized and preserved ginger and some of the nut and berry confections. Newly devised are recipes for marzipan, Chinese-style glazed nuts (including black walnuts, which would no doubt be news to cooks in China), cranberry Christmas candies, cranberries dried with a touch of sugar or alternative sweetening, classic toffee, and some sublimely rich truffles made variously with dark and white chocolate.

For more confections—especially several sweets that I think of as honorary cookies—look in the following chapter, "Great Cookies & a Cake or Two."

Almond Paste or Marzipan: "Play-Dough" for Pretty Confections

You may call this goodie either almond paste or marzipan, as the differences are slight. The term "almond paste" is sometimes limited to a preparation of almonds used in baking (especially when it's commercially made) and as the beginning of marzipan, which is often sweeter and smoother and is most often used to make confections. This recipe produces almond paste that can be used in either way. To create pretty candies, see the tips on the facing page.

There are several schools of almond-paste creation, but I remain loyal to this general way of proceeding. Using the hot syrup and a food processor seems to me to produce a smoother product than other methods. Although home-crafted paste will never have the flawless smoothness (or certain extra ingredients) of the commercial product, it will taste better, according to me, if you start with excellent almonds.

2¼ cups almonds, blanched (page 295)
3 to 4 tablespoons cold water, as needed for grinding the nuts
2 cups granulated sugar
⅓ cup water, for the syrup
¼ cup light corn syrup
1 teaspoon pure almond extract or 8 drops oil of bitter almonds (see sidebar)
½ teaspoon pure vanilla extract
1 cup sifted confectioners' sugar, or more if needed

Makes about 2 pounds

1. Heat the oven to 250°F. Spread the almonds on a baking sheet and warm them thoroughly, stirring them often until they are hot but not at all browned, about 15 minutes.

2. Transfer the nuts to a food processor. With the motor running, gradually trickle in 3 tablespoons of cold water through the feed tube. Process the nuts, scraping down the sides of the bowl several times, until you have a quite smooth paste (pinch a sample to check its texture). If the paste seems too dry, add the remaining tablespoon of water. Processing will take several minutes—just hang in there. Set the paste aside in the processor.

3. Combine the sugar, ⅓ cup water, and corn syrup in a large saucepan. Bring to a boil, stirring until the sugar has dissolved, then

Bitter Almonds—The Lowdown

*Botanically of the same species (*Prunus amygdalus*) as the familiar sweet almond, bitter almonds are quite different in character. Unlike common almonds, bitter almonds pack a wallop, tasting like a strong almond extract, or like peach or apricot kernels. Expectably so, because the kernels of all fruits of the* Prunus *genus contain greater or lesser amounts of the makings of the distinctive "bitter almond" flavoring as well as prussic (hydrocyanic) acid, which sounds (and is) poisonous. However, after bitter almonds have been commercially treated to produce intensely flavorful bitter-almond oil (available from sellers of baking supplies) or much milder almond extract for use in foods, neither flavoring poses a danger*

to consumers. It's the raw nuts (and the raw kernels of apricots, plums, cherries, and peaches) that should be eaten warily if at all. However, cooking a few kernels of plums, peaches, or apricots with stewed fruit or in jam is perfectly safe—the cooking deals with the undesirable stuff.

Making Pretty Sweets From Almond Paste

Almond paste is much used as a cake filling and in pastries and confections, but it's most fun to transform it into festive little marzipan sweets, particularly at Christmas and Easter.

Use your fingers to shape small fruits, vegetables, birds, Easter eggs or bunnies, or other shapes, let them air-dry until firm, then tint them with food coloring, using small watercolor brushes. Let dry again and voilà—a set of edible ornaments to hang on the tree (attach loops of thread while molding), or a bowlful of confections almost too pretty to eat.

boil without further stirring until the syrup reaches a temperature of 235°F on a candy/jelly thermometer, or until a little of the syrup forms a soft ball when dropped into cold water. Remove from the heat.

4. Start the food processor, then slowly pour the hot syrup through the feed tube. Continue to run the machine for several minutes, scraping down the sides of the bowl occasionally, until the paste has cooled a little. The mixture will be somewhat loose, but push on. Uncover the bowl and let the paste cool for a few minutes, then add the almond and vanilla flavorings and pulse the machine briefly.

5. Sprinkle about half the confectioner's sugar on a kneading surface. Scrape the paste onto the sugar and leave it to cool until tepid. Then scrape, fold, and knead it for a few minutes, using a bench knife (pastry scraper) if you have one, or a pancake turner if you must improvise. Continue to work the paste, adding more confectioner's sugar from time to time, until you have a fairly firm mass that holds the imprint of a finger when pressed.

6. Form the almond paste into a thick round, dust it with confectioners' sugar, wrap it securely in two layers of plastic, and refrigerate it until needed. If possible, let it ripen for at least a day—better several days—before using it. The paste will keep indefinitely if not allowed to dry out. If it should become too firm to shape easily, soften it by warming in the top of a double boiler.

Candied Cranberries

Cranberries candied in this fashion will keep perfectly in a glass jar, at room temperature, for many months, not that there is likely to be a need for such longevity. In color they are even brighter than cherries, so they make a pretty holiday garnish for either sweet or savory things. To serve them on their own as a sweetmeat, drop them into tiny bonbon cups, three or four to each. I also like to use them in baking in place of candied cherries.

There are more complicated ways to candy these tiny native fruits, but the method of Imogene Wolcott, which she credits to Cape Cod, is hard to beat. Here it is, adapted from the 1971 edition of her delicious *Yankee Cook Book*.

1½ cups large firm cranberries, picked over, any stems removed
1½ cups sugar, plus additional for coating
1¼ cups water

Makes about 1¾ cups

1. Rinse the cranberries and drain them. Prick each one completely through with a coarse needle, then dry them thoroughly on a towel.

2. Combine 1½ cups sugar and the water in a 10- or 12-inch sauté pan or skillet (you need to cook the berries in a single layer). Bring the mixture to a boil over high heat, stirring until the sugar has dissolved. Boil the syrup until it forms a soft ball when a small amount is dropped into ice water (the reading is 234°F on a candy/jelly thermometer).

3. Add the cranberries to the syrup and boil them rapidly, shaking the pan often, until the syrup reaches the hard-ball stage (250°F), 6 to 10 minutes. The berries will burst their skins and look rather messy, but this does not affect the final result.

4. Immediately lift the berries from the syrup with a wire skimmer or slotted spoon and scatter them on a nonstick or lightly oiled cookie sheet. The cranberries will be lying there in clumps; as soon as they have cooled enough to be touched comfortably, separate them with your fingers or two small forks and let them cool completely.

5. Place about ½ cup of additional granulated sugar in a bowl. Pick up a cranberry, together with any cooled syrup around it, and reshape it quickly; drop the now globelike berry into the bowl of sugar and roll it around to coat it well, then lift it onto a baking sheet to dry for a few hours. Do the rest of the berries in the same fashion and leave them on the pan until they are no longer sticky.

6. Store the sugared cranberries at room temperature in a tightly closed jar; they will keep indefinitely. If desired, sugar them again at serving time.

Cranberries Another Way

Candied Cranberries are sweet enough to be considered confections. For cranberries sweetened more delicately, see page 323 for Dried Cranberries Lightly Sweetened with Sugar, plus the directions for using alternative sweetenings for the sugar-shy.

Chinese-Style Glazed Walnuts, Pecans, or Black Walnuts

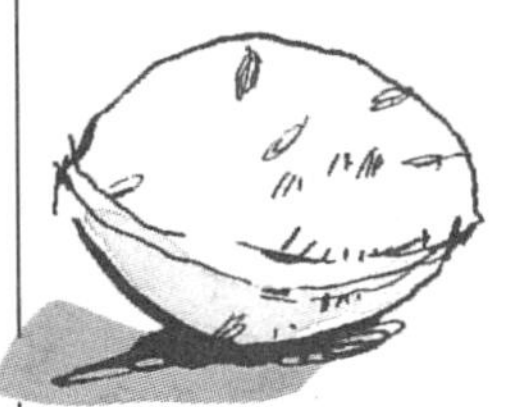

First tasted at the table of a Chinese hostess who was writing a now-classic cookbook, these walnuts sugared and fried in the fashion of Hunan have been in our repertory of treats ever since. Though nuts done this way are somewhat sweet (mostly they're nutty), they are wonderful with all manner of drinks, and are a traditional appetizer at Chinese banquets.

Walnuts are most often used in the recipes I've researched, but pecans are also favored. I've found black walnuts are terrific, too, especially if you can obtain them in big chunks, either by using a heavy-duty nutcracker or by purchasing them from a specialist.

2 cups walnut or pecan halves, or the largest available black walnut chunks
4 cups water
⅔ cup sugar
2 cups peanut oil

Makes about 2 cups

1. Rinse the nutmeats in a bowl of water to rid them of any small fragments or bits of shell, then drain in a sieve and combine with the water in a saucepan. Bring to a boil and simmer the nuts briskly for 3 minutes. Meanwhile, measure the sugar into a mixing bowl.

2. Drain the nuts, shaking the sieve to free them of as much moisture as possible, then spread them on a fresh tea towel (or a double layer of paper towels) and blot them quickly and lightly. Put the nuts into the bowl of sugar and stir thoroughly to coat each piece—the coating should look syrupy. Cover the bowl with a lid for a minute or two, then stir the nuts again. Spread the nuts on a baking sheet or platter and leave them to dry for at least 15 minutes, better 1 hour.

3. Set a wok or heavy saucepan over medium heat and pour in the oil. Heat it to about 300°F (if you're using a candy/jelly thermometer) or until a coated nut sizzles lazily when dropped in, then begins to float after a moment. (Don't let the oil get too hot or the nuts will blacken and be ruined.) Add a third or half of the nuts to the oil and stir them to keep them separate; fry them just until the sugar caramelizes to golden-brown, which will take 3 minutes or so if the heat is right. The instant they are ready, scoop them out with a wire skimmer and spread them to drain on plain brown paper or paper towels. Fry the remaining nuts in the same way.

4. As the nuts cool, separate them if they have formed clumps. When they are completely cool and crisp, serve them, or seal them airtight in a jar for future use. Refrigerated and kept airtight, they'll keep for at least a month. They may also be frozen for longer storage.

Black Walnuts

Those who would willingly walk the woods or roadsides to harvest these native American nuts (as we do whenever there's a good autumn crop) can save shoe leather, and people who live beyond black walnut country can enjoy good fresh nuts, by mail-ordering them. (See Mail-Order Sources, page 390). The firm we buy from knows how to shell out pieces of maximum size and how to keep the nuts fresh while in their custody (they're unusually perishable because of their high oil content). Be sure to store black walnuts in a capped jar in the freezer or, at the very least, in the refrigerator.

Waste-Not

When the oil has cooled, strain and bottle it for reuse if you belong to the waste-not school of cookery.

Crystallized Ginger

A favorite sweet in Britain and America for centuries, crystallized ginger was formerly always imported, usually from China, at considerable cost. Now that fresh ginger is available almost everywhere in the United States, thanks to shipments from Hawaii, other Pacific islands, Australia, and the other Americas, you can candy your own instead of shelling out many dollars for a ginger fix.

For candying, try to get the tender young ginger, called "stem ginger," which comes to Asian-oriented markets around July. It is much juicier and milder than the mature rhizomes; it can be identified by its white, smooth, translucent skin and the pink stubs of leaf sheaths left when the above-ground stems were trimmed away. Mature ginger can be satisfactory when candied, too, but it is much more fibrous and several times as fiery as stem ginger. In shopping for mature ginger, look for silky-skinned, unwithered rhizomes. The two kinds of ginger need to be treated differently, as described in the recipe.

1 pound fresh stem ginger or smooth-skinned, juicy mature ginger
3 cups sugar
3 cups water
2 tablespoons light corn syrup
Additional sugar for coating

Makes about 1¼ pounds

1. ***Preparing stem ginger:*** Break the rhizomes apart at the joints and scrape off the thin skin, using a small sharp knife. Trim off the leafy stem bases and any bruised or discolored ends. Slice the sections slightly on the bias into pieces about ¼ inch thick. Place the ginger in a large saucepan, add cold water to cover the pieces by 2 inches, and bring to a boil over medium heat. Lower the heat, cover the pot, and simmer the ginger for 2½ hours. If the liquid level drops below the ginger at any point, add boiling water. Drain the ginger, add fresh water to cover, and simmer for another hour, or until the slices are very tender. Drain the ginger.

2. ***Preparing mature ginger:*** Scrape, trim, and slice the rhizomes as described for stem ginger. Place the ginger in a bowl, add cold water to cover the pieces by 2 inches, and let stand overnight. Drain the ginger and place in a large saucepan. Add water to cover the pieces by 1 inch and bring to a boil over medium heat. Lower the heat, cover the pan, and simmer the ginger for 10 minutes. Drain the ginger, cover it with fresh water, and repeat the simmering and draining at least three times; after the fourth simmering, taste a scrap of ginger to see whether its hotness suits you. If the flavor is still too strong, change the water and repeat the simmering once or twice more. Continue cooking the ginger in the final water until the pieces are very tender, 2 to 3 hours, adding boiling water as necessary to keep the ginger covered with liquid. (This cooking can be done in several bouts, if that's more convenient.) Drain the ginger.

3. ***Candying either stem or mature ginger:*** Combine the 3 cups sugar, 3 cups water, and corn syrup in a large saucepan. Bring the mix-

Enjoying Ginger

Candied ginger is a lively nibble with a cup of tea or after-dinner coffee. Chopped, it's wonderful in ice cream (soften a quart of vanilla, add a handful of ginger bits, and refreeze). Also great in dessert sauces, shortbread (see the Index), other cookies, or in a pound cake.

For an especially elegant sweet to take to a hostess, consider the Chocolate-Coated Ginger on page 318.

ture to a boil over medium-high heat and boil it 2 minutes. Add the ginger slices. Heat the syrup again to boiling, shaking the pan often, and boil it hard for 1 minute. Remove the pan from the heat; let it stand until the ginger and syrup are completely cool, or as long as overnight.

4. Return the pan to the heat and again bring the syrup to a boil. Adjust the heat and simmer the ginger, covered, until the pieces are translucent and very tender, which can take from 1 hour to 3 hours; stir occasionally. If the syrup becomes too thick before the ginger is translucent, add a little hot water to restore its consistency.

5. Finally, cook the ginger uncovered, shaking the pan often, until the syrup is reduced to a spoonful or two. Remove the pan from the heat and let it stand for a few minutes.

6. Fork the ginger pieces onto a wire rack and leave them to dry at room temperature, a matter of an hour or two. When they are no longer sticky, roll the pieces in additional sugar to coat them well. Store the ginger in a covered container at room temperature. It keeps indefinitely.

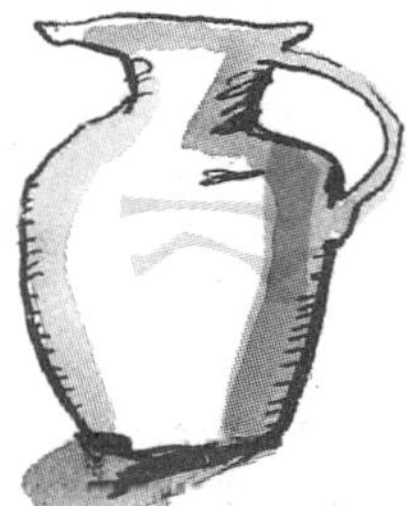

Ginger Preserved in Syrup

A little of this preserved ginger, chopped and mixed with some of the syrup, makes a luscious topping for ice cream; or fold chopped ginger and a little of the syrup into whipped cream and fill dessert crêpes with the mixture.

Use either tender young stem ginger—the preferable kind—which is available from midsummer until fall, usually in Asian markets, or mature ginger.

Prepare the ginger as described in steps 1 through 3 of the preceding recipe for Crystallized Ginger. If stem ginger is what you have, you may want to cut it into knobs or joints about the size of a thumb tip instead of slices. Complete step 3 of the recipe.

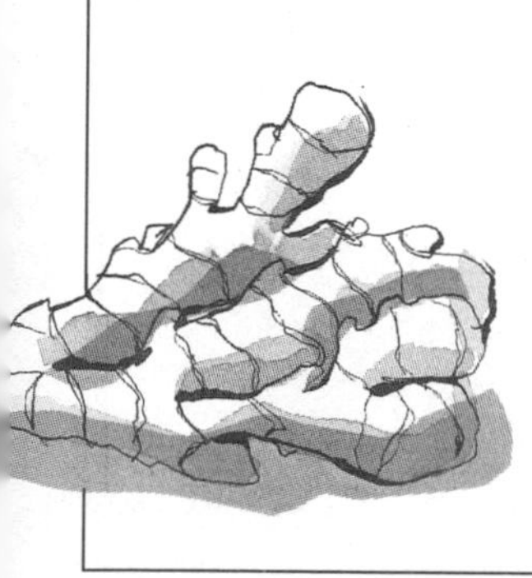

Ladle the boiling-hot ginger and syrup into a sterilized jar (page 282), let it cool, and cover it with a sterilized lid. If the syrup should be insufficient to cover the ginger pieces, make a little additional plain syrup in the original proportions and add it to the ginger while it is hot.

Pantry storage is fine if the ginger is kept for a few weeks, but refrigeration is recommended for longer storage. The ginger keeps indefinitely when refrigerated.

Chocolate-Coated Ginger

4 ounces fine-quality dark bittersweet chocolate, chopped up, or 3 ounces semisweet chocolate plus 1 ounce unsweetened chocolate, both chopped
½ teaspoon sweet (unsalted) butter
3 dozen pieces Crystallized Ginger (page 315) or the same quantity of purchased candied ginger
About ½ cup blanched almonds, toasted (page 349) and chopped medium-fine, or ½ cup chopped crystallized ginger

Makes 3 dozen candies

1. Cover a baking sheet or tray with waxed paper or foil.

2. Melt the chocolate in the top of a double boiler over barely simmering water, stirring until it has melted smoothly. (Or use your microwave, following the manufacturer's recommendations.) Stir the butter into the chocolate and scrape it into a small bowl or cup.

3. Rub off any loose sugar from the pieces of ginger. Dip each slice about halfway into the chocolate, shake off surplus into the bowl, then flip the little "tail" of chocolate back onto the top surface as decoration; set the piece on the prepared baking sheet. Repeat until all the pieces have been dipped.

4. Carefully sprinkle a pinch of chopped nuts or chopped ginger over the chocolate coating, keeping the decoration light. Leave the confections at room temperature until the chocolate has set. Store in layers, separated by waxed paper or plastic wrap, in a covered container. The confection will keep for 2 weeks or more but will be prettiest when freshly made.

A Smashing Sweet

The quality of the chocolate used to make this confection will make a difference between simply good and smashing. Although the recipe offers the choice of using a fine dark chocolate or a mixture of grocery-store kinds, finding good chocolate is worth the pain and suffering of sampling various brands of chocolate until you find the kind(s) you like the most. For some specialists in baking/confectionery supplies, see Mail-Order Sources, page 390.

Cranberry Christmas Gummies

Real cranberries star in these Christmassy candies made by the improbable-sounding process of boiling a gelatin mixture for quite a long time. Don't worry, it works.

First, prepare the cranberry juice. (If necessary, frozen cranberry juice concentrate may be used. Dilute it with only half to two-thirds of the water recommended on the label.) If the red tint of the mixture doesn't seem vivid enough when the candy has been cooked, stir in a very few drops of red food coloring before molding the candy.

3 cups sugar
4½ tablespoons (4½ envelopes) unflavored gelatin
2 cups Cranberry Juice (recipe follows)
2 tablespoons strained fresh lemon juice
About ¼ teaspoon orange oil or ½ teaspoon orange extract, optional
Pinch of salt, optional
Few drops red food coloring, optional
Additional sugar for coating the candies

Makes about 2 pounds

1. Stir together the sugar and gelatin powder in a large stainless-steel or other nonreactive saucepan. Stir in 1 cup of the cranberry juice, mixing thoroughly. Set over medium heat and bring to a boil, stirring constantly with a whisk or flat-ended spatula until the sugar and gelatin dissolve. Maintain a rolling boil (a boil that can't be stirred down), stirring almost constantly, for 15 to 20 minutes, until the mixture spins long threads when the whisk is lifted. Remove from the heat.

2. Add the remaining 1 cup cranberry juice, the lemon juice, orange oil or extract (if using), and optional pinch of salt. Skim off the foam. If you like, stir in a very little red food coloring. (Without it, the candies will be garnet-colored, which I like.)

3. Rinse an 8-inch square baking pan, preferably made of oven glass, with cold water. Pour in the candy mixture and leave at room temperature or in the refrigerator until very firm, at least 4 hours or up to overnight.

4. Scatter sugar generously on a work surface. Run a wet knife blade around the edges of the block of candy and cut the first strip needed for dividing the block into pieces. With a thin metal spatula, pry out the strip with a scraping motion and transfer it to the sugared surface. The remainder of the block may now release readily onto the work surface; if not, remove it a strip at a time. Dipping the knife blade often into hot water, cut the candy into small squares, rectangles, triangles, or diamonds.

5. Roll the pieces around in enough additional sugar to coat all surfaces—you can do this with a firm hand without risking damage. Set the "gummies" on a cake rack and leave them at room temperature to develop a crisp sugary shell, which may happen overnight or take two days or longer in humid weather.

6. Roll the candies in sugar again and store them in a cardboard box or a canister with its cover left open just enough to permit air to enter and preserve the crisp outsides. These keep well for many weeks or even months, becoming a bit chewier with time.

Cranberry Juice

1 package (12 ounces) cranberries, fresh or frozen
4 cups water
Pinch of salt, optional

Makes about 3 cups

1. Pick over and rinse the cranberries. Combine with water and the optional salt in a saucepan. Cook over moderate heat, stirring and mashing often, until all the berries have popped and become very soft, 5 to 10 minutes.

2. Pour into a sieve lined with two layers of fine cheesecloth and set over a bowl. Let the juice drain, pressing very lightly on the pulp toward the end.

To the Last Drop: Cranberry Juice

Here's one recipe in which frozen cranberries work marginally better than fresh fruit. Because freezing breaks down the cell walls, cranberries from the deep-freeze yield more juice than a fresh batch.

The leftover pulp, sieved and sweetened, makes a little batch of cranberry spread or "butter," either as is or with an added pinch or two of ground cinnamon and a smaller amount of ginger. To store, refrigerate.

Dried Cherries, Blueberries, Cranberries, & Others of That Ilk

Preparing for yourself today's newly popular (and very good) dried fruits—cherries, blueberries, or cranberries, as well as other berries—is quite simple and rewarding. You don't need an electric dehydrator, although you can speed up the drying by using such an appliance; just follow the manufacturer's directions.

To add some other small fruits to your repertory, follow the cherry directions below for such berries as red and black raspberries, blackberries, youngberries, boysenberries, loganberries, tayberries, and olallieberries. (Drying strawberries isn't a good idea, as they lose much of their flavor.) If you should be able to obtain fresh currants, whether red, black or white, use the blueberry directions. Cranberries have a method to themselves, as they require light sweetening to be palatable.

Dried Sweet or Sour Cherries

These drying directions give fine results with sweet cherries, the only kind available to most of us. However, if you can find fresh sour (pie) cherries, they are even more flavorful than the sweet fruit after drying.

9 pounds firm-ripe sweet or sour cherries
Sugar, if desired

Makes about 2 cups, loosely packed, of pitted cherries; more if unpitted

1. Stem, rinse, drain, and pit the cherries, trying to lose as little juice as possible. If sweet cherries are very large, halve them. If you are drying sour cherries and wish to leave in the pits for the almond-like flavor they contribute, place the cherries in a sieve and plunge them into boiling water for 30 seconds, then cool them in a bowl of ice and water and drain them well.

2. Fasten cheesecloth smoothly over two large oblong cake racks or an oven shelf, using paper clips or staples; or, if you have them, use three round cake racks made of closely set concentric wires (these require no cheesecloth).

3. Arrange the cherries, cut sides up if they have been halved, close together on the racks. If you like, sprinkle them very sparingly with sugar, using no more than a tablespoonful in all. (This helps to start the emergence of juice, the first step in the drying process.)

Oven-drying method: Preheat the oven to 200°F. Set the racks on foil-lined baking sheets (to catch any drips) and place the sheets in the oven. Leave the cherries for 20 minutes. Turn off the heat and let the oven cool with the door closed. Reset the control to between 120°F and 140°F (the lower the better), turn on the oven, and dry the cherries for 2 to 4 hours more (for halves) or for as much as 5 or 6 hours for whole cherries. The fruit is dry enough when it is leathery but pliable, like raisins from a freshly opened box; don't leave the cherries until they get hard. During drying, once no more juice is being exuded, the process can be speeded up by removing the baking sheets under the racks. If you have a convection oven, the job will take less time than a conventional oven requires; consult the oven manufacturer's instructions. Lacking instructions, set the convection oven temperature somewhere between 120° and 140°F.

Sun-drying method: Set the racks of fruit in full sun, protecting the cherries from insects with cheesecloth stretched over improvised props so it doesn't touch the fruit. Leave the cherries in the sunlight as long as it lasts, turning them when the upper sides begin to become leathery. Take the trays indoors overnight and resume drying the next

How Do I Use Them? Let Me Count the Ways

Eat your "super-raisin" cherries out of hand for a nibble of concentrated fruitiness; or use them in place of commercial raisins in puddings, pies, fruit or spice cakes, Irish soda bread, muffins, scones, or cookies. Include them in homemade mincemeat, too, if you indulge in making a seasonal supply of that goodie.

day. Turn the cherries twice a day for the 2 to 4 days (depending on weather) the drying will take. If dark or damp weather comes along, switch to the oven at the settings given above.

4. Cool the cherries completely, then store them airtight in a dry sterilized (page 282) jar. Leave the capped jar on the kitchen counter out of sunlight for 2 or 3 days and inspect it daily; if any fogging appears inside, oven-dry the cherries further, then return them to the jar and repeat the check for moisture. Store for up to a year in a cool cupboard.

To use the cherries: Soak them until soft in warm or hot water to cover: this will take an hour or more. Drain them well and pat them dry before using them in any way raisins are used. They are especially good in fruitcakes and other baking.

Blueberry or Huckleberry Raisins

The Native Americans knew a thing or two about preserving wild foods for winter use, and early settlers from Europe were quick to learn from them. Lacking such imported luxuries as genuine raisins, the colonists adopted dried blueberries with enthusiasm. Dried huckleberries, possible only if you have a wild patch within reach, are also quite flavorful, though seedy.

2 pint baskets (about 6 cups) firm-ripe blueberries or huckleberries

Makes about 1½ cups

1. Pick over the berries, then place half of them in a sieve and plunge it into a potful of boiling water to blanch for 20 to 30 seconds; remove the sieve and drop the berries into a bowl of water and ice. Repeat with the rest of the berries. Drain the berries well.

2. Cover two very large cake racks or oven shelves with tightly stretched cheesecloth and pin or staple it in place; or use several round wire cake racks made of closely set concentric wires (these require no cheesecloth). Spread the berries in a single layer on the racks.

3. *Sun-drying method:* Follow the directions in step 3 of the preceding directions for cherries, turning the berries at least once a day. Count on at least 2 days for thorough drying, which has been achieved when the berries are very firm, almost hard, yielding no moisture when squeezed. If the sunlight fails, switch to the oven method.

Oven-drying method: Follow the directions given for cherries in step 3 of the preceding recipe.

4. When the berries are ready, transfer them to a jar and test for residual moisture as described in step 4 of the directions for drying cherries. Store for up to a year in a cool cupboard.

SWAPS

Consider popping dried berries or dried berries other than cranberries into Cranberry Biscotti (see the Index), or swap any of these dried small fruits for raisins in a cookie, cake, or muffin batter that's usually raisin-studded. Cranberries needn't be soaked or otherwise prepared before use; however, sweet or sour cherries, home-dried fresh currants, blueberries, huckleberries, or any of the other berries recommended for drying on page 322 should be soaked in warm water until they plump up. Drain them, pat them dry, and they're ready to go into the batter bowl.

To use dried blueberries or buckleberries: Cover them with hot water and soak them until they have plumped up and softened, which usually takes a few hours. Drain them well and use them exactly like commercial raisins or currants.

DRIED CRANBERRIES

Light sweetening is needed if these extra-tart berries are to be palatable after drying, so cranberries must be handled differently from other, sweeter fruits. I've worked out a dual recipe for these delicate nuggets, offering a choice of sweetening with granulated sugar or a heat-stable noncaloric sweetener. Using such a substitute for sugar is a boon to calorie- and carbohydrate-watchers, as dried cranberries sweetened this way can be used in baking in place of high-carbohydrate raisins and can be enjoyed as a confection by the dietarily challenged, as they score close to zero on the "carb" scale.

DRIED CRANBERRIES LIGHTLY SWEETENED WITH SUGAR

3 packages (12 ounces each) fresh cranberries
2½ cups water
1 cup sugar

Makes about 4 cups

1. Pick over the cranberries, getting rid of any stems and soft berries. Meanwhile, bring 2 quarts of water to a boil in a saucepan.

2. Drop in enough cranberries to cover the surface and leave them just until the skins crack, a matter of a minute or so—popping sounds will be heard. Scoop out the berries onto a platter or baking sheet to cool. Repeat until all the berries have been treated. (Cracking the skins speeds up the drying.)

3. *Drying the berries, first phase:* Use an electric dehydrator according to the manufacturer's instructions, if you have one. If not, use cheesecloth-covered racks and your oven as described in the directions for Dried Sweet or Sour Cherries (page 321), omitting the sprinkling of sugar and the use of pans under the racks. Dry the cranberries until they have shrunken by half and become leathery. Check them from time to time; if any berries have puffed up because their skins haven't cracked, prick them with a thin skewer or coarse needle.

4. *Sweetening and redrying the berries:* Bring the water and sugar to a boil in a wide skillet or sauté pan and boil the syrup for 3 minutes. Add the cranberries and leave the pan over the heat until the syrup boils again, pushing the berries under the surface as they heat. Pour the whole business onto a platter or into a nonstick jelly-roll pan large enough to hold the fruit in one layer. Cover lightly with a cloth and leave the berries to imbibe all the syrup, which will take from 1 to 3 days, depending on the humidity of the room. When all the syrup has been absorbed, repeat the drying process in step 2, this time putting foil-lined baking sheets under the racks to absorb any stray drips. Stop the drying when the cranberries are again leathery but still pliable—don't let them get hard.

5. Store the berries and check the moisture level as described in step 4 of the recipe for dried cherries. They will keep for at least a couple of months in a cool cupboard, or for a year or more in a tightly capped jar in the freezer.

To use the berries: They are ready to eat, or to use in baking or cooking, just as they come from the jar.

For Nearly-Seedless Dried Cranberries

This little caper exchanges some extra work—halving the cranberries with a small sharp knife—for quicker drying and a final product that has almost no seeds. When you have finished the knife work, shake the berries in a sieve to free them of seeds; then proceed with the drying as described, beginning with step 3.

Dried Cranberries with Alternative Sweetening

There are many sugar substitutes (Sweet 'n' Low, Equal, Sunette, Sweet One, and so on), but not all of them retain their sweetness after being heated beyond a certain point, so it's vital to use a heat-stable sweetener if you plan to use dried cranberries in baking or other cooking. Read the labels.

Makes about 4 cups

Follow the preceding directions for sugar-sweetened dried cranberries, substituting for the 1 cup sugar the equivalent amount (check the label) of a heat-stable sugar substitute. Dissolve the sweetener after bringing the water to a boil, but do not boil the mixture. Add the cranberries to the hot liquid after their first drying and pour them onto a platter or pan to absorb the liquid, as described above. When most or all of the "syrup" has been imbibed, return the berries to their dehydrator racks or oven racks (I put foil-lined baking sheets under oven racks to catch the likely drips) and dry them again until leathery but still pliable.

These sugar-free cranberries can't be stored very long at room temperature, as their sweetening is not a preservative, so I freeze them in any clean, dry screwtop jar I have on hand. They keep for a year or more and can be poured from the container without thawing.

SUGARED & SPICED NUTS

Crisp-coated frivolities, pecans or walnuts gussied up with a little sugar and a little spice are nibbles for dessert time. Also recommended with a cup of cappuccino or other exotic (or basic black) coffee.

The fourth spice to enliven these nuts is coriander, which adds a subtle orangelike freshness to the familiar tastes of cinnamon, ginger, and allspice. Ground coriander can be bought, but as it becomes stale quickly it's better to grind the seeds in a little spice mill when they're wanted. First shaking them in a skillet over medium heat just until they're heated through will perk up their flavor.

1 large egg white
1 tablespoon water
1 pound pecan or walnut halves, or half a pound of each
⅔ cup superfine sugar
1 teaspoon salt
2 teaspoons ground cinnamon
¾ teaspoon ground ginger
¾ teaspoon ground allspice
½ teaspoon ground coriander

Makes about 1⅓ pounds

1. Preheat the oven to 250°F, with a shelf in the upper third and one in the lower.

2. In a bowl whisk the egg white and water together until the mixture is foamy. Stir in the nuts; mix well. Pour into a sieve and drain for 3 minutes.

3. Combine the sugar, salt, cinnamon, ginger, allspice, and coriander in a paper bag; gather the neck of the bag and shake the bag to mix everything. Add the drained nuts and shake the bag vigorously to coat them with the sugar and spice. Spread the nuts on two baking sheets, making sure they do not touch.

4. Bake the nuts for 15 minutes, then stir them and spread them out again. Lower the oven temperature to 225°F and continue to bake the nuts, stirring them occasionally, until they are well dried and crisp, about 1¼ hours longer; midway, switch the shelf positions of the two pans. Turn off the oven and let the nuts cool with the oven door open.

5. *To store:* Store the completely cooled nuts airtight. They keep well for a few days at room temperature, for 3 weeks refrigerated, or for 3 months frozen. Thaw frozen nuts unopened, then spread them on a baking sheet and refresh them for 10 minutes or so in a 200°F oven. Let them cool again before they're served.

NUTS, ELSEWHERE

Plain old pecans or English walnuts are handsomely served by this sugar-and-spice transformation into a confection, but that isn't the end of the nut story: Other nutty pleasures are to be found throughout the Index. For serving with cocktails or other preprandial drinks, see Curried Peanuts, or perhaps Deviled Peanuts or Almonds. For a substantial dish, see the nutted pastas—Peanut Pasta, or Hazelnut or Black Walnut Pasta. For a classic sweet, there's Almond Paste or Marzipan (and a number of macaroons). For a crisp, sweet-savory snack good at any hour, see Chinese-Style Glazed Walnuts, Pecans, or Black Walnuts.

Classic Toffee & Fancy Toffee Bars

A candy the unpracticed cook can succeed with, buttery, crisp English-style toffee has an undying charm whether devoured plain or topped with chocolate and almonds. It's not essential to use a candy/jelly thermometer when you make this, as it's feasible to fall back on the old-fashioned cold water test for the right stage of doneness of the candy mixture.

¾ cup (1½ sticks) sweet (unsalted) butter, sliced
2 cups sugar
2 tablespoons corn syrup, light or dark
2 tablespoons cider vinegar
⅛ teaspoon salt

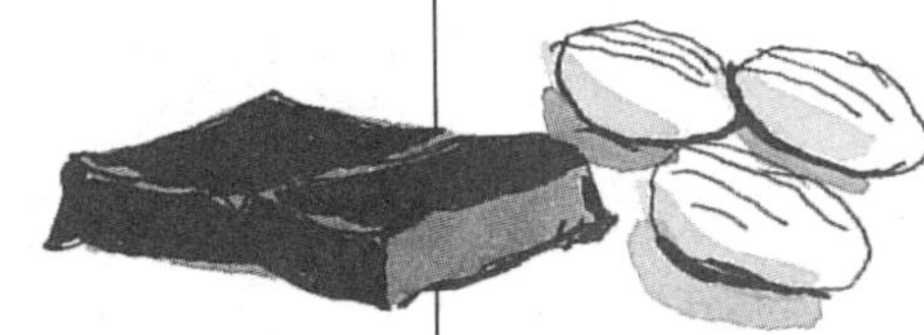

TOPPING (OPTIONAL)
4 ounces fine-quality dark sweet or bittersweet chocolate
2 teaspoons sweet (unsalted) butter
½ cup blanched almonds, toasted (page 349) and finely chopped

Makes about 1 pound plain toffee, or 1⅓ pounds when topped with chocolate and almonds

1. Butter a large baking sheet (not a nonstick baking sheet, which might be damaged by cutting the candy on its surface) and the bottom surface of a metal spatula quite liberally.

2. Combine all the ingredients in a heavy 2-quart saucepan and stir over medium heat until the butter has melted and the sugar has dissolved. Raise the heat to medium-high and boil the mixture, stirring it and scraping down the sides of the pan often until the reading on a candy/jelly thermometer reaches 290°F, or until a little of the mixture dropped into a glass of cold water turns glassy and hard. At once pour the mixture onto the prepared baking sheet (it can overbrown very quickly at this temperature), spreading it with the buttered spatula into a rectangle about ¼ inch thick. Let the candy cool slightly, tidying and straightening the edges with the spatula as it cools.

3. When the candy has set but is still malleable, use a heavy knife to cut it into small rectangles, about 1½ by 2 inches. (If you're adding the topping, you may want to make larger oblongs to resemble small candy bars). Use the edge of the blade to push the pieces slightly apart. Leave the candy to cool.

Sugar Is as Sugar Does, Usually

When granulated sugar is called for in a recipe, it makes absolutely no difference whether cane or beet sugar is used. If another sugar is specified—light or dark brown, superfine, confectioners' ("powdered"), raw, maple, and so on—that kind should be used.

4. ***If the toffee will be eaten straight,*** pack the pieces in a canister or metal box, separating the layers with waxed paper or plastic. Store, covered, at room temperature for as long as candy lasts at your house.

For fancy toffee bars: When the candy is completely cool, add the topping. Melt the chocolate with the butter over simmering water, stirring (or melt it in the microwave, using the manufacturer's recommended power setting). Push the cooled pieces of toffee back into their original rectangle. Using the back of a spoon, spread the chocolate over the assemblage, then sprinkle on the chopped almonds and brush them into an even layer with a pastry brush. Press the nuts lightly into the chocolate with a rubber spatula and leave the candy until the chocolate has set, which may take a few hours. When it is firm, pack the pieces in a canister in layers separated by waxed paper. If the candy isn't consumed within a week or so, you may want to refrigerate it to preserve the freshness of the nuts.

CHOCOLATE TRUFFLES, BLACK & WHITE

Black truffles and white truffles—the fungi—are morsels coveted by gastronomes, but they aren't to everyone's taste (or purse), happily for the survival of the wild supply. However, everyone likes the French confections called *truffes en chocolat*, which are shaped to resemble the black truffles for which they're named.

Classic truffles are richly compounded of chocolate, heavy cream, and/or butter, plus, sometimes, more sugar, various flavorings, nuts, egg yolks, coffee, or liqueurs or other spirits. The usual earthy-looking finish is a coat of cocoa, but truffles are often dipped into dark or white melted chocolate.

Chocolate truffles are shockingly easy to make. For smashing results, start with really fine chocolate; shop for bittersweet (my choice) or semisweet chocolate of the highest quality you can find, and you'll be rewarded with results worthy of a fancy confectioner. For the white truffles below (my own variation on the theme), look for a reputable label in order to be sure you're getting a bar of excellent "white chocolate," which isn't chocolate at all but is nevertheless very nice to eat if it's of high quality.

If you lack a supply of good chocolate but yearn for truffles anyway, try the cocoa-based Instant Truffles on page 373, made from the rich mixture called Chocolate Butter, Nutted or Otherwise.

White Truffles with Hazelnuts

These sandy-colored nuggets are nutty and delicate in flavor, in contrast to the bittersweet flavor impact of traditional truffles. I like to arrange both kinds on a pretty plate to be passed as dessert, with coffee.

¾ cup hazelnuts, toasted and skinned (page 372)
⅓ cup confectioners' sugar
8 ounces high-quality white chocolate, cut up
⅓ cup heavy (whipping) cream
1 tablespoon sweet (unsalted) butter, diced
1 tablespoon Frangelico (hazelnut liqueur) or Amaretto (almond liqueur)
1 teaspoon pure vanilla extract

FOR COATING:
Sifted confectioners' sugar, preferably vanilla-flavored (see sidebar)

Makes 3 to 3½ dozen truffles

1. Combine the hazelnuts with the ⅓ cup confectioners' sugar in the bowl of a food processor and grind the nuts fine, scraping down the workbowl as necessary; the mixture should be the texture of cornmeal. Remove and reserve.

2. Place the chocolate in a food processor; chop it fine with on-off bursts of the motor. Leave the workbowl in place on the machine.

3. Heat the cream just to the boiling point. With the motor running, pour the cream through the feed tube of the food processor and process the chocolate until smooth, scraping down the bowl as necessary. Add the butter and process until mixed. Add the hazelnut mixture, the hazelnut liqueur, and the vanilla; mix briefly, just until blended.

4. Scrape the truffle mixture into a bowl, cover, and chill for 1 hour, or until somewhat firm.

5. Scoop out rounded teaspoonfuls of the mixture (a melon baller is useful for this) and place the mounds on a baking sheet covered with waxed paper. Cover with plastic wrap and refrigerate again for several hours, or until very firm.

6. Sift a generous amount of confectioners' sugar into a small bowl and roll the truffles in the sugar, shaping them into irregular balls as you coat them. Pack the truffles in a refrigerator box or other plastic or glass container, separating the layers with waxed paper, and refrigerate them again. The truffles will keep for a week or two if kept cold. For longer keeping, pack them for the freezer and freeze for up to sev-

Vanilla-Flavored Confectioners' Sugar

Slit one or more vanilla beans open and bury the halves in a jar or canister of confectioners' sugar. Cover and store in a cool cupboard. Stir the sugar occasionally, and as you use it, add more sugar as long as the scent of the vanilla beans remains strong.

Recycling note: *Instead of starting with a pristine bean, recycle vanilla beans that have been used to flavor ice cream, custard, or stewed fruit. Rinse the pieces to remove any clinging cream or syrup, pat them dry, and add them to the sugar jar, where they will continue to do their bit for a considerable time.*

eral weeks. Thaw them in the refrigerator and treat them to a second coat of powdered sugar shortly before serving time.

Chocolate-Mocha Truffles with Rum

Compounded with both chocolate and cocoa, not to mention a touch of strong coffee and rum, these delectables are special favorites of the many fans of bittersweet chocolate.

6 ounces fine-quality bittersweet chocolate, cut up
6 tablespoons sifted fine-quality unsweetened Dutch-process cocoa powder
½ cup confectioners' sugar, sifted
¼ cup brewed espresso or other strong coffee
½ cup heavy (whipping) cream
2 tablespoons dark rum (Cognac or other good brandy can be substituted)

FOR COATING:
Unsweetened Dutch-process cocoa powder

Makes about 3 dozen truffles

1. Combine the chocolate, cocoa, and confectioners' sugar in a food processor. Run the machine in on-off bursts until the chocolate is chopped very fine. Leave the workbowl in place on the machine.

2. Heat together the coffee and heavy cream, just to the boiling point. With the motor running, pour the mixture through the feed tube of the food processor. Blend until very smooth, scraping down the sides of the bowl as necessary. Cool the mixture to lukewarm, then blend in the rum.

3. Scrape the truffle mixture into a bowl, cover, and chill until firm enough to shape, at least 1 hour.

4. Scoop rounded teaspoonfuls of the mixture (I use a melon baller) and place the mounds on a baking sheet covered with waxed paper. Cover with plastic wrap and refrigerate again for several hours, or until very firm.

5. Sift the cocoa for coating into a small bowl. Roll each truffle in the coating, shaping it into a knobbly little ball. Arrange them in a refrigerator box or similar container, separating the layers with waxed paper. Cover and refrigerate until needed. The truffles will keep for a week or two. They may be freezer-wrapped and frozen for several weeks' storage. Thaw frozen truffles in the refrigerator, then roll them in cocoa again just before serving time. (Refrigerated truffles may need a fresh powdering of cocoa, too.)

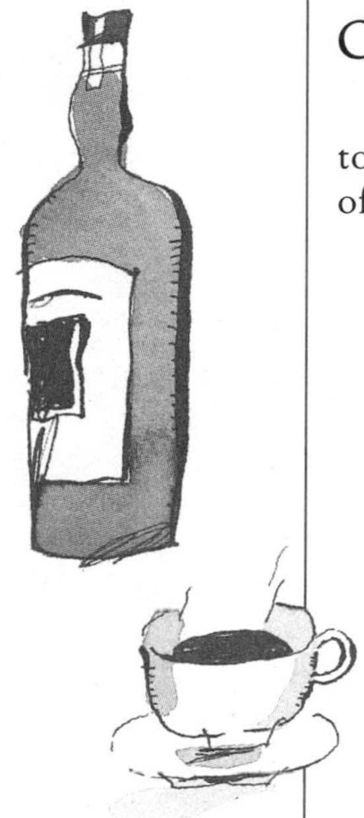

Going Dutch

Cocoa that has been given the alkali treatment called "Dutching"—so named because it was invented by Conrad van Houten, a Netherlander—is known as Dutch-process cocoa and is the cream of the crop for most uses. Compared to standard cocoa powders, it is superior in flavor, darker in color, and easier to blend with liquids. Unless a recipe says otherwise, it's what I use.

SUGAR BAKING

Great Cookies and a Cake or Two

The ebb and flow of food fashion, the kitchen gods be thanked, hasn't dislodged cookies from their special place in our hearts, although new nibbles do come into vogue now and then. Among newly noticed cookies are biscotti, which have long been with us in modest association with Italian cuisine; they've now come into their own as luxurious little bars that are fun to make and reliable keepers, too.

Half a dozen kinds of biscotti (chocolate/pepper, almond/orange/ginger, cranberry, and honey/spice, among them) aren't the only new cookies in this chapter. There's a small shopful of chewy macaroons plus Amaretti, the airy (not chewy) almond macaroons most familiar in commercial versions, and crisp double-baked sponge biscuits made from a cake that may also be served as a cake. Two cookies—Florentines and Improbable Almond Bars—teeter on the line between candies and cookies. Then there's Panforte, "strong bread," a baked Italian confection that's as far from "bread" as can be imagined. To round off, you'll find a range of shortbreads expanded from *Fancy Pantry*, plus Christmas Pfeffernüsse, Arrowroot Biscuits, Panettone—festive at any season—and a Holiday Keeping Cake, based on cranberries, that's a world away from the hackneyed fruitcakes we all know and some of us loathe.

Almond Macaroons, with Chocolate, Pecan, & Hazelnut Variations

The almond macaroons most of us know are soft and chewy, the kind produced, in a generous batch, by the main recipe below. One variation gussied up with chocolate and another made with either hazelnuts or pecans follows the classic version. (For the crisp and airy dry macaroons commonly called Amaretti, see page 336.)

Oil of bitter almonds: The oil of bitter almonds listed as an alternative to standard almond extract is worth seeking out for general baking use, not just for these cookies. (It's sold by specialists in baking supplies.) It is much stronger as well as different in character from almond extract—I add a drop or two to almost anything that depends on almonds for flavor, as run-of-the-orchard nuts can be lamentably bland.

Almond Macaroons

2 cups almonds, blanched (page 295) and well dried
1 cup granulated sugar, preferably superfine
Big pinch of salt
2 large egg whites, beaten just until foamy
¾ teaspoon pure almond extract or 3 or 4 drops oil of bitter almonds
Confectioners' sugar for dusting

OPTIONAL DECORATION:
Halves of candied cherries or cubes of candied orange peel, or additional almonds, slivered

Makes about 3 dozen cookies

1. Cover two baking sheets with aluminum foil; grease the foil or spray it with pan coating.

2. Working in two batches, grind the nuts to a coarse powder (about like cornmeal) in a food processor, gradually adding a little of the granulated sugar to each batch as the machine runs. (Alternatively, use a nut grinder, but don't try grinding the nuts in a blender.) Combine the batches in a mixing bowl and stir in the remaining granulated sugar, the salt, and almond flavoring. Work in about half of the beaten egg whites, mixing thoroughly, then add more egg white, up to the entire quantity, if needed. Stop adding egg white when the paste holds together when you pinch a sample between your fingers.

Macaroon Troubleshooting

Even slight overbaking can cause macaroons to become discouragingly hard. If this should happen, don't give them to the cats to play hockey with. Just pack them into a canister or a jar with two or three wedges of raw apple and close the container. Within 24 hours they should have rehydrated and become properly chewy. If they should still be too dry, replace the apple chunks and give them a little more time.

I've also revived overbaked macaroons by wetting a crumpled paper towel and parking it on a square of foil atop the cookies, then closing the container tightly.

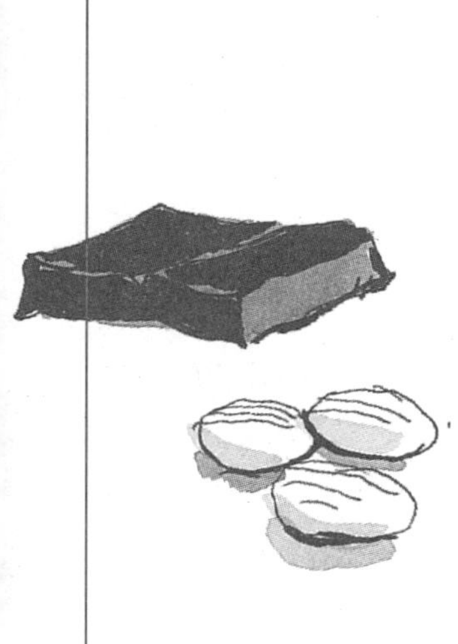

3. Scoop the paste into a pastry bag or cookie press fitted with a large plain or star tip and shape tall macaroons about 1 inch in diameter on the prepared pans, spacing them at least an inch apart. Alternatively, form rounded teaspoonfuls of the paste into balls and shape them with your fingers so they are a bit higher than they are wide; or push spoonfuls of paste onto the pans with the tip of a second spoon, then shape the cookies with your fingers.

4. Dust the macaroons lightly with confectioners' sugar and leave them uncovered for 1 to 2 hours, or until they feel dryish to the touch. Decorate the tops, if you wish, with candied fruit or slivered nuts.

5. Preheat the oven to 325°F, with a shelf in the upper third and one in the lower. Bake the macaroons for about 15 minutes, exchanging shelf positions midway in the baking; they are done when they are very lightly browned and still soft when touched. (For the correct chewy texture, it's important not to overbake them.) Remove from the oven, slip the foil from the pans, and let the cookies cool on the foil for a few minutes, then peel away the foil and cool them completely on a rack.

6. Store the macaroons in an airtight canister at room temperature for up to a week, or refrigerate them for longer storage. They'll keep for several weeks, suitably packaged, in the fridge.

Chocolate Macaroons

2 cups almonds, blanched (page 295)
1 cup sugar, preferably superfine
Big pinch of salt
½ cup (lightly packed) sifted fine-quality unsweetened Dutch-process cocoa powder
2 large egg whites, beaten just until foamy
⅓ teaspoon pure almond extract or 2 or 3 drops oil of bitter almonds
½ teaspoon pure vanilla extract

OPTIONAL DECORATION:
Additional almonds, slivered, or small chunks or chips of bittersweet chocolate

Makes about 3 dozen cookies

1. Follow the directions for making Almond Macaroons, adding the cocoa with the remaining sugar and salt after grinding the nuts.

2. After shaping the macaroons, decorate the tops, if you wish, with slivered almonds or a bit of chocolate. (Note that these macaroons do not receive a powdering of confectioners' sugar.) Let the unbaked cookies dry uncovered for 1 to 2 hours at room temperature.

3. Bake at 325°F for 12 to 15 minutes, exchanging shelf positions of the pans midway in the baking. The macaroons are done when they no longer feel tacky to the touch but are still a bit yielding, neither soft nor firm when pressed lightly. Let them cool on the foil sheet for 5 minutes, then remove, cool, and store them as described for Almond Macaroons.

Pecan or Hazelnut Macaroons

2¼ cups hazelnuts, toasted and skinned (page 372) or pecans, lightly toasted (page 302)
1 cup granulated sugar, preferably superfine
¼ cup (packed) sifted dark-brown sugar
⅛ teaspoon salt
2 large egg whites, slightly beaten

OPTIONAL DECORATION:
Halved candied cherries or cubes of candied orange peel
Confectioners' sugar for dusting

Makes about 3 dozen cookies

Make the dough, shape the cookies, and let them stand to allow the surface to dry as for Almond Macaroons, but leave a little more space between them on the baking pans and omit the initial dusting of confectioners' sugar. Decorate, if you like, with the candied fruit or peel.

Baking will require about 15 minutes; the macaroons are done when they have browned a little and feel only slightly soft when touched. Cool briefly on the foil, remove the foil, cool, and store the cookies as described for Almond Macaroons. If you like, dust these with confectioners' sugar when completely cool or just before serving.

Almond, Orange, & Ginger Biscotti

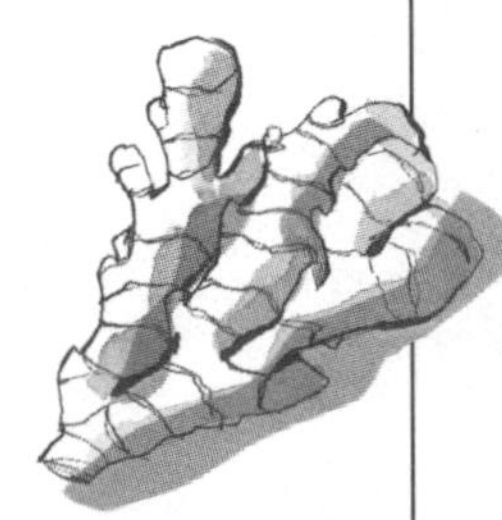

Crisp and subtly flavored, these gently sweet, twice-baked biscuits go with coffee or tea, or a glass of sweet wine, or a simple dessert of ice cream or fruit compote. Like all biscotti they keep beautifully, but if your family is like my family, you may find yourself making them quite often.

AN ANCIENT COOKIE

Biscotti, say food historians, are descended from the rudimentary rations—the hard biscuits, whose name means "twice-baked"—that kept together the bodies and souls of Roman soldiers and other fighting men of antiquity. After the Roman legions passed into history, rocklike biscuits of one sort or another were the rations of armies, ships' crews, and explorers for many centuries. Not found in those morsels were the almonds, sugar, eggs, and other goodies that make modern biscotti such popular delicacies. Such "rations" as Almond, Orange, & Ginger Biscotti and the other twice-baked cookies in this section, and several savory biscotti to go with drinks (see the Index) would amaze the Romans, the seamen, and soldiers who subsisted upon the "biscuits" of times gone by.

⅔ cup almonds, blanched (page 295) and well dried
2½ cups sifted all-purpose flour
3 teaspoons baking powder
¾ teaspoon salt
¼ teaspoon ground mace
½ cup (1 stick) sweet (unsalted) butter, softened at room temperature
¾ cup sugar
½ teaspoon pure vanilla extract
¼ teaspoon pure almond extract or 2 or 3 drops oil of bitter almonds (page 332)
2 large eggs
3 tablespoons chopped Crystallized Ginger (page 315) or drained Ginger Preserved in Syrup (page 317)
1 tablespoon finely chopped candied orange peel

GLAZE:
2 teaspoons milk
Sugar

Makes about 3 dozen biscotti

1. Preheat the oven to 350°F, with a shelf in the center position. Spread the almonds on a baking sheet and toast them, stirring every 2 or 3 minutes, until they are pale gold, about 10 minutes. Remove the nuts and raise the oven setting to 375°F. Cool the nuts and chop them coarsely; reserve. Cover the baking sheet with foil.

2. Sift together the flour, baking powder, salt, and mace; set aside.

3. Cream the butter in the large bowl of an electric mixer. Beat in the sugar until fluffy. Beat in the vanilla and almond extracts, then beat in the eggs one at a time. Stir in the dry ingredients, then the almonds, crystallized ginger, and candied peel. Mix the dough well, or knead it a few strokes on a lightly floured work surface. The dough should be firm; if it is not, knead in a little additional flour, up to 3 tablespoons.

4. Mold the dough firmly into two narrow loaves on the prepared baking sheet, making each about 12 inches long and 2½ inches wide and placing them 4 inches apart; the centers should be slightly higher than the sides. Smooth the surface of the strips with a pastry brush dipped in the milk, then sprinkle them lightly with sugar.

5. Bake the loaves until they are firm to the touch and colored pale gold, 20 to 25 minutes. Remove the baking sheet from the oven and lower the oven setting to 300°F.

6. Cool the loaves on the pan for 5 minutes, then carefully remove them from the foil and place them on a wire rack; cool 15 minutes longer.

7. Move the loaves to a cutting surface, and using a sharp serrated knife, slice them crosswise at a slight diagonal into ½-inch slices. Lay the slices flat on the baking sheet. Bake the slices for 10 minutes, then turn them and bake them 10 minutes longer. Turn off the heat and let the biscotti cool in the oven, with the door open.

8. Store the completely cooled biscotti in an airtight canister at room temperature; they will keep for at least 3 weeks. Alternatively, package them for the freezer and freeze them for up to 3 months. Thaw frozen biscotti in their wrappings, then refresh them on a baking pan in a 325°F oven for about 10 minutes. Cool before serving.

Amaretti

(Crisp & Airy Almond Macaroons)

These almond cookies are crisp and dry, the ultimate crunch, though they start out with more or less the same ingredients as chewy Almond Macaroons (page 332). A lot of trial and error (with *flat* results) finally produced this recipe for upstanding and airy little cakes. If you like the imported *amaretti* that come wrapped in pairs in tissue paper, you'll be glad to know how to make these respectable replicas.

Professional bakers of amaretti include in the dough the flavorful kernels of apricots, which are almost impossible to find as a stand-alone ingredient. If you should get your hands on some, you may substitute 3 tablespoons of the kernels for 3 tablespoons of the almonds. The oil of bitter almonds listed as alternative flavoring in the recipe (try a supplier of special ingredients for this) is worth searching for; a very few drops will back up the flavor of ordinary almonds in an extraordinary way.

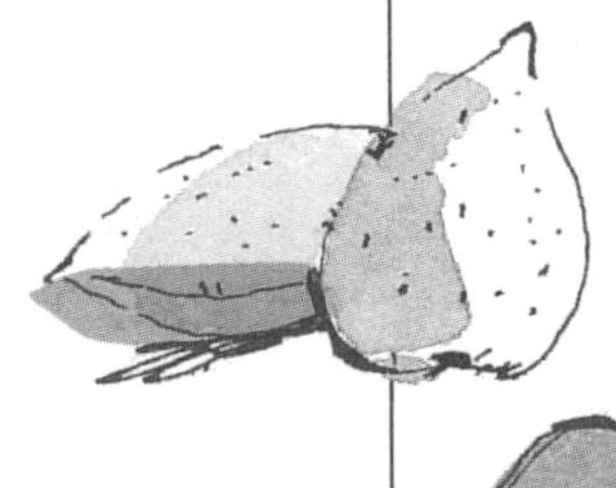

1 cup almonds, blanched (page 295) and toasted (page 349)
1 cup confectioners' sugar
3 tablespoons all-purpose flour
¼ teaspoon baking powder
⅛ teaspoon salt
4 large egg whites, at room temperature
½ to ¾ teaspoon almond extract (depending on its quality), or 5 drops oil of bitter almonds

Makes about 40 amaretti

THE DIFFERENCE IS WHAT?

All macaroons are amaretti, according to one school of thought, but in American usage, at least, "macaroons" means chewy almond cookies (sometimes made with coconut or some other nut than almonds), whereas "amaretti" generally designates dry, crisp little cookies like those produced by this recipe. Amaretti (and the smaller amarettini) are imported from Italy in great quantities.

1. Preheat the oven to 300°F, with a shelf in the upper third and one in the lower. Butter and flour two baking sheets.

2. Chop the almonds coarsely in a food processor (or use a nut grater). Add ¼ cup of the confectioners' sugar, the flour, baking powder, and salt. Run the machine in bursts, stirring the mixture several times, until its texture is like that of cornmeal. Pour the mixture into a bowl and whisk to break up any lumps.

3. Sift the remaining ¾ cup of confectioners' sugar. Beat the egg whites with an electric mixer at medium speed until they are foamy, then beat in the sifted sugar gradually. Add the almond extract and beat at high speed until the mixture forms well-defined but not dry peaks when the beater is lifted. Scatter the almond mixture over the top and fold everything very gently together with a rubber spatula.

4. Scrape the meringue gently into a pastry bag fitted with a large plain tube or rosette tip. Pipe tall mounds about 1¾ inches wide on the baking pans, spacing them 1 inch apart.

5. Bake the amaretti on two shelves of the preheated oven for 15 to 18 minutes or until light gold and somewhat firm, exchanging shelf positions midway. Remove the pans from the oven and let the cookies cool for a few minutes, then remove them to wire racks and cool them completely. (They won't be crisp at this point.) Meanwhile, turn off the oven and let it cool with the door open.

6. Return the racks of amaretti to the oven and turn the setting to about 150°F (or to its "warm" setting, usually about 140°F). Rebake the cookies for about 1½ hours, checking them every 20 minutes and shifting rack positions if necessary, until they are a lovely rich golden shade and dry throughout. (To be sure of this, you may have to consume a cookie, but someone has to do these jobs.) Cool completely.

7. Store the amaretti in an airtight canister or closed plastic bag. They keep well for weeks in a cool spot if not allowed to become damp. If they should become at all chewy, treat them to a brief spell in a warm oven, as described in step 6. The cookies may also be frozen for longer storage. Thaw them in their wrappings, then refresh them in a warm oven to ensure crispness.

ARROWROOT BISCUITS

(NOT FOR INFANTS ONLY)

If you have ever sneaked a nibble from a baby's box of arrowroot crackers, you know the insidious charm of those mild-mannered bites. This recipe adds lemon and anise to an eggy, buttery dough to make a grown-up treat.

The requisite arrowroot can be bought in the quantity you'll need most reasonably from specialty suppliers of spices, grains, and flours; the price for even a tiny jar is ridiculously high on grocery-store spice racks. (Arrowroot is great to have on hand as a thickener for bright, clear sauces and gravies, and for old-fashioned puddings and Scandinavian fruit soups and such.)

Another listed ingredient, ammonium carbonate or hartshorn, makes very crisp cookies, but it isn't found in supermarkets. If you can't get it from a specialty baking supplier or a druggist, just use the baking powder.

1½ cups all-purpose flour or unbleached pastry flour
1 cup arrowroot
⅔ cup superfine sugar
¼ teaspoon salt
⅛ teaspoon ammonium carbonate (baking ammonia or hartshorn), or substitute ½ teaspoon baking powder
½ cup (1 stick) sweet (unsalted) butter
½ teaspoon finely grated lemon zest (outer peel only, no white pith), or a drop or two of lemon oil (be sparing)
¼ teaspoon very finely crushed anise seed (use a mortar and pestle or a rolling pin), or more to taste
2 large eggs, well beaten
1 to 2 teaspoons milk, if needed

Makes about 1¾ pounds of cookies

1. Preheat the oven to 325°F, with a shelf in the center position.

2. Sift together very thoroughly the flour, arrowroot, sugar, salt, and ammonium carbonate or baking powder. Cut in the butter, lemon zest, and anise seed until the mixture is as fine as flour. (The sifting and cutting in are most efficiently done in a food processor.) Mix in the eggs to make a firm dough; if mixing with the processor, run the motor until the dough forms a ball on top of the blade. If the dough is crumbly, mix in a teaspoonful of the milk; if more is needed, add it cautiously, but don't make the dough oversoft or it will be hard to handle.

3. Divide the dough into two portions. Cover a baking sheet with aluminum foil and place one half of the dough on it. Cover the dough with a large sheet of plastic wrap and roll out the dough ⅛ inch thick with a rolling pin, keeping the shape as close to a rectangle as possible. Remove the plastic and cut the dough into oblongs or diamonds with a serrated pastry wheel (or a plain pizza cutter), using a ruler to keep lines straight; a good size is about 1½ by 2½ inches. Lift off the trimmings around the edges and reserve them for rerolling. Prick each cookie several times with a fork.

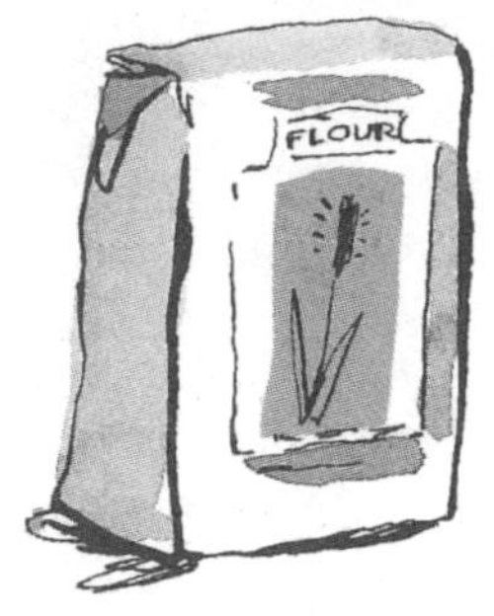

A Victorian Bequest

Arrowroot pudding was a staple food for the sick back in the days of Florence Nightingale because the starch is considered very easy to digest. From pudding it was no doubt a short step to inventing bland arrowroot baby biscuits, which are still baked commercially. Genuine arrowroot is a fine-grained starch extracted from the tubers of Maranta arundinacea, *and it comes from the West Indies. Other starchy roots native to other regions are also called "arrowroot" and yield starches used in much the same way as the genuine article.*

An Uncommon Ingredient & Why It's Still Used

Ammonium carbonate (or baking ammonia or hartshorn) was much used before baking powder came along. It's still the fussy baker's choice for cookies that should be exceptionally crisp. Best source: a specialist supplier of baking ingredients.

4. Bake the cookies until they are firm but not at all browned, 10 to 13 minutes. Remove the pan from the oven, go over the cutting lines again with the pastry wheel, and lift the cookies onto a rack to cool.

5. While the first batch is baking, shape the second half of the dough, plus the trimmings of the first panful, on a second sheet of foil. When the baking pan has cooled, slip the foil onto it and bake the cookies as described. Cool the second batch.

6. For extra-crisp cookies, place them, still on the racks after cooling completely, in the oven set at its lowest heat (or at "warm," about 140°F) and leave for 5 minutes or so. Turn off the oven, open the door slightly, and leave the cookies until almost cool. Cool them completely at room temperature, then store them in an airtight canister for up to a month at room temperature. They may also be packaged for the freezer and stored frozen for 2 months or more. Frozen cookies, or cookies that may have softened in the canister, should be refreshed with a few minutes' stay in a low (300°F) oven. Cool them again before serving.

Cranberry Biscotti

Festive in looks and flavor because they're freckled with tart-sweet dried cranberries, here are biscotti for any season, not just for the holidays. The recipe is flexible—either store-bought or custom-dried cranberries, blueberries, cherries, or currants may serve as the fruity element.

3 large eggs
⅓ cup granulated sugar
3 tablespoons vegetable shortening, regular or butter-flavored, melted and cooled
1 teaspoon pure vanilla extract
¾ teaspoon pure orange or lemon extract
1⅔ cups all-purpose flour
1 teaspoon baking powder
¼ teaspoon ground mace
¼ teaspoon salt
½ cup (about 3 ounces) dried cranberries, slightly chopped (see page 323 for directions for drying your own)

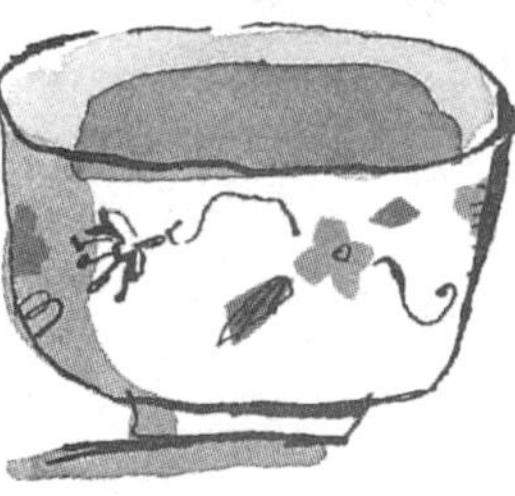

GLAZE:
2 teaspoons milk
Sugar

Makes about 3 dozen biscotti

1. Preheat the oven to 350°F, with a shelf in the center position. Grease a large baking sheet.

2. Beat the eggs until foamy in the large bowl of an electric mixer; gradually beat in the sugar, then beat at high speed until pale and light. Beat in the cooled shortening, vanilla, and orange or lemon extract.

3. Sift together the flour, baking powder, mace, and salt. With the mixer running at low speed, add the dry ingredients to the egg mixture and mix the dough well. Mix in the cranberries. (The dough will be somewhat soft.)

4. Spoon half of the dough onto the prepared baking sheet, making a strip about 10 inches long. Repeat with the second half, leaving 3 inches between the strips. Using your fingers lightly moistened with water, form each strip into a loaf shape 2½ inches wide and slightly higher in the middle than at the sides. Smooth the surface with a pastry brush dipped into the milk; sprinkle the loaves lightly with sugar.

5. Bake until firm to the touch and golden brown, about 25 minutes. Remove the baking sheet from the oven and lower the oven setting to 300°F.

6. Cool the loaves on the pan for 5 minutes, then carefully remove them from the foil to a rack and cool 10 minutes longer.

7. Move the loaves to a cutting surface, and using a sharp serrated knife, cut them crosswise at a slight diagonal into slices between ⅓ and ½ inch thick. Lay the slices flat and close together on the baking sheet.

8. Bake the slices for 10 minutes, then turn them over and bake 7 to 8 minutes longer, checking once or twice to avoid overbaking—the slices should be light gold in color.

9. Cool the biscotti completely on a rack and store in an airtight canister at room temperature; they'll keep for 2 or 3 weeks. Alternatively, wrap the biscotti for the freezer and freeze them for up to 3 months. Thaw frozen biscotti in their wrappings, then refresh them, spread on a baking sheet, for about 10 minutes in a 325°F oven. Cool before serving.

A Cranberry Choice

Cranberries dried with a little sugar or with a noncaloric sweetener work beautifully in these biscotti, but if you'd like more sweetness, try using Candied Cranberries. See the Index for directions for preparing these.

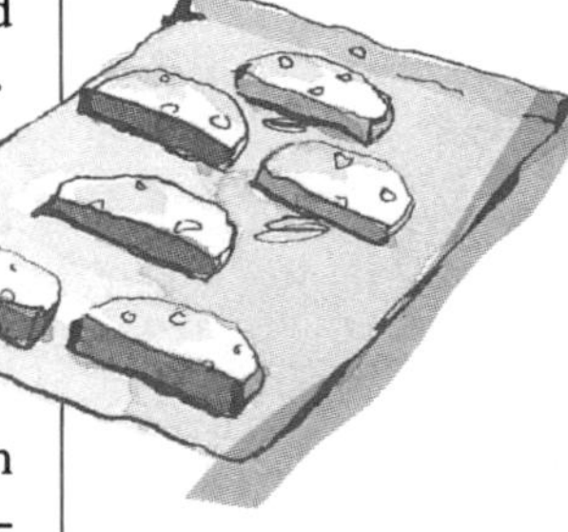

Crisp Sponge Biscuits

Golden, eggy sponge cake batter is baked twice to make these delicate bars, perfect as a crisp bite with tea, coffee, or a glass of wine. Their simplicity makes them a good accompaniment for dessert, too, especially if it's something soft and/or creamy.

To change the flavor of a batch, use 1 teaspoon vanilla in addition to the almond extract and omit the spices.

Sweet (unsalted) butter and confectioners' sugar for the pan(s)
1 cup all-purpose flour
½ teaspoon baking powder
¼ teaspoon salt
¼ teaspoon ground cinnamon
⅛ teaspoon freshly grated nutmeg
⅛ teaspoon ground mace
5 large eggs, separated
2 tablespoons cold water
1 cup plus 2 tablespoons granulated sugar
1 tablespoon (packed) grated or very finely chopped lemon zest (outer peel only, no white pith)
¼ teaspoon pure almond extract

Makes 4 to 5 dozen biscuits

1. Preheat the oven to 325°F, with a shelf in the center position. Butter the bottom only of a 13 x 9-inch baking pan or two 8-inch square baking pans and dust the buttered surface with confectioners' sugar. Knock out any surplus sugar.

2. Sift together twice the flour, baking powder, salt, cinnamon, nutmeg, and mace. Reserve in a small bowl.

3. Separate the eggs. Reserve the whites in a large mixing bowl. Place the yolks in the large bowl of an electric mixer and beat them on medium-high speed until thick. With the mixer running at the same speed, add the water and beat the mixture until thick, about 3 minutes. Continuing to beat, gradually add the granulated sugar, scraping the mixture down from the sides of the bowl once or twice. Add the lemon zest and almond extract and beat 1 minute longer.

4. Mixing at the lowest speed of the mixer or folding by hand, add the dry ingredients one third at a time, mixing after each addition only until no streaks of flour remain.

5. Beat the egg whites until they are stiff but still glossy and not dry. Add the whites to the batter and mix them in on the lowest speed of the mixer (or fold them in by hand) just until no streaks of white show.

6. Gently scrape the batter into the prepared pan or pans, smoothing it only enough to fill the corners (it will even out as it bakes).

7. Bake the cake in the center of the oven until it is golden, firm to the touch in the center, and has pulled away slightly from the pan sides, about 60 minutes for one large panful, 40 minutes for two pans.

8. Invert the pan(s) onto a wire cake rack and let the cake cool, still in the pan, upside down. Loosen the cooled cake all around with the tip of a sharp serrated knife and turn it out onto the rack. Using a sawing motion, cut the cake in half (lengthwise for the long pan), then slice each half crosswise into ½-inch slices.

SHORTCUT TO CRISP BISCUITS

Airy, twice-baked sponge biscuits made this way, rather than by shaping little cakes individually on a pan, are quicker to produce in the home kitchen. This recipe is popular at our house because it yields either cake or cookies, and the baked cake layers freeze well.

9. Lay the slices flat on wire cake racks (or you can use baking sheets) and place them in the oven, preheated to just under 200°F. Bake the slices, turning them once, until they are a slightly deeper gold in color and crisp throughout, 40 to 60 minutes; if you are using two shelves of the oven, exchange shelf positions of the racks once or twice.

10. Cool the biscuits completely on the racks, then store them in an airtight canister at room temperature for up to 3 weeks. Suitably packaged, they can be frozen for up to 3 months. If they have been frozen, spread them on a baking sheet and refresh them with a few minutes' stay in a 300°F oven, then cool them again. Do the same if humid weather causes the biscuits to soften in the canister.

Simple Sponge Cake

To use this recipe for a sponge cake rather than biscuits, bake the batter in two round or square 8-inch pans. The baking time may be shorter if round pans are used; check the layers for doneness after 35 minutes and frequently thereafter until the cake tests done (a cake tester piercing the center will emerge clean, and the sides will pull away slightly from the pan). Cool in the pans and unmold and cool as described in the main recipe.

Fill, frost, or dust with confectioners' sugar, or top with whipped cream and fruit as your fancy may prompt you.

The cooled layers, well wrapped, may be frozen for up to 3 months. Thaw them in their wrappers.

Florentines: A Cookie-Confection

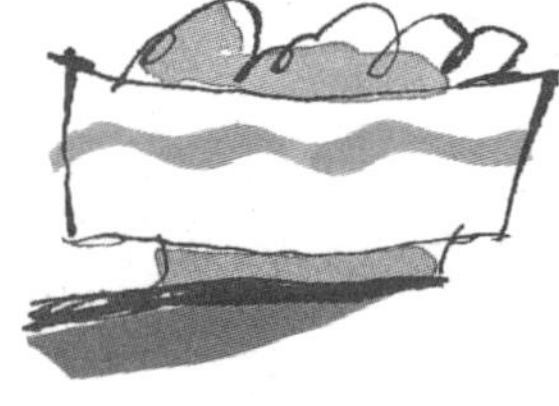

Whether you call them cookies or consider them the next thing to candy, these lacy rounds glossed with chocolate are to everyday cookies as truffles are to toadstools.

An ancient sweet known in Europe in many versions, Florentines are increasingly appreciated here. They appear in several guises, but candied fruits, cream, and almonds, plus a chocolate glaze, are constants. (Except in one "healthful" but unrecognizable version I once came across.) Florentines are especially happy companions for a cup of really good (straight, not exotically flavored) coffee, and they taste wonderful with tea, too.

DESPERATELY SEEKING CITRON

*Browsing in a Sicilian cookbook, especially one devoted to sweets, arouses a longing to taste candied citron (*Citrus medica*) on that sun-soaked Mediterranean island. Citron is an uncommon citrus fruit that resembles a very large and rough-skinned lemon. Its peel and the aromatic oil it contains are the only parts of culinary interest. Candied citron peel is aromatic and flavorful and is treasured for baking; the oil is used in liqueurs. Try to find genuine candied citron, which will contribute more to Florentines than the little cubes of some translucent, greenish, sweet substance sold in supermarkets. (I've never figured out what the processors of supermarket "citron" begin with; or, if it's actually citron, what they do to it to remove almost all flavor. Best bet: specialist suppliers of good stuff for bakers—see Mail-Order Sources, page 390.)*

1½ cups blanched almonds (page 295)
⅓ cup candied orange peel
⅓ cup candied citron or mixed candied citron and candied cherries
¼ cup sifted all-purpose flour
1 cup granulated sugar or ¾ cup sugar plus ¼ cup honey
⅔ cup heavy (whipping) cream
4 tablespoons (½ stick) sweet (unsalted) butter
Pinch of salt

FOR THE GLAZE:
4 to 6 ounces fine-quality bittersweet chocolate
2 to 3 teaspoons butter or vegetable shortening

Makes 3 to 3½ dozen Florentines

1. Chop 1 cup of the almonds to the size of rice grains. Sliver the remaining ½ cup. Chop the candied peels to the size of rice grains and add to the nuts. Stir in the flour thoroughly and reserve.

2. Preheat the oven to 325°F, with a shelf in the center position. Grease and flour two baking sheets, preferably nonstick, or spritz them with pan coating. (As each cookie requires a lot of space, you'll need to cool the pans between batches and reuse them, unless you can start with four baking sheets.)

3. Combine the sugar, cream, butter, and salt in a heavy saucepan and bring to a boil over moderate heat, stirring often. Boil, stirring often, until the mixture forms a soft ball when a little is dropped into cold water or until the temperature reaches 238°F on a candy/jelly thermometer. Remove from the heat and stir in the nut and fruit mixture.

4. Using a scant tablespoonful of dough per confection, place mounds on the baking sheet, spacing them a good 3 inches apart to allow for spreading. Flatten the dough with the back of a spoon, or your fingers, dipped into water.

5. Bake one panful at a time for 5 minutes, then remove the pan from the oven and inspect the cookies, which will have bubbled and spread amazingly. Use a round 3-inch cookie cutter (or the tip of a flat-ended spatula) to pull in the sprawling dough to make symmetrical rounds. Continue baking for another 3 to 5 minutes, until the cookies are golden and the dough has stopped bubbling (the bubbles will leave holes); check progress during baking and remove the pan from the oven at once if overbrowning is threatened. Leave the Florentines on the pan for about 3 minutes or until they can be lifted with a spatula without damage, then move them to a rack to cool completely. (If it should happen that some of the cookies cling desperately to the pan, return it to the oven for a minute or two to soften them slightly, then try again; this is unlikely to occur with nonstick pans.) If you want to make lacy tube shapes, immediately roll cookie while still soft around the handle of a wooden spoon.

6. *Preparing the glaze:* For a drizzling of chocolate over the tops of the cookies (my choice), use the 4 ounces of chocolate. If you want to coat the bottoms of the cookies in the traditional way, increase the chocolate to 6 ounces and add another teaspoon of butter. Melt the chocolate with the butter in a double boiler over hot water or, more quickly, in the microwave, following the manufacturer's recommendations.

Decorating the tops: Scrape the chocolate into a small pastry bag fitted with a small plain tip and drizzle a spiral or zigzag over each cookie. (Lacking a pastry bag, put the chocolate into a plastic sandwich bag and zip the top closed. Snip a tiny bit of one corner and squeeze the bag to make the squiggles.)

Glazing the bottoms: Use a pastry brush or small spatula to coat the surfaces evenly with chocolate, then inscribe wavy lines with a fork (or an icing comb, if you possess one). Leave the cookies undisturbed until the glaze has set.

7. Store the Florentines for up to a week in an airtight canister in a cool spot (not the refrigerator), or freeze them, without the chocolate glaze, for up to a month. Thaw them in their wrappings and, if they are at all soft, reheat them on a baking sheet in a 300°F oven just until they have warmed thoroughly, then cool them on a rack before adding the glaze.

Holiday Keeping Cake

When it's autumn and the calendar says it's time to make a holiday cake that will mellow and improve until Christmas, this spicy, fruity cranberry loaf is just the ticket. It can include nuts or not, but either way it's less rich (and we've found it more popular) than traditional fruitcakes. Swedish food expert Anna Olsson Coombs inspired this cake, which is an adaptation of "Norrland's Cake" in her long-out-of-print *Smörgasbord Cookbook.* I particularly like her method of putting the cake together.

If you prefer not to use fresh cranberries, the cake can also be made with good (meaning dense) canned cranberry sauce, or with the preserved lingonberries or lingonberry jam specified in the original recipe.

BOG HARVEST

Near our house are sandy bogs among the Atlantic dunes where cranberries grow wild, and it's a special autumn pleasure to gather our own crop for this cake as well as for Cranberry Preserves with Orange & Cardamom, Cranberry & Currant Relish, and Cranberry Ketchup. (See the Index for any or all recipes.) In lean seasons, we gather our cranberries at the supermarket, bringing home a few extra bags for freezing. Tossed into the freezer without any special wrapping, the berries keep beautifully for a year or more, remaining separate even when frozen hard.

2½ cups fresh or frozen cranberries, rinsed and drained
⅔ cup granulated sugar
1 teaspoon (packed) finely grated orange zest (outer peel only, no white pith)
½ cup (1 stick) sweet (unsalted) butter
2¼ cups all-purpose flour
2 cups (lightly packed) light brown sugar
2 teaspoons ground cinnamon
½ teaspoon ground coriander
½ teaspoon ground cardamom
¼ teaspoon ground cloves
¾ teaspoon salt
2 eggs
¾ cup dairy sour cream
2 teaspoons baking soda dissolved in 2 teaspoons water
⅔ to 1 cup coarsely chopped pecans (or butternuts, if you're fortunate enough to have some), optional

Makes 2 loaves, about 1½ pounds each

1. Grease two 6-cup (8½ x 4½ x 2½-inch) loaf pans, line them with baking parchment, grease the lining, and set them aside.

2. Combine 1½ cups of the cranberries with the granulated sugar and the orange zest in a saucepan. Bring the mixture to a boil over medium heat, stirring it often, and cook it, stirring occasionally, until the berries have popped and the syrup has thickened, about 5 minutes. While these cranberries cook, chop the remaining cranberries coarsely. Add them to the cooked berries and set the mixture aside to cool.

3. Melt the butter over low heat just until it is creamy, not liquid; set it aside to cool. Preheat the oven to 350°F, with a shelf in the center.

4. Sift together the flour, brown sugar, cinnamon, coriander, cardamom, cloves, and salt.

5. Beat the eggs well in a mixing bowl or the large bowl of an electric mixer; beat in the sour cream, then the dissolved baking soda. Beat in the sifted dry ingredients just until mixed, then beat in the melted butter. Mix in the cranberry mixture and the nuts, if they are used, just until the ingredients are blended.

6. Divide the batter between the prepared pans and smooth the tops; lift each pan a few inches from the work surface and drop it to settle the batter. Bake the cakes in the center of the preheated oven until a cake tester emerges dry after probing the center, or until the center springs back when pressed lightly; this will take about 1 hour.

7. Set the pans on wire racks and let the cakes cool for 15 minutes, then remove them from the pans and cool them completely on the racks, still encased in baking parchment.

8. Remove the paper from the cooled cakes and wrap the cakes closely in foil or plastic. Store them in a cool cupboard or the refrigerator for up to 3 months, or wrap them for the freezer and freeze them for up to a year. The cakes are ready to serve after a few days, but they continue to improve for weeks. Frozen cranberry cake should be thawed in its wrapper to prevent sogginess.

9. *Decorating a loaf for serving:* Brush the top very lightly with light corn syrup and arrange on it a wreath or other design of Candied Cranberries (page 313) or candied cherries or other glazed fruit plus a sprig of fresh holly; or use leaf shapes cut from candied angelica or green-tinted marzipan. Surround the cake with seasonal greenery, or brush the sides with corn syrup and decorate them in the same fashion as the top.

To Wrap a Decorated Loaf as a Holiday Gift

Set it on stout cardboard cut to size and covered with foil; enclose the sides in a "fence" of pleated foil or metallic gift wrap that is slightly higher than the cake, with pinked edges if you have pinking shears. Tape the pleated strip around the cake and overwrap the whole pretty thing with cellophane or clear plastic.

Classic Almond & Hazelnut Biscotti for Dunking

"Classic," here, means the recipe honors the Italian pattern for these twice-baked slices studded with two kinds of nuts. Substantial enough to dip into coffee or wine with abandon, they make wonderful dunkers—they won't fall apart in a hurry. They are, in fact, *hard.*

1 cup natural (unblanched) almonds
1 cup whole hazelnuts
3 cups all-purpose flour
1 cup granulated sugar
2 teaspoons baking powder
½ teaspoon baking soda
½ teaspoon salt
½ teaspoon ground mace
3 large eggs plus 1 large egg yolk
2 tablespoons water
1½ teaspoons pure almond extract

GLAZE:
1 large egg white, lightly beaten

Makes about 4 dozen biscotti

1. Preheat the oven to 350°F, with a shelf in the center position. Grease and flour a large cookie sheet.

2. *Toasting the nuts:* Spread the almonds on an ungreased baking pan and toast them in the preheated oven about 8 minutes or until they are hot and fragrant, stirring them often. Pour the nuts onto a plate and cool them completely. Toast the hazelnuts the same way for a slightly longer time, then rub them while hot in a towel to remove as much as possible of the outer skins. Cool them completely. Meanwhile, raise the oven setting to 375°F.

3. Sift together the flour, sugar, baking powder, baking soda, salt, and mace, then sift again into a mixing bowl. Make a hollow in the center of the ingredients.

4. In another bowl, whisk the eggs and egg yolk together with the water until frothy; beat in the almond extract. Pour into the well in the dry ingredients and stir from the center with a fork until mixed. Stir in the nuts, then knead the dough briefly in the bowl, turning and pressing it until it is firm.

5. Spoon half of the dough onto the prepared baking sheet, making a strip about 14 inches long. Using first your fingers or a rubber spatula, shape and smooth the strip into a loaf about 2½ inches wide and slightly higher in the center than at the sides. Smooth the surface firmly with a pastry brush dipped in the beaten egg white. Form and smooth the second loaf in the same way, leaving about 3 inches between the loaves on the pan.

6. Bake the loaves until golden and firm to the touch and colored pale gold, 25 to 30 minutes. Cool them completely on a rack, allowing about an hour.

7. Preheat the oven to 325°F.

8. Move the loaves to a cutting surface. Using a sharp serrated knife and long, firm strokes, saw the loaves slightly on the diagonal into slices between ⅓ and ½ inch thick. Lay the slices flat on ungreased baking sheets and bake them for 12 to 15 minutes on two shelves of the oven, exchanging shelf positions midway and turning the biscotti twice; they are done when they have turned light golden brown here and there and dried out a bit.

9. Cool the biscotti completely on a rack, then store them in an airtight canister at room temperature; they will keep for several weeks. Alternatively, wrap them for the freezer and store them for up to 3 months. Thaw frozen biscotti in their wrappings, then refresh them by warming on a baking sheet in a 325°F oven for about 10 minutes. Cool them before serving.

LESS FAT PER COOKIE

If counting fat grams is a dietary point of interest, note that Classic Almond & Hazelnut Biscotti for Dunking are baked without shortening. (But they do contain nuts and egg yolks, so they're not low low-fat.)

Honey Biscotti with Sweet Seeds & Nutmeg

Especially good with cheese, crisp biscotti lightly flavored with spices and honey are also welcome, as is, with wine, coffee, or tea. Versatile because they're not especially sweet, they may be made more cookie-like by doubling the quantity of sugar as suggested in the recipe.

For biscotti with plenty of flavor but no whole seeds (disliked by some), reduce the celery seed to ½ teaspoon and grind both the celery and caraway seeds in a spice mill.

3½ cups all-purpose flour
2 tablespoons sugar (double the amount for sweeter biscuits)
4 teaspoons baking powder
¾ teaspoon salt
1 tablespoon caraway seed, slightly bruised
¾ teaspoon celery seed
½ teaspoon freshly grated nutmeg or ground mace
2 large eggs
2 tablespoons milk
⅓ cup honey
½ cup (1 stick) sweet (unsalted) butter, melted

Makes about 3½ dozen biscotti

1. Preheat the oven to 325°F, with a shelf in the center position. Cover a baking sheet with aluminum foil.

2. Sift together the flour, sugar, baking powder, and salt into a medium-size bowl. Stir in the caraway seed, celery seed, and nutmeg.

3. Beat the eggs and milk together in a mixing bowl to blend them, then beat in the honey until it disappears. Stir in the melted butter, then the dry ingredients. Mix the dough well with a spoon, then knead it a few strokes by hand, working in the bowl; it should be quite compact.

4. Divide the dough into two parts. Form each into a firm loaf on the foil-covered baking sheet; make the loaves about 12 inches long and 2½ inches wide, slightly higher at the center than at the sides. Place them well apart on the sheet.

5. Bake the loaves until they are firm to the touch and colored pale gold, about 20 minutes. Remove the baking sheet from the oven and lower the oven setting to 275°F.

Honeys to Hunt For

Among the hundreds of kinds of honey available, you can choose for intensity of flavor (which also means fragrance) and/or color, which ranges from almost clear to near-black, with unlikely tints in between. Some honeys are very mild and therefore good for cooking—clover honey is one such; some, notably orange-blossom and other honeys with a strong floral character, taste extra sweet. Some are strong and "dry" in taste (buckwheat); some (like the rare fir blossom) taste both dry and delicate; and others, notably Hymettus honey from Greece, made by bees fed on thyme and other wild herbs, are both herbal and delicate. For general sweetening when the honey will be heated (as in the biscotti here), supermarket honey or whatever a local beekeeper sells will do very well, as the cooking would drive off the aroma of a special honey in any case.

6. Cool the loaves on the pan for 5 minutes, then carefully remove them from the foil to a rack and cool 15 minutes longer.

7. Move the loaves to a cutting surface, and using a sharp serrated knife and firm strokes, cut them crosswise at a slight diagonal into ½-inch slices. Lay the slices flat and close together on the baking sheet.

8. Bake the slices for 10 minutes, then turn them over and bake 10 minutes longer, until they are crisp and golden. Turn the oven off and let the biscotti cool in the oven, with the door open.

9. Store the completely cooled biscotti in an airtight canister at room temperature for several weeks. Alternatively, freezer-wrap and freeze them for up to 3 months. Thaw frozen biscotti in their wrappings and refresh them, spread on a baking sheet, for about 10 minutes in a 325°F oven. Cool before serving.

Improbable Almond Bars

Called "improbable" because they contain only three ingredients, not counting the touch of almond extract, these cookies (or confections?) are nevertheless surpassingly scrumptious. Cathy Lipkin, friend and fellow cookie fancier, remembers them from her school days, when her grandmother faithfully dispatched fresh-baked supplies to her.

Reconstructed from Cathy's recollections, this recipe has been in constant service at our house for several years, and I'd bet money that it will be equally popular far and wide after it appears in print. (As far as I have been able to discover, no such recipe has appeared so far, at least in English-language sources.)

If hazelnuts or pecans are the nuts for you, they will work, too. Omit the almond extract, substituting a little maple flavoring if you wish, or vanilla.

1½ cups natural (unblanched) almonds, toasted and cooled (see sidebar)
1 cup (packed) dark or light brown sugar, or a mixture of light and dark
1 large or extra-large egg, lightly beaten
¼ teaspoon pure almond extract or 3 drops oil of bitter almonds (page 332)

Makes 18 bars

To Toast Almonds, Blanched and Unblanched

Spread the almonds, blanched or natural (unblanched), on a cookie sheet and bake them in a preheated 350°F oven, stirring them every 2 or 3 minutes, until they smell toasty and a sample is golden inside; this should take no more than 10 minutes. The brown skin of unblanched almonds makes it hard to judge doneness by looking, so toast with care.

1. Preheat the oven to 350°F.

2. Combine the nuts and sugar in a food processor. Pulse the machine on and off just until the nuts are coarsely chopped. If any whole or overlarge chunks remain, divide them with a knife.

3. Stir in the egg by hand. (The mixture will be stiff.) Spread the nut batter in an ungreased 8-inch square baking pan; if there are a few gaps in coverage, they won't matter.

4. Bake in the center of the oven for 20 minutes, then check; the top should have deepened to a rich caramel color and become crusty. If this is true only of the edges, lower the oven setting to 300°F and bake another 5 minutes or so, until the top is crusty over a soft inside and the edges have begun to shrink from the pan a little. (If in doubt about doneness, choose to underbake rather than overbake, or the bars will be dry.) Remove from the oven.

5. Cool the panful for 3 to 5 minutes, then loosen the edges with a metal spatula and cut down through the confection to mark out 18 bars. (Don't worry if the cuts have crumbly or ragged edges.) Let cool until comfortable to touch, then cut through the markings again and remove the bars to a cooling rack. If necessary, mold the edges with your fingers to attach loose bits.

6. When cold and crisp, store the bars in an airtight canister at room temperature. They keep beautifully for several weeks. For longer storage, they can be freezer-wrapped and frozen for up to 3 months. Thaw frozen bars in their wrappings.

PANETTONE FOR THE HOLIDAYS

The Italian cake/bread called *panettone* is imported from Europe by the ton every winter holiday season; with its light, delicately sweet and fragrant crumb studded with raisins and candied fruit, this is the rare kind of sweet bread that tastes just right from breakfast to midnight, particularly with fine coffee or a glass of wine.

Those who enjoy panettone need not choose between packaged loaves, some of which are better than others; anyone who has ever made a loaf of bread can turn out a wonderfully fresh home version. If you opt for the classic appearance of the loaf, your panettone will be unadorned, although nuts, sugar, or both are often scattered on the loaves, as the recipe indicates.

PANS FOR PANETTONE

A deep pan is essential if panettone is to be properly light and correctly crowned with a smoothly rounded dome almost as tall as the base of the loaf. If you have springform or plain cake pans about 7 inches in diameter and 4 inches deep, they are perfect for the two loaves made by this recipe. If you can't lay hands on such pans, it's time to improvise.

- *Coffee cans of the 2-pound size (recommended by Carol Field, author of the masterly book* The Italian Baker*) can be used, as can charlotte molds (although their slightly flaring shape isn't quite right) or soufflé dishes. Either of the last two needs to be fitted inside with a collar of doubled heavy foil to increase its depth to 6 to 7 inches.*
- *When using springform pans, charlotte molds, coffee cans, etc., line the bottoms with rounds of parchment (or two layers of waxed paper) and grease the lining. Grease the inside of the collar, too.*

(cont.)

Some bakers like to put almonds or hazelnuts into panettone. If you follow suit, be careful not to use more than 2 cups, give or take, of fruits and nuts combined, lest you overload the delicate structure of the dough. In the fruit department, you might replace the traditional candied citron and citrus peels with chopped dried fruits—cherries, cranberries, apricots, peaches, pears, and/or pineapple are good. If dried fruits are substituted for candied citron and citrus peel, it's a good idea to double the quantity of grated lemon or orange zest.

2 packages active dry yeast, or 2 tablespoons bulk dry yeast
¾ cup lukewarm (110° to 115°F) water
1 cup sugar
6 cups all-purpose flour, stirred before measuring, plus additional flour for kneading
2 large eggs, at room temperature
4 large egg yolks, at room temperature
1 teaspoon coarse (kosher) salt
2 teaspoons pure vanilla extract
Finely grated or minced zest of 1 lemon, or ½ to 1 teaspoon lemon oil
Finely grated or minced zest of 1 orange, or 1 teaspoon orange oil
2 sticks (1 cup) sweet (unsalted) butter, softened at room temperature, cut up
1 cup dark or golden raisins
1 to 1½ cups diced candied fruit (citron, orange peel, and lemon peel), or any desired combination of dried and glazed fruits, plus the added lemon zest, as discussed in the recipe introduction

OPTIONAL GLAZE:
1 large egg yolk, beaten with 2 teaspoons milk

OPTIONAL TOPPING:
Coarse sugar and/or blanched almonds or skinned and chopped hazelnuts (page 372)

Makes 2 cylindrical loaves, about 2 pounds each

1. Sprinkle 2 tablespoons of the sugar, then the yeast, over the lukewarm water in a mixing bowl; stir, then leave until foamy, 5 to 10 minutes. Beat in 1 cup of the flour to make a smooth batter. Cover and leave until the sponge has doubled in volume and just begun to subside, 45 minutes to 1 hour.

2. In the large bowl of an electric mixer fitted with the paddle attachment, beat the eggs and egg yolks to combine. Beat in the remaining sugar, the risen sponge, salt, vanilla, and lemon and orange zest (or lemon and orange oils). With the mixer running at moderate speed, add the flour and beat until incorporated. Mix in the butter until it disappears. Change to the dough hook and knead the dough for 3 to 5 minutes, until it is smooth and elastic; if the dough doesn't clean the surface of the bowl shortly after kneading begins, sprinkle in a little flour and continue; repeat if necessary. Optionally, finish the kneading with a few strokes on a lightly floured work surface.

3. Form the dough into a ball and place it in a very large, lightly buttered or oiled bowl, cover it snugly with plastic, and let it rise until it has tripled in volume. This is likely to take 4 to 5 hours at ordinary kitchen temperature, so you may want to plan to let it rise overnight if the room temperature is low enough, no more than about 65°F.

4. Toward the end of the rising time, cover the raisins with cool water and let them soak for at least ½ hour, then drain them and pat them dry. Toss the raisins and the candied or dried fruits with a sprinkling of flour and set them aside. Prepare the molds for the panettone (see "Pans for Panettone," page 351).

5. Turn the risen dough onto a lightly floured surface and cut it in half. Pat each half out about ¾ inch thick, sprinkle with half of the fruit mixture, and fold and knead the dough gently to incorporate the fruit. Form each piece into a smooth ball and place it in a prepared mold or pan.

6. Let the loaves rise, covered with towels, until very light, almost tripled again in volume (the print of a finger will remain when the dough is pressed lightly). Shortly before rising is complete, preheat the oven to 375°F.

7. Optionally, brush the egg glaze over the tops of the loaves and sprinkle them, if you wish, with sugar and/or nuts. Using a razor blade (or a very sharp, thin knife), cut a large cross in the top of each loaf.

8. Bake the loaves for 20 minutes at 375°F, then lower the oven setting to 350°F and continue baking the loaves for 30 to 40 minutes longer, or until a cake tester emerges clean after piercing the center (or check the internal temperature with an instant-reading thermometer; it should be between 190° and 200°F). If the loaves are browning too rapidly at any point, cover them loosely with a sheet of foil.

9. Allow the loaves to cool in their molds for 20 to 30 minutes, then turn them out carefully and stand them on a wire rack to cool completely. When completely cooled, peel off any clinging parchment or waxed paper, wrap the loaves individually in foil or plastic, and store them at room temperature. This sweet bread is famous for keeping well, but its fragrance as it bakes and cools (or when sliced and toasted) makes it difficult to repel raiding parties, and because it's delightful at any meal, including breakfast, elevenses, and teatime, its keeping qualities may not be very severely tested at your house.

(cont.)

• *If no suitable containers are on hand, it's the work of a few minutes to make baking rings from heavy-duty foil 18 inches wide. To make 2 panettone molds about 7 inches in diameter, cut 2 strips of heavy-duty 18-inch aluminum foil 24 inches long. Fold each strip lengthwise in thirds to make a strip 6 inches wide. Form the strip into a ring 7 inches or thereabouts in diameter, overlapping the ends by 2 inches or so, and staple the ends together top and bottom (or use straight pins or paper clips). With your hands inside the ring, make it into a symmetrical circle and set it on a baking sheet covered with foil or parchment. Spritz the inside of the newly created molds with baking spray or oil, and there you are.*

Panforte Not from Siena

Our Christmas list includes the names of friends who adore this "strong bread," a rich confection made most famously in Siena, so in the past we've regularly made December searches for a source of supply. We haven't always been successful because imports are irregular, so I've worked out the how-to's of making this fruity, nutty, chewy, honey-sweet delight at home.

This recipe borrows a bit here, a bit there, from the experts, and the result is terrific. I've learned that panforte can be made with or without cocoa, with one kind of nuts or another, with a lot of spices or none, with several kinds of dried or glazed fruit or none at all. So this version isn't the last word. Feel free to have fun with it. You might even brush the top of the cooled round with melted bittersweet or dark chocolate, if delightful excess is your cup of tea.

½ cup all-purpose flour
⅓ cup (lightly packed) fine-quality Dutch-process cocoa powder, sifted
½ teaspoon ground cinnamon
¼ teaspoon freshly grated nutmeg or ground mace
Pinch of ground cloves
Big pinch of freshly ground white pepper
2 cups coarsely chopped walnuts or blanched almonds, or a combination of coarsely chopped walnuts, toasted and skinned hazelnuts (page 372), and blanched almonds in any preferred proportions
1 cup (lightly packed; about 6 ounces) chopped dried figs (¼-inch pieces)
½ cup (lightly packed) chopped candied orange peel (¼-inch pieces)
½ cup (lightly packed) coarsely chopped (¼-inch pieces) candied citron, or ¼ cup each chopped citron and candied lemon peel, or an additional ½ cup chopped candied orange peel sprinkled with either 1 tablespoon grated lemon zest (outer peel only, no white pith) or ¼ teaspoon lemon oil (not lemon extract)
⅔ cup granulated sugar
⅔ cup honey
Confectioners' sugar for dusting the finished panforte

Makes a 9- to 11-inch round, about 2 pounds

Citrus Interchange

If finding good candied citron is a chore (see page 343), note that you can omit it and play around with the kinds and proportions of the citrus peels used in Panforte. A trick worth noticing is the reinforcement of the flavor of orange peel by adding a little lemon oil.

1. Preheat the oven to 300°F. Coat with pan spray (or grease) the bottom of a springform pan 9 to 11 inches in diameter. Cut a round of baking parchment or waxed paper to fit the bottom, put it in place, and coat it with pan spray, or grease it.

2. Sift together the flour, cocoa, cinnamon, nutmeg, cloves, and pepper into a mixing bowl. Add the chopped nuts, figs, and candied peels; mix very well to separate any stuck-together bits.

3. Stir the sugar and honey together in a heavy saucepan and boil over medium-high heat, stirring, until a little of the mixture makes a medium-firm ball when dropped into cold water; boiling will take only a minute or two. Remove immediately from the heat and pour into the bowl of ingredients; stir fast with a wooden spatula until blended. Working quickly, press the mixture into a uniform layer in the prepared pan, using the spatula and/or your hands.

4. Bake the panforte for about 35 minutes (for an 11-inch pan) or 5 minutes or so longer for a smaller and thicker round. At the end of baking it won't look particularly "done," but the shiny surface will turn dull and darken a bit when it has baked long enough. Cool in the pan on a rack, then remove from the pan, invert the confection, and peel the paper from the bottom.

5. Allow to mellow at least overnight before dusting the top with confectioners' sugar and serving in slim wedges as a dessert or refreshment. ("Slim" because panforte is intensely sweet.) If you'll be keeping it for a while, cut the panforte into wedges and wrap them individually, or wrap the whole round closely in plastic for airtight storage. Kept cool or refrigerated, the panforte will keep for weeks. In the freezer, it keeps almost forever. For looks, sprinkle the panforte again with confectioners' sugar at serving time.

PFEFFERNÜSSE~SPICY CHRISTMAS COOKIES

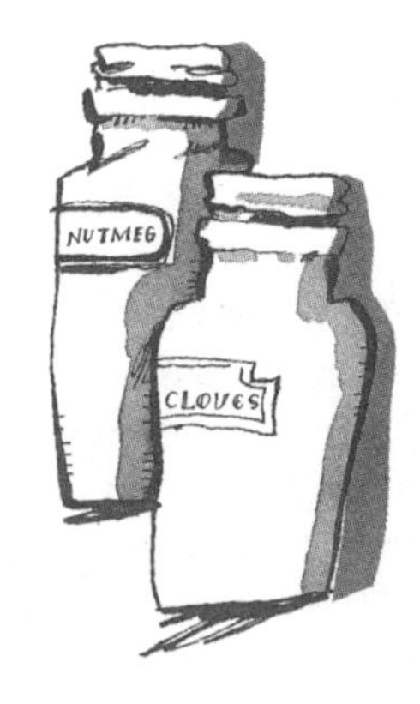

Let us not count the Yuletides during which these "peppernuts," redolent of many spices (including pepper), have been made with pleasure at our house and consumed with good appetite. One of their many charms is keepability—I've stored samples for months, in the spirit of culinary inquiry, and found them as delicious afterwards as before. So, do-aheaders, take note: Pfeffernüsse, unlike many holiday treats, needn't (shouldn't) be made at the last minute, and they're great for shipping, surviving without a crumble. Further note: This is a two-day (part-time) operation, as the shaped cookies must dry overnight before they're baked.

The recipe is more or less the one published in *Mrs. Witty's Home-Style Menu Cookbook.* It has evolved a bit since then, as recipes will (I put in more pepper and anise and lemon than I used to), but the essential cookie is one that has been in the family for a long time.

½ cup solid vegetable shortening
2½ cups granulated sugar or half granulated and half (packed) light brown sugar
5 large eggs
1 tablespoon ground cinnamon
1 tablespoon freshly ground cardamom (home-ground is better than store-bought)
1 teaspoon ground cloves
1 teaspoon freshly grated nutmeg
1½ teaspoons anise seed, lightly crushed, ground in a spice mill, or left whole
1 teaspoon coarsely ground fresh pepper, black or white
1½ tablespoons (packed) finely grated or minced lemon zest (outer peel only, no white pith)
4 cups all-purpose flour
1 teaspoon salt
½ teaspoon baking soda
½ to ¾ cup natural almonds, toasted (page 349) and chopped, or half almonds and half skinned hazelnuts
1 container (3½ ounces) candied citron, chopped
1 container (3½ ounces) candied orange peel, chopped (or use half orange peel and half candied lemon peel)

GLAZE:
2 tablespoons hot milk mixed with 1 cup sifted confectioners' sugar

Makes 10 to 12 dozen, depending on size

1. Cream the shortening in the large bowl of an electric mixer, then gradually beat in the sugar; beat until very fluffy and smooth. Add the eggs one at a time, beating well after adding each. Beat in the cinnamon, cardamom, cloves, nutmeg, anise seed, pepper, and lemon zest.

2. Sift together the flour, salt, and baking soda into a medium bowl. Stir in the nuts, citron, and candied peel. Stir the dry ingredients into the creamed mixture. Bundle the dough onto a sheet of plastic, wrap it, and refrigerate it until it's stiff, which will take an hour or two. (It may be left overnight if that's more convenient.)

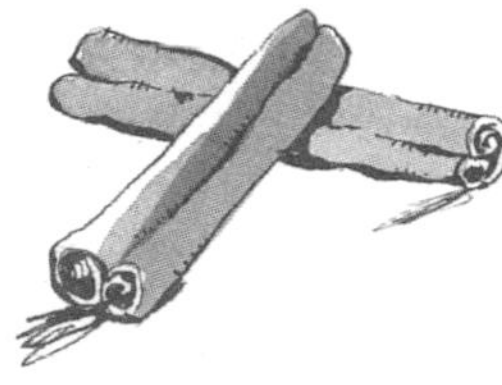

HIDDEN HEAT

The use of pepper in sweet things, for example Pfeffernüsse, isn't all that unusual in food history, although the notion may seem startling at first. The presence of pepper can be difficult to detect when it's used to back up and lend warmth to a medley of other spices, but without it, these beloved traditional cookies would lose something.

3. Prepare several baking sheets by spraying them with pan coating or greasing and dusting them with flour. If you don't have enough pans to accommodate all the cookies, lay out sheets of foil and pancoat (or grease and flour) them.

4. *Shaping the cookies:* This may be done with lightly floured hands or lightly moistened hands—try both ways and see which works better for your dough. Shape the dough into ¾-inch egg shapes (tall rather than round) and stand them on end on the prepared pans, leaving 1½ inches between cookies. When your pans are full, place cookies on the prepared foil in the same fashion. Leave the cookies uncovered at room temperature overnight to let the outsides dry (this leads to the attractive crackled finish that develops in the oven).

5. Preheat the oven to 350°F, with a shelf in the upper third and another in the lower. While the oven heats, prepare the glaze and brush each cookie lightly with it.

6. Bake the cookies two pans at a time for about 12 to 15 minutes, exchanging shelf positions midway. They are done when the surface has crackled and browned lightly.

7. Cool on wire racks, or loosen the cookies with a spatula and let them cool on the pans. Slip the foil sheets of cookies onto completely cooled pans and bake them when their turn comes; they may require an extra minute or two because of the insulation provided by the foil.

8. Store the peppernuts at room temperature in an airtight canister. They really come into their own in terms of flavor after mellowing for a few days, but they are edible (though hard) when fresh from the oven.

Shortbread—the Best Cookie There Is

(Theme & Variations)

Baker's choice: Make any of these versions of the most subtly delicious cookie or small cake in the Western repertoire as a single round to be cut into wedges, as in the first recipe below, or shape the shortbread as fingers or as round cookies, as described on page 359, following the recipe and its variations.

The Classic Shortbread that comes first is traditional except for tiny liberties taken with flavorings. The recipes for the variations move farther away from the original Scottish sphere, but the cookies remain

RICE FLOUR—FOR A TEXTURAL CHANGE

Some Scottish recipes for shortbread call for rice flour, for which cornstarch is commonly substituted (as in the adjacent recipe). Rice flour creates a unique texture in shortbread, making it subliminally gritty in a pleasing way. If you'd like to try using it, don't look high and low for a supply. Just grind raw white rice to powder in a well-cleaned spice or coffee mill. You can also use a blender or food processor, which will take a bit longer to deal with the grains.

members of the shortbread family, at least according to me. Afterthought: Two other wrinkles I like are adding either a handful of chopped candied ginger or chopped black walnuts to the dough for the classic version.

CLASSIC SHORTBREAD

½ cup (1 stick) sweet (unsalted) butter, at room temperature
½ cup confectioners' sugar, sifted
½ teaspoon pure vanilla extract
3 or 4 drops pure almond extract, optional
1 cup all-purpose flour
2 tablespoons cornstarch
⅛ teaspoon salt

Makes about 1 pound

1. Preheat the oven to 325°F, with a shelf in the center position.

2. Cream the butter in the large bowl of an electric mixer or in a mixing bowl, then add the sugar and beat them together until the mixture is fluffy; beat in the vanilla and almond extracts.

3. Sift together the flour, cornstarch, and salt. Work the dry ingredients into the creamed mixture, using the paddle attachment of an electric mixer or, if working by hand, a pastry blender; the mixture will be crumbly. Gather the dough lightly into a ball.

4. Place the dough in an ungreased 10-inch pie pan or 9- or 10-inch loose-bottomed tart pan. Using the fingers, press the dough into a layer of uniform thickness (this is made easier by covering the dough with a piece of plastic wrap); be sure the dough is well pressed down at the edges as well as the center, and push it firmly into the flutings if you are using a tart pan. If using a pie pan, use a narrow spatula to draw the dough slightly away from the sides of the pan all around, then decorate the edge by pressing it with the tines of a fork. Prick the dough deeply all over with a fork, then mark it into 12 or 16 wedges with a sharp knife, cutting almost through.

5. Bake the shortbread in the center of the oven until it is very pale gold and feels firm when touched lightly, about 40 minutes. Do not let it brown; if during baking it is still soft but beginning to take on color, lower the oven setting to 300°F.

6. Cool the shortbread in its pan on a wire rack. While it is still warm, go over the markings again with a sharp knife, separating the wedges completely.

7. Store the completely cooled shortbread in an airtight canister at room temperature for up to 2 weeks, in the refrigerator for several weeks, or, freezer-wrapped, in the freezer for several months. Chilled or frozen shortbread benefits from a short but refreshing stay, unwrapped, in a 250°F oven. Leave it until it has warmed through, then cool it on a rack before serving it.

Chocolate Chip Shortbread

Make Classic Shortbread (above), omitting the almond flavoring and reducing the vanilla extract to ¼ teaspoon. When the dough has been mixed, work in ⅓ cup miniature chips of real chocolate. Bake the shortbread at 300°F instead of 325°F; it is done when it is pale golden and firm, about 40 minutes.

Double Chocolate Shortbread

Reduce the flour in the Classic Shortbread recipe to ¾ cup; reduce the cornstarch to 1 tablespoon; sift 3 tablespoons fine-quality Dutch-process cocoa powder with the other dry ingredients. When the dough has been mixed, work in ⅓ cup miniature chips of real chocolate. Bake as for Chocolate Chip Shortbread just until firm.

Whole-Wheat Shortbread

In the recipe for Classic Shortbread, replace the confectioners' sugar with ¼ cup (packed) light brown sugar; sift the sugar before creaming it with the butter. Reduce the vanilla extract to ¼ teaspoon; omit the almond flavoring. Substitute 1 cup whole-wheat pastry flour for the all-purpose flour. Bake the shortbread at 325°F for 20 minutes, then lower the oven setting to 300°F and bake the shortbread 20 minutes longer, or until it feels firm to a light touch.

Whole-Wheat Pecan Shortbread

Follow the directions for Whole-Wheat Shortbread, stirring ¼ cup of very finely chopped pecans into the creamed mixture before adding the dry ingredients. Bake as for Whole-Wheat Shortbread.

Rosemary & Honey Shortbread

Make Classic Shortbread, with these changes: Cream 2 tablespoons of full-flavored honey (such as wild flower) with the butter. Omit the vanilla and almond flavorings; cream in 3 drops lemon oil (or ½ teaspoon finely grated lemon zest, no white pith) and 1½ teaspoons very finely minced fresh rosemary leaves. Bake the shortbread at 300°F until firm to a light touch; be careful not to let it overbrown.

If dried rosemary is used, measure about ⅔ teaspoon of the leaves, soak them for at least 10 minutes in warm water to cover, then drain and mince them.

Making Other Shortbread Shapes

Instead of pressing the dough into a round baking pan, roll it out ¼ inch thick between sheets of plastic wrap. Peel off the upper sheet of wrap and use a pastry wheel to cut it into fingers measuring about 2½ x 1 inches; or make oblongs of any size you like; or cut the dough into rounds with a cookie cutter.

Transfer the cutouts to an ungreased baking sheet, placing them an inch apart; prick them all over, sprinkle with coarse sugar if you like, and bake them at the temperature specified for each kind of shortbread. The baking time will be about 10 to 15 minutes less than for large rounds of shortbread; watch the cookies to prevent overbaking. (If shortbread actually browns, the flavor suffers.)

Peppery Chocolate-Nut Biscotti

Fresh-ground pepper secretly enlivens these dark, crisp, pecan-studded chocolate slices that are decidedly not your everyday biscotti. The gentle afterglow of the spice—which is not at all identifiable as pepper—makes them an especially good match for a glass of red wine.

1¼ cups pecan or walnut halves
1¾ cups all-purpose flour
⅔ cup sugar
½ cup (lightly packed) fine-quality Dutch-process cocoa powder
1 teaspoon fresh, coarsely ground pepper, black or white
½ teaspoon baking powder
½ teaspoon baking soda
¼ teaspoon salt
¼ teaspoon ground cinnamon
3 large eggs
3 tablespoons sweet (unsalted) butter, melted
1½ teaspoons pure vanilla extract
Water, if necessary
Milk for glaze

Makes 3 to 4 dozen biscotti

Chocolate—Trial & Error

When chocolate came to the Old World in the fifteenth century it was first consumed as an unsweetened but spiced and peppered beverage like that of the Aztec court where the Spaniards found it. Matters didn't rest there: the bitter beverage was gradually smoothed and sweetened and chocolate was solidified into a confection. While all that was slowly proceeding, the "food of the gods" was a seasoning for savory dishes. Most of the old recipes are now curiosities, but some have interest. Among them are Mexican mole sauce, invented for turkey, but good for rabbit, pork, and chicken; several Sicilian dishes, including versions of caponata (see the Index), a caponata-like sauce for rabbit, and a pork- and tomato-based pasta sauce served at Christmas; certain versions of the odd American dish called Cincinnati five-way chili; European game sauces; those rye breads in which cocoa

(cont.)

1. Preheat the oven to 350°F, placing a shelf in the center position. Grease and flour a large cookie sheet, or spray it with baker's pan coating.

2. Spread the nuts on an ungreased baking sheet and toast them in the oven for about 8 minutes, stirring them several times. Cool, then chop about two-thirds of the nuts coarsely (each half should end up in about three pieces) and chop the remainder to the consistency of very coarse meal.

3. Sift together the flour, sugar, cocoa, pepper, baking powder, baking soda, salt, and cinnamon into a mixing bowl. Stir in the nuts and make a well in the center of the ingredients.

4. In a small bowl, whisk the eggs until foamy; whisk in the melted butter and vanilla. Pour the mixture into the center of the dry ingredients and stir from the center with a fork, gradually drawing in the dry mixture. If the dough becomes too stiff to stir, knead it in the bowl until it is thoroughly mixed, if necessary adding a few drops of water to make a workable but not soft consistency.

5. Divide the dough into two parts. Form each into a rough log about 12 inches long, placing them on the prepared baking sheet about 3 inches apart. Shape into loaves about 2½ inches wide, slightly higher at the center than at the sides. Smooth the surface with a pastry brush dipped in milk.

6. Bake the loaves until firm but not visibly darkened in color, 18 to 20 minutes.

7. Remove the baking sheet from the oven and lower the oven to 300°F. Cool the loaves on the pan for 5 minutes, then carefully transfer them to a rack and cool 10 minutes longer.

8. Move the loaves to a cutting surface, and using a sharp serrated knife and long, firm strokes, cut them at a slight diagonal into slices ⅓ to ½ inch thick. Lay the slices flat on one or two ungreased baking sheets.

9. Bake the slices for 5 minutes, then turn them and bake 5 minutes longer. Check them by touch—they have baked long enough when the outside feels dry. If they need to be baked a little longer, first turn them again.

10. Cool on wire racks and store in an airtight canister at room temperature. These keep well for a couple of weeks in that fashion, or they may be freezer-bagged and frozen for up to 3 months. Frozen biscotti should be thawed in their wrappings, then refreshed by rewarming them in a 325°F oven for about 10 minutes. Cool the biscotti again before serving.

(cont.)
is a colorant; and, in the sweet sector, a few fruitcakes and forms of panforte (see the Index) in which the dusky taste of cocoa undergirds spices and fruits to excellent effect.

THE PAVLOVA & OTHER MARVELOUS MERINGUES

A Pavlova is a crisp, round meringue shell heaped with whipped cream and topped with fruit, traditionally a tropical kind. The dessert was invented (and called a "cake") by someone in Australia (or was it New Zealand?) in honor of the ballerina Anna Pavlova during a tour Down Under early in the century.

Like cream puffs, the free-standing confections called meringues (we're not talking pie toppings here) are sweet deceivers. They look as if they'd be complicated to make, but they are basically nothing more than whipped egg whites, sugar, and flavoring formed into shapes simple or baroque and baked very, very slowly until completely dry, airily crisp, and still ivory pale in color.

Because of the long baking, meringues won't be ready to serve the day they're begun unless the cook hops into the kitchen at dawn. But meringues may be made days ahead of time if you're careful to keep them free of any humidity thereafter—something best done by storing them in a turned-off oven kept slightly warm (and quite dry) by the viewing light. It is impossible for a meringue to become too dry.

My meringue/Pavlova recipe is not traditional—it employs an offbeat formula I like a lot and have published before (in my *Menu Cookbook,* where it becomes a pie topping). Feather-light and delicately crunchy when baked to utter dryness, the meringue shrinks less in the oven than other types and it is not oversweet.

The size of meringues is up to you: Make a big shell for a Pavlova as described first, or fashion the mixture into individual nests for ice cream, fruit compote, or chestnut puree, or for whipped cream plus exotic fruit (individual Pavlovas), or shape small heaps of the mixture into delicate little "cookies."

FOR AIRY EGG WHITES

Even a slight trace of grease on a spotless-looking bowl or beater will prevent egg whites from reaching maximum volume when they're beaten, so it's a good idea to wash the equipment with detergent, rinse, and dry it before it is used. Similarly, even a speck of (fatty) egg yolk that strays into the whites to be beaten will affect volume adversely.

½ cup plus 1 tablespoon water
4 teaspoons cornstarch
½ cup superfine sugar (see sidebar page 362)
½ teaspoon pure vanilla extract
¼ to ½ teaspoon almond extract, to taste
4 large egg whites, at room temperature
Pinch of salt

Makes a meringue shell to serve 6 as a Pavlova, or 6 individual meringue shells, or several dozen small "cookies," the total depending on their size.

1. ***Preparing the pan and the oven:*** Cover a baking sheet or pizza pan with foil, folding it under the edges of the pan so it won't slide off. Grease the foil generously with vegetable shortening. Set a 10-inch pot lid or round baking pan on the foil and draw around it with the end of a spatula handle or other blunt object. Set the marked pan aside. Turn on the oven at its lowest setting—for my oven, that's "warm"—and check the temperature with an oven thermometer if you can; you want a reading well below 200°F, the lower the better. (If the oven is too hot, the meringue will become undesirably brown before it's dry throughout.)

2. ***Preparing the meringue:*** Blend the water with the cornstarch and 2 tablespoons of the sugar in a small saucepan. Cook, stirring, over medium heat until the mixture boils and becomes clear (this can be done, in a microwave-safe bowl, in the microwave). Scrape into a bowl and allow to cool until barely warm. Stir in the vanilla and almond extracts.

Place the egg whites in the scrupulously clean and dry bowl of an electric mixer and add the salt. Begin beating at medium-low speed; when the whites have become foamy and the volume has almost doubled, without stopping the beaters add the cornstarch mixture a little at a time. Increase the speed to high and begin adding the remaining sugar a tablespoonful at a time. If necessary, scrape down the sides of the bowl, but don't stop beating. Continue until the mixture is very fluffy—the pattern left by the beaters will stay firmly in place, and a sample will hold a peak when spooned from the mass.

3. ***Shaping the meringue:*** Scoop a portion of the meringue gently into a pastry bag fitted with a large plain or rosette tip, filling the bag no more than three-fourths full. Pipe a ring of meringue over the circle marked on the foil, then fill up the round with concentric rings, refilling the bag as necessary. Pipe a raised border over the outside ring; then add a parapet of close-set globes or rosettes of meringue. If any mixture remains, pipe small shapes onto the vacant areas of the foil to make little cookies.

4. ***Baking the meringue:*** Bake the shell in the preheated but extra-cool oven for as long as it takes for it to become completely dry and firm throughout, which may be as much as 12 hours, depending on the thickness of the shell. When the upper surface is firm and seems dry, try to pick up the shell; if it's rigid, turn it over carefully and continue the drying. If the shell is browning at all—it should stay as pale as possible—turn off the oven, open the door, and let the oven cool, then turn it on again at its lowest setting and continue to bake with the door partly open. The shell is done when it is completely dry; test by picking it up and knocking on the bottom.

SUPERFINE SUGAR

Superfine sugar, or a reasonable facsimile, can be made from granulated sugar in a food processor. Just keep the machine running until the texture is quite fine, which will take a few minutes. Keep the machine going considerably longer if powdered sugar is what you want. Cover the feed tube in either case, as clouds of sugar dust will be produced.

CRISP OR CHEWY?

It isn't always easy to be sure about fabled dishes such as the Pavlova, but a fully baked, dry shell appears to have been the original idea. Travelers to the Antipodes report encountering soft-hearted Pavlovas there, and some Australian and New Zealand recipes call for baking times that could not produce a crunchy texture. So it's baker's choice, and when we're baking we come down firmly for crisp.

5. Keeping the shell crisp: To keep the shell crisp until serving time, it's safest, unless you live in an area of practically no humidity, to store it in the turned-off oven with the viewing light turned on; a meringue will keep for many days this way. If you choose another method of storage and the shell should soften, return it to the oven, at its lowest setting, and dry it again.

To Make a Pavlova "Cake"

At serving time, beat 1 cup heavy (whipping) cream until it holds soft peaks; add a little sugar or not, according to taste. Heap the cream in the meringue shell and top it with sliced, crushed, or sectioned fruit, preferably of an exotic kind.

Topping suggestions: Passion fruit puree was the original Pavlova topping; try sliced, fully ripe (and therefore fragrant) kiwi fruit, or strawberries, raspberries, or other berries; or use beautifully ripe and lightly sweetened peaches or nectarines; and on and on through the seasons of fruits.

Individual Dessert Meringues

Mark six 4-inch circles on two foil-covered and greased baking sheets (a standard coffee can is a good guide for the circles). Using a medium-size rather than large tip on the pastry bag, pipe a ring of the meringue mixture over each pattern, then proceed to fill in the rings and add low edgings as described for a large meringue shell. Bake and store as described. Fill the shells just before they're served to preserve their crunch.

To serve: A filling of ice cream plus a great sauce comes first to mind; see the Index for the whereabouts of dessert toppings involving raspberries, many forms of fudge, oranges, blueberries, chestnuts, cherries, rum plus raisins, and other fruits and nuts. Or fill the meringues with whipped cream and fruit exactly as for a Pavlova. In summer, I like to heap the shells with a "fool"—sweetened pureed or cooked berries or other fruit, blended into whipped cream or chilled custard with gentle strokes that leave streaks of color throughout.

Meringue Cookies

To make a whole basketful of tiny meringue mouthfuls, pipe small rosettes or globes of the mixture onto baking sheets covered with greased foil. Bake and store as described. Baking time will be much shorter—keep an eye on them.

The Making of Many Desserts

TOPPING OFF WITH DESSERT~

SAUCES & BEYOND

For grown-up people whose inner child is alive and well, beginning dinner with the really good stuff—*dessert*—is a secret dream that seldom comes true (except perhaps on an occasional birthday?), but no one can keep children of any age from dreaming.

For all the dessert-dreamers out there, we have kept for this last chapter the luxurious toppings and other goodies meant for the grand finale of the feast. When you have cannily stashed away such saucery as Chocolate Butter, or White Chocolate & Hazelnut Sauce, or any of the many fudge sauces, or Chestnuts in Cointreau Syrup, or Caramel-Mocha Ice Cream Sauce, or Jubilee Cherries, Melba Sauce, or Nesselrode Sauce, all you need for a festive dessert is a supply of fine ice cream. (If you've made the white chocolate sauce, *very* dark chocolate ice cream is the ticket.) Or you might just choose to spoon your topping over a simple pudding or a slice of angel or pound cake or, in a pinch, a scoop of plain frozen yogurt.

There are also some complete desserts here—for instance, pears or prune plums richly poached in wine, and a tart made from the plums; those decadent dainties Nesselrode pie, pudding, and sauce; and Chestnut Puree, together with half a dozen ways to turn it into memorable desserts. Come the holidays, Cumberland Rum Butter is commended for adding distinction to any steamed pudding or, for that matter, to squares of warm, homey gingerbread served for supper.

Blueberry Syrup or Sauce

Whether it is to be enjoyed as the base for a nonalcoholic cooler (pour over ice, add club soda) or as a royal-purple topping for ice cream, a waffle, or a stack of griddlecakes, blueberry syrup is exceptionally good when made with wild blueberries. These are often available frozen, a boon to those who can't get them fresh.

The short fermentation intensifies the flavor of the berries and the color of the syrup. There is no alcohol in the finished syrup.

2 pint baskets (about 6 cups) ripe blueberries
6 cups sugar
3 cups water
⅔ cup strained fresh lemon juice

Makes 3 pints

1. Pick over the blueberries to get rid of stems, leaves, and any soft specimens. Rinse and drain well.

2. Puree the berries, using a food processor, a blender, or a food mill fitted with the fine disk. Pour the puree into a ceramic, glass, or stainless-steel bowl, cover with a terry towel or other thick cloth, and leave at room temperature for 36 hours to undergo a mild fermentation. Stir after 2 or 3 hours' standing and again several times during the fermentation period. A crusty-looking cap will form at first; later the puree will become foamy, all as it should be.

3. Line a sieve with one thickness of dampened very fine nylon net or two layers of dampened fine cheesecloth and set it over a bowl. Pour in the puree and let it drain freely until the flow of juice slows. At that point twist the corners of the cloth together tightly and press on the pulp to extract all possible juice. Discard the pulp. You should have about 2⅔ cups of juice.

4. Combine the sugar and water in a nonreactive large saucepan. Bring to a boil over high heat and boil uncovered until the syrup will form a soft ball when a little is dropped into ice water, or until the syrup registers about 235°F on a candy/jelly thermometer. (It isn't important to achieve an exact reading.) Add the blueberry juice and lemon juice, stir, and return to a boil. Lower the heat and simmer the syrup for 5 minutes. Remove from the heat.

5. *For refrigerator storage:* Cool the syrup, then funnel it into dry sterilized (page 282) bottles or jars. Cover the containers with sterilized

Huckleberry Summers

Wild huckleberries don't grow everywhere in the country, but where they do grow these rather seedy little purple-black berries, borne on knee-high bushes, are well worth picking in the years when they deign to appear. (They are intermittent bearers, at least around here.) Huckleberries are often confused with blueberries—which generally have larger, softer, paler fruit, with soft seeds—but they're botanically a different kettle of fruit. They're equally good, though, for making Blueberry Syrup. If your huckleberry harvest isn't large enough to use this way, enjoy the little fruits fresh on breakfast cereal, or add them to muffin batter.

lids or caps and refrigerate. The syrup will keep for several months under refrigeration.

6. *For pantry storage:* Ladle the syrup while boiling hot into hot, clean pint-size canning jars, leaving ¼ inch of headspace. Seal the jars with new two-piece canning lids according to manufacturer's directions and process for 15 minutes in a boiling-water bath (page 283). Cool, label, and store the jars. The syrup will keep for a year in a cool cupboard.

Caramel-Mocha Ice Cream Sauce

This starts out to be creamy caramel candy, changes its mind with a little help from the cook, and ends up as an amber-brown, luscious caramel-mocha topping for ice cream. You can also spoon it over a pudding that needs a lift, or deploy it to create a complete dessert from a slice of sponge, angel, or pound cake. For sauces including pecans or walnuts and/or Cognac, see the variations following the main recipe.

Can Do

Canned evaporated milk is such a handy pantry item that one could wish that it tasted more like fresh milk—its characteristic "cooked" flavor isn't always what's wanted for a dish. Here, however, for this dessert sauce its taste is exactly right when paired with the caramel and mocha elements. Cream or half-and-half could be used instead of evaporated milk, in which case the amount of butter should be reduced a little.

¾ cup light corn syrup
¼ cup water
1 cup sugar
4 tablespoons (½ stick) sweet (unsalted) butter
1 cup evaporated milk
¾ cup triple-strength (or stronger) hot brewed coffee, or ¾ cup boiling water plus at least a tablespoonful (depending on the brand) of freeze-dried instant regular or espresso coffee
½ to 1 teaspoon pure vanilla extract, to taste
¼ teaspoon salt

Makes about 2½ cups

1. Measure the corn syrup, water, and sugar into a large saucepan. Heat the mixture over medium-high heat, stirring it with a straight-ended spatula, until it boils vigorously. Dip a pastry brush into cold water and wash down any sugar crystals clinging to the sides of the pan. Add the butter. When boiling resumes, begin adding the evaporated milk very gradually, stirring all the time. Continue to boil the caramel, stirring it constantly to prevent scorching, until it is thick and pale

golden-brown, about 10 minutes; if you use a candy/jelly thermometer (recommended), cook it to a reading of about 230°F, or until a little of the mixture dropped into ice water forms a soft ball that can be molded in the fingers. Remove the pan from the heat.

2. Stir in the coffee. (Don't be concerned if the whole business looks dreadfully curdled, as it probably will after the milk is added, if not before. The sauce will end up quite satiny.) Stir in ½ teaspoon of the vanilla and the salt.

3. Scrape the mixture into the container of a blender and blend, starting on low speed and gradually speeding up, until it is smooth. Taste the sauce and add more vanilla, if you like. For more mocha flavor, add more grains of instant coffee, either regular or espresso, and blend briefly.

4. Store the sauce, covered, in the refrigerator, where it keeps indefinitely. It will thicken somewhat upon chilling, so you may want to let it come to room temperature before serving it.

Caramel-Mocha Sauce with Pecans or Walnuts

To 1 cup of Caramel-Mocha Sauce add ¼ to ⅓ cup of lightly toasted (page 302) and chopped pecans or walnuts.

Brandied Caramel-Mocha Sauce

At any point before serving either the plain or nutted caramel-mocha sauce, stir in Cognac to taste. Start with a tablespoonful of brandy to a cup of sauce, blend, taste, and add more if you wish.

Chestnut Puree

(Crème de Marrons)

Now *here's* an autumn luxury for the dessert lovers out there: Chestnuts are poached in syrup with a vanilla bean, then pureed to make the foundation of a whole collection of elegant desserts. Some ways to use the puree, impromptu and otherwise:

• *Sweet & simple:* Serve the puree mounded in dessert glasses, topped with softly whipped cream or with heavy sweet cream poured around. (For looks, you may like to push the puree through a potato ricer into swirly mounds in the glasses.)

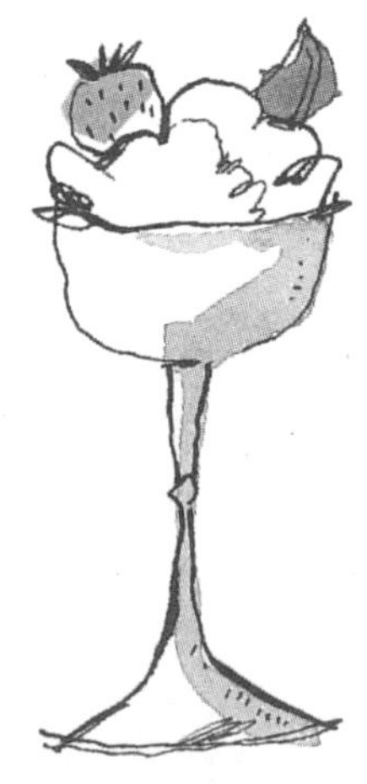

USING DRIED CHESTNUTS

Fresh chestnuts have a short season and are often hard to find, so dried chestnuts are a great fallback staple to keep on hand. Although I've used dried chestnuts in poultry stuffings and other savory preparations for a long time, not until lately have I discovered that they make a highly acceptable crème de marrons, *too, if well soaked to remove their characteristic smokiness. Chinese or other Asian groceries are the best source of supply. Stored in a glass jar, they keep for months at room temperature, almost indefinitely in the freezer.*

To make about 5 cups of puree: *Soak 1 pound of dried chestnuts in plenty of cold water for 12 to 18 hours, changing the water twice. Scrape off any bits of brown skin clinging to the chestnuts, rinse them well, then proceed with the Chestnut Puree recipe.*

• *Chestnut fool:* Swirl spoonfuls of puree into a rich egg custard (*crème anglaise,* to be found in any big cookbook); leave the mixture streaky. Chill in a crystal bowl or individual dishes, then top with lightly whipped cream sweetened and flavored with vanilla.

• *Chestnut topping:* Stir in a flavoring of dark rum, or Cognac, or an orange-flavored liqueur such as Triple Sec, Cointreau, Curaçao, or Grand Marnier; spoon over fine vanilla ice cream.

• *Chestnut and cream topping:* Blend the puree with a little fresh cream (and, if you like, a touch of rum or rum-based liqueur) as an ice-cream sauce. (Try it over chocolate ice cream.)

• *Parfait art:* Alternate spoonfuls of the puree in tall glasses with lightly whipped cream that has been sweetened and flavored with vanilla (or substitute spoonfuls of vanilla ice cream). Top with a final tuft of cream and a drizzle of warm fudge sauce (see page 376).

• *Chestnut and chocolate sauce:* Warm chestnut puree in a double boiler, stirring in about one quarter as much whipping (heavy) cream and a handful of chopped bittersweet chocolate; stir until smooth. Serve warm over ice cream.

3 pounds fresh chestnuts
1 vanilla bean, split
Boiling water as needed
1 cup sugar, or more to taste

AT SERVING TIME:
Any of the additions suggested in the headnote

Makes about 6 cups

1. Chop each chestnut in half with a cleaver or heavy knife (lay them flat side down on a cutting board for easy chopping).

2. Place the nuts in a heavy saucepan, add water to cover by 1 inch, and bring them to a boil over high heat. Boil the nuts, uncovered, 3 minutes, then drain them, Pry or pop the halves out of the shells. The skin will usually remain in the shell; scrape off any bits that adhere to the nuts. Halve each piece.

3. Return the nuts to the rinsed-out saucepan; add cold water to cover, the vanilla bean, and the sugar. Bring to a boil, lower the heat, and simmer the nuts gently, partly covered, until they are translucent and very tender, which may take as long as 2 hours, depending on the quality of the nuts. When necessary, add boiling water to keep the nuts covered; as they approach doneness, uncover the pan and let the syrup reduce and thicken somewhat. Cool the nuts in the syrup.

4. Remove the vanilla bean (don't forget to rinse it and air-dry it for reuse). Puree the chestnuts and syrup in a blender or a food processor until fairly smooth. Taste for sweetness and blend in additional sugar if you wish (or use honey or corn syrup). At the time of use, the puree may be thinned with light cream or milk if it's too thick for the use you're planning.

5. Pack the puree into clean, dry jars, cover, and refrigerate for up to 2 weeks. For longer storage, freeze the puree; it keeps for many months.

Chestnuts in Cointreau Syrup

Quartered chestnuts are poached in a rich syrup to make this chunky autumn delicacy. Two kinds of citrus, plus the Cointreau added at the end, do good things for the mealy nuts.

For a dessert, spoon chestnuts and syrup into stemmed glasses and add a crest of lightly whipped cream, or serve them as a topping over the best vanilla ice cream you can find. For another versatile chestnut sweet, see the preceding recipe for Chestnut Puree. That recipe also includes information on substituting dried chestnuts for fresh, when the latter are not to be had.

1½ pounds fresh chestnuts
Peel of 2 large fresh tangerines, all stringy pith scraped from the inside, torn into large chunks
Boiling water as needed
¾ cup sugar
1¼ cups water
⅓ cup light corn syrup
1 tablespoon finely slivered orange zest (outer peel only, no white pith)
⅓ cup Cointreau or other orange-flavored liqueur

Makes about 2½ cups

1. Chop each chestnut in half with a cleaver or heavy knife (lay them flat side down on a cutting board for easy chopping).

2. Place the nuts in a heavy saucepan, add water to cover by 1 inch, and bring them to a boil over high heat. Boil the nuts, uncovered, 3 minutes, then drain them. Pry or pop the halves out of the shells. The skin will usually remain in the shell; scrape off any bits that adhere to the nuts. Halve each piece.

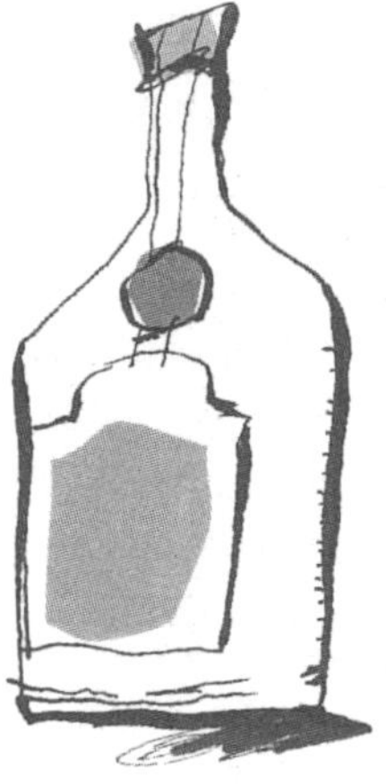

Orange Liqueurs

Cointreau and other intensely orange-flavored liqueurs are wonderful flavor enhancers when used in modest quantities in fruity or nutty desserts as well as in other dishes both savory and sweet. Often liqueurs may be purchased in small bottles, which is convenient for your wallet if you'd like to compare them. Among many orange-flavored possibilities are Grand Marnier, Triple Sec (several brands), Curaçao, and Van der Hum.

3. Return the nuts to the rinsed-out saucepan; add the prepared peel of one tangerine and enough cold water to cover the nuts. Bring to a boil, lower the heat, and simmer the nuts gently, partly covered, until they are translucent, about 1 hour. If necessary, add boiling water to keep the nuts covered.

4. Using a slotted spoon, lift the nuts from the cooking liquid, leaving any scum behind. Discard the liquid and tangerine peel.

5. Combine the sugar, the 1¼ cups water, and the remaining tangerine peel in the rinsed-out saucepan and bring the mixture to a boil. Simmer the syrup 10 minutes, then add the chestnuts. Bring the syrup to a boil again, then lower the heat and simmer the chestnuts, covered, for 15 minutes. Remove the pieces of tangerine peel. Add the corn syrup and the slivered orange zest; return the sauce to boiling and simmer it for 3 minutes.

6. Ladle the nuts and syrup into a sterilized storage jar and add the orange liqueur. Cap the jar, give it a shake or two, then cool and refrigerate it. The chestnuts and sauce mellow and improve for several weeks (but can be used at once) and will keep for up to a year under refrigeration.

Going Dutch—Cocoa with a Difference

Cocoa powder made by the so-called "Dutching" process is worth every penny when a recipe calls for it. Dutch-process cocoa (which is labeled as such, or as "Dutched cocoa") is darker and richer in flavor than standard grades of cocoa, as a result of an alkali treatment; it is available from specialist suppliers in degrees of richness ranging from low-fat upwards. If you must substitute, standard supermarket cocoa may be used.

Chocolate Butter, Nutted & Otherwise

Made with dark, very chocolaty Dutch-process cocoa, a jar of this velvety spread/sauce/confection has many uses. A lot of it has been consumed at our house while we have counted the ways we like it and also tried to decide whether we like it better with or without nuts.

Some of the ways to enjoy Chocolate Butter:

- Warm it slightly by setting the jar in quite warm water; stir it occasionally as it warms, then spoon it over ice cream.
- Add a tablespoonful of Amaretto liqueur to a cupful of warmed nutless Chocolate Butter; top chocolate, coffee, or vanilla ice cream with the now almond-scented sauce.
- Let Chocolate Butter soften slightly at room temperature, then spread it as a filling for a gold, white, or chocolate layer cake, or as a glaze for the top of a single-layer fudge cake or a panful of brownies.

• For chocolate cookie sandwiches, spread Chocolate Butter on the bottoms of thin vanilla or chocolate wafers, make sandwiches with more wafers, then wrap and freeze them. Serve these frozen.

• Spread Chocolate Butter, with or without nuts, on thin slices of pound cake, top the filling with another thin slice, and cut the sandwiches into fingers for sweet teatime nibbles. For less sweet but intriguing sandwiches, use thin-sliced, lightly buttered white bread, trim the edges and cut the sandwiches into strips.

• For instant "truffle" candies, see the variation following the recipe.

¾ cup (lightly packed) fine-quality Dutch-process cocoa powder
1 cup sugar
¼ teaspoon salt
½ cup hot water
¾ cup (1½ sticks) fine-quality sweet (unsalted) butter, at room temperature
½ to 1 teaspoon pure vanilla extract, to taste
⅛ teaspoon pure almond extract

FOR NUTTED CHOCOLATE BUTTER:
1 cup toasted and coarsely chopped walnuts or toasted, skinned, and coarsely chopped hazelnuts (see the accompanying sidebar for how-to's)

Makes about 2½ cups with nuts, 1¾ cups without

1. Combine the cocoa, sugar, and salt in the top pan of a double boiler (or use a heatproof bowl that can be placed over a saucepan containing simmering water). Stir the mixture with a whisk until it is thoroughly mixed, then mix in the hot water thoroughly. Set the pan over simmering water and stir the contents until the sugar has completely dissolved and the mixture is hot, about 3 minutes. Remove the top from the base and set it aside; cool the contents to lukewarm.

2. Cream the butter together with the vanilla and almond extracts in the small bowl of an electric mixer, or use a food processor to beat the butter with the flavorings just until it is light. With the motor of either machine running, gradually add the lukewarm chocolate mixture, continuing to beat just until everything is well combined. Let the chocolate butter cool completely, stirring or whisking it occasionally to lighten its texture. Add the nuts, if you're making the nutted version, then scrape the chocolate butter into a clean, dry storage jar, cover it tightly, and refrigerate it. The butter will keep perfectly for at least 6 weeks.

To Prepare Walnuts or Hazelnuts

Spread the nuts on a baking sheet and place them in an oven preheated to 350°F. Toast them 8 to 10 minutes, stirring them every two minutes or so. Walnuts are done when they are crisp and fragrant; hazelnuts are ready when they smell toasty and their skins have loosened.

Roll hazelnuts in a towel while they are hot and rub off as much of their skin as possible. Walnuts may be given the same rubdown (it removes their slight tinge of bitterness), but it's not essential. Cool the nuts and chop them into coarse chunks. Shake them in a sieve to remove the powdery bits before adding them to the other ingredients.

For Truffle-Hounds

More chocolate truffles, both dark and light, are to be found in the chapter that deals with confections—check the Index.

Instant Truffles

To make these confections, scoop up small spoonfuls of chilled Chocolate Butter, with or without nuts, and form them into knobby balls—don't try to make smooth spheres, as they're supposed to look like the dark, bumpy fungus they're named for.

Roll the truffles in sifted cocoa powder and refrigerate them, lightly covered, until wanted. If they're not to be served within a few hours, they may be wrapped and frozen and served without thawing.

At serving time, dust the truffles with more cocoa and, if you like, arrange them in frilly little paper cups.

Cumberland Rum Butter & Its American Cousin

For those who cherish tradition, it's pleasant to discover that "our" hard sauce for steamed Christmas puddings is descended from a delectable compound that takes its name from the beautiful Cumberland region of England.

At home, Cumberland Rum Butter is (of course) a pudding sauce, but it's also spread as a filling for cakes and sweet wafers; and following an especially charming tradition, it is prescribed as the first taste of solid food to be laid upon the lips of a newborn child.

To convert this old "receipt" into one for hard sauce, see the variation following the recipe.

Rum Around the Kitchen

If a good, dark, flavorsome rum isn't kept on hand for judicious use in cooking, bottled "rum" flavorings may be resorted to, but the taste won't be as lively and good. Among rums, the dark Jamaican rums, such as Myers', get the nod in our kitchen because a small amount does a better job than an equal measure of one of the blander rums meant for tall summertime drinks.

1 cup (2 sticks) lightly salted butter, or sweet (unsalted) butter plus ¼ teaspoon salt, at room temperature
1 pound (2¼ cups packed) light brown sugar, sifted
⅓ cup, or more to taste, dark rum, preferably Jamaican
¼ teaspoon freshly grated nutmeg
A pinch or two of ground cinnamon, optional
Additional freshly grated nutmeg, for topping

Makes about 2½ cups

1. Cream the butter in a mixing bowl with a wooden spoon, or beat it in the large bowl of an electric mixer until it is very light. Gradually beat in the brown sugar, then continue to beat the mixture until it is smooth and light. Beat in the rum gradually, then add the nutmeg and, if you include it, the cinnamon.

2. Pack the rum butter firmly into a bowl, smoothing the top. Cover it tightly with foil or plastic wrap and refrigerate it for at least overnight before serving it. It will keep in the refrigerator, tightly covered, for many weeks.

3. To serve the rum butter, let it soften at room temperature, then fluff it with a fork, pile it in a serving dish, and grate a little nutmeg on top. If you like the contrast of cold sauce with hot Christmas pudding (or even warm gingerbread), return it to the refrigerator until serving time.

American-Style Hard Sauce

Follow the Cumberland Rum Butter recipe, but substitute sifted confectioners' sugar for the brown sugar, omit the cinnamon (the nutmeg is still a good idea), and replace the rum with Cognac or other good brandy. Some like to include a little vanilla in place of or in addition to the brandy. Beat well, chill, and serve on a hot steamed pudding or on warm apple or mince pie.

European-Style Red Raspberry Syrup

Thanks to the mild fermentation this syrup undergoes, it is brilliant in color and rich in flavor, a wonderful thing to have on hand for desserts and beverages. The method is basically European, a way of intensifying the flavor of fruit; no alcohol remains in the finished syrup. In this recipe, instead of relying on nature to plant the yeasts that carry out the fermentation, I add a little active dry yeast to the raspberries. Works like a charm.

If you live where red raspberries are sold in stingy little trays and priced like jewels, this recipe may be of only academic interest. But if you can pick your own or otherwise obtain raspberries reasonably, it's a small treasure.

Ways to use the syrup: Mix it with chilled club soda or dry white wine, plain or sparkling, for a tall drink; sauce ice cream or pudding with a spoonful; sweeten sliced strawberries or a bowl of mixed fresh or frozen fruit with it; use it to sweeten any beverage that would be all the better for a touch of intense raspberry flavor.

Extending the Method

The time-honored trick of fermenting raspberry pulp before making it into syrup can be used with other fruits and berries, too. Just follow the basic proportions of this recipe and handle the fruit or berry pulp in the same fashion and you'll be rewarded with a syrup that is wonderfully deep in flavor.

5 pint baskets (about 2½ pounds) red raspberries
5 cups water
1 teaspoon active dry yeast
¾ cup strained fresh lemon juice
4 cups sugar

Makes about 7 cups

1. Sort the berries and rinse them quickly in a colander only if they seem dusty, then crush them thoroughly. (Processing them briefly in batches in a food processor is the quickest way.)

2. Pour the berry pulp into a large ceramic, glass, or stainless-steel bowl and add 1 cup of the water and the yeast. Cover the bowl with a cloth and let it stand at room temperature for about 3 days, stirring the pulp twice a day; fermentation is complete when the mixture is no longer bubbly when its top crust is stirred in. At this point it won't look especially appetizing, but press on.

3. Set a colander over a large bowl and line it with two layers of dampened fine cheesecloth or a single layer of dampened very fine nylon net. Alternatively, arrange a jelly bag in its frame over the bowl. Pour in the fermented mash and let the juice drain. If you are using a lined colander, when the juice flow slows down, tie the corners of the cloth to make a bag and hang it above the bowl to drip. After the juice has dripped undisturbed for several hours, it's permissible to press and squeeze the contents of the bag to extract the last drops of liquid, which will be murky.

4. Combine the juice in a stainless-steel or other nonreactive large pot with the remaining 4 cups of water, the lemon juice, and sugar. Bring the mixture to a boil over medium-high heat and simmer it briskly, stirring occasionally, until it has reduced to approximately 7 cups. Skim the syrup and let it cool, then skim it again.

5. *To bottle and store:* Funnel the cooled syrup into dry, sterilized bottles (page 282). Cap or cork the bottles (use new corks only and sterilized caps only) and store the syrup in the refrigerator, where it will keep indefinitely.

For pantry storage: Dip the necks of corked or capped bottles repeatedly into melted paraffin wax to form a snug seal. Refrigerate after opening.

To seal in jars instead of bottles: Reheat the syrup to simmering and seal it in sterilized (page 282) canning jars with sterilized new two-piece canning lids following manufacturer's directions. Refrigerate the syrup after it's opened. Unopened, it keeps for at least a year.

Fudge Sauce: Theme & Variations

Whether we're nominal adults or actual kids, most of us love an occasional indulgence like a hot fudge sundae. Twice a year can't hurt, can it?

For such occasions, or for an ice cream party where a choice of toppings is offered—this is sure-fire entertainment for all ages—here is our family fudge sauce, the product of years of self-sacrificing and public-spirited experimentation. It's properly dense and clingy when spooned over ice cream, and it can be used either at room temperature or after it has been warmed. You can vary this sauce, too—try the Amaretto, peppermint, mocha, and rum variations. If you're in a hurry, try the lazybones version, which uses the microwave to produce a silky sauce in next to no time.

If you use premium-quality chocolate for fudge sauce, you'll be glad.

Hot Fudge Sauce

1 cup evaporated milk or light cream
2 cups sugar
¼ teaspoon salt
¼ cup light corn syrup
6 tablespoons (¾ stick) sweet (unsalted) butter
4 ounces (4 squares) fine-quality unsweetened chocolate
2 ounces (2 squares) fine-quality semisweet chocolate
2 to 3 teaspoons pure vanilla extract, to taste

Makes about 3 cups

1. Combine the evaporated milk, sugar, salt, corn syrup, butter, and chocolates in the upper pan of a double boiler, or use a heatproof bowl that can be set over a saucepan containing simmering water.

2. Set the pan over simmering water in the double-boiler base and heat the contents, stirring occasionally, until the butter and chocolate have melted. Stir the sauce thoroughly and continue to cook it until it is smooth and slightly thickened, about 10 minutes.

3. If any lumps are seen, strain the sauce. Let it cool for 5 minutes or so, then stir in the vanilla extract. Scrape the sauce into a clean, dry jar or jars, cool it completely, then cover and store in the refrigerator, where it will keep for at least 3 months. For freezer storage for up to 6 months, freeze the sauce in a tightly covered container, preferably of glass, allowing at least ½ inch of headspace.

To serve the sauce: Thaw it unopened and let it come to room temperature if it has been frozen, or let refrigerated sauce come to room temperature. To warm the sauce, set the jar in a bowl of hot water and stir it occasionally until it has relaxed enough to flow smoothly when spooned over ice cream.

Fudge Sauce with Amaretto

Replace the vanilla extract with Amaretto liqueur, adding about 2 tablespoons, or the amount that pleases you.

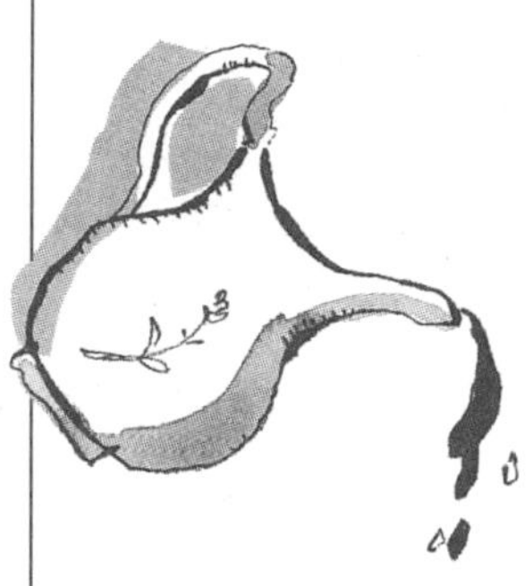

Chocolate Peppermint Fudge Sauce

Replace the vanilla extract with a small amount of peppermint extract or a spoonful or two of crème de menthe or other peppermint-flavored liqueur—start with ½ teaspoon of peppermint extract or a tablespoonful of liqueur, then taste and cautiously add more flavoring if it is needed; peppermint can be overpowering.

Mocha Fudge Sauce

While the basic fudge sauce is still hot, stir in 1 to 1½ tablespoons of freeze-dried coffee crystals, either regular or dark roast. If you want to flavor only part of the batch, figure on 2 teaspoons of crystals to a cup of sauce. If you have instant coffee powder rather than crystals, reduce the measurement by about one third.

Fudge Sauce with Dark Rum

When adding the vanilla to the basic fudge sauce, stir in 2 tablespoons of dark rum, preferably Jamaican. Taste and add a little more if more rumminess seems a good idea.

Lazybones Fudge Sauce

Inspired by a second-hand version of a third-party recipe that came my way, this is a shortcut I've found to be a gem when there's no time to make fudge sauce in the authentic fashion. Just be sure to use *good* dark chocolate. (I'm a Merckens fan.)

To make about 2¼ cups of sauce, stir together in a roomy microwavable container 12 ounces of cut-up bittersweet chocolate, ½ pint of heavy (whipping) cream, 2 to 4 tablespoons of sweet (unsalted) butter, and a pinch of salt. Microwave at moderate power (about 70% power for a large microwave) for 1 minute, stir well, and then continue microwaving in 20-second increments, stirring after each, until the chocolate is smooth; this should happen within a total of about 2 min-

Finding Work for the Microwave

The microwave needn't just sit there waiting for a leftover to be reheated—it deserves to be called on for a lot of jobs that would be more laborious to do on the stovetop. Case in point: Making Lazybones Fudge Sauce. (Or melting chocolate for any other use.) Once you're used to the very short "takes" involved in microwave cooking, preparing many dishes (not all are suitable for microwaving) in the conventional way begins to look like a poor idea.

utes. (Be careful not to overheat.) Stir in your choice of flavorings from the preceding recipes: start with 1¼ teaspoons vanilla; or 1½ tablespoons Amaretto; or ¼ teaspoon peppermint extract or 2 teaspoons crème de menthe; or 1 tablespoon freeze-dried coffee crystals; or 1½ tablespoons dark rum. Taste after adding the flavoring and dollop in some more if it is needed. My vote? Vanilla extract, if you have used wonderful chocolate.

Refrigerate in a glass jar, closely covered, for up to a month. Warm the sauce until it's pourable before serving; half a minute or so in the microwave should do it. Alternatively, set the container of sauce in a bowl of quite hot water and stir it occasionally until it has softened sufficiently.

JUBILEE CHERRIES

The flambéed dessert called cherries Jubilee, an elegant artifact of the Victorian table, remains a pleasure to those who like to climax a special dinner with flaming tabletop drama. In cherry time, it's the work of moments to seal into jars a supply of the liqueur-spiked fruit, ready to serve over ice cream at short notice. A pint jar is enough for 6 servings.

Here's another way to enjoy cherries preserved in a high-spirited syrup: Make a Black Forest cake by sandwiching lightly drained cherries between dark chocolate layers; top the cake with whipped cream and more cherries.

RETRO DRAMA

Cherries Jubilee tastes wonderful, but beyond that, the dessert is a link to a time when Sunday suppers were planned around that marvelous new appliance, the chafing dish (sweetbreads in cream, that sort of thing). Perhaps, today, the prospect of dark, sweet cherries being flamed in brandy will lead the owners of chafing dishes to dig them out, as it' s a pity to conduct this ceremony out of view of the diners.

4 pounds dark sweet cherries (about 9 cups after pitting)
2¼ cups sugar
¾ cup Cointreau or other orange-flavored liqueur
Brandy or kirsch, for flaming at serving time

Makes about 3 pints

1. Stem, rinse, and pit the cherries, saving any juice.

2. Combine the cherries and their juice with the sugar in a stainless-steel or other nonreactive large pan. Heat the mixture over medium heat, stirring it gently or shaking the pan occasionally, until the sugar has dissolved into a smooth syrup and the cherries are hot through; the mixture should not actually boil. Remove the pan from the heat.

3. Divide the liqueur among 3 hot, clean pint canning jars. Lift the cherries from the syrup with a slotted spoon and distribute them among the jars, leaving ½ inch of headspace. Reheat the syrup to boiling and fill the jars with it, leaving ½ inch of headspace. Remove any air bubbles by running a long thin knife blade or a cooking chopstick around the inside walls of the jars and add more syrup, if necessary. Seal the jars with new two-piece canning lids according to manufacturer's directions and process for 15 minutes in a boiling-water bath (page 283). Cool, label, and store the jars in a cool cupboard for at least 2 weeks before opening. The cherries will keep, unopened, for at least a year.

4. *To serve:* Add more liqueur to the sauce, if you like. Then reheat the cherries and syrup, preferably in a chafing dish so that the sight can be enjoyed at the table. For a pint of cherries, warm ¼ cup of brandy (or kirsch, if you prefer) in a small saucepan over low heat (be careful not to let it catch fire), pour it over the heated sauce, and set the brandy on fire—use a long match, and be careful. Spoon the flaming mixture over vanilla or peach ice cream that has been scooped into individual serving dishes. Crisp sweet wafers are a pleasant accompaniment for this festive dessert.

MME. MELBA LIVES

Dame Nellie Melba (1859–1931, née Helen Porter Mitchell), who took her stage name from Melbourne, her Australian home town, was toasted in both Europe and America throughout a long opera career. Now she is perhaps thought of most often as the inspiration for one of Auguste Escoffier's 10,000 culinary inventions—peach Melba, a dessert of fruit and vanilla ice cream bathed in raspberry sauce. (Escoffier later marketed Melba sauce—see my version, page 384— to the public.) Ultra-thin Melba toast was named for the diva, too, and so was an elaborate garnish for meat that committed the cook to preparing stuffed tomatoes, fluted mushrooms, and truffles, plus a sauce.

A WHITE CHOCOLATE & HAZELNUT SAUCE

Because white chocolate isn't dark in color and in fact isn't chocolate at all, don't assume it lacks character. More delicate in taste than true (dark) chocolate, it derives its flavor from cocoa butter and a touch of vanilla rather than what's called "chocolate liquor," the soul of the cocoa bean. In short, it's a "chocolate" with a difference.

White chocolate tastes especially marvelous combined with hazelnuts and cream, as in this luxurious sauce recommended for spooning over extra-dark chocolate ice cream. If you can't find ice cream that's dark and bittersweet, it's worth while to make your own.

½ pound white chocolate, broken into small chunks
¾ cup heavy (whipping) cream
½ cup sugar
Pinch of salt, optional
2 tablespoons sweet (unsalted) butter
½ cup toasted, skinned, and coarsely chopped hazelnuts (page 372)
A little hazelnut liqueur (Frangelico), if you like

Makes about 2 cups

1. Working in batches, grate the white chocolate in a blender. When all the chocolate has been grated, return all batches to the blender.

2. Combine the cream with the sugar, the optional salt, and the butter in a small heavy saucepan. Set the mixture over low heat and heat it, stirring, until the sugar and butter have melted and the mixture is piping hot.

3. Start the blender motor and pour the hot liquid through the opening in the cover. Blend the sauce until it is thick and smooth, stopping the motor once or twice and scraping down the sides of the container. Scrape the sauce into a bowl.

4. Stir in the hazelnuts. If you like (it isn't essential), stir in a tablespoon or two of hazelnut liqueur.

5. Store the sauce in a clean, dry jar, tightly covered, in the refrigerator for 2 months or more.

To serve: Let the sauce return to room temperature, or warm it slightly by setting the container in quite warm water and stirring it once or twice as it warms. If the sauce still seems too thick, add a little more cream.

Finding Quality

White chocolate is available under many labels (it's even bagged in morsel form), and, expectably, its quality corresponds to its price. Good white chocolate bars are available in fancy-food shops, but for serious cooking you may want to order white chocolate in larger quantities from a supplier of baking and candy-making ingredients. Bargain chocolate of any kind is no bargain at all.

Prune Plums Poached in Wine

Prunes we have always with us, so the famous *pruneaux du pichet* devised by the French gastronome Fernand Point and described in his book *Ma Gastronomie* know no season. The fresh plums that turn into wrinkly-faced prunes when dried—they're logically enough called prune plums, or blue or Italian plums—are available only while late summer is changing into autumn, and a new way to enjoy them in their brief season (in addition to tortes and tarts and just-plain-stewed) is offered here to fans of the fruit. The recipe copycats M. Point's transformation of dried prunes, which is reprised in the second recipe; the fresh-plum version is as smashing as the original and a bit less sweet. A refrigerator stash of either will provide a memorable dessert on less than a moment's notice.

For either recipe I use a decent domestic port and any light red wine good enough for drinking; vintage bottles aren't required.

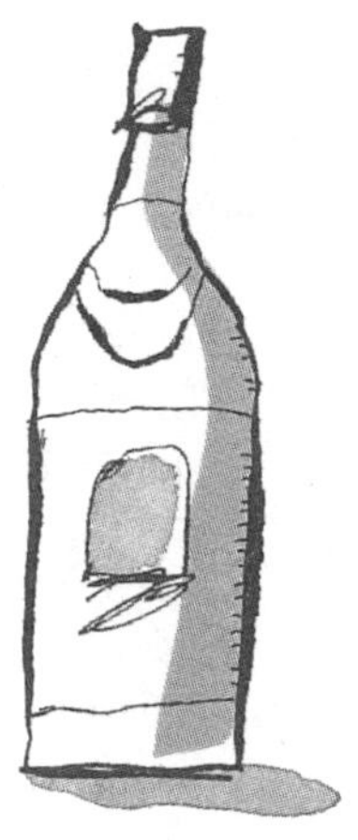

2 pounds (2 to 3 dozen) ripe but firm prune plums (blue or Italian plums)
2 or 3 wide strips of lemon zest (outer peel only, no white pith) (or substitute about 3 drops of lemon oil), optional
½ vanilla bean
1 cup red port wine
2 cups light, dry red wine, or enough just to cover the fruit
¾ cup sugar, or to taste

Makes about 8 servings

1. Rinse the plums and pat them dry. Place them in a stainless-steel or other nonreactive saucepan just large enough to hold them with a couple of inches to spare, tucking in the lemon zest or adding the lemon oil, if you are using either, and the vanilla bean, split open lengthwise. Add the port, red wine, and ½ cup of the sugar.

2. Set over medium heat and bring slowly to a boil, then reduce the heat to low, partially cover the pan, and poach the fruit very gently until the plums are completely tender to a probing knife tip. The cooking time will depend on the shape of the saucepan and the level of heat; the more slowly the plums are cooked the better, as you want them to retain their shape.

3. Lift out the plums with a slotted spoon and place them in a bowl. Discard the lemon zest. Fish out and recycle the vanilla bean (rinse, pat dry with a paper towel, and leave to dry at room temperature, then put away until needed for another dish).

4. Simmer the syrup rapidly until it has reduced by about half, to a little over 1 cup. Taste the syrup and add some or all of the remaining sugar, if you wish. Pour the syrup over the plums, cool, cover, and refrigerate for at least 24 hours.

5. Serve the plums and a share of syrup very cold, with a splash of heavy cream to set off their sweet wininess (for a less rich spoonful, use drained and thickened plain yogurt—see the Index for yogurt how-to's). The winy plums keep in their syrup for weeks in the refrigerator, increasing in delectability as they rest in a well-capped jar.

Point's Prunes~A Reprise

Fernand Point started with 36 fine big French prunes (but California prunes will be fine), soaked them for 24 hours in 2 cups of red port, then simmered them in that liquid plus an equal amount of light Bordeaux, half a vanilla bean, and a scant cup of sugar. The prunes were served very cold with cream and slices of brioche. Scrumptious.

These keep as long as you're willing to leave them in peace in the refrigerator.

MELBA SAUCE

This crimson raspberry sauce shouldn't be reserved for the classic "Melba" dessert, which is a poached fresh peach half bedded on vanilla ice cream. It makes a distinguished topping for the darkest possible chocolate ice cream, or a slice of any simple cake (add a tuft of whipped cream), or a pristine rice pudding flavored with vanilla rather than cinnamon. When you have poached some pears in vanilla syrup, cloak the fruit in a spoonful of this sauce at serving time.

The currant jelly in the sauce permits the berry puree to be cooked only briefly, which preserves both flavor and aroma and eliminates the starch thickening used in some adaptations of Escoffier's invention.

At serving time, you may want to add a nip of spirits to the sauce. First choice is framboise, but crème de cassis, cherry brandy, or any of the orange-flavored liqueurs will be complementary. A tablespoonful of liqueur to a cup of sauce is enough.

6 cups (about 2 pint baskets) fresh raspberries, picked over, rinsed, and drained
1 cup sugar
1 cup currant jelly, preferably "pure" (made without added pectin)
3 tablespoons strained fresh lemon juice

Makes about 4 cups

1. Puree the raspberries in a blender or food processor; pour the puree into a fine-meshed sieve set over a bowl. Press the puree through the sieve with a rubber spatula to remove all possible seeds. Discard the seedy pulp, or see page 301 for using it to make vinegar.

2. Stir the raspberry puree, sugar, currant jelly, and lemon juice together in a stainless-steel or other nonreactive large saucepan over medium heat until the ingredients are completely blended. Raise the heat to high and boil the sauce, stirring it constantly, for 2 minutes. Remove from the heat.

3. Skim off any foam and ladle the sauce, boiling hot, into hot, clean half-pint canning jars, leaving ¼ inch of headspace. Seal the jars with new two-piece canning lids according to manufacturer's directions and process for 10 minutes in a boiling-water bath (page 283). Cool, label, and store the jars. The sauce will keep for at least a year in a cool cupboard.

Alternative storage: If you prefer not to seal the sauce for storage, pour it into clean, dry jars, let it cool, cover it tightly, and refrigerate it. It keeps for months.

SUNDAY BREAKFAST SAUCE

Maple syrup isn't the only game in town when it comes to topping waffles, pancakes, or French toast. Orange, Lemon & Pineapple Dessert Sauce (page 385) should probably be renamed, as it seems to be poured at breakfast time as often as for desserts. The same goes for Blueberry Syrup or Sauce (page 366), and there's no reason why this Melba Sauce shouldn't be drizzled over a waffle.

Nesselrode Sauce

Once the peak of fashion—the Victorians knew very well how to enjoy the sweet course—this opulent compound, the basis of famous desserts, seems to have been originated by one M. Mony, the chef of Count Nesselrode, a nineteenth-century Russian diplomat. Over the years, the sauce and the derivative desserts bearing Nesselrode's name have been considerably altered by shortcuts and commercialization; the recipes that follow try to preserve the spirit of M. Mony's culinary invention and his period.

Making Nesselrode Sauce from scratch involves several simple but time-consuming procedures, so it might make sense to produce a double batch while you're about it. The sauce keeps (and improves) indefinitely, and a jar makes a luxurious gift.

1 pound fresh chestnuts
4 cups water
1¾ cups sugar
1 tablespoon strained fresh lemon juice
½ vanilla bean
½ cup light corn syrup, or more if needed
¼ cup dark rum, preferably Jamaican, or more if needed
¼ cup golden raisins
¼ cup dried currants
¼ cup seeded muscat raisins (or use dried cherries, if you have them)
½ cup coarsely diced candied cherries, or use part (or all) drained maraschino cherries, if you don't mind their artificial coloring
¼ cup finely diced candied citron
2 tablespoons finely chopped candied orange peel, preferably homemade
¼ cup maraschino liqueur, or more if needed

Makes about 6 cups

1. Chop each chestnut in half with a cleaver or a heavy knife (lay them flat side down on a cutting board for easy chopping).

2. Place the nuts in a heavy saucepan, add water to cover by 1 inch, and bring them to a boil over high heat. Boil the nuts, uncovered, 3 minutes, then drain them. Pry or pop the halves out of their shells. The skin will usually remain in the shell; scrape off any bits that adhere to the nut. Cut or break the nuts into quarters or sixths, depending on the

Replacing Fresh Chestnuts

The season for fresh chestnuts is so fleeting, and the price of canned chestnuts is so high, that using dried chestnuts in this recipe is a good option. Soak them for at least 12 hours, better 18, changing the water at least twice, before simmering them in fresh cold water to cover until they are barely tender. Then proceed with step 3 of Nesselrode Sauce. To replace 1 pound of fresh chestnuts in the recipe, about 6 ounces of dried nuts should be enough.

size of the nuts. Return the nuts to the rinsed-out saucepan, cover them with cold water, bring them to a boil, and simmer them, uncovered, until they begin to be tender, about 30 minutes. Drain the chestnuts, discarding the liquid.

3. Combine the 4 cups water, 1½ cups sugar, and lemon juice in the rinsed-out saucepan; split the piece of vanilla bean lengthwise and add it. Bring the mixture to a boil and boil it, uncovered, 3 minutes, then add the chestnuts. Lower the heat and simmer the chestnuts, uncovered, until they are transparent and very tender and the syrup has thickened, 30 to 45 minutes; stir them occasionally and skim off the foam. (It doesn't matter if some of the nuts break.) Add ½ cup light corn syrup and remove from the heat. Set the chestnuts and syrup aside until the fruits for the sauce are ready (overnight is fine).

4. Combine the golden raisins, currants, and muscat raisins in a saucepan. Add water to cover and bring to a boil; boil the fruit for a moment, then remove the pan from the heat and let the fruit cool completely.

5. Stir the rum with the remaining ¼ cup sugar until the sugar is dissolved. Drain the cooled fruit thoroughly and place in a bowl. Add the sweetened rum, stirring the mixture well. Let it stand at room temperature, tightly covered, for at least 2 hours and as long as overnight. In another bowl, combine the cherries, citron, and candied orange peel with the maraschino liqueur. Cover the bowl tightly and let the fruits stand, covered, for at least 2 hours and as long as overnight.

6. When you're ready to compound the sauce, remove the vanilla bean from the chestnut syrup. (Rinse, air-dry, and save it for a second use.) Scoop out about a third of the chestnuts and mash them, then return them to the syrup. Stir together the chestnuts and their syrup and the two batches of fruit and their liquid. Check the consistency of the sauce, which should be somewhat dense. If you'd like a more pourable sauce, add a little more corn syrup plus a little more rum and/or maraschino liqueur.

7. Store the sauce in sterilized (page 282), tightly covered jars in the refrigerator. It will be mellow enough for use in 2 weeks or so, but it keeps (and improves) indefinitely. Stir it before use.

Nesselrode Saucing

Without prompting, you'll scoop this delectable mixture over ice cream. Or spoon a little into a meringue case or over pound cake. If people still made old-fashioned cottage pudding (a plain cake served warm, in squares), they would love Nesselrode Sauce as a topping. The classic Nesselrode dishes are the original pudding, ice cream, and a tall, rich, creamy pie; read on for how-to's.

Defining Zest

Zest, an ingredient whose identity sometimes puzzles inexperienced cooks, is simply the oil-rich, flavorful outermost skin layer of a citrus fruit. To prepare it for use, shave broad strips of zest from the fruit with a swivel-bladed peeler, leaving all the white, bitter pith behind; or grate it off, carefully, again to avoid the pith; or use the small tool called a zester, which strips off the zest in tiny shreds. Citrus oil—orange, lemon, or lime—may be substituted for zest in recipes. Add these oils in mere drops, not dollops, as they pack a lot of authentic citrus flavor. Fancy-food shops and mail-order suppliers sell the oils.

NESSELRODE PUDDING

If you'd like to taste the modern counterpart of Chef Mony's original pudding, drain some of the sauce briefly, not completely (save the syrup), and fold the chestnuts and fruits into a rich Bavarian cream mixture before you add the whipped cream (see a good general cookbook for a Bavarian recipe). Chill the pudding well.

NESSELRODE ICE CREAM

Fold briefly drained fruits and chestnuts from the sauce (return the syrup to the jar of sauce) into softened vanilla ice cream and refreeze it. Serve it with the reserved syrup as topping.

NESSELRODE PIE

Erase all memories of the puffy travesties served in restaurants and described in some cookbooks. Instead, follow food writer Craig Claiborne's suggestions, quoted here with thanks:

Add a cupful of fruit and chestnuts drained from Nesselrode Sauce to a stovetop custard (1½ cups milk, 3 large egg yolks, ¼ cup sugar, ½ teaspoon vanilla) that has been reinforced, so to speak, by cooking 1 tablespoon plain gelatin with the other ingredients. Let the custard and fruit cool, then fold in, first, 3 large egg whites beaten until stiff with ⅓ cup sugar, then ½ cup chilled heavy (whipping) cream, whipped until stiff. Pile the filling *high* in a baked 10-inch pie shell, chill it well, and there you have it.

ORANGE, LEMON & PINEAPPLE DESSERT SAUCE

Evolution was probably discovered by the first cook, not Darwin, because ways (a.k.a. recipes) of cooking *anything* just don't stay put. This particular delectability began its public life in my *Home-Style Menu Cookbook* as Chunky Orange Syrup or Sauce, and very good it was (and is) in that reading. After several seasons of making it with the fine oranges of winter, the recipe method has been simplified and other fruits added, but the sauce is still a deep-gold syrup studded with tender shreds of orange zest. It may become lightly jellied, thanks to the pectin in the fruit.

The sauce keeps very well, refrigerated, so it's a good thing to have at hand to gild waffles or pancakes for a fancier-than-usual breakfast, or to spoon over ice cream or a chunk of unfrosted cake for an unfancy dessert. Drizzle the sauce over cultivated blueberries, too, to add both sweetness and a citrus counterpoint to their rather bashful persona.

3 large, bright-skinned winter oranges (navels for choice)
2 large, juicy lemons
Additional oranges or orange juice, as needed
1 cup pineapple juice
3½ cups sugar
About ¼ teaspoon butter
A few drops of orange oil and/or lemon oil, optional

AT SERVING TIME, OPTIONAL ADDITION:
Orange-flavored liqueur (Cointreau, for example) or kirsch, about 2 tablespoons per cup of sauce

Makes about 4 cups

1. Wash and dry the oranges and the lemon. Using a citrus-zesting gadget that removes the zest (outer skin) in several tiny slivers at a pass, remove the layer of zest from the fruit. Lacking such a gadget, use a swivel peeler to cut off the outer layer of peel in the thinnest possible sheets, then sliver the peel on a cutting board with a sharp knife. The finer the slivers, the better.

2. Cover the slivered peel with cold water in a saucepan, bring to a boil, and simmer 5 minutes. (This is a good job for the microwave, too; cook each time for 2 minutes after boiling starts.) Drain, add fresh water, and repeat this procedure twice, but reserve the liquid as well as the peel after the third simmering. While the peel cooks, squeeze and strain the juice from the oranges and lemons. If you don't have 3 cups of juice, pour in enough additional orange juice to make that amount.

3. Combine the peel, 1 cup of the cooking liquid, the combined orange and lemon juice, pineapple juice, sugar, and the dab of butter (which will help prevent boiling over) in a very large stainless-steel or other nonreactive saucepan or preserving pan. Bring to a boil, stirring until the sugar has dissolved, then boil at a moderate rate, stirring occasionally, for 10 to 15 minutes, until the syrup has thickened a little. (It will be thicker after cooling.) Taste the sauce and add a little more lemon juice if you wish. Optionally, add a very few drops of orange oil and/or lemon oil if you judge the citrus flavor needs support.

4. Pour the sauce into a sterilized (page 282) jar or jars, let it cool, then cover and refrigerate for storage. It keeps for months. At serving time, add orange liqueur or a little kirsch, if you like.

5. *Pantry strategy.* Make a double batch of the sauce and seal some for cupboard storage (see Preserving Notes, page 281). Leave ¼ inch of headspace in the jars and complete the sealing, cooling, and testing of seals as described.

Pears in Port

Firm winter pears are the right stuff for this wine-rich dessert, but fall pears (Bartletts, for instance) are fine, too, if that's what you have. It's lovely served chilled, a little crystal bowlful per person, with a benison of heavy cream or a tuft of Crème Fraîche (see Index).

The pears keep very well in their syrup, a merit that should place them on the "in case of company" shelf of the refrigerator. When company is expected and there's time for a bit of baking, see the elegant Pear Tart that follows the main recipe.

6 firm-ripe winter pears (Bosc, Anjou, etc.)
3 tablespoons fresh lemon juice, or as needed
1½ cups decent (it needn't be costly) red port, or combined port and full-bodied red table wine
1½ cups water
Zest of ½ lemon, pared in paper-thin strips from the fruit, no white pith
3 whole cloves
6 tablespoons sugar, as needed

Serves 6 or more, depending on size of pears

1. Pare the skin from the pears, quarter and core them, and drop them into cold water acidulated with 1 tablespoon lemon juice.

2. Combine the port with the 1½ cups water in a stainless-steel or other nonreactive saucepan or sauté pan Add the lemon zest, 2 tablespoons lemon juice, the cloves, and 6 tablespoons sugar. Heat, stirring, until the sugar has dissolved and the syrup is simmering.

3. Drain the pear quarters and add them. If the liquid doesn't cover the fruit, add water as necessary. (The syrup will be reduced later, so don't worry about loss of flavor.) Simmer the pears, partly covered, just until tender to a probing knife tip; don't let them become mushy. Uncover and cool in the syrup.

4. Lift the pear sections from the syrup into a bowl. Boil the syrup, stirring often, until it has reduced and become quite thick. Taste

How to Pick a Pear

At the market, that is, not from the tree. When shopping look for pears that are unbruised, if possible unblemished, and still firm. (Pears need to be harvested while unripe and allowed to come to eating condition indoors.) Leave them in the fruit bowl until the flesh yields slightly to gentle pressure near the stem; don't wait for them to become soft all over, at which stage they will have begun to spoil. When ready to eat or cook, pears may be refrigerated for a day or so if necessary, preferably enclosed in a paper (not plastic) bag.

for sweetness and tartness and add sugar and more lemon juice if necessary. Fish out and discard the strips of lemon zest and the cloves.

5. Pour the syrup over the pears, cool, cover, and refrigerate for at least 24 hours before using. The fruit will keep, chilled, for 2 weeks or so.

Pear Tart

Serves 6 to 8

If Pears in Port (above) are on hand and you'd like to serve a fancier dessert than pears with cream, this is a handsome way to dress up the fruit.

Bake a 9-inch tart shell just until lightly colored (use a recipe from any good general cookbook). Preheat the oven to 375°F.

Drain about 12 quarters of Pears in Port (you may need 2 or 3 more sections if the pears were small) and slice them lengthwise into 3 wedges each. Arrange the wedges in concentric circles in the tart shell.

Beat together 1 cup heavy cream or half-and-half, 2 egg yolks, 2 tablespoons sugar, ½ teaspoon pure vanilla extract, and 3 or 4 drops of lemon extract (optional). Pour the mixture over the fruit and bake the tart in the center of the preheated oven until only the center of the custard is jiggly when the pan is shaken lightly, about 30 minutes.

If you like, drizzle a little of the syrup drained from the pears over the top of the tart. Serve the tart while still warm, or at room temperature.

Rummy Raisin Ice Cream Sauce

Lean and mean as our diets may try to be nowadays, desserts have never really dropped off the menu, and in fact the revival of sweet stuff seems to be a permanent phenomenon. Old-fashioned rum raisin sauce is herewith nominated for attention as a luscious way to transform vanilla or chocolate ice cream into a special dessert. It's good on pound or sponge cake, too, when just-plain-cake isn't quite up to the occasion. Because it keeps like a charm, a prettily packaged jarful makes a welcome hostess gift.

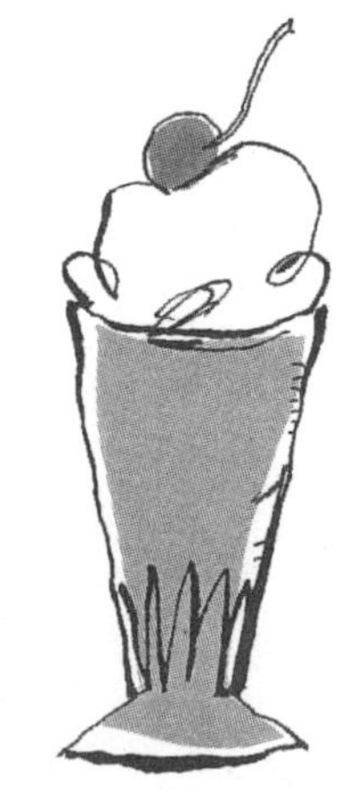

Custom-tune the recipe to suit: You can add a handful of coarsely chopped pecans or walnuts, and/or a scarlet scattering of that most retro ingredient, the maraschino cherry. If you have dried cherries on

OTHER RAISINS

Either dark or light commercial raisins will do very well when gussied up for this sauce, but any other favorite kind—especially Malaga raisins, which are especially flavorful—may be used.

hand (see the Index for how-to's), you could replace up to half of the raisins with dried cherries at the start of the proceedings.

1 cup seedless raisins, either dark (more flavorful) or light, or half and half (or use half raisins and half dried cherries)
½ lemon, sliced thin, seeds removed
Pinch of salt
1 cup (packed) light brown sugar
½ cup light corn syrup
2 tablespoons sweet (unsalted) butter
2 tablespoons cornstarch stirred with 3 tablespoons water
⅓ to ⅔ cup excellent dark rum, preferably Jamaican, to taste
1 teaspoon pure vanilla extract

Makes about 4 cups

1. Cover the raisins with water in a stainless-steel or other nonreactive saucepan, add the lemon slices and salt and bring to a boil. Cover, lower the heat to a simmer, and cook the raisins until very tender, almost falling apart; this may take up to an hour, depending on how dry the fruit was to start with. If the liquid reduces too much, add boiling water to keep the raisins covered. (This whole job is ideal for the microwave, used at medium or low power.)

2. Remove the debris of the lemon slices. If you like, mash or puree part of the raisins to add body to the sauce. Add the brown sugar, corn syrup, and butter and return to a simmer over direct heat. Gradually stir in enough of the cornstarch mixture to thicken the sauce lightly; continue to cook and stir until the liquid has clarified. Remove from the heat. Cool to lukewarm.

3. Stir in the rum and vanilla. Cool completely, then spoon into clean, dry jars and cover tightly for refrigerator storage. The sauce keeps for a month or more.

4. To serve, warm the sauce slightly and stir it well.

Mail-Order Sources

Unless otherwise noted, a catalog or price list is available. A few sources that do not issue catalogs are included because they're worth a telephone call or a visit.

American Spoon Foods:
Dried mushrooms, sour cherries, berries, and persimmons; native nuts, maple syrup, wild rice, preserves. 411 East Lake St., Petoskey, MI 49770. Phone: 616 347-9030.

Aphrodisia Products:
Comprehensive source for herbs, spices. No catalog. 282 Bleecker St., New York, NY 10014. Phone: 212 989-6440.

The Baker's Catalogue:
Published by the King Arthur flour people, this is the baking maven's delight for equipment, books, and (especially) hard-to-find ingredients, including but not restricted to King Arthur flours, meals, and grains. P.O. Box 876, Norwich VT 05055-0876. Phone: 800 827-6836.

Ball Canning Catalog:
Preserving, canning, and pickling utensils, ingredients, and supplies. Ball Home Canning Catalog, Direct Marketing Dept., Alltrista Corp, P.O. Box 2005, Muncie, IN 47307-0005. Phone: 800 240-3340.

The Bean Bag:
Their "beans, rice, grains and lots of other neat stuff" include unusual varieties; also spices, herbs, sun-dried tomatoes. Bean Bag Mail Order Co., Housewives Marketplace, 818 Jefferson St., Oakland, CA 94607. Phone: 510 839-8988.

Bland Farms:
Sweet Vidalia onions and Georgia peaches in season; also condiments. Bland Farms, P.O. Box 506, Glennville, GA 30427-0506. Phone: 800 843-2542.

Burgers' Smokehouse:
Nostalgia-rousing cured and smoked delicacies—hams and bacon in various styles; sausages; fresh beef and buffalo meat; smoked poultry and pork chops. California, MO 65018. Phone: 800 6224-5426.

Cabot Creamery:
Fine Vermont Cheddars, including excellent low-fat Cheddars for those who count fat grams; also flavored cheeses, gift packs. P.O. Box 128, Cabot, VT 05647. Phone: 800 639-3198.

Chef's Catalog:
Cookware, appliances, tools, and gifts sold here include many items of professional quality. 3215 Commercial Ave., Northbrook, IL 60062-1900. Phone: 800 338-3232.

CHILI PEPPER EMPORIUM:
Ristras of chilies, plus a pungent potpourri of other chilies, beans, and seasonings. P.O. Box 7397, Albuquerque, NM 87194. Phone: 505 839-7252; to order, 800 288-9648.

CORTI BROTHERS:
Fine grocers and wine merchants, the Cortis issue a newsletter about selected offerings; call to ask about hard-to-find items. P.O. Box 191358, 5810 Folsom Blvd., Sacramento, CA 95819. Phone: 916 736-3800; to order, 800-509-3663.

D'ARTAGNAN:
Such rarities as moulard and muscovy ducks; goose and duck foie gras; also game birds, meats, organic poultry, and charcuterie. 399 St. Paul Ave., Jersey City, NJ 07306. Phone: 800 327-8246.

DEAN & DELUCA:
Exotic food specialties and ingredients; also kitchenware and gifts. Catalog Dept., Dean & DeLuca, 560 Broadway, New York, NY 10012-3938. Phone: 800 221-7714.

EL PASO CHILE CO.:
Hot stuff and Southwestern specialties, both ingredients and packaged products; cookbooks, too. 909 Texas Ave., El Paso, TX 79901-1524. Phone: 800 274-7468.

FOUR RIDGE ORCHARDS:
They grow and sell Oregon hazelnuts and walnuts; also roasted and candied nuts. 13455 SW Brown's Drive, Hillsboro, OR 94123. Phone: 503 628-2721.

FRIEDA'S INC.:
A frequent answer to "Where can I buy it?" Unusual fruits, vegetables, herbs, and fungi in variety, from Asian pears to Seville oranges. 4465 Corporate Center Dr., Los Alamitos, CA 90720-2561. Phone: 800 421-9477.

KALYUSTAN:
Specialists in Middle Eastern foods, with such offerings as *lupini* beans, pomegranate juice and molasses, an array of halvahs, tamarind, almond oil, rose jam, and chapati flour. 123 Lexington Ave., New York, NY 10016. Phone: 212 685-3451.

KAM MAN:
An Oriental supermarket that for some rates a special visit to Manhattan's Chinatown. No catalog. 200 Canal St., New York, NY 10013. Phone: 212 571-0330.

KATAGIRI & CO.:
Japanese groceries and supplies, including unusual vegetables, beef for sukiyaki. 224 East 59th St., New York, NY 10022. Phone: 212 755-3566.

KING ARTHUR FLOUR:
See The Baker's Catalogue.

LE JARDIN DU GOURMET:
Herb, vegetable, and flower seeds and plants; sets for garlic, shallots, rocambole, uncommon onions; also books and some foods. P.O. Box 75, St. Johnsbury Center, VT 05863. Phone: 800 659-1446.

MAID OF SCANDINAVIA:
Now a division of Sweet Celebrations, this familiar firm is famous for special ingredients and tools, notably for cake baking and decorating and for confectionery; good list of cookbooks. Sweet Celebrations Inc., P.O. Box 39426, Edina, MN 55439-0426. Phone: 800 328-6722.

MILAN LABORATORY:
Everything for making wine and beer, and everything, including "mothers" (starters) and barrels, for making vinegar from wine or cider. Send stamped self-addressed envelope for a price list. 57 Spring St., New York, NY 10012. Phone: for information, 212 226-4780; to order, 800 233-7534.

MISSOURI DANDY PANTRY:
Spanking-fresh nuts, notably black walnuts and other fine native nuts; also such exotica as pistachios, macadamias. 212 Hammons Dr. East, Stockton, MO 65785. Phone: 417 276-5121.

NEW ENGLAND CHEESEMAKING SUPPLY COMPANY:
Kits, supplies, books, and equipment for making cheeses, buttermilk, crème fraîche, sour cream, and yogurt. Publisher of *The Cheesemakers' Journal.* 85 Main St., Ashfield, MA 01330. Phone: 413 628-3808.

NICHOLS GARDEN NURSERY:
Besides herbs and much else to interest a gardener, food items are also on offer. 1190 North Pacific Highway, Albany, OR 97321. Phone: 503 928-9280.

PENDERY'S:
Billing themselves as "the world of chiles and spices," this firm offers a huge list of hot sauces, ristras of chiles, many spices and herbs, plus nonedibles (tableware, gifts, clothing, and cookbooks). 1221 Manufacturing, Dallas, TX 75207. Phone: 800 533-1870.

PENZEYS:
Spices and herbs in variety; spice and herb blends, rubs, other seasonings. Informative catalog. Penzeys, Ltd., P.O. Box 1448, Waukesha, WI 53187. Phone: 414-574-0277.

PHIPPS COUNTRY:
Full of beans, including rare kinds; also bean and grain flours, uncommon grains and rices, herbs, spices. P.O. Box 349, Pescadero, CA 94060. Phone: 800 279-0889.

THE SAUSAGE MAKER:
Everything the creator of sausages or smoked meats, poultry, or fish might need, from sawdust to seasonings; equipment, too. 177 Military Rd., Buffalo, NY 14207. Phone: 716 876-5521.

SHEPHERD'S GARDEN SEEDS:
Excellent source of unusual seeds, plants, and supplies for the serious gardener; attractive and informative catalogue. 6116 Highway 9, Felton, CA 95018. Phone: 860 482-3638.

SUNNYLAND FARMS:
Nuts, most notably pecans (pecan meal, too); also dried and fresh fruits, confections, fruit cakes. Albany, GA 31706-8200. Phone: 800 999-2488.

SUR LA TABLE:
The stock of equipment, tableware, and books is no less than splendid. Store (worth a visit): 84 Pine St., Pike Place Farmers' Market, Seattle, WA 98101. Catalog division: 410 Terry Ave. N, Seattle, WA 98109-5229. Phone: 800 243-0852.

SWEET CELEBRATIONS:
See Maid of Scandinavia.

UWAJIMAYA:
Asian foods—Japanese, Chinese, Korean, Philippine, Thai—and possibly more besides; also cookware, from rice steamers to sesame-seed poppers. 519 6th Ave. S, Seattle, WA 98104-2812. Phone: 206 624-6248.

VELLA CHEESE CO.:
Famous for California handmade cheeses, especially their aged dry Monterey Jack; also Oregon blue cheese, fresh Jacks, and Cheddars. P.O. Box 191, Sonoma, CA 95476-0191. Phone: 800 848-0505.

VERMONT COUNTRY STORE:
Grains, cereals, flours, confections, maple specialties, plus a homey array of hard-to-find personal and household items and clothing. P.O. Box 3000, Manchester Center, VT 05255-3000. Phone: 802 362-2400.

WALNUT ACRES:
Known for organically produced grains and flours, cereals, nuts, beans, dried fruit, honey, spices and herbs, olives, sugars, and more, plus prepared foods. Walnut Acres Organic Farms, Penns Creek, PA 17862. Phone: 800 433-3998.

WILLIAMS-SONOMA:
Fine ingredients and specialty foods in addition to excellent cookware and tableware are available in branch stores over the U.S. or by mail order. P.O. Box 7456, San Francisco, CA 94120-7456. Phone: 800 541-2233.

THE WOODEN SPOON:
Excellent specialty cookware, some ingredients and seasonings. P.O. Box 931, Clinton, CT 06413-0931. Phone: 800 431-2207.

ZABAR'S:
A unique emporium dear to the hearts of New Yorkers; a huge selection of food and deli specialties (including genuine lox), ingredients, and groceries; large cookware department. 2245 Broadway (at 80th St.), New York, NY 10024. Phone: 212-496-1234.

D

E

F

G

N

O

P, Q

T

V

W